Advances in Modelling, Animation and Rendering

Springer
London
Berlin
Heidelberg
New York
Barcelona
Hong Kong
Milan
Paris
Singapore
Tokyo

John Vince and Rae Earnshaw (Eds)

Advances in Modelling, Animation and Rendering

These proceedings were published under the sponsorship of Silicon Graphics Inc.

 Springer

John Vince, PhD, FBCS, CEng
School of Media, Arts and Communication, Bournemouth University,
Talbot Campus, Fern Barrow, Poole, BH12 5BB

Rae Earnshaw, BSc, MSc, FBCS, CEng
Department of Electronic Imaging and Media Communications,
University of Bradford, Bradford, BD7 1DP

British Library Cataloguing in Publication Data
CG International 2002 (Conference)
   Advances in modelling, animation and rendering
   1.Computer graphics - Congresses
   I.Title II.Vince, John, 1941- III.Earnshaw, R.A. (Rae A)
   006.6
ISBN 1852336544

Library of Congress Cataloging-in-Publication Data
A catalog record for this book is available from the Library of Congress.

Apart from any fair dealing for the purposes of research or private study, or criticism or review, as permitted under the Copyright, Designs and Patents Act 1988, this publication may only be reproduced, stored or transmitted, in any form or by any means, with the prior permission in writing of the publishers, or in the case of reprographic reproduction in accordance with the terms of licences issued by the Copyright Licensing Agency. Enquiries concerning reproduction outside those terms should be sent to the publishers.

ISBN 1-85233-654-4 Springer-Verlag London Berlin Heidelberg
a member of BertelsmannSpringer Science+Business Media GmbH
http://www.springer.co.uk

© Springer-Verlag London Limited 2002
Printed in Great Britain

The use of registered names, trademarks etc. in this publication does not imply, even in the absence of a specific statement, that such names are exempt from the relevant laws and regulations and therefore free for general use.

The publisher makes no representation, express or implied, with regard to the accuracy of the information contained in this book and cannot accept any legal responsibility or liability for any errors or omissions that may be made.

Typesetting: Camera-ready by editors / colour section typeset: electronic text files prepared by editors
Printed and bound at The Cromwell Press, Trowbridge, Wiltshire
34/3830-543210 Printed on acid-free paper SPIN 10878463

Foreword

This volume is sponsored by Computer Graphics International 2002 and has been made possible by the collective effort of all the contributing authors. We would also like to thank everyone who assisted by reviewing the material and for editorial advice. It represents a snapshot of current research advances in the fields of modelling, animation, rendering, interaction, and visualisation.

We gratefully acknowledge the sponsorship of Silicon Graphics, Inc.

Rae Earnshaw
John Vince

Table of Contents

INVITED PAPERS

Problems and Solutions for the 3D Accurate Functional Modelling of the Hip and Shoulder
Nadia Magnenat-Thalmann, MyungJin Kang and Taro Goto *3*

Simulating a Human Society: The Challenges
Daniel Thalmann.. *25*

Content-based Image Indexing and Retrieval in Compressed Domain
J. Jiang... *39*

Visual Data Navigators " Collaboratories "
Mikael Jern, S. Palmberg and M. Ranlöf................................ *65*

What is Your Relationship with Your Information Space?
Jim J. Thomas, David R. McGee, Olga A. Kuchar, Judith W.Graybeal Dennis L. McQuerry and Pamela L. Novak7........................... *79*

State of Art in Digital Media
Jon Peddie.. *93*

MODELLING

A Body and Garment Creation Method for an Internet Based Virtual Fitting Room
Dimitris Protopsaltou, Christiane Luible, Marlene Arevalo and Nadia Magnenat-Thalmann *105*

Procedural Simulation of Interwoven Structures
Frederic Drago and Norishige Chiba..................................... *123*

An Approach to Blend Surfaces
Vladimir Savchenko and Nikita Kojekine................................ *139*

Borders, Semi-Sharp Edges and Adaptivity for Hexagonal Subdivision Surface Schemes
Koen Beets, Johan Claes and Frank van Reeth *151*

Mesh Smoothing with Shape or Feature Preservation
Hao Zhang and Eugene Fiume... *167*

Reconstructing Surface Discontinuities by Intersecting Tangent Planes of Advancing Mesh Frontiers
Luping Zhou, Indriyati Atmosukarto, Wee Kheng Leow and Zhiyong Huang .. *183*

Progressive Gap Closing for Mesh Repairing
Pavel Borodin, Marcin Novotni and Reinhard Klein *201*

An Isosurface Continuity Algorithm for Super Adaptive Resolution Data
Robert S. Laramee and R. Daniel Bergeron *215*

Acceleration of Elastic Model's Motion Computation Based on Elastic Element Reduction
S. Miyazaki, J. Hasegawa, T. Yasuda and S. Yokoi *239*

Explosive Impact on Real-time Deformable Terrain
Tao Ruan Wan and Wen Tang *247*

Image-Based Modeling Using Viewpoint Entropy
Pere-Pau Vazquez, Miquel Feixas, Mateu Sbert and Wolfgang Heidrich *267*

ANIMATION

Automatic Generation of Non-Verbal Facial Expressions from Speech
Irene Albrecht, Jörg Haber and Hans-Peter Seidel *283*

Experimental Investigation of Linguistic and Parametric Descriptions of Human Motion for Animation
Jason Harrison, Kellogg S. Booth and Brian D. Fisher *295*

A Novel Multi-resolution Anthropometrical Algorithm For Realistic Simulation and Manipulation of Facial Appearance
H.K. Hussein, A. Bastanfard and M. Nakajima *315*

Real Time Animation of Running Waters Based on Spectral Analysis of Navier-Stokes Equations
S. Thon and D. Ghazanfarpour *333*

RENDERING

Factoring a Specular Reflection Field Into Added Diffuse Reflection Fields
A.L. Thomas *349*

A Hardware Based Implementation of the Multipath Method
Roel Martínez, László Szirmay-Kalos and Mateu Sbert *377*

Fuzzy Random Walk
Francesc Castro, Miquel Feixas and Mateu Sbert *389*

Shadow Mapping for Hemispherical and Omnidirectional Light Sources
Stefan Brabec, Thomas Annen and Hans-Peter Seidel *397*

A Sky Light Illuminational Model in Specular Environment
Tomohisa Manabe, Kazufumi Kaneda and Hideo Yamashita *409*

High Quality Final Gathering for Hierarchical Monte Carlo Radiosity for General Environments
Frederic Pérez, Ignacio Martín and Xavier Pueyo *425*

New Contrast Measures for Pixel Supersampling
Jaume Rigau, Miquel Feixas and Mateu Sbert *439*

Visibility Maps: A Topological Structure for Fast Antialised Ray Tracing
J. Grasset, D. Plemenos and O. Terraz *453*

Realtime Shading of Folded Surfaces
B. Ganster, R. Klein, M. Sattler and R. Sarlette *465*

Rendering Natural Waters: Merging Computer Graphics with Physics and Biology
E. Cerezo and F.J. Serón *481*

A System for Image Based Rendering of Walk-throughs
Gaurav Agarwal, Dinesh Rathi, Prem K. Kalra and Subhashis Banerjee *499*

VISUAL INTERACTION

Interaction in Virtual Worlds: Application to Music Performers
J. Esmerado, F. Vexo and D. Thalmann *511*

Enhancing Archive Television Programmes for Interactivity
Mark Carey, Alf Watson and Dave Paget *529*

Author Index 549

Invited Papers

Problems and solutions for the accurate 3D functional modelling of the hip and shoulder

Nadia Magnenat-Thalmann, MyungJin Kang, Taro Goto
MIRALab, CUI, University of Geneva
24, rue du General Dufour, Geneva, Switzerland

Abstract

This paper presents the state-of-the-art on the 3D functional modelling of the hip and shoulder, and analyses critical aspects on this subject. For the accurate human hip and shoulder model, we need to pay a careful consideration to the correct material properties about organs (bones, cartilages, ligaments, muscles, and skins) and joint mechanics. The survey of functional modelling and our proposal, in order to obtain individual accurate model from MR Image dataset of several living people, are described.

Keywords: 3D functional modelling, Hip, Shoulder, 3D reconstruction, Magnetic Resonance Imaging, Deformable model, Registration

1. Introduction

Computer support is increasingly necessary for medical operations, for both preoperative planning and postoperative guides. For preoperative planning, a 3D functional model is created of the patient (or rather a specific part of the patient) with the aid of a computer. In this case, the accuracy of the 3D functional model has an enormous effect on the preoperative evaluation and task analysis that must be made by the surgeon. If the accuracy is sufficient, a surgeon can examine the 3D models prior to surgery, obtain a good visual result, and generally reduce the overall time of the surgical operation. However, software of this kind is still in its infancy and needs to be developed from the aforementioned conceptual stage, to a practical reality.

Patients with musculoskeletal disorders throughout the world are the most notorious and common causes of severe long-term pain and physical disability, affecting hundreds of millions of people across the world. An advanced understanding of musculoskeletal disorders, through research and in-depth examination, are absolutely necessary to improve their prevention and treatment [71]. This is yet another area in which these kinds of 3D modelling tools can be of major benefit is in the diagnoses and treatment of patients. In fact, surgeons are slowly, but surely, coming to expect computers to provide huge benefits for many areas of the medical profession. Therefore, it is evident that 3D functional modelling is moving from a general interest and teaching tool, that it once was, into the domain of aiding surgery, diagnosis and many other areas besides.

3D functional modelling is a multidisciplinary approach that requires system theory, mechanical engineering, mechanical design, human-machine interface, optimisation, medical knowledge, anatomy, orthopaedics, and radiology. In this paper, we introduce the state-of-the-art in 3D functional modelling of the hip and shoulder and propose critical aspects on this subject; 3D surface modelling, kinematic joint motions, material properties, and planning system, and give a solution for individual accurate surface models by using an inter-patient registration method.

2. Previous work

2.1 Introduction

Previous work has concentrated on two main body parts, the hip and shoulder, due to the fact they are the most sensitive areas for many disorders. The following sections detail previous work that has been performed in these two areas.

2.2 Shoulder Modelling

As one of the main joints of the human body, the shoulder has received a great deal of attention in literature and research. In summary, the focal points concerning the shoulder are:
- Bone and Joint Modelling
- Soft Tissue Modelling
- Kinematic Modelling

These specific areas are discussed in detail in the following sections.

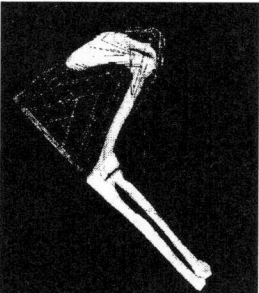

Fig. 1. Biomechanical shoulder model

2.2.1 Bone and Joint Modelling

The international shoulder group is a collaboration of mostly biomechanical oriented research groups, whose main interest is in the shoulder [81]. Resulting from the simulations of joint motions, they provide a standardization of shoulder joint rotations [59] and morphological parameters for modelling the human shoulder and arm [73].

The Delft shoulder group has developed a functional model of the shoulder and elbow. They have presented research on the control of human arm motions, including the proprioceptive feedback and the development of new measurement methods [80].

2.2.2 Soft Tissue Modelling

The Delft shoulder group has also concentrated on soft tissue modelling, by developing computer models based on a finite-element theory [58][59]. For an extension of this shoulder model, Breteler et al measured a set of muscle and joint parameters of the right shoulder of a male [10].

2.2.3 Kinematic Modelling

Bao et al focused on kinematic modelling and the parameter estimation of the human shoulder. They have estimated the components of the position vectors for each of the joint characteristic points [5]. Engin et al modelled the shoulder as a sequence of three spherical joints and measured the maximum movement for these three joints, assuming a minimum rotation criterion for the clavicle, scapula and humerus [24][25] [26]. Maurel et al proposed an extended shoulder model including scapulo-thoracic constraint and joint sinus cones [41] [42]. Charlton et al proposed spherical and wrapping algorithms in a musculoskeletal model of the upper limb instead of a straight-line muscle from origin to insertion [16].

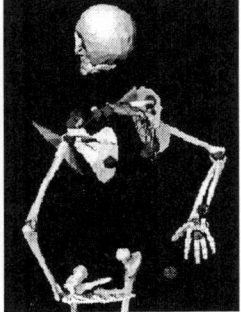

Fig. 2. *Elevation* and *extension* conic bounding with inventor model

Some researchers have provided information on ligament element function within the glenohumeral capsule by selective cutting [16] [46] and on joint contact areas [52][63]. Novotny et al. developed an analytical model of the glenohumeral joint to investigate how the glenohumeral capsule and articular contact between the humeral head and the glenoid stabilize the joint [45].

With respect to rotation, Karduna et al presented research on the effects of altering the Euler angle sequences of rotations. The result significantly alters the description of motion, with differences up to 50° noted for some angles [33].

2.3 Hip Modelling

Many people suffer from hip joint disorders as they have only a limited range of motion. Thus some hip joints do not move like others. In these cases, the head of the femur hits the acetabular rim and the joint starts to destroy itself. For such a reason many research teams work on the hip joint. The crucial points concerning the hip joint are one is hip joint range of motion to find the amount of limited range compared to normal hip joint movement, and the other is hip contact forces to detect the high-pressure region on the hip joint acetabulum and to give less pressure by altering the orientation of the acetabulum. Researches on soft tissues and musculoskeletal modelling have been carried out to find the influence of soft tissues on the hip movement. And more, hip navigation systems are developed to examine the effects of implant and alignment during total hip replacement surgery. These specific areas are discussed in detail in the following sections.

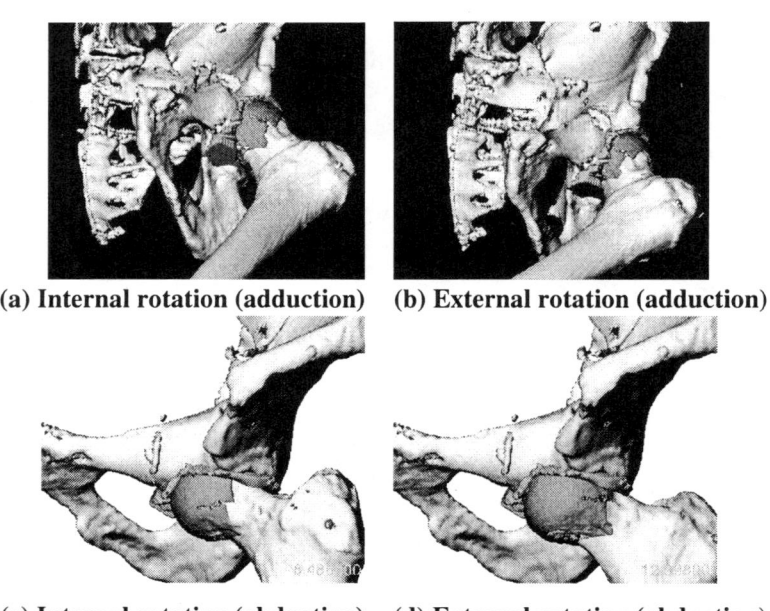

(a) Internal rotation (adduction)   (b) External rotation (adduction)

(c) Internal rotation (abduction)   (d) External rotation (abduction)

Fig. 3. Maximum hip range of motion

2.3.1 Hip Range of Motion

Hip pain, related to the acetabular rim and labrum, has received increased attention in orthopaedic literature. Despite the current concept of osteoarthrosis originating within the hip joint, a recent concept states that this condition often originates at the acetabular rim instead [57]. Genoud et al calculated the mean hip range of motion of the hip joint in the sagittal and frontal planes from five frozen cadaver hips and they found elements affecting the hip range of motion, i.e. impingement and capsule-ligament [29]. Teschner et al. determined the hip range of motion of a patient using reconstructed 3D models, and found a method to wide the range of motion by changing hip joint centre [53]. Jaramaz et al. also presented a work on hip range of motion for a preoperative planning system that helps surgeons choose the proper orientation of a hip implant prior to the patient entering the operating room [32].

Ferguson et al researched the influence of the acetabular labrum on the consolidation of the cartilage layers of the hip joint. A plane-strain finite element model was developed, which represents a coronal slice through the acetabular and femoral cartilage layers and the acetabular labrum. The labrum provided some structural resistance to lateral motion of the femoral head within the acetabulum, enhancing joint stability and preserving joint congruity [27]. According to several other studies, it is known that the association between labrum excision or pathology of the intact labrum and joint changes consistently [30][44].

2.3.2 Hip Contact Forces

Chao et al. presented a research on a pre-operative planning of femoral and pelvic
osteotomies. They noted the high-pressure zone in acetabulum as a preoperative planning and showed improved pressure distribution after the bone rotation and replacement as a postoperative planning [78]. Bergmann et al measured hip contact forces with instrumented implants and synchronous analyses of gait patterns and

 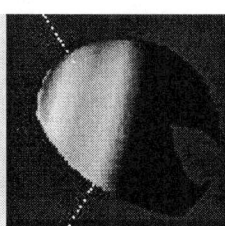  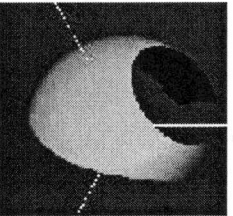

(a) Preoperative   (b) Postoperative

Fig. 4. Pressure zone in hip acatabulum: (a) Preoperative-note the high-pressure zone in acetabulum (b) Postoperative- improved pressure distribution after rotational osteotomy

ground reaction forces were performed in four patients during the most frequent activities of daily living; from the individual datasets, an average patient was calculated [9].

2.3.3 Soft Tissue Modelling

Ferguson et al employed a two-dimensional finite element model of the hip femoral and acetabula cartilage with labrum [27][28]. Hirota et al applied a finite element method for elastic solid deformation. They focus on the simulation of the mechanical contact between nonlinear elastic objects. The mechanical system used as case study is the human leg, more precisely, the right knee joint and some of its surrounding bones, muscles, tendons and skin (taken from the Visible Human Dataset) [31].

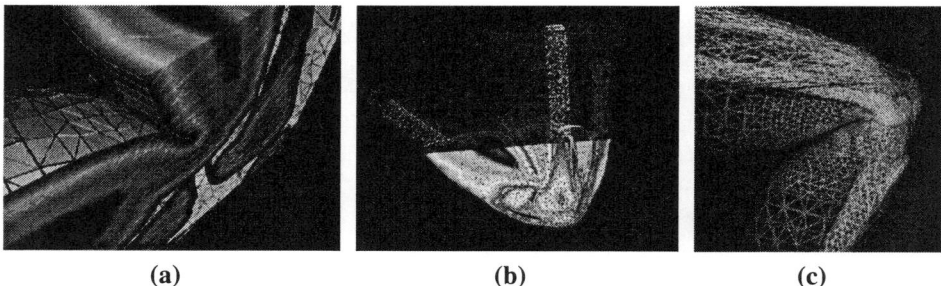

(a) (b) (c)

**Fig. 5. Implicit finite element method for elastic solids in contact:
(a) Cross section view (b) Sliding contacts between organs
(c) Wire frame rendering (skin, muscles, and bones)**

2.3.4 Musculoskeletal Modelling

Arnold et al have shown musculoskeletal modelling that provides a means of estimating muscle-tendon lengths and moment arms [1][2]. Other researchers have also made a generic model representing the musculoskeletal geometry and estimate the length of hamstrings and psoas muscles during normal and crouch gait [21][49][56].

For the rotational moment of the hip, Delp et al experimented with hip flexion in four cadavers [20], and Mansour et al quantified the rotational moment of the muscles about the hip. Van Sint Jan et al presented research on the joint kinematics of the hip motion and a method for registering 3D goniometry [60].

2.3.5 Hip Navigation Modelling

In the field of hip surgery navigation modelling, there are several approaches. DiGiola et al are developing a hip navigation system to help reduce the risk of dislocation after total hip replacement surgery. Their system included patient-specific location of the acetabular and a safe range of motion; guiding the surgeon to achieve the desired placement during surgery [22][23]. Mayo clinic has a virtual reality assisted surgery planning system for surgical planning and rehearsal, based on Analyze [73]. This virtual reality system transforms patient specific volumetric data, as obtained from CT (Computer Tomography) and MRI (Magnetic Resonance Imaging) scanners, into reasonable geometric (polygonal) models. For the hip implant, Bergmann et al. measured the implant temperatures and determined the temperature distribution in the hip joint region under varying conditions. A finite element study, based on the measurements, was used to calculate temperatures in and around the implant and to analyse the influence of different implant materials and mechanisms of heat transfer [7][8]. In a commercial context, 2C3D SA and Medivision provide navigated operation systems based on CT datasets [67][75].

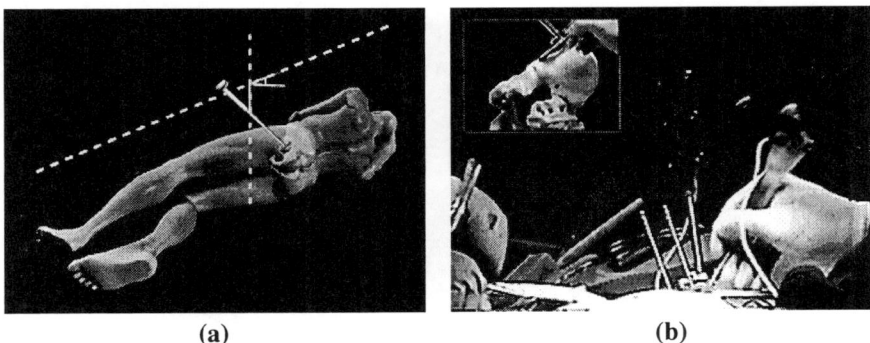

Fig. 6. Hip navigation system: (a) Test for cup alignment (b) Registration of collecting points from the patients pelvis with bony surface geometry

2.4 3D Surface Modelling

To create a three-dimensional functional model, a 3D model as a volume model or a surface model is needed. Recently, the surface models are widely used for the purpose of kinematic simulations because of the lack of geometry for the volume model.

A general method for creating a 3D surface model is to reconstruct 3D surfaces from the 2D contours of image datasets using specific algorithms [2][37][50][82]. 2D contours are obtained using manual segmentation for each image set or automatically by segmentation software. In the case of CT image datasets, automatic segmentation is made without difficulty. However, MRI data is difficult to segment automatically as MRI can produce a very noisy image and can result in a lot of missing information, therefore it is very slow to segment and results vary between expert interpretations. For this reason model based methods, that provide prior knowledge of the topology and geometry of the target object, are widely used [11][19][65]. Schiemann et al used a deformation method to register atlases with patient images; after an affine transformation, they used thin-plate-splines for the adaptation of a local shape [51].

Some commercial and non-commercial software can be used; for example, 3D-Doctor, 3D Slicer, Amira, Analyze, and Materialize are candidates for creating three-dimensional surface models even though they require a lot of manual work to produce an accurate 3D model [68][77][69][73][74].

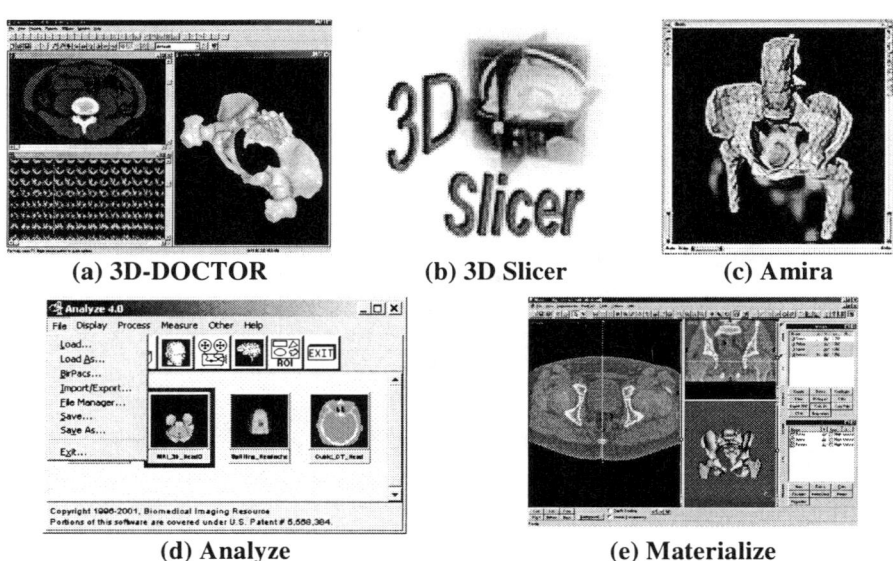

(a) 3D-DOCTOR   (b) 3D Slicer   (c) Amira

(d) Analyze   (e) Materialize

Fig. 7. 3D surface modelling software

3. What is the research still to be done?

We have found plenty of research on the 3D functional modelling of the hip and shoulder. With this enormous amount of literature, what other research needs to be done in order to obtain 3D accurate models of the hip and shoulder from MRI data? Specific research areas are discussed in detail in the following sections.

No single research alone can accomplish all desired benefits for patients who are suffering from bone and joint disorders. It is needed to create an integrated planning system to improve prevention, diagnosis and treatment for all patients and to empower patients to make decisions about their care [70].

3.1 Patient Specific Datasets

First of all, datasets are required to create 3D surface models. Visible human data, published by the National Library of Medicine, has been used in many research institutes, because these datasets provide complete high-resolution body data, and it is simple to distinguish between organs. However, although many research laboratories use these datasets [76], the datasets are of cadavers. In order to make an individualised accurate 3D model of a living person, the datasets also need to come from a living source, i.e. we require a method to create patient specific anatomical models.

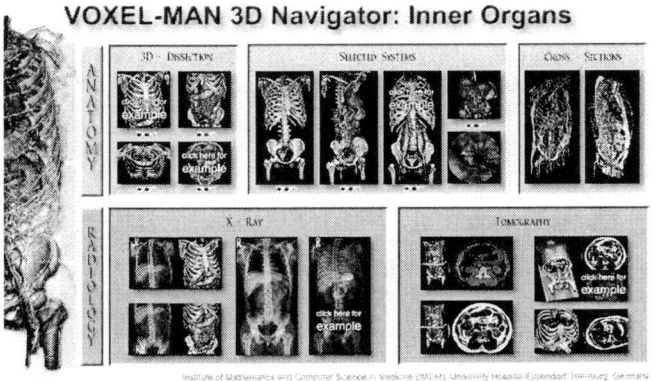

Fig. 8. VOXEL-MAN 3D-Navigator: Inner Organs

3.2 Obtaining Datasets

For an accurate 3D functional modelling, CT Images and MR Images are good candidates for obtaining individualised datasets. In the case of CT data, the difficulty is that patients are exposed to radiation; high photon energy may cause disease and is not permitted for healthy people. In the case of MR Images, problems arise in the segmenting of the initial images; high sensitivity to noise and missing information are two of the main problems. In addition, the segmentation of MR Images is extremely slow, time consuming work, as it currently can only be done manually.

3.3 Joint Reconstruction

The size of resulting 3D surface mesh is another problem when presented using the graphical system. For accurate functional modelling, the 3D surface model should also be very accurate, especially at the joint. The more accurate the surface model, the better the result. Creating an accurate surface model for a joint, but only a rough approximation for all others parts can be useful in reducing this complexity problem.

3.4 Organ and Joint Properties

To show the 3D surface model in a realistic way, the illumination model of human organs need to be considered. Datasets are always provided as grey-scale images;

hence the real colour of the living body itself is lost. Therefore, we need to have the real physical shape and colours of a subject in order to obtain a 3D model. In fact, in an ideal situation the material properties, their effects on the functionality of the joints, and the organ geometries must all be considered.

Generally these material properties (the density and strains of bones, labrums, cartilages, ligaments, muscles, and skin) can be applied in order to check the wearing of acetabular rim and bones. The accurate computation of stress in the acetabular rim is useful for the pre- and post-operative planning. The role of ligaments in motions would be useful in making models. It is unknown, especially for the hip model, if the role of the ligaments is mechanically limited, or the internal forces and muscular forces limit the motion.

3.5 Validation of Model and Motion

In addition, even after the 3D model has been produced, it is often difficult to validate whether the result is accurate, especially as each patient is different (i.e. there is no consistency between patients).

For accurate hip and shoulder modelling, the calculation of the centre of rotation and the range of motion should be found and then validated. It should not be estimated from the surface points, but by determining it from the all range of motions that are possible. This kind of study would require statistics compiled from authentic sources depending on age, gender, race, and pathology. For the surgical planning and the functional simulation, all the motions of the hip and shoulder have to be accurately captured from several people.

In the following section, one of the suggested research subjects, we propose an inter-patient registration method in order to obtain individual accurate surface models using MR Image dataset of several living people. It starts from the notation of registration.

4. Registration

Automatic methods for the segmentation of MRI are not common if at all realistically feasible. Our research is geared towards using an inter-patient registration technique to generate a surface model of a bone: i.e. to deform a generic bone model and fit this to an individual shape.

4.1 Classification of registration

Image registration is defined as a mapping between two images. Registration can be replaced with the problem of the task finding these transformation functions. Maurer et al and later Maintz et al categorized the registration including all the actual technical approaches [38][39][43]. Ritter et al explained for which context registration must be used [47]. This classification is not sufficient because individual modelling and analysis are not included in their description. Thus, we propose a new classification of registration purposes as follows:

- Patient image registration
    o Multi-modal registration, register same object by different sensors
        ▪ CT / MRI / SPECT / PET
        ▪ 2D and 3D
    o Viewpoint registration, register same object from different view
    o Temporal registration, register same object at different time
    o Template registration, specify features on the image
- Motion analysis, register sequential images to make the motion
- Inter-patient registration
    o Study the similarity and difference of patients
    o Making averaged template
    o Individual modelling

Multi-modal registration (in the case of medical imaging, CT, MRI, SPECT and PET are used) is a method to register the same subject using different types of sensors. Images from the same body part, taken from these sensors, need to be merged. The most well known case is in brain surgery. MR images are used to register with PET images. Malandian et al. and West et al classify the combination of these sensors and each one provides a description of this combination form different cases [40][64].

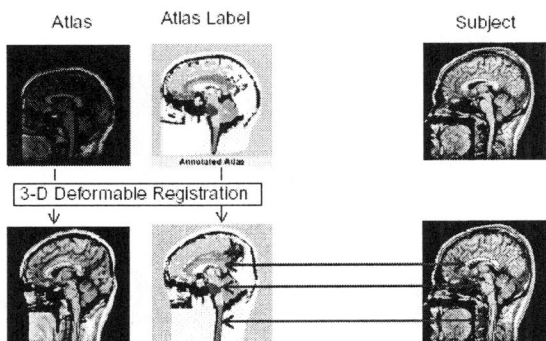

Fig. 9. Non-rigid registration of brain

There is also a classification of 2D and 3D registration included in this category. Bansal et al described 2D images and 3D volume registration [4]. While using CT scans, a simulation image is taken with weak energy. Due to the high photon energy, portal images are intrinsically of low contrast and poor sharpness. However, many treatments are moving to offer 3D conformal treatments. Thus, registration of the 3D images set to 2D portal images is necessary to quantify a 3D patient set-up before treatment. Viewpoint registration is a method used to register an image of the same scene taken from different viewpoints with same kinds of sensors, much like stereo imaging. Temporal registration is a method to register the same scene from the same viewpoint taken at different times. This method is used to create accurate image for surgery or noise reduction. Template recognition is a method to recognize the location of specific features or objects on the image. A reference image and a subject image are used. Chen et al use 3D hierarchical deformable registration algorithm and register features of the brain for MRI (Fig. 9) [15]. Davatzikos et al use a deformable surface model for MRI of the brain [17] including the classification by Ritter et al.

Registration techniques are not only used for these classical purposes but have been used recently for wider fields. Klein et al. use PET data and analyse heart motion [34] with energy minimization of corresponding voxels. This work is more like an image tracking or an image deformation than a registration technique. Another specific topic is inter-patient comparison, a method that takes two different patients and registers the images. This inter-patient registration method has several purposes to be used in medical field. One is the statistical study or statistical modelling. Warfield et al analyse anatomical variability of brain using MRI [61]. Ritter et al study optic nerve head and retina [47]. Another sub-item is to propose an averaged template model as Rueckert et al has made for the brain (Fig.10) [48]. Yao et al made a pelvis and femur model from CT images [66].

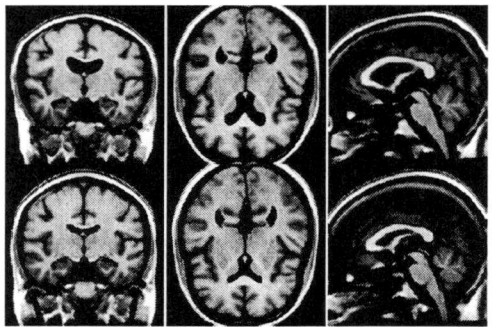

Fig. 10. Averaged model of a brain

The average model can be used to study the appearance of anatomical structure. It is also possible to deform the averaged template and build a patient model. This work will help image segmentation to be automated and it is the reason why we considered using registration. However, few researchers have worked in this field and we must further investigate which kinds of techniques are applicable to this field.

4.2 Registration techniques

Registration techniques for modelling individual body from MRI are not widely used due to the difficulty in obtaining data validation. However, other works of non-rigid inter-patient registration is applicable to our methods. There is a lot of previous work on non-rigid deformation. Maintz et al use cross-correlation for an elastic model deformation [39]. Davatzikos et al use elastic curve deformation in 3D volume [17]. These methods can be classified into: point based, line based, and surface based methods. Point-to-point registration is widely used [6][55]. Declerck et al used line-to-line registration [18]. Considering volumetric deformation, these methods are commonly used. Since our aim is to deform volumetric data and make an individual shape, point-to-point registration will not provide accurate result without using some landmark points. Line-to-line registration introduces a new difficulty, which is how to treat the line in volumetric space. If the line is kept within the 2D surface, the detail of the shape will be lost. Also, shape deformation after line registration is not an easy task.

B-Spline is widely used to deform 3D volume. Kybic et al used a B-Spline technique to deform the line and minimize the intensity level [35]. Thevenaz et al deformed the line in Parzen window density [54]. Leventon et al use Gaussian and Parzen window density for registration [36]. Chen et al use statistics of pixel intensity and the deformation is calculated by the probabilistic factor [15]. Internal energy will be the pixel intensity or gradient level in most cases of registration. Minimal entropy [62] or minimal potential energy [40] is used for the pixel comparison. Demons algorithm, to find where the boundary exists, is presented by Cachier et al [13].

4.3 Our work

For the purpose of inter-patient registration, information of intensity level is not kept constant for each individual. Therefore, the gradient will give better results. On the other hand external energy, to keep lines in certain shape, is also required for volumetric deformation.

In our case, the first goal of our project [83] was to create, from CT and MRI images, a few generic models of the hip that are animatable, i.e. with the topological information. The second long-term goal of our project is to be able, from any individual CT and MRI image data of the hip, to reconstruct an individual hip from the generic models. Since few researchers are working to create individual 3D models, we must decide which method is suitable for our purpose. The registration condition and techniques that we propose are as follows:

- Dimension: 3D
- Subject: Inter-patient MRI data
- Image: Theoretically any.
- Data: Two targets have different number of pixels for each axis
- Registration basis: Edge
- Global transformation: Affine transformation (rigid)
- Local registration: Non-rigid grid based
- Deformation: Edge based B-Spline

The reason why we use edge-based registration is because the pixel intensity of MR image is different for each scan. For inter-patient registration, the edge-based method is commonly used. An affine transformation is necessary because no landmarks are used for the deformation. Grid-based registration is an easy method to keep the anatomical structure of image volumes.

The registration method is examined at the femoral head from MR images. Fig.11 shows femoral head MRI volumetric data of a patient and the registration process. Fig.11(a) shows the femoral head parts extracted from the MR scan. Fig.11(b) image is B-Spline grid prepared in 3D space of the volumetric data. An averaged femoral head model is used to register to this patient model. Fig. 11(c) image is the 3D surface result that is generated from the deformed volume calculated by this registration.

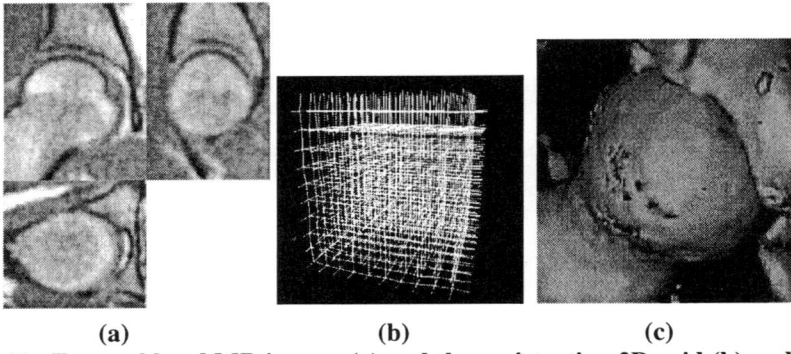

(a)　　　　　　　　(b)　　　　　　　　(c)
Fig. 11. Femoral head MR images (a) and the registration 3D grid (b) and the result (c)

To obtain an accurate model from the registration, the techniques should be validated using precision, accuracy, and stability. There are some validation methods for registration result [39]. However, our work does not need to be validated at twisting shape error or a point accuracy, because what we require is an accurate surface model of a bone to determine the anatomical structure. Accurate surface registration method and its corresponding validation method will be our future research.

We need to validate our bone model to determine if it is accurate enough for surgery. Other organs, such as muscle, cartilage and so on, will be added to the individual model. Motion of the bone depend on the range of motion should be accurate. This enormous amount of work should be done in order to create an accurate 3D functional model.

This survey will be an orientation of the medical modelling towards what kind of work has been made and what needs to be done.

Acknowledgement

This work is supported by CO-ME (Computer Aided and Image Guided Medical Interventions) project funded by Swiss National Research Foundation.

References

[1] A.S. Arnold, D.J. Asakawa, S.L. Delp, "Do the hamstrings and adductors contribute to excessive internal rotation of the hip in persons with cerebral palsy?", Gait and Posture Vol. 11, pp 181–190, 2000a.

[2] A.S. Arnold, S. Salinas, D.J. Asakawa, S.L. Delp, "Accuracy of muscle moment arms estimated from MRI-based musculoskeletal models of the lower extremity", Computer Aided Surgery Vol. 5, pp 108–119, 2000b.

[3] A.S. Arnold, "Quantitative descriptions of musculoskeletal geometry in persons with cerebral palsy: guidelines for the evaluation and treatment of crouch gait", Ph.D. Thesis, Northwestern University, Evanston, IL, 1999.

[4] R. Bansal, L. Staib, Z. Chen, A. Rangarajan, J. Knisely, R. Nath, J.S. Duncan, "A novel approach for the registration of 2D portal and 3D CT images for treatment setup verification in radiotherapy", MICCAI' 98, pp1075-1086, 1998.

[5] H. Bao, P.Y. Willems, "On the kinematic modeling and the parameter stimation of the human shoulder", Journal of Biomechanics, Vol. 32, pp 943-950, 1999.

[6] M. Betke, H. Hong, J.P. Ko, "Automatic 3D Registration of Lung Surfaces in Computed Tomography", Fourth international conference on medical image computing and computer-assisted intervention MICCAI 2001, pp 725-733, Utrecht, The Netherlands, October 2001.

[7] G. Bergmann, F. Graichen, A. Rohlmann, N. Verdonschot, G.H. van Lenthe, "Frictional Heating of Total Hip Implants, Part 1. Measurements with Patients" Journal of Biomechanics Vol. 34, pp 421-428 , 2001a.

[8] G. Bergmann, F. Graichen, A. Rohlmann, N. Verdonschot, G.H. van Lenthe, "Frictional Heating of Total Hip Implants, Part 2. Finite Element Study", Journal of Biomechanics Vol. 34, pp 429-435, 2001b.

[9] G. Bergmann, G. Deuretzbacher, M. Heller, F. Graichen, A. Rohlmann, J. Strauss, G. N.Duda, "Hip contact forces and gait patterns from routine activities", Journal of Biomechanics Vol. 34, pp 859-871, 2001c.

[10] M.D.K. Breteler, C.W.Spoor, F.C.T. Van der Helm, "Measuring muscle and joint geometry parameters of a shoulder for modeling purposes", Journal of Biomechanics Vol. 32, pp 1191-1197, 1997.

[11] M. Bro-Nielsen and S. Cotin, "Real-time volumetric deformable models for surgery simulation using finite elements and condensation", Computer Graphics Forum. Vol. 25, No. 3, pp 57-66, 1996.

[12] L.G. Brown, "A Survey of Image Registration Techniques", ACM Computing Surveys Vol. 24, No. 4, pp 325-376, December 1992.

[13] P. Cachier, X. Pennec, N. Ayache, "Fast non rigid matching by gradient descent: Study and improvements of the idemonsj algorithm", Technical Report 3706, Institut national de recherche en informatique et en automatique, June 1999.

[14] M. Capek, L. Mroz, R. Wegenkittl, "Robust and fast medical registration of 3D-multi-modality data sets", Medicon 2001, IX Mediterranean conference on medical and biological engineering and computing, Pula, Croatia, Part I, pp 515-518, June 2001.

[15] M. Chen, T. Kanade, D. Pomerleau, J. Schneider, "Probablistic registration of 3-D medical images", Technical report, CMU-RI-TR-99-16, Robotics Institute, Carnegie Mellon University, July 1999.

[16] I. W. Charlton, G. R. Johnson, "Application of spherical and cylindrical wrapping algorithms in a musculoskeletal model of the upper limb", Journal of Biomechanics Vol. 34, pp 1209–1216, 2001

[17] C. Davatzikos, "Spatial normalization of 3d brain images using deformable models", J Comput Assist Tomogr, Vol. 20, pp 656-665, July-August 1996.

[18] J. Declerck, G. Subsol, J.P. Thirion, N. Ayache, "Automatic retrieval of anatomical structures in 3D medical images", Proc. of Computer Vision, Virtual Reality and Robotics in Medicine, LNCS 905, pp153-162, Nice France, April 1995.

[19] H. Delingette and J. Montagnat, "General deformable model approach for model- based reconstruction", Proc. of the IEEE International Workshop on Model-based 3D Image Analysis, Bambay, India, January 1998.

[20] S.L. Delp, W.E. Hess, D.S. Hungerford, L.C. Jones, "Variation of hip rotation moment arms with hip flexion", Journal of Biomechanics Vol. 32, pp 493–501, 1999.

[21] S.L. Delp, J.P. Loan, M.G. Hoy, F.E. Zajac, E.L. Topp, J.M. Rosen, "An interactive graphics-based model of the lower extremity to study orthopaedic surgical procedures", IEEE Transactions on Biomedical Engineering Vol. 37, pp 757–767, 1990.

[22] A.M. DiGioia, III, B. Jaramaz, M. Blackwell, D. Simon, F. Morgan, J. Moody, C. Nikou, B. Colgan, C. Aston, R. LaBarca, E. Kischell, and T. Kanade , "An Image Guided Navigation System for Accurate Alignment in Total Hip Replacement Surgery", Tech. report CMU-RI-TR-98-18, Carnegie Mellon University, 1998a.

[23] A.M. DiGioia, D.C. Bruce, K. Nancy, "Computer Aided Surgery. Cybersurgery: Advanced Technologies for Surgical Practice", ed. R.M Satava, pp 121-139, 1998b.

[24] A.E. Engin, S.T. TuK mer, "Three-dimensional kinematic modeling of human shoulder - Part I: Physical model and determination of joint sinus cones", Journal of Biomechanical Engineering Vol. 111, pp 107-112, 1989.

[25] A.E. Engin, S.-M. Chen, "Statistical data base for the biomechanical properties of the human shoulder complex - I: Kinematics of the shoulder complex", Journal of Biomechanical Engineering Vol. 108, pp 215-221, 1986.

[26] A.E. Engin, R.D. Peindl, N. Berme, Kaleps, I., "Kinematic and force data collection in biomechanics by means of sonic emitters - I: Kinematic data collection methodology", Journal of Biomechanical Engineering Vol. 106, pp 204-211, 1984.

[27] S.J. Ferguson, J.T. Bryant, R. Ganz, K. Ito , "The influence of the acetabular labrum on hip joint cartilage consolidation: a poroelastic finite element model", Journal of Biomechanics Vol. 33, pp 953-960, 2000a.

[28] S.J. Ferguson, J.T. Bryant, K. Ito, "An investigation of the function of the acetabular labrum using a poroelastic finite element model", Journal of Bone and Joint Surgery [Br] 81-B (Suppl.1), pp 69, 1999.

[29] P. Genoud, H. Sadri, C. Dora, L. Bidaut, R. Ganz, P. Hoffmeyer, "The hip joint range of motion: a cadaveric study", 12th Conference of the European Society of Biomechanics, Dublin, pp 137, 2000.

[30] P.H. Gibson, M.K. Benson, "Congenital dislocation of the hip. Review at maturity of 147 hips treated by excision of the limbus and derotation osteotomy", Journal of Bone and Joint Surgery 64-B, pp 169-175, 1982.

[31] G. Hirota, S. Fisher, A. State, C. Lee, H. Fuchs, "An implicit finite element method for elastic solids in contact", Computer Animation 2001, November 2001.

[32] B. Jaramaz, C. Nikou, D. Simon, and A.M. DiGioia, III , "Range of Motion After Total Hip Arthroplasty: Experimental Verification of the Analytical Simulator", Tech. report CMU-RI-TR-97-09, Carnegie Mellon University, 1997.

[33] A.R. Karduna, P.W. McClure, L.A. Michener, "Scapular kinematics: effects of altering the euler angle sequence of rotations", Journal of Biomechanics Vol. 33, pp 1063-1068, 2000.

[34] G.J. Klein, "Forward deformation of PET volumes using non-uniform elastic material constraints", Information processing in medical imaging, 16th Annual Conference, Vol. 1613, A. Kuba, Ed.: Springer, pp 358-363, 1999.

[35] J. Kybic, P. Thevenaz, M. Unser, "Multiresolution spline warping for EPI registration", Proc. of the SPIE conference on mathematical imaging: Wavelet applications in signal and image processing VII, Denver CO, USA, Vol. 3813, pp 571-579, July 1999.

[36] M.E. Leventon, W.E.L. Grimson, "Multi-modal volume registration using joint intensity distributions", In Proc. MICCAI'98, pp 1057-1066, Cambridge, Massachusetts (USA), October 1998.

[37] C. Lorenz, N. Krahnstöver, "3D statistical shape models for medical image segmentation", Proc. of the second international conference on 3-D digital imaging and modeling (3DIM) '99, Ottawa, Canada, October 1999.

[38] J.B.A. Maintz, E.H.W. Meijering, M.A. Viergever, "General multimodal elastic registration based on mutual linformation", Image Processing, 1998.

[39] J.B.A. Maintz, "Retrospective registration of tomographic brain images", PhD Thesis, Utrecht University, December 1996.

[40] G. Malandain, S. Fernandez-Vidal, J.M. Rocchisani, "Physically based rigid registration of 3-D free-form objects: application to medical imaging", Rapport de recherche no. 2453, Institut National de recherche en informatique et en automatique, Sophia-Antipolis, 1995.

[41] N. Magnenat-Thalmann, F. Cordier, Construction of a Human Topological Model from Medical Data, IEEE Transactions on Information Technology in Biomedecine, Vol. 04, No. 2, p137, June 2000.

[42] W. Maurel, D. Thalmann, "Human shoulder modeling includng scapulo-thoracic constraint and joint sinus cones", Computers and Graphics, Vol. 24. pp 203–218, 2000.

[43] C. Maurer, J. Fitzpatrick, "A Review of Medical Image Registration", pp 17-44, Amer association of neurological surgeons, 1993.

[44] J.C. McCarthy, B. Busconi, "The role of hip arthroscopy in the diagnosis and treatment of hip disease", Canadian Journal of Surgery Vol. 38 (Suppl. 1), pp S13-17, 1995.

[45] J.n E. Novotny, Bruce D. Beynnon, Claude E. Nichols, "Modeling the stability of the human glenohumeral joint during external rotation", Journal of Biomechanics Vol. 33, pp 345-354, 2000.

[46] S.J. O'Brien, R.S. Schwartz, R.F. Warren, P.A. Torzilli, "Capsular restraints to anterior-posterior motion of the abducted shoulder: a biomechanical study". Journal of Shoulder and Elbow Surgery Vol. 4, pp 298-308, 1995.

[47] N. Ritter, R. Owens, J. Cooper, R. Eikelboom, K. Yogesan, P. Van Saarloos, "Registration of stereo and temporal images of the retina", IEEE Transactions on medical imaging, Vol. 18, No. 5, pp 404-418, May 1999.

[48] D. Rueckert, A.F. Frangi, J.A. Schnabel, "Automatic construction of 3D statistical deformation models using non-rigid registration", Medical image computing and computer-assisted intervention, MICCAI'01, W.J. Niessen and M.A. Viergever (Eds). Lecture Notes in Computer Science, vol. 2208 - Springer Verlag, Berlin, Germany, pp 77-84, 2001.

[49] LM Schutte, SW Hayden, JR Gage, "Lengths of hamstrings and psoas muscles during crouch gait: effects of femoral anteversion", J Orthop Res Vol. 15, pp 615–621, 1997.

[50] W. Schroeder, K. Martin, W. Lorensen, "The Visualization Toolkit" (2nd ed.), Prentice-Hall, New Jersey, 1997.

[51] T. Schiemann, K.H. Höhne, C. Koch, A. Pommert, M. Riemer, R. Schubert, and U. Tiede, "Interpretation of tomographic images using automatic atlas lookup", Visualization in Biomedical Computing III, Proc. SPIE 2359 Rochester, MN, pp 457-465, 1994.

[52] L.J. Soslowsky, E.L. Flatow, L.U. Bigliani, V.C. Mow, "Articular geometry of the glenohumeral joint". Clinical Orthopaedics and Related Research 285, pp 181-190, 1992a.

[53] M. Teschner, J. Richolt, R. Kikinis, B. Girod, "Computer-assisted analysis of hip joint flexibility", Proc. of Image and Multidimensional Digital Signal Processing '98, pp 63-66, Alpbach, Austria, July 12-16, 1998.

[54] P. Thevenaz, M. Unser, "Spline pyramids for intermodal image registration using mutual information", In SPIE conference proc. on wavelet applications in signal and image processing V, Vol. 3169, pp 236-247, 1997.

[55] J.Ph. Thirion. "New feature points based on geometric invariants for 3D image registration", International Journal of Computer Vision, Vol. 18, No. 2, pp 121-137, May 1993.

[56] N.S. Thompson, R.J. Baker, A.P. Cosgrove, IS Corry, HK Graham, "Musculoskeletal modelling in determining the effect of botulinum toxin on the hamstrings of patients with crouch gait", Dev Med Child Neurol Vol. 40, pp 622–625, 1998.

[57] C H Tschanauer et al. Hip International, Vol 8. pp 233-238, 1998.

[58] F.C.T. Van der Helm, "Analysis of the kinematic and dynamic behavior of the shoulder mechanism", Journal of Biomechanics Vol. 27, pp 527-550, 1994a.

[59] F.C.T. Van der Helm, "A finite element musculoskeletal model of the shoulder mechanism", Journal of Biomechanics Vol. 27, pp 551-569, 1994b.

[60] Van Sint Jan, "The VACKHUM project: Presentation and preliminary results", Poster, ISB2001 Congress, Zurich, July 2001.

[61] S.K. Warfield, J. Rexilius, P.S. Huppi, T.E. Inder, E.G. Miller, W.M. Wells III, G.P. Zientara, F.A. Jolesz, R. Kikinis, "A binary entropy measure to assess nonrigid registration algorithms", MICCAI 2001, pp266-274, 2001.

[62] S.K. Warfield, F. Jolesz, R. Kikinis, "A high performance computing approach to the registration of medical imaging data", Parallel Computing, Vol 24, pp 1345-1368, September 1998b.

[63] J.J.P. Warner, M.K. Bowen, X.H. Deng, J.A. Hanna, S.P. Arnoczky, R.F. Warren, "Articular contact patterns of the normal glenohumeral joint". Journal of Shoulder and Elbow Surgery Vol. 7, pp 381-388, 1998.

[64] J. West, M. Fitzpatrick, "Comparison and evaluation of retrospective intermodality brain image registration techniques", Journal of Computer Assisted Tomography, Vol. 21, pp 554-566, July-August 1997.

[65] C. Xu, D.L. Pham, J.L. Prince, M.E. Etemad, and D.N. Yu. "Reconstruction of the central layer of the human cerebral cortex from MR images", Proc. of first international conference on medical image computing and computer-assisted intervention, W. M. Wells, et al. (Eds.), Springer Verlag, Berlin, pp 481-488, 1998.

[66] J. Yao, R. Taylor, "A bone density atlas based on tetrahedral meshes", Fifth annual North American program on computer assisted orthopedic surgery, CAOS/USA, 2001.

[67] http://www.2c3dmedical.com/
[68] http://www.ablesw.com/
[69] http://www.amiravis.com/
[70] http://www.bonejointdecade.org/
[71] http://www.bonejointdecade.org/organisation/default.html

[72] http://www.fbw.vu.nl/research/Lijn_A4/shoulder/Mayo_study_intro.htm
[73] http://www.mayo.edu/
[74] http://www.materialise.com/
[75] http://www.medivision.ch/
[76] http://www.nlm.nih.gov/research/visible/animations.html
[77] http://www.slicer.org/
[78] http://swallow.monument1.jhmi.edu/
[79] http://www.uke.uni-hamburg.de/institute/imdm/idv/vm3dn/innerorgans.en.html
[80] http://www.wbmt.tudelft.nl/mms/dsg/index.htm
[81] http://www.wbmt.tudelft.nl/mms/dsg/intersg/isg.html
[82] http://www-sop.inria.fr/prisme/logiciel/nuages.html.en
[83] http://www.co-me.ch/prj10.html

Simulating a Human Society: The Challenges

Daniel Thalmann

**Computer Graphics Lab
EPFL
CH 1015 Lausanne
Daniel.Thalmann@epfl.ch
http://ligwww.epfl.ch**

Abstract

Simulating a human society is a very complex interdisciplinary problem. In this paper, we try to show some important aspects to create inhabited worlds where virtual people can interact, co-operate, perceive the world and the society. Main aspects are flexible motion control, perception of the real and the virtual world, and high-level behavior. Concepts are illustrated in the case-study of emergent crowds.

Keywords: Virtual Human, perception, emergent crowd, motivation, virtual sensors

1. Introduction

Our ultimate research objective is the simulation of Virtual Worlds inhabited by a Virtual Human Society, where Virtual Humans will co-operate, negotiate, make friends, communicate, group and ungroup, depending on their likes, moods, emotions, goals, fears, etc. But such interaction and corresponding groups should not be programmed. Behaviour should emerge as a result of a multi-agent system sharing a common environment, in our case, sharing a virtual environment. For example in a panic situation we do not model the group behaviour, because each human reacts differently depending for example on its level of fear. If we model the individual entity, there will be groups of different behaviours (not programmed explicitly) as result of the interaction of common individual behaviours. Our simulations consist of group of autonomous virtual human agents existing in dynamic virtual 3D environment. Virtual humans have some natural needs like hunger, tiredness, etc. which guide selection of their behaviours. In order to behave in believable way these agents also have to act in accordance with their surrounding environment, be able to react to its changes, to the other agents and also to the actions of real humans interacting with the virtual world. Our aim is to develop a behaviour model that is simple enough to allow for real-time execution of group of agents, yet still sufficiently complex to provide interesting behaviours. We extend the concepts we have developed for multi-agent simulations to encompass more autonomy at the level of individuals. We enhance our current multi-agent model with artificial life concepts, which will allow virtual humans to live and work autonomously in virtual environment. Virtual actors have their own motivations and needs, are able to sense and explore their environment, and their action selection mechanism determine suitable actions to take at any time. For this purpose, architecture allowing merging of individuals' artificial life simulation with the current multi-agent model is developed.

One important point in the simulation is the believability of the individual virtual humans, they should behave as real humans, including capabilities such as: perception, language understanding and generation, emotions, goal-driven behaviour, reactivity to the environment including with other virtual humans (Fig.1), memory, inference, appearance of thought and personalities, interpersonal interactions, social skills and possibly others.

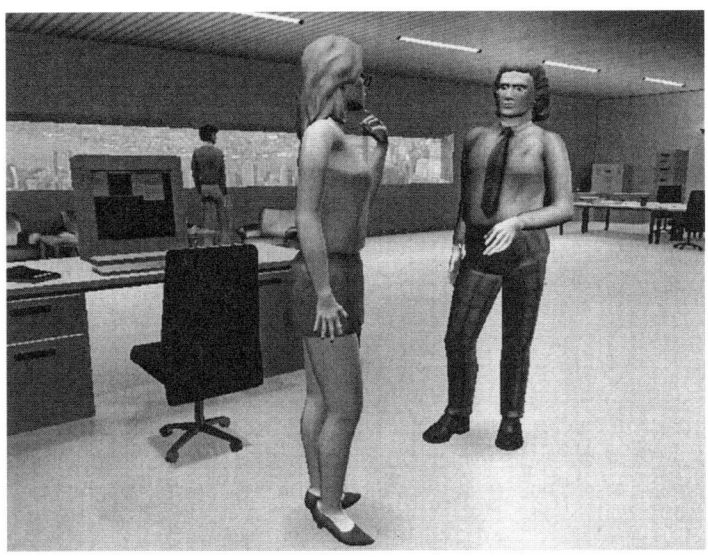

Figure 1. Communication between Virtual Humans

Virtual Humans in a society require four main ingredients:

1. High-level behavior, which concerns decision-making and finally intelligence, motivation, and social behavior
2. Perception: virtual sensors (for Virtual Worlds) and real sensors (for Real Worlds)
3. Animation: Flexible motion control
4. Graphics: Realistic aspect

We will not discuss in this paper the graphics part but emphasize the three other key topics, starting from the animation to end with high-level behaviors. Then, we will consider the case of emergent behavior for crowds.

2. Flexible motion control

The main goal of computer animation is to synthesize the desired motion effect which is a mixing of natural phenomena, perception and imagination. The animator designs the object's dynamic behavior with his mental representation of causality. He/she imagines how it moves, gets out of shape or reacts when it is pushed, pressed, pulled, or twisted. So, the animation system has to provide the user with motion control tools able to translate his/her wishes from his/her own language.

In the context of Virtual Humans, a Motion Control Method (MCM) specifies how the Virtual Human is animated and may be characterized according to the type of information it privileged in animating this Virtual Human. For example, in a keyframe system for an articulated body, the privileged information to be manipulated is the angle. In a forward dynamics-based system, the privileged information is a set of forces and torques; of course, in solving the dynamic equations, joint angles are also obtained in this system, but we consider these as derived information. In fact, any MCM will eventually have to deal with geometric information (typically joint angles), but only geometric MCMs explicitly privilege this information at the level of animation control.

But, how to do it ? A database of motion capture sequences is not the solution, key frame is not the solution, inverse kinematics is not the solution. But, they are part of the solution. Once an acceptable motion segment has been created, either from keyframing, motion capture or physical simulations, reuse of it is important. By separating motion or skeleton generation into a time-consuming preprocess and a fast process based on efficient data representation, it fits well to real-time synthesis for applications such as game and virtual reality while taking advantage of a rich set of examples. Much of the recent research in computer animation has been directed towards editing and reuse of existing motion data. Stylistic variations are learned from a training set of very long unsegmented motion-capture sequences [1]. An interactive multi-resolution motion editing is proposed for fast and fine-scale control of the motion [2]. Whereas most of other methods may produce results violating the laws of mechanics [3], an editing method maintaining physical validity is suggested [4].

In order to deal with these problems, our work is based on a multi-step function approximation for the interpolation with motion data compressed by principal component analysis. Then, basis functions less than the number of examples can be used, no global linear system needs to be solved and only a few dozens of real-valued interpolations have to done even if densely sampled data of motion capture are used. This enables motion models constructed out of a rich set of examples and fast computed. Therefore, motion models can be controlled by attributes invariant for each individuals such as age, gender, height and weight, which require many of example motions from different individuals: for instance, male-female walks and young-old walks. Differences in age, gender, height or weight lead into not only different motions but also different skeletons. To be complete, hence, parametric skeleton models are also necessary, which are constructed by the same technique of the function approximation. In our approach, out of 8 people varying in age, gender, height and weight, we captured 68 motion data of 'punching' over various target positions and also measured skeleton data such as lengths of arms and legs. After being aligned with respect to time, motion data went through PCA for the dimension reduction. The first 24 eigenvectors were enough to describe 99% variations among the motion data so that these data were represented in a 24-dimensional coordinate systems formed by the eigenvectors. Interpolation functions are constructed in the iterative way both for the motion model and the skeleton model. Once constructed, these models can compute and synthesize corresponding motion and skeleton data upon a set of the control parameters for age, gender, height, weight and target location: an articulated body structure is modified according to data computed by the skeleton model. The quality or precision of these parametric models degrades smoothly with decreasing number of Gaussians used in the interpolation functions.

But in the future, we need more powerful models and/or methods to dynamically generate movements.

3. Perception and sensors

Perception is the primary cause of action in the society. This means that we cannot build a Virtual Human society without considering the way Virtual Humans perceive the world and the society in particular. Moreover, we should consider the interaction with a virtual human as: triggering some meaningful reaction in the environment in response actions such as body, social gestures or verbal output from a participant, To realize this perception, Virtual Humans should have sensors, mainly for vision, audition, and tactile sensation. Now, we have to consider two cases:

- From the Virtual World: everything is available but it should be filtered for believability
- From the Real World: it takes devices: camera, microphone, haptic devices and recognition algorithms

In the first case, Virtual Humans should be equipped with synthetic or virtual sensors [5] like visual, tactile and auditory sensors. These sensors should be used as a basis for implementing everyday human behaviour such as visually directed locomotion, handling objects, and responding to sounds and utterances. The actor-environment interface, or the synthetic sensors, constitute an important part of a behavioral animation system. As sensorial information drastically influences behavior, the synthetic sensors should simulate the functionality of their organic counterparts. Due to real-time constraints, we did not think that it is necessary to model biological models of sensors. Therefore, synthetic vision [6] only makes efficient visibility tests using powerful graphics engine that produce a Z-buffered color image representing an agent's vision. A tactile point-like sensor may be represented by a simple function evaluating the global force field at its position. The synthetic "ear" of an agent will be represented by a function returning the on-going sound events. What is important for an actor's behavior is the functionality of a sensor and how it filters the information flow from the environment, and not the specific model of the sensor.

In the case of perception of the real world, the information is not part of the Virtual World. It takes real devices to "capture" this information and bring it to the Virtual World, that is to the Virtual Humans. Their natural interaction with objects will change the state of simulation and trigger some meaningful response. A good example for becoming part of the environment is shown in Figure 2 where a user's actions are captured by a magnetic tracking system, and a posture recognition is performed [7]. In this system participant uses his own body to interact with the virtual environment. An autonomous virtual human responses according the result of a gesture/posture recognition algorithm.

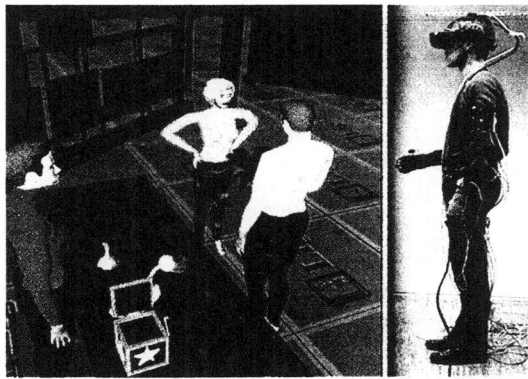

Figure 2. Action recognition using magnetic trackers

To have a similar interactive application in a mixed environment without any cumbersome tracking device, requires a real-time noninvasive tracker for complete human body. Only a computer vision based tracking system would fit this specification, however current vision trackers are not up to full body tracking and giving similar results like a magnetic tracker. To overcome this limitation we should track simpler objects than a human, but still having a large range of interaction possibilities. In our approach, tracked objects have semantic values known to real humans and to the mixed environment simulation. We made several experiments [8] to test the robustness of our algorithm before using it in a large-scale application. Figure 3 presents a snapshot of tracking experiments in the case of checkers. To develop our checkers game simulator we need to track real pieces and to place correctly a virtual human and virtual pieces we need to track the board. Tracking the board is performed by our model-based tracker, the result is used to track the camera movements.

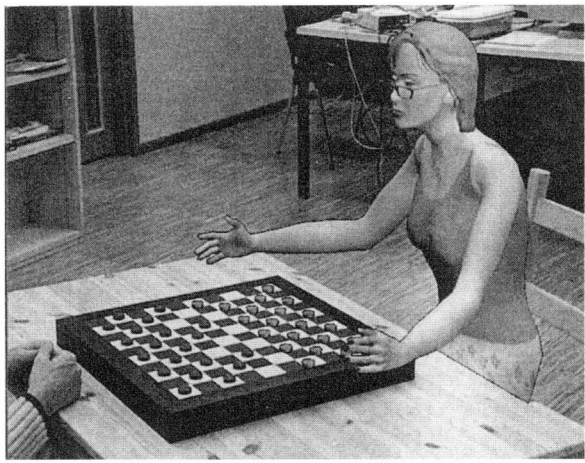

Figure 3. Tracking of real checker pieces in a mixed environment

4. High-level behaviors

To model human society, it is important to consider motivations and social behavior. Interesting implication of introducing communication abilities for agents could be in modelling of emergent collective behaviour. Emergent crowds (see next Section) can be formed based on transfer of both emotional states and behaviours for example by verbal and non-verbal communication between physically close agents. Such transfer can depend on personalities of involved agents, where charismatic persons will be more easily able to affect others, or where some agents with high level of dominance will be resisting to adopt crowd behaviour. Further possibility of such emotional and behavioural influences can be used to indirectly control the crowd, where one of the agents would be externally guided by real human user.

What is a complex behavior is not really clear. We could find in daily life a lot of examples of simple but complex situations. Let's take two examples.

1. Suppose a pedestrian walking along a boardwalk, suddenly he perceives another pedestrian coming exactly on the same line. What to do ? This is a common problem that we solve without expliciting the strategy, this is dependent on psychological factors.

2. How to make realistic people eating ? Some specific behavior have to be taken into account, like for example eating a T-Bone steak. In this case people generally (when they are rightist) use the right hand for the knife and the left for the fork when they cut their steak, but then they move their fork into the right hand to eat.

4.1 Motivations

Motivation is also a key cause of action and we will consider basic motivations as essential to model in the Virtual World, providing a true Virtual Life. We adapt basic actor motivations and needs to urban situations, where most actions involve interactions with the environment, especially manipulation of objects in natural situations like eating or drinking. We focus on common-life situations, where the actor senses and explores his environment, and following an action selection mechanism, determines the suitable actions to take. For this, we consider a mechanism of action selection based on a free flow hierarchy associated to a hierarchical classifier. The hierarchy of our model will contain four levels (depicted in Figure 4):

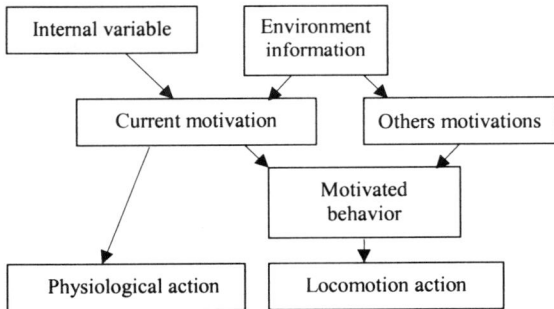

Figure 4. Simplified motivational model of action selection for virtual humans

The free flow hierarchy [9] permits to take into account different types of motivations and also information coming from the environment perception. The key idea is that, during the propagation of the activity in the hierarchy, no choices are made before the lowest level in the hierarchy represented by the actions is reached. The hierarchical classifier [10] provides a good solution to model complex hierarchies by reducing the search domain of the problem, and using rules with weights. Also, we can easily make behavioural sequences (composed by a sequence of actions). As a result, the virtual character can move to a specific place to perform a physiological action and satisfy the motivations no matter where it is. In another words, the main role of the action selection mechanism is to maintain the internal variables under the threshold by choosing the correct actions. Actions involving interactions are preferably chosen because they are defined to be directly beneficial for the virtual human. Otherwise, the virtual human is instructed to walk and reach the place where the motivation can be satisfied. During the simulation, the model is fed with parameters describing the current state of the actor concerning each of the motivations, and by flowing inside the hierarchical structure, will correctly trigger the concerned actions. After an action is selected as a response to satisfy one of the actor's motivations, the state parameter of the internal variable is adapted accordingly. An example is shown in Figure 5.

Fig. 5. Virtual life simulation: by default, the Virtual Human is working, waiting for a motivation (for instance, drinking) to be activated. The food is kept into the kitchen, as seen in the background.

4.2 Social behavior

In order to realistically simulate how humans interact in a specific social context, it is necessary to precisely model the type of relationship they have and specify how it affects their interpersonal behaviour. Sociologists have identified several dimensions that are important to provide for the simulation of any group behaviour: 1) power (dominance and submissiveness of the agents), 2) attraction (friendliness and unfriendliness), 3) instrumental control (hierarchical rank) and 4) emotional expressiveness. For the development of the agents' behaviour in an organizational context, taking into account the hierarchical relationship is of course crucial, but the importance of the more informal dimensions should not be underestimated.

The agents' behaviour within a group is highly dependant on their location in the sociometric structures but also on their own social identity. This social characterization should be done using social-statistical variables, 1) culture, 2) gender and 3) age, and taking into account the agent's roles within the group. A distinction between 4) task roles (e.g. function), and 5) socioemotional roles (e.g. confident) is often used. An additional 6) status rating (prestige) can also be introduced. Social interactions requires to reproduce verbal communication. In such a graphical environment, inter-agents communication would be more than just an exchange of messages. We need to create models for sound propagation, which should be suitable for verbal communication.

To increase the believability of behaviors resulting from emotions we include nonverbal communication elements. A nonverbal communication is concerned with postures and their indications on what people are feeling. Postures are the means to communicate and are defined by a specific position of the arms and legs and angles of the body. .It is also essential to notice that the effects of nonverbal communication, though unconscious, are nevertheless important. Let us have an example: two persons communicating with each other (Fig.6) and rejecting a third one. The first two persons are standing in an open triangle formation commonly used for friendly conversation. It leaves a potential opening for a third person to join them. Such a person attempts to join the group, but the first two respond by rejecting him out. One raises his left arm, forming a barrier. The other deliberately avoids making eye contact with the newcomer. They have formed a closed formation, suppressing any possibility for a new person to join them. The newcomer feels rejected and leaves unhappily.

Figure 6. Intercommunication

5. Emergent Crowds

Our work aims at simulation of larger number of virtual human agents for interactive virtual environments such as virtual reality training systems [11]. Compared to the other crowd modeling approaches we are focusing on more complex behaviors of many agents in dynamic environments with possible user interaction. In previous works crowds have been considered as already formed units with more or less uniform behavior placed in particular environments corresponding only to limited purpose of the simulation e.g. pedestrians just fleeing from burning building [12] or marching crowd during demonstration the crowd assigning people to particular groups and determining their behaviors. Collective behavior emerges from interaction of individuals [13], crowds are dynamically assembled and disassembled and over the time they change their behavior. We take inspiration from the field of sociology: [14] argues that members of a gathering don't act as a whole but rather that subsections of the number assembled react in similar way, which, when observed externally appears as a collective behavior. In our system crowd is modeled as collection of individuals, which react to the environment, other agents and real human participants of the simulation and can have very different behaviors both for one agent in different situations and for many agents in the same situation.

Figure 7. Crowd in virtual park: a) before emergency, b) after gas leak happened

We used implementation of our emergent crowd system to reproduce simple mulation consists of group of autonomous virtual human agents existing in dynamic virtual 3D environment. In order to behave in believable way these agents have to act in accordance with their surrounding environment, be able to react to its changes, to the other agents and also to the actions of real humans interacting with the virtual world. Agents contain set of internal attributes corresponding to various psychological or physiological states (e.g. level of curiosity, tiredness, etc.), set of higher-level complex behaviors and set of rules determining selection of these behaviors. Events provide way of agents' interaction with their environment, other agents or human participants of the simulation. Each agent is able to receive events from the environment objects, other agents or user interface. Combinations of different received events and different levels of agent's attributes produce both changes of its internal attributes and change of the overt behavior.

Our behavior model is based on combination of rules [15],[16] and finite state machines [17] for controlling agent's behavior using layered approach. First layer deals with the selection of higher-level complex behavior appropriate to agent's situation, second layer implements these behaviors using low-level actions provided by the virtual human [18]. At the higher level, rules select complex behaviors (such as flee) according to agent's state (constituted by attributes) and the state of the virtual environment (conveyed by events). In rules we specify for who (e.g. particular agent, or agents in particular group) and when the rule is applicable (e.g. at defined time, after receiving event or when some attribute reached specified value), and what is the consequence of rule firing (e.g. change of agent's high-level behavior or attribute). Example of such rule is:

FOR ALL
WHEN EVENT = in_danger_area AND ATTRIBUTE fear > 50%
THEN BEHAVIOR FLEE

At the lower level, complex behaviors are implemented by hierarchical finite state machines. Each behavior is realized by one FSM which drives selection of the low-level actions for the virtual human (like move to location, play short animation sequence), manages connections with the environment (like path queries, or event sending) and also can call other FSMs to delegate subtasks such as path following. There are two types of complex behaviors. First we can specify scripted behavior which is more precise, but less autonomous and with less environment coupling by using explicit sequences of low-level actions. Or second we can let agents perform autonomously complex behaviors with the feedback from the environment. Examples of such autonomous behaviors are wandering, fleeing, neutralizing the threat, or help requesting and providing.

6. What do we need more to model a believable human society ?

This is an extremely complex question. But there are some avenues we can explore. In particular, we could suggest to take into account the following aspects:

- It is important in some simulations to add basic needs to Virtual Humans, they should be hungry, thirsty or even have sexual desires.
- Virtual Humans should never do nothing, this means that we should add nervous gestures. Moreover, Virtual Humans should breathe to be human.
- We can expect that Virtual Humans can remember facts of their life and can also forget about them, this means that a realistic memory should be modeled.
- Unfortunately, real humans are never perfect, in particular, they make a lot of mistakes. So Virtual Humans should also commit errors in their life. But, this is a challenge because, computers are better for modeling perfection than imperfection.
- Emotional aspects should be emphasized, for example, it is essential to introduce stress when Virtual Humans act in certain conditions.
- Why Virtual Humans should be always fair when real people are not ?
- Virtual Humans should not always stop to speak when others speak, the y should be less polite to be believable
- Finally, Virtual Humans will be more believable when they will be conscious if ever they can be conscious

Does it mean that Virtual Humans should tend to become complex like real humans ? This is an important question. In fact, this is context-dependent. As a guide to find information on the Web: we just want an efficient agent. However, we are not interested to deal with an agent that has problem with his wife or complains about his/her headaches.

But, in a simulation of behavior in case of emergency, we want believable humans: panic, stress, leadership are the key issue. It is essential to take into account psychological aspects.

Finally, the goal of our research effort is to develop a behavioral model for animation of believable virtual humans (actors) in virtual environments. In this context, believability means that the behavior of a synthetic actor has to be indistinguishable from that of a human. For instance, an actor inhabiting a typical virtual environment composed of objects and other actors, only concerned to perform a given task without reacting to objects or actors it encounters or to what these actors are doing would not look believable. The behavior of these actors would be more that of a robot than that of a human. To be believable, an actor has to be affected by what takes place around it and needs to engage in social behaviors with other actors. Therefore, the behavioral model of an actor needs to be versatile enough to allow a change of behavior, the emotional state of the actor must be reflected and must affect its behavior, the interpersonal relationships with the other actors must be taken into account and possibly bring the actor to engage in social interactions.

7. Conclusion

The simulation of the dynamics of human societies is not an easy task, and we propose a bottom-up approach, which consists in defining the human entity as a single, autonomous and independent entity (called Agent), and then immerse many of them in a common environment to let them interact and co-operate as the environment evolves.

To achieve our goal and create Virtual Human societies, we try to extend the concepts we have developed for crowd simulations to encompass more autonomy at the level of individuals. For interactive training simulations such as modelling of crowd responding to emergency situations we extend our current crowd model with inclusion of multiple dynamic physical and emotional attributes for individuals in crowds. Such attributes are used to represent various states of agents such as levels of fear, aggressivity, tiredness or injuries on different body parts affecting both agents behaviours and rendering of agents appearances. Agents are able to access states of other agents and have possibly influence on it, e.g. for modelling of people calming down other people in panic decreasing thus their fear level.

Acknowledgments

The author is grateful to the people who contributed to this research, especially Jean-Sebastien Monzani, Etienne De Sevin, Anthony Guye-Vuillème, Ik Soo Lim, Branislav Ulicny, and Soraia Musse, and Mireille Clavien for the design of images. The research was sponsored by the Swiss National Research Foundation.

References

[1] M. Brand and A. Hertzmann, "Style machines", Proc. SIGGRAPH 2000, 2000, pp. 183 – 192.

[2] J. Lee and S. Y. Shin, "A hierarchical approach to interactive motion editing for human-like figures", Proc. SIGGRAPH 1999, 1999, pp. 39 –48.

[3] A. Witkin and Z. Popovic, "Motion warping" in Proceedings of SIGGRAPH '95, 1995, pp. 105 – 108.

[4] Z. Popovic and A. Witkin, "Physically based motion transformation", Proc. SIGGRAPH 1999, 1999, pp. 11 – 20.

[5] D. Thalmann, "A New Generation of Synthetic Actors: the Interactive Perceptive Actors", Proc. Pacific Graphics '96 Taipeh, Taiwan, 1996, pp.200-219.

[6] O. Renault, N. Magnenat-Thalmann, and D. Thalmann, "A Vision-based Approach to Behavioural Animation", Journal of Visualization and Computer Animation, Vol.1, No1, 1990, pp.18-21.

[7] L. Emering, R. Boulic, and D. Thalmann, "Conferring Human Action Recognition Skills to Life-like Agents", Applied Artificial Intelligence Journal, Special Issue on 'Animated Interface Agents: Making them Intelligent,Vol.13, No4-5, 1999, pp.539-565.

[8] S. Balcisoy, M. Kallmann, R. Torre, P. Fua, and D. Thalmann, "Interaction Techniques with Virtual Humans in Mixed Environments", Proc. International Symposium on Mixed Reality, Tokyo, Japan, 2001

[9] T. Tyrrell. "The use of hierarchies for action selection", 1993.

[10] J. Y. Donnart, and J. A. Meyer, "Learning Reactive and Planning Rules in a Motivationally Autonomous Animal". IEEE Transactions on Systems, Man, and Cybernetics, part B: Cybernetics, June, 1996, 26(3), pp. 381-395.

[11] B. Ulicny and D. Thalmann., "Crowd simulation for interactive virtual environments and VR training systems", Proc. Eurographics Workshop on Animation and Simulation'01, Springer-Verlag, 2001.

[12] D. Helbing, I. Farkas, and T. Vicsek, "Simulating dynamical features of escape panic", Nature, 407:487-490, 2000.

[13] N. Gilbert, "Simulation: an emergent perspective", 1996. http://www.soc.surrey.ac.uk/research/simsoc/tutorial.html

[14] McPhail, C., "The Myth of Maddening Crowd", NY:Aldine De Gruyter, 1991.

[15] D. Kalra and A. H. Barr, "Modeling with Time and Events in Computer Animation", Proc. Eurographics'92, pp. 45-58, Blackwell, 1992.

[16] P. S. Rosenbloom, J. E. Laird, A. Newell, "The Soar papers: Research on Artificial Intelligence", MIT Press, 1993.

[17] J. Cremer, J. Kearney, and Y. Papelis, "HCSM: Framework for Behavior and Scenario Control in Virtual Environments", ACM Transactions on Modeling and Computer Simulation, 5(3):242-267, 1995.

[18] R. Boulic, P. Becheiraz, L. Emering, and D. Thalmann, "Integration of Motion Control Techniques for Virtual Human and Avatar Real-Time Animation", Proc. VRST '97, pp. 111-118, ACM Press, 1997.

Content-based Image Indexing and Retrieval in Compressed Domain

J. Jiang, Department of Electronic Imaging & Media Communications
University of Bradford, United Kingdom

Abstract

As millions of images are being created and stored in computer networks and more and more images are already presented in compressed format at the source, it becomes increasingly important to consider direct image indexing and retrieval in compressed domain rather than in pixel domain. In this paper, we describe a range of such algorithms out of our recent research work to provide a platform for further research and further development of robust, efficient and effective software tools for many applications in the community of IT and computer science. As worldwide efforts for practical image compression are represented by JPEG international standardization activities, this presentation will focus on automatic image indexing directly in the compressed domain via: (a) DCT-based JPEG; (b) wavelets-based JPEG-2000; and (c) prediction-based JPEG-LS. Since human interpretation of image content is characterized by high level activities, attempts by the community of image processing and computer vision in extracting low-level features in pixel domain invites many questions about the accuracy of image indexing and retrieval. To this end, feature-extraction approach or automatic signatures of images often fail to produce satisfactory solution for retrieving images based on their content. As a result, pixel values are often desired for such content analysis or visual inspections. Therefore, one section out of this paper is contributed to the description of our work towards extracting not only features, but also a complete image for such content access. Compared with full decompression, the image extraction technology described features in low computing cost and low complexity, which essentially bridges the gap between the compressed domain and the pixel domain.

Keywords: image indexing and retrieval, image compression and JPEG

1. Introduction

Content-based image indexing and retrieval has attracted strong interests from a range of different research communities, including computer science, information systems, image processing and software engineering. While existing active research has produced a large number of such content-based image retrieval systems [1-8], the major challenge comes from the fact the low-level feature extraction approaches fail to match the high-level content interpretation and understanding activities inside the human vision. In most of the systems, such as QBIC[1], Photobook[2], SWIM[3], Virage[4], Visualseek[5], Netra[6], MARS[7] and WEBimager[8], image content is primarily characterized by a set of attributes or features including color[17], texture[10,11,22], shape[24,35] etc. and image retrieval is performed by matching the features of the query with those inside the database via some certain distance measurement or statistics approaches[16]. The main problem, however, is that the users often do not interpret the content in terms of those low-level features. As a result, poor performances are encountered for most of these existing systems. This is particularly true for those semantic queries. On the other hand, almost all visual information are stored in compressed formats, among which the format defined by Joint Picture Expert Group (JPEG) is one of the most popular formats widely used on either Internet or image databases [33]. Following this trend, a wave of new research on direct feature extraction from the compressed images is now gathering momentum in world-wide research communities. In this paper, we report our recent efforts in developing efficient algorithms in direct image indexing and retrieval in compressed domain, which covers three major international image compression standards, including JPEG-LS[28] for lossless image compression, JPEG[33] for lossy image compression and the emerging JPEG-2000[9] for wavelets-based progressive image compression. The rest part of the paper is organized as follows. Section 2 describes image indexing in the process of lossless image compression via JPEG-LS, Section 3 presents our work on image indexing in DCT-based JPEG domain, Section 4 reports shape-based image retrieval in JPEG-2000 domain, and finally Section 5 covers direct image extraction from compressed domain, providing a new paradigm for cases where features do not satisfy the needs of users, and manual browsing or further feature extraction and content analysis in pixel domain are required.

2. Integration of Image Indexing and Compression via JPEG-LS

2.1 Review of JPEG-LS

The latest JPEG efforts in new international standards for lossless and near lossless image compression is represented by JPEG-LS[28], in which the main compression techniques proposed can be summarised by (i) run-length coding, (ii) non-linear prediction, (iii) context based statistics modelling; and (iv) entropy coding. Following the input source image, JPEG-LS encodes each pixel in one of the two modes, run mode or regular mode. Run mode is characterised by run-length coding where a sequence of pixels with the same intensity value is identified and the length of the sequence is encoded. In regular mode, a prediction is made from a neighbourhood of three pixels to estimate the value of the pixel to be encoded and the predictive error is then entropy encoded, based on its context and the statistics modelling.

The mode selector decides whether the input pixel should be encoded by run-length coding or prediction-based entropy coding through a template of four neighbouring pixels. The template is illustrated in Figure 2.1. To reduce the computing cost for statistical modelling and the mode selection, JPEG-LS proposed the following three delta values to implement relevant operations.

$$\Delta_1 = d - b; \quad \Delta_2 = b - c; \quad \Delta_3 = c - a; \qquad (2.1)$$

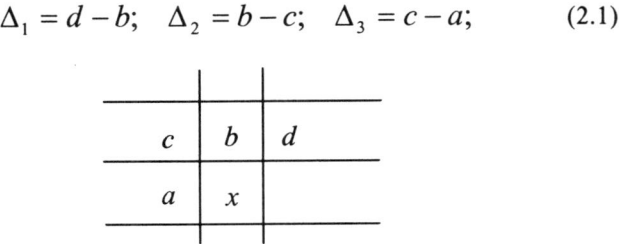

Figure 2.1 JPEG-LS predictive template

In order to accommodate near lossless compression, JPEG-LS defined an information loss parameter *NEAR*, which is a small integer, to allow for introduction of small distortion and maximise the compression efficiency. Specifically, if all the four neighbouring pixel values are the same (lossless) or their differences are less than *NEAR* (near lossless), it would be regarded as a good indication that the local region surrounding the pixel to be encoded is of smooth texture. Hence, run-length coding is applied for encoding the next sequence of pixels until the run is broken by a different one. Otherwise, a prediction based entropy coding should be selected. This can be summarised as follows:

$$coding\_mode = \begin{cases} run-length & if\ \Delta_1, \Delta_2\ and\ \Delta_3 < NEAR \\ predictive\ coding & otherwise \end{cases}$$
(2.2)

In regular mode, prediction is designed by exploiting a simple local texture analysis among three pixels inside the predictive template. All the relevant operations can be described as follows:

$$if\ (c \geq \max(a,b))\ predictive\_value = \min(a,b);$$
$$else\{$$
$$\quad if\ (c \leq \min(a,b))\ predictive\_value = \max(a,b);$$
$$\quad else\ predictive\_value = a + b - c;$$
$$\}$$
(2.3)

After the prediction is made, the predictive error is then further corrected and mapped into a non-negative range determined by the maximum intensity value. The statistics modelling is called upon to estimate the statistics of such mapped error, based on its context, to determine an appropriate code-word length for its final representation.

2.2 Algorithm Design

By further examination of JPEG-LS predictive coding design, it can be revealed that the prediction is designed based on a local texture analysis. This prompted us to extract those local texture features from the predictive coding process, and hence a content-based key can be constructed to index the input image.

Essentially, when a pixel x is encoded, it firstly goes through the prediction process, in which a coding mode is selected and in the regular mode, a predictive value is produced. Depending on the context analysis, the possible cases can be summarised as follows:

(i)   Regular mode: A horizontal edge is detected;
(ii)   Regular mode: A vertical edge is detected;
(iii)   Regular mode: Self-adaptive prediction by *a+b-c*;
(iv)   Run mode: run-length extracted and the point of run broken determined;

According to the above variations, texture features can be extracted from the coding process by a number of possible designs. Correspondingly, we have three texture extraction algorithms designed to do the content-based image indexing.

The first algorithm is to consider each pixel inside the predictive template as a target for encoding, and its code-word is determined by the above four possibilities. To describe the algorithm design, we encode the above four cases by two bits: $\{x_1x_2\}=\{00, 01, 10, 11\}$ Let the predictive template and the pixel to be encoded be represented as: *P{c, b, d, a, x}*, containing five elements. The whole process of compressing the image can be regarded as moving the window of predictive template along raft-scanning order to the end of image. Therefore, as the window moves, the outcome of encoding each element inside the window will capture the texture feature of the entire image. Since the encoding of each element will have four possible cases, the total number of combinations inside the window can be denoted as:

$$\Omega = c \in \{x_1 x_2\} \cap b \in \{x_1 x_2\} \cap d \in \{x_1 x_2\} \cap a \in \{x_1 x_2\} \cap x \in \{x_1 x_2\}$$
(2.4)

and the total number of elements inside Ω can be determined as $4^5 = 1024$.

As each pixel is compressed, its predictive template and the pixel itself would form a window, and the outcome of encoding all the pixels inside the window corresponds to one of the above 1024 elements or states. During the compression process, if we count the total number of each state that indicates how the pixels inside the window are being encoded, a histogram will be produced to represent the content or the texture of the input image. This give us:

$$H(c,b,d,a,x) = \frac{\Gamma(p\{c,b,d,a,x\} = i)}{N \times M} \qquad \forall i \in \Omega$$
(2.5)

where Γ represents a counting operation, in which the total number of the states: $p\{c,b,d,a,x\} = i$ is calculated throughout the whole image, and $N \times M$ stands for the size of the input image.

As the size of Ω is 1024, the state of $p\{c,b,d,a,x\}$ can be represented by 10 bits, and the value of i can be made to vary from 0 to 1023. This gives us a complete histogram, where the horizontal axis represents the 1024 states, and the vertical axis records the number of counts for each state generated during the compression process by JPEG-LS. If we use the histogram as the key to index every input image during the population of the database and the process of target retrieval, all images will automatically be compressed on lossless basis before they are stored inside the database.

In the above design, a window of five pixels is used to extract texture features from the entire image. As the window moves along the course of image compression, redundancy exists in the way that the same pixel could stay inside the window for a maximum of three times. This only happens to pixel d, as illustrated in Figure 2.1. To reduce such redundancy in producing histograms, the algorithm can be revised by excluding d from the window and thus equation (2.4) will only involve c, b, a, and x and the size of Ω will be $4^4 = 256$. Accordingly, equation (2.5) becomes:

$$H(c,b,a,x) = \frac{\Gamma(p\{c,b,a,x\} = i)}{N \times M} \qquad \forall i \in \Omega = [0,255] \qquad (2.6)$$

In fact, prediction in JPEG-LS only involves c, b, and a before x is predicted and the error being entropy encoded. Hence, this seems to be a more logical option. As a result, the size of Ω is reduced to 256, and the number of states can be encoded by 8 bits. We regard this variation as our second algorithm design for image indexing in the process of lossless image compression.

To further reduce redundancy and the size of Ω, the texture feature can be considered in terms of how the current pixel, x, is encoded in JPEG-LS. Specifically, before each pixel is encoded, a texture smoothness is tested by examining all the three delta values, based on which a decision would be made whether the pixel should be encoded in regular mode or run-length mode. With regular mode, prediction is the first step to reduce the pixel intensity value to the level of predictive error to remove the correlation among neighbouring pixels. As described in the previous section, the predictive value is produced corresponding to four cases. These include: (a) vertical edge detected, (b) horizontal edge detected, (c) a+b-c prediction and (d) run-broken prediction. In run-length mode, no prediction incurs and only the run-length is to be produced by testing a sequence of pixels until the run is broken by encountering a different pixel. To this end, the current pixel can be classified into three texture types which could be a good indication about the image content. These include vertical edge detected, horizontal edge detected and self-adaptive prediction by $a+b-c$. As the edges directly relates to the interpretation of image contents by human beings, we expect that this arrangement of texture feature extraction will give us a better result in retrieving images based on their content. Since run-broken prediction indicates the end of run-length mode and the predictive value is produced by excluding the pixel a, this type of texture information can be classified into the same range as that of run mode. In this circumstance, pixel x alone will not be sufficient to characterise the local feature, since its encoding involves a sequence of pixels as well as those neighbouring ones around x. Consequently, whenever such a case is detected during the encoding process, feature extraction can be directed to examine the context of three surrounding pixels, a, c, and b to see in what mode, and what context they are encoded. Since each pixel could be encoded with one out of five possible cases, the total number of cases for the context would be $5^3 = 125$. Adding the three states identified for x, the total number of states can be derived as 128. Hence, during the process of image compression, the state upon which the current pixel is encoded can be determined as follows:

$$state(x) = \begin{cases} 0 & \text{horizontal edge detected} \\ 1 & \text{vertical edge detected} \\ 2 & \text{prediction by } a+b-c \\ [3-127] & \begin{cases} a \text{ examined} \\ b \text{ examined} \\ c \text{ examined} \end{cases} \text{run mode or run broken} \end{cases} \quad (2.7)$$

The histogram can be constructed by the equation given below:

$$H(x) = \frac{\Gamma(state(x) = i)}{N \times M} \qquad \forall i \in \Omega = [0,127] \qquad (2.8)$$

We regard this design as our third algorithm for image indexing in the process of compression.

To retrieve a target image, similarity is calculated between histograms of the query and those inside the database. Given an image database with a set of histograms $\psi = \{H_1^ت, H_2^ت, ... H_i^ت ...\}$ and $H_i^ت = \{h_1^ت, h_2^ت, ... h_M^ت\}$, where M stands for the number of elements inside each histogram, the similarity between the query image, Q, and the possible target image, I, inside the database can be determined by calculating the following distance:

$$d(Q,I) = \frac{1}{M} \sum_{i=1}^{M} |h_i^ت - h_i^q| \qquad (2.9)$$

Each time the whole database is searched, the display of those retrieved images is designed as such that only ξ images are displayed, which also means that ξ minimum distances are selected to retrieve the target images. When all the ξ distances are arranged into an ascending order, the rank of each displayed image inside the set of display is the position of its corresponding distance.

2.3 Evaluations and Experimental Report

To test the performance of all the proposed algorithms described in the previous section, the first thing needed is an existing algorithm, which can be used to benchmark the proposed. The benchmarking scheme must satisfy the conditions as such that: (a) it has similar level of complexity in algorithm design and (b) it also uses texture-based feature extraction to do the image indexing. This is required to secure a fair comparison between the proposed algorithms and the existing techniques. Among all the possible candidates[10-12,15,22,30], it is verified that the 8-pixel texture extraction[15] is the closest algorithm and hence an appropriate to be used as the benchmark.

Although the 8-pixel texture-based indexing works in pixel domain and no compression involved, it satisfies the two conditions and meet the requirement for fair comparison in terms of the issues relating to content-based indexing and retrieval. For each pixel x inside the image, the 8-pixel technique simply examines all the eight surrounding pixels by comparing their intensity values. Corresponding to each pixel inside the surroundings, a single bit can be allocated to indicate whether the intensity value of x is greater than that of its neighbor or not. When all the eight bits are considered, a total number of 256 states can be formed to characterize the texture feature inside the input image. The corresponding histogram can be produced by the following equations:

$$state(x) = b_7b_6b_5b_4b_3b_2b_1b_0 \text{ and } b_k = \begin{cases} 1 & \text{if } x \geq y_k \\ 0 & \text{else} \end{cases} \quad \forall k \in [0,7]$$
(2.10)

$$H(x) = \frac{\Gamma(state(x) = i)}{N \times M} \quad \forall i \in \Omega = [0,255]$$
(2.11)

Altogether, four indexing algorithms are implemented in C++ to complete the experiments, which are carried out in a database containing about 8000 images. These include the benchmarking 8-pixel algorithm, and the proposed three schemes inside JPEG-LS. Apart from the fact that our proposed algorithms have the advantage of embedded image compression on lossless basis, our major concern is to see if any improvement can be achieved in terms of retrieving accuracy. In other words, we would like to see if the retrieved images provide any better interpretation of their contents, and make the interpretation closer to human understanding.

It is understood that content-based image indexing has a wide range of uncertainty and human interpretation of image content could vary. In order to provide a comprehensive evaluation for the performance of all algorithms tested, and an indication of how close each retrieved target image is to the users' desire of the image content, we follow two stages to carry out the experiments. The first stage is to retrieve 8 target images with the smallest distances according to the similarities estimated by equation (2.9) and their rank values determined from all those distances searched and arranged in the ascending order. The second stage involves a psyco-physical test[16] to evaluate each target image and interpret its rank value in terms of human understanding of the image content. Specifically, a group of users is drafted to carry out the first stage test for the same query image and each user is requested to score the displayed image by indicating whether the retrieved image is close to the query or not according to his or her understanding and the desire of the image content. A percentage is then calculated to indicate how many of them think that the image retrieved is close to his or her desire of the image content. This process applies to all 8 images at different ranks. Table 2.1 illustrates such arranged test results to cover the complete experiments. From the figures given in Table 2.1, it can be seen that the proposed algorithms, the first and the third, outperforms the existing non-compressed one in terms of such psyco-physical test for almost all ranks. The second proposed algorithm, however, fails to provide better performance. This explains that window-based scanning fails to extract good texture features, which could reveal the content of image as users desired. When the number of states inside the histogram is increased dramatically such as that given in the first proposed, the features extracted start to produce better keys for image content representation and reflection. This is evidenced by the test results in the first proposed. The third proposed algorithm, however, only has 128 states inside its histogram. Yet the performance achieved is the best among all the algorithms tested, although its histogram size is only half of the benchmark and the second proposed, and one eighth of the first proposed.

Table 2.1: Summary of Experimental Result

Schemes Tested	1st rank	2nd rank	3rd rank	4th rank	5th rank	6th rank	7th rank	8th rank
8-pixel	43	39	36	38	26	33	29	19
Proposed 1	51	44	31	38	36	33	32	30
Proposed 2	40	32	21	21	20	22	19	16
Proposed 3	54	40	41	39	24	33	34	25

3. Image Indexing and Retrieval in JPEG Compressed Domain

3.1 Direct Moment Extraction from DCT Domain

JPEG lossy image compression can be briefly summarized by three operational stages, block-based discrete cosine transform, quantization and entropy coding[33], among which the DCT consumes the major computing cost. In the existing research on image retrieval in pixel domain, Hu [40] first derived results illustrating the algebraic invariant of 2-dimensional moments. Thereafter, it is widely applied in feature detection and representation in image processing and pattern analysis because of its nice properties of being invariant to size, position, and orientation [13]. Following this work, we propose to compute those moments directly in DCT domain as given below.

Assume $X=x(i,j)$ ($i,j \in 0,1, \ldots$ N-1) are intensity values in a $N \times N$ block (N=8 in JPEG). If X is regarded as a random variable inside the block, the kth moment ($k \in [1,2,\ldots]$) of X in this block can be defined as the expectation of X^k, which is given as follows.

$$m_k = E(X^k) = \frac{1}{N^2} \sum_{i=0}^{N-1} \sum_{j=0}^{N-1} x^k(i,j)$$

(3.1)

As a result, its kth central moment, μ_k of X, is $E[(X-E(X))^k]$ by definition. Its specific equation can be worked out as the following:

$$\mu_k = E[(X - E(X))^k] = \frac{1}{N^2} \sum_{i=0}^{N-1} \sum_{j=0}^{N-1} [x(i,j) - E(X)]^k$$

(3.2)

From statistics mathematics, it is known that the 1st order moment m_1 and the 2nd order central moment μ_2 are also called mean and variance in this block, where m_1 essentially represents the average intensity of the pixel block, and μ_2 represents the difference of intensity values among the pixels inside this block. Further, μ_2 and m_1 satisfy the following relationship:

$$\mu_k = m_2 - m_1^2 \qquad (3.3)$$

On the other hand, a 2D DCT for this block can be defined as:

$$C(u,v) = \frac{1}{4} \alpha(u)\alpha(v) \sum_{i=0}^{7} \sum_{j=0}^{7} x(i,j) \cos\left(\frac{(2i+1)u\pi}{16}\right) \cos\left(\frac{(2j+1)v\pi}{16}\right)$$

(3.4)

where $\alpha(u) = \begin{cases} \sqrt{\frac{1}{2}} & \text{for } u=0 \\ 1 & \text{otherwise} \end{cases}$ and $C(u,v)$ are DCT coefficients at (u,v) ($u,v=0,1,\ldots,7$). Its corresponding inverse transform is:

$$x(i,j) = \frac{1}{4}\sum_{u=0}^{7}\sum_{v=0}^{7}\alpha(u)\alpha(v)C(u,v)\cos\left(\frac{(2i+1)u\pi}{16}\right)\cos\left(\frac{(2j+1)v\pi}{16}\right)$$
(3.5)

From both DCT definition and the moment definition, it can be seen that when both $u=0$ and $v=0$, we have:

$$m_1 = \frac{1}{8}C(0,0)$$
(3.6)

$$m_2 = \frac{1}{64}\sum_{i=0}^{7}\sum_{j=0}^{7}C^2(u,v)$$
(3.7)

and

$$\mu_2 = \frac{1}{64}\left(\sum_{i=0}^{7}\sum_{j=0}^{7}C^2(u,v) - C(0,0)\right)$$
(3.8)

In other words, equations (3.6)-(3.8) show that the mean m_1 can be directly derived from DC coefficients, and the variance μ_2 is just the average summation of all squared AC coefficients. Therefore, by applying (3.6)-(3.8), we can extract the moment features directly in DCT domain without going back to pixels via full decompression. In this way, computational cost can be seen significantly less than that of the existing work in pixel domain. In addition, the number of multiplication and addition in practical computation of μ_2 can be further reduced since $C(u,v)$ in the bottom-right region of the block are normally close to zero and thus are ignored in JPEG compression. To exploit this characteristics of JPEG, we can achieve further savings on computing cost without compromising performance by using only the first 32 DCT coefficients along the zigzag route to extract the moment features. Apart from the obvious advantage of avoiding full decompression, such moment extraction algorithm also achieves significant savings on computing cost through the effective exploitation of JPEG compression. A specific comparison of the computing cost between the existing algorithm and the proposed is given in Table-3.1.

Table 3.1. Computation Cost Comparison

moment	Compute directly from pixel domain			the proposed algorithm	
	addition	multiplication	decoding required	addition	multiplication
m_1	63	1		0	1
μ_2	64	66		≤62	≤64

3.2 Content-based Retrieval of JPEG Compressed Images

According to the JPEG compression standard, its decoding steps include: (a) Entropy decoding via the Huffman table, (b) dequantization, and (c) IDCT (inverse DCT). In the existing content-based image retrieval (CBIR) systems, these operation would become an overhead before any content key can be constructed. From our analysis given in previous section, the content key can be constructed from the moment parameters m_1 and μ_2, which are directly extracted in DCT domain as given in equations (3.6)-(3.8). Specifically, the mean m_1 represents average intensity of the 8x8 block. Yet the variance μ_2 or standard deviation σ ($=\sqrt{\mu_2}$) is regarded as a character being abundant in texture information, which is often used in image segmentation [14, 18]. Theoretically, m_1 and σ can also be used to establish a 2-D m_1-σ space, which satisfies $0 \le m_1 \le 255$ and $0 \le \sigma < 128$. Therefore, we design the following steps to construct the indexing keys by using the two moment parameters extracted in DCT domain:

i) Divide m_1-σ space into 28 unequal partitions (or subspaces), among which, the value of intensity mean m_1 is equally divided into 4 non-overlapping regions. Those regions can be indexed as 0, 1, 2,3 respectively. When the value of parameter σ is divided unequally into 7 non-overlapping regions, they can also be indexed via [0, 6]. By combining the two divisions together, a histogram of 28 elements can be constructed when the occurrence of each m_1 and σ is counted.

ii) For a given JPEG image, decode it into 8x8 blocks of DCT coefficients as described in Figure 1. Calculate m_1 and σ of all blocks according to equation (3.6) and (3.8), and count the number of their occurrences inside the 28 regions. As a result, 28 counters are set up to construct the indexing key and they can be represented as f_i (i=0,1,...,27).

iii) To achieve robust retrieval through the histogram comparison, the vector $\{f_0, f_1, ..., f_{27}\}$ is further normalized by dividing the total number of counts $\sum_{i=0}^{27} f_i$. In this way, the indexing key can finally be worked out as:

$$\frac{1}{\sum_{i=0}^{27} f_i} \{f_0, f_1, ... f_{27}\}.$$

3.3 System Performance Evaluation

Along with the above design, a content based image retrieval system (CBIR) is implemented by using C++. In normal practice, there are two factors to evaluate the performance of a CBIR system [54]. One is the retrieval efficiency, which focuses on the speed of retrieval. The other is the retrieval effectiveness, which emphasizes the accuracy of the retrieval. From the above discussion, it has been illustrated that the proposed system eliminated the need of IDCT in JPEG decoder, and directly generates the indexing keys from DCT domain. Consequently, the proposed system reduces the computing cost significantly in comparison with that of conventional systems for databases of JPEG compressed images. With our proposed algorithm, the key generation for a database of 500 JPEG compressed images takes only 23 seconds on a Pentium II PC platform with 350 MHz CPU, while it takes 51 seconds for the same operation in pixel domain, where full decompression is required. Therefore, our technique achieves more than 50% savings in terms of computing cost.

In addition, we also design the following two experiments to demonstrate the system's effectiveness.

The First Experiment: Following Faloutsos' work [54] on a variation of normalized precision to assess the performance of any image retrieval system, we employ parameters AVRR, IAVRR, and the ration of AVRR to measure our proposed system.

i) *AVRR* is a parameter to measure the average rank of all relevant images (the first position is 0th).

ii) *IAVRR* is the ideal average rank, in which all of the relevant images rank on the top. Obviously, $IAVRR = \dfrac{Number\ of\ relevant\ images - 1}{2}$

iii) Ratio of *AVRR* is defined as the ratio of *AVRR* to *IAVRR*, which gives a measure of the effectiveness of the retrieving system. When the ratio is equal to 1, the result of retrieval is the most ideal.

In our experiments, we selected 5 query images from a database of 500 images to carry out the test. The experimental results are summarized in Table 3.2. Notice the AVRR =5.68, and Ratio of AVRR=1.84, which is better than that given in [54].

Table 3.2 The measurement of the retrieval effectiveness

Query image	1	2	3	4	5	Average
Number of the relevant images	4	8	5	4	16	
AVRR		9/4	39/8	13/5	19/4	223/16	5.68
Ratio of *AVRR*	1.50	1.39	1.30	3.17	1.86	1.84

The Second Experiment: To investigate at which rank the first relevant image is retrieved, we randomly selected 32 images from a database of 524 images as query images, and record the total number of the retrieved images in each rank from 0 to 7 (excluding the query image). Two parameters are computed to assess the system's performance. One is the ratio of retrieval (*RR (r)*) which is defined as the number of retrieved relevant images at the rth rank divided by the total number of retrieved images. The other is the accumulated ratio at rank r (*AR(r)*) which is defined as

$$AR(r) = \dfrac{Number\ of\ found\ relevant\ image\ before\ rank\ (r)}{Total\ number\ of\ query\ image} \times 100\%$$

The experimental results are plotted as shown in Figure 3.1. The results show that: (a) the relevant images amass the front of ranks; (b) the probability of the relevant images retrieved at the 0th rank is over 80%; and (c) the probability of at least one relevant image being retrieved among the first 3 ranks is close to 97%. This means that the proposed system can retrieve at lest one relevant image within the first 3 ranks almost everytime. Figure 3.2 displays two typical examples for visual evaluation of those images retrieved by our proposed CBIR system.

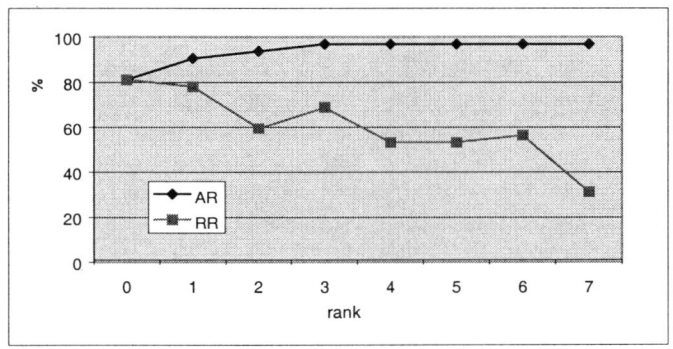

Figure 3.1 The Retrieval ratio and accumulation retrieval ratio

Figure 3.2 The two examples retrieved by the proposed algorithm

4. Feature Extraction in Wavelets Domain

Wavelets-based image compression proves to perform better that of DCT based by recent research investigations as well as international standardization activities[9,42,43]. Many researchers attempted extracting content features from wavelets domain and exploit wavelets theory[45] to develop algorithms for image retrieval[36,44,51]. In [19], a significant map of wavelet coefficients was used to represent object regions in their wavelet-based approach. For those images compressed with wavelets, the significant map can always be derived without full decompression. In this section, a description of our recent work on improving shape description for image retrieval is covered, which is mainly based on the work reported in [19]. Figure 4.1 illustrates a specific example to explain how a shape descriptor can be obtained starting from the existing shape feature extraction.

Motivated by an observation that those isolated significant points in wavelet coefficients domain may not represent region information of an object accurately and effectively, we introduce several simple but effective morphological operators to propose new algorithms and improve the existing moment-based shape descriptors in wavelet domain. The new shape description method is based on regions and proved to give a better capability to exploit its invariant features in comparison with the existing method proposed in [19]. In addition, since certain moments are invariant to rotation, we argue that it is rather inefficient to use multi-directional subbands of wavelet coefficients in the existing shape description. Therefore, a more compact and effective multi-scale moment representation method can be designed to interpret the shape information spread among those various directional wavelet coefficients.

4.1 Shape Description and Representation via Significance Map

From further examination of the work reported in [19], it is found that the significant map adopted in [19] contains many isolated points, which suggests that the significant maps may only be a coarse approximation of those object regions in the image. In [19], the moments of different subbands are directly computed based on their significant maps. These moment invariants are then used as the shape descriptors for image retrieval. However, since the moment invariant is defined on an object region rather than the significant map with isolated points, further improvement remains possible if such characteristics can be taken into consideration in formulating new shape descriptors.

Since different subbands of wavelet coefficients are produced via low-pass filtering and high-pass filtering along vertical and horizontal directions, the corresponding coefficients can be seen as values containing horizontal high frequency, vertical high frequency, and diagonal high frequency components. It is known that edge occurs in a place where its gray level or intensity values abruptly changes and its corresponding coefficient may belong to high frequency subband. Therefore, the coefficients with larger magnitude in these three subbands essentially represent a map of horizontal edges, vertical edges, and diagonal edges. Accordingly, the significant map adopted in [19] is an edge-oriented map of the original image, which could fail to reflect the region of objects or shapes inside the image. Further analysis also reveals that the significant map is only an approximation of the shaped region. To further improve the shape representation in wavelet domain, one of the possibilities is to extend those isolated edge-oriented significance points to a meaningful region representation. To this end, we propose to perform a series of morphological operations [48] over those isolated significant points before shape features are extracted. The specific process is illustrated in Figure 4.1, in which the improvement via the morphological operations is also shown. The original image is given in part (a), and the edge map extracted from wavelet coefficients is shown in part (b). After the closing and filling operations, the resulting images are shown in part (c) and part (d) respectively.

In order to generate a continued and closing object contour, closing operators [38] are used on the edge-oriented map extracted from the wavelet coefficients. The closing operator is simply performed by conducting dilate and erode operations [38], which is proved to be effective and efficient for simple objects as illustrated in Figure 4.1. As its computation is fast, only several simple steps are required. After the closing operation, the original isolated edge points are linked together to form contour curves of objects. To finalize the object region, a flood-fill algorithm[49] is further adopted in our scheme based on those closing edges. After the flood-fill operations, the task of extending isolated significant points to meaningful regions is completed successfully with only a small overhead computation cost. The result is also illustrated in Figure 4.1.

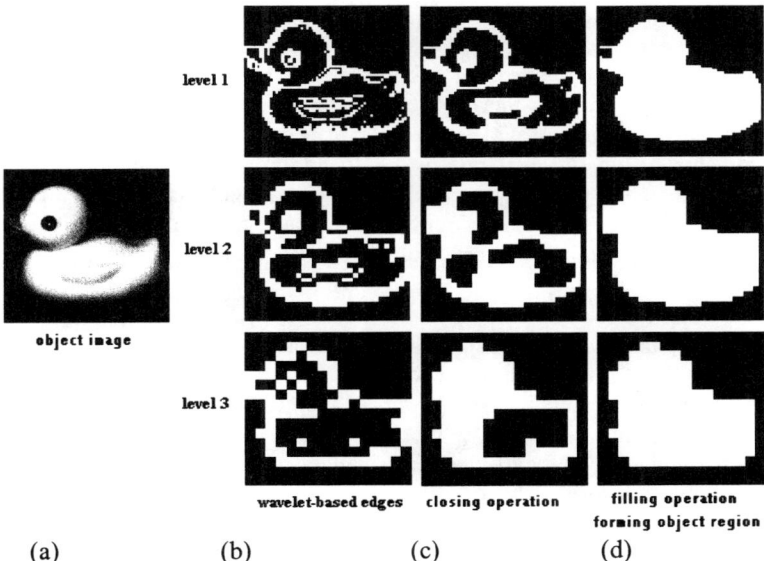

Figure 4.1 Significant points and mathematical morphological operations

4.2 Subband Representation in Wavelet Domain

By analyzing those specific circumstances for shape-based image retrieval and the properties of wavelet transform, we carried out some further testing, which reveals that further consideration is required on whether or not the multi-directional subbands should be included in shape analysis. This forms a strong argument that extraction of moment invariant in all multi-directional subbands may not always improve the performance, but may have potential to decrease the capability of moments to deal with rotational changes. Existing shape-based image retrieval methods in wavelet coefficients domain [19] often use all multi-directional subbands. Based on our further testing results and analysis mentioned above, we propose to combine various directional subbands into one single subband. The benefit of so doing lies in two aspects: (i) it avoids the problem caused by rotational changes; and (ii) it can significantly decrease the memory requirement for the storage of those feature moments. For example, in the method provided in [19], an image was decomposed into three level wavelet coefficients. Wavelet coefficients in every level have three directions, i.e., horizontal, vertical, and diagonal. If nine moment invariants are extracted from every subband, for example, a total of 81 moment invariants will be produced for an image. In our proposed method, however, three directional subbands in a level will be combined into a single one as illustrated in Figure 4.1(b).

4.3 Experimental results and assessment

Following the method proposed in previous sections, a series of experiments were carried out to evaluate its performances. The retrieval experiments are designed in a manner of query-by-example in wavelet compression domain, in which the Columbia Object Image Library (COIL-20) was chosen as our preliminary experimental data set (ftp site: zen.cs.columbia.edu). The images contained in this database have a wide variety of complex geometric and reflectance characteristics[37], which provides a useful test bed for evaluation of various shape descriptors for image retrieval purposes. In addition, there are large number of samples with different poses corresponding to every object. As a result, this database is suitable for testing on object recognition and shape-based image retrieval. COIL-20 database consists of 1440 grey scale images corresponding to 20 objects (72 image per object).

In our experiments, the database is compressed using a wavelet-based JPEG-2000 [9], in which three level pyramid decompositions are carried out. As a result, the whole wavelet coefficients consist of ten subbands. Moment-based shape feature vectors are computed via both the method described in WaveGuide [19] and the proposed method. We compare the performances of the two algorithms in retrieval precision, which is derived by computing an average retrieval precision from all individual testing. This is designed to reflect the overall retrieval performance of these two algorithms. The retrieval precision is defined as follows:

$$p = \frac{num_c}{num_c + num_f} = \frac{num_c}{M} \qquad (4.1)$$

where num_c, num_f, and M are the numbers of correct retrieval, false retrieval, and the first retrieval candidates with the smallest matching distance.

Based on the above design, all retrieval results are summarised in Table 4.1 and Figure 4.2.

Table 4.1: Overall retrieval precision comparison
(First matching number = 5)

WaveGuide[1] method	P = 27.40%
The proposed method	P = 41.44%

From the results given in Table 4.1, it can be seen that the overall retrieval precision of the proposed scheme is significantly higher than that of WaveGuide[19]. As analyzed earlier, this proves that the strategy of extending isolated significant points to meaningful regions indeed improves the shape characterization capability based on the moment invariant.

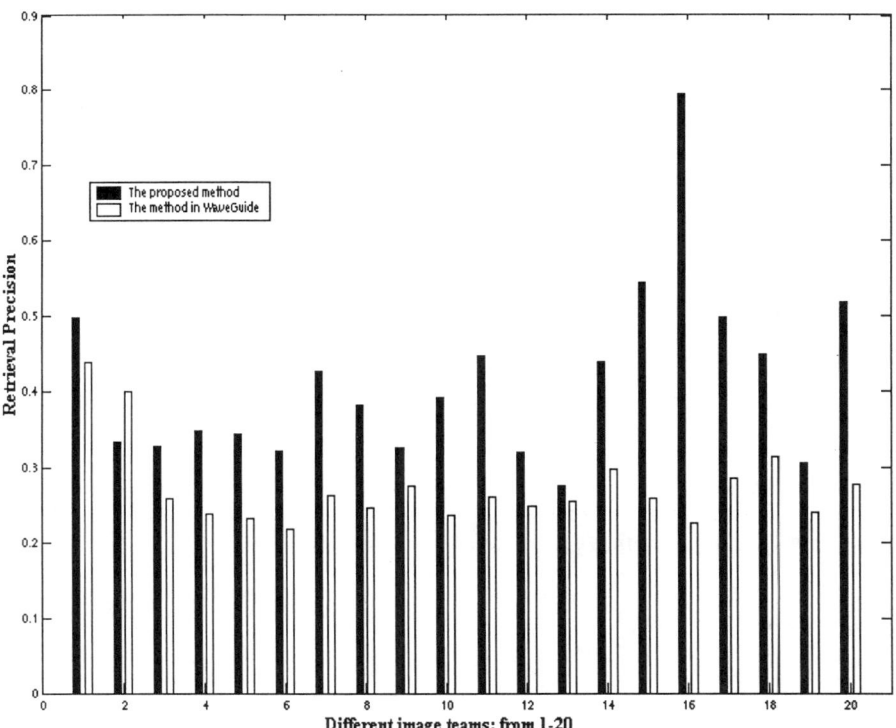

Figure 4.2 Experimental results summary

It should also be noted that the comparative results are achieved by the proposed algorithm with only one third of the memory required by WaveGuide [19]. In other words, the indexing keys for the proposed algorithm contains 27 elements instead of 81.

5. Image Extraction without Full Decompression

For image retrieval purposes, content access to compressed images is dominated by: (a) browsing of targeted images with limited numbers; (b) extraction of other features, which are not available inside the database; (c) some special content analysis or object recognition etc. All the above suggests that lower-resolution images maybe sufficient as long as the quality of image preserves all the content features. This prompted us to revisit the DCT-based JPEG standard compression techniques and see if a complete image with lower resolution can be directly extracted without full decompression. Specifically, starting from the full definition of IDCT as given in (5.1), it can be seen that the major factor in requiring multiplication is the cosine function. As the index value, u and v, which indicate the position of the coefficient, varies, the angle inside the cosine function changes correspondingly. However, observations from all the possible index values[53] reveal that no matter how the index value changes, the angle remains inside the first quadrant. Hence, if we expand the cosine function with Taylor series at $\pi/4$, a good approximation should be maintained for all the angles inside the first quadrant. This gives us the following equation:

$$\cos(x) = \cos(x_0) + \cos^{(1)}_{ij}(x_0)(x-x_0) + \frac{\cos^{(2)}(x_0)(x-x_0)^2}{2!} + ...$$
$$\frac{\cos^{(n)}(x_0)(x-x_0)^n}{n!} = \cos\frac{\pi}{4} - \sin\frac{\pi}{4}(x-\frac{\pi}{4}) + ... = \frac{\sqrt{2}}{2}\left(1-(x-\frac{\pi}{4})+...\right)$$

(5.1)

By ignoring all those terms with higher order than 1, we have:

$$\cos(x) \approx \frac{\sqrt{2}}{2}\left(1-(x-\frac{\pi}{4})\right)$$

(5.2)

As the DCT is orthogonal transform, the above operations can be perfectly applied to forward DCT transform, which is given below:

$$C(u,v) = \frac{1}{4}\alpha(u)\alpha(v)\sum_{i=0}^{7}\sum_{j=0}^{7}x(i,j)\cos\left(\frac{(2i+1)u\pi}{16}\right)\cos\left(\frac{(2j+1)v\pi}{16}\right)$$

(5.3)

Considering only the variables, $j, v \in [0,7]$, and the approximation given in (5.2), we have:

$$\sum_{j=0}^{7} x(i,j)\cos\left(\frac{(2i+1)0\pi}{16}\right) = x(i,0) + x(i,1) + \ldots + x(i,6) + x(i,7)$$
(5.4)

$$\sum_{j=0}^{7} x(i,j)\cos\left(\frac{(2i+1)1\pi}{16}\right) \approx \frac{\sqrt{2}}{2}\left\{\left(1+\frac{3\pi}{16}\right)x(i,0) + \left(1+\frac{\pi}{16}\right)x(i,1) + \left(1-\frac{\pi}{16}\right)x(i,2) + \left(1-\frac{3\pi}{16}\right)x(i,3) - \left(1-\frac{3\pi}{16}\right)x(i,4) - \left(1-\frac{\pi}{16}\right)x(i,5) - \left(1+\frac{3\pi}{16}\right)x(i,6) - \left(1+\frac{3\pi}{16}\right)x(i,7)\right\}$$
(5.5)

$$\sum_{j=0}^{7} x(i,j)\cos\left(\frac{(2i+1)2\pi}{16}\right) \approx \frac{\sqrt{2}}{2}\left\{\left(1+\frac{2\pi}{16}\right)x(i,0) + \left(1-\frac{2\pi}{16}\right)x(i,1) - \left(1-\frac{2\pi}{16}\right)x(i,2) - \left(1+\frac{2\pi}{16}\right)x(i,3) - \left(1+\frac{2\pi}{16}\right)x(i,4) - \left(1-\frac{2\pi}{16}\right)x(i,5) + \left(1-\frac{2\pi}{16}\right)x(i,6) + \left(1+\frac{2\pi}{16}\right)x(i,7)\right\}$$
(5.6)

...
Observations of all the above equations reveal that after the approximation, the DCT forward transform becomes a weighted summation of all the pixel values. Since we are working on partial decoding with lower resolution, i.e., only 2x2 pixels reconstructed for each block of 8x8, all the 64 pixels can be merged together to form just 4 average pixels by adding $x(i,0)$, $x(i,1)$, $x(i,2)$, $x(i,3)$ to form $a(N,0)$, and $x(i,4)$, $x(i,5)$, $x(i,6)$, $x(i,7)$ to form $a(N,1)$. As a result, by considering $v = 0,1$ only along the j direction, equations (5.4-5.6) can be further simplified into:

$$\sum_{j=0}^{7} x(i,j)\cos\left(\frac{(2j+1)0\pi}{16}\right) \approx 4(a(N,0) + a(N,1)) \qquad (5.7)$$

$$\sum_{j=0}^{7} x(i,j)\cos\left(\frac{(2j+1)1\pi}{16}\right) \approx 2\sqrt{2}(a(N,0) - a(N,1))$$
(5.8)

The above equations essentially specify an average expansion along the j direction for $v \in [0,1]$, which plays the major role to approximate the forward DCT by four average pixel values $a(N,M)$ $(N,M) \in [0,1]$. As a matter of fact, similar conclusions can also be obtained for $\sum_{i=0}^{7} x(i,j)\cos\left(\frac{(2i+1)u\pi}{16}\right)$ for $u \in [0,1]$, or the above two equations can be applied to both column and row directions (i and j) according to the DCT definition. In other words, for both $u=0$ and $v=0$, we use (5.7) to expand its average forward DCT equation. For both $u=1$ and $v=1$, we use (5.8) to expand its average forward DCT equation. For example, to approximate $C(0,1)$, we get equation (5.8) along the j direction since $v=1$. Next, since $u=0$, equation (5.7) should be used to expand $a(N,0)$ and $a(N,1)$ respectively for $N \in [0,1]$ along i direction. Thus, while expansion of $a(N,0)$ gives us $4\{a(0,0)+a(1,0)\}$, the expansion of $a(N,1)$ would give us $4\{a(0,1)+a(1,1)\}$. Consequently, we have:

$$C(0,0) = \frac{1}{4} \times \frac{1}{\sqrt{2}} \times \frac{1}{\sqrt{2}} \times 4 \times 4\{a(0,0)+a(1,0)+a(0,1)+a(1,1)\}$$
(5.9)

$$C(0,1) = \frac{1}{4} \times \frac{1}{\sqrt{2}} \times 4 \times 2\sqrt{2}\{a(0,0)+a(1,0)-a(0,1)-a(1,1)\}$$
(5.10)

$$C(1,0) = \frac{1}{4} \times \frac{1}{\sqrt{2}} \times 2\sqrt{2} \times 4\{a(0,0)-a(1,0)+a(0,1)-a(1,1)\}$$
(5.11)

$$C(1,1) = \frac{1}{4} \times 2\sqrt{2} \times 2\sqrt{2}\{a(0,0)-a(1,0)-a(0,1)+a(1,1)\}$$
(5.12)

Solving the above four equations, the four average pixel values can be derived as follows:

$$a(0,0) = \frac{1}{8}\{C(0,0)+C(1,0)+C(0,1)+C(1,1)\}$$

$$a(0,1) = \frac{1}{8}\{C(0,0)+C(1,0)-C(1,1)-C(0,1)\}$$

$$a(1,0) = \frac{1}{8}\{C(0,0)-C(1,0)+C(0,1)-C(1,1)\}$$

$$a(1,1) = \frac{1}{8}\{C(0,0)-C(1,0)-C(0,1)+C(1,1)\}$$
(5.13)

With the four average pixels given in equation (5.13), an image of $\frac{W}{4} \times \frac{H}{4}$ can be directly extracted, where $W \times H$ represents the original image size. The significance of equation (5.13) lies in the fact that, given a JPEG compressed image, a fast image extraction can be implemented with only 8 additions, four right-shifting operations and no multiplication. A hardware implementation flow chart is described in Figure 5.1, from which it can be clearly seen that the hardware implementation architecture is indeed simple and symmetric in terms of those adder units. As a result, it would have significant advantages not only in terms of low-cost in computation, implementation and fabrication, but also in terms of processing speed and power consumption. Figure 5.2 illustrates a few image samples for quality comparison in terms of visual inspection, and Table 5.1 summarizes the quality measurement in

PSNR values benchmarked by the same image samples reconstructed via full decompression.

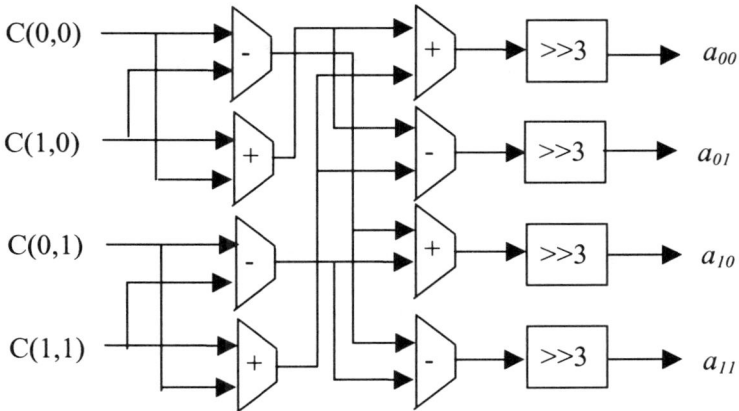

Figure 5.1. *The flow-chart diagram for image extraction*

Table 5.1 Summary of PSNR values for the assessment of quality of extracted images

Image Samples	PSNR (dB) for extracted images
Lena	27.25
Baboon	20.76
Boat	24.75
Truck	28.38
Zelda	30.65
Jet	24.59
Barb	23.28
Clown	22.48

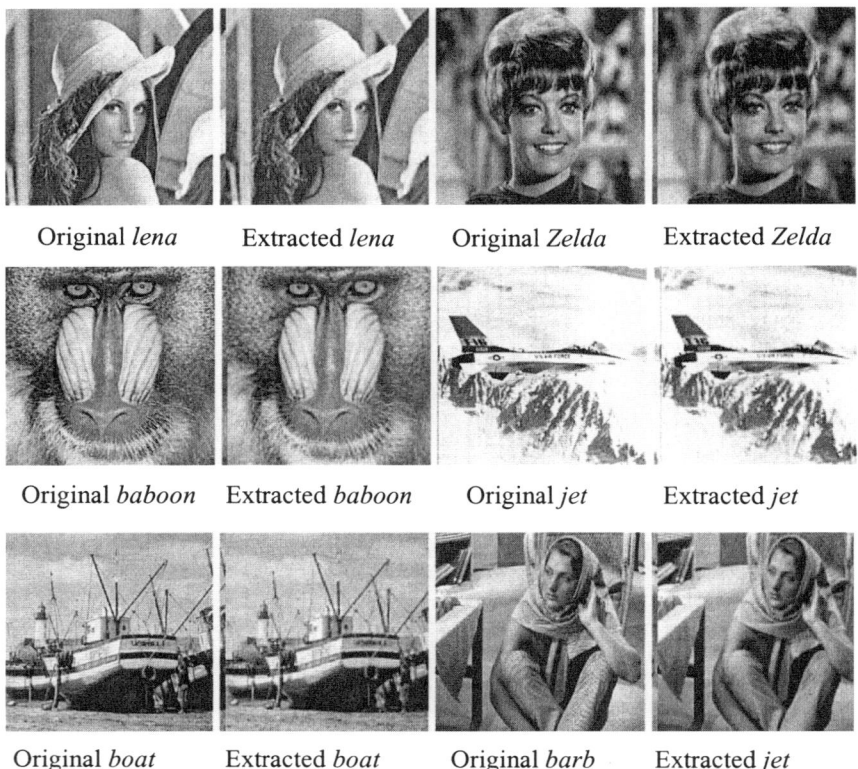

Figure 5.2 Visual inspection of extracted image samples

6. Conclusions

In this paper, an extensive discussion about image indexing and retrieval in compressed domain has been presented, which includes a range of popular image compression formats such as JPEG-LS for lossless image compression, JPEG for lossy compression and JPEG-2000 for both lossy, lossless and progressive image compression. While the big challenge still remains in image retrieval due to the fact that human interpretation varies and those low-level features extracted via automatic means fail to match the high-level content interpretation, the discussed work in the paper provides a pioneering view on the subject, which provide practical tools for visual information processing. This is especially useful as all the existing image processing techniques developed over the past decades are primarily developed in pixel domain, and the present trend for all digital images is to incorporate data compression to save the storage space and improve the processing speed.

The author wish to acknowledge the financial support from The Council for Museums, Archives & Libraries in the UK under the research grant LIC/RE/082.

References

[1]. Faloutsos C. et. Al 'Efficient and effective querying by image content' J. Intell. Inform. Syst. Vol 3, pp 231-262, 1994.

[2]. Pentland A., Picard R.W. and Sclaroff S., 'Photobook: Content-basd manipulation of image databases' Proceedings of SPIE storage Retrieval Image video databases, pp34-47, 1994.

[3]. Zhang H.J., et. Al 'Video parsing retrieval and browsing: an integrated and content-based solution, Proceedings of ACM Multimedia'95, 1995, p 15-24.

[4]. Hampapur A. et. Al 'Virage video engine' Proceedings of SPIE, San Jose, CA Feb 1997, pp 188-197;

[5]. Smith J.R. and Chang S.F. 'Visual seek: a fully automated content-based image query system', Proceedings of ACM Multimedia, Boston MA, Nov 1996, pp87-98;

[6]. Ma W.Y. and B.S. Manjunath, 'Netra: a toolbox for navigating large image databases' Proceedings of ICIP'97, Vol 1, Santa Barbara, CA, 1997, pp568-571;

[7]. Mehrotra S., Y.Rui et. Al 'Supporting content-based queries over images in MARS' Proceedings of IEEE International Conference on Multimedia Computing Systems, Canada, June 3-6, 1997, pp 632-633;

[8]. http://imaging.comp.glam.ac.uk/demonstration

[9]. Skodras A. et. Al 'The JPEG 2000 still image compression standard', IEEE Signal Processing Mgazine, September 2001, pp36-58;

[10]. Pichler O. et al. 'An unsupervised texture segmentation algorithm with feature space reduction and knowledge feedback' IEEE Trans. Image Processing, Vol 7, Jan. 1998, pp 53-61.

[11]. Wilson R. and Hsu T.I. 'A two-compnent model of texture for analysis and synthesis' IEEE Trans. Image Processing, Vol 7, No. 10, 1998, pp 1466-1476.

[12]. R. Brunelli, O. Mich, and C.M. Modena 'A survey on the automatic indexing of video data' Journal of Visual Communication and Image Representation, 78-112, 1999.

[13]. B. M. Methtre, M. S. Kankanhalli, and W. F. Lee, Shape measures for content based image retrieval: A comparison, *Information Processing & Management*, Vol.33, No.3, pp319-337,1997

[14]. R. Chantal and J. Michel, New minimum variance region growing algorithm for image segmentation, *Pattern Recognition Letters*, Vol.18, No. 3, pp.249-258, 1997

[15]. Berman and L. G. Shapiro 'A flexible image database system for content-based retrieval' Computer Vision and Image Understanding, Vol 75, No ½, 1999, pp 175-195.

[16]. I.J. Cox, M.L. Miller et. Al 'The Bayesian image retrieval system, PicHunter: theory, implementation, and psychophysical experiments' IEEE Trans. Image Processing, Vol 9, No 1 2000, pp 20-37.

[17]. Theo Gevers and Arnold W.M. 'PicToSeek: Combining color and shape invariant features for image retrieval' IEEE Trans. Image Processing, Vol 9, No 1, 2000, pp 102-119.

[18]. A.P.Mendonca and E.A.B. da Silva, Segmentation approach using local image statistics, *Electronics Letters,* Vol. 36, No. 14, pp. 1199-1201, 2000

[19]. K. C. Liang and C.C Kuo 'Waveguide: a joint wavelet-based image representation and description system' IEEE Trans. Image Processing, Vol 8, No 11, November, 1999, pp 1619-1629.

[20]. S.D. Servetto, and et al. 'Image coding based on a morphological representation of wavelet data' IEEE Trans. Image processing, Vol 8, No 9, 1999, pp 1161-1174.

[21]. M. Heath, et. Al. 'Comparison of edge detectors' Computer Vision and Image Understanding, Vol 69, No 1, 1998, pp 38-54.

[22]. B.S. Manjunath and W.Y. Ma 'Texture features for browsing and retrieval of image data' IEEE Trans. Pattern Anal. Machine Intell., Vol 18, pp 837-842, 1996.

[23]. M Beatty and B.S. Manjunath 'Dimensionality reduction using multi-dimensional scaling for content-based retrieval', IEEE Int. Conf. Image Processing, 1997.

[24]. B. Gunsel and A.M. Tekalp 'Shape similarity matching for query-by-example' Pattern Recognition, Vol 31, pp 931-944, 1998.

[25]. Rui Y., Huang T.S. and Metrotra S. 'Relevance feedback techniques in interactive content-based image retrieval', Proc. IS&T and SPIE Storage and Retrieval of Image and Video Databases VI, San Juan, PR, June 1997, pp762-768.

[26]. Minka T.P. and Picard R.W. 'Interactive learning with a society of models' Pattern Recognition, Vol 30, pp565-581, 1997.

[27]. Flickner M. *et. al.* 'Query by image and video content: The QBIC system', *IEEE Computer,* September 1995, pp 23-32.

[28]. http://www.jpeg.org/public/jpeglinks.htm: JPEG-LS ISO/IEC JTC 1/SC29/WG1, FCD 14495.

[29]. Weinberger M.J., Rissanen J. and Sapiro G. 'LOCO-I: A low complexity, context-based, lossless image compression algorithm', *Proceedings of Data Compression Conference,* Snowbird, Utah, April 1996, pp 140-149.

[30]. Salembier P. and Garrido L. 'Binary partition tree as an efficient representation for image processing, segmentation, and information retrieval' *IEEE Trans. On Image Processing,* Vol 9, No. 4, April 2000, pp561-576.

[31]. Lee C.S., Ma W.Y. and Zhang H.J. 'Information embedding based on user's relevance feedback for image retrieval', *SPIE Photonics East*, Boston, Sept. 20-22, 1999.

[32]. M.K. Hu, Visaul pattern recognition by moment invariants, *IRE Trans. in Information Theory*, Vol.8, 179-187, 1962

[33]. G. K. Wallace, The JPEG still picture compression standard, *Communication of the ACM*, Vol.34, No.4, pp31-45,1991.

[34]. R. Chantal and J. Michel, New minimum variance region growing algorithm for image segmentation, *Pattern Recognition Letters*, Vol.18, No. 3, pp.249-258, 1997

[35]. B. M. Methtre, M. S. Kankanhalli, and W. F. Lee, Shape measures for content based image retrieval: A comparison, *Information Processing & Management*, Vol.33, No.3, pp319-337,1997

[36]. M. K. Mandal, F. Idris and S. Panchanatha, A critical evaluation of image and video indexing techniques in the compressed domain, *Image and Vision Computing*, Vol.17, pp.513-529, 1999

[37]. Sammeer A. Nene, Shree K. Nayar, and Hiroshi Murase, "Columbia Object Image Library (COIL-20)," Technical Report No. CUCS-006-96, Department of omputer Science, Columbia University

[38]. J. Serra. Image Analysis and Mathematical Morphology. Academic Press, 1982.

[39]. Yong Rui, Thomas S. Huang, Shih-Fu Chang Image, "Retrieval: Past, Present, And Future," Proc. of Int. Symposium on Multimedia Information Processing, Dec 1997.

[40]. M. –K. Hu, "Visual pattern recognition by moment invariants." IRE Trans. Inform. Theory, vol. IT-8, pp. 179-187, Feb. 1962.

[41]. Ioannis Pitas, "Digital image processing algorithms," Prentice Hall International, 1993.

[42]. J. M. Shapiro, "Embedded image coding using zerotrees of wavelet coefficents," IEEE transaction on Signal Processing, Vol. 41, pp. 3445-3462, Dec. 1993.

[43]. Said and W. A. Pearlman, "A new, fast, and efficient image codec based on set partitioning in hierarchical trees," IEEE Transaction on Circuit and Systems for Video Technology, Vol. 6, No. 3, pp. 243-249, June 1996.

[44]. E. Jacobs, A. Finkelstein, and D. H. Salesin, "Fast multiresolution image querying," in Proc. SIGGRAPH Computer Graphics, Los Angeles, CA, 1995, pp. 278-280.

[45]. Stephane Mallat "Wavelet for a Vision", Proceedings of the IEEE, Vol. 84, No. 4, April 1996, pp. 604-614.

[46]. Milan Sonka, Vaclav Hlavac and Roger Boyle, "Image processing, analysis and machine vision," Cambridge University Press, 1996, Cambridge.

[47]. R. Courant and D. Hilbert, Methods of Mathematical Physics, Volume I and II, John Wiley and Sons, 1989.

[48]. J. Serra. Image Analysis and Mathematical Morphology. Academic Press, 1982.

[49]. Hearn and Baker, Computer Graphics -- C Version, 2nd ed. (1997), ISBN: 0-13-530924-7.

[50]. Sammeer A. Nene, Shree K. Nayar, and Hiroshi Murase, "Columbia Object Image Library (COIL-20)," Technical Report No. CUCS-006-96, Department of Computer Science, Columbia University.

[51]. X. S. Zhou, T. S. Huang, "Edge-based structural features for content-based image retrieval", Pattern Recognition Letters, 22 (2001), pp457-468.

[52]. A.A. Goodrum, "Image Information Retrieval: An Overview of Current Research", Information Science, Volume 3, No 2, pp63-67, 2000.
[53]. Jiang J. 'a generalized 1-D approach for paralled computing of NxN DCT', Applied Signal Processing, Vol 5, pp 244-254, 1998;
[54]. C. Faloutsos, R. Barber and M. Flickner et al, Efficient and effective querying by image content, *Journal of Intelligent Information System,* Vol.3, No.3, pp.231-262, 1994

Visual Data Navigators "Collaboratories"

M.Jern, S. Palmberg, M.Ranlöf
ITN, University of Linköping
Norrköping, 601 74 Sweden

Abstract

"Collaborative Visualization" refers to development of scientific understanding, which is mediated by scientific visualization tools in a collaborative context. A "Collaboratory" is a visual computing environment allowing project teams to collaborate and share data and insight while distributed over a network, using intuitive visual navigation techniques "Visual Conference Calls". The distributed architecture is based on Application Component Sharing and a network abstraction system for games providing real-time data interactivity. The innovation can be summarised as the integration of network technology used in collaborative games with 3D data navigation techniques and based on a low-level, fine-grained "atomic" component infrastructure, implemented and validated in real-world environments.

In this paper we focus on 3D medical imaging tools describing a collaboratory implementation of a "VolumeViewer". A Web based application component for 2D and 3D visualizations of MRI, CT and scientific 3D volume data that supports peer-to-peer collaborative sessions on PC desktops. The EC funded research project SMARTDOC proposes how collaborative visual data navigation technology, with Web-enabled application sharing, can be used routinely. The SMARTDOC project is also a blueprint to inform researchers and software engineers about the possibility to extend existing visualisation applications to support collaboration, e.g. making it easier to "collaboratize" visualization applications.

Keywords: collaborative visualization, volume visualization, visual user interface

1. Introductions and Background

Over the last decade a number of software frameworks for supporting collaborative computing and visualisation have appeared. These different frameworks are usually categorized depending on the creators' background and the target of the framework. These categories include among others terms like "team work", "group work", "Internet-based learning", "distance education" and "computer supported collaborative work", but they are all just names of more or less specialized software frameworks that underneath do the same thing. Unfortunately, almost all of these frameworks are realized using an architecture that makes them hard to modify, reuse, or extend with new functionality. SMARTDOC, a partly EC-funded research project, proposes a framework for supporting the design and realization of collaborative visualization with a special focus on scalability, extensibility, reusability and robustness. After providing a conceptual overview and brief background, we describe the application component of a collaborative Volume Viewer prototype.

In this paper we have focused on one of several SMARTDOC applications, "teleradiology", a science that has been in use for more than ten years and is the electronic transmission of radiological medical images and reports between distant groups. Teleradiology tools allow the radiologist to discuss a patient's case with colleagues remotely. Several research projects have been funded by the EC Commission [1] to visualize MRI and CT data. Although collaborative systems providing real time visualization and navigation exist in a broad range of usage areas, their appearance in the medical area is very limited.

SMARTDOC provides a framework for real time collaborative data visualisation and discovery among geographically distributed remote users, linking people and their desktops (collaboratories) in a worldwide "Virtual Data Environment". We define, develop and validate a conceptual distributed computing infrastructure required to support the development of real-time 2D and 3D visual data navigation "collaboratories" based on an "atomic" (low-level) component architecture. The atomic component technology and network infrastructure are based on available industry standard Microsoft technology COM, .NET and DirectX's network abstraction and distributed object system. The distributed architecture is based on "Application Component and Data Sharing" providing real-time data interactivity, reducing the load on the network and with zero administration client deployment. Currently, "peer-to-peer" collaboratories are supported. Figure 2 shows the overall architecture based on the Viewer, Communication Object and the Collaboratory application component. A client-side component "Collaborative Viewer", responsible for the graphics rendering and collaborative sessions, is developed and distributed free. This free Viewer can be compared with plug-ins such as the Adobe Acrobat Reader or VRML viewers.

Collaborative visualisation systems have been around for decades, but only recently did they start to gain ground outside academic and military units. This popularity increase is mainly due to the rapid development of computer power and network technologies. A number of challenges remain to be overcome:

- Management of network resources (concurrency, data loss, network failure, scalability, security issues such as with medical imaging, etc)
- Real-time visualisation applications (rendering OpenGL vs. DirectX vs. Java3D)
- Interactive multi-user applications (coordination mechanism, managing interdependencies, consistency among users, etc)
- Integration with Data Mining and large databases (geographic information, etc)

2. Collaborative Visualization of medical data

The clinical implementation of physiological imaging techniques requires new structures for data display and dissemination. The radical nature of these new techniques also demands that these structures encompass an inherent collaborative and educational function in order to optimise the understanding of the findings by all members of the multidisciplinary clinical team involved in the patients' management. In the early stages of clinical implementation this will be achieved by cascading of knowledge from specialist academic radiology centres to associated clinical departments and, in the later stages by dissemination from these to non-radiological members of the medical team.

Current medical data management systems fail to provide the flexibility to combine all the required visualisation and algorithmic technologies in a unitary framework. Most available systems are complex, difficult to use and expensive. The paradigm used by most manufacturers is to provide a broad range of functionality on a single platform that increases both complexity and expense. In addition, the use of these medical workstations in collaborative scenarios is relatively limited despite the increasing demand for "teleradiology" systems. SMARTDOC has developed a "VolumeViewer", that could offer potential solutions to some of these problems.

The VolumeViewer is a Web-enabled application component allowing collaborative examination of 3D MRI or CT data using standard volume visualisation techniques. For example, the use of atomic architecture offers the ability to "re-use" low-level algorithmic functions to produce application specific components for integration into custom user interfaces. Importantly, the SMARTDOC architecture also offers full collaborative interaction and the ability to use low-cost platforms. This approach to system architecture could, for the first time provide the infrastructure for affordable widespread medical image interpretation facilities available to any member of the clinical management team whilst allowing close collaboration between clinicians to optimise image interpretation and treatment planning. A doctor can visualize and analyse a volume dataset during any time away from the hospital.

The VolumeViewer has been developed as a stand-alone version, a network version, which provides collaborative sessions, and an ActiveX version that can be inserted into web documents as well as Microsoft Word or PowerPoint documents. The three versions cover the usage areas:
- Diagnosis
- Collaborative analysis
- Presentation and journaling

The user can interact with the volume by changing parameters such as isovalue, color, opacity, visibility etc. The volume can be scaled, rotated or translated by simple mouse moves and key presses. The graphics is immediately updated when any parameter is modified creating the effect of an animation. The 3D viewport contains the volume data represented as an isosurface and three movable orthoplanes that control the contents of two 2D viewports that display selected projected orthoslices. The orthoplane with a normal in the z-direction (xy-plane) is always displayed in one of these viewports, but the other viewport displays the xz- or the yz-orthoplane.

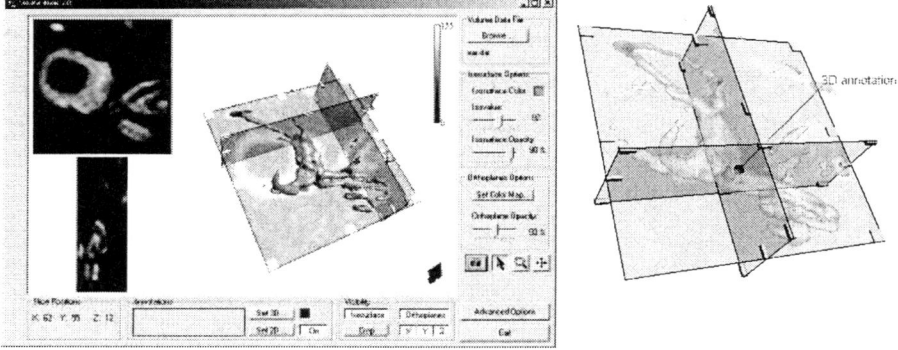

Figure 1: VolumeViewer – a "Collaboratory" for interacting and visualizing medical volume data and the 3D annotation tool in a teleradiology session.

2.1 Annotation

An annotation tool has been integrated to provide the ability to mark regions of interest in both the 3D isosurface and 2D orthoslice objects. Annotation is an important tool in a teleradiology system. 3D annotation is a challenging issue, since it is hard for the user to specify a position in three dimensions with only a simple mouse as a tool. VolumeViewer introduces a new 3D annotation method based on moving a 3D box in the scene where the movements are restricted to the normal direction of its faces, which limits its degrees of freedom but at the same time makes the process more intuitive. Only one user is allowed at a time to use the annotation tool, otherwise the behaviour of the VolumeViewer is undetermined. The underlying network system will solve this contention problem.

2.2 DICOM data interface

Digital Imaging and Communications in Medicine (DICOM) is a standard method for transferring images and associated information between different medical devices manufactured by various vendors [2]. DICOM is not an image format, but a set of protocols that an application, which claims to follow the standard, should conform to. One purpose of DICOM is to facilitate communication of medical digital images between different clinics etc. The standard is also meant for Picture Archiving and Communication Systems (PACS), which often have an interface to other parts of a hospital. Instead of developing a DICOM reader and interface, the project has demonstrated the scalability and extendibility of our component architecture and integrated a commercial DICOM component into the VolumeViewer. This means that the VolumeViewer can directly view and access patient data archives including the binary image data and attributes such as modality, patient ID, patient name, referring physician's name, study ID, study date, slice thickness and spacing between slices. The DICOM component is also responsible for the network security.

3. VolumeViewer based on a collaborative game architecture

The fundamental challenge when writing a networked, collaborative multi-user application is how to propagate state information to all the desktop computers in the session. The state of the session defines what users see on their desktops and what interactive actions they can perform. The session state is responsible for communicating the data navigation process and environment among the participant users. For example, the selection of multivariate data to be analysed, picking a special data object for additional metadata, correlation between data objects in 2D and 3D space and 3D viewing attributes including rotation, zooming and panning etc. Each user also has a state indicating the user's current properties. Actions performed by users of a data navigation application change the state of the session. When this happens the change will be propagated to the other desktops in the session through messages.

SMARTDOC is not the only web-based collaboratory system. There are multiple ongoing or completed projects in the area of Web-based distributed systems. The computer graphics research community has devoted many resources to collaborative visualisation. Research has focused on Java, VRML and the DIS protocol (IEEE Distributed Interactive Simulation) [4],[5],[6],[7]. Unfortunately, almost all of these systems are realized using architectures that make them hard to modify, reuse, or extend with new functionality.

The functionality and design of a collaborative environment depend on many different factors, such as location of data, available bandwidth and process distribution. One common solution is to divide the participants into one master and one ore more slaves and transmit changes of pixel values of the master screen to the slaves. This is for example how the Microsoft NetMeeting application works. Other solutions are based on a shared event model, where an event is generated each time a parameter on the host application is changed. The event can be multicasted to other participating applications without sending any pixel values. All parameters are then properly defined at each user's application unlike the master and slave solution. The collaborative solution suggested in this paper is based on the share event model, having the actual dataset stored locally.

An application area that heavily uses 3D graphics on networks is the computer gaming industry. Many of the games that work on ordinary PCs use the Microsoft DirectPlay API, a special library within DirectX that provides classes for networking facilities. Many of the visualization tasks that VolumeViewer handles are the same as the ones used by a traditional computer game, i.e. setting up a session, sending messages, player (user) management etc.

The network service provider architecture in all SMARTDOC components is based on Microsoft's DirectPlay API. The VolumeViewer integrates component-based visual data navigation tools and visual user interface methods with connectivity software based on emerging industry-standard network protocol for collaborative games. The project has learned from other research projects that have been dedicated to collaborative games [8]. The VolumeViewer supports most generalized communication capabilities shielding end users from the underlying complexities of diverse connectivity implementations, freeing them to concentrate on the real-time navigation scenario. The integration of a network abstraction system, "Application Sharing" and a "Data Navigation Protocol" provide the foundation for real-time collaborative visualisation. The VolumeViewer extends the Web collaborative paradigm to the domain of interactive data navigation in an integrated 2D and 3D worlds and visual user interface technology supporting large medical data sets. High performance is guaranteed through optimised coding with DirectX classes.

Our implementation of a collaboratory provides a layer that largely isolates the application component from the problems of an underlying network. With a multi-user application session, each user's VUI is synchronized with that of the other user(s) in the session [9]. A continual stream of messages flow to and from each user. For example, every time a user rotates a 3D object or changes an attribute, a message with the viewing matrix is sent to update that user's position on the other application client in the session. Our VolumeViewer collaboratory supports efficient and flexible messaging between all the computers in a session.

3.1 Overall architecture

From the system point of view, the system has a symmetric architecture. To initiate a collaborative session, one of the sites starts up its "Collaboratory" (for example the VolumeViewer). Other participants then start up their own Collaboratory to connect to the first participant that is acting as a "host" or "master". Each Collaboratory is identical to the others so that any of the applications can run as the "host" when the first participant decides to leave the session. Communication among participants is done through the Communication Object. This kind of "application component and data sharing" will provide a general-purpose networked environment with no bottlenecks.

The service provider architecture of the Communication Object insulates the application component from the underlying network abstract layer they are running on making it easier for the developer to extend any visualisation application component with collaborative activity. The Communication Object provides all tools needed to support a networked, collaborative data navigation session by providing the services to establish connection between desktops, create and joining sessions, manage single users or group of users, send messages between users, and automatically propagate the state among the computers.

3.2 Viewer Component

The SMARTDOC application component "Collaboratory" will be sharing an "engine" component responsible for visualisation, interaction, networking and rendering, called the SMARTDOC Viewer (see figure 2). The shared Viewer component connects directly into the window layout system of the parent application, and takes care of managing all of the visualisation inside the view including taking full advantage of and manage the complex interactions with high-performance graphics layer in OpenGL. The Viewer will not only be responsible for drawing and updating the charts and graphs but also for carrying out all mouse interactions and management of the viewing hierarchy.

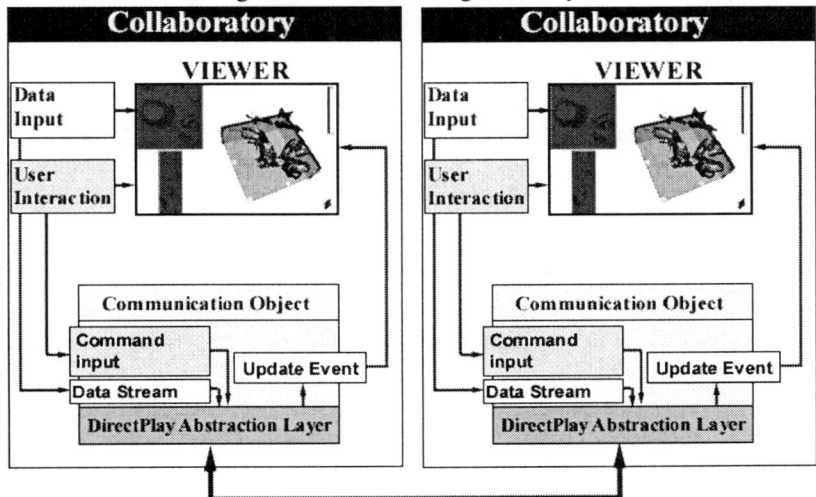

Figure 2 SMARTDOC collaborative architecture in "Peer-to-Peer" sessions with the central shared Viewer (Visualisation) component, Communications Object and the application component "Collaboratory".

The SMARTDOC architecture allows lightweight applications components to be deployed across the Web. Downloading the shared Viewer Plug-in (6Mb) to the client machine enables this and guarantees that the VolumeViewer has a small footprint (200Kb). The Viewer is distributed as "freeware" to allow free distribution of SMARTDOC collaborative applications on the network. The Viewer provides:
- Rendering of the output of the components in the Scene Tree to create the visualization
- Management of a system of attributes that control features of Viewer, including the color and shading of surfaces, projected images, line widths, styles and so on
- User interaction with the data in the view, including transformation, scaling, and picking

- Interface to the Communication Object responsible for the collaborative session management

4. VolumeViewer Collaborative methods

The VolumeViewer implements the DirectX classes to create a DirectX object that can start a DirectPlay peer-to-peer session with predefined parameters. The application must create a DirectPlay "player" (the API is originally meant for game play!) to be able to send and receive messages. All communication messages take place between different DirectPlay players and not between different computers. We call the players "members", who are identified by a unique ID-number assigned when the user connects.

When connecting, the members first have to select through which service they want to connect. The application enumerates the systems available service providers. IPX or TCP / IP on modem, LAN or serialconnections are supported. When the choice is made, the selected service provider is initialised. When the service provider is selected and successfully initialised the user can choose between joining a session or create a new session and wait for participants to join in. If the user decides to host a session, an instance of a DirectPlay session object, which is really a direct communication channel between the involved computers, must be created. The user that starts a session is called the host or the master and is the only one that can change session parameters. The VolumeViewer allows DirectPlay host migration. If the host decides to end the session, the other user overtakes the hosting of the session and other users can join it.

4.1 Active and Passive members

The host (master) is the only member that can interact with the VolumeViewer and change attribute and viewing parameters and is therefore the *"active member"* The other user(s) "Slaves" become the *"passive member"*. Although the underlying technology is peer-to-peer, we have used client-server philosophy when building the application. All interaction on the host side is briefly stored and sent to the passive member. The messages are received and the appropriate parameters are updated and the application is invalidated. The passive member is actually just a spectator watching the interaction by the active member.

The host, which is the active member of the session as default, has the ability to decide which one of the members that will work as the session's active member. When the host approves a passive member to be active, the host becomes a passive member but, unlike other passive members, has the ability to retake the active membership. The reason why the application has been implemented like this is to make sure that only one user can modify the graphics. The purpose of the application would be lost if multiple users affected the graphics at the same time. Too much flexibility and the users will get confused and there will so much divergence between the different clients that one will loose its collaborative nature.

A simple chat has been implemented so that communication between the users is possible. In further work, an implementation of for example DirectPlay Voice would be suitable for the application.

4.2 Messages

Message packages are sent to all participating members in a session and stored in a message receive queue. The application extracts the messages from the queue by an identifier that determines the type of message (Figure 4). A number of message types have been implemented, which are unique for the VolumeViewer application and are used to control the display of isosurface and orthoplanes. Examples of messages includes:
- *Matrix* message: Translation, rotation, zooming or panning.
- *Isosurface* message: Isovalue, surface opacity, surface color and visibility.
- *Orthoplane* message: Plane in the volume dataset, opacity and visibility.
- *File* message: Contains file name and size information of the host's dataset. The dimensions (x,y,z) and the filename are compared before another member can participate
- *FileOK* message: Sent by the member joining application when the comparison between the datasets is done. If the host dimension and name do not match, the joining member will automatically be disconnected.
- *2D and 3D annotation* message: Textual and polyline (only 2D) with array of X,Y coordinates, selected plane and color.

There are also other types of messages including background colour, viewport location and chat messages. The messages are built the same, but contain different data.

Figure 3: Example of a buffer in the message architecture

A message consists of a buffer that holds parameters stored as data or strings. The buffer starts with a "message type" that is checked when the message is received to ensure that the right action will be performed by the application. An offset variable is inserted after each data as a separator between the different message types (Figure 3). The system architecture provides full flexibility for the developer to remove or add new type of messages to the application.

4.3 Information Protection

During a session, the annotations made by the master and passive members are given a unique identity to avoid name conflicts and to make sure that only the user that created the annotation can remove or modify it. All annotations are displayed and updated. The integrated external DICOM component provides professional network security for medical data allowing SMARTDOC to focus on the visualization and collaboration features of the system [10]. Local client-side volume image data (figure 4) is anonymized.

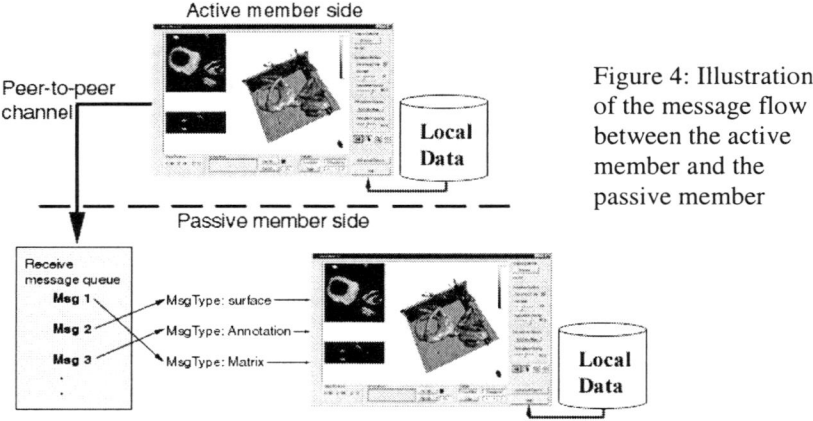

Figure 4: Illustration of the message flow between the active member and the passive member

4.4 Disconnection

When a passive member disconnects, the application stops receiving messages and looses references to the peer- and DirectX objects. If the user hosts a session, the DirectPlay host migration function checks if there is another user participating. If there is this user becomes the new host of the session and other users can now join the session. Any user can save and restore the contents of the VolumeViewer at any time allowing all members to have a collaborative session where the invocation parameters are shared, saved, and modified on each client.

5. Conclusion

There are multiple ongoing or completed projects in the area of collaborative visualization systems. Unfortunately, many of these frameworks are using an architecture that makes them hard to modify, reuse, or extend with new functionality. SMARTDOC are not trying to invent yet another collaborative system and network protocol, but have instead built on existing industry-standard network software in Microsoft's DirectX and demonstrated how this system originally developed for collaborative games can also be used for data visualization.
The SMARTDOC framework places a special focus on scalability, extensibility, reusability and most important robustness. The advantages and experiences from our implementation can be summarised:

Ease-of-use and robustness: A SMARTDOC collaboratory application provides a layer shielding end users from the underlying complexities of diverse connectivity implementations, freeing them to concentrate on image interpretation and treatment planning. Microsoft's DirectPlay provides license free, robust and easy-to-use visualisation collaboration. Clinicians can participate in an unconstrained process of group discovery with a minimum of previous network experience. The VolumeViewer has been tested and validated in a hospital network environment with real medical data and real doctors and was accepted as reliable and easy-to-use.

Easy-to-implement and reusability: The architecture of the Communication Object insulates the application components layer from the underlying DirectPlay network abstract layer they are running on. The Communication Object provides all tools needed to support a networked, collaborative data navigation session by providing the services to establish connection between desktops, create and joining sessions, manage single users or group of users, send messages between users, and automatically propagate the state among the computers. Any visualisation application component can be extended with these collaborative tools with a minimum of programming effort (a couple of days).

Component architecture provides scalability: Our system fuses 2D and 3D visualization, interactive visual data navigation and collaborative components into a VolumeViewer collaboratory application component. All components can be reused, refined or replaced. Data interaction, presentation styles, processing of large data sources and the network abstract layer are clearly separated from user interface, improving the lifetime of the application architecture. Microsoft's Visual Basic (VB) was used to design the user interface and embed the components. VB was also used for rapid prototyping in close collaboration with the end user.

Network and media independent: DirectPlay is media independent, which mean that sessions can be held no matter what types of networks that are used, including service providers such as TCP/IP, IPX on modem, LAN or serial connections. When DirectPlay is instantiated a virtual network connection is created between the application and the network, which enables the application to always, communicate in the same way regardless of which type of network that is used. Small state event messages during a VolumeViewer session reduce the amount of network traffic and thus visualisation performance is not restricted by use of low bandwidth.

Performance: 3D games must be interactive and high performance was guaranteed through our optimised coding with DirectX classes for both 3D rendering and network collaboration.

Small Collaboratories: A small footprint (200Kb) makes distribution of application components (application sharing) easy across the network.

Free sharing of a collaborative session: No licenses are required for the Web-based application component and network software.

The VolumeViewer has been evaluated by a group of clinicians. Systematic discussions about the security, functionalities and future possibilities have taken place, which have resulted in the implementation of additional features not available in the original design of the application. The lack of volume rendering in our application has been criticised by some academic reviewers. However, the clinicians agree that volume rendering is a technique not yet fully developed or trusted to be used in the diagnosis process. This visualization function is more important for initial guiding in the medical work and for the ability to do nice "scientific" presentations. Security was implemented through an external DICOM medical image access component [14] that was integrated with the VolumeViewer and thus shielding the security problems from the visualisation components.

The clinicians also agree on the SMARTDOC concept supporting three different stages: diagnosis, collaborative analysis and presentation/journaling. An innovative idea was discussed to extend the presentation/journaling part allowing the user to create and publish reports based on embedding a VolumeViewer ActiveX component. These "interactive" reports could be posted to a web server from which they could be easily accessed and downloaded. Such a solution could have great potential for education according to the end user.

Based on our work so far, we have identified the following research challenges that must be met to make effective collaborative visualization possible:

- Develop a theoretical understanding of the cognitive and social aspects of both local and remote collaboration mediated through display objects in a medical and other planned application context.
- Assess the advantages and disadvantages of extending methods of interactive 3D medical imaging and information visualization methods (developed for single users) to collaborative settings versus designing new methods to meet unique characteristics of group work.
- Implement client-server solutions for multi-user applications, e.g. for educational applications. An obvious drawback of peer-to-peer solutions is their scalability.

Acknowledgements

The SMARTDOC project is a collaboration between Linköping University, AVS, Unilever, AETmed, Intecs and Central Manchester Healthcare Trust. The project was partly funded by the EC Commission IST-2001-28137. The SMARTDOC web site can be found at: http://servus.itn.liu.se/smartdoc/.

References

1. L. Beolchi, "European Telemedicine Glossary, DG XIII-B1: Applications relating to Health", ISBN 92-828-7147-9,1999
2. DICOM Cook Book, for Implementations in Modalities, B Revet, PHILIPS Medical Systems, 1997.
3. Gabbard, J. L., D. Hix, and J. E. I. Swan. 1999. User-centered design and evaluation of virtual environments. *IEEE ComputerGraphics and Applications* Nov/Dec:51-59.
4. Wood, J., Wright, H. and Brodlie, K., 1997. Collaborative Visualization, Proc., IEEE information Visualization '97. IEEEComputer Society, Pheoniz, Oct. 19-24, 1997, pp. 253-259.
5. Roussos, M., Johnson, A., Moher, T., Leigh, J., Vasilakis, C. and Barnes, C., 1999. Learning and building together in an immersive virtual world. Presence, 8(3): 247-263.
6. Hindmarsh, J., Fraser, M., Heath, C., Benford, S. and Greenhalgh, C., 2000. Object-focused interaction in collaborative virtual environments. ACM Transactions on Computer-Human Interaction, 3(4): 477-509.
7. Padula, M. and Rinaldi, G.R., 1999.Mission critical web applications: A seismological case. Interactions, July-August: 52-66.
8. Collaborative 3D Visualization with CSpray; Alex Pang; www.computer.muni.cz/cga/cg1997/g2032abs.htm
9. Building Interactive Distributed Applications in C++ with The Programmers' Playground; Kenneth J.Goldman, Joe Hoffert, T. Paul McCartney, Jerome Plun, Todd Rodgers
10. Collaborative Visualization; Jason Wood; Leeds University PhD Thesis, February 1998. www.scs.leeds.ac.uk/kwb/publications95.htm#Love:98;
11. Di Benedetto, DirectPlay 8 Overview, Microsoft Corporation, May 2001,msdn.Microsoft.com
12. Jem, M., 1998. "Thin" vs. "fat" visualization client, Proc., Computer Graphics International. 772 -788.
13. SMARTDOC web site servus.itn.liu/smartdoc/
14. www.AETmed.com

What is Your Relationship with Your Information Space?

Jim J. Thomas, David R. McGee, Olga A. Kuchar, Judith W. Graybeal, Dennis L. McQuerry, and Pamela L. Novak
Pacific Northwest National Laboratory[1]
Richland, WA 99352
{firstname.lastname}@pnl.gov , www.pnl.gov/infoviz

Abstract
This invited paper describes a vision for a fundamentally new approach to finding the unexpected and verifying the expected in massive information spaces. Rather than communicate with our information spaces using abstractions, our relationship and interaction with our information spaces are that of a master to its slave. Today, we specify searches and our information resources respond to our specifically worded queries. However, when dealing with massive information spaces, determining how to construct the queries themselves is daunting. Instead, we argue that the information spaces themselves must be given sufficient latitude to support a human-information discourse, by (1) developing its own initiative and thereby supporting a more equal communication style, (2) presenting information within a context that can itself be relied upon as an artifact of communication, (3) while creating a two way dialogue for query and thought refinement. We will motivate the change from human-computer interaction into human-information interaction, discuss higher order interactions with information spaces, and address the technical challenges in achieving this vision.

Keywords: interaction, discourse, human-computer interface, massive data

1. Introduction and Background

1.1 Human Computer Interface Legacy and Beyond

For many years we have studied the Human-Computer Interface (HCI) [1,2]. This is mainly defined by the interactions between humans and their computer systems to include displays, keyboards, mouse, and even tactile and sound. This could be defined as the syntax of the interaction. Over the last few years of developing information analysis technologies [3-10] we have discovered the need for a deeper

---

[1] Pacific Northwest National Laboratory is managed for the U.S. Department of Energy by Battelle Memorial Institute under Contract DE-AC06-76Rl0-1830.

interface, the Human-Information Interface (HII). This interface defines the information flow, pace, contents within contexts, questions, and hypotheses, within a two-way dialogue between people and their information resources-- a discourse [11]. The contexts are the whole of the situations, backgrounds, or environments relevant to a particular event, personality, etc. The discourse is the active dialogue between the human and their information resources. This type of interaction implies what is sometimes called a "mixed initiative" [12] style where the information resources themselves can provide context and suggest avenues of study.

There is another entire field of study on the human - human interface (HHI) [13-17], how we communicate between people. This includes gestures, eye contact, as well as the verbal and visual. To help define the characteristics of the HII we ask, should the human-information interface take on many of the characteristics of the human - human communication? Our observations were that the HHI is unique and personal. Some will attempt to simulate this with avatars, but there is still a need for study towards discovering the semantics of discourse within the HII. What should be the content, form, style, and pace for the discourse between the human and our vast information resources? Certainly, these will be questions posed by many over the next few years.

Observations

- <u>Human/computer</u>
  - 2D
  - Bound by constraints of I/O
  - Keyboard/mouse/monitor
  - Harder to change
  - Syntactic
  - Master slave relationship
  - VR/AR may be different

- <u>Human/information</u>
  - Two way initiated communication
  - Teaching/suggesting
  - Mark progress
  - Understand my perspective
  - Shared assumptions and make new ones
  - Tools may modify behavior
  - Beyond technology today
  - Stories behind/within data
  - Multimodal

- <u>Human/human</u>
  - Convey semantics
  - Validation - trust
  - Relationship
  - Personal
  - Active listening
  - Experience driven
  - Multimodal

One of the distinctive characteristics of the human-human interface is that we convey meaning when communicating to another person; via voice, gesture, eye contact, and active listening. The degree of our meaning is often related to the degree of trust and understanding we have between ourselves and the listener. In direct contrast is the way that we communicate with computers – simple words, keystrokes, and mouse clicks. We feel that both perspectives, HCI and HHI, offer positive interactions for the HII. For example, the HII can become a two-way communication dialogue with the information resources suggesting clarification, different points of view, and setting contexts. The HII can solicit what the current problem is and use this to formulate responses during the interactions. In a way, we already do that today when we define a set of keywords and have systems scan news and push items of interest on a daily basis.

While there is still much to be developed, it is also plausible now to communicate with our information spaces with statements, hypotheses, questions, and have the response be directed towards multiple of these all the same time [8]. There will be multiple technical approaches to enabling such a dialogue from purely statistical to natural-language processing, and combinations of both.

The HII can become multimodal, whereby we use paper, voice, gesture, etc., within the interface. A recent series of publications on Conversational Interfaces [18,19] suggests the current state of the technology and advantages of this style of interaction.

The introduction of the core concepts within the human-information space has been strongly influenced by the challenges and opportunities posed by dealing with very large amounts of information.

1.2 Influences of Massive Data

One of the most compelling motivations for a different discourse between humans and their information resources is the influence of massive data. The terms large or massive are relative terms that change on a regular basis. Ten years ago a large data set might have been 100 Megabytes, now 100 Terabytes seems large. Even with modest size information spaces, the complexity of the relationships, often call the dimensionality, cause one to approach that analysis differently. A modest information space with high dimensionality can also then be perceived as large. Some say we are generating between one and two exabytes per year [20]. In addition, over 50% of the data in the world is stored on individual controlled computers vs. nicely organized databases [20]. We have a huge loose confederation of information spaces making up our information resources.

Both the size and the complexity of information spaces change how we approach and analyze the data in them. If we have 10 documents in our information space, we likely will just read them. However if we have 10,000 documents, we will take a very different approach. And if we have 10 million documents, then we will likely take yet another approach. It is the latter example that we define as massive and that drives some of the questions posed in this paper.

In any case the amount of information becoming available is by far outstripping our ability to manage and analyze it. There are real limitations to accessing and analyzing even small subsets of this information. In addition to these limitations we choose to look at this as an opportunity by asking: *what does large or massive information offer for the HII that is not achievable by smaller information spaces?*

For many years the statistical community has developed summary techniques for statistical databases while providing this as self-describing data. This might include: clusters, identification of outliers, distributions, ranges, embedded quality flags, graphics, or publications along with the more traditional metadata of field names, locations, sizes, etc. It is well within reason to develop analogous information for large information spaces dominated by text documents. This could then be played as the context of an information space when entering a new or updated information resource.

Large information spaces allow for the identification of associations and relationships within the data, through advanced data mining technologies. These can then again become part of the context that can be used during the HII.

Often information resources are collected from different sources, under different context, offering the opportunity to clarify issues of quality and uncertainty. If data from 6 independent locations all indicate an event is likely to happen, then one would have a higher level of confidence in expecting the event, (unless through a high-dimensional discovery one finds that a single source created the original information which was then copied by the others; a common situation in news reporting).

Another great advantage of large information spaces is that we can start to determine what is there as well as what is not there. What is not there is sometimes the solution to the problem. This also helps the human to establish a degree of certainty in their hypotheses and analysis.

In order to seize these advantages *and* overcome the limitations inherent in dealing with massive data, we present a vision for a future *human information interface*. However, before we attempt to further detail the components of our discourse and to help clarify the vision, we offer two scenarios of envisioned human-information interface influenced by access to large information spaces.

2. Example Scenarios of Interaction

The following are two example demonstration scenarios that illustrate some of the envisioned discourse between the human and his or her information resources.

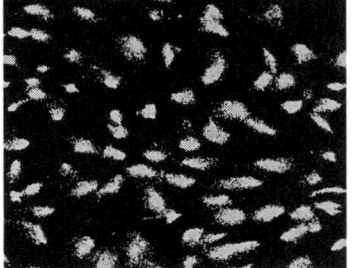

Scenario I: Blue November
Rianne Jackson is an analyst specializing in the Russian military. She begins the day by opening her interest profile; it visualizes recent

information, emphasizing themes and documents based on her prior analyses. One of the visualizations shows documents as graphical shapes, with clusters based on her interests and the key news topics of the day.

An e-mail requests a rush analysis: a new Russian submarine, the Blue November, is headed toward the U.S.; Rianne is asked to confirm a theory that the commander will launch a renegade attack. She reorganizes her information workspace for this analysis. She crosses out some clusters, eliminating many usual interests; she circles other clusters saying, "These are less important today." She starts the questioning on the Russian navy and the submarine commander by dragging the memo to the information space, highlighting parts of it, and saying, "Let's find out more about these." In response, her visualization shifts, emphasizing information related to those topics.

Rianne asks to see a temporal display of themes and events prior to the submarine launch. The system asks for clarification: "Include past years?" Rianne assents. The system asks further: "What classes of events?" It displays a drop-down list and Rianne selects several categories. Unexpectedly, she discovers that the sub's launch date is the anniversary of the death of the sub commander's wife. Rianne hypothesizes that the submarine commander's actions are an expression of anger—but against whom?

Rianne drags the name of the submarine commander to her relationship visualization tool, asking for a display of known political and military relationships. The tool displays an image of the commander, adds icons for other people and organizations, and shows arcs among the icons, using color, line pattern, and orientation around a horizontal  plane to portray the various classes of known relationships. The expected attack on the U.S. is also shown. She notices strong relationships among certain military officers. On a hunch, she circles the cluster of icons representing the biographies for the officers. The system responds, "Why are these interesting?" Rianne says, "I am looking for commonalities." "Which of these types?" Rianne answers, "Relationships." The visualizations confirm that the officers on the Blue November are longstanding colleagues of the commander. She asks to "See personal relationships;" several family arcs are shown for all of the people in the display, except for the sub commander and officers. None have surviving close family. Rianne considers a new hypothesis: they are all defecting. The visualization shows a hostile relationship between the sub commander and the fleet commander, reinforcing the hypothesis. Rianne says, "What if he is not attacking…" (the arc for the supposed attack disappears) "…but is defecting?" (She adds an arc representing a possible defection to the U.S.) The display shifts, and a checklist noting signs of defection comes up on the screen. A match.

Scenario II: Visualization Researcher in a Commercial Company

TJ, a visualization researcher, has proposed a new product concept for his company. Prior to getting his funding he first must find out if other companies are likely to have developed or are developing similar products and technologies and present his findings by 2:00pm that afternoon. TJ starts his quest.

TJ has developed a page of text describing his potential product idea. He opens his search and ingest agent in the morning. TJ transfers the description to the agent and asks for an information space to be established based on patents and publications. The agent remembers that his last search covered all references to multimedia and asked TJ if he wanted all those as well. TJ says no. The agent suggests a cup of coffee while the Search and Ingest takes place.

On return TJ finds an information space of 5,832 patents and 847 articles (about 200,000 pages of text and diagrams) related to the field of visualization and his potential product idea. TJ sees the overview summary of the entire space and asked for the context. As in a play, when you walk up into a theater, the context is set in a matter of minutes. There appeared a list of themes and topics on visualization, a distribution of patents by these themes over years with some outliers highlighted. TJ watched as the thematic changes took place of several years in an animation and much to his surprise found several portfolios of companies that had portfolios that may establish prior art with his idea.

TJ immediately noticed that the information retrieved included many patents on hardware rendering which had little relationship to the idea. On attempting to remove these from the information space he was cautioned that one such patent had a relationship, within a rare but identifiable common point with his idea. TJ examined the patent and found it had picked up one of his previous patents when rendering with almost the only thing going in graphics. His thinking and use of words in the description had flagged that patent as it was within context even though the word rendering was not used.

Now TJ realized his description conveyed old thinking and revised his description using more current technical terms for another Search and Ingest. This also encouraged him to provide alternate descriptions of a product to the search and ingest agent with varying capabilities. He also knew of a researcher in England who was doing something similar so gave the agent that information as well. It became clear that there were many ways to get similar products and each had to be evaluated.

TJ was presented with a series of thumbnails each having a context about the information provided. After playing the context he asked for what is common and different about each information space and determined most were on basic screen and window interaction with little on actual content visual approaches. TJ placed his descriptions in the middle of the display and asked to create the relevance map surrounding his different ideas and the name of the researcher in England. Some focused on very specific interaction technologies but there appeared to be a gap directly over two of his descriptions. The researcher in England had taken a different approach that looked very promising but did not overlap the description. He then proceeded to explore the patents most closely surrounding the two ideas in detail and found what was there and what wasn't there.

TJ had to give a confidence level on his findings to his manager. He considered that 4 of the companies had similar ideas but did not have any patents in the core mathematical approaches central to his ideas. However, one had a long standing patent that they might consider buying to secure an open patent space. His level of confidence was high based on the extent of the information analyzed and the dimensions of the information explored. He could not say his idea was completely unique but had enough confidence to proceed with initial investments.

TJ then attends his briefing where on completion he is asked to compare his product idea with from a new web technology that a manager read about on his Delta flight the day before. TJ captured the idea as a hypothesis and asked for a repeat analysis compared to his other statements. This was partially convincing and TJ was given conditional approval for his project startup; a typical response.

There are a lot of syntactic and visual details not present in these scenarios that can be inferred from references [3-11]. It is the flow of the discourse that we are attempting to illustrate.

Sample Requirements Learned from the Scenarios

Most of the underlying technology used in these scenarios is available today to find, within high-dimensional spaces, the information relationships based on some relevant statistics with clustering algorithms. (Natural language processing comment required here) However, the interaction, is not there in most systems. In summary we find that we need the following:

- Upon entering an information space, establishing the context for that space is critical. This becomes core when dealing with large and/or complex information. Knowing what is there and what is not helps define the analytic approach.

- Analyst-system joint determination of task and meaning of inquiries. The analyst and system negotiate the mutual understanding of the question, which may include identifying relations that the system was unable to discover alone.

- Extending "drill-down" by enabling the inquiry process to "breathe" (i.e., successively enlarging and narrowing its context and focus). The shifts in focus—whether to narrow in order to increase focus, or to enlarge in order to avoid a local minimum—can optimize the result of inputs from both analyst and system, which bring inherently complementary resources to the inquiry process.

- Fusing system knowledge (both statistical and propositional) with evolving analyst questions, assertions, interests, and analytical context. The system will provide constant feedback of shared understanding, primarily through visual means, suggesting alternative lines of inquiry and serendipitous, potentially useful information.

- Leveraging the development of contexts throughout the process. Multimodal manipulation of the visual feedback will allow analysts to develop individual contexts (or questioning frameworks) that will influence questions in a particular direction through contextual weighting.

- A multimodal framework for question positing. The interaction between analyst and system will include combinations of direct-manipulation and natural spoken language expressions. Propositions must take forms natural to the analysts and the tools they have at hand. Therefore, they will be necessarily multimodal.

These observations are just a small sampling, but can help to establish the vision of a human-information discourse.

3. Functional Components

To facilitate the relationship with information spaces through the envisioned discourse several functional capabilities will be required.

The first and central to all is a visual and highly interactive suite of paradigms. These will likely be augmented with other modalities while the dominant style well be visual. The forms of interactions are envisioned to be at a higher semantic level which we term Higher Order Interactions such as hypotheses and questions. These interaction will be captured within a dynamic, incremental, and reusable analytic process. One of the main influences on this discourse due to massive data, is that the discourse must be reusable within new contexts.

Indeed are many contexts that will have to be captured and factored into the discourse. These include the human's context such as a-priori and tacit knowledge, the information context (that which provides metadata about the many information resources, and the contexts for the situation to be accessed. The interactions of these contexts within the discourse will indeed be one of the grand challenges.

Accessing and ingesting information is a core challenge within massive information spaces. It is unlikely that one can see all the data at one time. So, we expect this to be an agent-driven retrieval process through the combined context. The motivation for having this being agent driven is that touching all ones information resources, especially those discussed as large, should be a well defined process that can be implemented within an agent framework.

Lastly we expect to have a modeling and plausible scenario generation component that would offer suggestions within the discourse. This is the formation of the theory aspect of discourse while the data/information provides the experiment. The interface between theory and experiment will become core to a highly interactive discourse. This happens naturally in human-human dialogue.

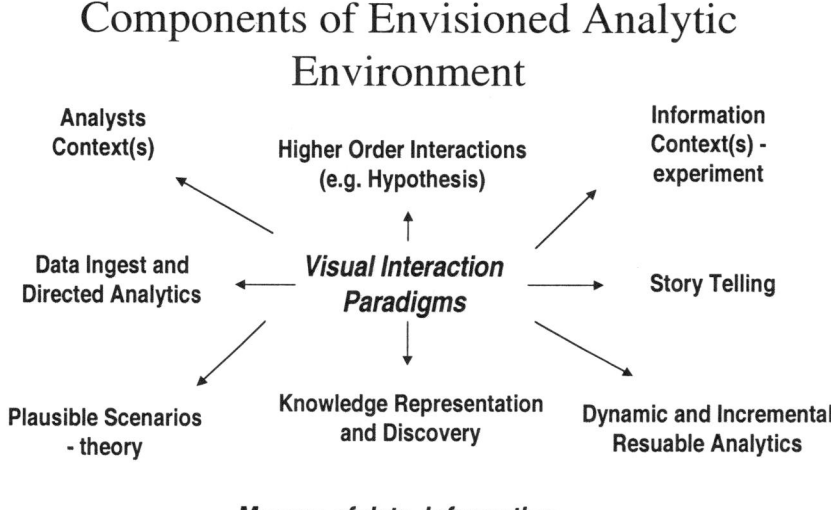

4. Higher Order Interaction Techniques

To further clarify our vision of higher order interaction techniques we offer some comparisons to interactions today. Currently we think in terms of concepts when communicating between humans, yet we decompose these into specific words or pickable objects when communicating with computers. These become the objects of our discourse. With higher order interactions one communications in concepts, phrases, questions, diagrams or even multiple hypotheses as seen in the scenario. This implies going from a syntactic dominant discourse to a semantic dominant discourse.

We expect the higher order interactions to include the functions of learning, remembered processes, to include the ability to capture and re-use processes as part of the knowledge discovery processes. The degree to which learning will be included is yet to be defined but the ability to capture the analysis process and reply it within another situation is strongly desired.

Today we have a master-slave relationship with our computer resources, whereas we envision a peer-to-peer relationship within this discourse. This implies a mixed initiative dialogue. Higher order interactions within information spaces are suggestive. As the user discovers themes, topics, and associations, the information space should contrast what it believes the user may have discovered to its knowledge of the analysts needs and suggest paths of study and refinement.

The pace of discourse and feedback within massive information spaces is critical. Humans expect some operations to take time while others must respond almost instantly. A search and ingest is one operation that one expects in general to take a longer, whereas a deletion of a cluster of already selected information should be instanteous.

We expect the functional balance of the different ontologies and contexts to become a core part of the discourse within analysis of massive information spaces. The discourse should indicate that "the tool understands me".

We would like to suggest a "relationship" criterion for the interface being called seductive. Today's interface does not encourage coming back for enjoyment. There are clearly games that have achieved this quality. However 90% of the tools we use today are work and not fun. There must be a balance between fun and work that would provide a discourse that encourages learning, exploring, and discovering within massive information spaces.

On a final note, one cannot describe a vision for dealing with massive information spaces to find the unexpected and verify the expected without depicting some of the physical aspects of human-information interaction. People interact with large information spaces to not only find an answer, but to explore and gain insight and knowledge about it. The mere presentation of information does not necessarily result in this process [21. 22. 23]. People need to be engaged with their information spaces.

For some time now, there has been a distinct preference for monomodality. For example, the most highly-valued novels came entirely without illustration, and had graphically uniform, dense pages of print. More recently this dominance of monomodality has begun to reverse. For example, novels have acquired colour illustrations and sophisticated layouts and typography. Another example is televisions that have evolved from viewers watching people speaking into a microphone to interactive TV. The world is hopefully moving towards multimodal communication. This multimodal supported discourse between the human and their information resources will become the source of several other papers.

5. Challenges and Conclusions

The technical challenges for enabling the desired vision are many and within reach given the technical foundations available to researches. There are:

- How do we deal with scale, distributions, and unassociated information? This will likely require the use and fusion of ontologies. This will also likely entail the creation of data signatures to represent the essense of the information in a mathematical form that can be fused across multiple contexts into the context for the situation under investigation.
- How do we introduce the context within an information space? This could be a 2 minute story of the sources, themes, topics, actors, and plausible events.
- How do we build and enable a discourse of communication between the human and their information resources? This must include a multi hypothesis and question driven investigation.
- How do we represent the uncertainty of the information, and the human given an information discourse, the user's tacit knowledge, and the situation under investigation?
- How do we capture and represent knowledge, human judgment, into reusable forms for use within other contexts and situations?
- How do we capture an investigative process for reuse within another study?

The relationship you have with your information space will be formed by a dialogue of interaction. We first presented the vision of moving from the human-computer interface into a *human-information interface* and compared that to human-human communication. The issues of massive and complex information within this dialogue have a direct impact and help suggest the need for a different style of communication. We then presented 2 sample scenarios that included some of the envisioned capabilities. This lead to the overview of the functional requirements and a further discussion of higher order interaction within the discourse.

We finally suggest that the human-information interface will become the driving technical agenda for several years to come as we discover how to create a relationship with our information spaces.

Acknowledgments

We gratefully acknowledge the contributions of our colleagues at the DOE Pacific Northwest National Laboratory in the Information Analytics and Rich Interaction Environment Groups. We especially what to thank Lucy Nowell, Beth Hetzler, Kris Cook, and Alan Turner for the many thoughts and contributions during the development of many of these concepts.

References

1. Card, S.K., T.P. Moran, and Newell, A., "The Psychology of Human-Computer Interaction," ISBN 0-89859-243-7, Lawrence Erlbaum Associates, 1983.

2. Schneiderman, Ben, "Designing the User Interface: Strategies for Effective Human – Computer Interaction," ISBN 0-2-1-69497-2, Addison Wesley, 1998.

3. Wise, James A., James, J. Thomas, Kelly Pennock, David Lantrip, Marc Pottier, Anne Schur, and Vern Crow: "Visualizing the Nonvisual: Spatial Analysis and Interaction with Information from Text Documents," Proc. IEEE Information Visualization '95, (1995), 51-58.

4. Thomas, James J., Kris Cook, Vern Crow, Beth Hetzler, Richard May, Dennis McQuerry, Renie McVeety, Nancy Miller, Grant Nakamura, Lucy Nowell, Paul Whitney, and Pak Chung Wong: "Human Computer Interaction with Global Information Spaces - Beyond Data Mining." Digital Media Futures: British Computer Society, International Conference April 13-14, 1999. Published by Springer, Digital Media, ISBN 1-85233-140-2.

5. Turner, A.E., and L.T. Nowell, "Beyond the Desktop, Diversity and Artistry," to appear CHI 2000 proceedings Spring 2000.

6. Hetzler, Beth, Paul Whitney, Lou Martucci, and James J. Thomas: "Multi-faceted Insight Through Interoperable Visual Information Analysis Paradigms." In Proc. of IEEE Symposium on Information Visualization, InfoVis '98, October 19-20, 1998, Research Triangle Park, North Carolina, pp.137-144.

7. Havre S.L., E.G. Hetzler, P.D. Whitney, and L.T. Nowell, 2002 "ThemeRiver: Visualizing Thematic Changes in Large Document Collections". IEEE Transactions on Visualization and Computer Graphics Vol 8, No 1, January 2002.

8. Havre S.L., E.G. Hetzler, K.A. Perrine, E.R. Jurrus, and N.E. Miller: "Interactive Visualization of Multiple Query Results." In Proc. of Information Visualization 2001. Pacific Northwest National Laboratory, Richland, WA.

9. Thomas J.J., P.J. Cowley, O.A. Kuchar, L.T. Nowell, J.R. Thomson, and P.C. Wong: "Discovering Knowledge Through Visual Analysis," Journal of Universal Computer Science, Springer, ISSN 0948-695x, International Conference on Knowledge Management, July 12-13, 2001. PP. 62-74.

10. Nowell LT, B.G. Hetzler, and T.E. Tanasse: "Change Blindness in Information Visualization." IEEE InfoViz Symposium 2001.

11. Thomas, J.J. and A.E. Turner: "Access and Retrieval of Digital Media," Digital Media Conference: BCS, April, 10-13, 2000, National Musuem of Photography,

Film, and Television, Bradford England, Published in book form by Springer, Oct. 2000.

12. de Beaugrande, R.: "New Foundations for a Science of Text and Discourse: Cognition, Communication, and the Freedom of Access to Knowledge and Society," Ablex Publishing Corp. (1996).

13. Novick, D. & S. Sutton: "What is mixed-initiative interaction?" Proceedings of the AAAI Spring Symposium on Computational Models for Mixed Initiative Interaction. Stanford University: AAAI Press. (1997).

14. Quine, W. V.: "Word & Object," MIT Press. (1964).

15. Eco, U.: "A Theory of Semiotics," Indiana University Press. (1976).

16. Habermas, J.: "The Theory of Communicative Action: Reason and the Rationalization of Society," Beacon Press. (1984).

17. Eco, U.: "Semiotics and the Philosophy of Language," Indiana University Press. (1986).

18. Habermas, J. and M. Cooke, M. "On the Pragmatics of Communication," MIT Press. (1998).

19. Lai, Jennifer, Guest Editor "Conversational Interfaces," Communications of the ACM, September, 2000.

20. Oviatt, Sharon: "Taming Recognition Errors with a Multimodal Interface," Communications of the ACM September, 2000.

21. www.sims.berkley.edu/now-much-info

22. Vygotsky, L.S. (1962) Thought and Language, MIT Press, Cambridge Books, New York

23. Piaget, J., and Inhelder, B. (1969) The Psychology of the Child, Basic Books, New York.

State of Art in Digital Media

Jon Peddie
Jon Peddie RESEARCH
Tiburon, California

Abstract
This paper focuses on the unrelenting push from the effects of Moore's law that are driving down size and cost and making new capabilities a practical and affordable reality. It's no longer a question about digital media; it's how much can I get, how soon, and for how much.

Keywords: Digital Media, MPEG-4, Handhelds, home gateways, miniaturization, Moore's Law

1. Introduction

Digital media was supposed to bring us untold hours of pleasure and ease. But what it seemed we got originally was untold hours of promises of pleasure and ease. And although things have not developed as quickly as some of the visionaries suggested, we have nonetheless witnessed and enjoyed some amazing new capabilities in digital media and its associated systems and content.

There have been two major leading and enabling technologies making this possible, semiconductors and the deployment of high-bandwidth; and there have been two trailing technologies, content, and rights protection.

1.1 Moore's Law and the miniaturization of the universe

Moore's Law, originally an observation about memory density, has become popularized to represent the unrelentless march of technology with a doubling effect every eighteen months. Since so much of new technology is based on semiconductors, this generalized application of Dr. Moore's observation[1] seems to work, and it is convenient shorthand for describing a rather complex processes.

With miniaturization comes more density within the same area. It is popular and convenient to characterize new circuits, processors, graphics and video controllers,

---

[1] Gordon Moore made his famous observation in 1965, just four years after the first planar integrated circuit was discovered. The press called it "Moore's Law" and the name has stuck. In his original paper (Electronics, Volume 38, Number 8, April 19, 1965), Moore predicted that the number of transistors per integrated circuit would double every 18 months. He forecast that this trend would continue through 1975. Through Intel's technology, Moore's Law has been maintained for far longer, and still holds true as we enter the new century.

communications, etc, in terms of the number of transistors within them. When processors are examined historically, this produces the famous Moore's law log curve, shown in the next diagram.

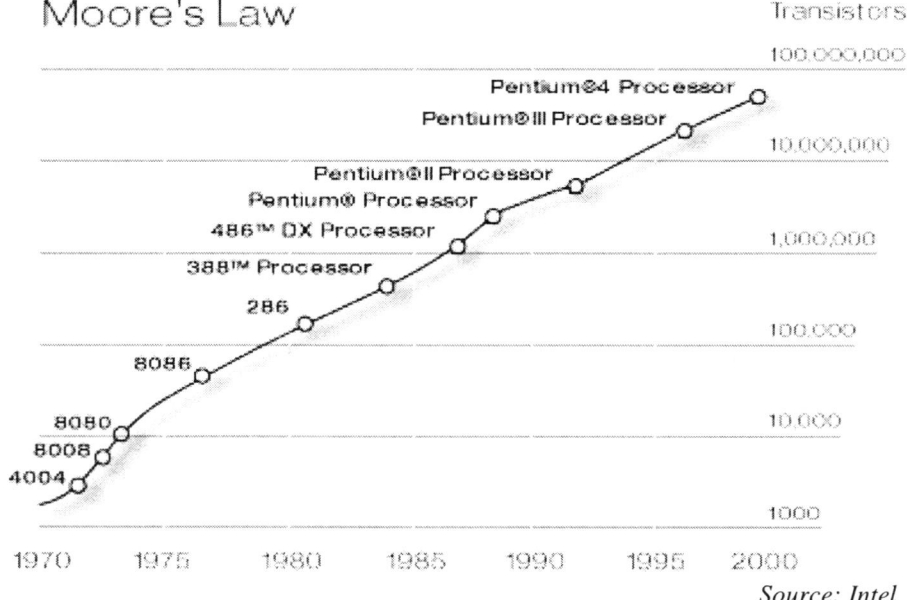

Figure 1. Moore's Law expressed with Intel processor advancement

Processors, however, are not the only devices to benefit from miniaturization, memory, graphics, communications and other system components also shrink in size and increase in density. This gives the designers a larger transistor budget to work with which means they can put more functions into the same space. That leads to either super powerful application specific circuits such as graphics processor units (GPUs) or more general purpose highly integrated parts know as systems on a chip (SOCs). SOCs are largely responsible for the new wave (and the next new wave) of super powerful, feature-rich consumer electronic devices like digital set-top boxes (STBs) for cable and satellite, digital video recorders (DVRs or PVRs), game consoles, DVDs, and the new wave of amazing video cameras.

In addition to the home digital entertainment boxes (DEBs) a new wave of personal mobile devices in the form of phones and personal digital assistants (PDAs) is emerging with full multimedia and wireless capabilities. And a third new digital media platform is emerging, the automotive entertainment system (AES).

With exception of the DVD and CD media (disc) all of the rich multimedia content that these platforms will make available to the user are being (or soon will be) delivered via high-speed, high-bandwidth communications systems. That's the good news. The bad news is there is such a plethora of communications delivery systems the user is confused and therefore intimidated, which results in slow acceptance of the technology. That feeds the cause-and-effect trap of content developers holding back until there is a sufficient installed base of users to justify the cost of development while the users hold back waiting for more or better content. This is one problem Moore's law can't solve.

But let's look at some of the technologies, infrastructure, and products impacting digital media that Moore's law has had an effect on.

2. Handhelds

When it comes to digital media that's mobile, we have seen several major developments: digital video cameras, multi-function mobile phones, 3rd generation PDAs, expanded MP3 players, and input/output devices.

2.1 Video Cameras. In late 2001 we saw the introduction of handheld consumer digital video cameras that can write directly to an on-board mini DVD disk that will store 30 minutes of MPEG2 video (2.3Gbytes) on each side of the disc in a format that can be read by almost all DVD players.

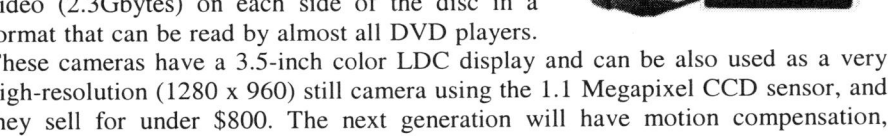

These cameras have a 3.5-inch color LDC display and can be also used as a very high-resolution (1280 x 960) still camera using the 1.1 Megapixel CCD sensor, and they sell for under $800. The next generation will have motion compensation, wireless connection capabilities, and more built-in video-editing functionality.

2.2 Multi-Function Mobile Phones. Phones are being developed and will soon be available (if not already) that have larger displays and added functionality. Your phone will become your PDA, and have a built-in camera, as well as play MP3 audio. The 3G phones, using MPEG-4, will usher in a new set of video conferencing users, which will (at long last) drive the market for even better video conferencing systems. As of the end of 2001, about 24 percent of the cumulative total of J-Phone's mobile phones in use had the function. The early units can only send still pictures, but the next generation (this year) will have low frame-rate video capability. Your telephone becomes a surveillance system, or a way to show people where you are either for entertainment or finding your way. And yes, you will watch movies, or at least commercials, on your phone, and play games—Everquest whilst commuting, can life get any better?

2.3 PDAs. The line between a PDA and mobile phone is becoming one of screen size, with the larger screen going to the PDA. PDAs with 802.11x are already in use and in addition to collecting e-mail, and becoming an always on Rim-like device, there are new models that will offer VoIP challenging the mobile phone. For example, Sharp will begin supplying personal digital assistant-type mobile phones to telecommunications companies in Europe this summer, and aims to ship the phones to the U.S. by year-end

Amazing high quality 3D games can now be played on PDAs, and they will, with their larger screen, probably become the platform of choice for the on the road game player. Newer models are also being equipped with MP3 player capability making the ever more ubiquitous device an portable entertainment center.

2.4 MPEG-4. The new MPEG-4 codec with its variable bit rate capability and foreground (object) extraction capabilities is one of the primary enabling technologies of this new revolution in handhelds. The MPEG-4 codec is being implemented in software for decompression in some cases (depending upon the processor and memory in the device) and hardware for encoding. Just three years ago an MPEG-4 codec took up a rack slot—Moore's Law in action.

3 Home Gateways

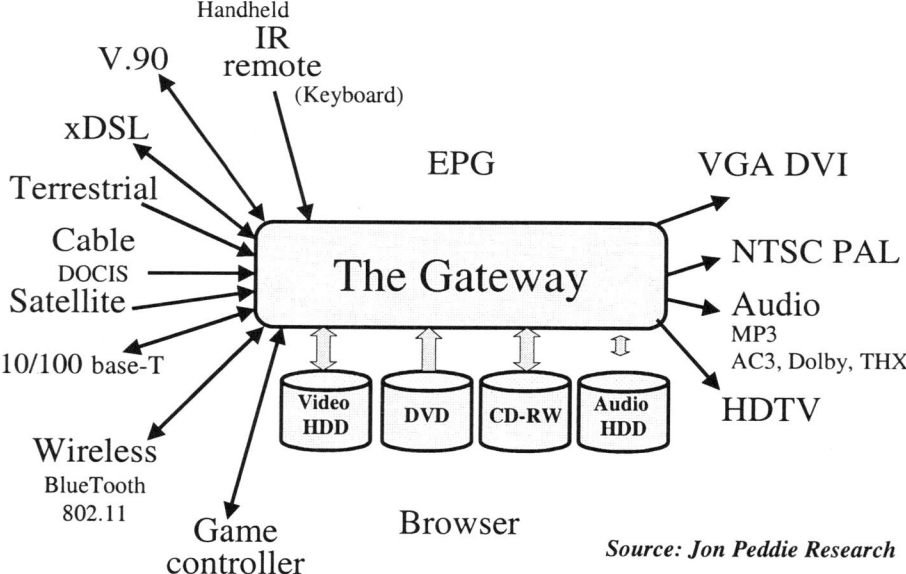

Figure 1. The fully configured home gateway system

One of the most exciting and poorly defined new digital media device categories is the new home gateway. A home gateway is exactly what the title suggests, a gateway to just about every form of digital media available, and distribution of that media to other devices within the home. As the following diagram shows, a fully equipped gateway would have all the various I/O ports, one or more disks, and video/graphics controller(s).

It's not likely anyone will build a system like this since it would expensive and difficult to sell. However, the problem the consumer electronics (CE) manufacturers face is trying to figure out which features to put in and which to leave out. And as soon as one of them decides, its competitors will leave off one to save costs, or add one more thing for upscale product differentiation. In the mean time we are seeing some of the gateway functionality being assimilated into DEBs, which is further confusing the category and consumers.

3.1 Cut the wires. Home gateways used to deliver digital media cannot rely on wires, so part of the digital media revolution is the move to wireless technology. Several companies like Broadcom, Cirrus Logic, Intel, Philips, and others are enabling the wireless revolution in home entertainment systems.

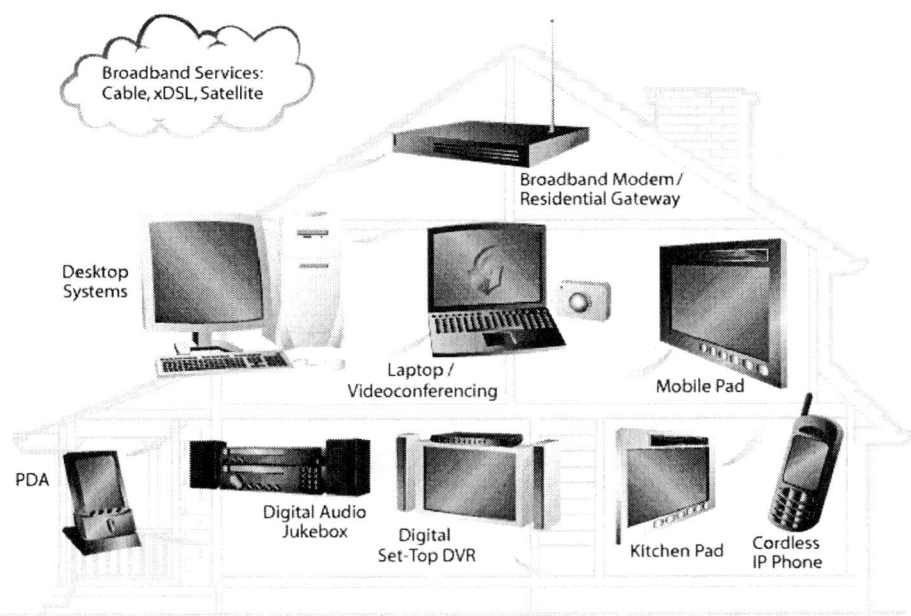

Source: Cirrus Logic

Figure 2. The home gateway challenge – wires

Possibly the first wave of home gateway systems with be audio jukeboxes from companies like Pioneer, HP, and Sonicblue.

4. Digital Entertainment Boxes

The category of digital entertainment boxes (DEBs) consists of several stand-alone CE devices. The following devices are DEBs:

- Cable STB
- Satellite STB
- Terrestrial HD receiver
- DVD player and recorder
- Internet TV ("WebTV")
- Digital TV (HD or SD)
- Game console
- Entertainment PC (AKA Virtual appliance)
- DVR/PVR

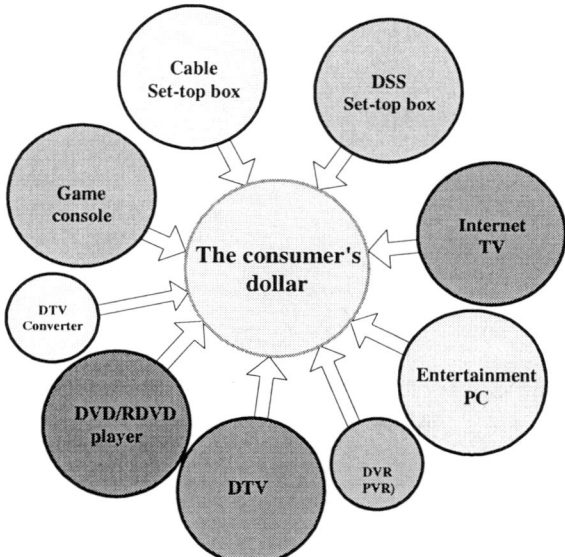

The stand-alone box functions are being assimilated into each other as CE manufacturers try various combinations. It is Darwinian in a sense in that all the combinations will be tried but only a few will survive and become successful and established species of CE devices. A few specific platforms have already become assimilated and lost their stand-alone attractiveness, such as the Internet TV. It's unlikely anyone will integrate a satellite STB into a cable STB; however, the DVR functionality has been integrated into both of them. Game consoles will remain a stand-alone platform for the foreseeable future, assimilating more functionality all the time.

4.1 Recordable DVDs. DVDs have become a new growth area and this year the recordable DVD is a practical reality having gotten below the $1,000 price level and standardization finally catching up. Recordable media has also come down in price and so, like the CD and CD/RW, we'll see RDVDs showing up in PCs which will impact the volume and drive down costs even further.

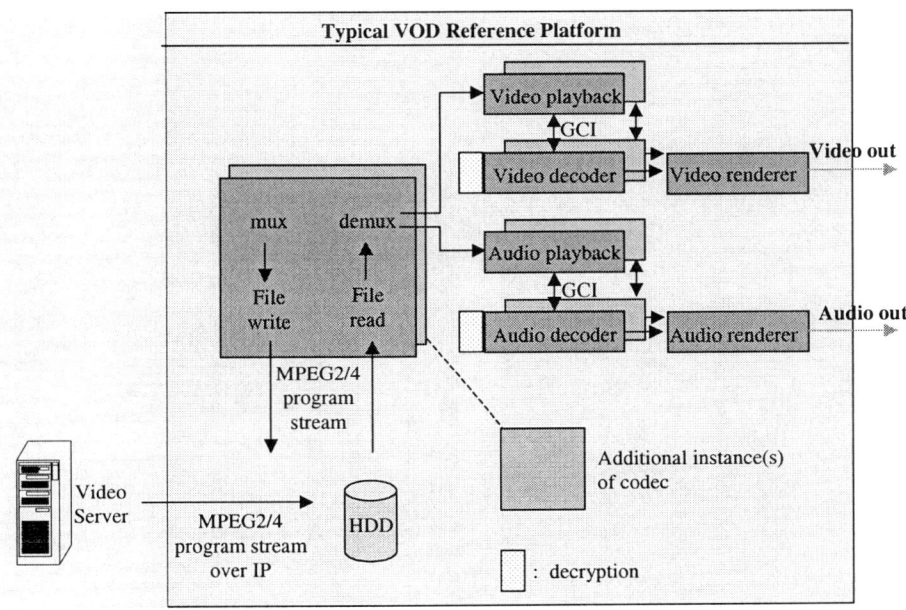

Source: Equator

Figure 2. Typical VOD reference platform

4.2 Entertainment PC. Not really a PC, but barrowing on the rich PC architecture and availability of low cost parts, new digital media platforms are being introduced as DEBs. Microsoft's Ultimate TV, a DVR, has PC architecture under it, as does the Moxi box. The Moxi box also incorporates many of the features of a home gateway. Apple computer has also been a leader in the entertainment PC area

4.3 VOD

The promise of VOD is almost with us, as DSL comes to more homes around the world. Semiconductor companies like National, Equator, and Broadcom are offering reference platform designs to the CE suppliers as enabling technology.

VOD has been limited by a delivery mechanism, and by the cost of the decoding and local distribution parts. Originally it was thought cable would be the delivery mechanism, or possibly satellite. Those delivery systems provide near video on demand (NVOD) by allowing the user to access entertainment within time segments. DVRs offer another form of VOD, with their time-shift capability.

In the case of true VOD again we see Moore's Law at work, bringing down the costs, and increasing the complexity of the SOCs and communications circuitry needed to implement it.

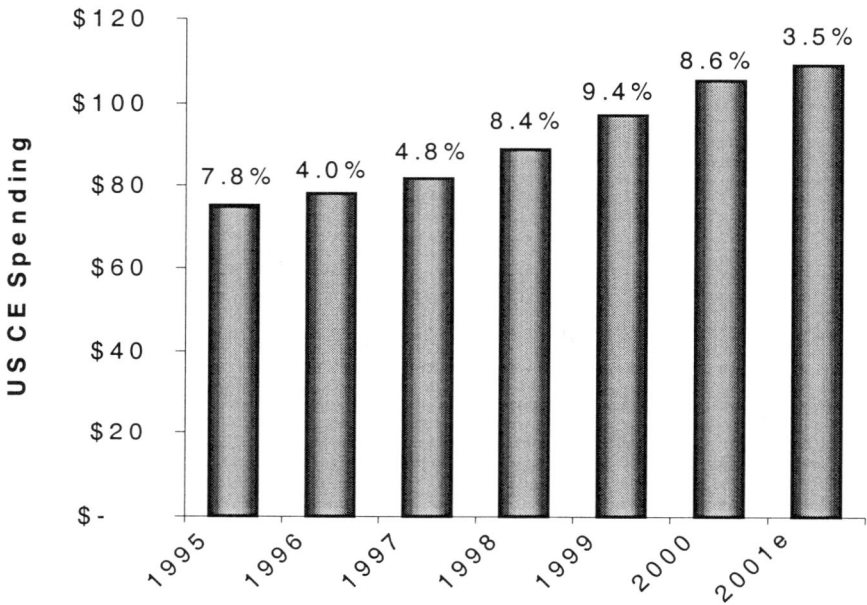

Source: CEMA

Figure 2. Rate of growth of CE market in U.S.

5. Input/Output devices

Input devices in the form of gloves, rings for the fingers, that allow typing in the air, and improved cameras for gesture recognition have been developed, as well as wireless headsets that use Bluetooth and incorporate voice recognition. Users can wander around their homes listening to MP3 music, and change channels with voice commands, never having to actually see the boxes that house the controls or the media. These devices contribute to the digital media experience, in both content creation, as well as use of the content.

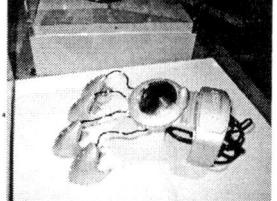

6. The Digital Media Market is Growing

Another cause-effect question that often gets asked is, is digital media enabling convergence, or is the development of convergence enabling digital media, and the answer is, yes. Naturally one cannot survive without the other, and it seems like a philosopher's riddle to try and figure it out else wise.

The experimentation on DEBs, gateways, and mobile devices is fueling some of the growth in CE market, which may have a negative effect if the products don't work out to expectation. Consumers may be unwilling to come back and buy yet another $300 to $600 box suspicious of it meeting their expectations.

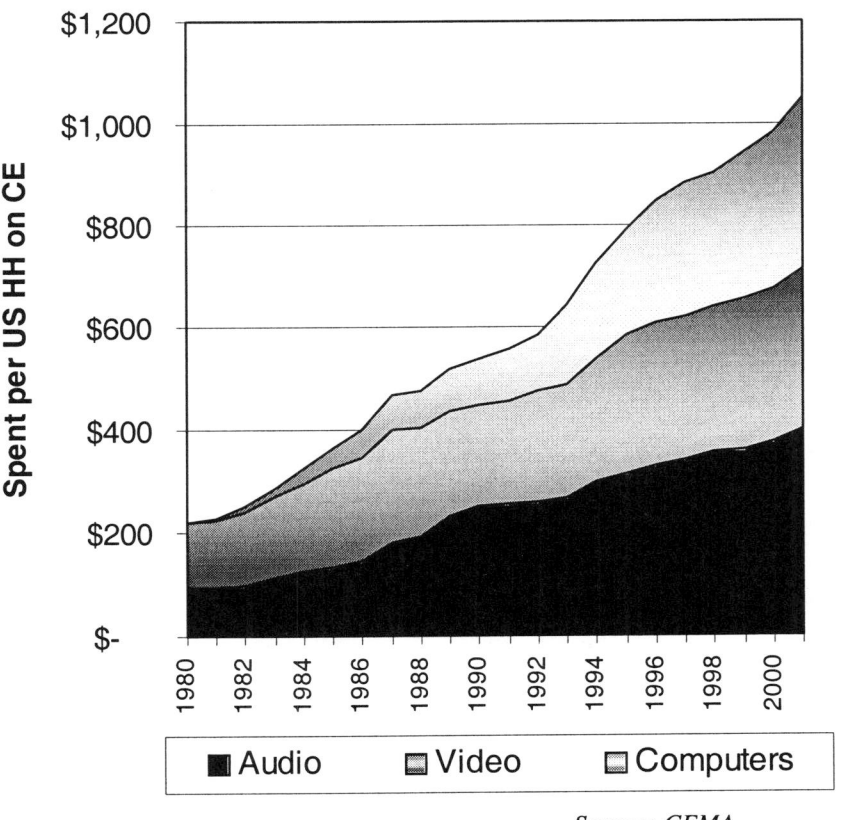

Source: CEMA

Figure 3. Audio, Video, and PC sales in the U.S.

However, the data clearly indicates the demand for audio is high, fueled to a large extent in the last couple of years by MP3, and the new jukeboxes. Video is also high, and were it not for the introduction of digital video in the form of satellite, cable, and DVD, the curve would have probably shown a decline.

Summary

Today's users are aware of and embracing digital media, in the home and on the go. The unrelenting push from the effects of Moore's law are driving down size and cost and making new capabilities a practical and affordable reality. It's no longer a question about digital media, it's how much can I get, how soon, and for how much.

Modelling

A body and garment creation method for an Internet based virtual fitting room.

Dimitris Protopsaltou, Christiane Luible,
Marlene Arevalo, Nadia Magnenat-Thalmann
MIRALab CUI, University of Geneva, CH-1211, Switzerland
{protopsaltou, luible, arevalo, thalmann}@miralab.unige.ch

Abstract

In this paper we present a new methodology for producing 3D clothes, with realistic behavior, providing users with an apposite feel for the garment's details. The 3D garments that are produced, using our methodology, originate from 2D CAD patterns of real garments and correspond to the regular sizes that can be found on a shop floor.

Our aim is to build a compelling, interactive and highly realistic virtual shop, where visitors can choose between many different types of garments designs and proceed to simulate these garments on virtually animated bodies. By merging the approach often used by the fashion industry, in designing clothes, and our own methodology for creating dressed virtual humans, we present a new technique providing trouble-free and straightforward garment visualization.

The entire process starts from the creation of virtual bodies (either male or female), using standard measurements, which form the basis for garment modeling. Using splines, the 2D garment patterns are created and then seemed together around a virtual human body, providing the initial shape. A simulation is made using the seemed garment by applying physical parameters based on real fabric properties. Once the garment has been created, a real time platform, which has been embedded inside a web browser, is used as an interface to the Internet. We extend the web interface to add interactivity and the ability to dynamically change textures, clothes, body measurements, animation sequences and certain features of the virtual environment.

The whole methodology does not aim to build only a virtual dressing room, where customers can view garments fitted onto their own virtual bodies but to visualize made-to-measure clothes, animate them, visualize the cloth behavior and to add interactivity. The entire Virtual Try-On experience is a process of targeting the clientele, designing the clothing collection, dressing the virtual models and then using the web as a virtual shop floor.

Keywords: Virtual Try On, 3D clothes, physical behavior, generic bodies

1. Introduction

The Internet has emerged as a compelling channel for sale of apparel. Online apparel sales exceeded $1 billion in 1999 and are expected to skyrocket to over $22 billion by 2004 (Forrester Research) [1]. While a significant number of apparel sold over the Internet still this number only represents less than 1% of all apparel sold in the United States and significantly lags Internet penetration in other consumer goods markets (e.g. books and music). A number of recent studies identified the causes for consumer hesitancy. Online shoppers were reluctant to purchase apparel online in 1999 because they could not try on the items. Furthermore of particular note is the consumer's overwhelming concern with fit and correct sizing, concerns with having to return garments and the inability to fully evaluate garment (quality, details, etc.) [2].

Consumers that purchase apparel online today base their purchase and size-selection decisions mostly on 2D photos of garments and sizing charts. Recognizing the insufficiency of this customer experience, e-tailers have begun to implement improved functionalities on their sites. Recently introduced capabilities allow the customer to view items together, such as a blouse and a skirt, enabling the mix and match of color/texture combinations, and zoom technology, to give the customer a feel for garment details. LandsEnd.com [3] uses **My Virtual Model**, which provides a virtual mannequin, adjusted to the shopper's proportions. In the same manner, Nordstrom [4] is using 3D technology from California based **3Dshopping.com**, which offers 360 degree viewing, enabling complete rotation of the apparel item. Even with these improvements in product presentation, a number of things can go wrong when the consumer pulls the apparel item out of the box. Although there are a number of solutions available, the problem of a realistic "Virtual mirror" still remains one of the main impediments. The most common problems include poor fit, bad drape, or unpleasant feel while wearing the item, or surprise as to the color of the garment. Customer dissatisfaction in any of these areas drives returns, a costly occurrence for e-tailers, and creates lost customer loyalty, an even more costly proposition.

Our work proposes an implementation of a simple and fast cloth simulation system that will add to the Virtual Fitting Room the feature of realistic cloth behaviour something that is missing today from the existing Virtual Try On (VTO) solutions in the market. Macy's Passport 99 Fashion Show [5] is one of the most high quality VTO show room that has been created so far. The primary benefit of Macy's VTO was to introduce dressed bodies animated in real time on the web. Although the user interactivity has been of primary focus, the actual content lacks of realism. The content is highly optimized and although it is optimal for web application, real cloth behavior is not visible.

Besides realism, modern applications require cloth simulation to accommodate modern design and visualization processes for which interactivity and real-time rendering are the key features. We propose an adaptation of Macy's approach to web visualization that provides a decent cross-platform and real-time rendering solution. However this defines major constraints for the underlying simulation methods that should provide high-quality results in very time-constrained situations, and therefore with the minimal required computation. We additionally propose a scheme that brings to the cloth exact fit with the virtual body and physical behavior to fully evaluate the garment. Our work uses a practical implementation of a simple and fast cloth simulation system based on implicit integration [6].

Along the evolution of cloth simulation techniques, focus was primarily aimed to address realism through the accurate reproduction of the mechanical features of fabric materials. The early models, developed a decade ago, had to accommodate very limited computational power and display device, and therefore were geometrical models that were only meant to reproduce the geometrical features of deforming cloth [7]. Then, real mechanical simulation took over, with accurate cloth models simulating the main mechanical properties of fabric. While some models, mostly intended for computer graphics, aimed to simulate complex garments used for dressing virtual characters [8, 9, 10], other studies focused on the accurate reproduction of mechanical behavior, using particle systems [11] [12] or finite elements [13]. Despite all these developments, all these techniques remain dependent on high computational requirements, limiting their application along the new trends toward highly interactive and real-time applications brought by the highly spreading multimedia technologies. While highly accurate methods such as finite elements are not suitable for such applications, developments are now focusing toward approximate models, that can render, using minimal computation, approximate, but realistic results in a very robust way.

This paper is composed of two main sections. The first section is a description of the research methodology we used to develop the complete chain of processes for the making of bodies and clothes for a Virtual Fitting Room. The second section is a case study presenting the Virtual Try On developed by MIRALab.

2. Research Methodology

2.1 Generic Bodies Approach

With virtual bodies we consider mainly two issues. The first issue is that bodies should correspond to real human body shapes, in order for a user to relate his own body with the virtual body on the screen. The second issue is that virtual bodies should have an appropriate 3D representation for the purpose of cloth simulation and animation.

The first phase of our methodology is based entirely on the generation of human body models that are immediately animatable by the modification of an existing reference generic model. This tends to be popular due to the expenses of recovering 3D geometry. Based on adding details or features to an existing generic model, such approach concerns mainly the individualized shape and visual realism using high quality textures. We propose the creation of five generic bodies, for each sex. Every single generic body corresponds to a different standard size: Extra Small, Small, Medium, Large, Extra Large (plus top model shape).

However the definition of body shape is dependent on many factors, not just simply the standard sizes. It is a complex application dependent task. General anthropometric classifications (somatotyping) are based on specific sets of measurements with specialised instruments (the ordinary tape being just one of them). Many of these measurements relate to the physical identification of anatomical landmark. Existing descriptions of body shapes in the specific application domain (garment design and fitting) are predominantly qualitative (based on the perception of a human body from experts, e.g. fashion designers, or tailors), or quantitative, based on empirical relationships between body shapes – patterns (basic blocks) and garment drape. The primary data used for the character modeling of the generic bodies were collected from sizing surveys results prepared by the Hohenstein Institute [14].

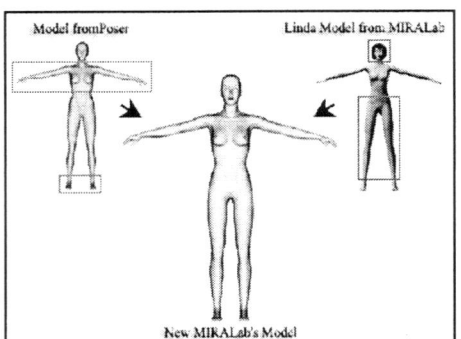 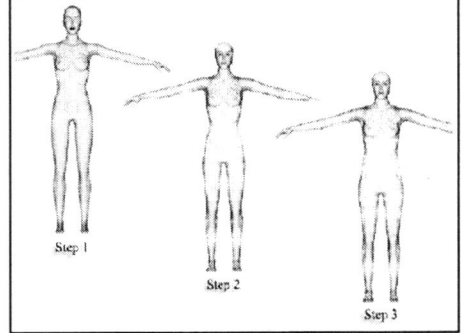

Figure 1 – Reference generic body

The reference generic model (Figure 1) is sliced into a set of contours with each contour corresponding to the set of the measurements as described in the table below (Table 1). To generate a body shape according to the sizes specified, we warp each contour to fit the given measurement and then warp the mesh to interpolate the warped contours. In our approach we take into account only the primary measurements, however manipulation of the secondary body measurements can be facilitated following the same methodology described above.

	Female Standard Body Sizes	XS/34	S/36	M/38	L/40	XL/42
	Primary Measurements					
1	Height	168	168	168	168	168
2	Bust girth	80	84	88	92	96
3	Under-bust girth	71	74	77	80	84
4	Waist girth	65	68	72	76	80
5	Hip girth	90	94	97	100	103
6	Inside leg length	78.3	78.3	78.1	77.9	77.7
7	Arm length	59.6	59.8	60	60.2	60.4
8	Neck-base girth	34.8	35.4	36	36.6	37.2
	Secondary Measurements					
9	Outside leg length	106	106	106	106	106
10	Back waist length	41.4	41.4	41.6	41.8	42
11	Back width	33.5	34.5	35.5	36.5	37.5
12	Shoulder slope	72	74	76	78	80
13	Shoulder length	12	12.1	12.2	12.3	12.4
14	Front waist length	41.9	42.8	43.7	44.6	45.5
15	Girth 8cm below waist	81	84	88	92	96
16	Waist to Hips	21	21	21	21	21
17	Thigh girth	52	53.8	55.6	57.4	59.2
18	Head girth	55.4	55.6	55.8	56	56.2
19	Upper arm length	34.8	35	35.2	35.4	35.6
20	Upper arm girth	26.2	26.8	28	29.2	34
21	Wrist girth	15	15.4	15.8	16.2	16.6
22	Neck shoulder point	25.5	26.5	27.5	28.5	29.5
23	Knee height	45	45	45	45	45

Table 1 – Body Measurements of standard female bodies [14]

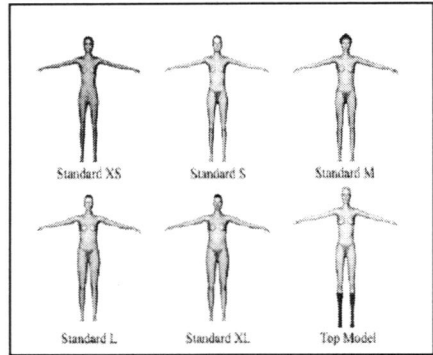 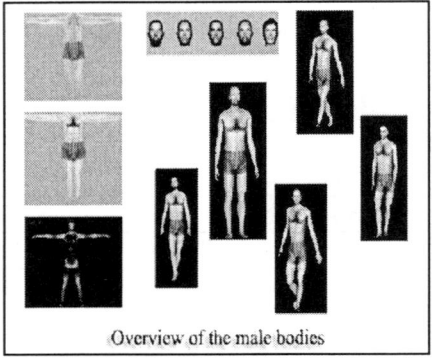

Figure 3 – Overview of the standard female (left) /male (right) bodies modeled according to sizes

The standard male bodies are created using the same methodology as in the case of the female bodies (Figure 3).

2.2 Animation of Generic Bodies

Human Motion Capture [15] techniques necessitate strong competences in Virtual Human modelling and animation as well as thorough knowledge of hardware and software pipelines to transform the raw data measured by the hardware into parameters suited for virtual models (e.g. anatomical angles). We used Optical Motion Capture based on markers [16,17].

The typical pipeline production for optical motion capture begins with camera volume calibration, where the relation between all the cameras is computed using recording of dedicated calibration props (assuming the volume set-up [where the cameras are properly aimed at the captured volume] has already been achieved). Then the subject, wearing optical markers (e.g. spheres of 25mm diameter for body capture), is recorded in a static posture so that the operator can manually label all the markers. The operator gives/selects names for each marker in this static pose, usually using anatomically relevant labels (e.g. LKNE for the left knee marker). The information gathered at this stage will be used by the system to label the trajectories automatically during post-processing of dynamic movements.

Figure 4 – Technical skeleton

The post-processing of motion sequences primarily involves the following two stages: trajectory reconstruction and labelling of markers/trajectories. Once those two steps have been completed, it is possible to visualize the technical skeleton (Figure 4) obtained by drawing segments between the marker positions. From this information the subject skeleton and its animation are derived [18].

It is relatively easy to construct the subject skeleton (or its approximation) from the markers. However, the problem becomes much more complex when considering the body meshes and its deformation parameters. Skin deformation (or skinning) is based on three inter dependant ingredients. First the skeleton topology and geometry, second the mesh or surface of the body, and third the deformation's own parameters (very often consisting of vertex-level ratios describing the scope of deformation with relation to joints). Good skinning results are achieved by a careful design of these three components, where positions of joints inside the body surface envelope and attachments ratios are very important issues.

2.3   Cloth Simulation and Animation

For the simulation of clothes we use MIRACloth as the 3D garment simulator that was developed by the University of Geneva. This engine includes the modules of mechanical model, collision engine, rendering and animation. The algorithms have been integrated in a 3D design framework allowing the management of complex garment objects in interaction with animated virtual characters[19]. This integration has been carried out in the form of a 3DStudio Max plugin (Figure 5). The cloth simulation process has two stages:

1. The garment assembly stage, where the patterns are pulled together and seamed around the body. This is a draping problem involving to obtain a rest position of the garment as quickly as possible.

Once the 2D patterns have been placed around the body, a mechanical simulation is invoked, forcing the patterns to approach along the seaming lines. As a result the patterns are attached and seamed on the borders as specified and attain a shape influenced by the form of the body. Thus the garment is constructed around the body (Figure 5). The seaming process relies on a simplified mechanical simulation, where the seam elastics pull the matching pattern borders together. Rather than trying to simulate the exact behavior of fabric, the simplified model optimizes seaming speed using parameters adapted for that purpose, that is to say no gravity, no friction, etc.[20]

2. The garment animation stage, where the motion of the garment is computed as the body is animated. The dynamical motion of the cloth is important here.

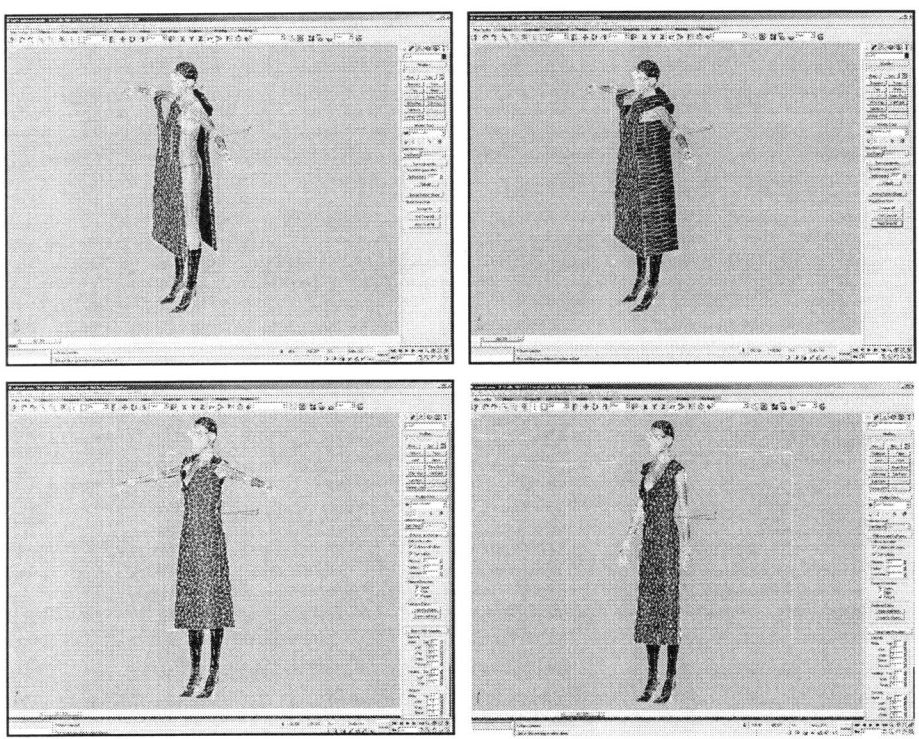

Figure 5 – 3D simulation of cloth

The mechanical parameters of the actual fabric are set, as well as gravity, in order to put the cloth into actual mechanical conditions. Animation of a garment here pertains to its movements along with the virtual body. This is accomplished with collision response and friction with the body surface. At this stage the mechanical parameters are set and tuned with visual feed back. The setting of the parameters may be different from what was used during the process of seaming and construction garments. The mechanical simulation then gives the animation of the garment on a virtual body.

The animation parameters, and particularly the mechanical simulation parameters, are adjusted through the parameters panel. It features two categories: environment (global parameters) and object (local parameters). On one hand, among the global simulation parameters, we will find gravity and finally collision distance and detection modes. On the other hand, the local parameters include elasticity, surface density, bending rigidity, friction values, Poisson coefficient, as well as viscosity and non-linear elasticity values, which are the mechanical properties of objects.

At this stage we aim to quantify precisely the mechanical parameters that are relevant for the perceptual quality of cloth animation for simulated cloth. Starting from the measured parameters, additional parameters (viscosity, plasticity, non-linearity) are also investigated in order to match the simulated deformations with the real values (Table2,3). The experiments involve a 40x40 cm fabric square maintained by the two corners opposite to the attachment line, and distant by 5 cm from the line (the edge length), giving an initial curved loop shape to the fabric. The validation of the experiments was to perform the constrained fall tests and to compare them to reality using two criteria: the time taken for the fabric to reach vertical position in its initial motion, and the damping of the residual motion. [20]

PARAMETERS	Linen	Cotton	Tencel
ELASTICITY			
Weft elasticity	50 $N.m^{-1}$	16.67 $N.m^{-1}$	25 $N.m^{-1}$
Warp elasticity	50 $N.m^{-1}$	16.67 $N.m^{-1}$	25 $N.m^{-1}$
Shear G	55 $N.m^{-1}$	60 $N.m^{-1}$	86 $N.m^{-1}$
Weft bending	208.1 10^{-6} N.m	10.5 10^{-6} N.m	25 10^{-6} N.m
Warp bending	153.9 10^{-6} N.m	6.7 10^{-6} N.m	14.8 10^{-6} N.m
VISCOSITY			
Weft elasticity	50 10^{-2} $N.m^{-1}.s$	16.67 10^{-2} $N.m^{-1}.s$	25 10^{-2} $N.m^{-1}.s$
Warp elasticity	50 10^{-2} $N.m^{-1}.s$	16.67 10^{-2} $N.m^{-1}.s$	25 10^{-2} $N.m^{-1}.s$
Shear G	55 10^{-2} $N.m^{-1}.s$	60 10^{-2} $N.m^{-1}.s$	86 $N.m^{-1}$
Weft bending	208.1 10^{-6} N.m.s	10.5 10^{-6} N.m.s	25 10^{-6} N.m.s
Warp bending	153.9 10^{-6} N.m.s	6.7 10^{-6} N.m.s	14.8 10^{-6} N.m.s
DENSITY	310 10^{-3} $Kg.m^{-2}$	310 10^{-3} $Kg.m^{-2}$	327 10^{-3} $Kg.m^{-2}$

Table 2 – Example of fabric parameters[1]

PARAMETERS	
GRAVITY	10 m.s^{-2}
AERODYNAMIC VISCOSITY	
ISOTROPIC (Damping)	0.1 N.m^{-3}.s
NORMAL (Flowing)	1 N.m^{-3}.s
	1 10^2 m^{-1}
PLASTICITY (f/h)	f = 10 m^{-1} et h = 0.1

Table 3– External parameters[2]

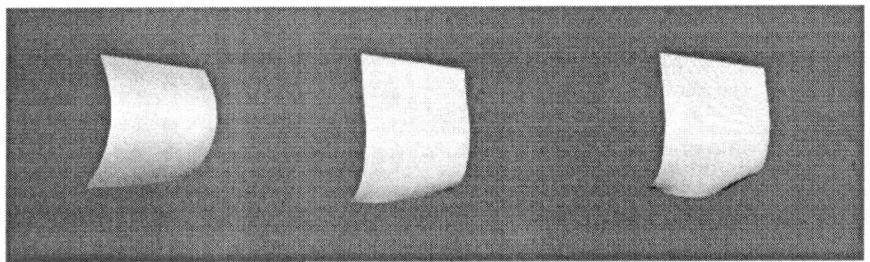

Figure 6 –Example of fabric parameters: Linen/Cotton/Tencel

The effects of additional parameters (viscosity, plasticity, non-linearity) are further investigated through simulation and perceptual assessment. Finally, complete garments are simulated with the cloth simulation system that integrate the accurate model found relevant and defined from the previous study.

---

[1] Metric elasticity: measurement of the fabric elongation elasticity (N.m^{-1})
–*Weft and Warp elasticity*: elasticity along the Weft and Warp directions
–*Shear elasticity*: elasticity for a shearing deformation between weft and warp directions
Bending elasticity: measurement of the fabric bending elasticity (N.m)
–*Weft and Warp bending*: bending along the Weft and Warp directions
Viscosity parameters: defined for each elastic parameter
Density: mass per surface unit of the fabric (Kg.m^{-2})
[2] Gravity: nominal acceleration of objects left at rest (9.81 m.s^{-2} > ~10 m.s^{-2})
Aerodynamic viscosity: aerodynamic force exerted on a fabric per surface unit and per velocity unit between the fabric speed and the air speed:
–*Normal* (*Flowing*: N.m^{-3}.s) and *Isotropic* (*Damping*: N.m^{-3}.s) components relative to the orientation of the fabric surface

2.4 Web Interface and User Interactivity

There is a considerable number of 3D technologies that can be used for the Virtual Fitting Room implementation. Of all the available technologies, VRML (Virtual Reality Modeling Language) [21] is the most established and widely used (ISO standard). Its latest version, VRML97 supports animation and advanced interaction. We used Shout3D [22] as a 3D player/viewer that is implemented using Java taking as input VRML exports from the cloth simulator.

The integrated solution is a cross-platform application/viewer accessible by nearly all web browsers. Such application/viewers provide extensibility via APIs, which means that additional desired features can be programmatically added in them. Shout3D is, at bottom, a Java class library. The methods of that library constitute the Shout3D Application Programming Interface (API). We went further and extended this class library to create a new class with new methods. The primary means of utilizing the API is through direct Java programming. We extended the basic Shout3D Applet and Panel classes to create a new class that implement interactivity using the methods in the API. The methods that extend the basic class library aim to control mainly the user interaction with the 3D viewer. That involves input when the user requires changing the cloth on the animated body, body size, background images and scene rotation. This approach is suitable for commercial-quality work that will run reliably on all platforms. It is also possible to use JavaScript to call the methods in the API. The latter approach, while convenient for testing ideas, will not generally be satisfactory for commercial work and will not be functional on all platforms.

The Virtual Try On is composed mainly of two web pages, where one contains the 3D viewer and the other the cloth catalogue. The 3D viewer (MIRALab Generic Viewer) after initialization loads the default 3D scene where the dressed models will appear. The generic viewer is an extended version of the basic Shout3D applet. Most interactivity programming is implemented in an extended Panel class. The extended class can implement the **DeviceObserver** interface to handle mouse and keyboard events from the user. These events are handled in a method named **onDeviceInput()**. The extended Shout3DPanel class can also make use of the render loop through the **RenderObserver** interface. This interface consists of the **onPreRender()** and **onPostRender()** methods, which are automatically called immediately before or after each render cycle. Initialization duties, such as obtaining references to objects in the scene, are handled by overriding the **customInitialize()** method of the Shout3DPanel class.

The default scene loaded initially is composed of an empty VRML Transform Node namely "emptymodel" that will act as the container where the dressed bodies will load. To implement such interactivity we control the values of class objects that represent nodes in the 3D scene graph. For example, a visitor can manipulate a geometric model only if the panel class has access to the Transform node controlling that geometry. The panel class must therefore create a Transform class object reference variable, and must obtain a reference to place in that variable. Once the reference is obtained, the fields of the Transform node can be changed by means of the reference. The primary means of obtaining such a reference is the **change_model()** extended method of the **miralab_generic class**. This method takes the DEF name "model" of the desired node in the VRML scene file as an argument, and returns a reference to the Java class object. With most (but not all) browsers, JavaScript in an HTML page can be used to call methods in the Shout3D API and therefore implement interactivity and procedural animation without writing and compiling extended Shout3DApplet and Shout3DPanel classes. In order to obtain references to objects in the scene, we used the standard **change_model()** method of the **miralab_generic class**. This method necessarily requires a reference to the **miralab_generic** object.

Apart from the 3D viewer an important part of the Virtual Try On is the catalogue of the different clothes. We use one of the new features introduced in Microsoft® Internet Explorer 5.5, that is Dynamic HTML (DHTML) behaviors. DHTML behaviors are components that encapsulate specific functionality or behavior on a page. When applied to a standard HTML element on a page, a behavior enhances that element's default behavior. As encapsulated components, behaviors provide easy separation of script from content. This not only makes it easy to reuse code across multiple pages, but also contributes to the improved manageability of the page. The MPC behavior is used to add both the multipage container and the individual page tabs. We use the MPC behavior to create two clothes catalogues (male & female) as shown in the figure 7.

Individual page tabs implemented with DHTML help significantly to download a lightweight web page.

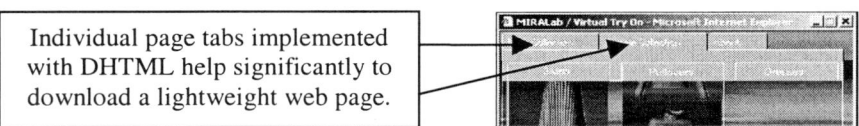

Figure 7 – The online cloth catalogue implemented with DHTML MPC behavior

3. Case Study – MIRALab's Virtual Try On

3.1 Preparation of generic bodies

The generic model is composed of an H-Anim LoA 2 [23] skeleton hierarchy and a skin mesh. The skin surface is a combination of a Poser character and body models created at the University of Geneva. A proper skin attachment was essential for the skeletal deformation. The attachment is considered as assigning for each vertex of the mesh its affecting bones and corresponding weights. To say that a vertex is "weighted" with respect to a bone means that the vertex will move as the bone is rotated in order to stay aligned with it. At 100 percent weighting, for instance, the vertex follows the bone rigidly. This method combines for each vertex the transformation matrix of the bones in accordance to their weight. Once the skin is properly attached to the skeleton, transformation of the bone automatically derives transformation of the skin mesh [24].

To animate the virtual bodies we used Optical Motion Capture (VICON system at the University of Geneva). To obtain a realistic animation sequence, we hired two professional fashion models (Guido Frauenrath & Sarah Stinson) to simulate a catwalk (Figure 6). The captured animation from the models was applied to the H-Anim skeleton to obtain the animated generic body.

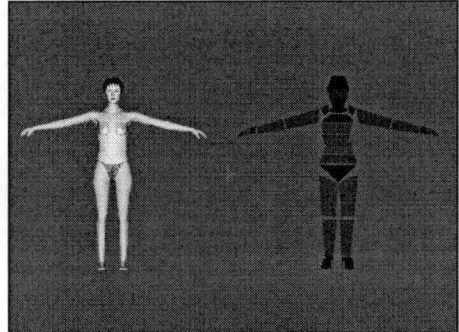

Figure 8 – Motion Tracking with VICON(left) and H-ANIM skeleton (right)

3.2 Cloth creation and simulation

Garments are designed using the traditional 2D pattern approach. We use the Modaris software [25] package to create the patterns. The functionality of the software allows us to simulate the approach of a traditional cloth designer (Figure 9).

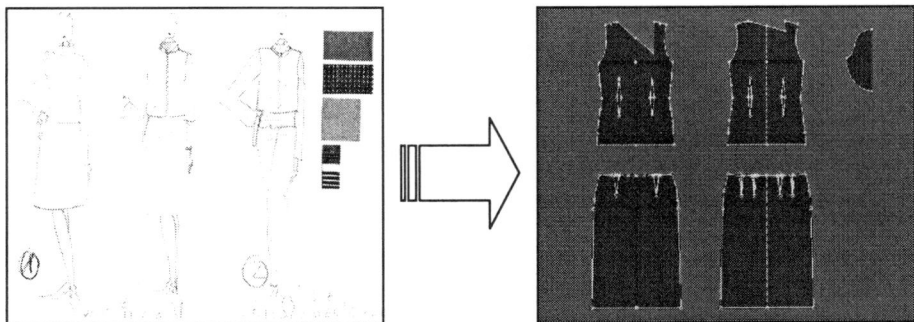

Figure 9 – 2D patterns creation import in CAD software

The patterns then are discretized into a triangular mesh. Following that we place the planar patterns automatically around the body with the use of reference lines (Figure 10). These 2D patterns are constructed and imported in the MIRACloth garment simulator.

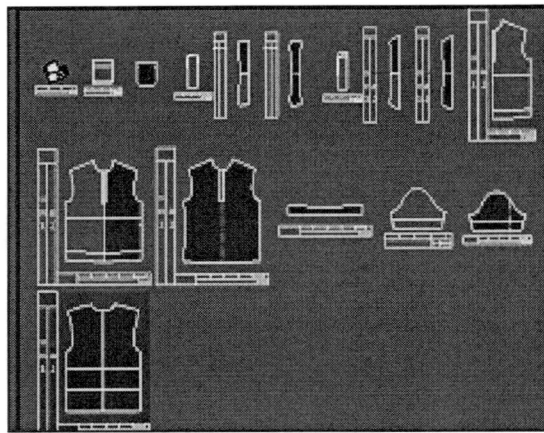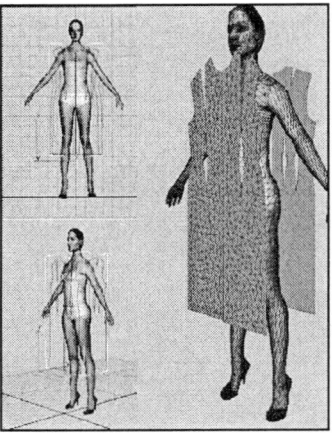

Figure 10 – 2D patterns creation and positioning around generic body

We simulated three different types of clothing for the female bodies (skirt, pullover and dress) each one applied with different fabric properties.
- The skirt and the pullover was simulated with the cotton properties (Section 2.3) and
- The dress with the tencel properties (Section 2.3)

(For the male bodies we applied the same methodology)
Since the final models must be optimized for usage on the Internet, each garment was composed of only 1000 polygons. A second step was performed to decrease the weight of the textures, in order not to overload the video memory during the real time visualization on the web, keeping sizes to 512x512 pixels. The final output was exported in VRML. 3DSMax like all 3D animation packages, offers spline interpolation. To approximate the smooth curvature and subtle speed changes of spline interpolated function curves, the 3Dsmax VRML exporter provides a sampling mechanism for linear key frame animation. The greater the number of frame samples, the closer the linear interpolated result approximates the spline interpolated original.

3.3 Web Interface

The outcome of the overall methodology is an approach to online visualization and immersion that lets any standard web browser display interactive 3D dressed bodies without the need for extra plugins or downloads. For the purposes of wide public Internet access, the first VRML97 output directly from the garment simulator (MIRACloth - 3DSMax plugin) is used. Therefore, it is possible to view it locally or across the network without any special dedicated viewer. This allows a large-scale diffusion of the content over the W.W.W without increasing the cost of distribution. The models performed satisfactory in Internet Explorer with a rendering performance of 20 to 35 frames per second. A snapshot is shown in Figure 11.

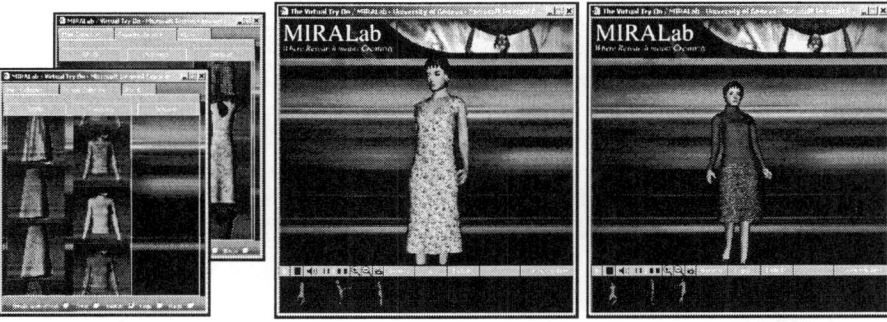

Figure 11 – The Virtual Try On: The online cloth catalogue (left) and the 3D viewer/extended java class (right)

The models exported from the 3D Garment Simulator described before were integrated in the Virtual Try On suite to offer a Virtual Fitting Room service. The major considerations that determined the quality of the Virtual Fitting Room application were:

- The high quality *rendering realism*: (The geometry of the object was correctly perceived to include all its desired features). Additionally, antialiasing techniques, smooth shading and texture mapping were the most important factors that improved the rendering quality.
- The high *quality of the animation*, depending largely on the number of frames that can be redrawn on the display during a unit of time. (We keep in mind that while correct motion perception starts at 5 frames per second, good animation contains at least 15 frames per second).
- The *interactive possibilities*, these are related to how the user can move around the scene and visualize the objects through modification of viewing parameters (spins, body sizes, change transforms etc.)
- The *response time* that should be minimal. (The user is not willing to spend more than a few minutes in the Virtual Fitting Room). The whole process of dressing the customer and displaying the animations was fast enough.

4. Conclusions

With respect to Macy's fashion show, the high-end interactivity that they introduced was unparalleled till now. They have included virtual humans and several cloth catalogues, so that the viewer's sense of participation and interaction is increased. We have introduced a new methodology to create step by step a Virtual Try On, starting from the creation of standard bodies, animating them, dressing them and then creating an interface to make them available on a Virtual Try On on the Internet.

Based on realistic properties the behavior of our cloth simulation is highly realistic and this is visibly evident when viewing our VTO and comparing our results with previous work. We have succeeded to introduce a complete chain of processes for making bodies and clothes optimized for Internet usage in a Virtual Fitting Room. The bodies created with our approach correspond to real human body shapes as the human body measurements were derived from anthropometric sizing surveys and were modeled appropriately to be entirely animatable. The approach to design the clothes was merged with the fashion house approach to address the requirements of a cloth designer. Furthermore we simulated the physical parameters of the garments aiming to give to the user the feeling of the cloth behavior in order to be as close as possible to reality.

5. Future work

The next goal, for several researchers in MIRALab, is to dynamically change the body measurements of a virtual human in order to move from the existing dressed bodies according to sizes to dressed bodies according to individual measurements. We have already decided to use the standard open specifications and we have opted for the H-Anim format that is part of the MPEG4 and X3D specification. The main issue is the implementation of realistic deformations, as H-Anim bodies are segmented, as well as animation file format. We are currently working on an in-house solution in the form of an API that allows for virtual human real-time deformation, animation and integration with the 3D environment.

6. Acknowledgements

This work is supported by the IST European project 'E-TAILOR'. We like to thank Pascal Volino and Frederic Cordier for the development of the MIRACloth software, Tom Molet for the development of the motion tracking software, and our partners in E-TAILOR for the business analysis of the market. We like to thank Sabine Schechinger for her contribution in the making of the male, body and cloth, collection. Special thanks are due to Chris Joslin, Pritweesh De and George Papagiannakis for proof reading this document.

References

[1] Forrester Research, Apparel's On-line Makeover, Report, May 1999, http://www.forrester.com/ER/Research/Report/0,1338,5993,00.html

[2] Brian Beck, Key Strategic Issues in Online Apparel Retailing, yourfit.com, 2000, Version 1.0

[3] Welcome to My Virtual Model(TM), http://www.landsend.com/

[4] NORDSTROM, http://www.nordstrom.com

[5] Macy's Passport 99 Fashion Show
http://www.shoutinteractive.com/Fashion/index.html

[6] Volino P., Magnenat-Thalmann N., Implementing Fast Cloth Simulation with Collision Response, Computer Graphics International 2000, June 2000.

[7] Weil J., "The Synthesis of Cloth Objects", Computer Graphics (SIGGRAPH'86 proceedings), Addison-Wesley, 24, pp 243-252, 1986.

[8] Yang Y., Magnenat-Thalmann N., *"Techniques for Cloth Animation"*, New trends in Animation and Visualisation, John Wiley & Sons Ltd, pp 243-256, 1991.

[9] Carignan M., Yang Y., Magnenat- Thalmann N., Thalmann D.,*"Dressing Animated Synthetic Actors with Complex Deformable Clothes"*, Computer Graphics (SIGGRAPH'92 proceedings), Addison-Wesley, 26(2), pp 99-104, 1992.

[10] Volino P., Courchesne M., Magnenat-Thalmann N., *"Versatile and Efficient Techniques for Simulating Cloth and Other Deformable Objects"*, Computer Graphics (SIGGRAPH'95 proceedings), Addison-Wesley, pp 137-144, 1995.

[11] Breen D.E., House D.H., Wozny M.J., *"Predicting the Drap of Woven Cloth Using Interacting Particles"*, Computer Graphics (SIGGRAPH'94 proceedings), Addison-Wesley, pp 365-372, July 1994.

[12] Eberhardt B., Weber A., Strasser W., *"A Fast, Flexible, Particle-System Model for Cloth Draping"*, Computer Graphics in Textiles and Apparel (IEEE Computer Graphics and Applications), pp 52-59, Sept. 1996.

[13] Eischen J.W., Deng S., Clapp T.G., *"Finite-Element Modeling and Control of Flexible Fabric Parts"*, Computer Graphics in Textiles and Apparel (IEEE Computer Graphics and Applications), pp 71-80, Sept. 1996.

[14] HOHENSTEIN (DE), Workpackage 7 Input, Project No: IST-1999-10549, Internal Project Consortium document, July 2001

[15] Molet, T., Aubel, A., Çapin, T. et al (1999), *ANYONE FOR TENNIS?*, Presence, Vol. 8, No. 2, MIT press, April 1999, pp.140-156.

[16] Oxford Metrics (2000) *Real-Time Vicon8 Rt*. Retrieved 10-04-01 from:
http://www.metrics.co.uk/animation/realtime/realtimeframe.htm

[17] MotionAnalysis, (2000) Real-Time HiRES 3D Motion Capture System. Retrieved 17-04-01 from:
http://www.motionanalysis.com/applications/movement/research/real3d.html

[18] Bodenheimer B., Rose, C., Rosenthal, S., & Pella, J. (1997). The Process of Motion Capture: Dealing with the Data. *Eurographics workshop on Computer Animation and Simulation'97, Springer-Verlag Wien*, 3-18.

[19] Volino P., Magnenat-Thalmann N., Comparing Efficiency of Integration Methods for Cloth Simulation, Proceedings of CGI'01, Hong-Kong, July 2001.

[20] Volino P., Magnenat-Thalmann N., Virtual Clothing Theory and Practice, ISBN 3-540-67600-7, Springer-Verlag, Berlin Heidelberg, New York

[21] VRML97, The VRML97 The Virtual Reality Modeling Language International Standard ISO/IEC 14772-1:1997, http://www.vrml.org/Specifications/VRML97/

[22] Polevoi R., Interactive Web Graphics with Shout3D, ISBN 0-7821-2860-2, Copyright 2001 SYBEX Inc. Alameda

[23] Babski C., Thalmann D., A seamless Shape For HANIM Compliant Bodies

[24] Seo H., Cordier F., Philippon L., Magnenat-Thalmann N., Interactive Modelling of MPEG-4 Deformable Human Body Models, Postproceedings Deform 2000, Kluwer Academic Publishers. pp. 120~131.

[25] LECTRA SYSTEMS – MODARIS V4
http://www.lectra.com/dyna/produits/modarisv4gb3ac477f005907.pdf

Procedural Simulation of Interwoven Structures

Frédéric Drago   Norishige Chiba

University of Iwate*

Abstract

We present a convenient method to simulate the geometry and appearance of interwoven structures for the production of complex scenes. This solution is based on procedural texturing and shading techniques, the macro and micro geometry of materials being simulated by procedural displacement. We demonstrate that in the case studied, displaced surfaces offer a number of benefits over complete geometric modeling or bitmap mapped textures. The system proposed is efficient and easily integrated to the general CG production pipeline.

Keywords: Interwoven materials, Procedural textures, Displacement mapping, Textile modeling, Visual simulation.

1. Introduction

Structures made of interlaced or interleaved parts are present everywhere in our daily lives: woven fabrics, knitwear, wire netting or fishing net are just a few examples that come to mind. In this paper, we took the liberty to call this whole family of materials "interwoven structures" due to failing to find a better or more accurate word in English. Because most of these structures are made of a simple loop repeated over and over, they should be easy to model and render; indeed they are, but the basic loop needs to be instanced or worse copied many times resulting in a huge number of parts all dynamically related. This complexity is generally not implementable when objects made of these materials need to be part of a scene involving other models with different characteristics. Moreover, animation of such models requires a complex dynamic calculation and expensive collision detection among its parts. We present a simple and efficient procedural technique that allows a visually appealing simulation of this family of materials in 3D.

A basic geometrical model is offset by procedural displacements to form the macroscopic structure of fibers. Surface reflectance characteristics, also based on procedures, can be physically or artistically simulated. Our implementation offers significant possibilities and advantages, such as geometric simplicity, scalability, and ease of animation, parametric choice, implicit representation, realistic results and a good integration to the general computer graphics production pipeline.

This paper is divided in three main parts. Section 2 introduces the reader to previous research in the areas of procedural shading and texturing, cloth modeling and dynamic simulation, micro-geometry and surface reflectance of fabrics, all of which are domains related to this work. Section 3, a step-by-step explanation of our scheme, presents the curve drawing process, displacement of the surface, construction of the yarn profile, some possible shading models and finally the assembling process of the structure. A dynamic simulation of a piece of fabric is presented in section 4. Some examples and particular characteristics of three different structures, canvas (figure 13), knitwear (figure 1, 12) and wire-net (figure 11) are shown to illustrate the versatility of the technique.

Figure 1 Pullovers textured with a displaced knitwear pattern, the one on the left is made of twice as many stitches as the other one.

2. Background

Our method for simulation of three-dimensional textures of interwoven structures reposes essentially on procedural texturing techniques. Procedures to simulate the realistic appearance of natural materials started to appear long ago [3] but widespread use of the procedural paradigm started in the 1980s when essential algorithms were published by Ken Perlin [16], Cook [7] and many other renowned researchers. The development of the RenderMan[1] shading language permitted everyone with sufficient knowledge to use procedural methods to create photo-realistic scenes. Because surface details and characteristics are introduced only during rendering, the use of procedures (programming codes and algorithms specifying the material and/or geometry of a model or phenomenon), greatly simplifies the task of modelers and animators. A major drawback of procedural textures is their difficulty to program and antialias in non-trivial cases. In the book "Texturing & Modeling" [9], Ebert gives three essential words to summarize the

---

[1]RenderMan is a registered trademark of Pixar.

power of procedural techniques. Abstraction: the complexity of a model is stored in a function and evaluated only when needed; parametric control: a few parameters affect the intrinsic characteristics of a model; flexibility: the designer or programmer is not bound to physical accuracy but has freedom to simulate any desired characteristics or artistic effects.

Our implementation can be used to represent many kinds of fabrics and knitwear. The representation and animation of clothing is an extensive research subject, presented in many papers and books [23]. The complex draping behaviour of woven fabrics was successfully implemented in [5] by representing the microstructure of the fabric with interacting particles. The involved process of physically animating the macrostructure of knitwear was presented by Nourrit [15] and Rémion [20]. Research on deformation, wrinkling and interaction of clothes with the body to realistically animate humans in their garment [6, 2, 23] came to a relative maturity, allowing commercial clothing simulation systems involving complex dynamics simulations. The study of surface light scattering characteristics revealed some significant differences among fabrics, mostly dependent upon the quality of the fiber and microstructure. Most woven fabrics have been represented by microfacet-based BRDF [21, 24, 26]. In the case of knitwear different approaches are usually taken. Volumetric rendering was considered by Gröeller et al. [10, 11], resulting in a very detailed representation of knitwear. Zhong et al. [27] modeled the yarn microstructure along a network of 3D interlocking curves, and further development led to photo-realistic rendering [25] using a radiance description of a cross section of the yarn.

Since implementation of complex algorithms and rendering techniques for accurate simulation of these materials is not always practical, their visual aspect is usually simulated by texture mapping; a bitmap representation of the color, bump, and opacity of the material is applied to a simple geometric model, while reflectance characteristics can be simulated using empirical or very elaborate surface shaders [24]. For a close up view or fly-through scene, building the complete macro-geometry is sometimes necessary, but animation, dynamic simulation and previewing in realtime remain a major problem. For example, the author found an average of 12 stitches by cm^2 on a handmade jersey, the total surface without sleeves was approximately 2700 cm^2, if one sweeps a cylinder along the curve of a stitch, a minimum number of 132 triangles would be necessary to obtain a smooth Gouraud shaded surface. A rapid calculation show that this technique would result in a model made of more than 8.5 million polygons!

Figure 2 Three interwoven materials, from left to right, simple woven fabric, wire-net, and simple knitwear pattern. The wire-net is a hybrid of the first and third 3D texture.

We propose a simple framework to implement the 3D textures of interwoven materials. Although not dictated by physically accurate simulation, our method implicitly contains many characteristics of the real material.

The images presented were rendered using ray tracing, shaders were written using the RenderMan shading language, and geometric modeling and dynamic simulations done using of-the-shelf software. Our results should be applicable to a broad range of procedural shading languages and modeling/animation software.

3. Construction of the structure

Our implementation to simulate interwoven structures in 3D roughly follows this step by step summary (illustrated in figure 3): The weave of the texture is created by procedurally displacing the geometry, and the loop is defined by a 2D polygonal curve repeated as many times as needed to form a pattern on the surface. The loop is displaced along the new surface normals to form a semi circular indent, giving the 3D characteristics of the yarn. Finally the

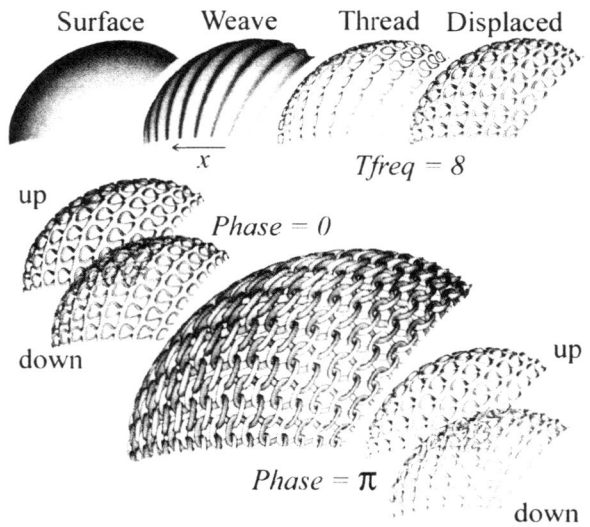

Figure 3 Building process of the interwoven structure from left to right, and assembling of the four surfaces.

underlying model is copied four times and textured with different parameters that define orientation and direction. Interwoven materials can be divided into two categories: woven materials made by interlacing or weaving a straight thread, and knitted materials generated by interleaving a loop. Simple knitwear patterns such as presented on the right side of figure 2 and 3 are constructed by rows of consecutive loops. Each loop is generated by pulling the yarn through the holes of the two corresponding loops of the preceding row. We simulated this technique by interlacing complete rows of loops at once. The following subsections present the pattern building and assembling process, most explanations and demonstrations of which are based on but not limited to the case of knitwear.

3.1. Weaving the surface

We used displacement shaders to simulate the macroscopic structure of the materials. The concept of displacement was introduced by Cook [7] in the Shade Tree system, it is closely related to bump mapping [4] but in the former case, instead of simply modifying the normal to give an effect of surface perturbation, the surface is actually moved, changing also the silhouette and allowing effects like self occlusion and self shadowing.

Displacement mapping is a convenient technique to add details, such as dent and scratches or to simulate complex organic elements like bark or wavy surfaces like water without the cost of actually modeling the geometry and with the advantage of only adding details adaptively during the rendering process.

Displacement maps perturb surface position in a given direction [8] often the normal vector of the point on the surface being shaded. The surface is subdivided into a grid of sub-pixel sized patches or micropolygons, and displacement is calculated at the vertices of the grid to evaluate a new position for each vertex within a bound.

Offset values can be given by a procedural function such as Perlin noise [17] darkness variations of a bitmap or, in our case, by a set of explicit mathematics functions. Because displacement generates a huge number of elements, it is not always practical in raytracing where all the objects in a scene need to be diced and displaced in a prepass and extra geometry kept available during the whole rendering time. For example, the sphere in figure 6 was rendered at 400*400 pixels, it was diced in 1310720 elements and 124Mb were necessary in contrast with 25Mb used to render the same view with surface shaders only. Since dicing resolution is evaluated in function of screen space size and occupancy, bigger objects will generate more geometry. This is a drawback of our method in the case of raytracing. REYES [8] rendering engines or similar micropolygon based scanline algorithms subdivide all the geometric primitives into grids anyway, but to limit memory usage divide the screen into buckets individually rendered. These limitations of raytracing are addressed in recent papers [12] offering different solutions such as caching a subset of the geometry created and rendering it in a coherent manner [18].

In our scheme, we use two or three successive displacements before calculation of the final surface normals. The surface is offset along its geometric normals by the amplitude of a sinusoidal function. The thread is then modeled by a second displacement ideally along new normals generated during the previous step. A third optional displacement models the micro characteristics of the yarn and adds necessary details. Our simulation is based on the functionality and requirements of the RenderMan shading language, often considered the most flexible and popular language for procedural shading. Detailed explanations of RenderMan built-in functions are beyond the scope of this paper but are wildly available [1, 19]. To model the weave of the material variations the following sinusoidal function was used.

$$Weave(x) = \cos(2 * \pi * x * T_{freq} + Phase) * Height$$

A few parameters determine the characteristics of the weave. The curve created is function of x that we ideally choose in the direction of the parameters s or t the surface shading directions in the RenderMan shading language. T_{freq} is the number of thread requested; it determines the coarseness of the structure and will dictate other parameters characterizing weaving attributes. *Height* is the total amplitude of the weave, which should ideally be twice the radius of the yarn. The *Phase* constant is either 0 if the geometry represents even rows of threads or π for odd rows. This function is not a physically accurate representation of the weaving pattern, but it satisfies our purpose and some variations can be applied to different kinds of materials regardless of the number of repetitions required. Different weaving patterns can be implemented using more complex functions, for example to simulate traditional Italian painting canvas, which has sextupled weft threads.

3.2. The guiding curve for the loop

An arbitrary shaped loop is drawn with a postscript drawing software (figure 4 left). We parse the saved file to extract the guiding points of the two dimension Bézier curves which are processed using a variation of the Bézier curve drawing algorithm proposed by Miller [14] resulting in an array of points adaptively sampled on the curve. The loop is drawn on the surface by computing the distance of the shaded point to the nearest point on a segment of the curve, points farther than the requested width defining surface transparency. This same technique will be used to determine offset values of the yarn. At this stage, a reader might think that our presentation does not follow a logical order and the curve drawing should have been explained first. In fact, the

Figure 4 Drawing the initial loop of knitwear. The Bézier curve on the left is adaptively transformed into a polygonal curve (middle, here with 10, 16, 30, and 72 segments), and a pattern is generated by a modulo function.

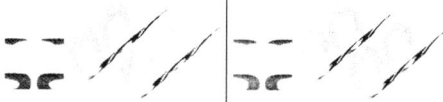

Figure 5 The width of the segments of curve is stretched because of the surface elongation in one direction, as seen on the left. An adaptive reparation scheme is applied on the right side.

previous weave displacement increased the length of the surface in the frequency direction of the sinusoidal curve, but initial surface shading coordinates remained unchanged, affecting the width of the segments forming the loop according to their angle with the curve direction (figure 5 left). To remedy this situation we need to adaptively calculate an appropriate width for each segment. Using the following equation, we add a minimum constant to the angle between the considered segment and the direction of the rows of thread, taking into account the relative length of the surface in the weave direction.

$$W = W_{min} + k(\arccos \| \mathbf{S} \bullet \mathbf{dir} \|) \| 1 - \int_0^t \sqrt{1 + \left(\frac{dWeave}{dx}\right)^2} dx \|$$

W is the adaptive width value we try to find for each segment of the loop, and W_{min} is an arbitrary minimum width. $\mathbf{S}$ is the normalized vector, which characterizes the direction of the considered segment of loop. The vector **dir**, follows the rows of loops or threads, as such it is perpendicular to the weaving direction. We assume in this equation that texture shading coordinates s and t is between 0 and 1. When the vectors **S** and **dir** are parallel, or in the hypothetical case of the arc length of the weave being equal to one, W is equal to W_{min} since the right part of the equation is zero. Since the polygonal curve of the loop is continuous on both sides it can be instanced seamlessly by a modulo function taking the appearance of a periodic curve. A pattern is created by division of the shading space in as many cells as wanted (Figure 4 right side). Contrary to physically modeling the yarns, our approach does not tax geometry with new polygons for every stitch used and rendering times are not linked to the coarseness of the structure. The graph on the right side of figure 7 demonstrates the independence between rendering times and texture frequency. A difference of 42 seconds or 16% only was observed by rendering the sphere of figure 6 with different numbers of stitches.

After using a texture frequency of 128, effectively generating a knit like pattern on a sphere made with 128*128*6 stitches, the rendering time slightly decreases probably because at this resolution and antialiasing level, offset distances are

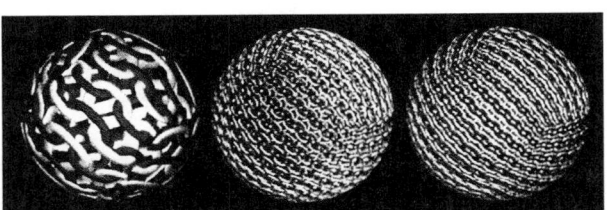

Figure 6 A sphere made of 6 nurbs patches copied four times. In this image, surface reflectance is based on the Phong model.

negligible and the rendered image presented a noisy surface. Repeating the experiment at higher resolution confirmed this tendency. It is also interesting to note that the memory used and the number of microelements generated by displacement mapping remained constant. However, the number of segments of the primary loop linearly increases pre-processing time of the geometry, and using curves with different coarseness is the base for an adaptive level of detail (LOD) implementation of the texture. The figure 7 illustrates this phenomenon. To obtain visually satisfying

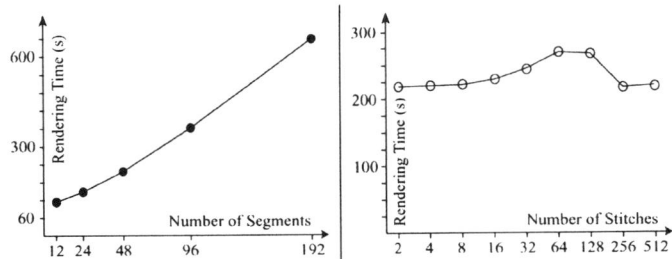

Figure 7 Left, effect on rendering times of doubling the number of segments of the primary loop. Right, dependency of rendering times and number of stitches. The sphere in figure 6 was used in both cases.

results, the primary knitting loop of the pullovers of figure 1 is generated with only 30 segments. In figure 6 the loop of the knit pattern used to build the middle sphere is made of 48 segments, but the one on the right has only 12 and the difference between the 2 patterns is very noticeable. In the case of woven materials, only one segment is used to form a complete row, but subsequent subdivision with point placement generated by a semi random noise can give a wavy aspect to the thread.

3.3. Construction of the threads profile

The half section of the yarn is modeled by an explicit curve giving relief to the surface. We implemented a simple procedure which evaluates for each point, its distance to the centre of a considered segment of the loop; if the point being shaded falls outside the requested bound, it is rejected and will not be offset; otherwise its coordinates are passed to the displacing function and offset distances are returned. We usually used a semi circle modeled from the explicit equation $y = \sqrt{1-x^2}$, where x represents the point being shaded as a ratio of its distance from the considered segment of the loop and the segment's width previously calculated. Simply changing the returning function of the procedure can generate different profiles. While simpler to implement, offset along original surface normals does not produce a satisfying profile since width varies with the slope of the weave (figure 8 left). We rely on an explicit formulation of new normals based on original geometry and on the equation for the weave (figure 8 right). This produces a correct profile and avoids possible displacement cracking caused by discontinuous grid boundaries of software-calculated normals. The self-intersection of the half thread on the right is a minor problem, which never occurred in simulation where much smaller weave amplitude is needed. A

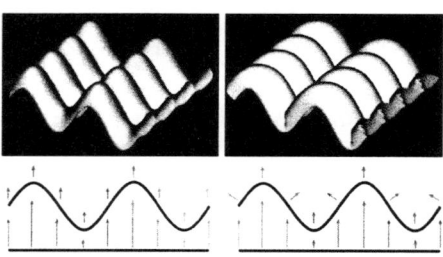

Figure 8 Two types of displacement, the image on the left was displaced twice following geometric normals, on the right, a first displacement along geometric normals is followed by a second along the newly calculated normals, resulting in a suitable profile for the upper part of the thread

third displacement can be implemented to simulate the micro geometry of the material. The yarn of fabrics is usually made of micro-fibers twisted around the yarn axis, often resulting in a rough helicoids aspect. The quality and nature of the fiber employed which relates to the spatial density and regularity of the weave determines the fabric aspect and fuzziness. By offsetting the points of the yarn by a chosen angle and distance, combined with a semi random noise function, many different procedural microstructures can be created.

When necessary we also use a bump mapping function following the shading characteristics because it is easier to antialias properly. We did not try here to match the impressive results obtained in [11, 25] both algorithms are highly specialized and hard to integrate in our production pipeline, the former also succeeded only in the case of a flat surface. Figure 9 shows a comparison of a smooth model and a woollen piece of cloth. Adding transparency, fuzziness and a procedural noise displacement to the model simulates the visual aspect of the wool.

Figure 9 A woollen piece of textile. Comparison of the material before (left) and after (right) micro-structural modelization.

3.4. Surface shading

We also rely on procedural methods for surface shading. The variety of interwoven structures that can be simulated leads to a "case-by-case" situation. Moreover physically or artistically based models of light scattering and surface characteristics can be used or combined when appropriate. The metallic wire-netting surface of figure 11 necessitated only a simple metal-like BRDF combined with an environment-mapped reflection. A function based on Fresnel equations was used to simulate propagation of light in textile. Reflectance characteristics of dielectric materials like fibers are known but a truly realistic rendition of the translucency and fuzziness requires multiple scattering and self-shadowing [13] among fibers.
Our model, to reproduce the aging process of painting canvas does not yet take these phenomenon into account, since we do not physically model the fibers an explicit BDRF model would have to be based on numerous assumptions.

3.5. Assembling the interwoven structure

Only parts of the material were considered thus far, but in this section the final assembling of the structure is explained. For any given coordinate on the surface a new value is calculated by displacement; the result of moving one point in any direction will always result in only one point. For example, we cannot displace a flat surface to generate many cylindrical shapes to construct yarns (we could fold it like a sheet of paper, but obtain only one thread). Our approach requires copying and offsetting the geometry in different directions. We effectively use four copies of the same model. Parallel threads or even rows in the case of knitwear are made of two surfaces offset with positive and negative values, another two surfaces are necessary to model odd rows or perpendicular threads for woven materials. This displacement in two opposite directions is a drawback of our method, since gaps may appear at the junction of the top and bottom half thread. This situation arose during animation of the top part of figure 10. Stitches are submitted to consequent torsion of the underlying surface and disturbing visual artefacts had to be corrected by using different thread width for surface and displacement.

A summary of the steps involved in simulating interwoven materials follows:
- Geometric modeling, lighting and texturing of the scene. To model interwoven objects, polygons, nurbs, subdivision surfaces, and other known techniques can be used, topological continuity of surfaces is not a necessity but offers a seamless shading, this artefact became apparent on the left pullover of figures 1 and 12 modeled with Bézier patches and textured with twice as many stitches as the one on the right side.
- Keyframe animation and/or dynamic simulation of the scene. Since only the underlying surface is animated, realtime animation and preview of the geometry is possible. Dynamic simulation is also conducted with a simple model for which the animator decides the parameters necessary to simulate different behaviour for each material. The relative width of the structure needs to be considered to avoid surface penetration during collision detection.
- Exporting the frames to RIB (RenderMan Interface Binary) format. The RIB files are parsed and the archive of the interwoven structure called four times, each with different displacement parameters. Rendering of the scene does not require any particular treatment and is done in a straightforward manner.

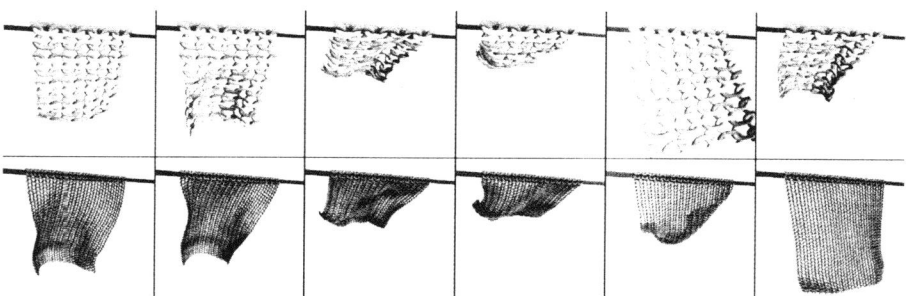

Figure 10 Simulation of a hanging piece of fabric with a simple knitwear material applied reacting to a gust of wind. The top row shows extreme torsion of the structure made with only four loops, and the bottom row, made of 16 loops reacts in a more realistic way. Shadows were applied only in the second row.

4. Animation

Physically based animation of textile requires a complex dynamic system taking into account at least the properties of the fiber, the forces of friction among threads, and the geometry of the structure. To animate knitwear, Nourrit [15, 20] relies on a complex set of Lagrangian equations considering constraints and forces such as gravity, viscosity, and other less influencing forces among yarns. To test the dynamic behaviour of our scheme, we animated the reaction of a piece of fabric swept by a gust of wind (figure 10). A dynamic cloth simulation engine, based on a mass/spring system, was used. Constraints and forces exerted among stitches were not considered, but the model was set to "approximately" match the dynamic behavior of a knitted scarf, and the animator could estimate parameters such as drag, stiffness, and damping and collision radius. We cannot pretend to a physically accurate simulation, but we think that a visually believable and pleasant result was obtained. Because animation is based on the underlying simple geometry, the response is very fast, almost real time in the example presented in figure 10. Once the shaders properties are set, yarns are "locked" in position avoiding the need to rely on expensive collision detection and friction calculation at a macro structural level. This last point is also the main drawback toward more realistic results, because stitches do not react freely but are stretched with the surface. Our system inherited the advantages and inconveniences of texture-mapped objects, but the level of realism obtained at a medium or close range is a significant step forward from bitmap textures. The speed and ease of animation of our approach is undoubtedly quite advantageous compared to a complete modeling of the macro structure.

5. Conclusions

We have presented a flexible and convenient scheme to visualize the texture of interwoven materials. A given surface is offset by a sinusoidal function, the threads are represented by a pattern based on adaptive polygonal curves generated from Bézier curves, the 3D representation of thread profiles is generated by an explicit function, finally the surface is shaded and repeated three times using different offset parameters. Based on procedural texturing and shading techniques, this implicit method does not require to generate the complex macro and micro geometry of the objects until rendering times, and most of the necessary physical features to animate the model are naturally embedded in the procedure. Unfortunately, surface displacement is an expensive technique in a raytracing context, and almost impossible to incorporate in a global illumination rendering because of the high number of micropolygon generated. Interactive visualization of the complete texture is not possible, but remains straightforward with the initial geometry. Future developments involve a better integration of the postscript drawing technique with RenderMan, and implementation of complex weaving pattern to visually simulate different kind of canvases (figure 13). We are planning to use some of the techniques presented here in other cases of macro structural modeling such as the simulation of crack patterns on aged paintings.

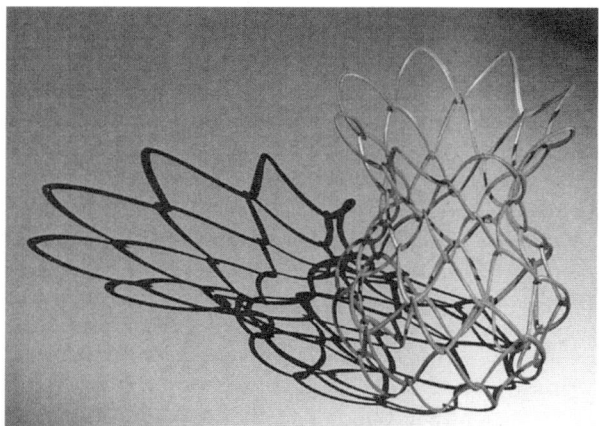

Figure 11 Wire netting simulation on the geometry of a vase.

Figure 12 Detail of the knitwear structure.

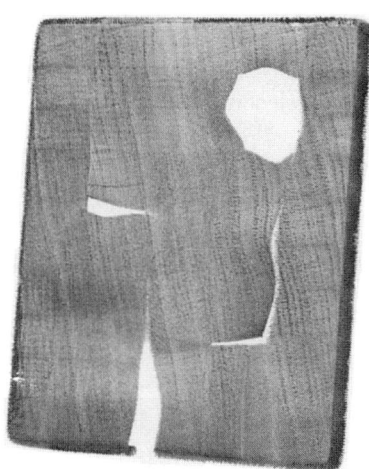
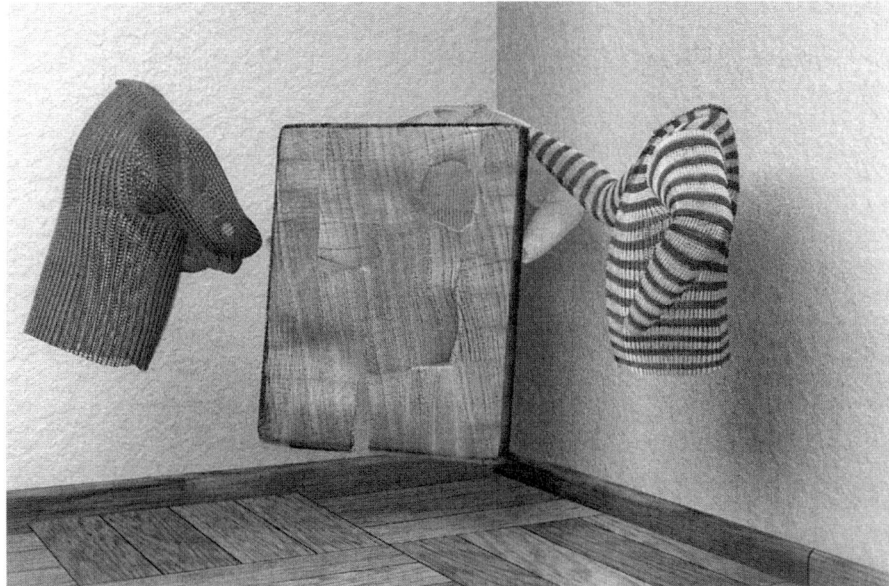

Figure 13 Top: Canvas fabric used in painting conservation. A scanned piece of painting canvas is compared to our simulation. On the right side, a procedurally aged version is applied to the geometry.

Bottom: Presentation of a "chef d'oeuvre". Two different types of interwoven structures are put in context.

Acknowledgement

This work was supported partly by "A Support System for Region-specific R&D Activities" of Telecommunications Advancement Organization of Japan.

References

[1] Anthony A.Apodaca and larry Gritz. Advanced RenderMan. Morgan Kaufmann, December 1999. ISBN 1558606181.

[2] David Baraff and Andrew P. Witkin. Large Steps in Cloth Simulation. Proceedings of SIGGRAPH 98, pages 43-45, July 1998. ISBN 0-89791-999-8. Held in Orlando, Florida.

[3] J. F. Blinn and M. E. Newell. Texture and Reflection in Computer Generated Images. Communications of the ACM, 19:542-546, 1976.

[4] James F. Blinn. Simulation of Wrinkled Surfaces. Computer Graphics (Proceedings of SIGGRAPH 78), 12(3): 286-292, August 1978. Held in Atlanta, Georgia.

[5] David E. Breen and Donald H. House and Michael J. Wozny. Predicting the Drape of Woven Cloth Using Interacting Particles. Proceedings of SIGGRAPH 94, pages 365-372, July 1994. ISBN 0-89791-667-0. Held in Orlando, Florida.

[6] Michel Carignan and Ying Yang and Nadia Magnenat Thalmann and Daniel Thalmann. Dressing animated synthetic actors with complex deformable clothes. Computer Graphics (Proceedings of SIGGRAPH 92), 26(2):99-104, July 1992. ISBN 0-201-51585-7. Held in Chicago, Illinois.

[7] Robert L. Cook. Shade trees. Computer Graphics (Proceedings of SIGGRAPH 84), 18(3):223-231, july 1984. Held in Minneapolis, Minnesota.

[8] Robert L. Cook and Loren Carpenter and Edwin Catmull. The Reyes Image Rendering Architecture. Computer Graphics (Proceedings of SIGGRAPH 87), pages 95-102, July 1987. Held in Anaheim, California.

[9] David Ebert and Ken Musgrave and Darwyn Peachey and Ken Perlin and Steven Worley. Texturing and Modeling: A Procedural Approach. Academic Press, October 1994. ISBN 0-12-228760-6.

[10] E. Gröller and René. T. Rau and W. Straßer. Modeling and visualization of knitwear. IEEE Transactions on Visualization and Computer Graphics, 1(4):302-310, December 1995. ISSN 1077-2626.

[11] Eduard Gröller and René T. Rau and Wolfgang Straßer. Modeling Textiles as Three Dimensional Textures. Eurographics Rendering Workshop 1996, pages 205-214, June 1996. ISBN 3-211-82883-4. Held in Porto, Portugal.

[12] Wolfgang Heidrich and Hans-Peter Seidel. Ray-Tracing Procedural Displacement Shaders. Graphics Interface 98, pages 8-16, June 1998. ISBN 0-9695338-6-1.

[13] Tom Lokovic and Eric Veach. Deep Shadow Maps. Proceedings of SIGGRAPH 2000, pages 385-392, July 2000. ISBN 1-58113-208-5.

[14] Robert D. Miller. Quick and Simple Bézier Curve Drawing. Graphics Gems V, Chapter IV.8, pages 206-209, 1995. Academic Press.

[15] Jean-Michel Nourrit. Modélisation, animation et visualisation de textiles a base de mailles. Universite de Reims Champagne Ardenne, January 1999. Phd Thesis.

[16] Ken Perlin. An Image Synthesizer. Computer Graphics (Proceedings of SIGGRAPH 85), 19(3):287-296, July 1985. Held in San Francisco, California.

[17] Ken Perlin and Eric M. Hoffert. Hypertexture. Computer Graphics (Proceedings of SIGGRAPH 89), 23(3):253-262, July 1989. Held in Boston, Massachusetts.

[18] Matt Pharr and Pat Hanrahan. Geometry Caching for Ray-Tracing Displacement Maps. Eurographics Rendering Workshop 1996, pages 31-40, June 1996. ISBN 3-211-82883-4. Held in Porto, Portugal.

[19] Pixar. The Renderman Interface, Version 3.2 specification. July 2000.

[20] Yannick Rémion and Jean-Michel Nourrit and Didier Gillard. A dynamic animation engine for generic spline objects. The Journal of Visualization and Computer Animation, 11(1):17-26, February 2000. ISSN 1099-1778.

[21] Vladimir Volevich and Edward A.Kopylov and Andrei B.Khodulev and Olga A.Karpenko. An Approach to Cloth Synthesis and Visualization. Proceedings of The Seventh International Conference on Computer Graphics and Scientific Visualization, 1997. Graphicon-97.

[22] Pascal Volino and Nadia Magnenat Thalmann. Implementing Fast Cloth Simulation with Collision Response. Computer Graphics International 2000, pages 257-268, June 2000. ISBN 0-7695-0643-7.

[23] Pascal Volino and Nadia Magnenat-Thalmann. Virtual Clothing. Springer Verlag, December 2000. ISBN 2540676007.

[24] Stephen H. Westin and James R. Arvo and Kenneth E. Torrance. Predicting Reflectance Functions From Complex Surfaces. Computer Graphics (Proceedings of SIGGRAPH 92), 26(2):255-264, July 1992. ISBN 0-201-51585-7. Held in Chicago, Illinois.

[25] Ying-Qing Xu and Yanyun Chen and Stephen Lin and Hua Zhong and Enhua Wu and Baining Guo and Heung-Yeung Shum. Photo-Realistic Rendering of Knitwear Using the Lumislice. Proceedings of SIGGRAPH 2001, pages 391-398, August 2001. ISBN 1-58113-292-1.

[26] Takami Yasuda and Shigeki Yokoi and Jun-ichiro Toriwaki. A Shading Model for Cloth Objects. IEEE Computer Graphics & Applications, 12(6):15-24, November 1992.

[27] Hua Zhong and Ying-Qing Xu and Baining Guo and Heung-Yeung Shum. Realistic and efficient rendering of free-form knitwear. The Journal of Visualization and Computer Animation, 12(1):13-22, February 2001. ISSN 1049-8907.

An Approach to Blend Surfaces

Vladimir Savchenko
Faculty of Computer and Information Sciences,
Hosei University
3-7-2, Kajino-cho, Koganei-shi, Tokyo 184-8584, Japan

Nikita Kojekine
Faculty of Engineering, Tokyo Institute of Technology, 2-12-1,
O-okayama, Meguro-ku, Tokyo 152-8552, Japan

Abstract

In this paper, we present an application of a space mapping technique for surface reconstruction (more precisely: reconstruction of missing parts of a real geometric object represented by volume data). Using a space mapping technique, the surface of a given model, in particular tooth shape is fitted by a shape transformation to extrapolate the remaining surface of a patient's tooth with occurring damage such as a "drill hole." The genetic algorithm minimizes the error of the approximation by optimizing a set of control points that determine the coefficients for spline functions, which in turn define a space transformation. The fitness function to be minimized consists of two components. First one is the error between the blended surface of an object and the surface of the object to be blended in some predefined points. The second is a component that is responsible for the bending energy being minimized.

Keywords: Constructive solid geometry, volume modeling, space mapping, surface reconstruction, computer-aided restoration design

1. Introduction

This paper extends the work of Savchenko and Shmitt [1] where an application of 3D-space mapping technique and numerical optimization with a specially designed genetic algorithm to a problem concerning computer aided design (CAD) in dentistry was presented. The applications considered and approaches proposed in this paper and in the article [1] are sufficiently–different. In [1] the task was to find a functionally transformed occlusal surface (an inlay part) of a model tooth that best matches the remaining occlusal surface of a treated tooth. In this project, we attempt to approach the well-known problem of "fulfillment" of missing data. The surface reconstruction problem can be expressed as follows:

Given shapes $S_1, S_2, \ldots$, find a blending surface S_b that is a reasonable approximation of the surface satisfying a set of constrains.

Important examples of fitting surface data have been intensively investigated in the past few years. An overview can be found in the paper [2] by Hermann et al. Various strategies were proposed to minimize user interaction; however, it is noticed in [2] that surface fitting of complex free-form shapes still remains a largely unsolved problem of great practical importance.

Traditionally, constructive solid geometry (CSG) modeling uses simple geometric objects for a base model, which can be further manipulated by implementing a certain collection of operations such as set-theoretic operations, blending, or offsetting. Recently, a great attention was paid to new implicit surface creation methods based on the use of radial based functions (RBF) for interpolating scattered data. Like other implicit surfaces they can be used for CSG modeling. Whatever complex operations have been applied to a geometric object, which can be given by a voxel raster, by elevation data, or by interpolated data, an equivalent volume data can be generated. We use the term *volume model* to refer to the wide class of surfaces that like other implicit surface descriptions can be used for CSG [3]. Objects defined in this manner are not regularized solids, as is required in traditional constructive solid geometry modeling, but have a function description.

In this paper we propose that RBFs offer a mechanism to get extrapolated points of a blended surface for various parts of a reconstructed object that can be used as "CSG components" to design a volume model.

Here let us explain the motivation behind this project. In spite of a flurry of activity in the field of scattered data reconstruction and interpolation, this matter remains a difficult and computationally expensive problem. Many recent works have focused on simplifying large data sets and researchers usually state that RBF methods guarantee automatic mesh repair or interpolation of large irregular holes. Our experiments show that reconstruction of a hemisphere by using one pole point and points belonging two parallel cross sections gives a maximum error of about 20 percent. A vast amount of literature is devoted to the subject of scattered data interpolation. Different interpolations can generate very different output for the same data set. For example, grids interpolated by Shepard's method [4] miss some details of the original data. In most applications a Delaunay triangulation is used for object reconstruction. Unfortunately, this method has some serious drawbacks resulting in a confusing image because sometimes an object's features can be stretched and distorted. Even with the elimination of large triangles, the reconstructed shape remains convex-looking, as noted in [5].

Another approach to surface reconstruction is skeletal. An implicit surface generated by point skeletons may be fit to a set of surface points [6], but this method is rather time consuming.

One other approach is to use methods of scattered data interpolation, based on the minimum-energy properties [7], [8], [9], [10], [11], [12]. The benefits of modeling 3D surfaces with the help of radial basis functions (RBF) have been recognized in [13]. They were adapted for computer animation [14], and medical applications [15], [16] and were first applied to reconstruct implicit surfaces by Savchenko et al. [17].

However, the required computational work is proportional to the number of grid nodes and the number of scattered data points. Special methods to reduce the processing time were developed for thin plate splines and discussed in [18], [19], see also recent publications [20], [21], [22].

Terracing and ringing problems are well discussed in the literature concerning terrain reconstruction. Partial differential equations (PDE) are widely used to model surfaces subject to certain constrains, see [23], [24]. A well-founded mathematically set-level approach has found applications in shape design and data fitting. Whitaker and Breen [25] give a highly exhaustive overview of related to this matter works; their paper presents an improved numerical algorithm and solves particular problems in geometric modeling. In particular, level set models with a positive-curvature flow are used to create a smooth blend (fillet) between solid objects. Gousie and Franklin give an extended overview of PDE methods and present two new methods for approximating elevation data from contours data to a grid [26]. They tested various interpolation/approximation methods designed with the following properties: the ability to handle realistic amounts of data and to minimize artifacts (terracing and ringing). The intermediate contours method produces a new contour between existing successive contours and a thin-plate approximation is applied to complete the surface between the new contours. In the gradient lines method, gradient lines are calculated from the surface produced by the thin-plate interpolation. At the next step of interpolating elevations along the whole gradient, the RBFs or thin-plate approximation is applied once again. The proposed methods appear visually smoother, with undesirable terracing effects much reduced.

Among a wide array of various techniques and solutions, the most famous one is the snake model proposed by Kass, Witkin and Terzopoulos [27]. We refer the interested reader to the paper by Duan and Qin [28]. A technique presented in [28] is capable of recovering geometric shape of unknown topology either from volumetric data or from range data. However, it cannot overcome the problem of missing data; through the minimization process of the cost function, their model will inflate like a balloon until it reaches the boundary of the modeled objects.

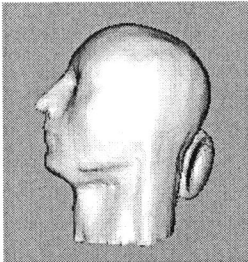

Figure 1. Illustration of an improper reconstruction by compactly supported RBFs

Recently special methods, so called compactly supported RBFs, aiming to reduce processing time were developed. For more references see [29]. However, if we have a gap in the data set, we face the problem of evaluating the functions at extra points; if the radius of support is quite large, then the cycle associated with the matrix of linear equations will include nearly all the points from the input data. For more references see [30]. Figure 1 illustrates an artifact (can be observed on the right-hand side of the reconstructed area) stipulated an inappropriate choice of the radius of support. Let us note that we have a lack of data in lower part of the "head." Thus, the work required for correct reconstruction of the object is becoming nearly proportional to number of all scattered data points. The amount of computations becomes significant, even for moderate number of nodes.

The goal in occlusal surface modeling for restoration is to reproduce a "reasonable" reconstructed shape surrounding a missing part of the restoration area. In [1], an example of applying a monotone formula [31] demonstrates how one can use an exact analytic description (a polygon) to reproduce inlay parts of treated teeth. A variety of techniques can be applied to let the user create volume models applying geometric operations. In this work, for simplicity we are using a "drill hole."

In what follows, we shall review a class of techniques that can be used in a variety of applications to reconstruct volume objects from scattered data and a 3-D space transformation technique. We then consider the so-called *tracking* or *correspondence problem* by applying genetic optimization for automatic correction of corresponding points to avoid superfluous folding over a blended area. The original surface and the restored surface must smoothly join along predefined boundary regions of the restoration area. Genetic optimization was used in the paper to illustrate the approach; nevertheless, other methods such as dynamic programming can be used.

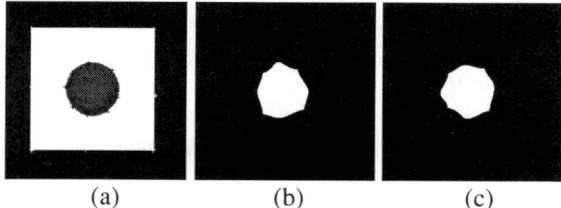

(a) (b) (c)

Figure 2. Tracking problem

To illustrate our approach and the tracking problem, consider the example in Figure 2(a): a black squire is used to "fill" the white area by contracting the white squire in eight directions for gluing black and red areas. Human knowledge and experience is necessary to assign correspondence points to compensate for the gap between the region of restoration and the existing part of the object. Figures 2(b) and 2(c) illustrate the fact that the result of restoration depends on a sufficiently good initial guess. An approach where the target landmarks or destination points are freed to slide along lines discussed by Bookstein in [32], [33] naturally can be used in such a simple case. Figure 2(c) illustrates an application of the weighted least squares technique to select destination points to adopt the configuration of minimum bending energy. In this paper, correction of coordinates of a limited number of corresponding points initially assigned by the user that define the space transformation is done by using a genetic algorithm. One of the most attractive features of genetic algorithms is that they are easy to interface to a model, thus we use genetic optimization as it was discussed in [1]. The book by Vose [34] and the article [35] provide an overview of theoretical aspects of genetic algorithms.

2. 3D-Reconstruction and transformation

In this paper we address the problem of reconstructing missing parts of a treated tooth represented by elevation data on an 2-dimensional grid where the surface is written as the graph of the function: $z - f(x,y) \geq 0$. We assume that due to continuity in the surface the boundary of an existing surface can be propagated to complete the missing part. In order to obtain the proper surface of a treated tooth, a dentist may choose to create and modify the surface in a CAD application interactively using his own experience. Actually, this approach is currently commonplace in dental CAD systems based on parametric representation. A different approach described in [1] is to use the displacement of• M control points between model tooth and treated tooth. Authors have shown and proved that they have a good alliance of geometric modeling and optimization techniques to determine the reconstructed surface and assure overall smoothness. Nevertheless, this approach has the defect that a generic tooth acquired from the library of standardized teeth should be used to reconstruct missing part of the treated tooth. This paper is concerned in an algorithm for multi-step extension of an original surface to construct discrete points needed for reconstructing missing part of volume object. After that, for instance finite element approximation [7] for 2D data set or compactly supported RBFs [30] for 3D case can be used. The automatic production of synthetic points reminds an extraction of edges that leads to the "filling" of absent space. Naturally, we do not expect to exactly reconstruct the missing part of an object; our goal is to get outlines that look reasonable. Under the term "reasonable outline" we imply first of all that we wish to extend local features of starting points as globally as possible, and secondly, to avoid superfluous folding over the blended area.

In this section, we shall give a short account of the shape transformation method used in the application considered in this paper. According to our knowledge, the first publication on using discrete landmark points is that of Bookstein [32], see also [33]. To interpolate the overall displacement, we use a volume spline based on Green's function. A detailed description of the method can be found in [10]. The problem is to find an interpolation spline function $U \in W_2^m(\Omega)$, where $W_2^m(\Omega)$ is the space of functions whose derivatives of order $\leq m$ are square-integrable over $\Omega \subset \mathbf{R}^n$, such that the following two conditions are satisfied: (1) $U(p_i) = h_i$, $i = 1,2, \ldots ,M$, and (2) U minimizes the bending energy, if the space transformation is seen as an elastic deformation, i.e.,

$$\Phi(U) = \int_\Omega \sum_{|\alpha|=m} m!/\alpha! \; (D^\alpha U)^2 \, d\Omega \to \min,$$

where m is a parameter of the variational functional. The minimization of the functional $\Phi(U)$ results in a system of linear algebraic equations for the spline coefficients. An increase in the parameter m essentially leads to an increase in surface rigidity. Our experiments have shown that using the parameter $m = 3$ leads to superfluous folding over the blended area.

A space mapping in $\mathbf{R}^n$ defines a relationship between each pair of points in the original and deformed objects. Let an n-dimensional region $\Omega \subset \mathbf{R}^n$ of an arbitrary configuration be given, and let Ω contains a set of arbitrary control points $\{\boldsymbol{q_i} = (q_1^i, q_2^i, \ldots, q_n^i) : i=1,2,\ldots,M\}$ for a non-deformed object, and $\{\boldsymbol{d_i} = (d_1^i, d_2^i, \ldots, d_n^i) : i=1,2,\ldots,M\}$ for the deformed object. It is assumed that the points $\boldsymbol{q_i}$ and $\boldsymbol{d_i}$ are distinct and given on or near the surface of an object. These points establish a correspondence between features of the two objects under consideration. The goal of the construction of the deformed object is to find a smooth mapping function that approximately describes the spatial transformation. The inverse mapping function that is needed to transform surfaces can be given in the form

$$\boldsymbol{q_i} = U(\boldsymbol{d_i}) + \boldsymbol{d_i},$$

where the components of the vector $U(\boldsymbol{d_i})$ are volume splines interpolating displacements of initial points $\boldsymbol{q_i}$.

3. Algorithm and results

Nowadays sheet stamping of parts with thin walls is a widespread technology based on finite element models of plastic deformation of sheet metal. To clarify our strategy let us discuss an analogy between our approach and simulation of a sheet metal forming process for a planar square:

- At first, boundaries of the objects and boundary conditions are setting up, see Figure 3(a); in this example red and yellow crosses define the boundaries and provide fixation of the displacement along the plain surfaces.

- Boundaries of surfaces are stretched in opposite directions that can add material in between the boundaries. Area in between of the boundaries is a blended area.

- The material of the sheet is assumed to be rigid plastic and its deformation is described by space transformation technique discussed above.

- The deformation process is regarded as taking place step by step so that the transition from a known state to a new state takes place with small increments in deformations.

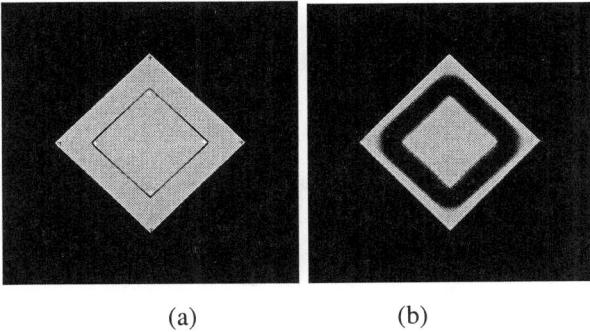

(a)   (b)

Figure 3. Illustration of stretching a plane squire sheet

The result of applying of two iterations is illustrated in Figure 3(b). Figure 4(a) presents another example - the treated tooth that has the drilled cavity. Besides, the user placed an additional volume object at the central part of treated tooth, that is, volume objects S_1, S_2 are given, thus we can

- Define control-mapping points q_i on the surfaces of S_1, S_2 objects and

- Define implicit functions for the objects S_1, S_2.

The dark blue area between the additional object S_2 and drill hole is a blended area. The user assigned 20 control points linked to features manually. The small crosses mark these points. Figure 4(d) presents the recovered area of treated tooth. In practice, one can apply several consecutive space mappings, i.e., one can sculpt the desired surface manually, by assigning control points. Unfortunately, smooth surface reconstruction is difficult to realize even for very similar surfaces; the generated surfaces will typically have a sufficiently rough reconstructed surface. To decrease this "roughness", we apply the following strategy to blend primary surfaces:

- Calculate a mapping function for the current step and apply it to boundary points according to the following procedure:

  - Define a point on the object that will be stretched. The point defines the origin of a coordinate system called the master coordinate system, which is used to calculate a stretching direction.
  - Features of volume representations are very suitable for calculating gradients. Any vector perpendicular to the surface gradient will define a floating direction, and it is possible to make the starting points float over the surface. The floating or stretching direction is calculated as a bisector direction for two adjacent edges defined by neighboring starting points.
  - The plain passing through the starting point and parallel to the vector of a stretching direction, and perpendicular to the floating plane is calculated.
  - The line segment is then scaled and x,y,z-steps are calculated. This step actually defines destination coordinates d_i that form boundary contours.

- Apply genetic optimization to avoid superfluous folding over a predefined area.

- For each iteration, calculate new destinations coordinates d''_i and apply the same space mapping technique for points d''_i.

- Repeat the loop.

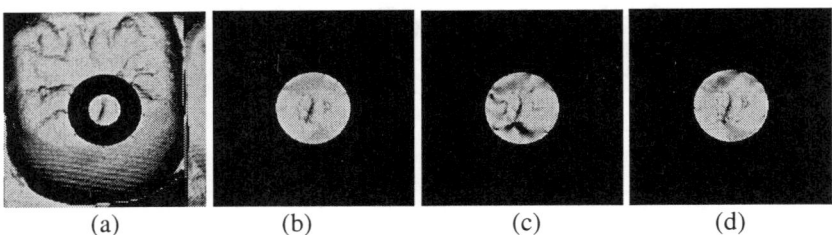

Figure 4. (a) Tooth to be treated. (b) Area reconstructed by RBFs; All interior boundary and points of central part were processed; (c) Result of reconstruction without optimization; (d) Result of reconstruction with optimization.

The application of the genetic algorithm starts with selecting a set of M variable control points $\{d_i=(d_1{}^i,d_2{}^i,d_3{}^i): i=1,2,\ldots,M\}$ for the definition of the space transformation generating the reconstructed object. (Actually, for the first iteration the user selects points q_i on the surfaces of the tooth.) The collection of coordinates of d_i defines a creature with 3M coordinates that are subject to correction. The algorithm begins by randomly distorting the initial creature, and generates s creatures, which are collected to form the initial population. Now, the genetic algorithm as described in [1] is applied to this initial setup to minimize the fitness function.

Our main premise here is to avoid superfluous folding over a predefined area where we calculate the fitness to get the "best approximated surface." Recall that the spline (determined by the set of variable control points d_i that constitute a creature) provides a minimization of the bending energy. We define the fitness function f as follows:

$$f(c) = \sum_{p=1}^{M} \sum_{i=1}^{k} \sum_{j=1}^{l} r_{ij} + h^t A^{-1} h \quad \text{for i,j} \in B_f,$$

where the first component of fitness function can be an arbitrarily chosen "gluing" area B_f (here we use small 5×5 pixels image spots), and r_{ij} are residuals (between interpolated and given surface) of elevation teeth data; the second component is the value of the bending energy, where A^{-1} is the bending energy matrix and h_i are so called heights, for the case of space transformations $h_i = q_i - d_i$. The first component of the fitness function expresses the idea that the more smoothly we glue a "sheet" of plastic to a surface, the fewer residuals of elevation data between the blended area and the remained area of treated one will be observed.

Let us note, since we know the new "state" of the surface, the strategy of calculating a stretching direction as a bisector direction for two adjacent edges can be replaced by a more promising approach where we can use geometric information for generating boundary contours.

4. Remarks

In this paper, we have presented an approach for surface reconstruction (more precisely, blending parts of a real geometric object represented by volume data) by employing a space mapping technique based on using RBFs. Figure 4(d) demonstrates the result of reconstruction of the missing part of the tooth according to presented technique. Calculation time is less then one minute on an SGI Octane workstation. We can state that proposed approach allows the design of a blended surface resembling the surface shown in Figure 4(b), reconstructed by using a "naive" RBFs approach. Let us note that processing 2000 points by "naive" RBFs methods takes two hours approximately, while processing of a fulfilled data set with the same number of points by compactly supported RBFs takes less then 10 seconds. There are several directions for future work. Chiefly, we anticipate that modifying the procedure of finding stretching directions by the process of birth and death of destination control points according to the curvature at the point will improve results of reconstruction. It might be a good idea to explore ways in which we will be able to find a good alliance between our approach and a method [36] to design nonlinear splines via curve evolution driven by curvature. While many challenges remain, we believe that the presented approach for recovering missing parts of geometric objects provides an important direction for research and practical applications.

References

[1] V. Savchenko and L. Schmitt, *"Reconstructing Occlusal Surfaces of Teeth Using a Genetic Algorithm with Simulated Annealing Type Selection"*, Proc. 6th ACM Symposium on Solid Modeling and Application, Sheraton Inn, Ann Arbor, Michigan, June 4-8, 39-46, 2001.

[2] T. Hermann, Z. Kovacs, and T. Varady, *"Special applications in surface fitting"*, Geometric Modeling: Theory and Practice, W. Strasser, R. Klein and R.Rau (Eds), Springer, pp 14-31, 1997.

[3] M. Chen, A. Kaufman and R. Yagel (Eds), "Volume Graphics, Springer", 2000.

[4] R. Franke and G. Nielson, *"Scattered Data Interpolation and Applications: A Tutorial and Survey, Geometric Modeling, Methods and Applications"*, H. Hagen and D. Roller (Eds.), Springer-Verlag, pp 131-160, 1991.

[5] S. Djurcilov and A. Pang, *"Visualizing Sparse Gridded Data Sets"*, IEEE Computer Graphics and Applications, Sept/Oct, pp 52-57, 2000.

[6] S. Muraki, *"Volumetric Shape Description of Range Data Using "Blobby Model""*, Computer Graphics, Proc. SIGGRAPH 91, Vol 25, No 4., pp 227-235, 1991.

[7] V. Savchenko and S. Sedukhin, *"Pattern Dependent Reconstruction of Raster Digital Elevation Models from Contour Maps"*, Proc. Visualization, Imaging, and Image Processing conference (VIIP'2001), Marbella, Spain, September 3-5, pp 237-244, 2001.

[8] J. H. Ahlberg, E. N. Nilson, J. L. Walsh, "The Theory of Splines and Their Applications", Academic Press, New York, 1967.

[9] J. Dushon, *"Splines Minimizing Rotation Invariants Semi-Norms in Sobolev Spaces, Constructive Theory of Functions of Several Variables"*, W. Schempp and K. Zeller (Eds.), Springer-Verlag, pp 85-100, 1976.

[10] V. A. Vasilenko, "Spline-functions: Theory, Algorithms", Programs, Novosibirsk, Nauka Publishers, 1983.

[11] R. M. Bolle, B. C. Vemuri, *"On Three-Dimensional Surface Reconstruction Methods"*, IEEE Transactions on Pattern Analysis and Machine Intelligence, 13(1), pp 1-13, 1991.

[12] G. Greiner, *"Surface Construction Based on Variational Principles"*, Wavelets, Images and Surface Fitting, P. J. Laurent et al. (Eds), AL Peters Ltd., pp 277-286, 1994.

[13] V. Savchenko, V. Vishnjakov, *"The Use of the "Serialization" Approach in the Design of Parallel Programs Exemplified by Problems in Applied Celestial Mechanics"*, Performance Evaluation of Parallel Systems, Proc. PEPS'93, University of Warwick, Coventry, UK, 29-30 Nov., pp 126-133, 1993.

[14] P. Litwinovicz, L. *"Williams, Animating Images with Drawing"*, Computer Graphics, Proc. SIGGRAPH'94, pp 409-412, 1994.

[15] J. C. Carr, W. R. Fright and R. K. Beatson, *"Surface Interpolation with Radial Basis Functions for Medical Imaging"*, IEEE Transaction on Medical Imaging, 16(1), pp 96-107, 1997.

[16] F. L. Bookstein, *"Principal Warps: Thin Plate Splines and the Decomposition of Deformations"*, IEEE Transactions on Pattern Analysis and Machine Intelligence, 11(6), pp 567-585, 1989.

[17] V. Savchenko, A. Pasko, O. Okunev and T. Kunii, *"Function representation of solids reconstructed from scattered surface points and contours"*, Computer Graphics Forum, 14(4), pp 181-188, 1995.

[18] R. K. Beatson and W. A. Light, "Fast Evaluation of Radial Basis Functions: Methods for 2-D Polyharmonic Splines", Tech. Rep. 119, Mathematics Department, Univ. of Canterbury, Christchurch, New Zealand, Dec. 1994.

[19] W. Light, "*Using Radial Functions on Compact Domains*", Wavelets, Images and Surface Fitting, P. J. Laurent et al. (Eds), AL Peters Ltd., pp 351-370, 1994.

[20] B. Morse, T. S. Yoo, P. Rheingans, D. T. Chen, and K.R. Subramanian, "*Interpolating implicit surfaces from scattered surface data using compactly supported radial basis functions*", Shape Modeling conference, Proc SMI'2001,Genova, Italy, May, pp 89-98, 2001.

[21] J. C. Carr, T.J. Mitchell, R.K. Beatson, J.B. Cherrie, W. R. Fright, B. C. McCallumm, and T.R. Evans, "*Reconstruction and representation of 3D Objects with Radial Basis Functions*", Computer Graphics, Proc. SIGGRAPH'2001, August, pp 67-76, 2001.

[22] L. Greengard and V. Rokhlin, "*A Fast Algorithm for Particle Simulation*", J. Comput. Phys, 73, 325-348, 1997.

[23] M.I.G. Bloor and M.J. Vilson, "*Spectral Approximation to PDE surfaces*", CAD, 28(2), pp 145 – 152, 1996.

[24] J.A. Setian, "Level Set Methods: Evolving Interfaces in Geometry, Fluid Mechanics, Computer Vision, and Material Sciences", Cambridge University Press, 1996.

[25] R. T. Whitaker and D E. Breen, "*Level-set Models for The deformation of Solid Objects*", Proc. Implicit Surfaces'98, June 15-16, Seattle, USA, pp 19-35, 1998.

[26] M.B. Gousie and W.R. Franklin, "*Converting Elevation Contours to a Grid*", Proc. Eighth International Symposium on Spatial Data Handling (SDH), Vancouver BC Canada, July 1998. Dept of Geography, Simon Fraser University, Burnaby, BC, Canada, 1998, http://www.ecse.rpi.edu/Homepages/wrf

[27] K. Kass, A. Witkin, and D. Terzopoulos, "*Snakes: Active Contour Models*", International Journal of Computer Vision, pp 321-331, 1988.

[28] Y. Duan and H. Qin, "*Intellegent Ballon: A Subdivision-Based Deformable Model for Surface Reconstruction of Arbitrary Topology*", Proc. Sixth ACM Symposium on Solid Modeling and Applications, Ann Arbor, Michigan, June6-8, pp 47-58, 2001.

[29] H. Wendland, "*Piecewise polynomial, positive defined and compactly supported radial functions of minimal degree*", AICM, 4, pp 389-396, 1995.

[30] N. Kojekine, V. Savchenko, D. Berzin, I. Hagiwara, "*Software Tools for Compactly Supported Radial Basis Functions*", Computer Graphics and Imaging, Proc. IASTED CGIM'2000, Hawaii, USA, August 13-16, pp 234-239, 2001.

[31] V.V. Savchenko, A.A. Pasko, A.I. Surin, T.L. Kunii, "*Volume Modeling: Representations and advanced operations*", Proc Computer Graphics Int. Conf., F. Wolter and N.M. Patrikalakis (Eds.), Hannover, Germany, IEEE Computer Society, June 22-26, , pp 4-13, 1998.

[32] F.L. Bookstein, "Morphometric Tools for Landmark Data", Cambridge University Press, 1991.

[33] F.L. Bookstein, *"Two Shape Metrics for Biomedical Outline Data: Bending Energy, Procrustes Distance, and The Biometrical Modeling of Shape Phenomena"*, Proc. Shape Modeling Conference (SMIA`97), March 3-6, Aizu-Wakamatsu, Japan, pp 110- 120, 1997.

[34] M. D. Vose, "The Simple Genetic Algorithm: Foundations and Theory (Complex Adaptive Systems) ", Bradford Books, 1999.

[35] L.M. Schmitt, *"Theory of Genetic Algorithms"*, to appear in Theoretical Computer Science, 2001, 61p. (available as preprint from the author).

[36] A. Belyev, E. Anoshkina, and S. Yoshizawa, *"Nonlinear Spline Generation with Curve Evolutions Driven by Curvature"*, Proc. Shape Modeling Conference (SMIA`99), March 1-4, Aizu-Wakamatsu, Japan, pp 146- 153, 1999.

Borders, Semi-Sharp Edges and Adaptivity for Hexagonal Subdivision Surface Schemes

Koen Beets, Johan Claes, Frank Van Reeth

Limburg University Centre - Expertise Centre for Digital Media, Belgium

{koen.beets, johan.claes, frank.vanreeth}@luc.ac.be

Abstract

In recent research, hexagonal subdivision schemes for meshes with an arbitrary topology have been introduced. They can either be viewed on their own or be combined with their dual triangular counterparts to generate surfaces with high degrees of continuity, similar to the earlier approaches with quadrilateral schemes. For practical applications, however, a major obstacle is the lack of good algorithms to generate borders and to adaptively subdivide meshes up to user-controlled criteria.

As hexagonal schemes operate on dual meshes with constantly changing positions of vertices, defining borders and corners is less straightforward than for primal schemes. In this paper, we describe an elegant method based on half polygons to create such borders, which also can be adapted to create sharp and even semi-sharp edges.

Adaptive techniques are a necessity to manage the exponential growth of the number of new polygons created by the subdivision process. Existing techniques for dual subdivision schemes lead to quite difficult implementations, and would be impractical to extend to hexagonal schemes. Where earlier approaches are face centered, we view the problem in a dual way, focusing on whether or not to subdivide around the vertices of the precedent subdivision steps. This allows for crack-free tessellations with deeply subdivided portions closely bordering much coarser regions.

Keywords: Recursive subdivision surfaces, hexagonal subdivision, primal dual schemes, adaptive subdivision.

1. Introduction

Subdivision surfaces define a smooth surface as the limit of a series of refinements, starting from a polygonal control mesh. Nowadays, they are popular for many kinds of applications, such as in geometric modeling, and their study is still gaining interest due to their close relation to wavelet and multi-resolution analysis [22].

Chaikin was one of the first to suggest the principle of repeated refinements to generate smooth curves [3], later advanced by Lane and Riesenfield, analyzing subdivision methods to create B-spline curves of any degree [11]. In 1978, Catmull and Clark generalized these ideas to surfaces, not only for regular quadrilateral meshes, but also for meshes exhibiting an arbitrary topology [2]. They generated a smooth limit surface by recursively splitting quadrilaterals into four. Doo and Sabin introduced a dual to Catmull and Clark's scheme, interchanging the role of vertices and faces [6]. Later, subdivision schemes which operate on triangular meshes were proposed, such as Loop's scheme [13] generalizing a quartic box-spline and Kobbelt's Sqrt(3) scheme [10].

For a recursive subdivision surface scheme to be based on a mesh of one type of polygons, triangles, quadrilaterals or hexagons have to be considered. These are the only types of polygons that allow a regular tiling of an infinite 2D plane. Schemes that operate on the dual of triangular meshes – namely, hexagonal meshes – were investigated very recently by Claes et al. [4]. Subdivision for regular hexagonal meshes has also been analyzed by Jiang and Oswald [9]. Oswald and Schröder investigated a family of subdivision schemes for triangular and hexagonal meshes [17]. These papers are a continuation on the work of [25] and [21], who describe how to generate surfaces with a high degree of continuity by repeated averaging, combining primal and dual subdivision schemes.

For greater acceptance in modeling applications, extra features, such as vigorous support for borders and adaptive subdivision, are highly desired.

1.1 Borders and sharp edges

To model open surfaces, a robust algorithm for borders is a necessity. Most of the existing research on borders concentrates on primal subdivision schemes. In such primal schemes, new faces are generated by dividing existing edges and relaxing the existing vertices. Therefore, it suffices to define special relaxation rules to define good-behaving boundary edges. For dual subdivision schemes, the existing edges are constantly cut away, urging the need for more complicated measures. An interesting approach comes from Nasri, who describes methods to create creases and borders for the dual Doo-Sabin scheme. He augments the object with polygonal strips, which converge to a specific B-spline [15, 16].

Hoppe et al. modified the subdivision rules to add borders to Loop surfaces [8]. They also provide support for creases, by uncoupling the crease curve from the surface from both sides [8], with special attention to extraordinary points. Schweitzer proves these rules result in C^1 continuous surfaces [19].

Sederberg et al. add support for sharp edges to the Doo-Sabin and Catmull-Clark schemes by introducing non-uniform knot vectors [20]. Sharp edges are created in Doo-Sabin surfaces by setting knot spaces along certain control edges to zero. Non-uniform subdivision rules, however, severely increase the complexity of the algorithm, and analyzing the behavior of the surface around extraordinary points becomes very complex.

Biermann and Levin extend this work and provide the Catmull-Clark and Loop schemes with flexible support for borders and normal control [12, 1]. They also observed that in certain situations it is interesting to employ different rules for convex and concave borders. Levin further extended the boundary to allow arbitrary parametric curves, removing the previous restriction to subdivision curves for B-splines.

Velho and Zorin add support for smooth borders to their 4-8 subdivision scheme [23]. These smooth borders are 5th degree B-splines, based on Lane and Riesenfields algorithm [11]. Just as in [1], they adapt their rules in the neighborhood of extraordinary boundary vertices to improve continuity at the boundary around extraordinary points. [25] suggests simplifying the algorithms and not implementing such special rules around extraordinary boundary points, as the defects at the boundary are not noticeable in practice.

DeRose et al. employ an elegant technique, which they called hybrid subdivision, to add support for creases of variable sharpness to the Catmull-Clark scheme [5]. First, a set of sharp rules is applied a finite number of times, followed by a set of smooth rules. Additionally, non-integer sharpness is supported through interpolation between sharp and smooth rules.

1.2 Adaptive subdivision

In any subdivision scheme, the number of faces grows exponentially. Due to memory and time restrictions, the number of subdivision steps that can be performed is relatively small. A solution to get good-quality surface approximations without too many faces, is to subdivide adaptively: regions where little detail is present are subdivided coarsely while regions with fine detail are subdivided much further. To determine which regions will be refined again, some specific criteria must be established. Such criteria are often based on the dihedral angle between adjacent faces and can be extended with view-dependent criteria.

Very important is a consistent way to guarantee a correct connectivity. In many cases, this means maintaining additional information in the mesh structure. In order to avoid surface artifacts, adaptive refinement is often limited to balanced meshes, where the subdivision level of adjacent faces differs by no more than one level [25].

For dyadic split refinement on triangular meshes, such as the Loop scheme, locally splitting faces causes gaps if their direct neighbors are not split. This can be avoided by replacing adjacent triangles with a triangle fan. When one subdivides further, these triangle fans have to be removed again. Red-green triangulation is a good example of such a technique, employing dyadic refinement, mesh balancing and gap fixing by triangle fans [10].

Kobbelt's triangular Sqrt(3) scheme supports adaptive refinement without adding extra information to the mesh since no edges are split [10]. As such, the localization is better than for dyadic refinement. The scheme also lends itself well to adaptive techniques because it limits the amount of overtesselation since the number of triangles is multiplied by three instead of four in every step, similar to our hexagonal scheme [4].

Velho and Zorin's 4-8 subdivision is a primal scheme, based on bisectional refinement [23]. The number of faces increases by a factor of two instead of four, which allows for better granularity in adaptive subdivision.

Zorin and Schröder present a method for adaptive subdivision for primal and dual quadrilateral subdivision, based on quad trees [25]. Besides the restriction that adjacent faces differ by no more than one subdivision level, they also pose the same restriction for faces adjacent to the same vertex. Their method for adaptive subdivision turns out to be very hard to implement in the case of dual schemes such as Doo-Sabin's.

Other methods for adaptive subdivision of the dual Doo-Sabin scheme have been described in [14] and [24]. Their approaches are limited to having a difference of maximally one subdivision level for adjacent faces.

The rest of this paper is organized as follows. Section 2 introduces rules and properties of the hexagonal subdivision scheme from [4]. As many common meshes found in computer graphics environments are triangular, section 3 proposes a construction to convert these meshes to hexagonal ones. Section 4 is dedicated to the creation of borders and their intrinsic relationship with quadratic curves, while section 5 presents our new technique for adaptive subdivision. Finally, section 6 presents some of our results, followed by our conclusions in section 7.

2. Stationary hexagonal subdivision rules

In this section, we briefly describe our hexagonal subdivision scheme. We refer the interested reader to [4] for more details. Similar to recursive subdivision schemes operating on other types of meshes, an initial hexagonal mesh is recursively subdivided into smaller hexagonal meshes.

The standard algorithm for hexagonal subdivision first calculates two new control points for every existing edge, one inside each of the two faces it is connected to. Then, two types of new faces are formed by connecting these new points: inside each face a smaller face is constructed and around every vertex new faces are added. The net result has the effect of recursively cutting away all corners of a polygonal mesh.

2.1 Subdivision rules in the regular case

When determining the rules and weights for new points, certain desirable properties are considered. First, the support area of the scheme should be small, such that every control point exhibits only a local influence. Symmetrical subdivision rules make sure all input polygons are treated in an equal way, independent from their position in the mesh. For the scheme to be invariant under affine transformations, the sum of these weights should equal one.

For an entirely regular mesh (consisting of hexagons with valence 3 vertices), these considerations lead to the existence of three different weights (see figure 1):

- one for the two points closest to the new point (a),
- another weight for the two points in the middle (b),
- and a third weight for the two furthest points (c).

Expressed using these factors, the equation for the new point is then written as:

$$P = aP_1 + aP_2 + bP_3 + bP_6 + cP_4 + cP_5 \qquad (1)$$

Taking into account all the previous considerations, we arrive at the following ideal weights in the regular case:

$$a = \frac{7}{18} \quad b = \frac{1}{18} \quad c = \frac{1}{18} \qquad (2)$$

Note that with these weights, for an input configuration entirely consisting of equal regular hexagons, the smaller hexagons in the refined configuration again all have exactly the same size. [4] and [9] show that these rules lead to the best continuity for the given stencil.

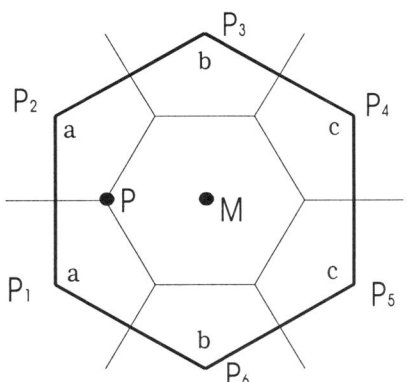

Fig. 1. The position of the new point P is a weighted average of the points of the surrounding hexagon.

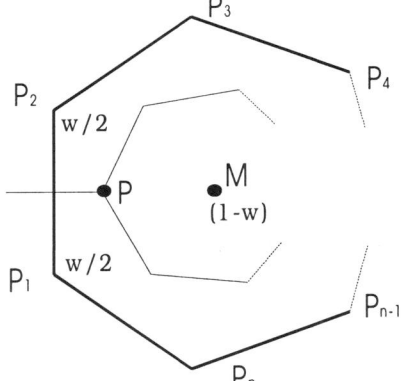

Fig. 2. Situation of a polygon in the extraordinary case. New points are a weighted mean between the ends of the nearby edge and the center of the polygon.

2.2 Rules for the extraordinary case

The rule for the regular hexagonal case can be viewed in another way. Instead of formulating it using the six points of the hexagon, we could see it as taking the uniformly weighted average of the two nearby points with the center of the hexagon.

A simple rule for the polygons of the old mesh that are not hexagons, is to use the same approach as for hexagons: just take the average of the center and the two nearby points. However, in this case the weights should be adapted to obtain a uniform shrinking between all types of polygons. If we stay with the idea that the new point should be an average (though not uniformly weighted) between the two nearby points and the center, we would get the following formula (see figure 2):

$$P = w\frac{P_1 + P_2}{2} + (1-w)M \qquad (3)$$

Here M is the center of the polygon, calculated as the weighted average of its n points. The only way to get the shrinking factor equal to the shrinking by one-third of the hexagon is for w to equal:

$$w = \frac{1}{\sqrt{3}\cos(\pi/n)} \qquad (4)$$

In the practical implementation we strongly depend on the formulation using the polygon center, but for use in matrix analysis, M should be replaced by its original components:

$$P = \frac{(n-2)w+2}{2n}P_1 + \frac{(n-2)w+2}{2n}P_2 + \frac{1-w}{n}P_3 + \frac{1-w}{n}P_4 + \ldots + \frac{1-w}{n}P_n \qquad (5)$$

3. Converting triangular to hexagonal meshes

Most polygonal meshes found in computer graphics environments mainly consist of triangles and quadrilaterals. Meshes that mostly contain hexagons are quite rare. The meshes obtained from 3D laser scanners, for example, are typically arranged in a triangular way, exhibiting an arbitrary topology. In this section, we describe ways of converting such triangular meshes to mainly hexagonal ones. Meshes containing polygons with more than three vertices can easily be triangulated using standard techniques.

[4] describes two suitable methods to convert a triangular to a hexagonal mesh: by cutting the corners of the triangles or by replacing the mesh by its dual. For the sake of simplicity, in this paper we will restrict ourselves to using the dual mesh for this conversion.

All triangles of the original mesh will be converted to vertices, and all vertices of the original mesh will be converted to polygons. For each vertex, the centers of the surrounding triangles are connected to form a polygon. The number of sides is determined by the valence of the original vertex. In figure 3, the vertices with the regular valence of six in the triangular mesh are converted to hexagons, while valence five vertices are converted to pentagons. While the polygons created by this process can have an extraordinary number of vertices, the newly created vertices themselves all have a valence of three, as would be needed for a regular hexagonal mesh. Luckily, for all subsequent subdivisions, the only newly created polygons will be hexagons.

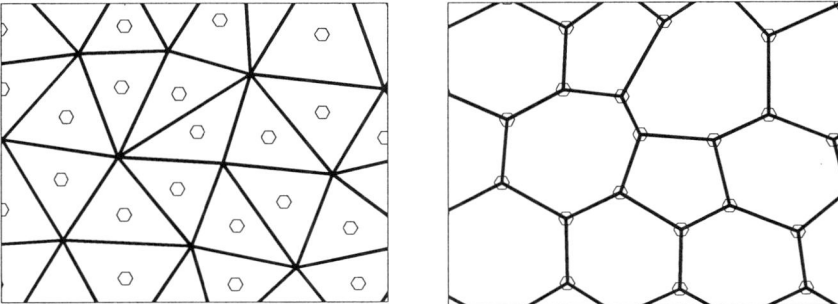

Fig. 3. Left: In an irregular triangular mesh the centers of the triangles are marked. Right: These centers are used to construct the dual hexagonal mesh.

4. Curves and borders

4.1 Ternary refinement of quadratic curves

By putting hexagons symmetrically around the control points of a quadratic subdivision curve, the resulting subdivision surface will interpolate that curve. Under these conditions, the subdivision rules mimic a ternary division of the quadratic curve. This is similar to how the four-point subdivision scheme for curves is embedded in the Butterfly scheme [7].

For a ternary refinement of a quadratic curve, Sabin derived the coefficients of equation 6 [18]. The first formula relaxes the position of an old control point, while the second and third define the position of the newly inserted vertices.

$$p_0' = \frac{1}{9}(p_{-1} + 7p_0 + p_1)$$
$$p_1' = \frac{1}{9}(6p_0 + 3p_1) \qquad (6)$$
$$p_2' = \frac{1}{9}(3p_0 + 6p_1)$$

4.2 Borders for hexagonal schemes

Our approach starts with a triangular mesh with a border. This mesh is converted to a hexagonal one. As no full hexagons can be created at the border, we decided to work with half hexagons near these borders. For the hexagonal scheme, the border will be formed by the edges that cut these half hexagons.

For clarity, we often refer to the input polygons of the hexagonal scheme as hexagons. In practice, these polygons can have any number of vertices, depending on the valence of the vertices in the original triangular mesh. Luckily, after the first step, newly generated polygons will only be hexagons.

4.2.1 Converting triangular meshes with borders to hexagonal ones

Figures 4 and 5 show an input mesh M_T of gray-colored triangles and its conversion to a hexagonal mesh. Little circles mark the centers of the triangles, which will be connected to form a mesh M_0 of mainly hexagons. At the borders of M_0, no full hexagons can be created. Therefore, we decided to use the middle points of the border edges of M_T, which are also marked in figure 5. These middle points of the triangle border will become the middle points of edges of a virtual full polygon in M_0. These polygons are drawn in thin lines in the figure. The actual data structure for M_0 contains only the half polygons that are inside the surface. In order to illustrate the nature of these half polygons, figure 5 also shows the outer half of the polygons.

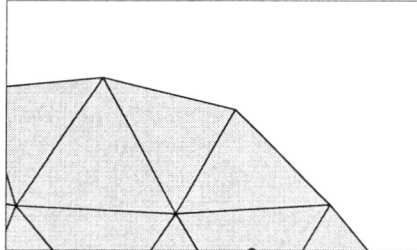
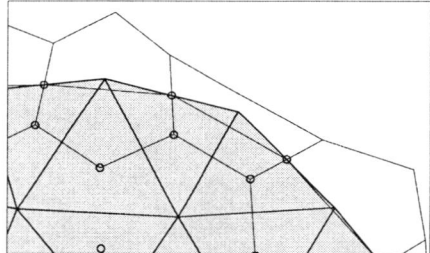

Fig. 4. An input triangular mesh M_T with border.

Fig. 5. Conversion of the triangular mesh M_T with border to a hexagonal mesh M_0. The border of M_0 consists of half polygons.

4.2.2 The first subdivision step near the border

The first subdivision step is depicted in figure 6. The initial polygons and half polygons for this step are colored gray and the new control points are again marked with little circles.

For most operations in the subsequent subdivision process, the half polygons and their vertices are treated just like the full polygons: new vertices are calculated around their internal vertices and connected to form new hexagons. Care has to be taken concerning the weights, as the formulas (equations 4 and 5) need to consider the number of vertices of the full polygon. Furthermore, the middle of the cutting edge is taken to be the center of the virtual full polygon.

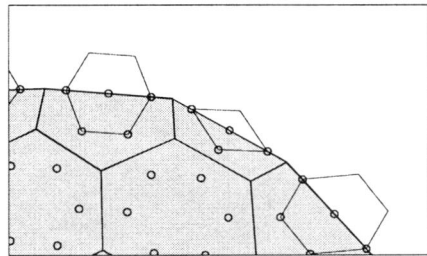
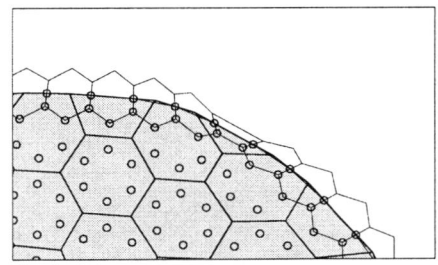

Fig. 6. The first subdivision step near the border, subdividing mesh M_0 to become M_1. The control points for M_1 are marked with circles and near the border the half polygons of M_1 are drawn using a thin line style.

Fig. 7. The second subdivision step near the border. Here the control points of the newly generated mesh M_2 are marked with circles and its half polygons are drawn using a thin line style.

At the border, again special control points are calculated. As our hexagonal subdivision is the dual of Kobbelt's Sqrt(3) scheme, the hexagons are rotated with 30° after each subdivision step. Therefore, the polygons at the border are now halved by cutting using the line connecting two opposite vertices (instead of the line connecting two edge centers).

Although only two new control points are strictly necessary in between two existing points P_n and P_{n+1}, we introduce three new points: Q_{3n}, Q_{3n+1} and Q_{3n+2} (see figure 8). Introducing three points has the benefit that the number of vertices of the half polygons does not alter with every subdivision step, which further helps to simplify the subdivision rules at the border. These three points are calculated as:

$$Q_{3n+1} = \frac{1}{2}(P_n + P_{n+1})$$

$$Q_{3n} = \frac{2}{3}P_n + \frac{1}{3}Q_{3n+1} = \frac{5}{6}P_n + \frac{1}{6}P_{n+1} \qquad (7)$$

$$Q_{3n+2} = \frac{2}{3}P_{n+1} + \frac{1}{3}Q_{3n+1} = \frac{5}{6}P_{n+1} + \frac{1}{6}P_n$$

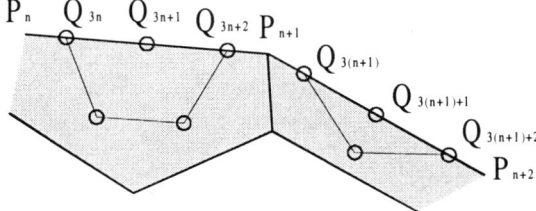

Fig. 8. The points P_i form the border of the even indexed meshes. Points Q_j are inserted to form the border of the next mesh.

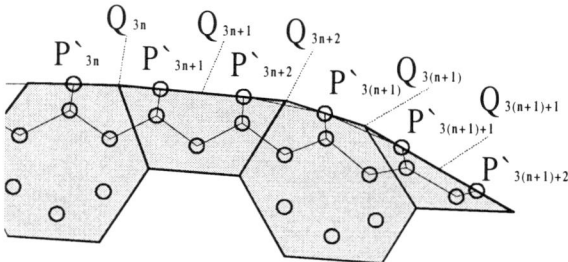

Fig. 9. In between each two points Q_j and Q_{j+1} of the odd indexed meshes, we insert a new control point P'_{j+1} for the border of the next mesh.

4.2.3 The second subdivision step near the border

In figure 7, mesh M_1 contains the initial polygons and half polygons that are used as input for the second subdivision step. The new control points for mesh M_2 are again marked with little circles. Two types of new half polygons are created at the border: one at the center of each old half polygon of the previous step and one around the old vertices (see figure 7). The net result is a configuration of half polygons similar to the configuration in M_0.

Thanks to the insertion of an extra point in the middle of the borders of M_1, only one new point P'_{j+1} for the border of M_2 needs to be inserted between two subsequent points Q_j and Q_{j+1} of M_1. The most straightforward approach would choose P'_{j+1} to be the middle of Q_j and Q_{j+1}. Taking a closer look at the relation between P'_{j+1} (forming the border of M_2) and the points on the border of M_0, reveals the following:

$$P'_{3n+1} = \frac{1}{2}(Q_{3n} + Q_{3n+1}) = \frac{2}{3}P_n + \frac{1}{3}P_{n+1}$$

$$P'_{3n+2} = \frac{1}{2}(Q_{3n+1} + Q_{3n+2}) = \frac{1}{3}P_n + \frac{2}{3}P_{n+1} \quad (8)$$

$$P'_{3(n+1)} = \frac{1}{2}(Q_{3n+2} + Q_{3(n+1)}) = \frac{1}{12}P_n + \frac{5}{6}P_{n+1} + \frac{1}{12}P_{n+2}$$

This resembles the formulas for a quadratic subdivision curve described in section 4.1, except for a small difference in the weights for $P'_{3(n+1)}$. In order to get a proper quadratic curve, we modify the formula for $P'_{3(n+1)}$ to:

$$P'_{3(n+1)} = \frac{1}{6}(Q_{3n+1} + Q_{3n+2} + 4Q_{3(n+1)}) = \frac{1}{9}P_n + \frac{7}{9}P_{n+1} + \frac{1}{9}P_{n+2} \quad (9)$$

4.2.4 The subsequent subdivision steps near the border

After the second subdivision step, the same situation as before the first subdivision step is reached. Therefore, both types of subdivision step can be used in alternating fashion. Every second subdivision step will be a ternary subdivision of the initial control polygon forming the border of M_0. In the limit, this leads to a continuous quadratic curve on the border. Figures 10 and 11 show the second and third subdivision of the initial mesh, illustrating the smoothening process on the border.

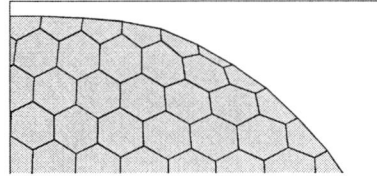

Fig. 10. The second subdivision step results in mesh M_2.

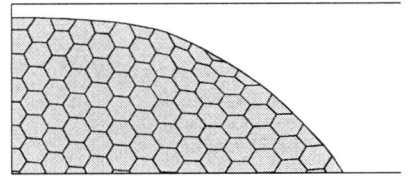

Fig. 11. Mesh M_3 is the result of the third subdivision step and illustrates the smoothness of the limit curve at the border.

4.3 Corners at the border of hexagonal schemes

A corner can be created by simply keeping one of the border points on its initial position. In our implementation, we let the user mark some of the border points to create a corner. As the hexagonal subdivision process constantly creates dual meshes, the even numbered meshes would not have a control point to represent the corner point. Therefore, we add an extra point in these even-numbered meshes. Figure 12 illustrates the subsequent steps of this process.

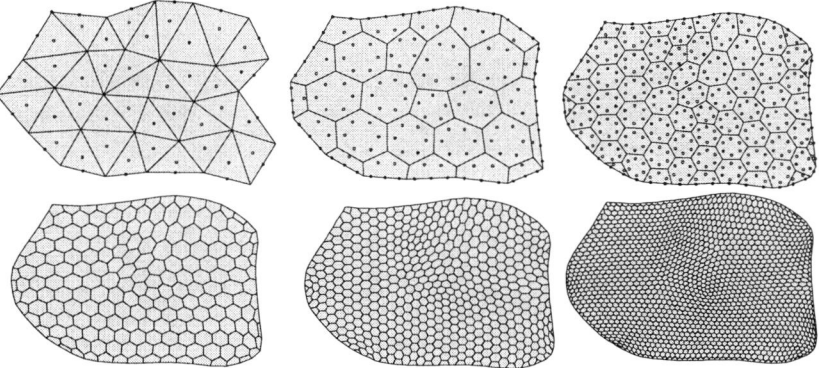

Fig. 12. The upper left point of a mesh was indicated as a corner, while the rest of the points at the border were treated using the standard border rules. The initial triangular mesh M_T and five subdivision steps ($M_0 \ldots M_4$) illustrate the algorithm. The partial polygon in the corner consists of five vertices in the even-numbered meshes and of four vertices in the other meshes.

5. Adaptive subdivision strategies

Although our hexagonal scheme has only a multiplication factor of three, the number of polygons generated grows exponentially, as in any subdivision surface scheme. Therefore, most practical implementations of subdivision surface schemes employ an adaptive subdivision strategy. Depending on user-controlled stopping criteria, the mesh will be subdivided less into regions that are relatively flat, and more into heavily curved regions.

Most techniques for adaptive subdivision are either quite complicated to implement, or oblige neighboring regions to differ no more than one subdivision level. Usually these techniques decide to subdivide a face less deep than one or more of its neighbors. As the points on the border of the deeper subdivided region do not fit the points of the less subdivided region, without additional measures, this results in gaps between neighboring faces. Typically, these gaps are filled using triangle fans or extra tessellation points.

Both for primal and for dual schemes, researchers define these stopping criteria on neighboring faces. We, on the contrary, view the problem in a dual way, and define these criteria on the vertices. The subdivision process around a vertex continues until the surrounding faces become close enough to be coplanar.

We designed the following algorithm for adaptively subdividing a hexagonal mesh, which is illustrated by figure 13.

Algorithm 1. Adaptive subdivision

1. At the start of the iteration, all vertices for which the stopping criterion holds are labeled as "stopping".

2. Then, new vertices are calculated on the edges, depending on the "stopping" labeling:

   2.A) If both vertices of an edge are labeled as "stopping", no new vertex is calculated.

   2.B) If none of the two vertices is labeled as "stopping", two new vertices are calculated, matching the setup of the standard subdivision process.

   2.C) If one vertex is labeled as "stopping" and the other one not, only one new vertex in the middle of the edge is calculated. Its position is the average between the two vertices that would be generated for this edge in the standard subdivision.

3. New faces are created:

   3.A) Inside the old faces, all vertices of step 2, together with the old vertices labeled as "stopping", are collected to form a new face inside the old one.

   3.B) Around every non-stopping vertex, all vertices of step 2 belonging to the surrounding edges are collected to form a new face around the old vertex.

   3.C) No new faces are created around the stopping vertices.

To guarantee that the adaptive points will be on the same position as they would be in the standard subdivision, for each of the polygons, its center is calculated separately and also its original number of vertices is stored. The original number of vertices determines the weights to be used (see equations 4 and 5 in section 2). A new face that is created inside an old face just inherits its center. For new faces that are created around old vertices, the center is a weighted mean between itself and the surrounding vertices.

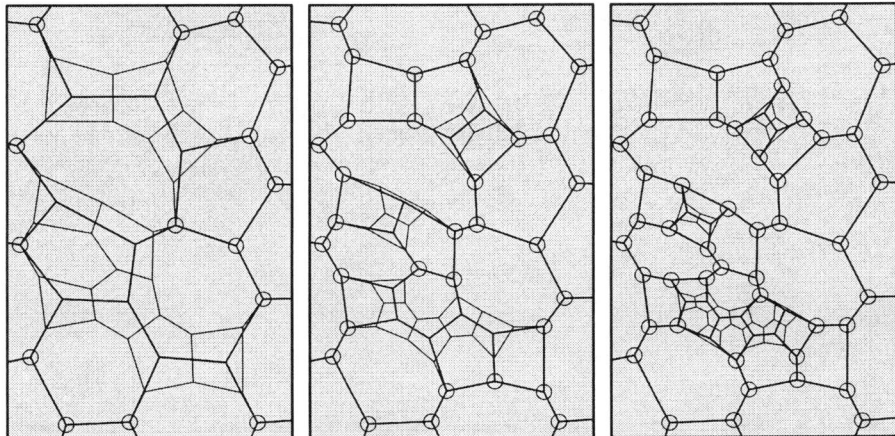

Fig. 13. Three steps in the adaptive subdivision of a mesh. For each step, the input mesh is drawn using thick lines and the more subdivided mesh using thinner lines. The stopping points are marked with a circle. New faces are created inside the existing faces and around the non-stopping vertices.

6. Results

We described adequate algorithms to add borders and adaptivity to the hexagonal subdivision scheme, enabling their use in practical applications, in a similar fashion as longer existing approximation subdivision surface schemes.

Figure 14 shows two subdivided objects. A sharp edge is created by fitting two open surfaces that share a common boundary (left image). Semi-sharp edges are created by starting with sharp rules and afterwards jump back to the smooth rules (right image), similar to the approach of DeRose et al. for Catmull-Clark's scheme [5].

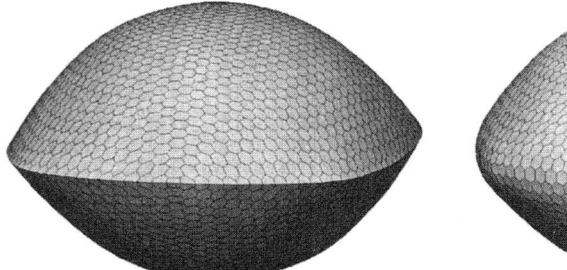 

Fig. 14. Sharp (left) and semi-sharp edges (right), extending the techniques of [5].

Figure 15 shows an adaptively subdivided cat model. Higher subdivision levels represent tinier features, for example around the ears of the cat. Figure 16 shows the same adaptively subdivided model, where the subdivision level is determined by a spatial threshold, illustrating how our algorithm allows highly subdivided regions to closely border much coarser regions.

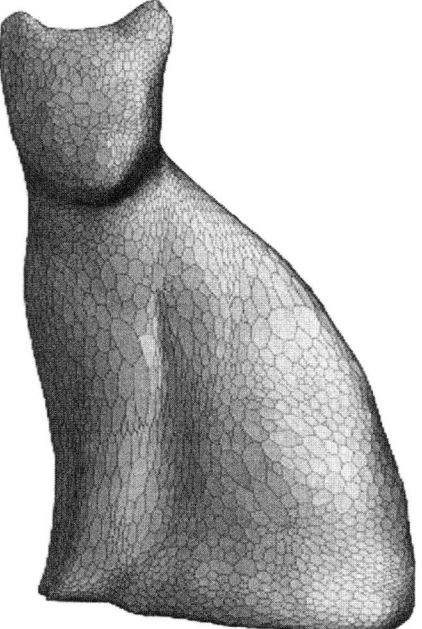 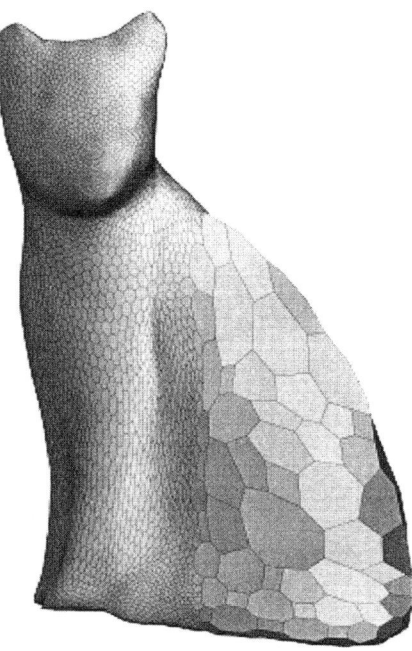

Fig. 15. Adaptively subdivided cat model, consisting of 4656 faces. More levels of subdivision were used in strongly curved regions.

Fig. 16. Here the subdivision level of the cat model is determined by a spatial threshold. This illustrates the algorithm's ability to swiftly join deeply and coarsely subdivided regions. The left side is subdivided four times.

7. Discussion

Recent research showed the importance of hexagonal subdivision schemes for creating smooth surfaces [17], extending the work of [25] and [21] about combining dual quadrilateral schemes to create high-continuity surfaces.

In this paper, we demonstrated how these hexagonal subdivision surface schemes can have similar extensions as the more conventional subdivision schemes, facilitating their use in applications such as surface modeling. When operating on a triangular input mesh, the mesh can be transformed to its dual by putting new faces at the position of old points and new points at the center of the old faces.

A new algorithm for borders is presented, relying on the close relation with a ternary subdivision for quadratic B-spline curves. To handle the problems arising from the continuous cutting away of existing edges, the use of half polygons turns out to be a very promising novel approach. By ensuring that the rules for the new boundary points do not rely on any interior point, sharp edges can be created on the joints of two surfaces sharing a common boundary. This approach can be extended to create semi-sharp edges thanks to an adequate combination of sharp and smooth rules.

Although the hexagonal subdivision algorithm has only a multiplication factor of three, adaptive subdivision techniques are a necessity to cope with the exponential growth of the number of faces. We propose a new algorithm based on subdividing around vertices instead of the traditional face centered approach. Besides the benefit of a straightforward implementation, the new algorithm also allows for large differences in subdivision levels between neighboring regions.

8. Acknowledgements

The authors are pleased to acknowledge that this work has been partially funded by the European Fund for Regional Development and the Flemish Government.

Reference list

[1] Biermann H., Levin A., Zorin D., "Piecewise Smooth Subdivision Surfaces with Normal Control", SIGGRAPH 00 Conference Proceedings, pp. 113-120, 2000.
[2] Catmull E., Clark J., "Recursively Generated B-Spline Surfaces on Arbitrary Topological Meshes", Computer-Aided Design 10 (Sept. 1978), pp.350–355.
[3] Chaikin G. M., "An Algorithm for High Speed Curve Generation", Computer Graphics and Image Processing, 1974, 3(4), pp. 346-349.
[4] Claes J., Beets K., Van Reeth F., "A Corner-Cutting Scheme for Hexagonal Subdivison Surfaces", to be published in the Proceedings of Shape Modeling and Applications (SMI '02), 2002.
[5] DeRose T., Kass M., Truong T., "Subdivision Surfaces in Character Animation", SIGGRAPH 98 Conference Proceedings, pp.85–94, July 1998.
[6] Doo D., Sabin M., "Behaviour of Recursive Division Surfaces Near Extraordinary Points", Computer-Aided Design 10 (Sept. 1978), pp.356–360.

[7] Dyn N., Gregory J. A., Levin D., "A Butterfly Subdivision Scheme for Surface Interpolation with Tension Control", ACM Transactions on Graphics, Vol. 9, No. 2, pp. 160–169, April 1990.
[8] Hoppe H., DeRose T., Duchamp T., Halstead M., Hubert J., McDonald J., Schweitzer J., Stuetzle W., "Piecewise Smooth Surface Reconstruction", SIGGRAPH 94 Conference Proceedings, pp. 295-302, 1994.
[9] Jiang Q., Oswald P., "On the Analysis of Sqrt(3)-Subdivision Schemes", Submitted, 2002.
[10] Kobbelt L., "Sqrt(3) Subdivision", in Proceedings of the Conference on Computer Graphics (SIGGRAPH 2000), pp.103-112, July 2000.
[11] Lane J., Riesenfield R., "A Theoretical Development for the Computer Generation and Display of Piecewise Polynomial Surfaces", IEEE Transactions on Pattern Analysis and Machine Intelligence, 2(1):35-46, 1980.
[12] Levin A., "Combined subdivision schemes for the design of surfaces satisfying boundary conditions", in Computer Aided Geometric Design, 16(5), pp. 345-354, 1999.
[13] Loop C., "Smooth Subdivision Surfaces Based on Triangles", Master's thesis, University of Utah, Department of Mathematics, 1987.
[14] Mueller H., Jaeschke R., "Adaptive Subdivision Curves and Surfaces", in the Proceedings of Computer Graphics International '98, pp. 48-58, 1998.
[15] Nasri A., "Interpolating Meshes of Boundary Intersecting Curves by Subdivision Surfaces", The Visual Computer, Vol. 16, No. 1, 2000, pp. 3-14.
[16] Nasri A., "Constructing Polygonal Complexes with Shape Handles for Curve Interpolation by Subdivision Surfaces", in Computer Aided Design 33, pp.753-765, September 2001.
[17] Oswald P., Schröder P., "Composite Primal/Dual Sqrt(3)-Subdivision Schemes", Submitted, 2002.
[18] Sabin M., "Subdivision: Tutorial Notes", tutorial of Shape Modeling International (SMI'01), May 2001.
[19] Schweitzer J., "Analysis and Application of Subdivision Surfaces", Ph.D. dissertation, Department of Computer Science and Engineering, University of Washington, Technical Report UW-CSE-96-08-02, August 1996.
[20] Sederberg T., Zheng J., Sewell D., Sabin M., "Non-Uniform Recursive Subdivision Surfaces", Computer Graphics Proceedings (SIGGRAPH), Annual Conference Series, 1998, pp. 387- 394.
[21] Stam J., "On Subdivision Schemes Generalizing Uniform B-Spline Surfaces of Arbitrary Degree", in Computer Aided Geometric Design. Special Edition on Subdivision Surfaces, Volume 18, 2001, pp. 383-396.
[22] Stollnitz E. J., DeRose T. D., Salesin D. H., "Wavelets for Computer Graphics", Morgan Kaufmann Publishers, San Francisco, 1996.
[23] Velho L., Zorin D., "4-8 Subdivision", in Computer-Aided Geometric Design, 18(5), pp. 397-427, 2001. Special Issue on Subdivision Techniques.
[24] Xu Z., Kondo K., "Adaptive Refinements in Subdivision Surfaces", in EUROGRAPHICS 1999 Proceedings.
[25] Zorin D., Schröder P., "A Unified Framework for Primal/Dual Quadrilateral Subdivision Schemes", in Computer Aided Geometric Design, Volume 18, Issue 5, pp. 429-454.

Mesh Smoothing with Shape or Feature Preservation

Hao Zhang   Eugene Fiume
University of Toronto
Toronto, Ontario, Canada

Abstract

In this paper, we develop mesh smoothing algorithms capable of retaining and even enhancing important shape characteristics of the original model. For a preservation of overall shape or low-frequency characteristics, we propose the simple idea of one-step shape restoration, which partially recovers the low-frequency contribution attenuated away by Laplacian smoothing.

To preserve the sharp features of a mesh, such as ridges and corners, we develop a geometric smoothing algorithm which minimizes a vertex-to-plane distance measure defined at the mesh vertices. Unlike previous feature-preserving algorithms, we do not identify features explicitly. Our algorithm can also be modified to obtain a feature-enhancing vertex flow.

Keywords: mesh smoothing, low-pass filtering, shape and feature preservation, feature enhancement

1. Introduction

Large and complex mesh models are often obtained from points sampled over real-world objects. With the advent and advances in 3-D scanning and acquisition technology [2], models obtained this way are becoming widely available. But due to the inevitable physical noise added by a scanning device, points sampled from a 3-D object often do not reflect their correct locations, resulting in meshes containing undesirable rough features.

Mesh smoothing, or denoising, is a process dedicated to the removal of these rough features. The ultimate goal of mesh smoothing is to produce highly smooth meshes efficiently, for rendering, modeling, and visualization, while still preserving the basic overall shape and important features of the original model.

1.1 Low-pass filtering with shape preservation

A signal processing approach to mesh smoothing was first proposed by Taubin [10] in 1995. Since the rough features over a mesh have an intuitive frequency-domain characterization, mesh smoothing can be reduced to *low-pass filtering* in the mesh spectrum [3, 7, 10, 11, 13], constructed by an eigenvalue decomposition of the mesh with respect to the umbrella operator [8]. Compared with smoothing techniques based on geometric optimization [3, 12], low-pass filtering is known for its simplicity and efficiency.

It is widely believed that an ideal low-pass filter provides an optimal scenario for mesh smoothing [3, 10], where frequencies within a pass-band defined by a tunable cut-off frequency are left unchanged, and all other frequencies are eliminated. For large mesh models however, computing their spectrum and realizing the ideal filter is a formidable task. Therefore in practice, we need to find an approximation using simple functions.

1.1.1 Previous work

Polynomial filters used in Laplacian smoothing [10, 11] attenuate all but the zero frequency. Since the overall shape of a mesh is characterized by the low-frequency contributions, Laplacian smoothing usually leads to shrinkage and visible shape distortion [3, 10, 11]. Taubin [10] remedies this problem using the λ-μ filter, where pass-band frequencies can be retained; but they are also *amplified* slowly as the degree of the λ-μ polynomial increases.

Vollmer et al. [11] tackles the shrinkage problem in the spatial domain. Using their HC algorithm, each vertex is moved back towards a weighted average of its original position and its previous position, after each step of Laplacian smoothing. A common drawback of the HC algorithm and λ-μ filtering is their slow smoothing speed for large mesh models.

Rational filters of the form $1/p(x)$, where $p(x)$ is a polynomial, offer an alternative approach to mesh smoothing [3, 13]. It has been shown that a Butterworth filter of relatively low degree, i.e., $4 \leq deg[p(x)] \leq 8$, already provides a very good approximation of the ideal low-pass filter [1], enabling us to produce highly smooth models, while still preserving the basic shape and features of the original mesh.

But the implementation of higher-order Butterworth filters, with $deg[p(x)] \geq 2$, requires the solution of a series of complex sparse linear systems, and the associated computational cost may still be undesirable. Geometric smoothing algorithms based on explicit minimization of surface energy [3, 5, 12] are often much more expensive. To achieve interactivity, we still need more efficient algorithms.

1.1.2 Our approach and contribution

In this paper, we propose the simple idea of *shape restoration*. It partially recovers the low-frequency contribution attenuated away by Laplacian smoothing. We demonstrate that the mesh models produced are both smooth and shape-preserving. Our method is trivial to implement and it is very efficient, especially for large models, for which existing methods [10, 11, 13] are often not fast enough. We also show that a scaling in the restoration operation can *enhance* the low-frequency characteristics of a mesh, creating some interesting effects at no extra costs.

1.2 Feature-preserving mesh smoothing

Important shape features such as ridges and corners often exist in mesh models tempered with random noise [1]. Low-pass filtering inevitably "blurs out" these sharp features, since they are constituted by *correlated* high-frequency contents. As a result, an ideal low-pass filter is only optimal in preserving the overall shape of a mesh, and the preservation of ridges and corners has to be achieved through a different approach.

1.2.1 Previous work

In the field of image processing, many techniques for edge segmentation and edge crispening have been developed [9]. These provide the bases for their 3-D counterparts [1, 4, 8]. Anisotropic curvature diffusion has been applied to height fields [4] and to general 3-D meshes [1]. In both cases, edges are detected *explicitly* and locally at each time step, using either an edge contrast parameter [4] or a principle curvature threshold [1]. In order to separate noise from true features of a model, low-pass prefiltering is often necessary [1]. For meshes with semi-regular connectivity, a combination of Gaussian scale mixture (GSM) and Wiener filtering is shown to be effective [8].

1.2.2 Our approach and contribution

In this paper, we take a different approach to feature-preserving mesh smoothing of arbitrary meshes. Our initial goal was to develop a smoothing algorithm based on the minimization of global bending energy. We would also like to work with the intrinsic geometry of a mesh for it is well known that parameterization-dependent smoothing algorithms often create various artifacts, e.g., tangential shift of vertices using the umbrella operator [3].

The smoothness measure we use is *integral mean curvature*, or *IMC*, a discrete measure of bending energy over a mesh with curvatures discretized at the edges. We develop a smoothing algorithm that approximates IMC by a sum of squared vertex-to-plane distances. Let us call it the MIN-DIST algorithm.

The MIN-DIST algorithm induces a *vertex flow* that performs rapid smoothing over homogeneous regions, and slow smoothing near ridges and corners. It differs from previous approaches in that there is no explicit edge detection. We can also modify the MIN-DIST algorithm to perform a *feature-enhancing flow*, so that gradual variations over a mesh surface can be concentrated. This would be difficult to achieve using local edge detection [1, 4].

Bending energy minimization has been used by others for mesh smoothing. For instance, Kobbelt et al. [7] adopt an isoperimetric parameterization and minimize the thin-plate energy discretized at the mesh vertices, while Guskov et al. [5] choose to minimize divided differences defined at the mesh edges.

Due to its assumption on isoperimetric parameterizations, thin-plate smoothing may produce very different results after processing the *same* mesh object with different sampling and connectivity. Our MIN-DIST algorithm, on the other hand, does not rely on any parameterization, and it does a better job in feature preservation than thin-plate smoothing. In Figure 1, we show the result of MIN-DIST flow and compare it with the thin-plate algorithm. The divided difference approach of Guskov et al. [5] is similar to ours and should produce similar results, but the minimization of divided differences is more expensive computationally than our method.

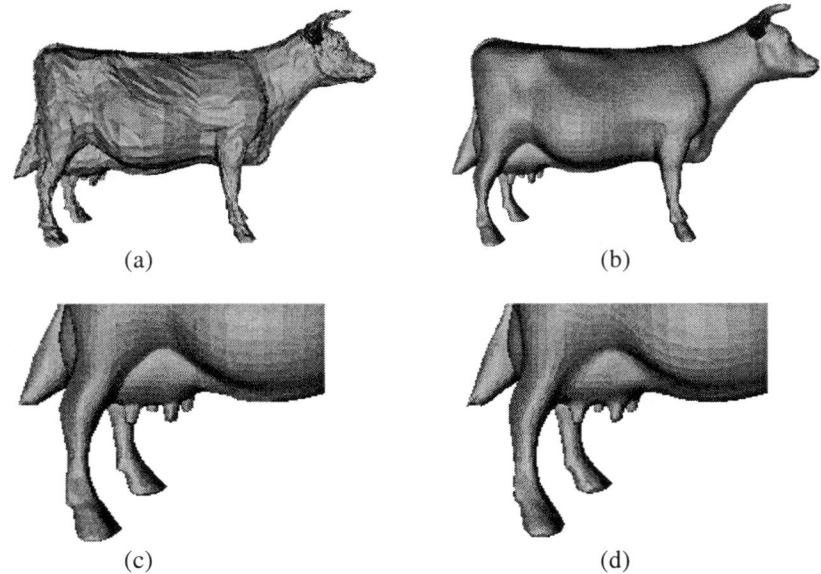

(a) (b) (c) (d)

Figure 1: (a) Original cow model tempered with artificial noise. (b) After 20 iterations of the MIN-DIST algorithm. (c) A close-up of (b) to shown feature preservation. (d) After 20 iterations of Kobbelt's thin-plate smoothing [7].

1.3 Organization of the paper

In the next section, we describe our shape restoration technique and compare it with existing methods [10, 11, 13] designed with a similar goal. The MIN-DIST and feature-enhancing flows are presented in Section 3, where we also explain why they work the way they do. Finally, we conclude in Section 4.

2. Mesh smoothing with shape restoration

In the signal processing framework, mesh smoothing or denoising is equivalent to low-pass filtering. Laplacian smoothing uses the filter $f_1(\sigma) = (1 - \lambda\sigma)^N$, where σ is the frequency and $0 < \lambda < 1$ is a time step parameter. Taubin's λ-μ filter is of the form $f_2(\sigma) = [(1 - \lambda\sigma)(1 - \mu\sigma)]^{N/2}$, where N is even, $0 < \lambda < -\mu < 1$, and the cut-off frequency $\underline{\sigma}$ satisfies $\underline{\sigma} = 1/\lambda + 1/\mu$. In Figures 2(a) and 2(b), we plot the two filters for the same degree N. Computationally, filtering with $f_1(\sigma)$ and $f_2(\sigma)$ corresponds to multiplying a sparse matrix to the mesh vertex vector N times.

Figure 2: (a) Laplacian smoothing filter with $N = 40$. (b) Taubin's λ-μ

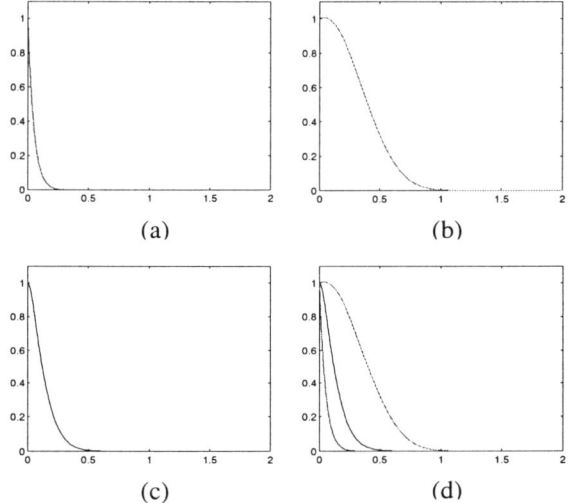

filter with $N = 40$. (c) Our p-q filter with $p = q = 20$. (d) Together.

2.1 Shape restoration with p-q filtering

To design an efficient filter that preserves shapes better than Laplacian smoothing, we complement Laplacian smoothing with *one-step shape restoration*. The resulting filter is $f_3(\sigma) = (1 - \lambda\sigma)^p + (1 - \lambda\sigma)^q - (1 - \lambda\sigma)^{p+q}$. For convenience and lack of a better term, let us refer to $f_3(\sigma)$ as the *p-q filter*. Observe that p-q filtering improves upon Laplacian smoothing in that it attempts to restore the overall shape of the mesh. It does so by partially recovering the loss of low-frequency contributions, given by $(1 - \lambda\sigma)^q - (1 - \lambda\sigma)^{p+q}$.

Since $f_3(0) = 1$, the p-q filter preserves the average position, or DC level in signal processing terms, of the mesh. As $p, q \to \infty$, $f_3(\sigma) \to 0$ if $\sigma > 0$, and the closer σ is to 2, the highest possible frequency, the faster $f_3(\sigma)$ converges to 0. As shown in Figure 2(c), the p-q filter is indeed low-pass. If q is sufficiently large, for which most of the high-frequency contents have already been attenuated away, our shape restoration does not affect the general smoothness of the mesh.

In Figure 2(d), we compare the three filters presented so far, where the same number of matrix-vector multiplications is required. This already provides a pretty good illustration of the advantage of p-q filtering, but let us demonstrate this further using our experimental results.

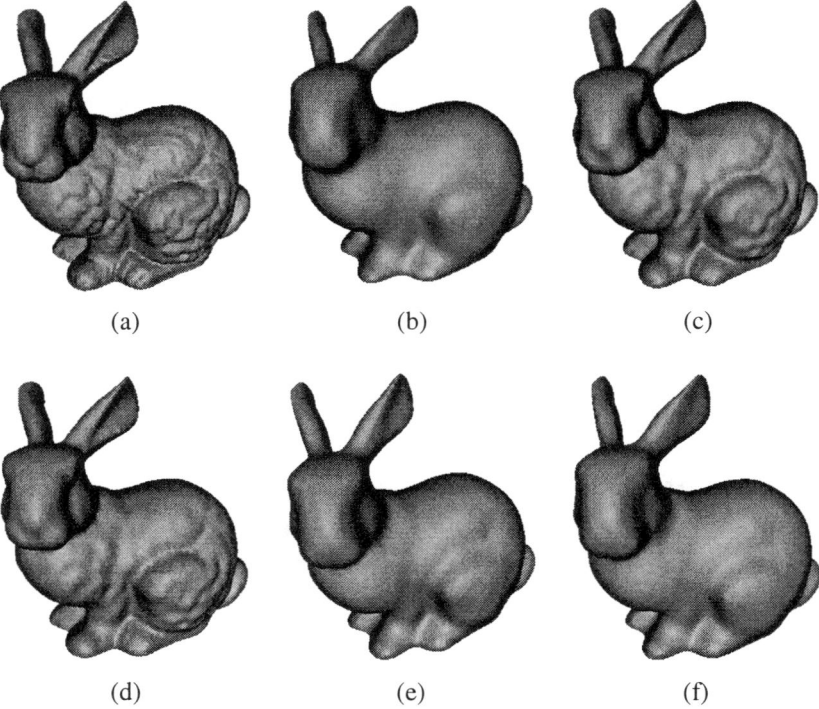

Figure 3: (a) Original bunny with about 70,000 triangles. (b) After 30 iterations of Laplacian smoothing. (c) After 60 iterations of Taubin's λ-μ filtering. (d) After 30 iterations of the HC algorithm. (e) After p-q filtering with $p = q = 30$. (f) After fourth-order Butterworth filtering.

2.2 Implementation of p-q filtering

In terms of mesh transformation, p-q filtering gives us $x' = (S^p + S^q - S^{p+q})x$, where x and x' denote the original and the transformed mesh, respectively; the matrix $S = I - \lambda L$ is the mesh smoothing operator, where I is the identity matrix and L is the umbrella operator [8], a sparse matrix with about seven non-zero entries per row. Note that the implementation of the mesh transformation requires only $p + q$ matrix-vector multiplications. To obtain x', we simply compute $S^{p+q}x$, and store $S^p x$ and $S^q x$ along the way. The cost of three extra vector additions is negligible.

2.3 Experimental results

In Figure 3, we show the original bunny model and meshes produced by a number of smoothing algorithms. For λ-μ filtering [10], HC algorithm [11], and p-q filtering, the same number of matrix-vector multiplications are performed, where we note that one iteration of the HC algorithm corresponds to about two iterations of p-q filtering. For Laplacian smoothing, we use half as many multiplications to achieve about the same level of smoothness as the result of p-q filtering. Additional steps of Laplacian smoothing will distort the shape further.

We set the time step $\lambda = 0.75$, where applicable. For the λ-μ filter and the fourth-order (rational) Butterworth filter [13], we choose a cut-off frequency of $\underline{\sigma} = 0.02$. Since λ-μ filtering creates frequency amplification within the pass-band, if $\underline{\sigma}$ is not chosen properly, ripples start to appear over the mesh surface; this intensifies as more iterations are applied. Our current choice of $\underline{\sigma}$ ensures that we have progressive smoothing using λ-μ filtering.

The parameters for the HC algorithm control the extent to which a vertex is to move towards its original and previous position after each step of Laplacian smoothing. These parameters are not easy to choose. In our experiments, we use trial and error to select a combination which gives us the highest level of smoothness.

The advantage of our shape restoration technique using p-q filtering is quite obvious. We have sufficient smoothing and better shape preservation than Laplacian smoothing; this is most visible around the ears, the face, and the legs of the bunny. For Taubin's λ-μ filter and the HC algorithm to achieve the same level of smoothness, several hundred iterations are required. So our approach is much more efficient. In terms of mesh quality, only the fourth-order Butterworth filter would appear to be the best, but it takes about four times as much time to execute. On the other hand, the smoothness quality of the meshes produced by p-q filtering and higher-order Butterworth filtering is quite close.

In Table 1, we provide some quantitative measures to support our visual findings. The running times are given in seconds. We report the change of IMC, as a percentage of the IMC of the original model. For a measure of shape distortion, we compute the sum of squared distances between vertices of the original model and the corresponding vertices of the transformed model. The change of volume, as a percentage of the original volume, is also given.

Table 1: Results from smoothing the bunny model.

Algorithm	Vol%	IMC%	Distortion	Time
LAP smoothing	−2.19%	−86.44%	38.69	4.91s
λ-μ filtering	+0.34%	−67.33%	9.72	10.34s
HC algorithm	+0.29%	−67.50%	9.60	11.19s
p-q filtering	+0.39%	−84.18%	22.58	9.02s
Butterworth	+0.75%	−84.73%	28.31	35.58s

2.4 Scaling and low-frequency enhancement

Let us note that the p-q filter still attenuates all but the zero frequency, since it is not possible to recover all the loss in low-frequency contributions. As a result, shrinkage may still occur. We can include a scaling parameter s in the p-q filter to prevent shrinkage completely. The modified filter is of the form

$$f_4(\sigma) = (1-\lambda\sigma)^p + s[(1-\lambda\sigma)^q - (1-\lambda\sigma)^{p+q}].$$

For $s > 1$, the recovered low-frequency contribution is amplified, so is the pass-band frequency in the final mesh. This is similar to what the λ-μ filter of Taubin [10] does, but the computational cost involved is considerably less. As shown by the plot in Figure 4, 60 iterations of p-q filtering result in more frequency amplification, when desired, than that of 400 iterations of λ-μ filtering.

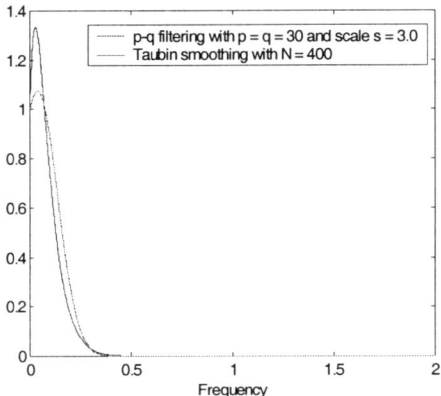

Figure 4: Pass-band frequency amplification by the p-q filter and the λ-μ filtering, with the same cut-off frequency.

We often do not find scaling to be necessary for the smoothing of large mesh models. But it gives us a trivial way of enhancing the low-frequency features of a model, creating some interesting effects. In Figure 5, we show that enhancements of this type can exaggerate certain features of a mesh, such as the size of the ears of the bunny and the "bulkiness" of the horse model. Such *global* effects would be hard to obtain through local editing or a uniform scaling in the spatial domain [3].

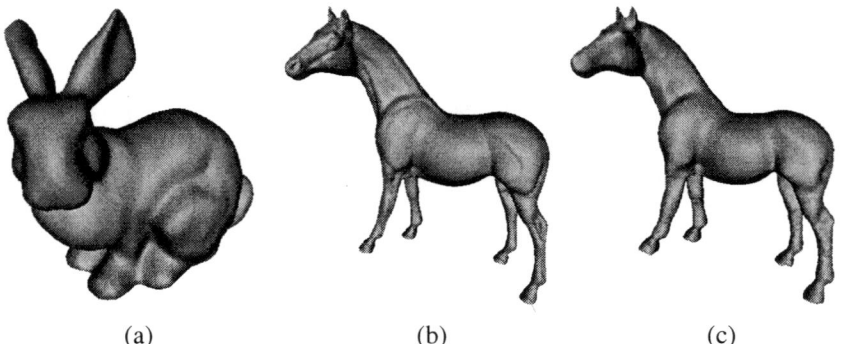

(a) (b) (c)

Figure 5: Low-frequency enhancements. (a) Enhanced bunny model. (b) Original horse model. (c) Enhanced horse model.

3. MIN-DIST and feature-enhancing flows

3.1 Some notations

Let us work exclusively with meshes composed of triangles. We use $V(M)$ and $E(M)$ to label the set of vertices and edges of a mesh M, respectively. Vertices are labeled as i, j, k, etc., and their 3-D positions are denoted by x_i, x_j, x_k. An edge joining vertices i and j is represented by $e_{ij} = (i, j)$. A face with vertices i, j, and k, in counterclockwise order, is denoted by Δ_{ijk}.

The *one-ring neighbor* $N_1(i)$ of a vertex i is defined to be the set of mesh vertices immediately adjacent to i, that is, $N_1(i) = \{j \in V(M) \mid e_{ij} \in E(M)\}$. Finally, we denote the interior dihedral angle between two faces adjacent to an edge e_{ij} by ϕ_{ij}.

3.2 Integral mean curvature

From differential geometry, the most natural energy functional used for surface smoothing is the total curvature,

$$E_T(S) = \int_S (k_1^2 + k_2^2) dS$$

where k_1 and k_2 denote the principal curvatures at a point on the surface S. The mean curvature at a point is defined to be $\rho = (k_1 + k_2)/2$. By the Gauss-Bonnet Theorem, if the topology of the surface does not change, then minimizing the total curvature $E_T(S)$ is equivalent to minimizing the total squared mean curvature,

$$\overline{E}(S) = \int_S (k_1 + k_2)^2 dS .$$

Since k_1 and k_2 depend non-linearly on the mesh geometry, we have to find an approximation that is easy to compute. In this paper, we measure mean curvature using dihedral angles, and approximate them using vertex-to-plane distances.

Consider an edge e_{ij}. The principal curvatures at any point along e_{ij} are zero and $\pi - \phi_{ij}$, where we recall that ϕ_{ij} is the dihedral angle at e_{ij}. The mean curvature at e_{ij} is then $\rho(e_{ij}) = (\pi - \phi_{ij})^2 / 4$. If e_{ij} is a boundary edge, then $\rho(e_{ij}) = 0$. The *integral mean curvature*, or *IMC*, of a mesh M is defined as

$$H(M) = \sum_{e_{ij} \in E(M)} \rho(e_{ij}) \cdot |e_{ij}| = \frac{1}{4} \sum_{e_{ij} \in E(M)} (\pi - \phi_{ij})^2 \cdot |e_{ij}|.$$

Note that the inclusion of edge lengths in IMC is crucial. In the same spirit, the divided difference defined by Guskov et al. [5] relates the bending energy at an edge to the area of its adjacent triangles.

3.3 The MIN-DIST flow

The main difficulty in minimizing $H(M)$ is that dihedral angles also depend non-linearly on mesh geometry. So we approximate $H(M)$ by a sum of squared distance measures. Minimizing these distances is a linear problem.

3.3.1 The distance measure

In a local optimization setting, we wish to move a mesh vertex i to reduce the total mean curvature at all the edges involved. The movement of i affects the mean curvature at edges adjacent to i, and at edges opposite to i. We approximate the total curvature by a squared distance measure to a set of mesh faces.

Let us call a plane determined by three consecutive vertices in vertex i's one-ring a one-ring plane, as shown in Figure 6 in light gray, and a plane determined by an edge in i's one-ring and the vertex opposite to i with respect to that edge a wing plane, as shown in Figure 6 in darker gray. Note that Guskov et al. [5] call the wing planes the flaps of the one-ring.

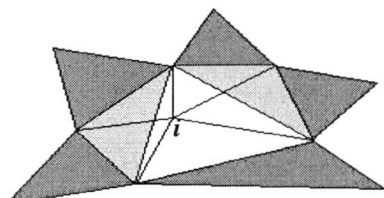

Figure 6: One-ring planes and wing planes.

If we were to move i close to the one-ring plane Δ_{jkm}, while keeping the length of e_{ik} about fixed, then the mean curvature at e_{ik} is reduced, as shown on the left side of Figure 7. The same holds for the mean curvature at e_{jk}, if we were to move i close to the wing plane Δ_{jlk} while keeping the length of e_{ij} and e_{ik} about fixed, as shown on the right side of Figure 7.

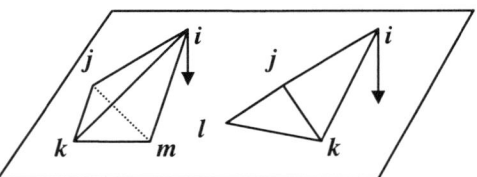

Figure 7: Moving vertex i to decrease total curvature.

Let us denote the set of wing planes and the set of one-ring planes around a mesh vertex i by $W(i)$ and $R(i)$, respectively. We define the measure $Q(x_i)$ as a weighted sum of squared distances from vertex i to the wing planes, the one-ring planes, and the centroid $g(i)$ of i's one-ring neighbors. That is,

$$Q(x_i) = \beta \cdot D(x_i, g(i))^2 + (1-\beta)(D_{wing} + D_{ring}), \quad (1)$$

where $D(x_i, g(i))$ is the distance from i to the centroid $g(i)$, β is a user-defined parameter in [0,1], D_{wing} is a weighted sum of squared distances from i to the set of wing planes, and D_{ring} is a weighted sum of squared distances from i to the set of one-ring planes. Specifically, we have

$$D_{wing} = \frac{\sum_{\Delta_{jlk} \in W(i), j,k \in N_1(i)} |e_{jk}| \cdot D(x_i, \Delta_{jlk})^2}{\sum_{j,k \in N_1(i), e_{jk} \in E(M)} |e_{jk}| + \sum_{j \in N_1(i)} |e_{ij}|}$$

and

$$D_{ring} = \frac{\sum_{\Delta_{jkm} \in R(i)} |e_{ik}| \cdot D(x_i, \Delta_{jkm})^2}{\sum_{j,k \in N_1(i), e_{jk} \in E(M)} |e_{jk}| + \sum_{j \in N_1(i)} |e_{ij}|}.$$

Note that the distance to the centroid must be included in (1) because otherwise, a vertex may move towards a mesh edge in order to minimize the vertex-to-plane distance involved. This could create ripples over the mesh surface. With $\beta > 0$, we punish such movements.

In practice, we find that the factor β can be made very small for our smoothing tasks. This ensures that the effect of Laplacian smoothing is small enough, and the minimization of total curvature is the dominant force behind the vertex flow. For all of our experiments, $\beta = 0.03$ proves to be a good choice.

3.3.2 The vertex flow

Since $Q(x_i)$ is quadratic in x_i, the minimization problem can be solved by direct differentiation, and is reducible to the solution of a system of three linear equations. If the optimal solution is x_i^* for vertex i, we can apply the following local update rule *simultaneously* for each iteration of the MIN-DIST flow:

$$x'_i = x_i + \lambda(x_i^* - x_i),$$

where λ is a damping factor. Our experiments show that $\lambda = 0.5$ gives the best result, and instability may occur if λ is close to 1.

3.3.3 Feature preservation

We now explain roughly why our MIN-DIST flow tends to preserve the *true* ridges and corners of the original model. Consider any mesh vertex k, and let $T_1, T_2, \ldots T_m$ be the mesh triangles adjacent to k, and F_i a flap of k's one-ring opposite to T_i, where $i = 1, 2, \ldots, m$. In the following analysis, let us consider the $2m$ pairs of triangles $P_i = \{T_i, F_i\}$ and $P_{m+i} = \{T_i, T_{i+1}\}$, where $i = 1, 2, \ldots, m$.

The key observation we make here is that the more pairs of triangles among $P_1, P_2, \ldots, P_{2m}$ are *collinear* or *close to collinear*, the more *unlikely* k is to move under the MIN-DIST flow. In particular, if k has a completely flat neighborhood including the flaps, then each pair P_i of triangles are collinear. On the other hand, if k lies on a ridge or corner with completely flat sides, then all but two or three pairs of triangles

are collinear. Although our arguments are quite informal, it should be intuitively clear that MIN-DIST flow tends to retain the position of a vertex k if
- k is on a flat region, along a ridge, or at a corner, and
- the one-ring neighborhood of k including the flaps is almost flat except at the edges of the ridge or corner.

The above situation is unlikely a result of random noise. Instead, we expect them to reflect the true features of the original model.

3.4 A feature-enhancing flow

The distance measure (1) to be minimized by the MIN-DIST flow has a component D_{ring} for the flatness of the one-rings. This ensures that in homogeneous regions, e.g., flat regions with uniform noise, MIN-DIST flow achieves rapid smoothing. Figure 8(a) illustrates such a situation for a cross section of the mesh. If we discard D_{ring} from the formulation, then only the flaps of a one-ring would dictate the flow of the center vertex. This could amplify the noise, as shown in Figure 8(b).

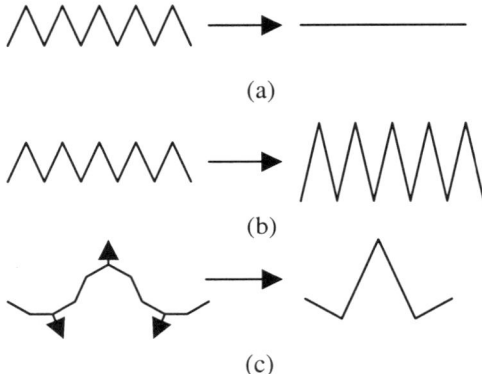

Figure 8: (a) Uniform noise under the MIN-DIST flow. (b) Uniform noise amplified if D_{ring} is ignored. (c) A feature-enhancing flow.

To avoid noise amplification and enhance the features of a mesh at the same time, we can substitute the one-ring planes used in (1) by the *triangles adjacent to the center vertex*. A vertex flow constructed this way should not enhance uniform noise, but it is able to "sharpen" the variations over the mesh surface. This is illustrated in Figure 8(c), where for vertices to be moved by the flow, we indicate the direction of its movement. As we can see, this flow is indeed feature-enhancing.

3.5 Experimental results

In Figure 9 and Figure 1 given earlier, we show how well MIN-DIST flow is able to smooth a mesh and preserve or recover the important features of the mesh. The thin-plate algorithm [7] is about twice as fast as MIN-DIST flow, but it blurs the ridges and corners more. If such feature degradation is tolerable, then we should really use Laplacian smoothing with shape restoration; it produces almost the same result as thin-plate smoothing, but in fraction of the time.

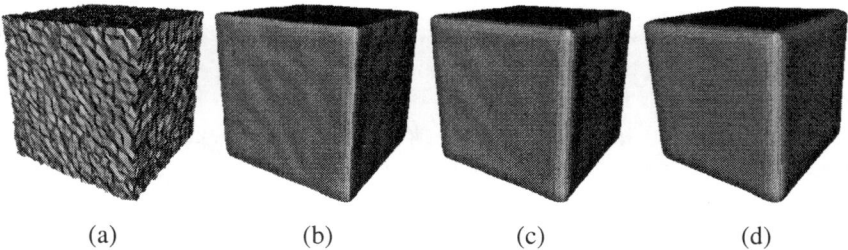

(a)   (b)   (c)   (d)

Figure 9: Smoothing a noisy cube. (a) The original cube. (b) After 50 iterations of MIN-DIST. (c) After 50 iterations of thin-plate smoothing. (d) After p-q filtering with $p = q = 10$.

Figure 10(a) shows the Isis model. As we can see, the facial features of the model are almost unrecognizable. In fact, a local edge detection scheme [1, 4] would unlikely find any features at all. However, if we apply our feature-enhancing flow on the Isis, we do get very encouraging results. This is shown in Figure 10(b). We can observe feature enhancement throughout, and that the smooth regions over the original model are only slightly perturbed. We can now apply our MIN-DIST flow on the enhanced model to remove these small perturbations and still preserve the recovered features.

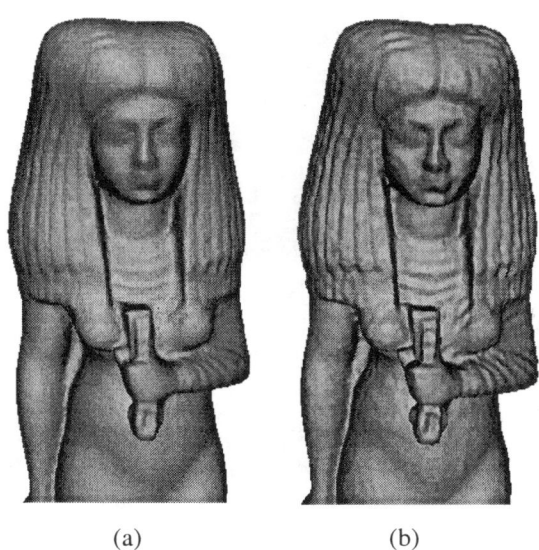

(a)   (b)

Figure 10: Result of feature-enhancing flow. (a) Original model. (b) Enhanced model after 20 iterations.

3.6 Multi-level smoothing

Like any other mesh processing algorithms based on geometric optimization [5, 12], our MIN-DIST and feature-enhancing flow algorithms are rather expensive computationally. To remedy this problem, we can either cast our approach into a multiresolution setting [5], or adopt the *multi-level smoothing* technique suggested by Kobbelt et al. [7]. In both cases, we can take advantage of the feature-preserving property of our vertex flow methods at low resolution.

We run the mesh decimation algorithm of Garland and Heckbert [6] once on the original bunny model to reduce the number of faces from 70,000 down to 5,000. We then apply MIN-DIST flow five times. The resulting mesh is then uniformly subdivided twice using 1-to-4 splitting of the triangles to increase resolution. Note that the newly inserted vertices are simply the midpoints of the mesh edges, and their final locations are computed by Laplacian smoothing with shape restoration. The total time taken by this combined approach is about 20 seconds. The final result is shown in Figure 11. As we can see, we achieve a good combination of speed, smoothness quality, and shape and feature preservation.

Figure 11: Result of multi-level smoothing.

4. Conclusion and future work

While the primary goal of mesh smoothing is to remove the undesirable rough features representing noise, important shape characteristics such as volume, ridges, and corners should also be preserved. Combining Laplacian smoothing and one-step shape restoration, we are able to smooth a mesh and preserve its overall shape efficiently. We also present feature-preserving and feature-enhancing methods based on geometric vertex flow, and show their effectiveness.

As for future work, we would like to investigate the possibly of having a *Gaussian curvature flow* for an arbitrary mesh. Our interest in this is motivated by two observations. On one hand, we note that the Gaussian curvature at a mesh vertex is zero if and only if its one-ring is flat or corresponds to a ridge with flat sides. On the other hand, Heckbert and Garlard [6] have been able to show that the minimization of a quadric at a mesh vertex x, defined as a sum of squared distances from x to a set of nearby faces, is related to the Gaussian curvature at x. We believe that our feature-enhancing flow may well be a good starting point of this investigation.

References

[1] U. Clarenz, U. Diewald, M. Rumpf. "Nonlinear Anisotropic Geometric Diffusion in Surface Processing," *Proc. IEEE Visualization 2000, pages 397-405*, 2000.

[2] B. Curless and M. Levoy, "A Volumetric Method for Building Complex Models from Range Images," *SIGGRAPH 96*, 1996.

[3] M. Desbrun, M. Meyer, P. Schröder, and A. Barr, "Implicit Fairing of Irregular Meshes using Diffusion and Curvature Flow," *SIGGRAPH 99*, pp. 317-324, 1999.

[4] M. Desbrun, M. Meyer, P. Schröder, A. Barr, "Anisotropic Feature-Preserving Denoising of Height Fields and Bivariate Data," In *Proc. Graphics Interface 2000*, 2000.

[5] I. Guskov, W. Sweldens, and P. Schröder, "Multiresolution Signal Processing for Meshes," *SIGGRAPH 99*, pp. 325-334, 1999.

[6] P. S. Heckbert and M. Garland, "Optimal Triangulation and Quadric–Based Surface Simplification," *J. Comput. Geom.: Theory and Applications*, 1999.

[7] L. Kobbelt et al., "Interactive Multi-Resolution Modeling on Arbitrary Meshes," *SIGGRAPH 98*, pp. 105-115, 1998.

[8] J. Peng, V. Strela, and D. Zorin, "A Simple Algorithm for Surface Denoising," In *Proc. IEEE Visualization 2001*.

[9] W. K. Pratt, *Digital Image Processing*, 2nd Ed., Wiley, 1991.

[10] G. Taubin, "A Signal Processing Approach to Fair Surface Design," *SIGGRAPH 95*, pp. 351-358, 1995.

[11] J. Vollmer, R. Mencl, and H. Muller, "Improved Laplacian Smoothing of Noisy Surface Meshes," *Proc. EURO-GRAPHICS 99*, 1999.

[12] W. Welch and A. Witkin, "Free-form Shape Design Using Triangulated Surfaces," *SIGGRAPH 94*, pp. 247-256, 1994.

[13] Hao Zhang and Eugene Fiume, "Efficient Mesh Fairing using Butterworth Filters," submitted, 2001.

Reconstructing Surface Discontinuities by Intersecting Tangent Planes of Advancing Mesh Frontiers

Luping Zhou, Indriyati Atmosukarto,
Wee Kheng Leow, Zhiyong Huang [*]
School of Computing, National University of Singapore
3 Science Drive 2, Singapore 117543, Singapore
zhoulupi, indri, leowwk, huangzy@comp.nus.edu.sg

Abstract

Reconstruction of surface discontinuities from unorganized 3D points is a difficult problem. Both the polygonization and surface fitting approaches to surface reconstruction face the same chicken-and-egg problem: to correctly reconstruct surface discontinuities, the points that lie on the same side of the discontinuities should be used to reconstruct the surfaces to form the discontinuities. However, to know whether the points lie on the same or different sides, the algorithm needs to know the locations and orientations of edge discontinuities, which are not directly available in the unorganized point set.

This paper presents an elegant method of overcoming the above problem. The method reconstructs an object's surface by constructing meshes at flat surfaces and advancing the mesh frontiers towards predicted surface discontinuities. As the frontiers of two or more meshes approach a discontinuity from its different sides, tangent planes at the mesh frontiers are estimated using the points within the frontiers, thus eliminating the problem of accidentally using points on different sides of the discontinuity to estimate a single tangent plane. Then, the tangent planes are intersected to form the discontinuity. Quantitative evaluation shows that this method can estimate the tangent planes very accurately, and can reconstruct surface discontinuities even when 3D points are not sampled at the discontinuities.

Keywords: polygonization, intersecting tangent plane, surface normal re-estimation.

---
[*] This research is supported by NUS ARF R-252-000-051-112

1. Introduction

In 3D model acquisition, an object is scanned and a large set of 3D points on the surface of the object are sampled. The object's surface can be reconstructed from the 3D points using one of two approaches: surface fitting and polygonization. The first approach accomplishes the task by finding a set of parametric surfaces to fit the 3D points as closely as possible [1, 8, 9, 11, 12, 14]. Typically, a single smooth, continuous surface is used to fit a subset of points, and neighboring surfaces are blended to form smooth joints. On the other hand, the second approach connects neighboring 3D points into triangles or polygons to approximate the object's surface [2, 3, 6, 7, 10].

These two approaches are different and each has its own strengths and weaknesses. Interestingly, when it comes to reconstructing surface discontinuities (i.e., edges, corners, etc.) from a set of unorganized points, both approaches face the same chicken-and-egg problem, which has not been solved in an elegant and efficient manner. For the first approach, 3D points lying on different sides of a discontinuity such as an edge should be fitted with different surfaces so that the discontinuity can be formed from the intersection of the surfaces. This approach thus requires knowledge about the location and orientation of the edge, which are not available in a set of unorganized points until the edge is reconstructed.

For the second approach, the frontier advancing algorithm that we proposed in [3] can be used to reconstruct a discontinuity as a natural consequence of meeting frontiers if 3D points on the discontinuity are sampled. The algorithm can estimate the location of the discontinuity but not the orientation of an edge. On the other hand, if the discontinuity is not sampled, the natural solution would be to estimate the tangent planes at the points near the discontinuity and to form the discontinuity by intersecting the tangent planes. The tangent plane can be estimated by computing its normal vector using the sample points. Now, we face the same problem: only the points lying on the same side of a discontinuity should be used to estimate a tangent plane, and this again requires knowledge about the location and orientation of edge discontinuity.

It turns out that this problem can be solved by performing tangent plane estimation and frontier advancing polygonization *at the same time*. Our frontier advancing polygonization algorithm has already been described in [3], with test results for general, irregularly shaped objects. A brief summary of the algorithm will be provided in Section 3. Complementing our earlier work, this article presents the method of reconstructing surface discontinuities by intersecting the tangent planes of advancing mesh frontiers. In particular, it focuses on the accurate estimation of tangent planes (Section 4), the formation of discontinuities by intersecting tangent plane (Section 5), and quantitative evaluation using synthetic 3D models (Section 6).

2. Related Work

Direct estimation of surface normals from unorganized 3D points is not a simple task. Although surface normals are inferred in some surface reconstruction algorithms, they are obtained mostly as by-products of the algorithms which depend on special reconstruction processes. For example, in Amenta's crust algorithm [2], surface normals are inferred from the Voronoi diagram built in previous stages of the algorithm. Nevertheless, there are several algorithms which directly estimate surface normals. These methods are discussed in this section.

Hoppe et al. [7] applied Principal Component Analysis on a small cluster of points to estimate the normal at the center of the cluster. It proves to be a robust method for points on smooth surfaces, but is not accurate at surface discontinuities because a cluster may contain points lying on different sides of a discontinuity (see Section 1 for details).

Hoppe et al. also made use of tangent planes in surface recovery. However, the tangent planes were used to define a signed distance for the sample points. A marching cube algorithm was then applied to compute the isosurface that formed the final polygonization result. On the other hand, we use the intersection of tangent planes to form surface discontinuities.

The method of Mediori [13] uses *Tensor Voting* to estimate surface normals. It is grounded on tensor calculus for data representation and tensor voting for data communication. The inputs of this method can be 3D points, 3D curve segments, or 3D surface patches. The possible surface normals at these input sites are represented as tensors. The actual normals at an input site is estimated according to a weighted sum of the tensors and the distance to its neighbor determines the weight of the contribution of the neighbor. Because the information about surface discontinuities is not available in the tensors, this method cannot accurately estimate surface normals at discontinuities.

Another general approach to estimating surface normals is to fit planar or quadratic surfaces to sample points [1, 8, 9, 11, 12, 14]. However, these methods suffer from the chicken-and-egg problem discussed in Section 1.

The method of Benko et al. [4, 5] is particularly interesting. First, it triangulates a point cloud to determine the neighborhood and connectivity of the sample points. Then, it segments the sample points into disjoint subsets such that the points in each subset can be fitted by one or more second order analytic surfaces. The surface normal at each sample point is then given by the normal of the fitted surface at the point. In addition, a least-square plane is fitted to each point and its neighbors. Points with large fitting errors are considered as lying on highly curved surfaces or at surface discontinuities. The triangles at these regions are removed. Next, an adjacency graph is constructed from the remaining fitted regions, which is used to determine the edges of the smooth faces (which consists of adjacent smooth regions). The edges are then constructed by intersections between the surfaces that represent the smooth faces.

This method consists of many stages, some of which are very complex. First, the region segmentation process involves complicated hypothesis testing. Second, at least three surface fitting processes are involved: one each for estimating surface normals, identifying surface discontinuities, and reconstructing complex smooth surfaces that cannot be fitted by a single second order surface. Moreover, the method requires an initial triangulation of point cloud which, as discussed in Section 1, may produce incorrect neighborhood and connectivity relationships between the points near surface discontinuities. The error incurred is expected to propagate to subsequent stages of the method, degrading the overall performance of the method.

In comparison, our method is simpler and more elegant. Moreover, as will be seen in Section 3, it can also accurately estimate surface normals at and near surface discontinuities.

3. Overview of Algorithms

The tangent plane intersection algorithm is built upon our frontier advancing polygonization algorithm described in [3]. Hence, it is useful to first provide a summary of the frontier advancing algorithm.

3.1 Summary of Frontier Advancing Polygonization Algorithm

The frontier advancing algorithm consists of the following stages:

1. Identifying reliable points

2a. Constructing a closed mesh around a point

2b. Merging meshes and advancing mesh frontiers

In stage 1, Principal Component Analysis (PCA) is used to estimate surface normals in a manner similar to [7]. Given a set of 3D points, PCA computes three eigenvectors e_i and eigenvalues λ_i, $i = 1, 2, 3$ in decreasing eigenvalue. If the set of points lie on a surface without discontinuity, the third eigenvector e_i would be parallel to the normal of the surface that best fit the points. However, when a surface discontinuity exists, points lying on different sides of the discontinuity may be used in the estimation. Consequently, the estimated normal would be an average of the normals of the different surfaces (Fig. 1).

If the set of points lie on a flat surface, the third eigenvalue λ_3 would be very small. These points are called *reliable points* because we are certain of the types of the surfaces at the points. For a set of points distributed near a surface discontinuity or a smooth curve surface with large curvature, λ_3 would be large compared to λ_1 and λ_2. Therefore, λ_3 can be used to distinguish between points lying on flat surfaces from other points. However, it cannot differentiate between points lying near discontinuities and those on smooth surfaces with large curvature. So, these points are called *ambiguous points*.

Stage 2a and 2b proceed simultaneously. After identifying reliable points, an initial mesh is first constructed around a randomly chosen reliable point based on the properties of Delaunay triangulation. It advances the mesh frontiers by adding neighboring reliable points until ambiguous points are encountered. This step is repeated for all reliable points.

After all the reliable points have been added to the mesh, there will be one or more disconnected meshes which are separated by ambiguous points. At this stage, the algorithm further extends the frontiers by completing the meshes around ambiguous points in increasing order of ambiguity. The mesh frontiers would finally meet at the most ambiguous points to form surface discontinuities. If 3D points along the edges and at the corners are sampled, then the algorithm will form an edge where two advancing frontiers meet and a corner where three or more frontiers meet. Otherwise, the algorithm will construct approximations of the edges and corners.

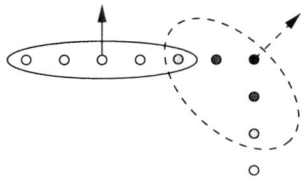

Figure 1. Third eigenvector (dashed arrow) of the points at the corner is not a correct estimate of the surface normals at the points. Darker points represent more ambiguous 3D points.

3.2 Overview of Tangent Plane Intersection Algorithm

As described in Section 3.1, the surface normals estimated by PCA may not be accurate for ambiguous points. To improve the estimation accuracy, surface normals at ambiguous points should be re-estimated and the re-estimation process should use only the points that lie on the same side of a discontinuity.

The basic idea of the tangent plane intersection algorithm is as follows. The first two stages (1 and 2a) of the algorithm are similar to those of the frontier advancing algorithm. The difference lies in how the two algorithms identify mesh edges. The frontier advancing algorithm uses a geometric approach to identify Delaunay edges whereas the tangent plane intersection algorithm uses the intersection of tangent planes. For sample points that lie on nearly flat surfaces, the tangent plane intersection algorithm reduces to the frontier advancing algorithm. Hence, tangent plane intersection is performed only for ambiguous points that are predicted to lie near surface discontinuities.

Before Stage 2b of the tangent plane intersection algorithm is executed, surface normals at ambiguous points must be re-estimated to obtain more accurate estimations. The re-estimation process first identifies sample points that are predicted to fall on the same side of a discontinuity as an ambiguous point near the mesh frontier (Section 4). The normals at these sample points are then used to estimate the normal at the ambiguous point. Once the normals of the ambiguous points near the mesh frontiers are re-estimated, tangent planes at the points are intersected to derive new mesh edges that are added to the mesh frontier (Section 5). Thus, the normals at the points in the mesh are reliable. In this way, normal re-estimation and frontier advancement alternate until all sample points are included in the mesh. With this concept in mind, we can now look at the normal re-estimation process in detail.

4. Surface Normal Re-estimation

Re-estimation of surface normals at ambiguous points proceed together with frontier advancement in increasing order of ambiguity. An ambiguous point next in queue at which the surface normal is to be re-estimated always lie just beyond a mesh frontier with no other intervening free points, which are the points not in the mesh. The surface normal re-estimation process consists of two steps:

1. Finding consistent neighbors
   Consistent neighbors refer to the points that are predicted to lie on the same side of a discontinuity.

2. Recomputing surface normals
   Normal re-estimation is performed only on consistent neighbors.

4.1 Determining Consistent Neighbors

Two methods of determining consistent neighbors have been investigated: point-based method and mesh-based method. The point-based method uses normals at the sample points whereas the mesh-based method uses the normals at the points that are inside the advancing mesh.

4.1.1 Point-based method

Conceptually, a point at a discontinuity has a locally maximum ambiguity. Therefore, a direct method of finding the consistent neighbors is to look for local maxima of ambiguity and collect consistent neighbors accordingly. However, this approach is computationally expensive.

An alternative method which is computationally more efficient is to first collect all the neighbors of a sample point p and then remove those points that are predicted to lie on different sides of a discontinuity as p. Because a discontinuity is a meeting of two or more surfaces, the difference in surface normal would be relatively large between points on different sides of the discontinuity. This could be used to predict whether two neighboring points are lying on the same surface.

Figure 2 illustrates this concept. Suppose that the neighbors p_1, p_2, and p_3 of an ambiguous point q are also ambiguous. Point p_1 has a similar normal as q, that is $||\mathbf{n} \cdot \mathbf{n}_1|| < \Gamma_n$, a fixed threshold, while points p_2 and p_3 have very different normals: $||\mathbf{n_2} \cdot \mathbf{n_3}|| \geq \Gamma_n$. We can draw a plane at p_2 orthogonal to the direction from q to p_2 and exclude all the points on the opposite side of the plane (Fig. 2, shaded area). Even if there is no discontinuity between p and p_2, it is still reasonable to exclude the points on the opposite side of the plane because their normals are very different from that of q. This method is repeated for each neighbor p_i whose normal $\mathbf{n}_i$ differs significantly from the normal $\mathbf{n}$ of q. The remaining neighbors are the consistent neighbors.

This method turns out to be not very accurate. As discussed in section 3.1, the initial PCA estimate at a discontinuity may include points on different sides of the discontinuity (Fig. 1). As a result, the initial estimates of the normals at ambiguous points may not be accurate. Without differentiating between accurate and inaccurate estimates, this method is therefore not expected to work well.

4.1.2 Mesh-based method

The mesh-based method is performed as follows. Given an ambiguous point q at which the normal is to be re-estimated, the mesh-based method first determines the

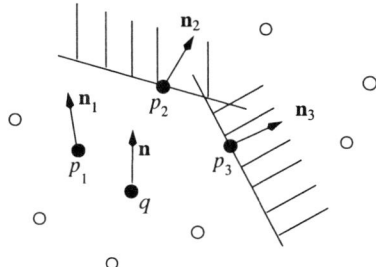

Figure 2. Using constraint planes to find consistent neighbors. Sample points on the shaded side are excluded because their normals are very different from the normal n of the sample point q. Dark points are ambiguous points while light points are reliable points.

neighboring points of q that are already in some meshes. Since normal re-estimation is performed together with frontier advancement, sample points that are already in the meshes always have accurately estimated normals. These neighboring points are grouped into clusters based on the similarity of their normals.

Next, for each cluster i, the point p_i nearest to the ambiguous point q are determined. Point p_i should be located near the frontier (Fig. 3). A pairwise intersection of the tangent planes at points p_i and p_j is performed. The resulting intersection line should be located near a discontinuity if one exists. Based on the resulting pairwise intersection lines, we determine on which sides of the intersection lines does q lie and collect the corresponding cluster of points (Fig. 3). The resulting cluster of points would be the consistent neighbors of q. If there is only one cluster after the grouping prorcess, then the points in this cluster are regarded as the consistent neighbors of q.

Instead of performing all $m(m-1)/2$ pairwise intersections of the tangent planes of m clusters, the consistent neighbors can also be determined by a more efficient $O(m)$ algorithm:

> Choose an initial cluster M_1 and set p_1 as point w.
> Repeat for each nearest neighbor p_i, $i = 2, \ldots, m$,
>   Intersect the tangent planes at w and p_i
>   to produce an intersection line L.
>   If q is on the same side of L as p_i then,
> $w = p_i$.

At the end of the algorithm, the mesh points in the cluster that contains point w are the consistent neighbors.

Consider Fig. 3 for example. Suppose p_1 is considered first, and the algorithm intersects the tangent planes at points p_1 and p_2 to produce an intersection line L_{12}. Since

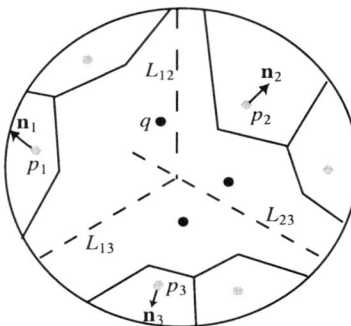

Figure 3. The mesh-based method for collecting consistent neighbors. There are three groups of mesh points in the neighborhood of the ambiguous point q. The consistent neighbors are those on the same side of the predicted discontinuity L_1 and L_2 as point q.

q lies on the same side as p_1, w is set as p_1. The algorithm continues by intersecting the tangent planes at points p_1 and p_3 and produces the intersection line L_{13}. Since q lies on the same side as p_1, w is set as p_1 and the mesh points in p_1's cluster are the consistent neighbors of q.

Now consider another possibility. Suppose p_2 is considered first, and the tangent planes at p_2 and p_3 are intersected to produce the intersection line L_{23}. Since q lies on the same side as p_2, w is set as p_2. Next, the tangent planes at p_1 and p_2 are intersected to produce the intersection line L_{12}. Because p_1 lies on the same side as q, w is set as p_1 and the mesh points in the cluster that contains p_1 are still considered the consistent neighbors. Therefore, the algorithm correctly identifies consistent neighbors regardless of the order in which the points p_i are considered.

4.2 Estimating Normal from Consistent Neighbors

A straightforward method to estimate the normal is to apply PCA on the consistent neighbors. This method is not accurate because PCA's estimate is correct for the normal at the centroid of the neighborhood but the ambiguous point tends to fall at the fringe of the neighborhood (Fig. 3). Therefore, a more accurate method is to perform linear extrapolation.

The linear extrapolation method uses both the positions and the normals of the consistent neighbors to infer the normals at the ambiguous point. To perform linear extrapolation correctly, the normals of the consistent neighbors must be pointing at similar directions, i.e, $\mathbf{n}_i \cdot \mathbf{n}_j \geq 0$ for consistent neighbors i, j. Since the normals are initially estimated using PCA (Stage 1) and PCA does not guarantee a consistent orientation of the estimated normals, a local alignment of normals similar to the approach of Hoppe et al. [7] is applied.

After aligning the normals, linear extrapolation is applied. Since the points p_i and ambiguous point q lie on the same side of a predicted discontinuity, the surface containing these points would be a plane or a small patch of a curved surface. Hence, $\mathbf{n}_i$ would be approximately linearly related to p_i:

$$\mathbf{n}_i = \mathbf{A}\mathbf{p}_i + \mathbf{B} \quad \text{for each } i \qquad (1)$$

where $\mathbf{A}$ is a 3×3 matrix and $\mathbf{B}$ is a 3×1 vector. The matrices $\mathbf{A}$ and $\mathbf{B}$ are computed by finding the matrices that minimize the error E

$$E = \sum_{i=1}^{n} \|\mathbf{n}_i - (\mathbf{A}\mathbf{p}_i + \mathbf{B})\|^2. \qquad (2)$$

After obtaining $\mathbf{A}$ and $\mathbf{B}$, the normal $\mathbf{n}$ at q can be computed as $\mathbf{n} = \mathbf{A}\mathbf{q} + \mathbf{B}$.

5. Computing Mesh Polygon

The polygonization process constructs a polygon around a sample point c, and merges the polygon into the existing mesh. The polygon consists of vertices v_i, $i = 1, \ldots, n$, with $v_{n+1} = v_1$. The polygon edges are contained in the intersection lines $L(c, p_i)$ produced by the intersection of the tangent planes at c and at its neigbor p_i. The vertex v_{i+1} is computed as the intersection of line $L(c, p_i)$ and $L(c, p_{i+1})$. In practice, it is easier to compute the vertex v_{i+1} by intersecting 3 planes, the tangent planes at c, p_i, and p_{i+1} instead of two 3-D lines. That is, v_{i+1} is the solution of the following equation:

$$\begin{aligned}
(\mathbf{x} - \mathbf{c}) \cdot \mathbf{n} &= 0 \\
(\mathbf{x} - \mathbf{p}_i) \cdot \mathbf{n}_i &= 0 \\
(\mathbf{x} - \mathbf{p}_{i+1}) \cdot \mathbf{n}_{i+1} &= 0
\end{aligned} \qquad (3)$$

In this polygon construction process, the first point p_1 is the sample point nearest to c. The algorithm determines the next point p_2 by finding a point whose intersection point v_2 is nearer to the line from c to p_1 than are any other possible intersections. All subsequent intersection points v_{i+1} are computed in a similar manner except they are the inersections that are closest to their predecessors v_i along the intersection lines $L(c, p_i)$ (Fig. 4).

The vertices v_i, $i = 1, \ldots, n$, make up the polygon which includes the sample point c within the polygon. Once a polygon is constructed around a point c, it is merged into the existing mesh frontier in the same way as the frontier advancing algorithm in [3].

6. Test Results and Discussions

In order to perform quantitative analysis of the normal estimation methods, synthetic data with known normals were used. These data points were sampled randomly from

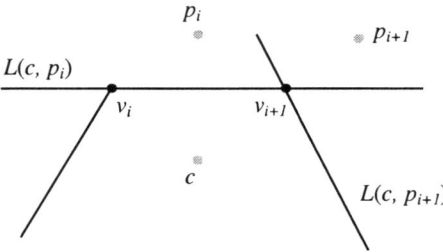

Figure 4. The next polygon vertex v_{i+1} is computed by the intersection between $L(c, p_i)$ and $L(c, p_{i+1})$, and v_{i+1} is nearer than other intersections are to v_i.

Table 1. Numbers of reliable and ambiguous points in each test case.

test case	reliable points	ambiguous points
cube	394	207
cylinder	894	258
hemisphere	690	171

the surfaces of a cube, a cylinder, and a hemisphere (Figs. 5, 6, 7). The 3 test data had different numbers of reliable and ambiguous points (Table 1). To test the reconstruction process, the edges and the corners were not sampled so as to demonstrate that surface discontinuities can be reconstructed using the tangent plane intersection algorithm. On the other hand, to assess the accuracy of normal estimations, points were sampled along discontinuities.

Five test cases were performed for each test data: (1) PCA: apply PCA on 3D sample points; (2) PCA/P: apply PCA on consistent neighbors obtained using the point-based method; (3) LE/P: apply linear extrapolation on consistent neighbors obtained using the point-based method; (4) PCA/M: apply PCA on consistent neighbors obtained using the mesh-based method, and (5) LE/M: apply linear extrapolation on consistent neighbors obtained using the mesh-based method. The mean error measured in terms of the angle between the actual and the estimated normals was computed. For points lying exactly on a surface discontinuity, the normals of the surfaces that form the discontinuity were taken as the possible normal vectors. So, an edge point would have 2 possible normals, and a corner would have more than 2 possible normals. The measured errors at these points were taken as the smallest error between the estimated value and the possible normals.

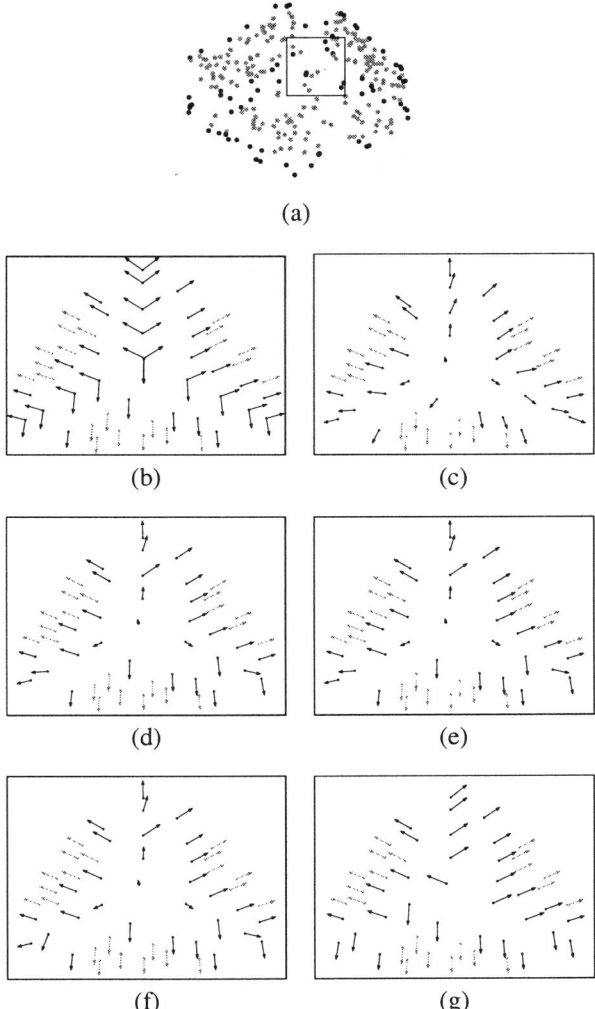

Figure 5. Visual comparison of normal estimation for the cube. Dark color denotes ambiguous points and light color denotes reliable points. (a) Random points sampled on the surface. (b) Actual normals. (c-g) Normal vectors estimated by (c) PCA, (d) PCA/P, (e) LE/P, (f) PCA/M, and (g) LE/M.

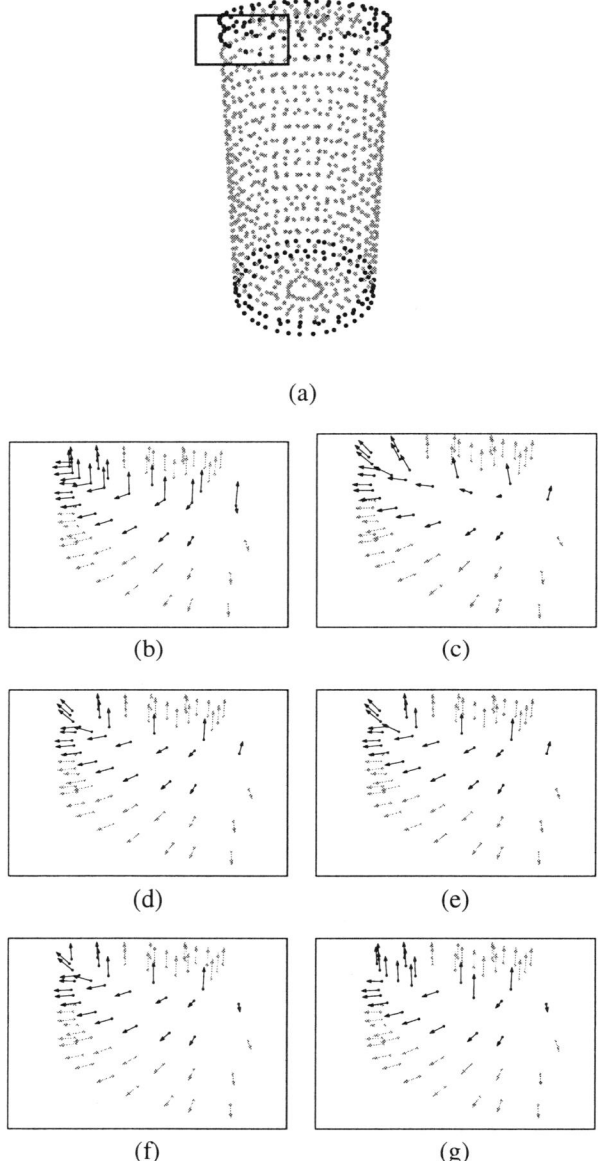

Figure 6. Visual comparison of normal estimation for the cylinder. (a) Random points on the surface. (b) Actual normals. (c-g) Normal vectors estimated by (c) PCA, (d) PCA/P, (e) LE/P, (f) PCA/M, and (g) LE/M.

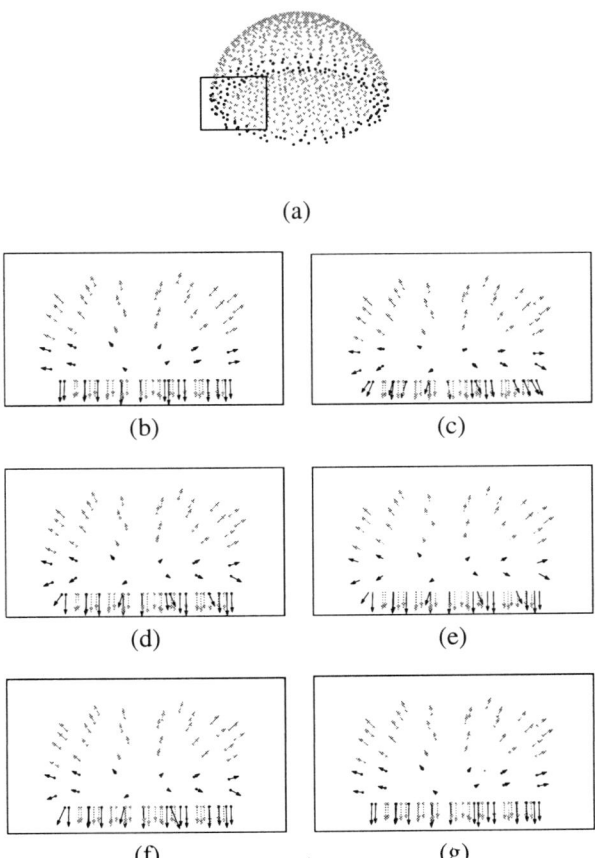

Figure 7. Visual comparison of normal estimation for the hemisphere. (a) Random points sampled on the surface. (b) Actual normals. (c-g) Normal vectors estimated by (c) PCA, (d) PCA/P, (e) LE/P, (f) PCA/M, and (g) LE/M.

Table 2 shows the results produced by five methods of normal estimation. The results show that both PCA/P and LE/P can produce more accurate normal estimation than PCA. LE/P's error estimation for reliable points is slightly larger than that of PCA/P. However, its estimation for ambiguous points is more accurate than that of PCA/P. This is because an ambiguous point tends to fall on one side of its consistent neighbors. As a result, the centroid of the consistent neighbors may not coincide with the position of the ambiguous point. However, PCA always computes the third eigenvector with respect to the centroid. Therefore, the normals at the ambiguous points estimated by PCA are less accurate than those estimated using linear extrapolation.

PCA/M's error estimation is better than both PCA/P and LE/P for reliable and am-

Table 2. Comparison of mean error (angle) of normal estimation. PCA: Principal Components Analysis on 3D sample points, LE: linear extrapolation, P: the point-based method for finding consistent neighbors, M: the mesh-based method for finding consistent neighbors.

methods	cube		cylinder		hemisphere	
	reliable points	ambiguous points	reliable points	ambiguous points	reliable points	ambiguous points
PCA	1.478	24.764	2.983	30.163	2.654	35.428
PCA/P	0.369	9.072	1.430	14.328	1.647	18.466
LE/P	0.369	9.069	1.468	13.621	1.832	16.545
PCA/M	0.115	5.433	0.953	7.877	1.430	10.326
LE/M	0.000	0.018	0.334	2.336	0.598	2.869

biguous points because the mesh-based method is more reliable than the point-based method in determining consistent neighbors. LE/M combines the strengths of both linear extrapolation and mesh-based method of determining consistent neighbors. Therefore, its estimation of surface normals is most accurate. In particular, its estimation of the normals at ambiguous point is roughly one order of magnitude better than those of PCA.

Visual comparisons of selected regions of the 3 test data are shown in Figs. 5, 6, and 7. These figures clearly show that the normals at the ambiguous points (dark arrows) estimated by PCA differ significantly from the actual normals. The normals estimated by PCA/P and linear extrapolation are more accurate than that of PCA and the estimation of mesh-based linear extrapolation is the most accurate. Zoom-in views of the reconstructed surfaces (Figs. 8, 9) show that the tangent plane intersection method can derive the points at the edges and the corners even though they are not sampled.

A comparison of the polygonization produced by the tangent plane intersection method with the frontier advancing Delaunay triangulation method [3] is shown in Figure 9. The curved edges produced by frontier advancing Delaunay triangulation (Fig. 9(c)) is jagged and is not as smooth as those constructed by the tangent plane intersection method (Fig. 9(a, b)). This result clearly demonstrates the strength of the tangent plane intersection algorithm.

Figure 10 shows the experiments conducted on the foot and the mannequin standard data points. The algorithm is able to derive the surface discontinuities on the foot such as the toes and on the face such as the eyes, nose, mouth, and ears.

Our tangent plane intersection method is similar in strategy to that of Benko et al. [4, 5], but is simpler and more elegant:

1. Our method uses linear estimation to determine ambiguous points and estimate surface normals. It is simpler than the second order surface fitting of Benko et al., and yet produces very accurate estimations as shown in the test results (Table 2). On the other hand, complicated region segmentation and hypothesis testing are

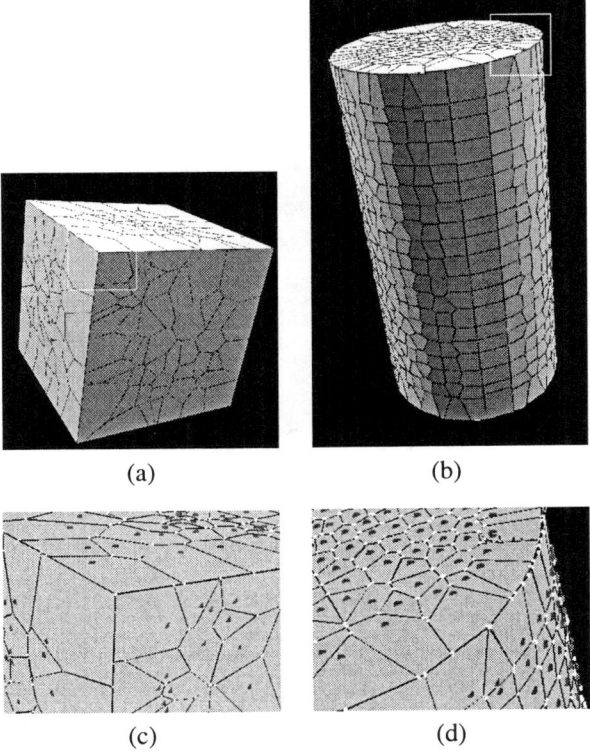

Figure 8. Polygonization of (a) a cube and (b) a cylinder. (c, d) Zoom-in views of surface discontinuities. Tangent plane intersection method could derive the points at surface discontinuities (light points) from the sample points (dark points) even though the discontinuity were not sampled.

required in their method.

2. In our method, surface normal estimation and polygonization, which includes reconstruction of surface discontinuities, are performed together in a single process, thereby completely resolving the chicken-and-egg problem. In contrast, the method of [4, 5] involves a lot of stages, and does not completely resolve the problem.

7. Conclusions

This paper presented a method of reconstructing surface discontinuities by intersecting the tangent planes of advancing mesh frontiers. The method incorporates intersec-

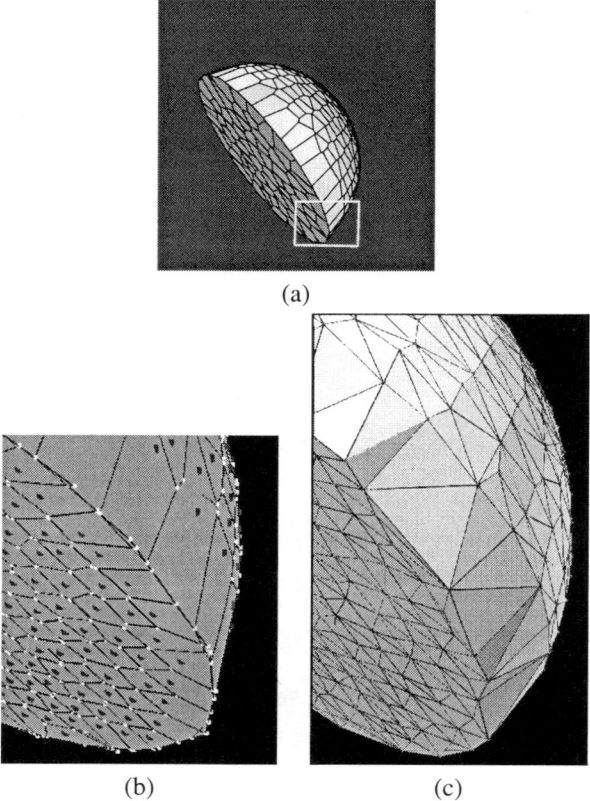

Figure 9. Polygonization of a hemisphere. Since the curve edges were not sampled, Delaunay triangulation produced jagged edges (c). On the other hand, the tangent plane intersection algorithm reconstructed smooth edges (a, b).

tion tangent planes into the frontier advancing algorithm. By performing surface normal estimation together with frontier advancement, the method can accurately estimate surface normals for points at and near surface disconituities. Quantitative evaluation shows that the normal estimation obtained is accurate. In particular, the combination of linear extrapolation and mesh-based method is roughly one order of magnitude more accurate than PCA. Using the accurately estimated normals, the method can accurately reconstruct sharp discontinuities even when they are not sampled.

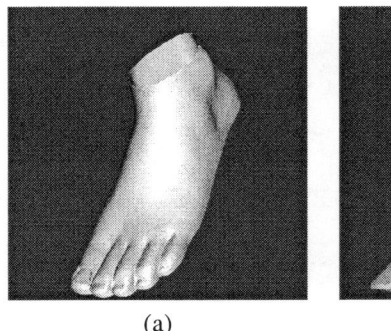
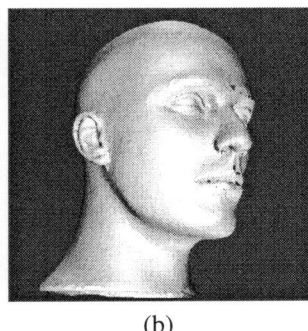

(a)   (b)

Figure 10. Polygonization of (a) the foot and (b) the mannequin standard data points.

References

[1] M.-E. Algorri and F. Schmitt. Surface reconstruction from unstructured 3D data. In *In Proc. Computer Graphics Forum*, pages 47–60, 1996.
[2] N. Amenta, M. Bern, and M. Kamvysselis. A new Voronoi-based surface reconstruction algorithm. In *Proc. SIGGRAPH '98*, pages 415–421, 1998.
[3] I. Atmosukarto, L. Zhou, W. K. Leow, and Z. Huang. Polygonizing non-uniformly distributed 3D points by advancing mesh frontiers. In *Proc. CGI '01*, 2001.
[4] P. Benko, G. Lukacs, R. R. Martin, and T. Varady. Algorithms to create B-rep models from measured point clouds. *Research Report of Geometric Modelling Laboratory, Computer and Automation Institute, Hungarian Academy of Sciences, Budapest*, 6, 1998.
[5] P. Benko, R. R. Martin, and T. Varady. Algorithms for reverse engineering boundary representation models. *Computer Aided Design*, 33(11):839–851, 2001.
[6] H. Edelsbrunner and E. P. Mucke. Three-dimensional alpha shapes. *ACM TOG*, 13:43–72, 1994.
[7] H. Hoppe, T. DeRose, T. Duchamp, J. McDonald, and W. Stuetzle. Surface reconstruction from unorganized points. In *Proc. SIGGRAPH '92*, pages 71–78, 1992.
[8] G. Kos, R. R. Martin, and T. Varady. Methods to recover constant radius rolling ball blends in reverse engineering. *Computer Aided Geometry Design*, 17(2):127 – 160, 2000.
[9] S. Lodha. Surface approximation with low degree patches with multiple representations. *Ph.D Thesis, Computer Science, Rice University, Houston, Texas*, 1992.
[10] C. Oblonsek and N. Guid. A fast surface-based procedure for object reconstruction from scattered points. *Computer Vision and Image Understanding*, 69(2):185–195, 1998.
[11] R. Poli, G. Coppini, and G. Valli. Recovery of 3D closed surfaces from sparse data. *Computer Vision, Graphics and Image Processing*, 60(1):1–25, 1994.
[12] D. Ruprecht and H. Muller. Free form deformation with scattered data interpolation methods. *In Proc. Geometric Modelling*, pages 171–200, 1995.
[13] C. K. Tang and G. Medioni. Inference of integrated surface, curve and junction descriptions from sparse 3D data. *IEEE Trans. PAMI*, 20(11), 1998.
[14] D. Terzopoulos, A. Witkin, and M. Kass. Constrains on deformable models: recovering 3D shape and non-rigid motion. *Artificial Intelligence*, 36:91–123, 1988.

Progressive Gap Closing for Mesh Repairing

Pavel Borodin, Marcin Novotni, Reinhard Klein
Computer Graphics Group
Institute of Computer Science II
University of Bonn
Römerstr. 164, D-53117 Bonn, Germany

Abstract

Modern 3D acquisition and modeling tools generate high-quality, detailed geometric models. However, in order to cope with the associated complexity, several mesh decimation methods have been developed in the recent years. On the other hand, a common problem of geometric modeling tools is the generation of consistent three-dimensional meshes. Most of these programs output meshes containing degenerate faces, T-vertices, narrow gaps and cracks. Applying well-established decimation methods to such meshes results in severe artifacts due to lack of consistent connectivity information. The industrial relevance of this problem is emphasized by the fact that as an output of most of the commercial CAD/CAM and other modeling tools, the user usually gets consistent meshes only for separate polygonal patches as opposed to the whole mesh.

In this paper we propose a solution, which interprets the above issue as a mesh boundary decimation task. As suggested by Garland and Heckbert [4] and Popovi• and Hoppe [12], adding a vertex pair contraction operation enables to join unconnected regions of the mesh. In addition to this and the usual edge-collapse operation, we introduce a new vertex-edge collapse operation. This provides extra support for closing gaps and stitching together the boundaries of triangle patches lying in near proximity to each other. In our method, the decimation process is error controlled and conducted in a progressive manner in terms of the error. Therefore, the user is enabled to visually inspect and interactively influence the procedure.

Keywords: mesh repair, gap closing, CAD, simplification

1 Introduction

Today, polygonal surfaces have become ubiquitous as three-dimensional geometric representation of objects in computer graphics and even in some engineering applications. The fact that this particular representation is arguably the most widespread one is due to its simplicity, flexibility and rendering support by 3D graphics hardware. Models of this type are used for rendering of objects in a broad range of disciplines like medical imaging, scientific visualization, CAD, movie industry, etc. Essentially, a set of polygons not containing consistent connectivity information suffices for rendering purposes. Since the generation of 3D models is application-driven, numerous models contain artifacts like T-vertices, degenerate triangles, gaps and holes.

However, as a natural consequence of recent advances in computer graphics field, we no longer want to be able only to render images of objects, but also to process and analyze the already available models. New demands and applications have arisen where *"better behaved"* polygonal models are desired, in a sense that they do not contain the above artifacts. Signal processing techniques on meshes aim at analyzing the geometry and improving the visual quality of models. Compression and progressive transmission facilitate robust transfer of 3D meshes through the Internet and their efficient storage. Mesh simplification algorithms reduce the complexity of highly detailed models by optimally approximating the geometry within a prescribed tolerance. An example of applying a common mesh decimation algorithm to a model containing gaps between the patches is demonstrated in Figure 1. Computing geodesic distances has gained a lot of attention in the last few years, since this numerical method was recently found very useful in a number of applications [11]. The effect of lack of consistent connectivity of vertices is depicted in Figure 2. There are numerous variants of these geometric modeling techniques, and some of them are applicable to meshes containing the artifacts described above. Generally however, in order to achieve optimal results, consistent vertex connectivity information is required.

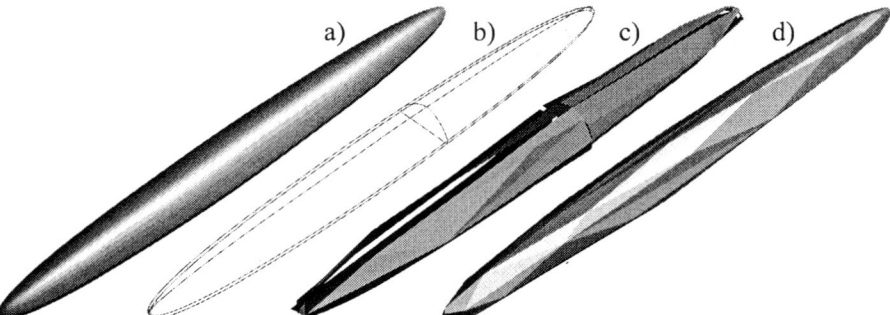

Figure 1: Result of applying mesh decimation to an unrepaired and repaired mesh. The original model is shown in a), it consists of 5500 faces. b) depicts the boundary, c) and d) demonstrate the result of the decimation applied to the unprocessed mesh and the repaired model, respectively. The simplified models contain 80 triangles.

Figure 2: Demonstration of the impact of inconsistent vertex connectivity on an algorithm computing geodesic distances on triangular meshes. The left side hippo's mesh is a closed watertight one, it can be seen that the algorithm produces appropriate wavefronts. In contrary, for the hippo on the right containing a long hole along its back, the wavefront breaks at the ends of the hole, thus producing erroneous results.

The aim of the work presented in this paper is to eliminate these artifacts and repair the input mesh by applying topological modifications while retaining the overall geometry.

In the proposed method we suggest to approach the problem of eliminating the artifacts listed above as a simplification task. Without loss of generality, we formulate our technique for triangle meshes. Since we intend to proceed by altering the topology of the triangle mesh, we clearly need topology modifying operators. Garland and Heckbert [4] and Popovi• and Hoppe [12] already generalized the common edge contraction operator, where two vertices lying on a common edge are contracted, to vertex contraction, where two vertices not necessarily connected by an edge are contracted. This way unconnected regions of the mesh can be joined. We further generalize this operation by introducing a *vertex-edge* contraction, where a vertex is unified with its projection on an edge. The intuition behind our algorithm is that the gap closing should proceed by attracting the boundaries of the mesh towards each other, which is achieved by utilizing the vertex-edge contraction operator. In other words, we apply the methodology of mesh decimation to the decimation of boundaries targeted at gap closing. Similarly to the common simplification methods, the procedure is error controlled as well; furthermore, it is performed in a progressive manner according to a monotonically increasing error. Our method essentially generates a sequence of meshes where the gaps and holes are progressively removed (see Figure 3). As explained in Section 2, the transition between the neighboring models in the sequence is accomplished very by applying a single contraction operator or its inverse. We enable the user to navigate between these meshes, thus facilitating the visual inspection of the results and interactive control of the process by determining a desired error tolerance. As pointed out by Weihe and Willhalm [15], stitching of mesh boundaries is a highly non-trivial process, since some of the gaps may be intentionally modeled, while others might be results of erroneous modeling or tessellation procedure. We take this issue into account by allowing the user to manually select/deselect areas to be considered during the stitching process.

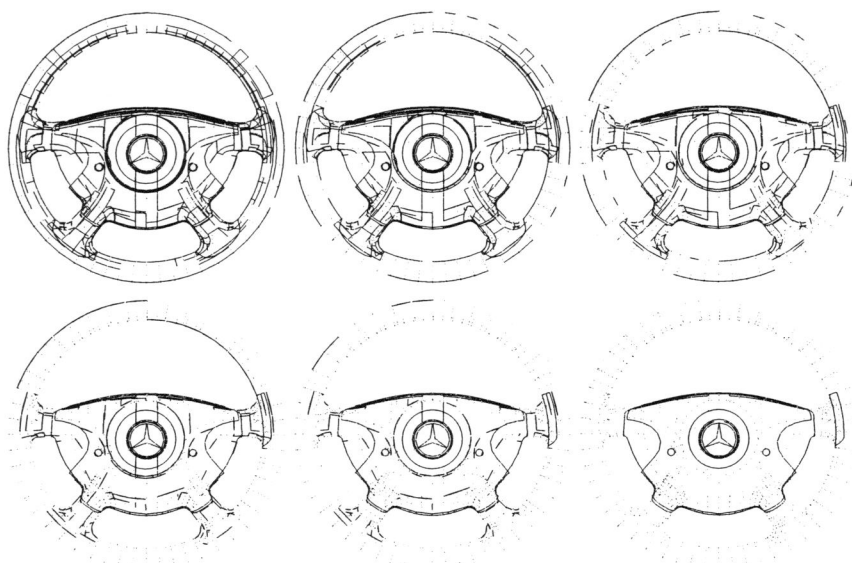

Figure 3: Representative stages of repairing a steering wheel model, demonstrating the progress of our algorithm. Only the boundary edges are rendered as wireframe. In addition the vertices of the mesh are rendered to give a feeling where the surface is. About 2700 models were generated in sequence between the leftmost original mesh and the rightmost final one. After the generation of this sequence, the user is free to navigate back and forth between the models and select the desired one; she/he can also choose to proceed further with the gap closing.

1.1 Related Work

Considerable amount of research and development has been conducted in the area of polygonal mesh and CAD data repairing in the recent years.

Mesh Reparation. Due to differences in inherent structures of meshes generated by various modeling tools and 3D acquisition techniques, the approaches handling the errors and degeneracies vary depending on the source of the data.

Turk and Levoy [14] generate polygonal models from registered range data, they remove overlaps by clipping them, utilizing a technique called mesh zippering. The meshes coming from 3D scanners and volumetric data often contain artifacts of the reconstruction process: small handles and tunnels. Guskov and Wood [6] conceptualized these as *topological noise*, identified and eliminated them by cutting and sealing the mesh, thus reducing the genus and topological complexity of the model.

Due to the industrial relevance of the problem, a lot of work has been devoted to repairing polygonal models generated by modeling tools, mainly CAD systems. Our algorithm differs from the available techniques as it employs a well established operation borrowed from mesh decimation field and as it is progressive. Barequet and Kumar [2] determine corresponding edges within an error tolerance and stitch them together in one pass. Butlin and Stops [3] present a method for repairing CAD data for analysis and exchange purposes. Guéziec et al. [5] generate manifold surfaces from non-manifold sets of polygons by identifying the topological singularities and decomposing the model into manifold components by cutting along these singularities. They also describe a stitching operation which allows to connect boundaries of the components, while guarantees the manifoldness. Murali and Funkhouser [9] first classify the regions of space as either solid or not, and generate a consistent set of polygons describing the boundary of the solids. Nooruddin and Turk [10] repair the polygonal models by converting them into volumetric representation; they subsequently eliminate the topological noise by morphological open and close operators, and finally reconstruct the polygonal mesh of the so-defined implicit function.

Simplification. Since the mesh simplification is one of the fundamental operations on polygonal meshes, there is an extensive amount of literature on this topic. However, we are interested only in methods allowing topology changes during the process. The *vertex clustering* family of methods has been introduced by Rossignac and Borrel [13] and has been refined in numerous more recent works (see e.g. [8]). The algorithms of this family essentially proceed by applying a 3D grid to the object and for each cell contracting all the vertices inside the cell. Although the degenerate faces are subsequently removed, it is difficult to influence the fidelity of the result due to lack of control over induced topological changes. The already mentioned *vertex contraction* operator [4, 12] offers more control over the topological modifications, however, without further processing it possibly generates non-manifold meshes.

1.2 Our Setting

The input of our algorithm is a general *polygon soup* – a set of unorganized polygons without any explicit topology information a la STL file format [1]. We assume the mesh to be composed of triangular faces. Notice that this does not imply any loss of generality, since the polygonal faces may easily be converted into triangular ones. The mesh to be processed by our method will possibly include the following artifacts:

- *degenerate faces* without finite area,

- unwanted *gaps* and *cracks* between regions of the mesh resulting from erroneous scan data reconstruction or modeling and/or tessellation of analytical surfaces,

- *holes* in the model due to missing polygons,

- *T-vertices* lying on interior of an edge of a face.

The vertex-edge decimation operator will possibly introduce non-manifold edges and/or vertices; therefore the output of our system will also be a non-manifold mesh in the general case. However, if a manifold surface is desired, the methods presented in [5] may be applied to our results, the mesh will be cut exactly along non-manifold features, thus preserving the consistent connectivity of the manifold components.

1.3 Paper Overview

The overview of the paper is as follows. In the next section we describe our new vertex-edge contraction operator, which is followed by the detailed description of the gap closing algorithm in the Section 3. We present and discuss the results in Section 4. Finally, we conclude and draft some directions for future research in Section 5.

2 Vertex-Edge Contraction

Let us describe our notation and terminology: ς is a set of N abstract vertices, $|\varsigma| = N$. The abstract polygonal surface $\Sigma(\varsigma)$ contains the topological information of the model, it is composed of subsets of ς. Since we work with triangle meshes, the subsets are vertices, edges and triangles. In order to embed the mesh into the three-dimensional space $\mathfrak{I}^3$, we assign a geometric position in space to each abstract vertex. Let $\Pi = \{ p_i \in \mathfrak{I}^3 \mid 1 \leq i \leq N \}$. We now define the triangular mesh M as the pair (Σ, Π).

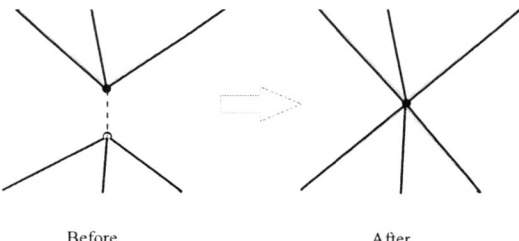

Before After

Figure 4: Vertex contraction operation

The decimation methods utilizing the *edge contraction* operator proceed by iteratively contracting edges. As already pointed out above, this operator does not provide enough topological flexibility during the decimation process. It is possible to close holes in the mesh by iterative application of the operator; however, the disconnected regions of the mesh will remain in separate components. The *vertex contraction* operator (cf. Figure 4) is a natural generalization of the edge contraction, and it seems to be the appropriate compromise between topological flexibility and control over the topological changes it induces. This operator contracts vertices not necessarily lying on a common edge, therefore it allows for stitching together the boundaries of the mesh. Note that we only want to process the boundaries of the mesh, in which case even the vertex contraction may be not flexible enough. In order not to introduce distortions in case of narrow gaps, it is sometimes more favorable to project a vertex directly onto an edge. We call this operator a *vertex-edge contraction*, which is made up of the sequence of following operations (cf. Figure 5):

1. Project the vertex v orthogonally onto the edge e.

2. Insert a vertex v' into the edge at the geometric position of the projection.

3. Split the triangle t_1 into two triangles $t'_1 = (v_0, v', v_2)$ and $t_2 = (v_1, v_2, v')$.

4. Perform a vertex contraction to v and v'. The new position of the vertex will be a convex combination of v and v', we move the new vertex v_{new} into position $\lambda v + (1 - \lambda) v'$.

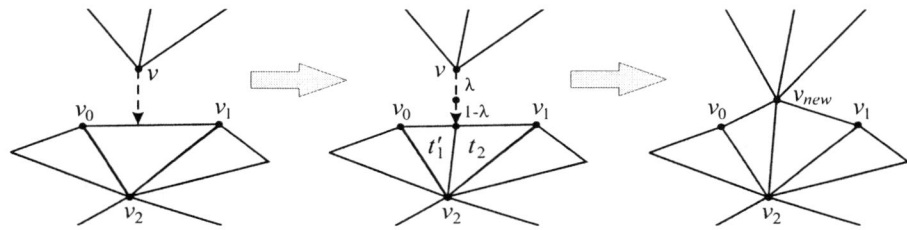

Figure 5: Vertex-edge contraction operation

At this point, it is necessary to mention that during the process we maintain for each boundary edge a list of vertices being projected onto it. In case the geometric position of the edge changes, the edge is destroyed or no longer belongs to the boundary due to modifications in its vicinity, we recompute the correspondences for all vertices in the list. Furthermore, note that if the vertex v is projected onto a vertex incident to the edge e, only a simple vertex contraction is performed. Thus, the vertex-edge contraction is a further generalization of the vertex contraction. The projection of vertices is conducted according to an error measure; see the next section for details on that.

The goal of our method is to construct a series of meshes $M_0, M_1, \ldots, M_M$ by incrementally applying the vertex-edge contraction operator, where M_0 is the input mesh. The user should be able to choose the desired model M_i, therefore we allow him/her to navigate between the meshes. Thus, we essentially generate a sequence of meshes in a sense of multiresolution representations (see e.g. [7]). The forward navigation is clearly accomplished by applying the contraction according to some well-defined order. However, in order to undo the operations during the backward navigation, we have to define an *inverse* vertex-edge contraction operator, and store some data during the generation of the sequence. The data to be stored and the inverse operators for vertex contraction are described in [4, 12]. We focus only on formulating an inverse operator of the vertex-edge contraction (see Figure 5):

1. Project v_{new} orthogonally onto the edge e determined by vertices v_0 and v_1,

this way we reconstruct the position of the vertex v'.

2. Compute v as follows: $v = \dfrac{v_{new} - \lambda v'}{1 - \lambda}$.

3. Delete the triangle t_2, which can unambiguously be determined, since we define it to be incident to v_1 and non-incident to v_0.

4. Restore the triangle $t_1 = (v_0, v_1, v_2)$. Note that v_2 can also always unambiguously be determined, since e is a boundary edge.

Note that we do not have to delete any vertex, since we reuse v to store v_{new}. Given a mesh M_i, $0 < i \leq M$, in order to fully restore the mesh M_{i-1}, we only need to store the indices of vertices v_0 and v_1 as "split information". The projection direction is the vector pointing from v_{new} towards v', in order not to be forced to recompute the projection, we additionally save the λ. We store the split information for each projected boundary vertex; to retain the ordering, we include the indices of vertices of this kind in an array as the decimation proceeds. Moreover, note that in order to navigate between the already generated meshes, it is not necessary to maintain for every boundary edge lists of vertices corresponding to it. The ordering of features to be contracted, which we store in an array during the procedure, fully determines the process for these cases. We only have to store this information for the mesh M_M, where M is the largest index in the mesh sequence, since the correspondences are needed only if the user chooses to continue to generate further meshes.

3 Gap Closing

The algorithm for gap closing essentially consists of a preprocessing phase and the boundary decimation process itself. The method proceeds according to an increasing error computed as distance between feature pairs that are possible candidates for a contraction operation. This in turn implies that our approach has the nice *progressive* property, which means that always the contraction corresponding to the smallest error is performed. The progressivity is not only a numerically pleasant feature, it is also greatly appealing on the user level, since the user can follow the process in an intuitive manner.

3.1 Preprocessing Phase

1. *Reading the mesh*: we first read the input triangle soup and convert it to an *indexed face set* representation where every vertex is stored only once, and the triangles are determined by the indices of according vertices. We accomplish this by lexicographically sorting the vertices in a priority queue. Let v_{stored} be a stored vertex and v_{input} the actual input vertex, in case the distance $d(v_{stored}, v_{input}) = \|v_{stored} - v_{input}\| < \varepsilon$ for some ε, the vertices are considered to be the same and v_{input} is not added to the priority queue.

2. *Identification of boundaries*: find all the edges *e* and vertices *v* that are elements of the boundary *B*. The boundary edges are those having only one incident triangle, the boundary vertices are simply the vertices incident to boundary edges.

3. *Identification of corresponding vertex-vertex and vertex-edge pairs*: in order to accomplish a pairing between vertices and edges to be contracted, for all boundary vertices we find the nearest boundary edge that is non-incident to the vertex. If an orthogonal projection of the examined vertex onto the corresponding nearest edge is possible, we store the edge as the paired feature; otherwise we store the nearest vertex of the edge. We additionally store all corresponding vertices for each boundary edge.

4. *Ordering of the pairs*: For each feature pair we compute the distance between the features as an error measure. We subsequently include all the pairs into a priority queue sorted by this error.

An example of the preprocessing phase is depicted in Figure 6.

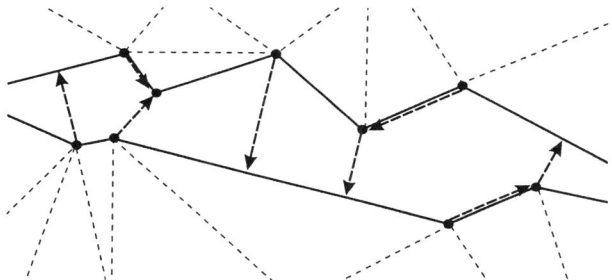

Figure 6: Result of the preprocessing step, the dashed arrows indicate the correspondences. Note that some arrows point along an edge, which possibly implies an edge contraction.

3.2 Decimation step

For a boundary decimation step we first pop the vertex with minimal error from the queue, then we perform a vertex or vertex-edge contraction depending on the type of the corresponding nearest feature. Finally we maintain the correspondences for each vertex corresponding to a modified edge; we accordingly maintain the priority queue as well. The pseudo code for the decimation step can be found in Algorithm 1.

Algorithm 1: Decimation step

1: Vertex v = pqueue.pop_min();
2: Feature f = v.nearest_feature();
3: **if** is_vertex(f) **then**
4:    vertex_contraction(v, f);
5: **else**
6:    vertex_edge_contraction(v, f);
7: **end if**
8: EdgeSet E = {modified_edges()};
9: **for all** Edge $e \in E$ **do**
10:    **for all** Vertex $v \in \{e$.corresponding_features()$\}$ **do**
11:      v.maintain_correspondences();
12:      pqueue.reinsert(v);
13:    **end for**
14: **end for**

Note that if a vertex v is projected onto an edge in the vicinity of one of its vertices v_i, it is reasonable to *snap* the projected vertex v' to the vertex v_i, this way creating triangles with very small edges will be avoided. In our implementation if $d(v', v_i) < \varepsilon$, where ε is the global error threshold, we snap the vertices v_i and v'. Thus, in this case a vertex contraction will be applied to v and v_i.

4 Results

The first example shown in this section demonstrates a steering wheel model kindly provided by DaimlerChrysler AG. As shown in Figure 8, this model gives an insight into artifacts resulting from tessellating a complex model of a tessellated trimmed NURBS surface. Every kind of artifact listed in the introduction can be a found in the model. As it can be seen in the close-up, there are holes even inside relatively flat triangular regions and narrow gaps between the original NURBS patches as well. We managed to close the undesired gaps and holes. Note however, that the gaps intentionally modeled by the CAD tool operator are preserved. The impact of the mesh repairing on performance of mesh processing methods is demonstrated by an example of triangle mesh simplification. The simplified original model is hardly recognizable even after a relatively small amount of decimation steps. In contrary, the repaired model retains the overall shape after a considerable reduction of number of triangles (the original model contains 6540 triangles, it has been simplified to consist of 1229 triangles).

An example of a different nature coming from a 3D acquisition tool is the 3D scan of a woman (see Figure 7). The model consists basically of one connected component, however, it contains holes with jagged boundary and T-vertices. As shown in Figure 7, our method succeeds to remove the artifacts from this mesh as well.

Figure 7: The results for a scan. The boundaries identified in the original model are depicted on the left side. Our procedure removed all the holes, the result can be seen on the right side.

5 Conclusions and Future Work

We presented an algorithm for repairing meshes containing various artifacts due to incorrect modeling or acquisition process. Our method removes the inconsistency of vertex connectivity and thus produces high fidelity models with properties, which are important prerequisites for most of the geometry processing and numerical simulation methods.

Essentially, our technique accomplishes the removal of undesired artifacts by simplifying the boundary of the mesh. For this purpose we generalized the vertex contraction operator into the vertex-edge contraction. The needed topological modifications were already possible by applying the vertex contraction, however, our vertex-edge contraction operator provides additional flexibility. Our system is capable of creating a sequence of meshes generated during the boundary decimation process, which allows the user to choose the desired model. With additional interactive functionality, the user is enabled to select the regions of the mesh she/he wants to repair.

As for further development, we see plenty of room to develop interactive tools facilitating the effective work with the system. A 3D brush for instance could be used to navigate along a narrow gap and selecting it for subsequent *zippering*.

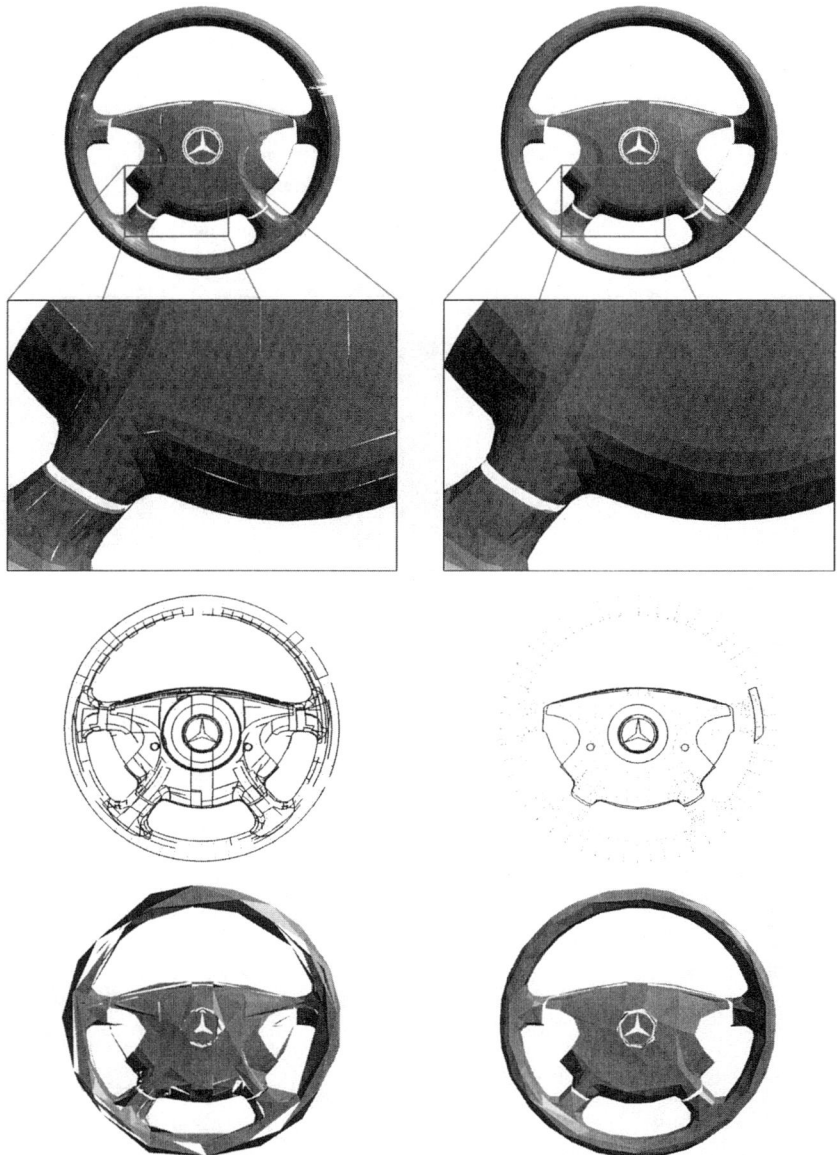

Figure 8: Results for a steering wheel. The images for original model are shown on the left and for repaired model on the right. The top image depicts the solid model, the one below shows a close-up on the highlighted region. Note the holes on the left side and that they have been removed by our procedure, which is even more obvious by looking at the boundaries. The bottom images demonstrate the impact of the decimation of models.

References

[1] Stereolitography interface specification. SLA CAD, 3D Systems Inc. (Valencia, CA), 1989, p/n 500650S01-00.

[2] Gill Barequet and Subodh Kumar. Repairing CAD models. In Roni Yagel and Hans Hagen, editors, *IEEE Visualization '97*, pages 363–370, 1997.

[3] Geoffrey Butlin and Clive Stops. CAD data repair. In *5th International Meshing Roundtable*, pages 7–12, 1996.

[4] Michael Garland and Paul S. Heckbert. Surface simplification using quadric error metrics. In *ACM SIGGRAPH Computer Graphics Proceedings*, pages 209–216, 1997.

[5] Andre Guéziec, Gabriel Taubin, Francis Lazarus, and Bill Horn. Cutting and stitching: Converting sets of polygons to manifold surfaces. *Trans. on Visualization and Computer Graphics*, 7(2), pages 136–151, 2001.

[6] I. Guskov and Z. Wood. Topological noise removal. In *Graphics Interface*, 2001.

[7] Hugues Hoppe. Progressive meshes. *Computer Graphics*, 30 (Annual Conference Series), pages 99–108, 1996.

[8] Kok-Lim Low and Tiow Seng Tan. Model simplification using vertex-clustering. In *Symposium on Interactive 3D Graphics*, pages 75–82, 188, 1997.

[9] T. M. Murali and Thomas A. Funkhouser. Consistent solid and boundary representations from arbitrary polygonal data. In *Symposium on Interactive 3D Graphics*, pages 155–162, 196, 1997.

[10] F. Nooruddin and G. Turk. Simplification and repair of polygonal models using volumetric techniques. Technical Report GITGVU -99-37, Georgia Institute of Technology, 1999.

[11] Marcin Novotni and Reinhard Klein. Computing geodesic distances on triangular meshes. Submitted for publication to Winter School on Computer Graphics 2002.

[12] Jovan Popovi• and Hugues Hoppe. Progressive simplicial complexes. In *ACM SIG-GRAPH Computer Graphics Proceedings*, pages 217–224, 1997.

[13] J. Rossignac and P. Borrel. Multi-resolution 3D approximations for rendering. In *Modeling in Computer Graphics*. Springer-Verlag, 1993.

[14] Greg Turk and Marc Levoy. Zippered polygon meshes from range images. *Computer Graphics*, 28 (Annual Conference Series), pages 311–318, 1994.

[15] Karsten Weihe and Thomas Willhalm. Why CAD data repair requires discrete algorithmic techniques. In *2nd Workshop on Algorithm Engineering*, 1998.

An Isosurface Continuity Algorithm for Super Adaptive Resolution Data [*]

Robert S Laramee [†]
VRVis, Center for Virtual Reality and Visualization
Donau-City-Strasse 1
A-1220 Vienna, Austria
laramee@vrvis.at

R. Daniel Bergeron [‡]
Department of Computer Science
Kingsbury Hall
University of New Hampshire
Durham, New Hampshire 03824, USA
rdb@cs.unh.edu

February 27, 2002

Abstract

We present the chain-gang algorithm for isosurface rendering of super adaptive resolution (SAR) volume data in order to minimize (1) the space needed for storage of both the data and the isosurface and (2) the time taken for computation. The chain-gang algorithm is able to resolve discontinuities in SAR data sets. Unnecessary computation is avoided by skipping over large sets of volume data deemed uninteresting. Memory space is saved by leaving the uninteresting voxels out of our octree data structure used to traverse the volume data. Our isosurface generation algorithm extends the Marching Cubes Algorithm in order to handle inconsistencies that can arise between abutting cells that are separated by both one and two levels of resolution.

Keywords: isosurface rendering, adaptive resolution visualization, marching cubes, uncertainty visualization, chain-gang

---

[*] The research presented here is supported in part by the National Science Foundation, grants IIS-9871859 and IIS-0082577 and the KPlus research program in Austria
[†] phone: +43 (316) 787-1740, fax: +43 (316) 787-777
[‡] phone: +1 (603) 862-3778, fax: +1 (603) 862-3493

1 Introduction

Data analysis in the scientific community often deals with volume data. The size of today's volume data sets continues to grow much faster than our ability to render that data in an effective interactive environment. One approach to handling these very large data sets is to represent them at multiple levels of resolution. A scientist can initially view and manipulate a relatively coarse version of the data in order to identify regions of interest which can then be viewed at a finer resolution. Alternatively, it is sometimes possible to create a single data set that retains fine resolution data in "interesting" regions (e.g. where the data is changing rapidly) while using coarse resolution data in other areas. This AR data representation can be more time and space efficient than multiresolution data, but it is more difficult to process. This paper describes the chain-gang algorithm: an extension of the Marching Cubes (MC) [9] isosurface volume rendering to support volume data defined with a super adaptive resolution representation. Unlike previous research, the chain-gang algorithm is able to resolve discontinuities in isosurfaces constructed from SAR volume data in which neighboring cubes can differ by two or more resolution levels.

2 Data Generation

In this section we describe our MR and SAR data sets which also include error data that can be included for uncertainty visualization.

2.1 Multiresolution Data

There are numerous techniques for generating a multiresolution representation (MR) of a volume data set. For the data sets shown in this paper we generate a hierarchy by subsampling attribute data. Subsampling chooses every other data point in each dimension to generate the next coarser resolution. This methodology for generating MR hierarchies has also been used in other applications [6]. We also tried another averaging technique, a wavelet approach [19], but we found subsampling to be more suited for this particular algorithm.

2.2 Super Adaptive Resolution Data

We use the term *super adaptive resolution* (SAR) data to describe a dataset that contains abutting neighbors that differ by *two* or more levels of resolution. An example of SAR data is shown in Figure 1. Cubes numbered 1 and 4 abut data that is two levels of resolution finer than themselves. Conceptually, this involves combining cubes whose vertex values are within a specified delta range. The SAR representations are decided by the change in values in a local area. We store a finer resolution representation in areas of rapidly changing sample data points, whereas areas with little change are stored with a coarser resolution representation. In other words, we can define a scalar value that represents an amount of change, δ, in the volume data set. When examining

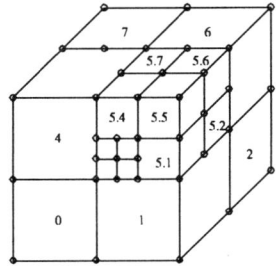

Figure 1: An example of a super adaptive resolution (SAR) data set with numbered octants. Cubes numbered 1 and 4 abut data that is two levels of resolution finer than themselves.

a volume cube, if the cube's vertices do not encompass a change greater than or equal to δ, the volume is represented by a larger cube (of coarser resolution). Each node of the octree includes a cube. If the difference between the maximum and minimum vertex scalar values is less than the threshold value, all of the octree node's children are pruned from the octree. The result is that the volume data is downsampled in areas of that are mostly flat and conversely maintains fine resolution in areas of high detail as in [13]. With this adaptive representation of the volume data, we do not save data which we may find to be uninteresting. In this fashion, we save both memory space resulting from a reduction in the amount of data stored and computation time during the rendering phase because many cubes have been eliminated from the data set.

SAR data gets its name from the amount of memory space that is saved relative to uniform resolution data. Our SAR data sets are only 1/5–1/10 the size of the full, uniform resolution data sets.

2.3 Uncertainty Data

In addition to the SAR data representation, we also generate a measure of the error introduced into the data by the SAR data generation. We assume that each point in the coarse data representation represents 8 points in the next finer resolution (the 8 child nodes in the octree). We compute the error of this point to be the average error representing the 8 original values. This error information can be included in the isosurface rendering [11]. One advantage to including the error data is that we can see which portions of the isosurface are generated from data with high error. These portions show up as yellow and red hue in the resulting images (see Results Section 5). One disadvantage to including the error data is that the rendering is no longer optimized with respect to time, since we are now processing multivariate data sets.

3 Related Work

Multiresolution data has been used to speed up isosurface rendering since early research showed that 30% to 70% of time spent rendering was spent processing empty cubes [17, 18]. Most of the approaches in this area rely on the creation of a single complete static MR representation of the data that is *adaptively traversed* to generate the isosurface. Some researchers have developed algorithms that generate isosurfaces from AR data including Engel et al. [3], Shekhar et al. [13], Shu et al. [14], and Westermann et al. [16].

3.1 Related Work in Isosurface Extraction

First we review some related work in the area of isosurface extraction. Livnat et al [8] presented an isosurface extraction algorithm for unstructured grids. The focus of their work was to minimize the search time for finding an isosurface over the value space and to extract the isosurface from an unstructured grid. A table of performance times is given only for the search phase of their algorithm. The focus of this paper is resolving the discontinuities that arise from SAR representations. In [8] the problem of discontinuities in an SAR representation is not addressed. Furthermore the preprocessing step of quick-sorting the data by both maximum and minimum coordinates is not a requirement of the chain-gang algorithm (as it is in [8]) since our representation is inherently structured. However, we can learn from their work that the search of the octree data structure has a maximum complexity of $O(k + k \log(n/k))$.

In the work done by Weber et al [15] a different problem is addressed. They are concerned with resolving the discontinuities between different levels in an Adaptive mesh refinement (AMR) hierarchy. The resolution takes place at the data set level, not the isosurface level. Sample AMR grids are stitched together with a refinement ratio of 2. Special stitch cells are generated using a case-table approach that bridges the gap between adjacent levels in the AMR hierarchy. The resulting computation is then used for isosurface extraction (for example). However, the results can also be used for other purposes such as direct volume rendering.

3.2 Static MR Representation

Cox and Ellsworth [2, 1] observe that the amount of data generated by a visualization algorithm is relatively small compared to the total amount of data. This implies that sparse traversal methods can be created that reduce the amount of data needed to be accessed [7]. In these approaches the entire octree is constructed and then traversed adaptively. In other words, the data is *not* adaptive but the traversal is. The isosurface value is examined inside blocks and the different resolutions are accessed adaptively. Isosurface traversal begins at the coarsest level of resolution. Whenever the isosurface value falls within the minimum-maximum boundary of a block of volume data, the next finer level of resolution in that block is traversed. If the isosurface value falls within the minimum-maximum boundary of one of those finer resolution blocks, again, the next finer level of resolution in the corresponding block is traversed. This procedure is applied recursively as long as the isosurface value is found within the bounds of the volume data or until the finest resolution block is reached. Given an isosurface value, if it's not within the minimum-maximum boundary of a block, then entire branches of the tree data structure are skipped.

One characteristic of this approach is that neighboring cubes used to generate the isosurface are always at the same resolution. When the isosurface passes from one cube to its neighbor, the neighbor is at the same level in the octree. This is a consequence of having a full MR representation to start with. However, the full MR representation also has disadvantages. In particular, the full MR representation takes up more storage space and requires more computation than AR or SAR representations. It is often the case that a full MR representation is not needed due to volume data redundancy and areas in the volume that are simply not the focus for a scientist. Furthermore, an isosurface *cannot* pass through a cube with 8 equal vertex values, therefore these cubes should be summarized with SAR representations.

The focus of the research presented by Shekhar et al [13] is to minimize the number of triangles needed for an isosurface. Discontinuities in the isosurface are resolved only as a result of their octree-based decimation of marching cubes surfaces, not of the SAR data representation itself. Again, the data is not adaptive but the traversal is. Access to the finest resolution data is always available. The approach is a bottom-up traversal of the octree that uses adaptive downsampling as a means to reduce the number of surface primitives. The volume data is downsampled in areas of the isosurface that are mostly flat and conversely maintains fine resolution in areas of high detail. There are some drawbacks to their approach:

1. The reported savings of up to 90% in the number of surface triangles is not much of an improvement over the 80-90% savings reported by Montani et al [10] in their discretized MC algorithm.

2. Several passes are required through their octree data structure in order to achieve a compact surface representation. In the chain-gang algorithm only one pass is made through the entire isosurface (phase I) and one pass is made through only the adaptive portions of the isosurface (phase II).

3. The user is required to choose a seed cell, that is, a cell having a piece of the desired isosurface. This can be a drawback in terms of the time required for user interaction. Also, the user may not know where an appropriate seed cell is.

4. Their approach generates a maximum of one isosurface even though there may be more than one surface with the same isovalue.

5. They use a crack-patching strategy to resolve discontinuities. Crack-patching does not take full advantage of the finer resolution data that is available at the

location of the discontinuity. However, the chain-gang algorithm does take advantage of the finer resolution data.

6. Not only does their patching scheme not take full advantage of all the data that is available, but it also introduces unnecessary error. Patching may move triangle vertices out of the cell from which it was generated. Since the patching sometimes moves points from a fine resolution edge more error is introduced, and the introduced error may exceed the user-specified error.

7. Although the authors claim to handle the case where a $4 \times 4 \times 4$ cell meets a $1 \times 1 \times 1$ cell, they do not present a clear explanation as to how this case is handled.

3.3 Adaptive Marching Cubes

Shu, Zhou, and Kankanhalli [14] were successful in speeding up the marching cubes algorithm with their version of an adaptive marching cubes (AMC) algorithm. Their goal was to bring the MC algorithm to interactive time. They reduced the number of triangles by up to 55% by adapting the size of triangles to fit the shape of the isosurface. Their research differs from ours in the following ways:

1. Their algorithm does not handle resolution transitions that are two or more levels apart as in Figure 2 (right). Our algorithm is able to resolve this type of discontinuity. Their algorithm only resolves discontinuities such as those found in Figure 2 (left).

2. They resolve discontinuities in the isosurface differently then we do. Cracks may appear between two different neighboring cubes at different levels of resolution. In what they called the "crack problem" [14], discontinuities in the surface are patched with polygons the same shape as those of the cracks. While crack patching is an efficient solution it does not take full advantage of the finer resolution data. In other words, the coarser resolution is left as is, with less accuracy. Our algorithm updates the coarser resolution data with the finest resolution data that is available from the neighbor, thus improving the accuracy of the isosurface.

3. Their cracks are abstracted into 22 basic configurations of different sizes, a solution that requires $O(n^2)$ of working memory space for an $n \times n \times n$ volume data set. Our algorithm only requires the working memory space necessary to hold the SAR data set. The amount of working memory space taken up by the SAR data set is flexible and is often 1/5–1/10 the size of the equivalent MR data set (as in Results Section 5).

4. Their algorithm uses a static uniform resolution representation with a dynamic MR traversal. Our algorithm uses an SAR representation of the data and does not require access to the original MR representation.

5. Their volume data is stored using a single level resolution representation with an MR traversal. Our data is stored using an SAR representation with an AR traversal.

Westermann, Kobbelt, and Ertl [16] achieved real-time exploration of regular volume data using adaptive reconstruction of isosurfaces. Their work differs from ours in the following manner(s):

1. Their algorithm does not handle resolution transitions that are two levels apart (as in Figure 2, right). Our algorithm is able to resolve this type of discontinuity. Their algorithm only resolves discontinuities such as those found in Figure 2 (left).

2. Their algorithm requires knowledge about the direction in which the resolution transition occurs. The direction in which the resolution transition occurs is defined as radially outward from a *focus point oracle* (at the center of interest). In other words, they can only resolve discontinuities when they know the transition direction is from the focus point oracle, where the fine resolution data resides, to the coarse resolution data (outside the *radius of interest*). We can handle discontinuities occurring from any direction and in *multiple* directions.

3. They use the *focus point oracle* to decide which portions of the data are rendered at the finest resolution [16]. In our case, the subset of data at the finest resolution is chosen automatically, prior to run time.

4. As a consequence of the focus point oracle, their algorithm also relies on having access to the entire, uniform resolution data set whereas we start with a static SAR data set. that is often 1/5–1/10 the size of the equivalent MR data set (as in Results Section 5).

It is important to note that the strategies used by Shu et al [14] and Westermann et al [16] to resolve discontinuities in AR data are based on case tables not unlike those used be the original MC algorithm [9]. A simple case table approach is not feasible nor extensible for resolving discontinuities that are separated by two levels of resolution. Also worthy of note is that we are implementing our algorithm in Java (not C++) taking advantage of it's platform independence.

3.4 Isosurface Discontinuities

Because we are dealing with adaptive resolution data, we may have a larger, unsubdivided volume with a triangle next to a smaller, neighboring cube with another triangle sharing a vertex with the larger triangle. This can introduce discontinuities in the isosurface. Looking at Figure 3a, we may generate a lower resolution triangle entirely in the larger voxel. Then we generate the triangles in the neighboring finer resolution voxel (entirely in the smaller cube). Another possible configuration is shown in Figure 3b. In both cases the two triangles introduce a surface discontinuity. The key to identifying this problem is recognizing that one or more triangle vertices are on the face of

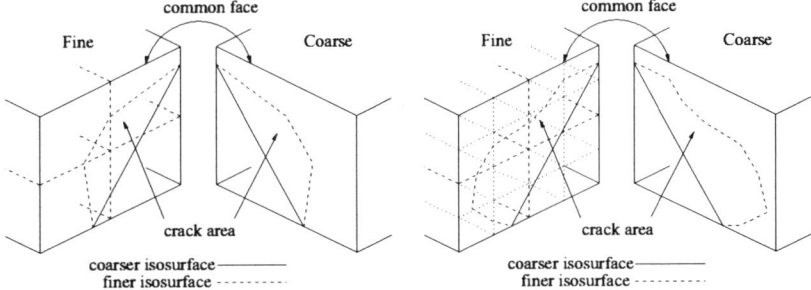

Figure 2: (left) An isosurface discontinuity that is resolved by Livnat [8], Shekhar [13], Shu [14], Westermann [16], and the chain-gang algorithm. (right) Another isosurface discontinuity that the chain-gang algorithm can resolve. The resolution of the neighboring data is separated by two levels.

the larger voxel. The difference between the two cases is that the first one has 2 cube vertices above the isovalue on the *edge* of its coarser neighbor, while the second case has an additional cube vertex (above the isovalue) on the *face* of its coarser neighbor.

The algorithms presented by Livnat [8], Shekhar [13], Shu [14], Westermann [16], and the chain-gang algorithm all resolve those discontinuities in which the abutting cubes are one level apart in resolution, as in Figure 2 (left). However, only the chain-gang algorithm provides a clear means by which to resolve discontinuities two levels apart in resolution as in Figure 2 (right).

4 The Chain-Gang Algorithm

The chain-gang algorithm consists of two phases. The first phase consists of identifying the AR and SAR portions of the isosurface. The second phase then resolves the discontinuities between resolution transitions. Our approach uses a static SAR representation and an AR traversal algorithm. Any value from the data set may be chosen to generate an isosurface. The basic goal of our algorithm is to identify isosurface intersections that can be chained together. Groups of chains form a gang. As a result we've named our algorithm the chain-gang algorithm.

4.1 Phase I, Identifying the Gang

Since we are rendering an adaptive representation of the volume data, complications arise from the adjacency of blocks at different levels of resolution. The elegance of the conventional MC algorithm is that each cube is treated independently. This elegance is lost when we render adjacent blocks at different levels of resolution. We must introduce additional methodology into the MC algorithm to overcome these complications.

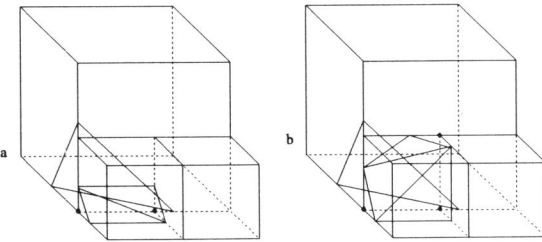

Figure 3: Two triangles generated at different resolutions that introduce isosurface discontinuity (a) the finer resolution cube has 2 cube vertices above the isovalue on the edge of its coarser neighbor (b) the finer resolution cube has 3 cube vertices above the isovalue on the edge and face of its coarser neighbor

Just as the MC algorithm acts conceptually as a filter applied to an input 3D data set and outputting an isosurface, the chain-gang algorithm acts as another filter applied on top of the MC algorithm. The input to the chain-gang filter is the isosurface output by the MC algorithm, with discontinuities, and the output is the same isosurface with the discontinuities resolved. Figure 2 shows two examples of these discontinuities.

In phase I of the chain-gang algorithm, the isosurface is separated into two portions: (1) the uniform resolution portion(s) of the isosurface and (2) the SAR portion(s) of the isosurface. The AR and SAR portions of the isosurface are defined as those where a resolution transition occurs from one cube to the next i.e. where a resolution transition occurs between two or more abutting cubes.

In phase I each cube generates triangles using the standard MC algorithm. In order to identify the SAR portions of the isosurface, each cube examines the resolution of its eight abutting face neighbors using an AR octree data structure. If a *coarser* neighbor is found then the *finer* resolution cube performs the following computation:

1. Each triangle computed by the MC algorithm is examined to see if one of its edges abuts the coarser resolution neighbor.

2. If a triangle edge is found that abuts the coarser resolution neighbor, that triangle segment is attached to the face of the coarser resolution face of the neighboring cube.

3. The coarser resolution neighbor is identified being part of the SAR portion of the isosurface and the triangle edge is identified as being a chain-link.

The computation of the chain-links is shown in Figure 4. We can see from the figure that whenever a finer resolution cube identifies one of its own triangle edges on the face of its coarser neighbor, the triangle edge forms a chain-link on the coarser resolution

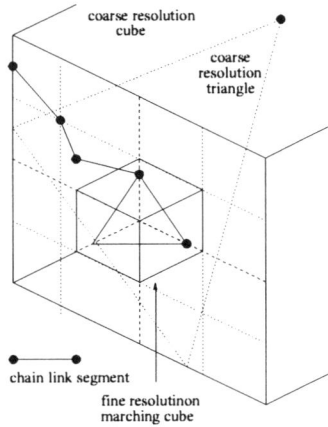

Figure 4: The first phase of the chain-gang algorithm: computing the chain links.

face. We can also note that the order in which the cubes are traversed is independent from the chain-links themselves. The same chains will be formed independent of the cube traversal order.

At the end of phase I, every cube has been identified as belonging to the uniform resolution portion of the isosurface or the SAR resolution portion. All of those cubes belonging to the adaptive portions will have a set of chain links on one or more of their faces.

4.2 Phase II: Assembling the Gang

Phase II of the chain-gang algorithm consists of assembling the chain-links into continuous chains and then using the chains as a basis for the triangle fans output by the algorithm.

At the beginning of phase II, each SAR cube has a set of chain links on one or more of its faces. For each face of the cube these chain-links are assembled one-by-one into coherent chains by joining the chain-links at their corresponding endpoints. At the end of this process, the SAR cube has a group of chains i.e. a chain-gang. When the chain-gang has been assembled, the cubes own triangles (computed from the standard MC algorithm) are then searched. The following computation is performed:

1. A coarse triangle (i.e., a triangle inside a coarse resolution cube) edge is matched with a chain. In order for there to be a match, a coarser triangle edge must be on the same cube face as the chain, as in Figure 4.

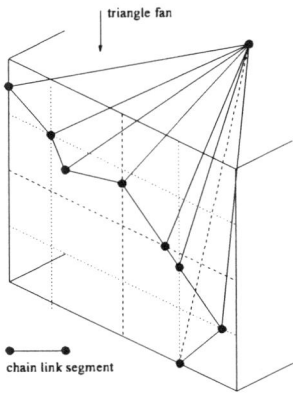

Figure 5: The second phase of the chain-gang algorithm: assembling the chain segments into chains and outputting the triangle fan(s).

2. If a matching coarse triangle edge has been paired with a chain, the coarse triangle edge is removed.

3. The coarse triangle edge is then replaced with the chain.

4. A triangle fan is formed by using each chain-link as the new base of coarser resolution triangle.

Figure 5 shows the chain-gang assembly. A coarser resolution triangle inside a coarser resolution cube is replaced by a triangle fan formed by the chain and one vertex from the original coarser resolution triangle. The coarser resolution triangle vertex remains if it is not on the same face as the finer-resolution chain.

There are cases when more than one chain is associated with only one coarse resolution triangle. Figure 6 shows how the chain-gang algorithm identifies chains on multiple faces of a coarse resolution cube. In Figure 6, there are two chains on different sides of a coarser resolution cube that create a discontinuity that must be resolved with only one coarser resolution triangle. These cases are handled by applying the chain-gang algorithm in an iterative fashion. In short, after phase I has computed all of the chain segments, we apply phase II, repeatedly, until the discontinuity is resolved. In this way, we show that this is not a special case.

First we apply phase II of assembling the chain-gang and outputting a triangle fan, ignoring any other possible chains. The result of this step is shown in Figure 7. Here we see one triangle fan generated thus resolving the discontinuity between one chain and one coarse resolution triangle (on the left hand side). However, this is only an inter-

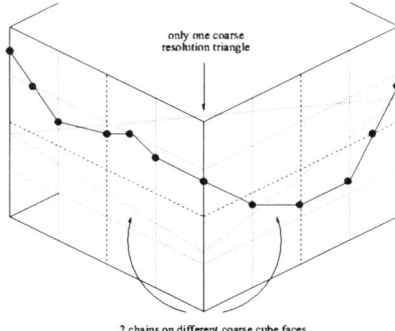

Figure 6: This figure shows the result of the chain-gang algorithm attach chain segments onto multiple sides of a coarse resolution cube.

mediate step. There is still a discontinuity between the second chain and the resulting isosurface on the inside of the coarser resolution cube (on the right). The chain-gang algorithm then uses the adjacent triangle in the triangle fan to resolve the discontinuity. This is the shaded triangle in Figure 7.

Figure 8 shows the result of the second application of phase II. A second triangle fan is generated using the vertex labeled B (as shown). If a coarse resolution triangle edge abuts the side of a cube before phase II is applied, a triangle edge is also guaranteed to abut the same side after phase II is applied. And this triangle edge can be used in another discontinuity resolution.

4.3 Special Isosurface Discontinuity Cases

There are special discontinuity cases that arise when three different resolution levels are allowed to meet in the same data set. One such case is shown in Figure 9. Figure 9 shows cubes from three different resolutions meeting along a common edge. The key to resolving this discontinuity is for the finest resolution cube to treat all of its coarser resolution neighbors the same. In other words, no distinction is made between a coarser neighbor that is one resolution level coarser or two resolution levels coarser. In both cases, the finer resolution cube attaches its own triangle edge to the face of its coarser neighbor.

Figure 10 shows how this type of discontinuity is resolved. Two chains and two triangle fans (at different resolutions) are computed. Note that there is one triangle vertex that is shared amongst triangles at 3 different resolutions. Normally this would result in a case of inconsistent interpolation between cube vertices. However, the chain gang algorithm can overcome this by assembling the chains in finest-to-coarsest order. Figure 10 shows

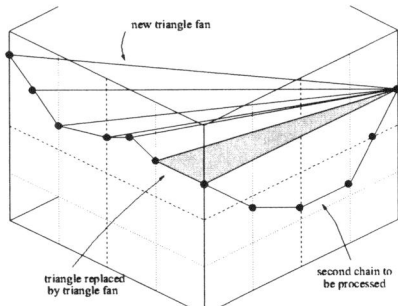

Figure 7: This is the intermediate result of resolving the discontinuity between one chain (on the left) and one side of a coarse resolution triangle. The shaded triangle shows which triangle is used to resolve the remaining discontinuity between the other chain (on the right) and the intermediate surface in the coarser cube.

the finer chain that is assembled first (the base of the first triangle fan). Then the chain gang algorithm assembles the chains on the coarsest cubes. Since all of the triangles point to a common shared triangle vertex list and each triangle vertex stores its resolution, the finer resolution triangle vertex position is used automatically. It is through this triangle vertex list that inconsistent interpolation is corrected.

4.4 Inconsistent Interpolation

The standard algorithm for computing the intersection of a surface with a cube edge is to compute the linear interpolation between the end points of the edge. In a conventional volume data set, all cells are the same resolution, hence all shared edges have the same vertex values and thus neighboring cells interpolate to the same position. However, in our data set, two neighboring voxels at different resolutions may compute different linear interpolations. This ambiguity is easy to resolve: we always use the interpolated point of the finer resolution voxel. In order to identify an instance of inconsistent interpolation, each octree node inspects the neighboring nodes that share the edge on which an edge intersection occurs.

5 Results

Our evaluation experiments were run on an HP PC with a 1 GHz Intel Pentium III Processor and 500 Mbytes of RAM running Red Hat Linux 6.2. We use Sun Microsystem's Java version 1.2 (ported to Linux by Blackdown.org) and utilizes Java 3D. The isosurface generation algorithm is an Adaptive Marching Cubes derived from *The Visualization Toolkit* by Schroeder, Martin, and Lorensen [12], The display algorithm uses

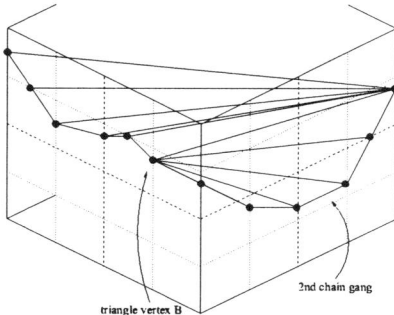

Figure 8: This is the result of phase II of the chain-gang algorithm being applied in an iterative fashion. A second triangle fan is generated using the shaded triangle shown in Figure 7. The vertex labeled B is used to form a triangle fan with the second chain (on the right-hand-side).

the VisAD [5, 4]. graphics library.

One of our test data sets is a $113 \times 256 \times 256$ slice CAT scan of a cadaver head taken on a General Electric CAT Scanner and provided courtesy of North Carolina Memorial Hospital and Siemens Medical Systems, Inc., Iselin, NJ. Figure 11 shows a 128^3 uniform resolution rendering of the medical image data with an isovalue of 0.185. The other data set is a $128 \times 128 \times 64$ slice CAT scan of a lobster.

The AR threshold, δ, is the difference between the minimum and maximum scalar vertex values of a node's cube and all of its children. For example, a δ value of 10% results in all octree nodes whose scalar vertex values vary by less than 10% being trimmed from the original, uniform MR representation. Occurrences of discontinuities are clearly a function of both δ and the isosurface value chosen. With a higher δ we are more likely to encounter discontinuities for a given resolution. Also, for a constant δ the number of discontinuities varies with isovalue. With the proper AR threshold, we can compare the chain-gang algorithm with other AR algorithms. With our data sets we found the values of δ that create both AR data sets and SAR data sets. This is the fundamental difference between the previous work and the work presented here. The higher δ is, the more often neighboring data will differ by two levels of resolution. The chain-gang algorithm amounts to the same as previous AR algorithms when run on AR data while the added functionality is seen only with SAR data sets.

We gain considerable savings in space from an SAR data representation. Table 1 compares the storage and processing requirements of an AR data set with an SAR data set. The adaptive measure column identifies AR data sets and SAR data sets. In this case the AR data sets for the cadaver were generated using a δ value of 5% while the SAR data sets were generated using δ values of both 10% and 15% (labeled SAR and SAR+

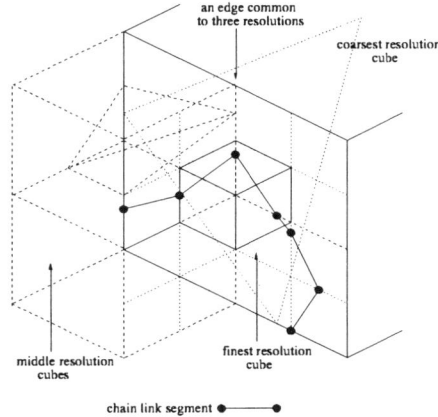

Figure 9: The chain gang algorithm also resolves discontinuities in which three different resolutions meet along the same edge. Phase I does not discriminate between neighbors that are one or two levels coarser in resolution.

respectively). The AR data sets for the lobster were generated using a δ value of 15% while the SAR data sets were generated using δ values of both 20% and 25% (labeled SAR and SAR+ respectively). The fourth column compares the storage requirements for each data set as a percentage of the original uniform resolution data set.

The AR cadaver head data set uses approximately 50% more storage space than the SAR data set and approximately 85% more storage space than the SAR+ data set. For the lobster data set the AR representation uses approximately 4% more storage space than the SAR data set and approximately 6% more storage space than the SAR+ data set.

The last column shows the number of cubes that were processed when generating the isosurface. With the AR cadaver head data, about 7% more cubes are processed in generating the isosurface than the SAR isosurface and about 17% more cubes that the SAR+ isosurface. For the lobster data, only about 1% more cubes are processed in generating the AR isosurface than the SAR or SAR+ isosurfaces (both of isovalue 0.185).

Table 2 compares some sample AR isosurfaces with sample SAR isosurfaces. The fourth column compares the number of triangles in each isosurface. The AR cadaver head isosurface generates approximately 1,330 more triangles than the SAR isosurface and approximately 14,000 more triangles than the SAR+ isosurface (for the isovalue 0.185). We note that for the lobster, the SAR lobster and the chain-gang algorithm retain approximately the same number of triangles as the AR lobster. We attribute this

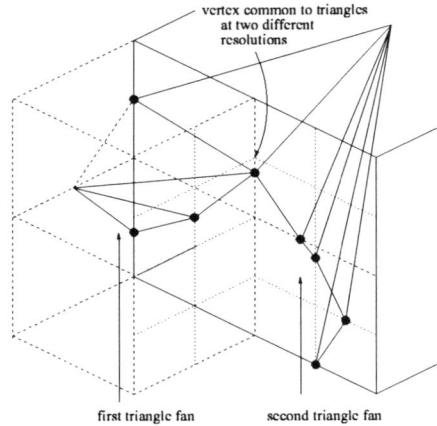

Figure 10: Here we illustrate how the chain gang algorithm resolves discontinuities in which three different resolutions meet along the same edge. Two triangle fans are created at two different resolutions. The inconsistent interpolation is also resolved.

data set	adaptive measure	isovalue	storage space (%)	no. of cubes in isosurface
head res 128^3	AR	0.185	28.3	338, 202
		0.408		158, 840
	SAR	0.185	18.8	316, 417
		0.408		156, 649
	SAR+	0.185	15.3	289, 751
		0.408		149, 068
lobster res 128^3	AR	0.185	11.5	77,918
	SAR		11.1	77,825
	SAR+		10.8	77,441

Table 1: This table compares the storage requirements of an SAR data set with an AR data sets.

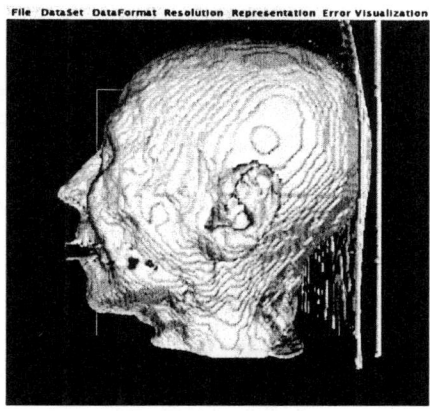

Figure 11: A 128^3 resolution rendering of the cadaver head data set with an isovalue of 0.185

the algorithm's ability to maintain high levels of detail in isosurfaces with high curvature.

The last column shows the number of abutting cubes that differ by two levels of resolution in the given isosurface (2RT -two resolution transitions). A requirement of the AR data sets is that there are none of these transitions. Whereas the sample SAR+ isosurface contains many of these transitions. However, from looking at Figures 12 through 14 we can see that the image quality remains intact throughout. The uncertainty visualization shows exactly where some of the 2RTs occur. We assign no error (mapped to green) to the original 128^3 resolution portions of the isosurface while error is accumulated for coarser resolutions (mapped to non-green hue).

6 Conclusions and Future Work

Our research has shown that isosurface rendering of an SAR volume data set using the chain-gang algorithm can lead to more efficient rendering with minimal loss to image quality. We can extend this research in several directions including: (1) improvements to the rendering algorithm, (2) handling a wider range of AR data representations, (3) rendering larger data sets, and (4) faster rendering time. Improvements to the rendering time can be made using a Just-In-Time compiler (JIT) or a Java compiler.

We would also like to explore SAR isosurface rendering cases where a finer resolution isosurface abuts two or more sides of coarse resolution cube, but no isosurface is computed inside the coarse resolution cube. From our initial experiments using the data sets in this paper, this appears to be a rare occurrence, however, we would like to

data set	adaptive measure	isovalue	no. of triangles in isosurface	no. of 2RTs
head res 128^3	AR	0.185	215, 713	0
		0.408	208, 710	0
	SAR	0.185	214, 375	106
		0.408	207, 912	260
	SAR+	0.185	201, 880	1, 163
		0.408	203, 874	977
lobster res 128^3	AR	0.185	96, 112	0
	SAR		96, 111	47
	SAR+		95, 644	222

Table 2: This table compares sample AR isosurfaces with sample SAR isosurfaces.

identify more precisely how often it occurs. Ideally we would handle these cases by connecting the the isosurface across the coarse resolution cube. However, whenever we encounter an unexpected case using the chain-gang algorithm, we simply subdivide the cube.

7 Acknowledgements

We would like to thank all those who have contributed to the finance of this research including: The NSF -National Science Foundation (grants IIS-9871859 and IIS-0082577), the VRVis Center for Virtual Reality and Visualization (www.vrvis.at) which is funded by both AVL (www.avl.com) and an Austrian Governmental research program called KPlus (www.kplus.at). We would also like to thank (1) Phil Rhodes and Ted Sparr of the University of New Hampshire for their valuable contributions, (2) Zoltan Konyha of VRVis for his valuable contributions and feedback, and (3) Bill Hibbard and the VisAD group for their technical support. And one final note: all of the programming code for this project is 100% open source. Anyone interested in obtaining the open source code can contact laramee@vrvis.at.

References

[1] Michael B. Cox and David Ellsworth. Application-controlled demand paging for out-of-core visualization. Proc. Of Visualization '97. IEEE Computer Society Press, October 1997.

[2] Michael B. Cox and David Ellsworth. Managing big data for scientific visualization. *ACM Siggraph '97*, 21, August 1997. Course #4 Exploring Gigabyte

Datasets in Real-Time: Algorithms, Data Management, and Time-Critical Design.

[3] Klaus Engel, Rudiger Westermann, and Thomas Ertl. Isosurface extraction techniques for web-based volume visualization. In *Volume Visualization*, Visualization 99, California, October 1999.

[4] William Hibbard. Connecting people to computations and people to people. *Computer Graphics*, 32(3):10–12, 1998.

[5] William Hibbard. The visad java class library developers guide. The World Wide Web, November 1999. http://www.ssec.wisc.edu/~billh/visad.html.

[6] Eric C. LaMar, Bernd Hamann, and Kenneth I. Joy. Multiresolution techniques for interactive texture-based volume visualization. In David Ebert, Markus Gross, and Bernd Hamann, editors, *IEEE Visualization '99*, pages 355–362, San Francisco, 1999. IEEE.

[7] C. Charles Law, Kenneth M. Martin, William J. Schroeder, and Joshua Temkin. A multi-threaded streaming pipeline architecture for large structured data sets. In *Volume Visualization*, Volume Visualization 99, California, October 1999.

[8] Yarden Livnat, Han-Wei Shen, and Christopher R. Johnson. A near optimal isosurface extraction algorithm for structured and unstructured grids. *IEEE Transactions on Visual Computer Graphics*, 2(1):73–84, 1996.

[9] William E. Lorensen and Harvey E. Cline. Marching cubes: a high resolution 3d surface construction algorithm. *Comput Graph*, 21:163–169, 1987.

[10] Claudio Montani, Riccardo Scateni, and Roberto Scopigno. Discretized marching cubes. In R. Daniel Bergeron and Arie E. Kaufman, editors, *Proceedings of the Conference on Visualization*, pages 281–287, Los Alamitos, CA, USA, October 1994. IEEE Computer Society Press.

[11] Alex T. Pang, Craig M. Wittenbrink, and Suresh K. Lodha. Approaches to uncertainty visualization. *The Visual Computer*, 13(8):370–390, 1997. ISSN 0178-2789.

[12] William J. Schroeder, Kenneth M. Martin, and William E. Lorensen. *The Visualization Toolkit*. Prentice-Hall, Inc, Upper Saddle River, New Jersey 07458, 1996.

[13] Raj Shekhar, Elias Fayyad, Roni Yagel, and J. Fredrick Cornhill. Octree-based decimation of marching cubes surfaces. In Roni Yagel and Gregory M. Nielson, editors, *Proceedings of the Conference on Visualization*, pages 335–344, Los Alamitos, October 27–November 1 1996. IEEE.

[14] Renben Shu, Chen Zhou, and Mohan S Kankanhalli. Adaptive marching cubes. *The Visual Computer*, 11:202–217, 1995.

[15] Gunther H. Weber, Oliver Kreylos, Terry J Ligocki, John M. Shalf, Hans Hagen, Bernd Hamann, and Kenneth I Joy. Extraction of crack-free isosurfaces from adaptive mesh refinement data. In D.S. Ebert, J.M. Favre, and R. Peikert, editors, *Data Visualization 2001 (Proceedings of VisSym 2001)*, pages 25–34, Vienna, Austria, 2001. Springer-Verlag.

[16] Ruediger Westermann, Leif P. Kobbelt, and Thomas Ertl. Real-time exploration of regular volume data by adaptive reconstruction of isosurfaces. *The Visual Computer*, 15:100–111, 1999.

[17] Jane Wilhelms and Allen Van Gelder. Topological ambiguities in isosurface generation. Technical report, University of California, Santa Cruz, California, December 1990. Extended abstract in ACM Computer Graphics. 2, 5 79–86.

[18] Jane Wilhelms and Allen Van Gelder. Octrees for faster isosurface generation. *ACM Transactions on Graphics*, 11(3):201–227, July 1992.

[19] Pak Chung Wong and R. Daniel Bergeron. Multiresolution multidimensional wavelet brushing. In Roni Yagel and Gregory M. Nielson, editors, *IEEE Visualization '96*, pages 141–148. IEEE, 1996.

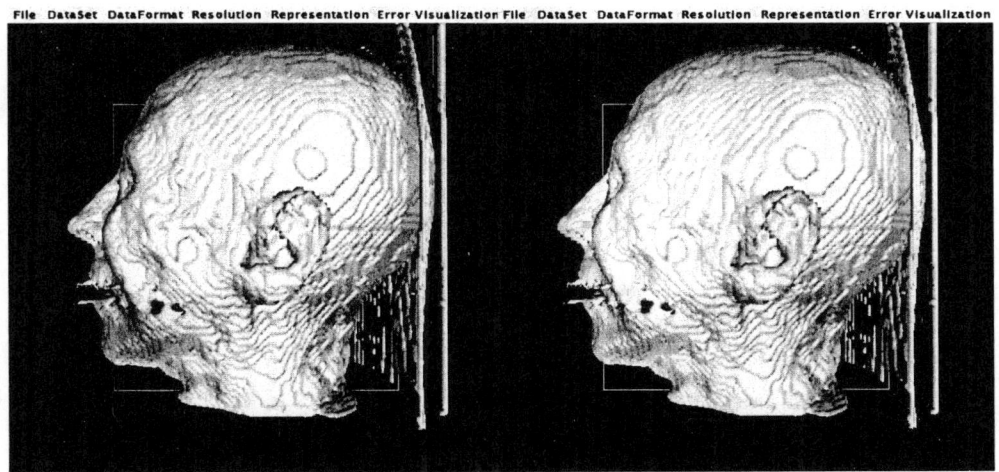

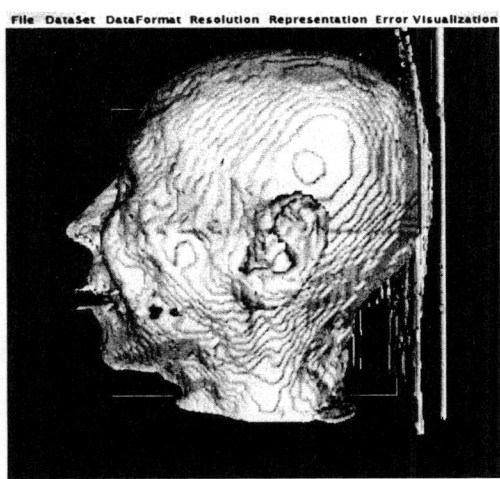

Figure 12: Three isosurfaces from the cadaver head data set, each with resolution 128^3 and an isovalue if 0.185: (top, left) a sample AR isosurface, (top, right) a sample SAR isosurface containing 106 2RTs, and (bottom, left) a sample SAR+ isosurface containing 1,163 2RTs. Yellow and red hue indicates SAR portions of the isosurface.

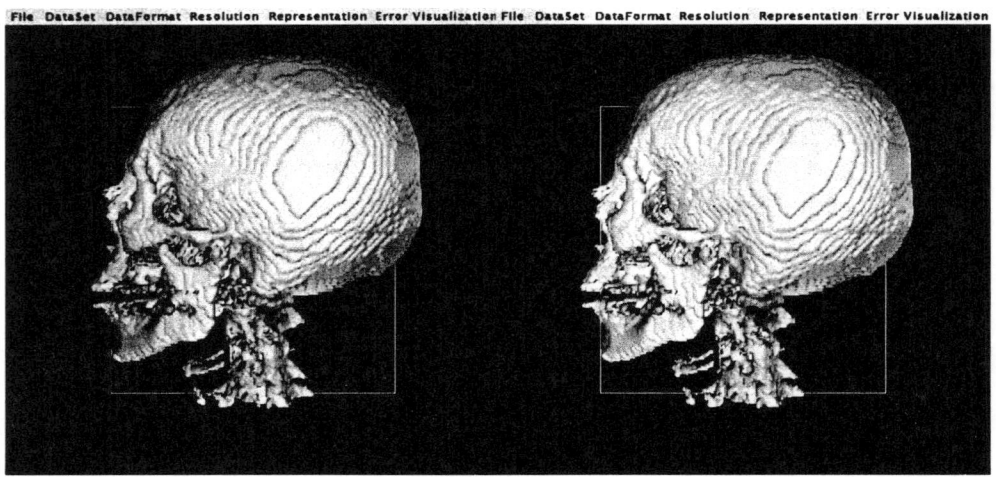

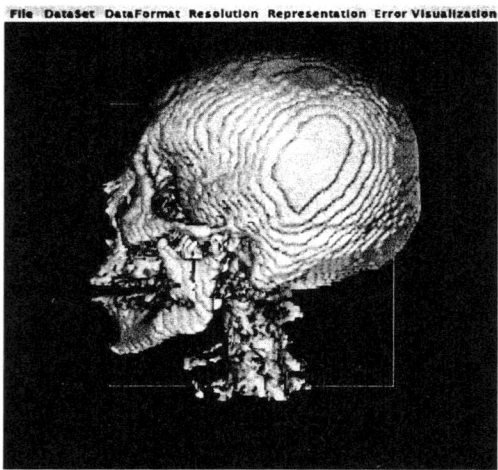

Figure 13: Three isosurfaces from the cadaver head data set, each with resolution 128^3 and an isovalue if 0.408: (top, left) a sample AR isosurface, (top, right) a sample SAR isosurface containing 260 2RTs, and (bottom, left) a sample SAR+ isosurface containing 977 2RTs. Non-green hue indicates occurrences of 2RTs.

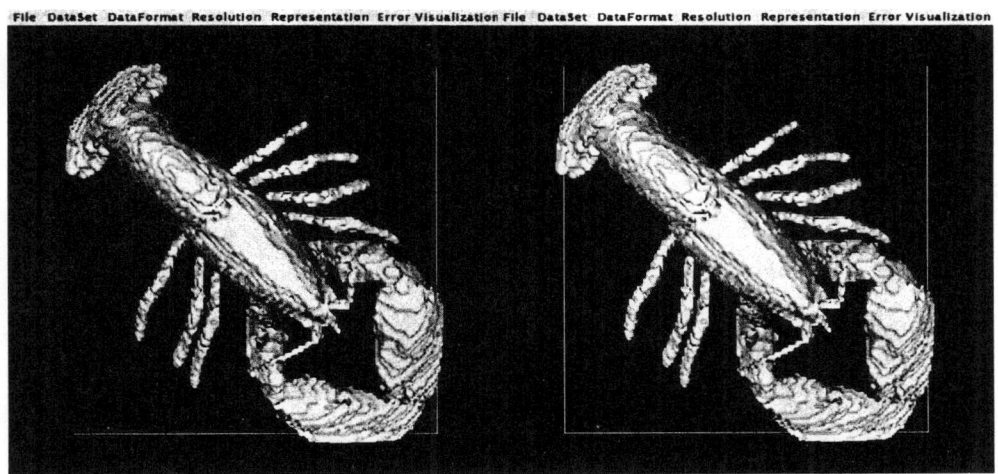

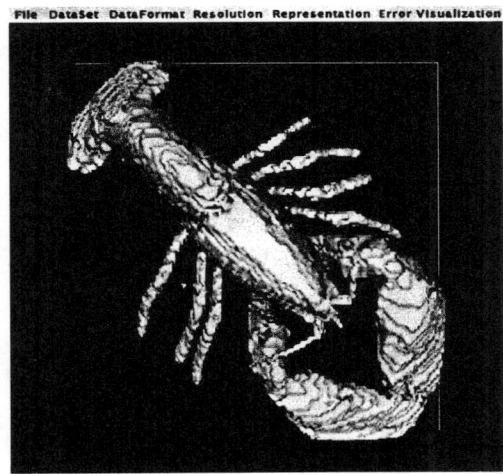

Figure 14: Three isosurfaces from a lobster data set, each with resolution 128^3 and an isovalue if 0.185: (top, left) a sample AR isosurface, (top, right) a sample SAR isosurface containing 47 2RTs, and (bottom, left) a sample SAR+ isosurface containing 22 2RTs. Yellow and red hue indicates occurrences of 2RTs.

Acceleration of Elastic Model's Motion Computation Based on Elastic Element Reduction

S. Miyazaki, J Hasegawa
Chukyo University
101 Tokodachi, Kaizu-cho, Toyota-city 470-0393, Japan

T. Yasuda, S. Yokoi
Nagoya University
Furo-cho, Chikusa-ku, Nagoya-city 464-8601, Japan

Abstract

This paper proposes a fast computation elastic model. It was constructed by a small number of elements. Elastic objects are constructed in various sizes of elements. Small elements are laid out on the surface and larger elements are confined to the center. A variety of element shapes and the way they fit into any voxel-based shape are presented here. It effectively reduces the number of elements, and saves computation time. This elastic element model is directed to the duties of real-time processing, performing consistent restoration, and being applicable to any shape of polyhedron elements.

Keywords: elastic object, deformable model, element reduction, acceleration, real time, computer graphics

1. Introduction

Physically-based modeling is an effective way to generate natural motion of deformable objects by defining a comparatively simple model that represents the local property of the object [1-3]. It has been developed in the field of computer animation for the purpose of generating real motion of deformation as an animation. Recently, its possibility is increasing to extend its real-time applications with high-resolution object models, thanks to great advances in computation performance. However, even with great advances in computation performance, if properties are limited to linear elasticity, high-resolution models are still hungry for computation power. It is necessary to construct objects with fewer elements.

Another function is to construct any shape of objects. Polygon-based models are popular ones in the field of real-time computer graphics. It can flexibly represent any shape with fewer elements. In general, the shape of elements should be equivalent in length in every direction for performing smooth deformation. It should be close to regular polyhedrons. Voxel-based models are another popular one which is often converted into polygon models for fast processing, if the object is non-deformable. However, it is suitable as deformable models, for it consists of the same size of cube. Conversions between polygon models and voxel ones have been studied for a long time and aren't complicated. Voxel models constructed from CT images are generally used in the field of medical imaging, one major field of study. Therefore, for now, the input shape is limited to a voxel model.

Constructing simple models suitable to its purpose is a necessity in real-time processing. For example, Promayon et al's model supposes elastic objects like a ball, in which an elastic surface like rubber surrounds air [4]. It consists of mass-and-spring lattice on the surface. In addition, the internal volume is constrained to be constant. As a result, this works to push every surface point to the outer sides. It really acts well with little computation. However, our interest is in the construction of general use and homogeneous elastic models rather than elastic models in which rubber-like models are arranged only on the surface. Then, in such models, elastic elements should be arranged in whole not only on the surface. Our study attempts the acceleration of computation in elements by employing variable sizes and reducing the number of elements.

2. Elastic Element

2.1 Overview

We also propose an original element model [5]. Many kinds of deformable models have been reported. Under the conditions of real-time processing, their foundations are classified into either mass-and-spring model or simplex element in Finite Element Method (FEM). Our model's criterion is different from those, but is derived from them. Restoration force is proportional to the displacements of vertices of the element from the reference position that gives its equilibrium shape. It is expanded from mass-and-spring models. In reference to displacement, its position is not given as a unit of length but as a unit of shape, this is common in FEM elements. These three models almost all similarly define the same force, when object deformation is small. However, our model does not have such serious problems like the other two models have, when object deformation is large.

2.2 Problems in Mass-and-Spring Models

Mass-and-spring model has an advantage that the implementation is easy, but the restoration force becomes more improper as the mass-and-spring lattice deforms. Especially, when the object is heavily compressed, almost all springs become parallel to each other. As a result, restoration force is depleted by competition among springs (Figure 1).

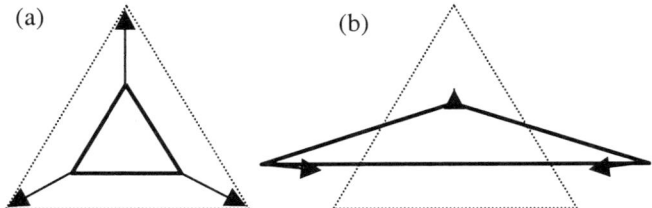

Figure 1 For mass-and-spring models, the bold lines represent the deformed state, the dotted lines represent the reference shape, and the arrows represent restoration force. In (b), you can see restoration force depleted in the vertical direction.

Promayon et al's model modifies this problem. They choose some neighboring vertices to define a base plane in elements and decide the force of some other neighboring vertices to keep location relative to the plane. This works well in their use of constructing elastic surfaces. Base planes should be laid along the object surface. However, applying the model in general to any shape element is not recommended. Deciding which vertices make the base plane is complicated.

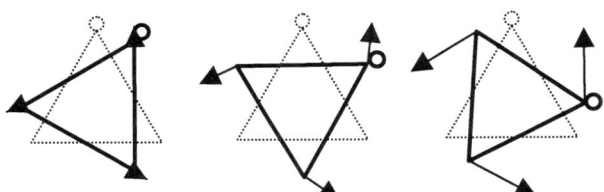

Figure 2 For simplex elements in FEM, unexpected force appears as large as its element rotation. Inadequacies have to be overcome in order to apply this to object rotating cases.

2.3 Problems in FEM Elements

FEM element's advantage is that physical properties of real material are directly reflected to the model. It works well in such cases when its usage is limited to static behavior in stable layouts. However, in general use, problems occur during the object's rotation around itself. If the reference shape is stable at all times, as rigid rotation deviates from the reference, force error rapidly becomes as large as the rigid rotation (Figure 2). This theory exists only under small deformative objects. This problem will be solved by finding the 'axis of principal stress' and also by employing dynamic reference shapes which can chase deformed elements like ones being used in our model. Even if this theory is considered, our model is superior in shape flexibility as shown in 2.4.

2.4 Shape Flexibility

Our model permits any shape of elements. It is a great privilege constructing the proposed elastic model. In FEM models, elements must be subdivided into the base shapes of triangle or tetra. Mass-and-spring model's problem, is how improper layout springs keep truss structure. The resultant force is often inadequate even if the layout is completed, because of competition among springs.

2.5 Stability

Elastic elements sometimes strongly deform by itself, especially when too strong a force acts upon it. It may cause an inconsistent state, in which an element turns itself inside out. Our model works to restore inconsistent states back to consistency, in any case. It is an unavoidable necessity for other models to detect inconsistent states and to cope with them. Although, this is not so easy, as computation time increases.

2.6 Implementation

This subsection easily explains our model. It decides elastic force only depending on a simple assumption. Elastic force is proportional to displacements of vertices; they are not ones in springs but ones from reference shapes. The reference shape's location is decided in each element as is; both the resultant internal force and the moment of force of the internal stresses are equal to zero vectors.

$$\sum_i r_i \times k(R_i - r_i) = k \sum_i r_i \times R_i = \vec{0} \quad (1)$$

Here, vector R_i and r_i are relative positions of vertex i in the reference shape and the deformed shape with respect to the center of gravity, respectively (Figure 3). Force is proportional to displacements with proportionality constant k.

In the implementation, the initial values of $\{R_i\}$ are registered as $\{Ro_i\}$, and $\{R_i\}$ is defined as a result of the rotation of $\{Ro_i\}$ around the center of gravity.

$$\sum_i r_i \times M\, Ro_i = \vec{0} \quad (2)$$

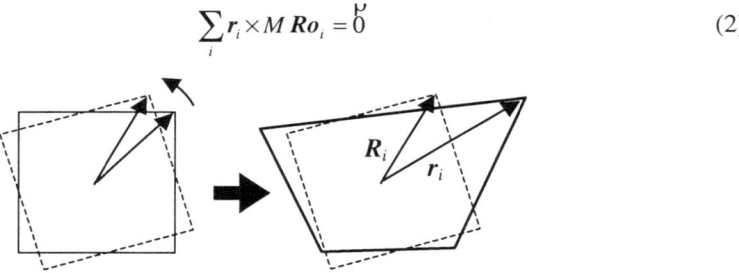

Figure 3 Position vectors have respect to the center of gravity, in the original reference shape, rotated reference shape, and in the deformed shape.

When deformed shape { r_i } and the initial reference shape { Ro_i } are given, rotation matrix M and the reference shape { R_i } are sequentially decided. It specifies a unique reference shape location. It means removing the rigid rotation component in deformation before deciding displacements. Ref [5] presents a fast computation method of Equation (2) for 3D models. This procedure has little complications, but as a result, its computation time is almost the same as mass-and-spring models.

It works equally as FEM elements when shapes are base ones, for exact compatibility, reference shapes should be distorted in Poison's ratio. More vertex shapes should be subdivided into base shapes, in every base shape, to evaluate distortions in more detail. Our model regards distortion as being constant in polygons. Preciseness is lost in deciding force, but it saves computation time.

3. Gradational Resolution Model

Considering that element reduction procedure is performed by replacing a few elements with one element that fills their domestic spaces. If this procedure can be applied only to elements whose deformations are comparatively small, this might be an effective element reduction. However, including procedures to search such elements spoils the acceleration of computation, because its computation time is proportional to the number of elements. It is difficult to predict deformation tendencies beforehand, but it can be said that deformation is large around contact points with rigid objects. External force from rigid objects is far larger than internal force in elastic objects, and it works directly on the surface of elastic objects. Element's sharing vertices also constrain neighboring elements' deformation. This works less on the surface where fewer neighboring elements are joined.

Based on the above considerations, here we propose a model whose element sizes can be gradationally increased from the surface to the center. It effectively saves computation time and maintains voxel's original resolution on the surface.

3.1 Implementation

Vertex density in elements should be higher on the surface side than in the center, like one shown in Figure 4. Followings simply explain construction procedure with this element model in a two dimensional case. In the first step, voxel data is scanned in every neighboring 2x2-voxels independently to find surface 2x2-voxel ones, which includes boundaries of voxel object surface. Figure 5 shows how to layout vertices on them, that has variation in the number of 1-voxels. Then, all of the surface unit's 1-voxels are changed into 0-voxels. This procedure simultaneously prepares us for the next step. After this procedure, 2x2-voxel-units consist of either four 0-voxels or four 1-voxels. Then, procedure is repeated and 2x2 units become one voxel in the next step. These procedures resulted in such a model shown in Figure 6. Figure 7 is an example of a manipulation environment.

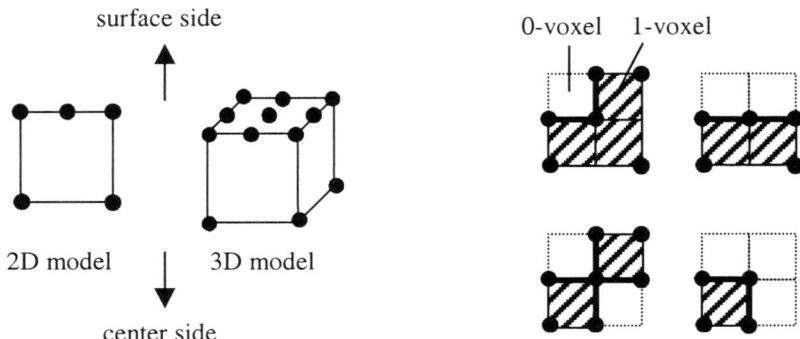

Figure 4 Elements in gradational resolution models.

Figure 5 Variations in vertex layouts. Bold boundaries represent voxel object surfaces.

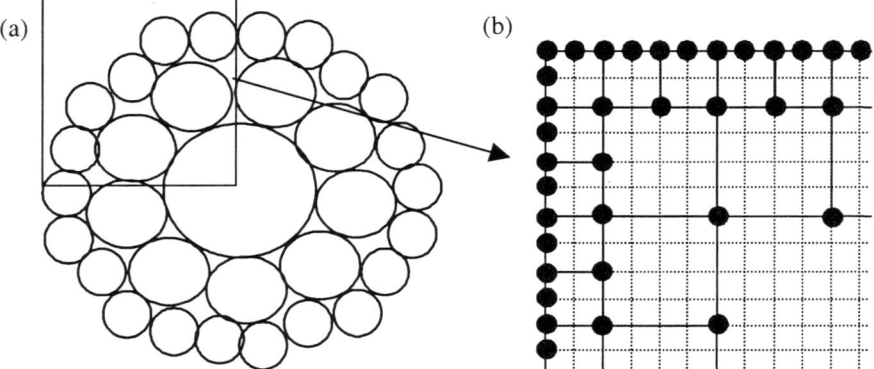

Figure 6 The image illustration (a), and the concrete image illustration (b) of a gradational resolution model. (b) is a magnified illustration of a corner of a cubic object.

3.2 Performance of element reduction

The number of elements increases proportionally to the third power of object resolution. Computation's size is roughly proportional to the number of nodes. A n by n by n cubic voxel object has 8 n^3 nodes. They are reduced into 26 n^2 by the gradational resolution model, which has the same resolution as the surface. In three dimensional cases, a sphere-like object, which has 552 voxel elements before reduction, can fit mostly into a 10x10x10 cubic volume. It was reduced into 74 elements in the experiment. Table 1 shows real computation time running at PCs highest performance. It can process about 100 element 3D objects in real time at this current performance speed ($k = 10000$).

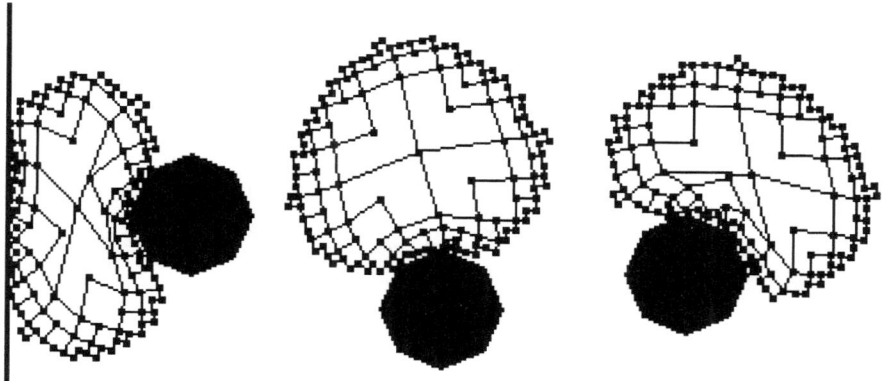

Figure 7 Implementation of manipulation environments. An elastic object can be manipulated by a rigid circle manipulator which is controlled by mouse.

CPU	Pentium4 (1.9G)	AthlonXP (1900+)
computation time per vertex(s)	7.06	4.22
max element number ($k=10000$)	68	114

Table 1 Real computation time and maximum element number available for real-time processing.

3.3 Advantage of discretization

The Euler method is a standard solution of motion computation, for it sequences dynamic motions, step by step. For fast computation, time steps should be as large as possible with consideration to the cycle of simple harmonic motion, performed by elastic elements. However, it delays internal force propagations in objects proportional to the number of medium elements. Our element reduction decreases this problem.

4. Conclusions

We proposed a fast computation elastic model constructed by a small number of elements. Elastic objects were constructed in various sizes of elements. Small elements were laid out on the surface and larger ones were confined to the center. A variety of element shapes and the way they fit into any voxel-base shape were presented here. It effectively reduced the number of elements, and saved computation time.

The elements in Figure 4 make too rapid a gradation for high resolution models. So, degrees in gradation should be controlled depending on applications.

Acknowledgments

We would like to thank Professor Teruo Fukumura of Chukyo University for his encouragement and assistance. Special thanks to Marvin Lenoar, a great English teacher and for English assistance on this project. This research was supported in part by the grant-in-aid for Private University High-Tech Research Center from the Ministry of Education, Japan.

References

[1] Terzopoulos D. Platt J. Barr A. Fleisher K. "Elastically Deformable Models", Computer Graphics, 21(4), pp.205-214, 1987.
[2] Terzopoulos D. Fleisher K. "Modeling Inelastic Deformation: Viscoelasiticity, Plasticity, Fracture", Computer Graphics, 22(4), pp.269-278, 1988.
[3] Norton A. Turk G. Bacon B. Gerth J. Sweeney P. "Animation of Fracture by Physical Modeling", The Visual Computer, 7, pp.210-219, 1991.
[4] Promayon E. Baconnier P. Puech C. "Physically-based Deformations Constrained in Displacements and Volume", In Computer Graphic Forum, 15(3), pp. 155-164, Eurographics96, 1996.
[5] Miyazaki S. Hasegawa J. Yasuda T. Yokoi S. "A Deformable Object Model for Virtual Manipulation Based on Maintaining Local Shapes", SCI2001, Orland, 2001, (URL : http://www.sccs.chukyo-u.ac.jp/~miyazaki/)

Explosive Impact on Real-time Deformable Terrain

Tao Ruan Wan and Wen Tang*

School of Informatics, University of Bradford
Bradford, BD7 1DP, UK

*School of Computing and Mathematics,
University of Teesside,
Middlesbrough, TS1 3BA, UK

Abstract

In this paper, we describe methods for real-time modelling explosions and their impacts on realistic deformable terrains. Our simulation method elaborates a strength and damage model for terrain material under explosion shock wave loading. The creation of the terrain deformation is tightly coupled with an adaptive mesh algorithm for dynamic level of detail terrain rendering to achieve both visual realism and frame coherences. A novel particle system is developed to model the effects of falling soil and rock masses distributed around the explosion area to create realistic variations. The techniques presented here can be adapted by the most of systems involving dynamic terrain rendering for modelling explosions and topology changes of the terrain for real-time interactive applications. The integrated terrain deformation also offers adaptive mechanisms for further system development.

Keywords: Real-time Deformable Terrain, Procedure Animation, Explosion and Shock Wave, Damage Loading, Explosive Impact, Adaptive Meshing

1. Introduction

Terrain is a centerpice in many virtual 3D applications. Deformable terrain is a feature rarely found in current Real-time simulation systems such as Real-time Strategy Games (RTS). A system that realistically simulates terrain deformations and the explosion impact in real-time not only increases the visual realism of the virtual environment but also alters actions and strategies within the environment. In many computer systems, the traditional isometric view has been changed into fully 3D environments [1,2]. Some of the interactions in the systems were of mass destructions and explosions causing damages and would destroy buildings and other objects, but the terrains in these systems could hardly be damaged by such shock wave loading.

Distractions and damages of explosion impacts are one of the most dramatic phenomena found in nature. An attempted description of explosions was given as: A sudden burst of energy from a mechanical, chemical, or nuclear source causes a pressure wave to propagate outwards. The blast wave "shocks up", creates a nearly discontinuous jump in pressure, density, and temperature along the wave front."[3].

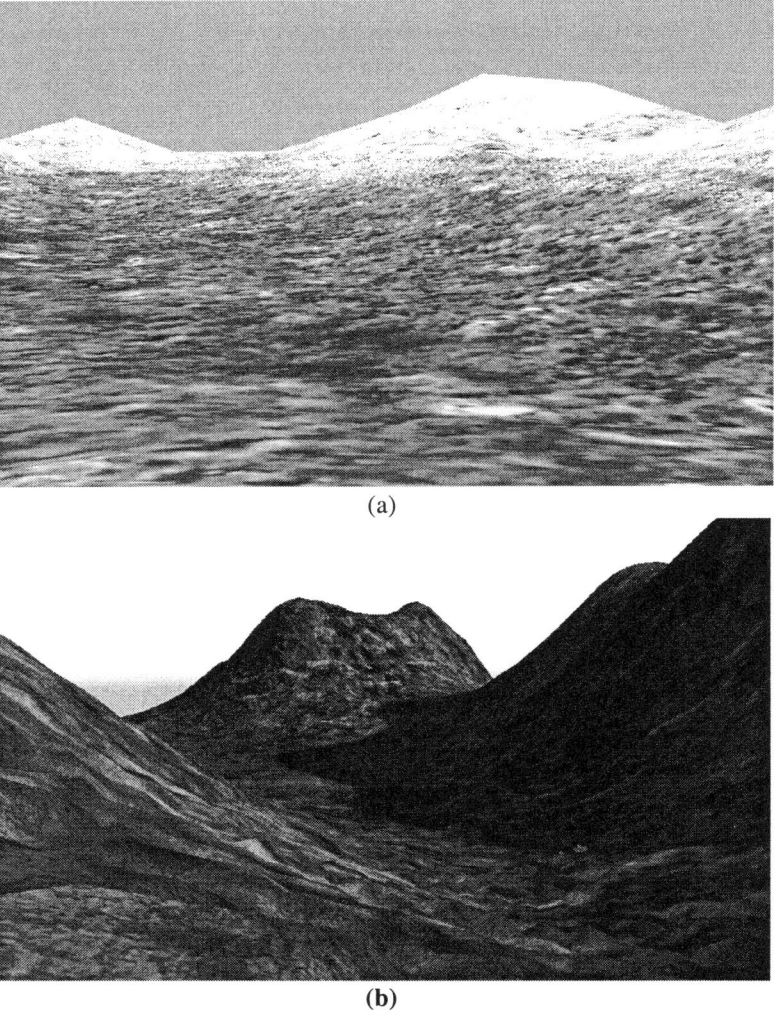

Figure 1: *Two example images of terrain generated by our system*

The complex special effects of explosions are dangerously recreated in much smaller scales for action films in Hollywood. Only limited achievements have been made to simulate those effects due to the incomplete discoveries of the explosion phenomena itself in science and engineering, and the computational complexity of the visual simulations. Recently, in the computer graphics community, a number of publications have particularly addressed the issues of modelling and simulating explosions based on physically based approaches [3, 4, 5]. For real-time interactive simulation systems, the limited computational resources for such special visual effects would impose extra constrains to the simulations. Particle systems and image based techniques are two commonly used methods for fire, explosions, and cloud simulations in real-time systems [6, 7].

Terrain deformations, fractures with the impact of explosions have been largely neglected in interactive systems, which would certainly add extra features and functions to the simulations. It is not surprising since modelling explosions and any gaseous phenomena is a difficult and time-consuming task for animators. It is also a challenge for procedure animations. Incorporating the impact of explosions in real-time systems demands simulation algorithms to be easy to use and be adaptable by the terrain rendering engine. Hence, a number of issues would be raised in both technique implementations and system design. From the point of view of terrain modelling, the design of the terrain structures should allow fast and efficient generations and deformations of the terrain on general PCs available to most users. The techniques should also enable the most terrain rendering tasks to be taken effectivly by graphics cards so that more CPU time available for other areas of the system such as 3D sound and artificial intelligence. The terrain deformation model should make the most use of the terrain internal structures so that the topology changes of the terrain after explosions can be adapted effectively by the system. The adaptation of the deformations is also important for further implementations for the dynamic object behaviours modelling within the system.

In this paper, we describe a procedure model to generate realistic explosions and terrain deformations in real-time. Our method simulates strength and damage model for virtual terrain material under explosion and shock wave loading. The generations of the terrain craters are tightly coupled with an adaptive mesh algorithm of the simulation system to achieve visual realism with high dynamic level of rendering. The techniques can be used to simulate explosions and the topology changes of virtual terrain for real-time applications.

The next section discusses related work in the field of simulating fire, gas, explosions, and as well as terrain modelling techniques. The following section introduces the method for terrain generation in the context of real-time adaptive rendering implemented in our simulation system. The section 4 discusses the explosion theory and blast wave pressure profile. We also present the details of our implementations for terrain deformation with explosion impacts in this section. Subsequently, section 5 outlines some simulation results, while section 6 concludes and discusses future work.

2. Related Work

In the past, many research attempts have been made to create realistic 3D terrains. Quite separately, simulating and animating gaseous phenomena such as fires, smokes, hot turbulent gases, and explosions, have also received much attention in the computer graphics community.

2.1 Simulating and Animating Gaseous Phenomena

There are generally two different classes of approaches in this area. Of which, particle simulation techniques have been used to generate visual effects of fire, smoke, and explosions with aid of texture mapping and advanced rendering techniques [7, 8, 9]. Fire, grass and trees have been simulated using the techniques in [6]. A procedure model was used to generate realistic 2D fires based on a noise function [23]. 3D procedure textures were generated for representing clouds [24]. Motion characteristics of smoke have been simulated using randomly generated velocity fields based on a Kolmogoroff filter [25]. Although the work mentioned above has not directly modeled the physical properties of the gaseous substance, particle systems with advanced texturing and rendering techniques have been widely accepted as fast visual simulation tools for the special effects in computer graphics (CG).

Recently, physically-based approaches have been taken in order to model the dynamic motions of fire, smoke, and explosions based on fluid dynamic models and numerical integration methods. Algorithms and numerical solving techniques were adapted and modified from the field of computational fluid dynamics (CFD). A visual simulation model of smoke has been presented based on Euler equations to describe the motions of coarse grids of smoke particles [26].

Simplified Navier-Stokes equations have been used to calculate computational fluid dynamics of hot turbulent gas [27]. More recently, three papers have particularly addressed explosions. Yngve, O'Brien, and Hodgins have simulated the propagation of an explosion through the surrounding air using a CFD model based on the equations for compressible viscous flow [3]. The system in [3] models the shock wave and surrounding air as a fluid discretized over a three dimensional rectangular linear grid. The system simulates the volume of an explosion and damaged objects by converting the objects from triangular mesh representations to voxels in order them to be displaced. Connected voxels have also been used in the work done by Mazarak et al. for animating exploding objects [4]. The explosion was simulated by the wave propagation based on a blast wave model. A visual model for blast waves and two-dimensional fractures was presented by Neff and Fiume [5]. The three simulations have referenced blast wave models found in material engineering and engineering studies [10, 11, 12, 13]. Different to previous work [7, 8, 9, 23, 24, 25], the papers [3, 4, 5] have addressed the modeling issues for blast waves and its impact to sounding objects. Although visually realistic, the physically-based simulations of this kind are generally requiring numerically solving the equations of the motions of the gas and waves. The computational processes have to be stable enough to produce animations therefore the simulations were generally not real-time. Achieved displacement animations of the damaged objects such as walls and glass were in relatively smaller scales. A simple and fast fluid solver based on the Fourier transform has also been presented, which simplifies many aspects of the fluid dynamic models [28]. This model was used to generate real-time fluid behaviours for computer animations at the cost of sacrificing the accuracy for speed and stability.

Our objective is to real-time simulate explosions and their impacts on terrain for interactive applications. Hence, there is a need to develop fast algorithm which is simple and easy to be implemented to model the physics properties of the phenomena realistically and effectively. Our implementation is coupled with a model to elaborate the damage and deformations of the terrain under shock wave loading. We introduce a novel particle system to model the after effects of an explosion on the ground by calculating the particle distributions on the ground.

2.2 Algorithms for Real-time Terrain Generation

An fast algorithm for terrain generation is one of the major concerns. There are a number of developed techniques for terrain generations. For example, voxel rendering method has been used in many interactive systems such as computer games for terrain generation [14, 15, 16]. The advantages of the method are that the landscapes are extremely detailed and have "organic" look due to the ray cast rendering. However, voxel rendering is very constraining and CPU intensive. It will result poor quality rendered terrain on low end computers. Some optimisation algorithms, such as the one introduced by Cohen-Or et al. [17], which is a form of level of detail (LOD), can be implemented to speed up the rendering process. Despite many advantages in voxel techniques and the advances of techniques in speed [18], voxel method remains too slow for today's graphics card. Determining where the ray intersects with objects is highly processor intensive and the algorithm also lacks support of hardware acceleration. Modern consumer level graphics cards only accelerate polygon data. With the huge difference that hardware acceleration can make, voxel rendering does not seem to be the way for our implementation purposes. On the other hand, polygon terrains are most used data structures in real-time applications due to the fact that polygon-based terrains with high level of details have become gradually achievable and feasible. Methods have been presented to generate terrains using height fields incorporated with defined polygon structures and Level of Detail (LOD) algorithms [18, 19, 20]. Duchaineau et al presented a ROAM (Real-time Optimally Adapting Meshes) algorithm for maintaining an optimal polygon mesh [20]. The method uses a set of heuristics to determine which part of a terrain should be rendered using more polygons than other parts. The method can also implemented with camera system to speed up the overall rendering process.

3. Terrain Modelling with Roam Algrithm

The local adaptive feature of the ROAM algorithm offers a coherent data structure suitable for modelling dynamical features of terrain topology in real-time. ROAM algorithm has been implemented in our system for dynamically updating the terrain deformations after explosions. The essence of the ROAM algorithm is the techniques to split and merge triangles wherever and whenever it is necessary according to terrain variations, distances from camera, and maximum polygon counts. Finally, as an added on advantage of the data structure, highly efficient frustum culling can also be achieved.

3.1 Binary Triangle Trees for Terrain Deformation

In our system, the terrain could be loaded from a height-map, converted to a polygon mesh and then, during the application process, be updated and continuously optimised. Figure 1 shows two examples of terrain generated by our system. The terrain system also allows users to configure the detail settings in order to run optimally on their personal machine. The algorithm could even be aware of current frame rates and consider this when optimising the terrain. The terrain generated in our system uses two types of image maps: actual height map for terrain topology and the terrain type map for example green represents grass, yellow represents rock and blue as water.

The binary triangle structure is the key component of the program. It deals only with right-angled isosceles triangles. The terrain is originally represented by two right-angled triangles. At the top level of a binary triangle tree, there is one triangle, which then has two descendants, and each of them have two descendants etc as shown in Figure 2. It is important to mention that since the structure contains only triangles, and the terrain to be built is square, there must actually be two trees at all times. Because each level of subdivision does not replace the level above, the number of triangles after n levels of division is: $2^{(n+1)} - 1$. Although this is quite a high number of triangles, only the bottom level are drawn while the rest can be used for frustum culling and collision detections.

Each triangle is stored as a node, with each node being aware of its 'parent' and its two 'children' as shown in Figure 3. These structures are linked together and are often treated as one. Each node has to keep track of several things in order for the structure to be maintained. Each node needs to know its three neighbours. These are highly important for coping when a triangle has to be split. The terrain system also allows triangle merging according to the distance to camera to accomplish rendering priorities.

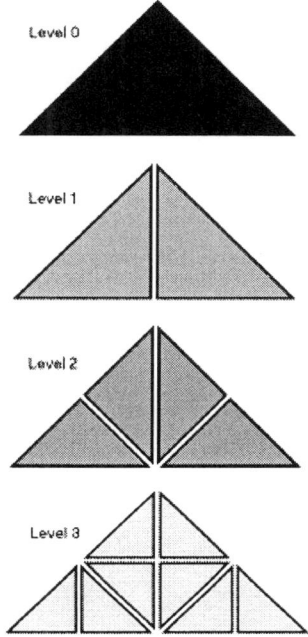

Figure 2: *The triangle split*

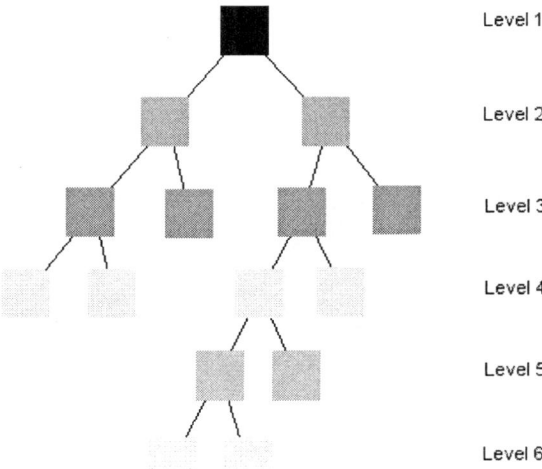

Figure 3: *The resulting tree structure*

3.2 Local Adaptive Meshing

Depending on the local variance of a particular area in a terrain, which is recorded in the terrain height map, the triangle node in our system would be further split to add more details locally until a visual tolerance has been reached. The local variance is the actual difference in height values of the interpolated midpoint for a triangle node and the height field sample at the point. A vertex in world space can be donated as $V_w(V_x, V_y, V_z)$, where V_z is the height at the domain coordinate of vertex v, which is defined by the value in height map, $V_z = Z(v)$.

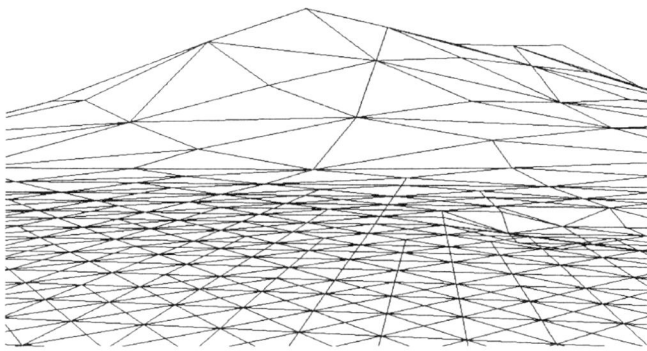

Figure 4.a: *A wire frame representation of the terrain with different mesh LODs*

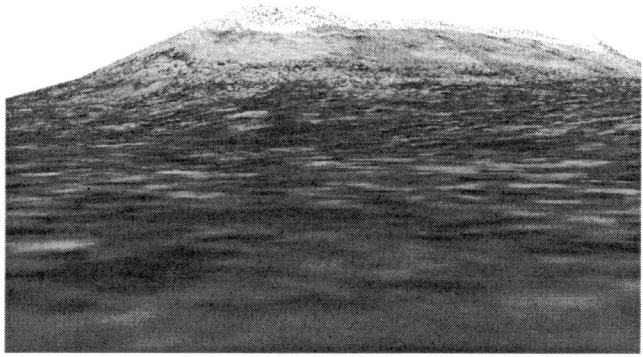

Figure 4.b: *A rendered terrain image with level of details*

The depth of the tree node to be further spilt is calculated by equation 1 where, δ is the visual tolerance.

$$\left| Z_{center} - (Z(V_{left}) + Z(V_{right}))/2 \right| \leq \delta \qquad (1)$$

When the terrain is to be deformed, the variance calculation would be required for each frame. Our procedure model that simulates a shock wave loading would automatically generate a local map for an exploded area. At the particular exploded location, the terrain will be regenerated locally. Figure 4.a shows the different polygon mesh details of a terrain in a wire frame representation. The same part of the terrain is shown in Figure 4.b in rendered image. The local mesh generations by the algorithm represent the local topology details according to the information from the terrain height map and the δ settings. Triangles are spit and merged at different locations of the terrain.

4. Modelling Explosive Impact on Terrain

4.1 Explosion Theory

Explosions rapidly release energies that generate shock waves. When a large quantity of energy is generated into a small volume, fireballs will develop and expand. A blast wave will form and propagate at supersonic speed. Blast wave physics accounts for the development and radiation of this directed explosion energy in terms of pressure changes across air and its impact on surrounding objects. Energy transfer of this kind is not by conductance of heat, but by shock. The initial pressure may increase thousand fold or more above the atmosphere pressure P_0 which violently forces objects within the wave front to be fractured and propelled outwards.

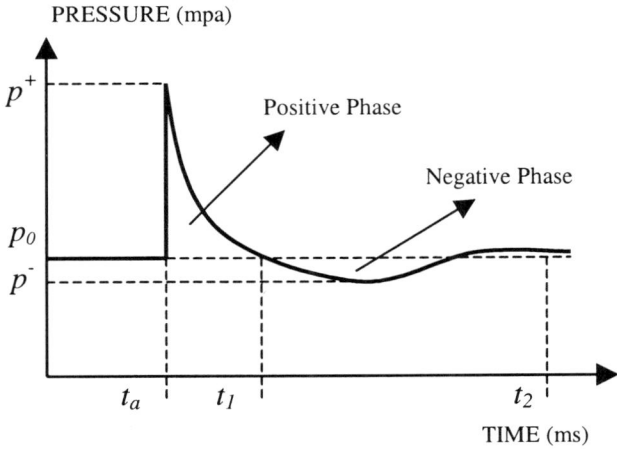

Figure 5: *An illustration of a time dependent blest curve*

The drastic increase of pressure at time t_a is normally referred as peak overpressure P^+. During a period of time t_1-t_a, wave pressure decays and approaches P_0 then starting a so called 'negative phase' with pressure below P_0. The negative phase ends with the pressure reaching back P_0 again during a period of time t_2-t_1. As an ideal shock wave front in air is spherical, the characteristics of the impact are functions of distance from the centre of the source R and explosion time t. The time dependent pressure profile of an ideal explosion is shown in Figure 5. The pressure profile can be described by the modified Friedlander equation [13].

$$P(t) = P_0 + P^+ \; (1-t/(t_1-t_a))e^{-bt/(t_1-t_1)} \qquad (2)$$

In equation 2, b is a customizable coefficient with values for different explosions.

The hydrodynamic quantities of objects in shock waves can be algebraically described to follow the general laws of conservation of mass, momentum, and pressure [29].

$$v_p = V_0 \bullet (P(t) - P_0)/D; \qquad (3)$$
$$V = (D - v_p) \bullet V_0/D; \qquad (4)$$
$$E = E_0 + 0.5 \bullet (P(t) + P_0)(V_0 - V); \qquad (5)$$

Where V_p is the mass velocity, i.e. the velocity of particles behind the shock, V is the specific volume, P is pressure, E is the internal energy, D is a material dependent constant, and the subscript '0' refers to the initial quantities of the parameters.

The spherical blast waves described above are in the states where the waves propagate freely through air. In practice, the waves are seriously modified when they encounter any solid or denser objects, as they reflect from the object or diffract around it [13]. As shown in Figure 6, there are three types of shock waves in propagation in terms of incident shock I, reflected wave R, and Mach wave ρ that connects the intersection of R and ρ to the ground surface S.

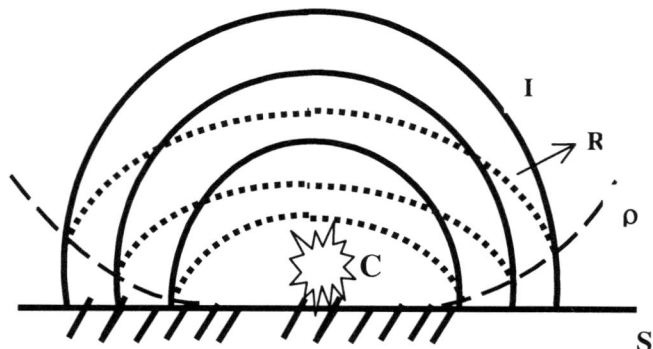

Figure 6: *Strong shock wave propagation*

The simulation of the explosions in our system is assumed to take a form of spherically symmetric flow. Therefore, an analytic solution can be found and adapted to the simulation.

4.2 Simulating Fireballs behind the Shock Wave

The shock waves of an explosion are normally invisible. During the explosion, fireballs will develop and grow, which can be simulated as a cloud of particles in very high temperatures for visual effects. Fireballs are forced or momentum-driven particle clouds that behave differently from buoyancy-driven flow such as smoke. The motion of the particle clouds is motivited by the shock wave initially and expands at a much slower speed than the shock wave propagation. In order to simulate the flow motion of these particles, the governing equations 2-5 are used. A combination of two types of fireballs is used to simulate the incident fireball flow propagation and reflected propagation from the ground surface.

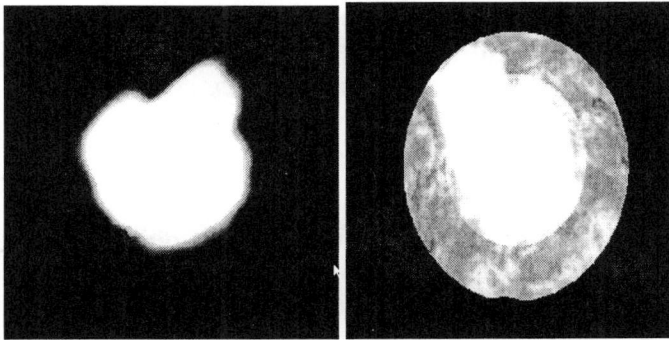

Figure 7.a: *Top down view of an explosion simulation*

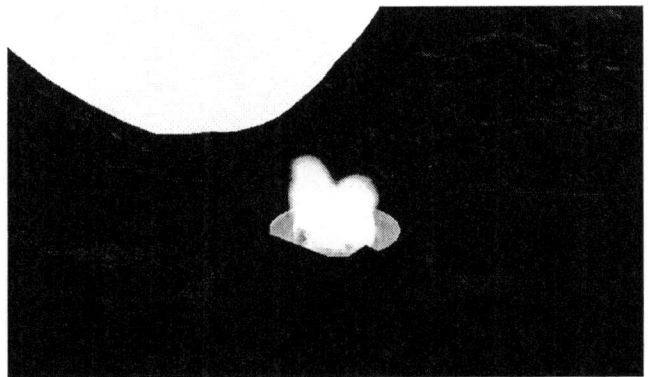

Figure 7.b: *Simulated fireballs at the starting state*

Figure 7.c: *Simulated fireballs in propagation*

At each time step t, acceleration on each particle is calculated by differentiating the equation 3. $a_t = \partial v/\partial t$ The velocity at the time step is calculated as $v_t = v_{t-1} + a_t t$. Using v_t for the particle velocity and update volume V by equation 4. In this way we can simulate the explosion fireball effectively. Figures 7.a, b and c show a number of snapshots of simulated fireballs.

4.3 A Model for Terrain under Shock Wave Loading

One of our objectives is to model the impact of explosions on terrain. Terrain deformation under shock wave loading is an issue concerned with modelling the dynamic response of the terrain material. In the field of engineering, dynamic response of material such as rock and soil in explosions is a challenging topic itself. Research studies in Geology physics and structure engineering have been developing empirical and theoretical models to describe the behaviours of different materials in explosions [21, 29]. This still, however, lacks strength and failure models for different materials which would reassemble the real life scenarios, because most of the existing models were developed under static conditions which did not account for the dynamic response of large scale and rate effects of masses, such as terrain mass displacements. The material response in an explosion generally consists three phases. During phase 1 the material is being compacted in shock loading. Bulking takes place after porosity of the material. Phase 2 begins after shock pressure reached the overpressure. In phase 2, the material would be damaged. In phase 3, velocities of masses are decreasing as inverse to the cube of the distance to the explosion source [21].

In the computer graphics simulations, much effort of the modelling tasks are emphasised on the visual effects and realism and therefore the simulation can be simplified using stochastic methods. As shown in Figure 8, from the centre of the explosion C, a volume with radius r_0 of the ground materials around the C is impacted by peak overpressure. The original ground structure is in a state of material failure which is being damaged and broken into particles by the violent shock forces when the peak shear strengths of the soil/rock materials are reached. Under the explosion forces, the damage materials are being pushed and propelled outwards outside of the area of the crater. The failure criterion τ_f of the materials can be described by following equation [30]

$$\tau_f = c_p + \sigma_n \quad (6)$$

where, c_p is the peak shear strength of the specific material and σ_n is the normal effective stress by the explosion.

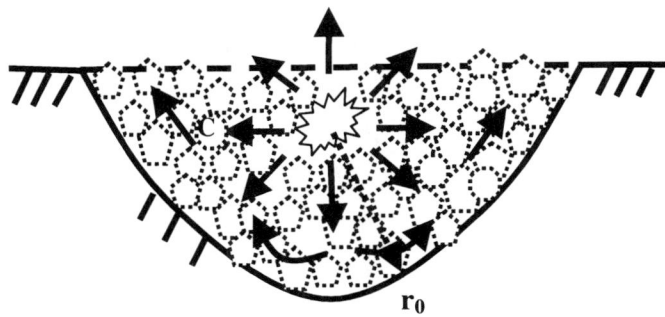

Figure 8: *Cross section view of the explosion impact on ground*

The forces exerted to the soil/rock particles can be estimated by equation 7.

$$f = p(r,t) S_{soilparicle} \quad (7)$$

where, p(r,t) is pressure received by a soil/rock element at a location from C with distance r over the time and S is the equivalent area of the element. Equation 2 and 7 are used to calculate the normal effective stress of an explosion. The impact strength of the explosion, the location of the charge C, and the resistance strength of the soil/rock materials determine the dimensions of a crater created by an explosion as indicated by Equation 8.

$$r_{max} = D \cdot L \cdot M \cdot P_{peak} \quad (8)$$

where D is dimension coefficient, L is the coefficient related to the location of the explosion charge C, M is the material resistant parameter and P_{peak} is the peak shear strength of the material. The cross section view of an explosion impact on terrain is illustrated in Figure 8.

5. Simulating the Accumulated Particle Displacement on the Ground

A particle system has been used in our work for simulating the accumulated displacements of soil/rock material masses after explosion. The damaged materials by the shock waves are displaced and accumulated in the areas around the explosion centre. The crater created on the ground and the effects of accumulation of falling soil/rock masses are finalised using a local adaptive re-meshing scheme to update the local topology of the terrain.

5.1 A Particle-based System for Modelling the Accumulated Effect of Soils/Rocks on the Ground

Under the explosion pressure, the original soil/rock structure of the ground is being damaged at the impact area. As a consequence, broken soil and rock masses were driven by the shock forces to fly over and accumulated in the vicinity area around the charge centre. In our system, the released soil and rock masses are represented by a system of particles that act following the physical law of motion. The effect of the mass displacement of terrain material is simulated using particle deposition.

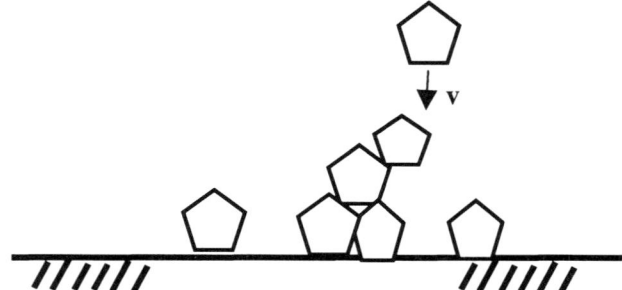

Figure 9.a: *Soil particles falling and accumulating*

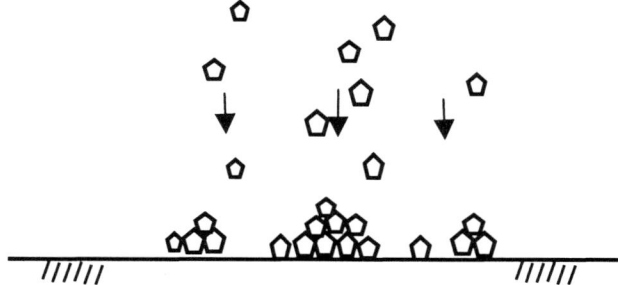

Figure 9.b: *Non-even distributions of the soil and rock masses*

Figure 9.c: *Cross section view of the final distributions*

As a general case, the locations of the falling soil and rock masses can be assumed as being to reach peak values at the location near the edge of the crater and gradually diminished along the direction of shock wave propagation. We developed a model to simulate and simplify this mass distribution by a two-dimensional probability density function to calculate the accumulated height field values. The height field value is estimated by equation 9.

$$h(x,y,t) = \int_0^t \frac{(x-r_0)^2 + (y-r_0)^2}{(\mu-r_0)^2} e^{-\frac{(x-r_0)^2+(y-r_0)^2}{2(\mu-r_0)^2}} dt \qquad (9)$$

where μ is the location of the peak value of the height field.

Furthermore, together with the emitting particles from the centre of the explosion, the particle system must also maintain the general law of conservation of mass, which is simplified as equation 10.

$$\Delta mass_{emitting} = \Delta mass_{accumulated} \qquad (10)$$

Figures 9.a and b show an illustration example, in which particles are falling down, set on the ground. Figure 9.c shows a cross section illustration of the final shape of the new ground formed by particle accumulation.

We generate dust particles using equation 9 and 10 and drop them on to the explosion spectrum map for local adaptive re-meshing.

5.2 Local Re-meshing

The simulation system detects the location of an explosion impact on the terrain ground. During the interaction process, if there is an impact or whatever change on the terrain, the system deforms the terrain by regenerating the local terrain structures around the effected area. Customisable parameters are assigned to terrain nodes according to the terrain type maps to record the local characteristics of the terrain based on the explosion information. The adaptive meshing algorithm integrated in our rendering engine is able to create the new ground by adaptively re-meshing the local terrain structure. The local variances created by the explosion are calculated as described in above sections. The adaptive mesh algorithm locally splits and merges the triangle nodes at real-time according to the regenerated variance values. The local topology of the terrain is hence being changed. Figures 10.a, b, and c show an example of an explosive impact on ground. Figure 10.a shows a ground, a part of the terrain undisturbed with mainly grass and soil features. Figure 10.b shows a rendered image of the damaged ground caused by the explosive impact. Figure 10.c shows a wire- frame image of the crater created. A top down view of the terrain is shown in Figure 10.d, which demonstrates the adaptive local level of details after an explosion.

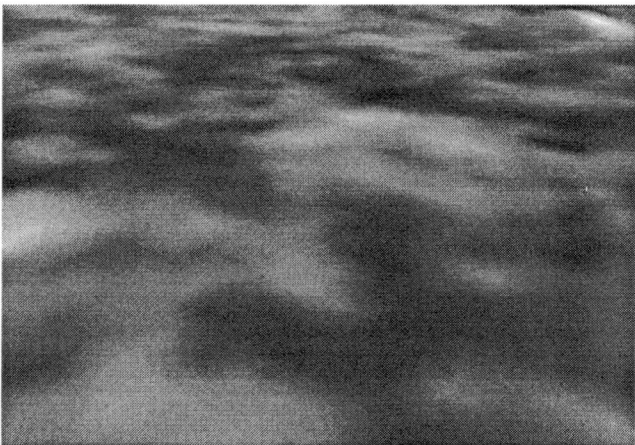

Figure 10.a: *Cross section view of the final distributions*

Figure 10.b: *Cross section view of the final distributions*

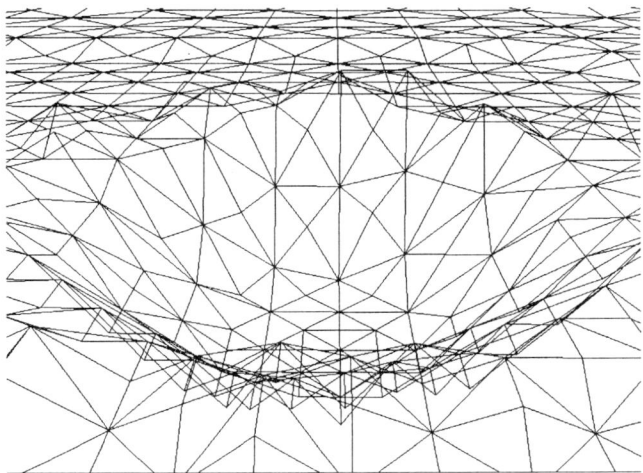

Figure 10.c: *Cross section view of the final distributions*

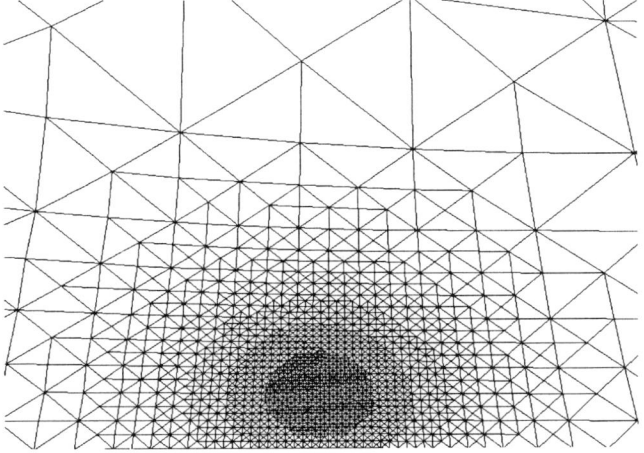

Figure 10.d: *Cross section view of the final distributions*

6. Conclusion

We have presented a real-time terrain deformation model with simulated explosion impacts to generate deformable terrain for interactive systems. Our goal is to simulate and model explosions and impacts on virtual terrain in real-time. By incorporating the adaptive meshing algorithm such as ROAM algorithm with a strength and damage model of terrain material, we are able to create local deformations under shock wave loading. The model is able to elaborate the physics properties of the explosions and the soil and rock materials in order to generate realistic simulation results. Practical modelling approached for explosion shock waves and soil mechanics are adapted from engineering field. A novel particle system has been introduced to model the effects of falling soil and rock particles distributed around explosions. Our simulation algorithm is fully integrated with the real-time terrain rendering techniques for polygon data structures so that one of the major advantages of our method is that it can be adapted by the most of interactive systems involving terrain rendering and polygon meshing. Algorithms described here are practical and easy to use. The generated results are effective and visually convincing.

However, since the simulation approach accounts for the most interactive applications, the polygon structures of the terrain would certainly impose constraints to the simulations. Similar to other real-time simulations, our simulation algorithm also has to sacrifice engineering accuracy for speed and visual realism. Further work should be concerning with implementing realistic adaptive object behaviours as the terrain is deformed.

References

[1] Ron Dulin, Total Annihilation, Review, *GameSpot UK*, http://www.gamespot co.uk/stories/reviews/ ,1997
[2] Ed Ricketts, Populous: The Beginning Game Review, PC Gamer Issue 65. http://www.pcgamer.co.uk/
[3] Yngve, G. D, O'Brien, J. F., and Hodgins, J. K. Animating Explosions, *Proceedings of SIGGRAPH 2000,* August 2000.
[4] Neff, M. and Fiume, E. A Visual Model For Blast Waves and Fracture, *Graphics Interface'99*, pages 193-2002, June 1999
[5] Mazarak, O., Martins, C., and Amanatides, J., Animating Exploding Objects, *Graphics Interface'99*, pages 211-218, June 1999.
[6] Reeves, W. T., Particle Systems – A Technique for Modeling A Class of Fuzzy Objects. ACM Transactions on Graphics, 2(2): pages 91-108, April 1983.
[7] Sims, K. Particle Animation and Rendering Using Data Parallel Computation. *Proceedings of ACM SIGGRAPH'90*, pages 405-413, August 1990.
[8] Witkin, A. and Kass, M. Reaction-diffusion Textures. *Proceedings of ACM SIGGEAPH'91*. pages 299-308, July 1987.
[9] Ebert, D.E., Texturing and Modeling: A Procedural Approach. Academic Press, 1994
[10] Kuethe, A.M. and Chow, C., Fundations of Aerodynamics: Bases of Aerodynamic Design. John Wiley and Sons, Inc.1998
[11] Kinney, G. F., Explosive Shocks in Air. The MacMillan Company. , New York, 1962

[12] Davison, L., Dennis E. Grady, and Mohsen Shahinpoor, Editors, High Pressure Shock Compression of Solids II: Dynamic Fracture and Fragmentation, Springer-Verlag, 1996.
[13] Baker, W. E., Explosions in Air, *University of Texas Press*, 1973
[14] Alan Watt and Fabio Policarpo, 2001, "3D Games Real-time Rendering and Software Technology", Addison-Wesley, 2001
[15] Foley and Van Dam et al., Computer Graphics – Principles and Practice, Addison-Wesley, 1996
[16] Champandard, A., " Voxel Landscape Engines", Daily Game Development News and Resources, http://www.flipcode.com/voxtut/.
[17] D. Cohen-Or, E. Rich, U. Lerner, V. Shenkar Real-Time Photo-Realistic Visual Flythrough. *IEEE Transactions on Visualization and Computer Graphics,* 2 (3) 1996, pages 255-265.
[18] Lindstrom, P., Koller, D., and Ribarsky, W., Real-Time, Continuous Level of Detail Rendering of Height Fields, Proceedings of *ACM SIGGRAPH 96,* pages. 109-118, August 1996
[19] Hoppe, H., Progressive Meshes, Proceedings of *ACM SIGGRAPH 96,* pages. 99-108, August 1996
[20] Duchaineau, M. Wolinski, M., Sigeti, D., Miller, M., Aldrich, C., and Mineev-Weinstein, M. ROAMinf Terrain: Real-time Optimally Adapting Meshes, In Proceedings *IEEE Visualization'97*, pages 81--88, 1997
[21] Vorobiev, O. Y., Antoun, T. H., Lomov, I. N., and Glenn, L. A, A Strength and Damage Model for Rock Under Dynamic Loading, Lawrence Livermore National Laboratory.
[22] Henrych, E., The dynamics of Explosion and Its Use. Elsevier Scientific Publishing Company, Amsterdam, 1979
[23] Perlin, K., An Image Synthesizer. In Proceedings of ACM SIGGRAPH'85, pages 287-296, July 1985
[24] Gardner, G., Visual Simulation of Clouds, In Proceedings of ACM SIGGRAPH'85, pages 297-303, July 1985
[25] Stam, J. and Fiume, E. Turbulent Wind Fields for Gaseous Phenomena, In Proceedings of ACM SIGGRAPH'93, pages 369-376, August 1993
[26] Fedkiw, R. Stam, J., and Jensen, H. W., Visual Simulation of Smoke, In Proceedings of ACM SIGGRAPH'2001, pages 23-30, 2001
[27] Foster, N. and Metaxas, D., Modeling the Motion of a Hot Turbulent Gas. In Proceedings of ACM SIGGRAPH'97, 58(5):pages 471-483, 97
[28] Stam. J, A Simple Fluid Solver based on the FFT, Journal of Graphics Tools 2001 (to appear), http://www.dgp.toronto.edu/people/stam/reality /Research/ pub.html
[29] Krasyuk, I.K. Application of Laser-driven Shock Waves in Studies of Thermal and Mechanical Material Properties, Conferences and Symposia, Physics-Uspekhi: 42(10), pages: 1056 – 1059, October, 1999.
[30] G. E. Barnes, Soil Mechanics; Principles and Practice, *MACMILLAN PRESS LTD*, 1995

Image-Based Modeling Using Viewpoint Entropy

Pere-Pau Vázquez[†] Miquel Feixas[†] Mateu Sbert[†]
Wolfgang Heidrich[*]
[†] Institut d'Informàtica i Aplicacions. Universitat de Girona
[*] University of British Columbia

Abstract

We present a new method to automatically determine the correct camera placement positions in order to obtain a minimal set of views for Image-Based Rendering. The viewpoints should cover all visible polygons with an adequate quality, so that we sample the polygons at enough rate. This allows to avoid the excessive redundancy of the data existing in several other approaches. The localisation of interesting viewpoints is performed with the aid of an information theory-based measure, dubbed viewpoint entropy. *This measure can be used to determine the amount of information seen from a viewpoint. We have also developed a greedy algorithm that aims to minimise the number of images needed to represent a scene.*

In contrast to other approaches, our system uses a special preprocess for textures to avoid artifacts appearing in partially occluded textured polygons. Therefore no visible detail of these images is lost.

Keywords: Image-Based Modeling, Image-Based Rendering, Viewpoint Selection, Entropy.

1 Introduction

Image-Based Rendering (IBR) [1, 2] has received a great interest since the last decade. It allows to compute realistic images at low cost thanks to the use of precomputed ones. However, most of the research has been focused on finding fast and reliable reconstruction algorithms instead of dealing with the important issue of correctly sampling the scene with the minimum number of images.

In this paper we present a new method to automatically select the camera positions that allow to minimise the amount of images used as representation. Such an algorithm should fulfill two conditions: all visible polygons must be covered, and the sampling rate should be high enough to allow for further reconstruction.

To decide which images are important we will use an information theory-based [3, 4] measure called *viewpoint entropy* [5]. This measure can be used to determine the amount of information captured from a viewpoint. Viewpoint entropy will be used together with a greedy algorithm to choose the minimal set of views that captures the maximum information on the scene. Moreover, we add a preprocess for textures that avoids visual artifacts produced when textured polygons are partially occluded in all available views.

The rest of the paper is organised as follows: In Section 2 we will present the previous approaches to this problem, Section 3 will present our method, in Section 4 we discuss the results, and finally, in Section 5 we conclude pointing out some lines of future research.

2 Previous Work

The problem of selecting an optimal set of images for Image-Based Rendering has not attracted much research. Most of the techniques use a fixed set of camera positions to capture the images of the scene (a notable exception is [6]). Then, these images are used to further rendering. Thus, in many cases the amount of redundant data is high, and being the capturing process costly, it becomes interesting to find a cheap way to determine which images are useful and which are not. This problem can be stated as trying to recover the maximum information of a scene with the minimum number of images. A similar problem has been examined by the robotics and AI communities, under the names of *sensor planning* or *next best view*.

2.1 Non Image-Based Modeling methods

The problem of finding a good view direction to help the user understand a scene has already been treated in Computer Graphics, but not with an Image-Based Modeling purpose in mind. Kamada and Kawai [7] consider a viewing direction to be good if it minimizes the number of degenerated faces under orthographic projection. This method fails when comparing scenes with equal number of degenerated faces and it does not ensure that the user will see a large amount of detail, as discussed in [8]. Barral et al [8] and Dorme [9] modify Kamada's coefficient in order to cope with perspective projections. Then they create a heuristic with some other parameters that weight both the number of faces seen from each point and the projected area, moreover they add an exploration parameter which accounts for the faces already visited. This way they define an evaluation function that allows to explore the scene in real time. However, they admit that they have not been able to determine a good weighting scheme for the different factors. This causes some problems with objects containing holes, as these are not captured properly by the algorithm.

In the robotics literature, the goal of selecting a small set of cameras which allow to observe all object surfaces has also been studied. Usually this problem is stated as: Determine where to place the $(N + 1)$st camera positions given N previous camera locations, for $N \geq 0$. Most approaches identify the next best view as the one that reveals the maximal amount of unknown detail of the scene being treated. Different assumptions are made in next best view systems in order to simplify the problem. Several systems require a CAD model of the scene to be known a priori. The two main approaches are: search-based and silhouette-based.

Search-based methods use optimization criteria to search a group of potential viewpoints of the next best view. Many of these methods employ range images to carve away voxels in a volumetric space. Wong et al [10] present an algorithm that searches all possible viewpoints, and selects the next best view as the one that can carve the most empty space voxels. This system is effective, but as pointed out by Massios and Fisher [11], such an approach may result in views that observe surfaces at very oblique angles, which is undesirable in IBR, as it yields poor sampling of colour in those surfaces.

Other approaches use the silhouettes of objects. For example, Abidi [12] develops a method that employs information theory. For a given view, a silhouette is divided into segments of equal lengths. Then, an information measure that computes the geometric and photometric entropy is found for each segment. The segment with the minimal entropy is chosen to select the next best view. This method assumes that by moving the camera to better observe the segment containing the least information, more information about the scene will be captured. Silhouette-based methods can often compute next best views more quickly than search-based approaches, however, it is not always possible to generate an accurate silhouete in an image for an arbitrary (for example indoor) scene.

2.2 Image-Based Modeling and Rendering

There are few papers which refer to the viewpoint selection process for Image-Based Modeling. Grossman and Dally [13] use 32 orthographic projections of an object. McMillan and Bishop [1] use cylindrical reference views placed on a regular grid in a scene. As none of these methods take care of sampling all surfaces, this can result in important regions of the scene remaining invisible to photographs, resulting in gaps or holes during the rendering process. Stürzlinger [14] creates a method for sampling all visible surfaces but does not address the problem of adequate coverage. Lischinski and Rappoport [15] use 6 perpendicular depth images placed on the boundaries of a cube (LDC). Fleishman et al [6] present an algorithm that adequately samples the surfaces visible from a certain walking region by placing the camera on a large number of positions on the boundary of the walking zone. The coverage quality criterion for a polygon is based on the projected area on a hemisphere for a camera position. The set of cameras is selected by choosing the cameras that sample a higher number of polygons at appropriate rate. Although this method is well-suited for the problem it addresses, the ordering of the cameras is guided by the amount of polygons sampled. If we had a scene with certain regions covered with a lot of very small polygons, this method could first sample parts of the scene that cover small areas instead of chosing other regions which cover larger portion of an image with less (or closer) polygons.

Hlavac et al [16] use a set of images to represent an object. Their objective is obtaining an IBR representation to be rendered by interpolation. Consequently they choose a set of reference images positioned around the object in intervals that guarantee error bounds below some threshold during reconstruction of intermediate views. However, this method only applies to single objects, instead of scenes, and their measure can only be used to compare two images, of the same object, and it is useless for views which show different parts of the same scene. Xiang *et al* [17] study the sampling of the plenoptic function for light fields from a spectral analysis of light field signals and using the sampling theorem. The authors determine the minimum sampling rate for light field rendering.

3 Automatic Camera Placement

In order to obtain a good set of cameras to sample a scene we need a measure of the goodness of an image. Fleishman *et al* [6] consider an image to be good if it samples a high number of surfaces with a certain quality. In contrast to this, we consider a view to be good if it shows a high amount of information coming from the surfaces that are covered with good quality. The amount of information can be measured with the use of *viewpoint entropy*. Viewpoint entropy has been successfully applied to compute the best views of an object and also to automatically determine a navigation path around an object or scene for Scene Understanding purposes [5]. We proceed now to describe viewpoint entropy measure.

3.1 Viewpoint Entropy

The *Shannon entropy* [3, 4] of a discrete random variable X with values in the set $\{a_1, a_2, ..., a_n\}$ is defined as

$$H(X) = -\sum_{i=1}^{n} p_i \log p_i,$$

where $p_i = Pr[X = a_i]$, the logarithms are taken in base 2 and $p_i \log p_i$ is equal to 0 for $p_i = 0$ for continuity reasons, as stated in [3, 4]. As $-\log p_i$ represents the *information* associated with the result a_i, the entropy gives the average *information* or the *uncertainty* of a random variable. The unit of information is called a *bit*.

To define the viewpoint entropy we use as probability distribution the relative area of the projected faces over the sphere of directions centered in the viewpoint (see **Figure 1**). Thus, the *viewpoint entropy* is defined [5] as

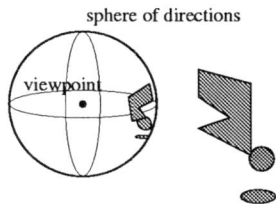

Figure 1: Viewpoint entropy is measured by projecting all the polygons in a bounding sphere centered in the viewpoint. The projected areas of every polygon are used as probability distribution of the entropy function.

$$H_p(X) = -\sum_{i=0}^{N_f} \frac{A_i}{A_t} \log \frac{A_i}{A_t},$$

where N_f is the number of faces of the scene, A_i is the projected area of face i, A_t is the total area covered over the sphere, and A_0 represents the projected area of background in open scenes. In a closed scene, or if the point does not *see* the background, the whole sphere is covered by the projected areas and consequently $A_0 = 0$. Hence, A_i/A_t represents the *visibility* of face i with respect to the point p. It is important to remark that the area A_i/A_t is proportional to the cosine of the angle between the normal of the surface and the line from the point of view to the object, and it is inversely proportional to the square distance from the point of view to the face. Therefore, A_i/A_t grows when the face is seen at a better angle and at a shorter distance.

The maximum entropy is obtained when a certain point can *see* all the faces with the same relative projected area A_i/A_t. So, if the object does not see the background, we will have a maximum entropy of $\log N_f$. By optimizing the value of entropy in our images, we are trying to capture the maximum number of faces under the best possible orientation. We define the *best* viewpoint as the one that has maximum entropy, i.e. maximum geometric information captured.

The computation of the viewpoint entropy can be done with the aid of graphics hardware using OpenGL, in a similar way to Barral et al [8]. The projected area of each face is computed by summing up all the pixels that belong to that face, weighted by the solid angle subtended by the pixel. To distinguish between the different polygons, the faces are colour-coded in an item buffer, and to cover all the surrounding of a viewpoint six different views are used. We can also restrict to compute the viewpoint entropy of a single projection [5], by using a perspective image and changing A_t by the corresponding value of the perspective frustra.

Figure 2: Scene of a classroom. The polyhedron in red depicts the walking region. The cameras are placed over its boundaries.

3.2 Image-Based Modeling using Viewpoint Entropy

In this Section we present an algorithm to select a set of images that accurately represent the scene to be rendered. As Fleishman et al [6] point out, it is important to notice that adequate coverage of every surface of a scene is only possible if we can restrict the user to walk in a region empty of objects. Otherwise, if the user can approach arbitrarily close to any surface no sampling rate can guarantee a lower bound on the coverage quality. We have also used a bounding box to define the walking region (see **Figure 2**). To determine a set of good viewing positions our algorithm uses three steps:

1. Select the positions of the camera on the bounding box representing the walking region.

2. Compute relative projected area of each polygon from all the camera positions using graphics hardware.

3. Select the best camera positions.

The first step consists in selecting a set of points placed in regular positions on the boundary of the walking region.

The most important step is the second one. We compute five projections from the selected viewpoints. These five views cover a cube all around the viewpoint but the view which points inside the waking region. Throughout all this process we store the contribution to entropy of every visible polygon seen from each camera. In addition to this, we also store in an array the maximum projected area of each face. This information will then be used to decide which cameras are chosen first. The maximum values array will be used to determine the coverage quality of a polygon in a certain view. For a concrete scene projection, the coverage quality Q of a polygon P will be computed as $Q = (A/A_{max}) * 100$ view, where A is the actual projected area and A_{max} is the maximum projected area of the polygon in all views.

The third step performs the actual selection of the best views. This is carried out with a loop iteration where viewpoint entropy is computed for each camera position, and taking the position with higher value, and masking out the already visited polygons. However, when computing viewpoint entropy, instead of considering all visible polygons, we only use the ones which present adequate coverage. That is, we compute the amount of information captured from each view coming from the polygons which are accurately sampled (i.e. their relative projected area is above a certain, user-defined, percentage of the maximum). This does not require any extra scene projection as we saved in step two the contributions to entropy of every polygon for each view. The loop stops when all visible faces have been captured. This algorithm is depicted in **Algorithm 1**.

Algorithm 1 Computes the minimum set of views which samples adequately all the polygons in a scene.

Select a set of points placed in regular positions on the boundary of the walking region
for all the points **do**
   Store an array with the projected area of each face from the point
   Update the array of maximum area projected for each face
end for
Recompute the entropies using *only the faces properly covered* according to the coverage quality given by the user
Select the point with maximum entropy
Accumulate the visited faces in a bitmap
while not finished **do**
   Recompute entropies using *only the faces properly covered* which *have not been visited* yet
   Select the point with maximum entropy
   Accumulate the visited faces in a bitmap
   finished $\leftarrow$ isFinished(numberofVisitedFaces)
end while

This method guarantees that we select first the camera positions which provide higher information on the scene. Previous methods [14] do not care on the accuracy of the views, or use as the best camera position the one which *sees* the higher number of polygons at good rate [6]. If some of the polygons appear small (are small or are far), this can lead to select an image which shows a high number of small polygons but which cover a small portion of the image, instead of choosing a different view with less but larger polygons. We can see

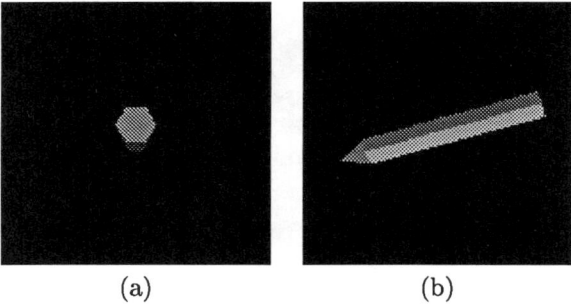

(a) (b)

Figure 3: Two different views of a pencil. In image (a), a higher number of polygons are captured properly, but the amount of information they provide is lower than in picture (b), where only two polygons are captured properly but they give higher amount of information on the object.

an example of this in **Figure 3**. **Figure 3a** shows a view of a pencil which sees several polygons at a good sampling rate, although the coverage of the image is smaller than in **Figure 3b** where only two of the polygons are captured with appropriate rate, but covering a larger portion of the image. Consequently, if the stopping condition is changed (for example we have a limited number of cameras, or we want to stop when a certain percentage of all visible faces have already been captured), the method ensures that the set of views will show a high amount of information on the scene. Notice that determining the optimal set is NP, as it is related to the Art Gallery problem [18]. With our method we obtain a good suboptimal, which is enough.

3.3 Texture sampling

Up to now we have seen how to select a minimum set of views which captures all visible polygons in a scene with adequate coverage. However, handling with textures is more difficult. When a polygon is partially occluded in all available views, our method guarantees that we are obtaining the best projection. As large polygons of the scene are first discretised, it is likely that the whole polygon will appear in any view. However, if this does not happen, the polygon will be undersampled. In this case methods such as splatting can fill the resulting holes, but the colour used will be roughly the colour of the nearest point belonging to the same polygon. If the undersampled polygon is textured, this can lead to creating visual artifacts, as the colours used to fill the gaps might be incorrect. We can see this with an example. We have built a scene with a textured polygon and an object. The camera moves in horizontal direction in front of the objects (see **Figure 4**), and the polygon is partially occluded in all views. **Figure 5** shows the captured set of views of this scene. If we were only considering the textured polygon, **Figure 5f** will be the one chosen to capture the polygon. However this would produce a hole as in **Figure 6**,

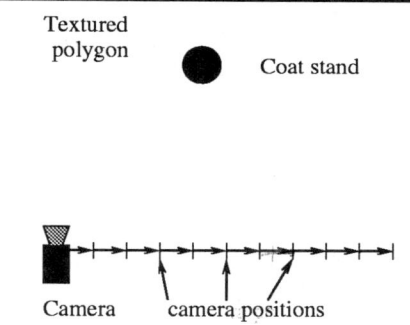

Figure 4: The path followed by the camera in front of the textured polygon and the object.

which is difficult to fill correctly. Although usually such a big polygon will be discretised, note that this situation can happen with densely populated scenes. Moreover, discretising the polygon according to the higher frequency of the texture a huge number of unnecessary very small polygons.

In order to avoid these artifacts we segment the texture using a region growing algorithm [19] and then colour code it. This results in a polygon that can be added to the rest of the scene. Then we use the algorithm described in the previous Section to ensure appropriate sampling for every region of the image. **Figure 7** shows an example. In **Figure 7a** the texture has been segmented using the region growing algorithm. The texture colour coded appears in **7b**. As a consequence, views **5f**, **5b** and **5j** are selected. The result combining the information of these views appears in **Figure 7c**.

4 Results

Texture segmentation can be done as a preprocess, although the region growing algorithm only takes some seconds. Colour-coding the texture is done while loading the segmented image. The number of new regions we achieve with this method is far below than the number of polygons that would produce a discretisation of the polygon according to the higher frequency of the texture. We have made several tests with our method and the results appear in **Figure 8**. For the classroom scene 51 camera postions were selected from the initial set of 150 possible views. The process takes less than two minutes in a Pentium III with 64 Mb of memory and a Nvidia TNT2 graphics card with 32 Mb of memory. **Figures 8a** to **8d** show different views of the classroom. The representation we store is a Layered Depth Image [20], which is computed with Render Park [21] and captured by using graphics hardware. The rendering method consists in a simple projection of the captured points using graphics hardware, but our output can also be rendered with more complex systems

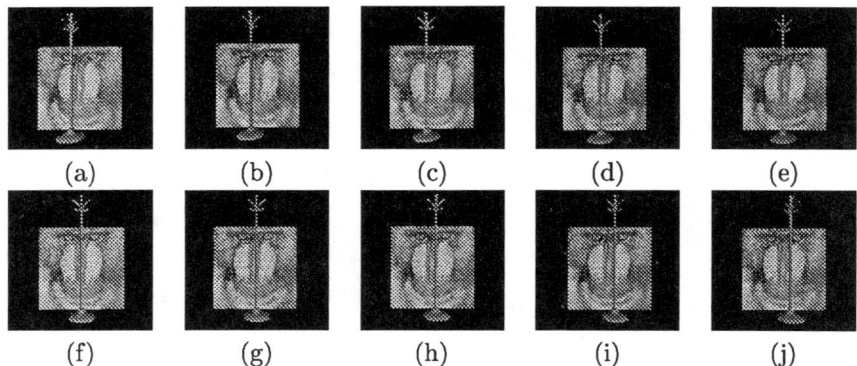

Figure 5: The ten initial images used to sample a partially occluded textured polygon. Figure (f) shows the better projection of the polygon, and will be the one selected to sample it if we do not take into account the texture. Note that there is no view showing the whole polygon without occlusions.

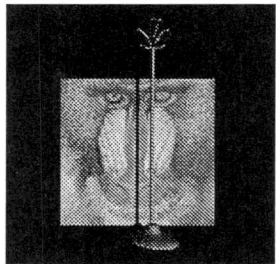

Figure 6: A hole appearing behind the coat stand. The gap is difficult to fill as we should use the correct colours appearing in the texture.

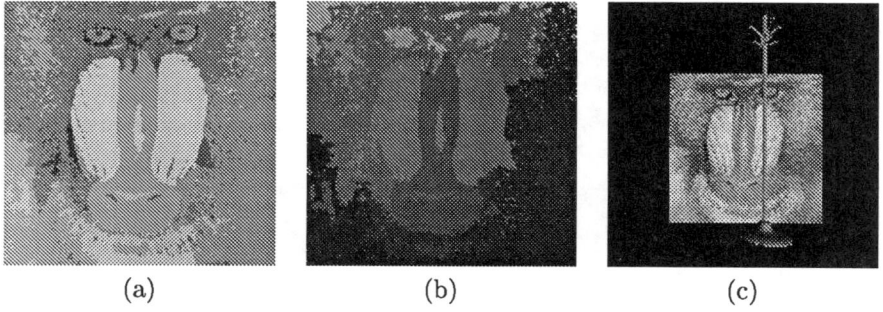

Figure 7: Processing the texture. Figure (a) shows the texture after being segmented with a region growing algorithm. (b) shows the colour-coded segmented texture. Finally, (c) shows the results. This figure has been created using the results of our algorithm with the colour-coded texture. Note that the gap behind the coat stand does not appear now.

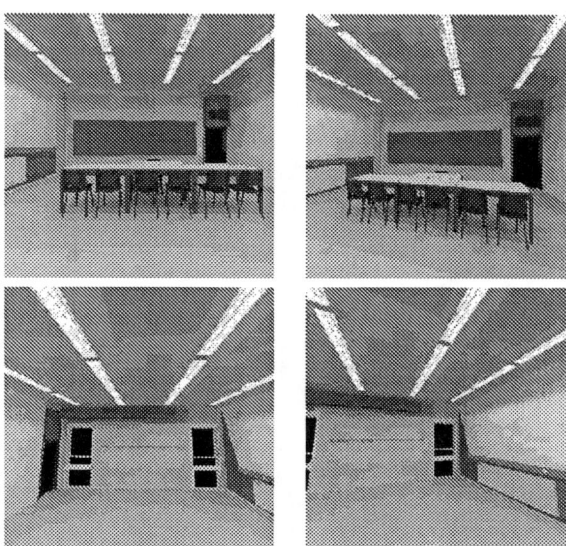

Figure 8: Examples of the classroom. The LDIs representation was created using the views selected with our method.

such as QSplat [22]. Note that the quality of the result is high with our simple rendering algorithm. Our quality criterion is a percentage of the maximum projected area in all views. Either the quality criterion or the maximum number of images to compute can be set by the user.

5 Conclusions and Future Work

We have presented a new method to automatically build an Image-Based model of a scene. We make use of a measure called viewpoint entropy that determines the amount of information seen from a point. Our system also takes care of textures by using a region growing segmentation and posterior colour coding of the regions of the texture. This way we avoid visible artifacts caused by polygons which are partially occluded in all views. This situation is likely to happen in very crowded scenes or when textured polygons are not sufficiently discretised. The selection of the most important views is carried out by a greedy algorithm that obtains a set of views which cover all visible polygons with a quality defined by the user. Our method avoids redundancy in the data and, as it works using an item buffer and hardware-acceleration, we save illumination computations, which are only calculated for the selected views.

In our Future Work we will focus view-dependent illumination. A new measure has to be defined in order to cope with photometric effects. This will make our system more general to cope with any kind of materials.

Acknowledgements

This work was partially supported by BR98/1003 grant of Universitat de Girona, SGR2001-00296 from Catalan Government, and TIC 2001-2416-C03-01 from the Spanish government. The authors want to thank Hartmurt Schirmacher for his valuable advice, and Jordi Freixenet from University of Girona for providing us with the code of region growing segmentation.

References

[1] L. McMillan and G. Bishop. Plenoptic modeling: An image-based rendering system. *Proc. of SIGGRAPH 95*, pages 39–46, August 1995.

[2] L. McMillan. *An Image-Based Approach to Three-Dimensional Computer Graphics, Ph.D. Dissertation*. PhD thesis, April 1997.

[3] R.E. Blahut. *Principles and Practice of Information Theory*. Addison-Wesley, 1987.

[4] T.M. Cover and J.A. Thomas. *Elements of Information Theory*. Wiley, 1991.

[5] Pere-Pau Vázquez, Miquel Feixas, Mateu Sbert, and Wolfgang Heidrich. Viewpoint selection using viewpoint entropy. In T.Ertl, B. Girod, G.Greiner, H. Niemann, and H.-P. Seidel, editors, *Vision, Modeling, and Visualization 2001*, 2001.

[6] S. Fleishman, D. Cohen-Or, and D. Lischinski. Automatic camera placement for image-based modeling. *Computer Graphics Forum*, 19(2):101–110, Jun 2000.

[7] T. Kamada and S. Kawai. A simple method for computing general position in displaying three-dimensional objects. *Computer Vision, Graphics, and Image Processing*, 41(1):43–56, January 1988.

[8] P. Barral, G. Dorme, and D. Plemenos. Scene understanding techniques using a virtual camera. In A. de Sousa and J.C. Torres, editors, *Proc. Eurographics'00, short presentations*, 2000.

[9] G. Dorme. *Study and implementation of 3D scenes comprehension techniques*. PhD thesis, 2001.

[10] L. Wong, C. Dumont, and M. Abidi. Next best view system in a 3-d object modeling task. In *Proc. International Symposium on Computational Intelligence in Robotics and Automation (CIRA)*, pages 306–311, 1999.

[11] N.A. Massios and R.B. Fisher. A best next view selection algorithm incorporating a quality criterion. In *Proc.of the Britsh Machine Vision Conference*, 1998.

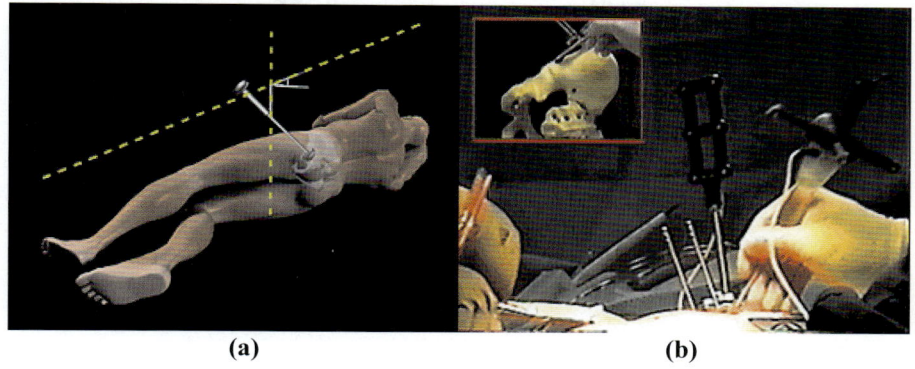

Figure 6 Hip navigation system (a) Test for cup alignment (b) Registration of collecting points from the patient's pelvis with bony surface geometry [26]

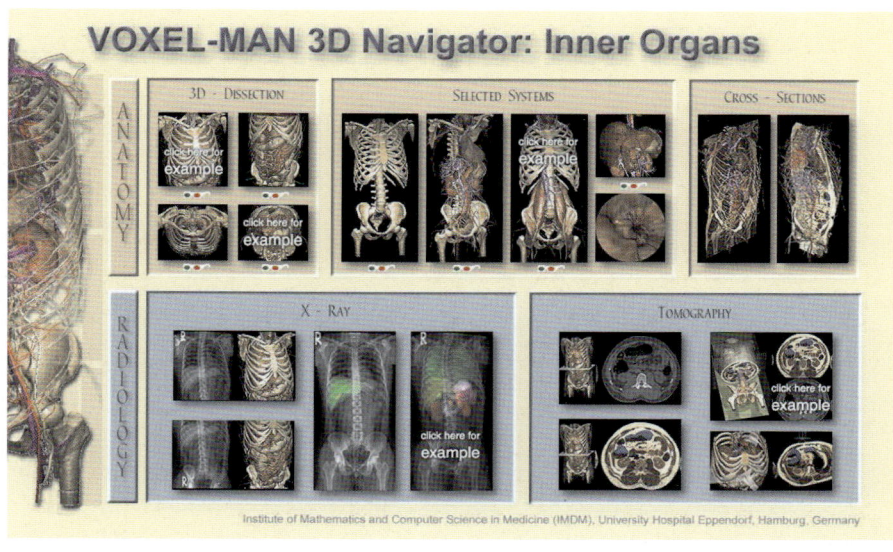

Figure 8 VOXEL-MAN 3D-Navigator: Inner Organs [94]

"**Problems and Solutions for 3D Accurate Functional Modelling of the Hip and the Shoulder**"

Nadia Magnenat-Thalmann, Myung Jin Kang and Taro Goto

Figure 13 Top: Canvas fabric used in painting conservation. A scanned piece of painting canvas is compared to our simulation. On the right side, a procedurally aged version is applied to the geometry. Bottom: Presentation of a "chef d'oeuvre". Two different types of interwoven structures are put in context.

"Procedural Simulation of Interwoven Structures"

Frédéric Drago and Norishige Chiba

Figure 10.a: *Cross section view of the final distributions*

Figure 10.b: *Cross section view of the final distributions*

"Explosive Impact on Real-time Deformable Terrain"

Tao Ruan Wan and Wen Tang

Figure 3 Left: Scene illuminated by an omnidirectional point light (located in the middle of the room). The two paraboloid shadow maps used (shown as grey scale images).
Right column: The two hemispheres as seen by the light source.

Figure 4 Left: Scene illuminated by a hemispherical point light.
Right column: Shadow map and light source view (paraboloid mapping).

"Shadow Mapping for Hemispherical and Omnidirectional Light Sources"

Stefan Brabec, Thomas Annen and Hans-Peter Seidel

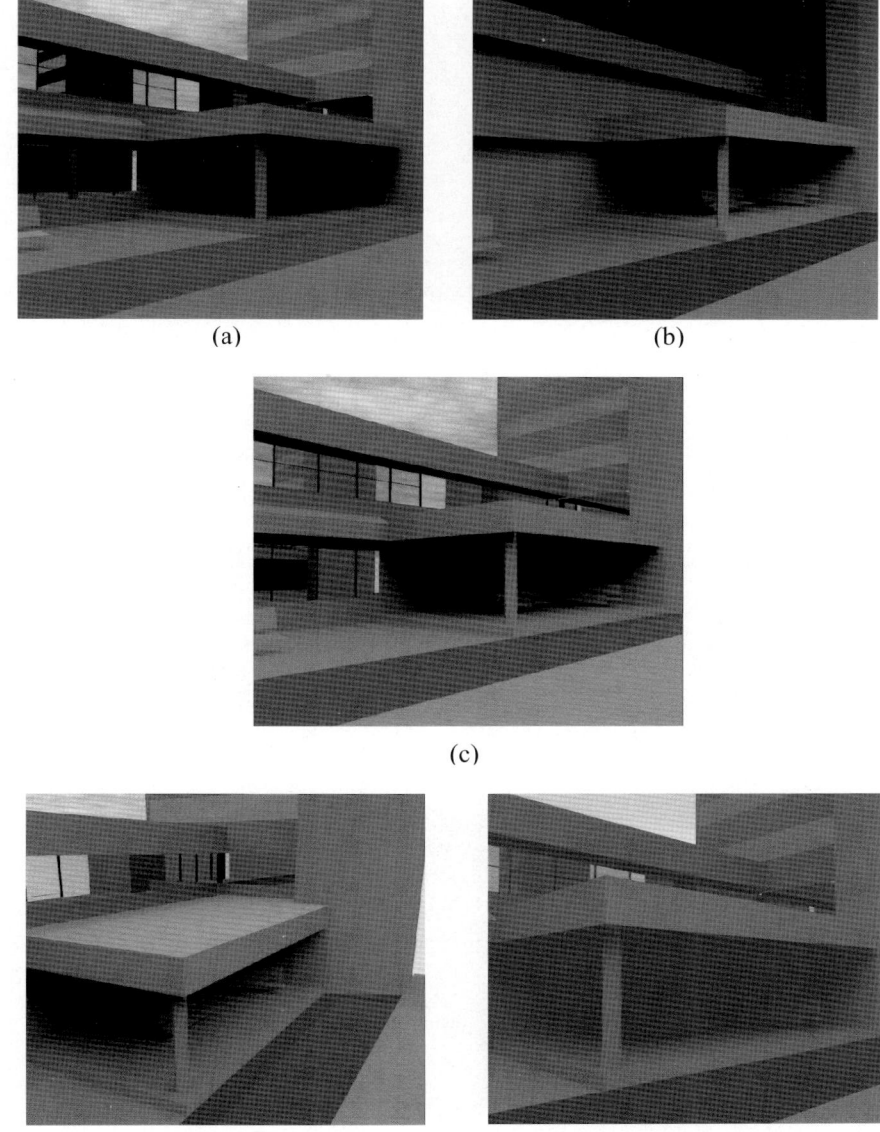

Fig. 14 Example images. (a) Traditional method; (b) Luminance due to reflected sky light; (c) The proposed method; (d) Different viewpoint; (e) Different solar position and weather condition.

"A Sky Light Illumination Model in Specular Environment"

Tomohisa Manabe, Kazufumi Kaneda and Hideo Yamashita

Figure 6: (From left to right and from top to bottom) Results of the second step using 4, 8, 16, 32, 64 and 128 samples per pixel for the room scene.

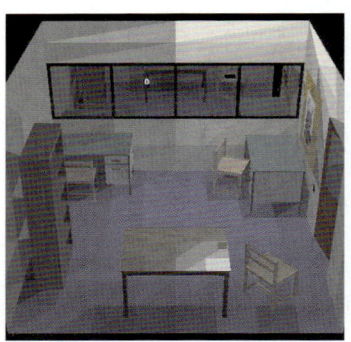
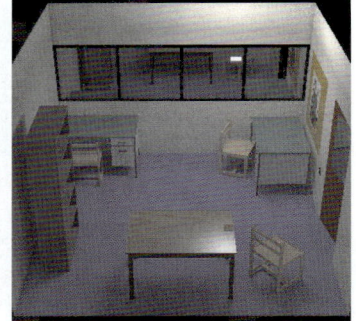

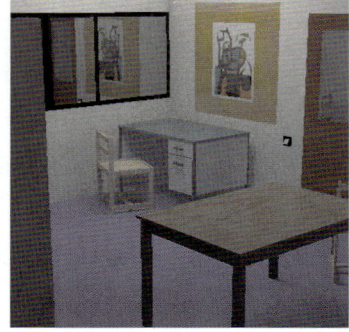

Figure 8: Office room with indirect illumination: (Left) The result of the HMCR step. (right) Solution after the second pass. (bottom) Solution after the second pass for a second view

"High-Quality Final Gathering for Hierarchical Monte Carlo Radiosity for General Environments"

Frederic Pérez, Ignacio Martin and Xavier Pueyo

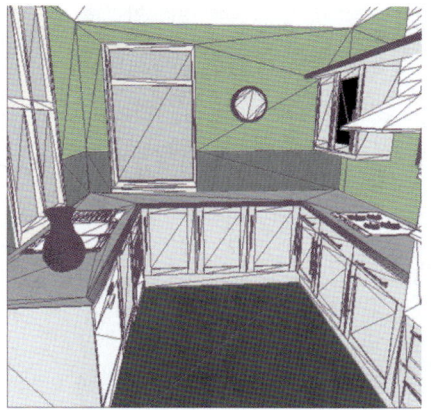

Figure 9 The global illumination is roughly computed for a kitchen model (left—courtesy of LightWork Design) with the extension of the HMCR algorithm (right—shown flat-shaded). Finally, with the use of our local gathering procedure, we obtain a high quality image (bottom).

"High-Quality Final Gathering for Hierarchical Monte Carlo Radiosity for General Environments"

Frederic Pérez, Ignacio Martin and Xavier Pueyo

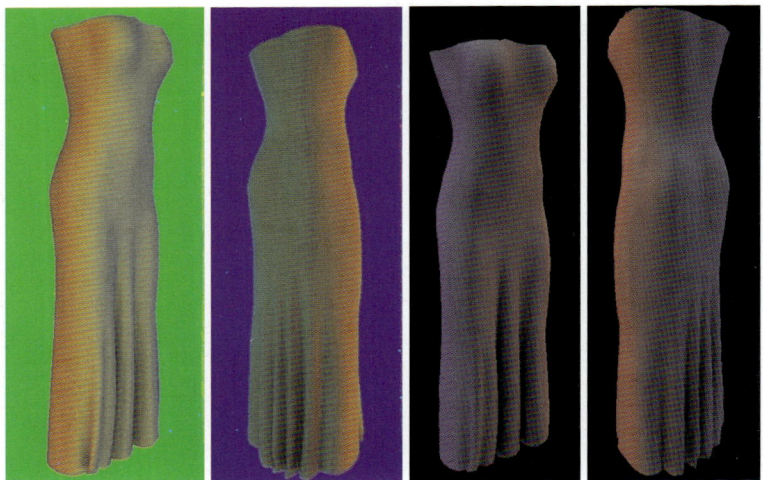

Figure 5 These images show the effects of the usage of the environment faces as coloured light sources. The mesh used, is the same as in figure 3. The corresponding environment maps are shown in figure 6. The reflection of the different light sources can be distinguished from each other in the folds.

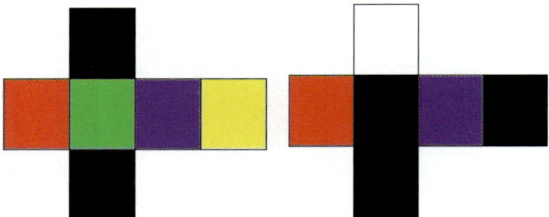

Figure 6 Environment cube maps used for the rendering of the above images. For the two left images top and bottom are black. Sides are red, green, blue and yellow. For the two right images left and right are blue and red, the top is white and the rest is colored black.

"Real-time Shading of Folded Surfaces"

B. Ganster, R. Klein, M. Sattler and R. Sarlette

[12] B. Abidi. Automatic sensor placement. In *Proc. Intelligent Robots and Computer Vision: Algorithms, Techniques, Active Vision, and Materials Handling*, pages 387–398, 1995.

[13] J.P. Grossman and William J. Dally. Point sample rendering. In George Drettakis and Nelson Max editors, editors, *Rendering Techniques '98*, pages 181–192. Springer-Verlag, 1998.

[14] W. Stuerzlinger. Imaging all visible surfaces. In I. Scott MacKenzie and James Stewart, editors, *Proc. of the Conference on Graphics Interface (GI-99*, pages 115–122, Toronto, Ontario, June 2–4 1999. CIPS.

[15] D. Lischinski and A. Rappoport. Image-based rendering for non-diffuse synthetic scenes. In George Drettakis and Nelson Max editors, editors, *Rendering Techniques '98*, pages 301–314, 1998.

[16] V. Hlavac, A. Leonardis, and T. Werner. Automatic selection of reference views for image-based scene representations. In *Lecture Notes in Computer Science*, pages 526–535, New York, NY, 1996. Springer Verlag. Proc. of European Conference on Computer Vision '96 (ECCV '96).

[17] Jin-Xiang Chai, Xin Tong, Shing-Chow Chan, and Heung-Yeung Shum. Plenoptic sampling. In *SIGGRAPH 2000, Computer Graphics Proceedings*, pages 307–318. ACM Press / ACM SIGGRAPH / Addison Wesley Longman, 2000.

[18] J. O'Rourke. *Art Gallery Theorems and Algorithms*. Oxford University Press, New York, 1987.

[19] Robert M. Haralick and Linda G. Shapiro. *Computer and Robot Vision, vol. 1*. Addison-Welsey: Reading, MA, 1992.

[20] L. He J. Shade, S. Gortler and R. Szeliski. Layered depth images. In *Computer Graphics Proceedings (Proc. SIGGRAPH '98)*, pages 231–242, July 1998.

[21] Philippe Bekaert, Frank Suykens de Laet, Pieter Peers, and Vincent Masselus. Renderpark: A testbed system for global illumination. available under http://www.cs.kuleuven.ac.be/cwis/research/graphics/RENDERPARK/.

[22] Szymon Rusinkiewicz and Marc Levoy. QSplat: A multiresolution point rendering system for large meshes. In Kurt Akeley, editor, *Siggraph 2000, Computer Graphics Proceedings*, Annual Conference Series, pages 343–352. ACM Press / ACM SIGGRAPH / Addison Wesley Longman, 2000.

Animation

Automatic Generation of Non-Verbal Facial Expressions from Speech

Irene Albrecht   Jörg Haber   Hans-Peter Seidel

Max-Planck-Institut für Infomatik
Stuhlsatzenhausweg 85, 66123 Saarbrücken, Germany
E-mail: {albrecht, haberj, hpseidel}@mpi-sb.mpg.de

Abstract

Speech synchronized facial animation that controls only the movement of the mouth is typically perceived as wooden and unnatural. We propose a method to generate additional facial expressions such as movement of the head, the eyes, and the eyebrows fully automatically from the input speech signal. This is achieved by extracting prosodic parameters such as pitch flow and power spectrum from the speech signal and using them to control facial animation parameters in accordance to results from paralinguistic research.

1. Introduction

While listening to another closely visible person, for instance in a dialogue or movie close-up, the main visual focus of the listener is on the mouth and the eyes of the speaker. But also non-verbal facial expressions such as movement of head and eyebrows or frowning play an important role during speech. They enhance understanding by emphasizing words and syllables of special importance. Speech synchronization for animated characters should thus not be restricted to mouth movements, but should rather include other speech-related facial expressions as well in order to render the animations more vivid and believable.

Speech-related facial animation is tightly coupled to the prosody of the utterance. Prosody, in turn, can be determined by the pitch of the signal. At the end of a question, the eyebrows raise and so does the pitch. In general, accented words and syllables come along with raised pitch.

The information that is not contained in the words themselves, but in the "acoustic packaging" of the utterance [2, p. 597], e.g. in prosody or frequency and duration of pauses, is referred to as *paralinguistic information*. Paralinguistic research provides valuable insights for the automatic generation of non-verbal facial expressions from speech: prosodic parameters of a speech signal such as slope and range of the fundamental frequency f0 are related to facial expressions. By extracting these prosodic parameters from

 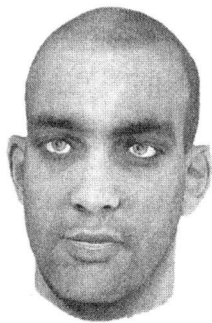

Figure 1. Snapshot of a reflective moment during speech synchronized facial animation. Left: only mouth movement is generated from the speech signal. Right: additional movement of head, eyes, and eyebrows is generated automatically from prosodic parameters.

the speech signal, we are able to automatically generate facial expressions that match the prosody of the utterance (see Figure 1).

We propose a method to automatically generate the following non-verbal facial expression from speech:

- head and eyebrow raising and lowering dependent on the pitch;
- gaze direction, movement of eyelids and eyebrows, and frowning during thinking and word search pauses;
- eye blinks and lip moistening as punctuators and manipulators;
- random eye movement during normal speech.

The intensity of facial expressions is additionally controlled by the power spectrum of the speech signal, which corresponds to loudness and intensity of the utterance.

2. Previous Work

2.1. Facial Animation

Many different approaches for facial animation have been presented in the last thirty years. A comprehensive overview of the field can be found in the textbook by Parke and Waters [20]. In particular, several facial animation systems for speech synchronization have been proposed. Automated speech synchronization for recorded speech using linear prediction has been presented by Lewis and Parke [17], while an automatic approach to synthesize speech by rules has been proposed by Hill et al. [11]. Both approaches consider the movement of jaw and lips only. Cohen and Massaro additionally included movement of the tongue and introduced a technique for modeling coarticulation [7]. To combine speech synchronization with facial expressions, script-based approaches have been presented by Pearce et al. [21] and by Ip and Chan [13]. Here, the user specifies the facial expressions that should be displayed during speech in an application-dependent script language. Kalra et al. describe a script-based multi-layered approach to specify facial animation [16].

The image-based facial animation system introduced by Brand [3] takes speech as input and generates corresponding mouth movements including coarticulation as well as additional speech-related facial animation as, for instance, eyebrow movement. The system learns facial dynamics and states during speech from video footage of real humans and applies its "knowledge" to novel audio input.

Animation systems for agents that interact and communicate with the user or other agents have been developed by Pelachaud et al. [22] and by Cassell and Stone [4]. In these systems, text-to-speech techniques are used to synthesize the agent's speech. The same component that generates the text for the agent's speech also generates the accompanying gestures based on the content of the text and additional knowledge of the structure of the utterance and the course of the dialogue.

Lundeberg and Beskow [18] have developed a spoken dialogue system featuring a character that was designed to resemble the famous Swedish writer Strindberg. Similar to the above approaches, the agent is capable of communicating using bimodal speech accompanied by simple punctuation gestures like nods or blinks as well as by more complicated gestures especially designed for certain sentences.

2.2. Paralinguistic Research

Ekman [9] was one of the first to systematically investigate speech-related eyebrow movement. He noticed that raising of both the inner and the outer part of the brows is most often used for accentuating particular words (*batons*) and for emphasizing greater parts of a sentence (*underliners*). Ekman reckons that the choice of movement depends mainly on the context. When the speaker experiences distress, perplexity, doubt or other difficulties, the brows will probably be lowered, otherwise they will be raised. Raised or lowered brows are also used as *punctuation marks*, i.e. they are placed where in written speech some kind of punctuation mark would be placed. Again, lowered brows indicate some kind of difficulty, doubt, or perplexity as well as seriousness and importance. In addition to the context dependent use of eyebrow movement, eyebrow raising is often used to indicate that a question is being asked. Lowered eyebrows were also observed during word search pauses, especially together with an '*errr*'. Raised brows do occur as well in this context accompanied by an upward gaze direction. It is also typical for word searches that the eyes look at a still object to reduce visual input.

Chovil [6] reports that *syntactic displays* (batons, underliners, punctuators, etc.) occur most often. Among these, raising or lowering of brows are most prevalent. Other important movements of the speaker are related to the content of the talk, e.g. facial shrugs or expressions while trying to remember something. Cavé et al. [5] found that eyebrow movement during speech is often (in 71 % of the cases) linked closely to pitch contour. Raising pitch is usually accompanied by a raising of the eyebrows, while lowering of pitch and lowering of eyebrows also coincide. Typically, 38 % of overall eyebrow movements occur during pauses or while listening. They are used to indicate turn taking in dialogs, assure the speaker of the listener's attention, and mirror the listener's degree of understanding (back-channel). House et al. [12] examined the importance of eyebrow and head movement for the perception of significance. They observed that both movements are weighty here. Perceptual sensitivity to timing is about 100–200 ms, which is about the average length of a syllable. Cosnier [8] investigated the relationship between questions and gestures. He found that, apart from a head raising at the end of a question, for informative questions (as opposed to questions related to the interaction itself) the facial expression is not different from the head and eyebrow movement during normal informative conversation. The gaze, however, is directed more often towards the listener than during statements. Relations between emotions (joy, fear, anger, disgust, sadness, boredom) and prosodic parameters (f0 floor/range/slope, jitter, spectral energy distribution, number of accentuated syllables) have been investigated by Paeschke et al. [19] and by Johnstone and Scherer [14]. Accordingly, they report that most of the measured prosodic parameters are suitable to classify emotions.

3. Generating Non-Verbal Facial Expressions

We have implemented our method for automatic generation of non-verbal facial expressions from speech as a module in our facial animation system [10]. In this physics-based animation system, deformation of the skin is controlled by simulated contraction of facial muscles [15]. The set of muscles used in our animations is shown in Figure 2. Speech synchronized movement of lips and jaw is generated automatically from an input speech signal [1]. In addition to the contraction values of the facial muscles, we employ the following parameters for facial animations:

- rotation of the eyeballs / looking direction;
- variable opening/closing of the eyelids;
- rotation of the head (roll, pitch, yaw).

The generation of both speech synchronized mouth movement and non-verbal facial expressions is carried out in a preprocessing step, which takes about one minute for a speech signal of ten seconds duration on an 800 MHz Pentium III PC. Once the speech synchronized animation parameters have been generated, the simulation and rendering of the animation performs in real-time at about 30–40 fps on the same hardware with a GeForce2 graphics board.

3.1. Facial Expressions from Pitch

To automatically generate head and eyebrow movement from a speech signal, we first extract the pitch values of the utterance at a sampling distance of 10 ms. To this end, we use the Snack Sound Toolkit developed by Sjölander [23], which contains a variety of procedure calls for speech analysis. Since the production of unvoiced phonemes such as /p/ or /f/ does not involve vocal chord vibration, the notion of pitch does not exist for these sounds. Hence the pitch value is zero, which leads to a very rugged appearance of the pitch curve in turn. Therefore we eliminate these zero values and approximate the remaining pitch values using a B-spline curve. Next, the local minima and maxima of this curve are determined. Their positions and values, however, do not correspond exactly to

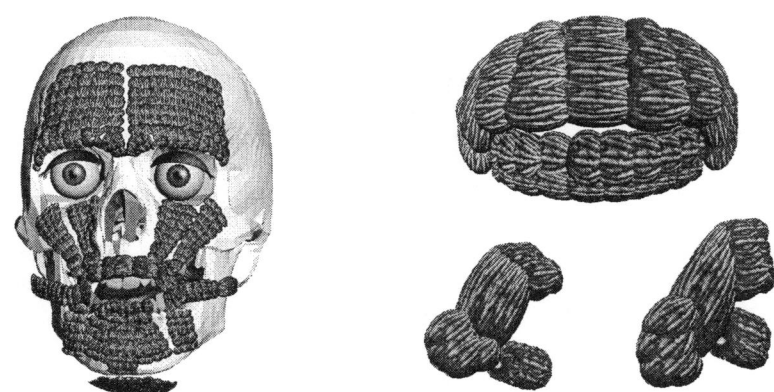

Figure 2. Left: layout of the facial muscles used in our animations (skin surface removed); right: orbicularis oris muscle, front view (no contraction), and side views for protrusion and retraction.

the minima and maxima of the original pitch curve. Thus, for every local maximum of the B-spline curve, position and value of the maximum of the original pitch data from the interval between the preceding and succeeding turning point of the B-spline curve are retrieved. An analogue process is performed for the local minima. The "reconstructed" original extrema are then used for the generation of head and eyebrow movement.

For each of the so determined maxima it is decided whether the differences between its value and the values of the preceding and succeeding minima exceed a given threshold. This threshold depends to a certain degree on the speaker due to the differences in voice melody: some people show greater pitch variations than others. For those maxima where the threshold is exceeded, the head is raised. The amount of head movement depends on the magnitude of the maximum. We typically generate head movements of at most three degrees rotation about the horizontal axis.

For each minimum, the difference values to the preceding and succeeding maxima are computed. Again, if the differences are larger than a given threshold, head movement is generated. In this case, the head is rotated back into its neutral position. This combination of upward and downward movement of the head supports accentuation of the speech. Figure 3 depicts different stages of the processing of the speech signal and the resulting animation parameters.

Both raising and lowering of the head are synchronized at the phoneme level, i.e. both beginning and end of head movements coincide with the closest phoneme boundary.

It is necessary to use only the most prominent maxima and minima, because otherwise too much head movement would be generated. In order to prevent monotony of the movement, the head is also randomly turned or tilted slightly to one side from time to time.

Head movement is often accompanied by analogue eyebrow movement: eyebrows are raised for high pitch and lowered again with the pitch. In our approach, eyebrow movement is generated using the same method as for the head rotations. Figure 3 (bottom) shows the eyebrow raising pertaining to the pitch.

According to Cavé *et al.* [5], only the magnitude of the left eyebrow's movement is related to the f0 pattern. This is taken into account by varying the degree of eyebrow raise for the left side according to the value of the current maximum. Cavé *et al.* also report that the duration of eyebrow raising is not correlated to the magnitude of the movement. This is inherently included in our implementation, since the duration depends only on the time step between the previous minimum and the maximum.

The only difference between questions and normal speech is that during questions the gaze of the speaker is directed towards the listener most of the time and always at the end [8], while for statements the speaker does not constantly look at the listener. If the speaker turns towards the listener, he either expects some feedback from the listener or wants him to take over the role of speaker. Since we do not model dialogues, this gaze behavior is not important for us.

3.2. Thinking and Word Search

During prolonged or filled pauses (e.g. " ... errr ... ") in a monologue, the speaker is typically either thinking about what to say next or searching for words. In both cases, similar facial expressions are exhibited: the gaze is directed at an immobile, fixed location to reduce input [9]. This location is usually either somewhere on the floor or up in the air. When people look up, they also raise their eyebrows. One possible explanation for this is an increase in the field of view when the eyebrows don't occlude part of the vision [9]. On the other hand, when people look at the floor while searching for answers, they often show a slight frown.

We have implemented this word search and thinking behavior during pauses. The duration of pauses that justify thinking and word search behavior seems to be speaker dependent and can hence be adjusted by a parameter.

3.3. Punctuators and Manipulators

Facial expressions that occur during speech at the same positions where punctuation marks occur in written text are called *punctuators*. They help to structure the flow of speech. A good example for such punctuators are eye blinks. In our implementation, we generate eye blinks at the beginning of pauses.

Movements that serve a physical need are called *manipulators* and are performed unconsciously. Eye blinks also serve the physical need to keep the cornea wet. Such additional blinks occur on average every 4.8 seconds [22]. To make our synthetic character more lifelike, we also include involuntary eye blinks: if the time elapsed between the previous and the next blink exceeds the threshold of 4.8 seconds, an additional blink is inserted.

As described by Pelachaud *et al.* [22], eye blinks consist of a closing interval (avg. duration: 1/8 s), the apex (avg. duration: 1/24 s), during which the eyes remain closed, and an opening interval (avg. duration: 1/12 s), where the eyes open again. Eye blinks are also synchronized to the speech: beginning of the closing, the apex, and the opening coincides with the nearest phoneme boundaries each. This behavior is simulated in our implementation.

Besides involuntary eye blinks, another example for a manipulator would be the moistening of the lips during extended speech periods. This can be implemented by letting the

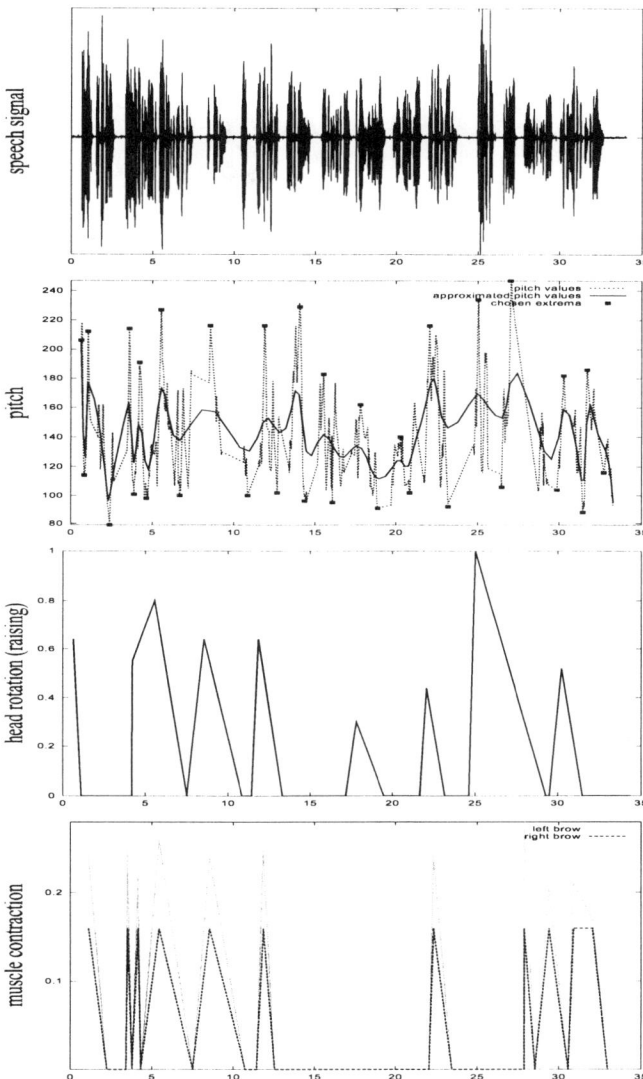

Figure 3. Processing the speech signal (cf. Sec. 3.1). Top to bottom: input speech signal (about 33 s); original pitch values (stippled) and corresponding B-spline curve (solid); resulting head movement; muscle contractions of the frontalis muscles, which are responsible for the eyebrow movement (grey: left brow, black: right brow). Note that the movement of the left brow is scaled according to the magnitude of the pitch value.

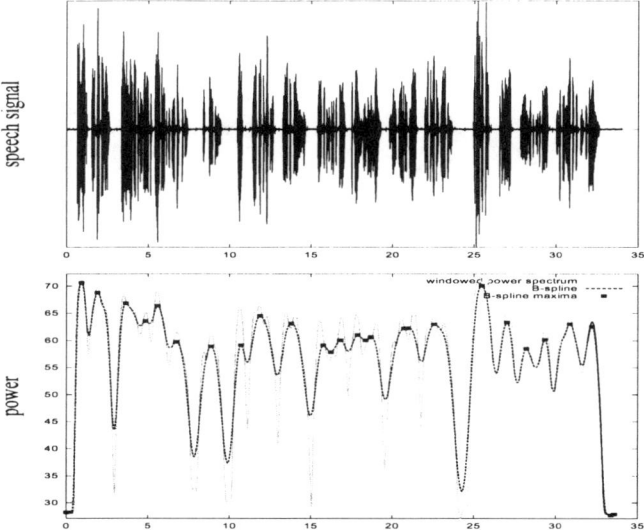

Figure 4. The windowed power spectrum. Top: input speech signal. Bottom: windowed power spectrum (grey), approximating B-spline curve (black), and maxima of the B-spline (black squares). This information is used for scaling facial expressions with respect to loudness.

synthetic character lick his/her lips during pauses that match the average lip moistening frequency best. During pauses where a thinking or word search expression is exhibited, the tongue motion should be slower, because the speaker is concentrating entirely on what to say next.

3.4. Random Eye Movement

During normal conversation, the speaker does not always look at the listener [8]. Moreover, eyes are almost constantly in motion. For an animated character lacking this behavior, the gaze is staring and dead. We have included additional random eye movement into our facial animations. Here it is important that the eye positions do not differ too much between two movements. Otherwise the movement would seem erratic and the character might seem agitated. As with all upward and downward eye movements, it is crucial that the lids accompany the eyeballs. If a person's gaze is directed downwards, the eyelids also close to a certain degree. Contrary, if one looks up, the eyelids open more to prevent an occlusion of the field of view.

3.5. Volume-controlled Intensity

Loudness primarily influences the magnitude of speech-related mouth movements for vowels. Additionally, it is also a good indicator for the distance of the person we are talking to. If somebody wants to pass on information to a person standing several meters away, he must speak louder in order to be understood. For the same reason he may also choose to intensify his speech-accompanying facial expressions. A very slight head movement, for example, is not perceivable at greater distances, so the speaker may want to nod more vigorously. Therefore we do not only scale the facial expressions pertaining directly to speech by the power of the signal, but it is also possible to do so for pitch related facial expressions. The extent to which this is done can be regulated by a parameter. This allows us to model differences in the behavior of the animated characters.

Using the Snack sound toolkit [23], we extract a windowed power spectrum of the speech signal and fit an approximating B-spline curve to it. An interpolating polynomial is fitted to the local maxima of this B-spline curve and normalized to a $[0, 1]$ range. It indicates the relative loudness of the speech signal. These relative loudness values are individually weighted for each animation parameter and used to scale the intensity of facial expressions. The weight for jaw rotation, for instance, is greater than the weight for eyebrow movement. As mentioned above, the weights can be modified to model characters with different tempers. Figure 4 shows the windowed power spectrum for an example sentence together with the approximating B-spline curve and their maxima.

4. Results

Incorporating non-verbal speech-related facial expressions into our facial animations definitely improved their naturalness and made them more convincing. Although the movements are generated by rules, random variations are taken into account to prevent the facial expressions from being entirely predictable. Some predictability, however, should remain indeed, since the accentuating facial expressions of humans tend to be predictable as well.

By specifying weights and frequencies for the movements of head, eyes, and eyebrows, different synthetic characters can be designed that exhibit different ways of visually accentuating their speech. This is also the case for real humans: some people tend to underline important parts of their utterances more by eyebrow movement, and some more by nodding. The frequency and amplitude of such movements depend highly on the temperament and culture of the individual as well. We would expect an Italian, for instance, to show much more facial and body gestures than a person from Northern Europe.

Figure 5 shows several snapshots from a facial animation sequence synchronized to a speech signal both with and without additional non-verbal facial expressions. The animation that includes non-verbal facial expressions looks clearly more convincing and lifelike. Since these enhancements are difficult to represent in still images, additional material including a movie can be found at http://www.mpi-sb.mpg.de/resources/FAM.

5. Conclusion and Future Work

We have presented a method to automatically generate non-verbal facial expressions from a speech signal. In particular, our approach addresses the movement of head, eyes,

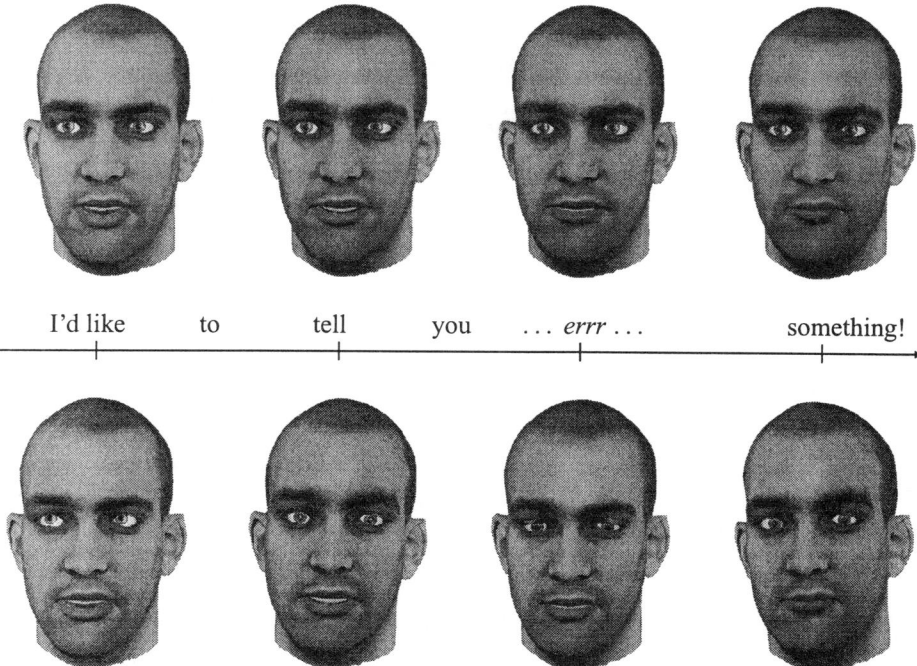

Figure 5. Snapshots from a facial animation sequence synchronized to a speech signal with the textual representation: "I'd like to tell you ... *errr* ... **something!**". Top row: movements of lips and jaw are generated from the speech signal. Bottom row: additional non-verbal facial expressions are created automatically from a paralinguistic analysis of the speech signal.

eyelids, and eyebrows depending on prosodic parameters such as pitch, length and frequency of pauses, and the power spectrum of the input signal. These parameters are extracted automatically from the speech signal and control our facial animation parameters in accordance to results from paralinguistic research. Resulting animations exhibit a definitely more natural and vivid character compared to speech synchronized animations that control mouth movements only.

We are planning to extent our repertoire of prosodic movements further in order to increase the diversity of our animations. For instance, females often use nose wrinkling for prosodically motivated movements [9], and many people additionally employ tightening or widening of the eyes [6]. Incorporating facial expressions that match the emotion conveyed by the speech signal would enhance the realism of our system considerably. Some sophisticated signal processing should be sufficient to extract the f0 attributes that are characteristic of the basic emotions joy, sadness, fear, anger, disgust, and boredom.

References

[1] I. Albrecht, J. Haber, and H.-P. Seidel. Speech Synchronization for Physics-based Facial Animation. In *Proc. WSCG 2002*, pages 9–16, 2002.

[2] D. Barr. Trouble in mind: Paralinguistic indices of effort and uncertainty in communication. In *Oralité et Gestualité. Actes du colloque ORAGE 2001*, pages 597–600, 2001.

[3] M. Brand. Voice Puppetry. In *Proc. SIGGRAPH '99*, pages 21–28, 1999.

[4] J. Cassell and M. Stone. Living Hand to Mouth: Psychological Theories about Speech and Gesture in Interactive Dialogue Systems. Technical Report FS-99-03, AAAI Fall Symposium on Psychological Models of Communication in Collaborative Systems, 1999.

[5] C. Cavé, I. Guaïtella, R. Bertrand, S. Santi, F. Harlay, and R. Espesser. About the relationship between eyebrow movements and f0 variations. In *Proc. ICSLP '96*, 1996.

[6] N. Chovil. Discourse-Oriented Facial Displays in Conversation. *Research on Language and Social Interaction*, 25:163–194, 1991.

[7] M. M. Cohen and D. W. Massaro. Modeling Coarticulation in Synthetic Visual Speech. In N. M. Magnenat-Thalmann and D. Thalmann, editors, *Models and Techniques in Computer Animation*, pages 139–156. 1993.

[8] J. Cosnier. Les gestes de la question. In Kerbrat-Orecchioni, editor, *La Question*, pages 163–171. Presses Universitaires de Lyon, 1991.

[9] P. Ekman. About brows: emotional and conversational signals. In M. v. Cranach, K. Foppa, W. Lepenies, and D. Ploog, editors, *Human Ethology: Claims and limits of a new discipline: contributions to the Colloquium.*, pages 169–248. 1979.

[10] J. Haber, K. Kähler, I. Albrecht, H. Yamauchi, and H.-P. Seidel. Face to Face: From Real Humans to Realistic Facial Animation. In *Proc. Israel-Korea Binational Conference on Geometrical Modeling and Computer Graphics*, pages 73–82, Oct. 2001.

[11] D. R. Hill, A. Pearce, and B. Wyvill. Animating Speech: An Automated Approach using Speech Synthesised by Rules. *The Visual Computer*, 3(5):277–289, Mar. 1988.

[12] D. House, J. Beskow, and B. Granström. Timing and Interaction of Visual Cues for Prominence in Audiovisual Speech Perception. In *Proc. Eurospeech 2001*, 2001.

[13] H. H. S. Ip and C. S. Chan. Script-Based Facial Gesture and Speech Animation Using a NURBS Based Face Model. *Computers & Graphics*, 20(6):881–891, Nov. 1996.

[14] T. Johnstone and K. Scherer. The Effects of Emotions on Voice Quality. In *Proc. XIVth International Congress of Phonetic Sciences*, 2000. in press.

[15] K. Kähler, J. Haber, and H.-P. Seidel. Geometry-based Muscle Modeling for Facial Animation. In *Proc. Graphics Interface 2001*, pages 37–46, June 2001.

[16] P. Kalra, A. Mangili, N. Magnenat-Thalmann, and D. Thalmann. SMILE: A Multilayered Facial Animation System. In *Proc. IFIP WG 5.10, Tokyo, Japan*, pages 189–198, 1991.

[17] J. P. Lewis and F. I. Parke. Automated Lip-Synch and Speech Synthesis for Character Animation. In *Proc. Graphics Interface '87*, pages 143–147, Apr. 1987.

[18] M. Lundeberg and J. Beskow. Developing a 3D-agent for the AUGUST dialogue system. In *Proc. Audio-Visual Speech Processing (AVSP) '99*, 1999.

[19] A. Paeschke, M. Kienast, and W. Sendlmeier. F0-Contours in Emotional Speech. In *Proc. International Congress of Phonetic Sciences '99*, pages 929–931, 1999.

[20] F. I. Parke and K. Waters, editors. *Computer Facial Animation*. A K Peters, Wellesley, MA, 1996.

[21] A. Pearce, B. Wyvill, G. Wyvill, and D. R. Hill. Speech and Expression: A Computer Solution to Face Animation. In *Proc. Graphics Interface '86*, pages 136–140, May 1986.

[22] C. Pelachaud, N. Badler, and M. Steedman. Generating Facial Expressions for Speech. *Cognitive Science*, 20(1):1–46, 1996.

[23] K. Sjölander. The Snack Sound Toolkit. http://www.speech.kth.se/snack/, 1997–2001.

Experimental Investigation of Linguistic and Parametric Descriptions of Human Motion for Animation

Jason Harrison   Kellogg S. Booth   Brian D. Fisher

Department of Computer Science
and
Media and Graphics Interdisciplinary Centre
University of British Columbia, Vancouver, BC Canada

Abstract

Computers process and store human movement in a different manner from how humans perceive and observe human movement. We describe an investigation of the mapping between the linguistic descriptions people ascribe to animated motions and the parameters utilized to produce the animations. The mapping is validated by comparing both the linguistic and parametric descriptions to similarity measures obtained during experiments in which subjects made judgements about the similarity of pairs of animated motions. Analysis of the experimental data revealed that similarity judgements are not true distances (they do not form a metric space), but statistical tests and principal component analyses of the linguistic and parametric descriptions indicate correlations with the similarity judgements that provide the basis for mappings between the two descriptions. Although there are significant individual differences in the mappings across subjects, there is some indication that our methodology can be extended to provide a more robust direct mapping from linguistic descriptions to at least initial approximations of the corresponding parametric descriptions of the motion for use in computer animation systems.

Keywords: Computer animation, human figure animation, human movement, judgement of human movement, description of human movement, movement perception.

1. Introduction and Overview

The leading paradigm used by computer animation systems employs three tightly coupled models. These models, used in movies such as *Toy Story*, *Final Fantasy: The Spirits Within*, and *Monsters Inc.*, are (1) a set of time signals $\mathcal{Q}(t)$ that specify the kinematics of the movement, (2) a mapping $\mathcal{A}$ between $\mathcal{Q}(t)$ and the position, orientation, and posture of the human figure, and (3) a "costume" or "visual appearance" that specifies the outer appearance of the human body.

In sharp contrast to the exactness of computers, it is not well understood how we visually perceive human movements. It is believed that we utilize the motor control centers of our brains to recognize and interpret the movements of others. However, we do not know how observed movements are encoded or how they are translated into linguistic descriptions. Neither do we understand the process we use to translate "mental images" of movements into physical movements.

In order to build higher-level computer animation tools for selecting, specifying, or modifying movements represented by computer models we need to know how the parameters of a movement, $\mathcal{P}(\mathcal{Q})$, affect our perceptions and judgements. We present results from two participant-based experiments that gathered information on the relationships between three motion spaces: the first motion space is the "mechanical motion space," a vector space of motion signals, $\mathcal{Q}(t)$; the second motion space is the "psychological motion space" in which humans encode and organize motions according to their features; and the third motion space is the "linguistic motion space" that humans use to describe movements using words.

In this paper we describe our initial findings about what we believe will eventually be a novel approach for specifying human motion in computer animation systems. Unlike traditional techniques that provide animators with tools that deal directly with the mechanical motion space in which motions are represented parametrically, our approach tries to bridge between the mechanical motion space and the more intuitive linguistic motion space in which motion is described using adjectives and adverbs. The bridging is accomplished using a hypothesized intermediate psychological motion space, based on human perception of motion and human judgements of motion similarity.

After providing a conceptual framework for relating the three motion spaces, we provide a brief summary of previous work including earlier attempts to provide animators with linguistically based tools for specifying motion. This is followed by a description of two experiments that were conducted to determine the nature of the mappings between the three motion spaces. The results of the experiments, and how those results provide a basis for future work that will refine our technique to produce practical tools for animators are then discussed.

The contribution of this work to the field of computer animation is three-fold:

(a) The conceptual framework relating the three motion spaces, as validated by our experiments, is a sound basis for mapping the more intuitive linguistic descriptions of motion to the commonly used parametric descriptions employed in many animation systems.

(b) The experimental methodology we have developed can be used to extend our preliminary findings to a more robust set of mappings covering a wider range of motions.

(c) The need to account for individual differences when calibrating the mappings suggests a number of research questions that should be pursued.

The conceptual framework and experiments reported in this paper were part of the research described in the first author's dissertation [9]. In this paper we describe the components of the conceptual framework, two experiments that were conducted to validate the framework, and the main conclusions that were drawn from the research.

2. Three Motion Spaces for Describing Human Movement

Many computer animation researchers focus on the technical aspects of computer animation systems such as increasing the realism of the visual models, refining techniques to record the movement of human actors, and building algorithms to assist in the editing of recorded movements. In other words, research has tended to focus on the limitations of computer based representations of human movement rather than on higher-level techniques for specifying and adjusting motions. For example, if an animator wanted to adjust the style of a movement while not affecting the gross path of the movement — making a movement more "happy," "awkward," "drunk," "graceful," or "fast" — almost none of the prior work in computer animation is applicable.

Our ultimate goal is to provide a direct and automatic mapping between everyday linguistic descriptions of human motion ("a sad, slouching man walking despondently down the road") to the mechanical (kinematic) description required by the underlying modeling and rendering software. This is beyond our current capability, but the work described here is a first step because it provides a framework for defining the mapping between the linguistic and mechanical motion spaces.

In order to build higher-level computer animation tools for selecting, specifying, or modifying movements represented by computer models we need to know how the parameters of a movement, $\mathcal{P}(\mathcal{Q})$, affect our perceptions and judgements. This requires knowledge of computer animation, human-computer interaction, and visual psychophysics. Thus, it is useful to introduce three different types of motion spaces to assist in our discussion of the relationship between the parameters of movement and the perceptions and judgements formed by a human observer.

The first motion space is the standard "mechanical motion space," a vector space of motion signals $\mathcal{Q}(t)$ that describes the kinematics of movement. Computer animation tools operate in this space. It remains an open problem as how to define a basis for $\mathcal{Q}(t)$ which would allow us to interpolate two motion signals while maintaining constraints such as foot contacts. Given this problem, we use the set of input parameters $\mathcal{P}(\mathcal{Q})$ to a kinematic walk generator that are used to define the motion signal $\mathcal{Q}(t)$. For example, if $\mathcal{Q}(t)$ is the motion signals for a walking motion, $\mathcal{P}(\mathcal{Q})$ includes joint angle limits, walking speed, step frequency, stride length, etc.

The second motion space is a hypothesized space in which humans encode and organize motions. We call this space the "psychological motion space." Although we know little about the structure or properties of this space, we can hypothesize that judging the similarity of two movements requires the computation of a "distance" between them. Although we consider this space to be pre-categorical, when we (as humans) categorize a movement as belonging to the class "running," "walking," or "throwing," we probably use the shortest distance between the movement and exemplars of these different classes [19].

The third motion space is also a conceptual space in which humans describe movements using words. This "linguistic motion space" contains attributes in which concepts such as "slower" and "bouncy" are defined. This is also the space used to interpret the labels on the user interfaces of computer animation tools, although there is little reason to believe that there is a solid basis for choosing the labels that are

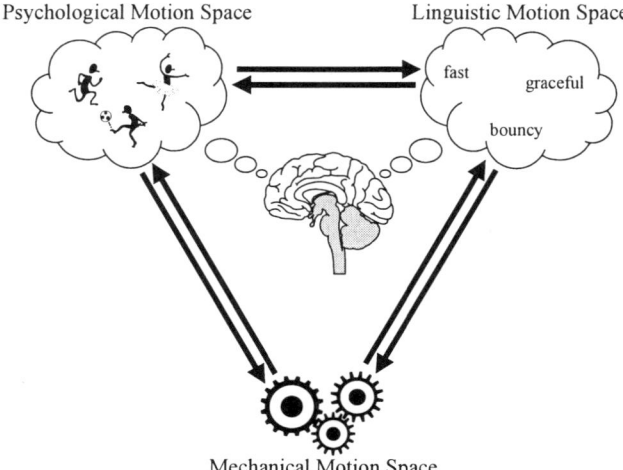

Figure 1: The three motion spaces used to discuss the relationship between the parameters of a movement and the perceptions and judgements formed by a human observer. Computer animation tools usually operate in the mechanical motion space, whereas humans perceive and code the features of movements in the psychological motion space and they describe movements with words in the linguistic motion space.

currently in use.

Figure 1 illustrates the relationships between these three motion spaces. One contribution of our work is the investigation of the form of the mappings between these three space. The mechanical motion space is a vector space, which makes it particularly amenable to computation — one of the main reasons it is used as the basis for most animation systems. The other two spaces are not vector spaces, but may have some structure that can be exploited. If they were vector spaces, the problem would be easy. We would simply choose convenient bases in each space and use those to define the mappings between them.

The linguistic space is defined by a number of categorical dimensions such as fast-slow, flexible-stiff, smooth-bouncy, etc. But these almost certainly do not form a vector space in the mathematical sense of the term. Even more problematic is the psychological space in which similarity-dissimilarity judgements are made. Ideally dissimilarity would have the properties of a distance measure, but it is not likely that human judgements form a metric space, much less a vector space. So we are left with the problem of determining the extent to which we can map between these three ways of describing motion in a manner that is useful for computer animation.

Computer animation programs represent human movement using a three-component model: time signals $\mathcal{Q}(t)$ specifying the movement of the figure, a mapping ($\mathcal{A}$)

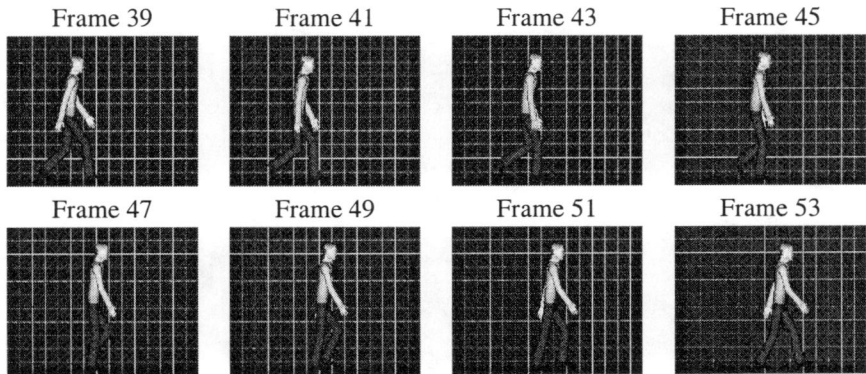

Figure 2: Sample frames from a computer animation display of a human walking movement.

between $\mathcal{Q}(t)$ and the position, orientation and posture of the human figure, and the visual appearance of the human figure (skin, clothing, and other surface attributes). This low-level representation is suitable for highly trained animators who are experienced at translating high-level natural language descriptions of motions (*e.g.*, scripts and storyboards) into manipulations of motion signals, but it is not very intuitive for non-animators.

Motion signals are transformed using the mapping $\mathcal{A}$ and the visual appearance of a human figure into a visual presentation termed a *computer animation display*. Computer animation displays of human figure animations rapidly create and present images ("frames") that show successive poses, positions and orientations of a human movement. Computer animation displays allow changes in viewpoint and arbitrary playback rates. Figure 2 shows eight frames from a computer animation display of a human walking movement.

As noted before, our ultimate goal is to allow animators to directly specify motion using the linguistic motion space, rather than requiring them to perform the tedious mapping to the less intuitive parametric description of the mechanical motion space. This is ambitious. It is likely that this will never be achieved in its entirety, but even a system that gets "most of it right" would substantially improve the process of computer animation. If skilled animators could get "first cut" motion sequences that were almost right, they could concentrate their efforts on the final tailoring of the details. This is a more achievable goal, and one that we believe we have made some progress on.

In the next section we survey earlier work on developing higher-level techniques for describing human motion for computer animation, emphasizing recent attempts to specify motion using linguistic or emotional descriptions.

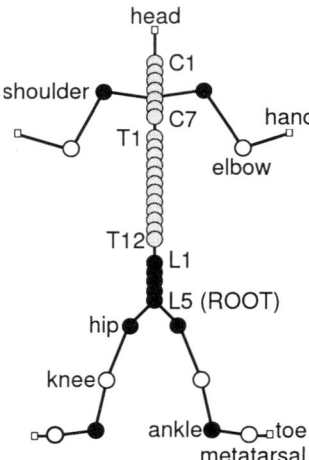

Figure 3: An articulation approximating the skeletal structure of the human body. Open (white) circles indicate hinge joints with only one rotational axis. Shaded (gray) circles indicate joints with two rotational axes. Dark (black) circles indicate joints with three rotational axes.

3. Related Work

In a computer program, the mapping $\mathscr{A}$ typically involves the specification of the jointed skeletal structure of a human. Originally suggested by Burtnyk and Wein [3], this structure is usually represented by an acyclic hierarchical articulation with the root at the hips, the approximate center of mass and movement. Zeltzer [23] presented a method for defining the articulation using a compact notation and Chadwick et al. [4] discussed the attachment of the visual form including deformable muscles, fat, skin, and clothing.

In computer animation applications, the human body requires from seventeen to over one hundred joints as illustrated in Figure 3. Some joints can be modeled as simple hinges with one rotational axis while other joints are modeled as "ball and socket" connections with three rotational axes.[1]

The movement of the human figure — that is the change in posture, position, and orientation of the articulation — is specified by the elements of $\mathscr{Q}(t)$, one function for each rotational or simple translational joint axis, and six functions specifying the position and orientation of the articulation as a whole. For classes of motions, such as cyclical symmetric straight-line walking motions, we can summarize the motion signals of a specific motion from the class with a set of motion parameters, $\mathscr{P}(\mathscr{Q})$. For walking motions, $\mathscr{P}(\mathscr{Q})$ includes parameters such as walking speed, stride frequency,

---

[1] Many of the joints are in the hands. Excluded from our definition of $\mathscr{A}$ is the ability to include facial expressions in $\mathscr{Q}(t)$ since these are not necessary for gross human body motions.

stride length, and joint angle limits of the arms, spine, hips, legs and feet.

For our work we used Bruderlin's `Walker` and his "Akira" visual form for the mechanical motion model [2]. Scaled values of `Walker`'s twenty-nine parameters were used to define $\mathscr{P}(\mathscr{Q})$. These parameters are: walk velocity, step length, step frequency, shoulder rotation, degrees of arm swing, angle arms are raised from the sides, elbow rotation (min, max), torso tilt (forward/backward), torso sway (side to side), torso rotation (left to right), lateral displacement, rotation of the pelvis about the vertical axis and list from side to side, bounciness on foot strike as the supporting knee bends, amount of over stride, hip flexion as leg swings forward, knee angle during swing, midstride and impact, stride width (distance left to right of foot placements), angle of foot with respect to straight forward ("pigeon or duck toes"), and whether the heel or toe strikes the ground first, as shown in Figure 4.

Bruderlin's `Walker` is one attempt to allow the specification of human movements at a higher level than a full specification of the motion signals, *i.e.*, a particular parameter set $\mathscr{P}(\mathscr{Q})$ for $\mathscr{Q}(t)$. Manipulations of `Walker`'s slider-based user interface produces walks with different styles that are always dynamically stable and physically plausible. Subtle constraints between the parameters are automatically adjusted by `Walker`, *e.g.*, increasing the walking speed increases the stride frequency and stride length, and leans the figure forward. Nevertheless, Bruderlin's description is still in a mechanical motion space.

We are interested in creating techniques that work at the level of movement quality and style. Other researchers have presented techniques for editing the quality of an existing motion or blending two motions with different styles to create intermediate styles. For example, Loomis *et al.* recorded the movements of native American Sign Language signers and then created synthetic signs and manipulated their movement quality independently of spatial path [13].

Much later, Unuma, Anjyo, and Takeuchi attempted to use Fourier analysis to represent cyclical motions such as running and walking [22, 21]. By interpolating and extrapolating between the Fourier coefficients they were able to create motions containing "emotive" content such as happy or sad walks, or normal and brisk walks. Their goal was to be able to extract the "briskness" factor from a walk and add it to a run to create a "brisk run." Along a similar line, Amaya *et al.* applied signal processing techniques to create an "emotional transform" capable of determining the difference between a neutral and emotional movement as contained in the timing and amplitude differences of the motions [1].

Rose and Cohen presented a system that parameterizes cyclical motion captured "verbs," such as walk, with "adverbs" that alter the motion, enabling them to create a continuous walking motion up and down hills, and turning left and right [20]. They could also add emotive variations such as happiness and sadness. The target application for their work was the real-time control of a digital puppet or video games character, with smooth transitions between motion verbs and adverbs.

Perlin presented a method to generate motion with "personality" by using expressions containing pseudo-random noise functions to generated the joint angle motions [16]. Also aimed at real-time motion generation, Perlin's system allows the operator to control a character while specifying particular moods and attitudes to be

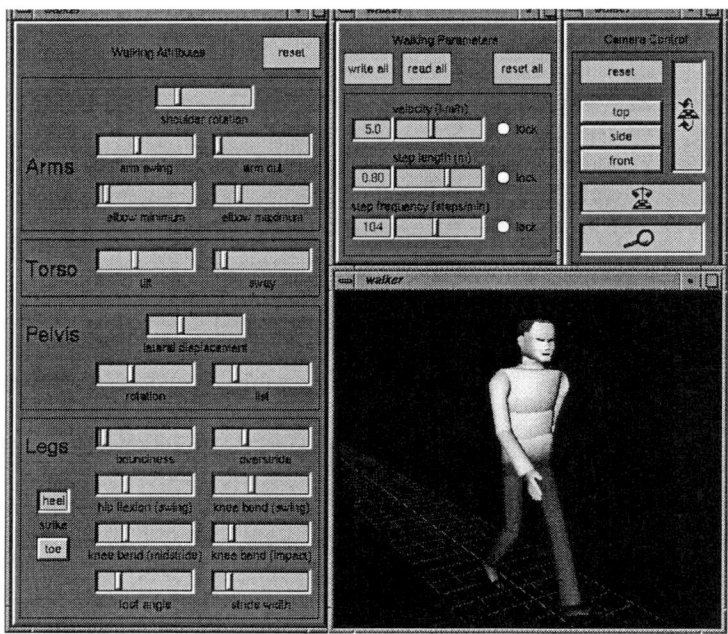

Figure 4: Screen shot of Bruderlin's Walker showing the output window and controls. The program uses twenty-nine inputs to vary the style of the walk by computing the motion of thirty-six joints totaling eighty-three degrees of freedom. The inputs are: walk velocity, step length, step frequency, shoulder rotation, degrees of arm swing, angle arms are raised from the sides, elbow rotation (min, max), torso tilt (forward/backward), torso sway (side to side), torso rotation (left to right), lateral displacement, rotation of the pelvis about the vertical axis and list from side to side, bounciness on foot strike as the supporting knee bends, amount of over stride, hip flexion as leg swings forward, knee angle during swing, midstride and impact, stride width (distance left to right of foot placements), angle of foot with respect to straight forward ("pigeon or duck toes"), and whether the heel or toe strikes the ground first.

conveyed. Kinematic constraints prevent "impossible" transitions.

All of these approaches use kinematics, as represented by the motion signals, rather than dynamics to model the motions. In contrast, Phillips and Badler presented a method of maintaining dynamic constraints such as balance and stability, which they consider "characteristics of human-like movement," while the animator specified goal-oriented motions [17]. Popovic and Witkin also employed dynamics rather than kinematics, but generally focused on manipulating the spatial path of a motion while maintaining it's existing movement qualities [18].

The weakness of these and similar techniques is that they are difficult to evaluate and there have been few attempts to validate the effects of the proposed manipulation methods. We are interested in descriptions of motion that are directly related to human perception of motion, and not tied to the underlying mathematics employed by the computational algorithms. One possible evaluation technique is to employ Certified Movement Analysts (CMAs) to estimate factors such as the Effort components of the resulting movements. CMAs are trained and certified by the Dance Notation Bureau [7], and employ a formal descriptive methodology developed by Rudolf von Laban [11, 12]. Laban's four effort elements[2] attempt to capture the interactions between the spatial path and temporal elements of a movement that often occur in coordinated movements of the whole body.

One of the few computer animation systems evaluated by CMAs is Chi's PhD Thesis on creating motion specified through a combination of keyframing and Laban's Effort descriptors [5, 6]. Chi created several video sequences of a character moving its arms, and then presented these sequences with and without effort components. Four CMAs viewed the video sequences twice, the first time to familiarize themselves with the character and its movement, and a second time to judge which of the four Effort elements were present in each segment to what extent (positive, not present, negative). The CMAs judged at least 53% of the Effort elements correctly — that is, in agreement with the input settings of Chi's system, with the in-house consultant judging 76.6% correctly. The majority of the incorrect judgements were "not present" judgements rather than opposite to the intended effort element.

Although Chi achieved moderate success with her system for interpolating keyframed movements, attempting to use Laban's effort system to translate between computer and human representations of motion is very difficult if not impossible. Because Laban's effort elements are a notational system used to communicate stylistic patterns of whole body movements between two humans they require experience of how humans move and code movement. While we can approximate the movement of humans by using $\mathcal{Q}(t)$ and $\mathcal{A}$ we do not yet know how humans code movements mentally or how much they rely on their own experiences of generating movement to code the observed movements of others.

Another technique is to have participants in an experimental setting categorize the resulting movements according to their emotional content. This technique has been used by Paterson and Pollick to determine the role of velocity in affect discrimination [15, 14]. Using both movements created by actors attempting to express different

---

[2]The elements are indirect versus direct, light versus strong, sustained versus quick, and free versus bound.

affects and neutral movements manipulated with signal processing similar to Amaya *et al.*'s techniques [1], Paterson *et al.* had participants name the resulting affects associated with each movement. Their results indicate a strong effect of velocity on the modulation of affect.

A final possible technique would be to obtain direct comparisons between two movements, one created by a computer and one recorded from natural human motion, and use these as a basis for mapping the linguistic descriptions of the natural human movement to the parametric description of the closest corresponding computer-generated movement. We have taken an approach that is related to this, but which adds a third motion space. Rather than assume that humans rely solely on either a categorical linguistic motion space — such as Laban's Effort model or Paterson and Pollick's emotional affects — we also assume the existence of a non-categorical non-linguistic psychological motion space in which observers code, compare, and analyse human movements.

The goal of our research is to eventually build higher-level computer animation systems by determining the structure and the bidirectional relationships between the three motion spaces. In the next section we describe the first steps in augmenting this basic framework with such mappings through the experimental collection and analysis of judgements made by human observers of computer-generated human motion.

4. Description of Experiments

We conducted two participant-based experiments to collect information about the relationships between the three motion spaces. The mechanical motion space is defined by Walker's parameters, $\mathscr{P}(\mathscr{Q})$. The psychological and linguistic motion spaces are unique to each participant and are defined by their descriptions and comparison of human motions. Although we analysed the relationships between the motion spaces within-participants, we also looked for commonalities between participants.

The psychological motion space of each participant is defined by their judgements of the similarity of pairs of motions. We used a method similar to those used by earlier researchers. In both experiments comparison trials presented on a computer monitor two walking motions, one after the other. A participant then recorded their judgement of similarity on a continuous scale with the "Similar" end of the scale coded as zero, indicating "no distance" between the two motions, and the "Dissimilar" end of the scale coded as one, indicating a "large distance" between the two motions. Figure 5 illustrates a motion comparison trial. Each trial took about ten seconds: seven seconds for the presentation of the gaits and two to three seconds for the participant to make a judgement and click on the "Finish Trial" button.

After completing all of the trials involving comparing motions the participants described each motion. These descriptions define the linguistic motion space of each participant. After presentation of a single walking motion the participant recorded a description of the gait on eight continuous scales labeled with pairs of words with opposite meanings: fast-slow, flexible-stiff, smooth-bouncy, young-old, energetic-tired, light-heavy, graceful-spastic, and normal-strange. Ratings on each scale were coded in the interval $[0, 1]$. Figure 6 illustrates a motion rating trial. Each trial took about

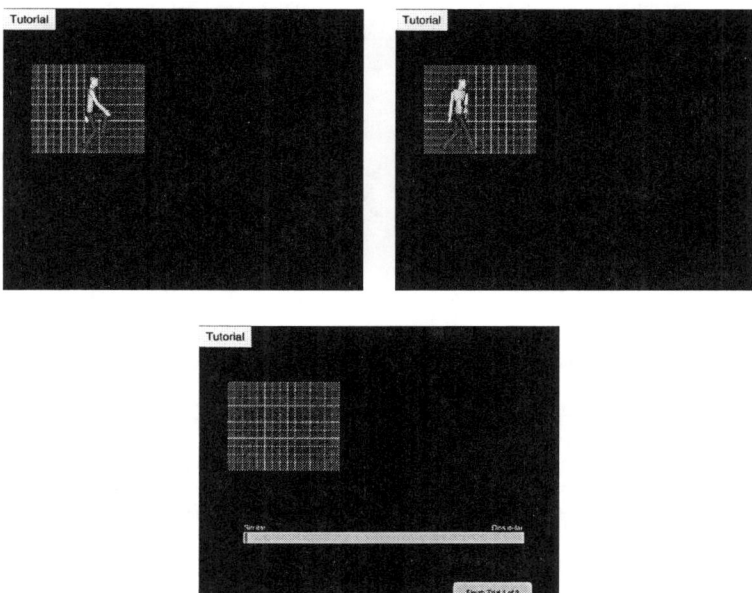

Figure 5: Three screen shots illustrating a motion comparison trial. *Top images*: The first gait is presented, then the second gait is presented. *Bottom image*: Next, the Similar-Dissimilar scale is displayed with the marker at the Similar end of the scale. After indicating a judgement of dissimilarity, the participant clicks on the "Finish Trial 1 of 3" button in the lower right hand corner of the screen. Participants were instructed to click on the "skip" button in the lower left hand corner of the screen only if they felt their attention drifted during the presentation of the stimulus and they failed to observe the walking motion. The "Tutorial" label in the upper left hand corner of the screen appears only during the training portion of the experiment.

fifteen seconds: four seconds for the presentation of the gait and about ten seconds for the participant to record ratings on each of the eight descriptive scales and click on the "Finish Trial" button.

All trials were replicated in random order in each of four blocks and participants were instructed to use the first block to learn the task of comparing or describing the gaits. Participants were shown all of the gaits used in an experiment as many times as they wished before beginning the first block of trials. Participants were naive to the hypotheses and were paid for their involvement.

Experiment One was a broad initial experiment performed to demonstrate the collection of similarity judgements and descriptions of the movements from human observers using a wide range of human walking movements. We systematically varied Walker's motion parameters to create twenty-six gaits with as wide a variety as possible of walking motions with the constraint that all gaits had the same walking

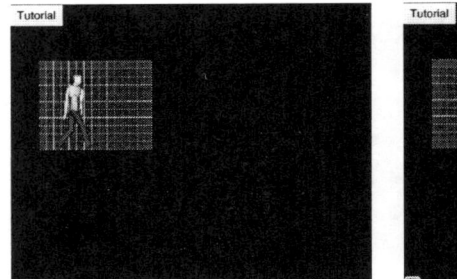
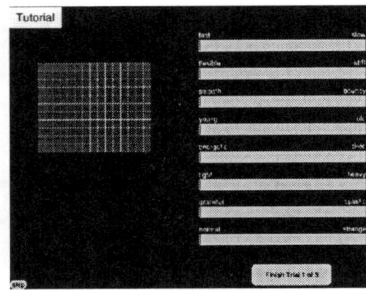

Figure 6: Two screen shots illustrating a motion rating trial. *Left to Right*: A gait is presented, then the eight rating scales were displayed. After indicating a description of the motion, the participant clicks on the "Finish Trial 1 of 3" button in the lower right hand corner of the screen. Participants were instructed to click on the "skip" button in the lower left hand corner of the screen only if they felt their attention drifted during the presentation of the stimulus and they failed to observe the walking motion. The "Tutorial" label in the upper left hand corner appears only during the training portion of the experiment.

velocity. Each gait was randomly paired with two other gaits to create fifty-two trials (repeated in each of four blocks). We recruited six participants: five were social dancers (three females and two males) chosen with the expectation that they would be able to apply their experience observing, imitating, and discussing human movements; the remaining participant was a non-dancer (male).

Experiment Two was an in depth experiment to determine the properties of the psychological motion space by using a narrower range of walking movements that included movements created by interpolating motion parameters. Figure 7 illustrates the two networks used to define the gaits. The first network is a triangle defined by three "primary" gaits, indicated with the filled circles. The gait parameters of the primary gaits were interpolated to create the gait in the center of the triangle. The second network is defined by two primary gaits on the ends of a line and the gait parameters of the primary gaits are interpolated to create three gaits along the line. The use of interpolation of gait parameters allows us to test the effect of interpolation in the mechanical motion space on proximities in the psychological motion space. Each gait was paired in both orders of presentation with all other gaits and itself within its network to create forty-one trials (sixteen plus twenty-five).

Reflecting our focus on the psychological motion space, we expanded the number and backgrounds of our participants to reflect the general population of individuals. We recruited thirty participants. They had experience in social dancing (seven females, one male), recreational running (nine females, eight males), or neither (one female, four males). We also introduced an additional experimentally controlled variable that specified the direction the figure walked across the screen: left to right — the same condition as in Experiment One (nineteen participants) — and right to left

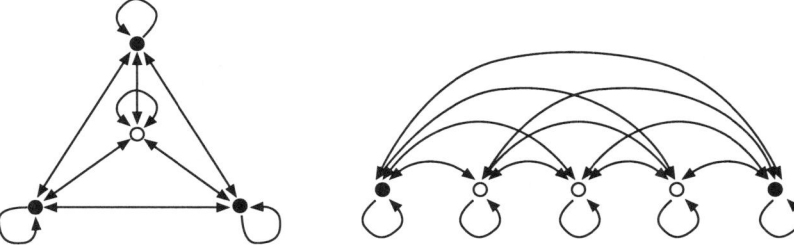

Figure 7: Networks of comparisons for primary gaits (filled circles) and interpolated gaits (unfilled circles). On the left, a triangle of three primary gaits with an interpolated gait in the center requires sixteen comparisons (arcs) to test the metric properties. On the right, two primary gaits are interpolated to create three new gaits, requiring ten comparisons to test metric properties and parameterization.

(eleven participants). We used a variety of measures, such as average judgement variance, badness of triangular fit, weirdness index (as computed using multidimensional scaling), and strength of correlation between similarity judgements and differences between ratings.

5. Analysis of the Properties of the Psychological Motion Space

The purpose of *Experiment Two* was to determine the properties of the psychological motion space — specifically by using networks of gaits which are compared in all possible combinations. By using interpolation of the motion parameters we sought to determine if the psychological motion space has metric properties. These properties are:

H_0^{1m} Non-degeneracy: only the self-distance is zero, and distances are never negative: $d(i,j) > d(i,i) = 0$.

H_0^{2m} Symmetry: distances between points are symmetric: $d(i,j) = d(j,i)$.

H_0^{3m} Triangular Inequality: sum of lengths of two sides of a triangle is never less than the length of the third side: $d(i,j) + d(j,k) \geq d(j,k)$.

If similarity judgements had the metric properties then we could continue to treat similarity judgements as approximations of the distance between motions. This would allow us to move beyond simple correlation between the spaces and begin to build models of how motion parameters are combined to form similarity judgements.

To test the first metric property we constructed trials in which each motion was compared to every motion within its network including itself. Our analysis of the motion comparison trials in which a motion was compared to itself revealed that the participants recorded a judgement more than one mark along the scale away from the similar end on average six times out of twenty-seven trials.[3] This indicates that $d(i,i) \neq 0$.

We also analysed the trials in which two different motions were presented and discovered an asymmetry in the pattern of judgements. We believe that if a participant recorded a similarity judgement for two different motions between the Similar end of the scale and the first mark on that scale that they thought that either they had seen the same motion twice or that they had seen two very similar motions. We term these judgements *mis-judgements*.

Participants tended to make a mis-judgement more frequently when the first motion was more "average" than the second. For example, when the center motion in the triangular network was presented first followed by one of the corner motions the number of mis-judgements was much higher — on the order of 50% — than the reversed order of presentation. These mis-judgements indicate that $d(i,j) = 0$ even when $i \neq j$.

We tested the symmetry of similarity judgements by testings if the average judgement $d(i,j)$ was equal to the average judgement in the reverse presentation order, $d(j,i)$ (within participants). The triangular network requires six of these comparisons, and the linear network requires ten. We used $\alpha = 0.05$ to indicate asymmetry of judgements. While each participant had at least one asymmetric average judgement, and the worst participant had four asymmetric average judgements, we did not feel that these asymmetries were strong enough to demonstrate violation of the symmetry property.

Finally, we tested the triangle inequality by counting the number of triangles formed using averaged similarity judgments that did not conform to the triangular inequality. We concluded that the triangular inequality did not hold because across the participants 14-30% of the triangles failed the triangular inequality.

We also compared groups of participants as defined by demographics (dancer/ runner/ neither, male/ female) and direction of walking according to the following measures: average judgement variance, badness of triangular fit, weirdness index (as computed using multidimensional scaling [8]), and strength of correlation between similarity judgements and differences between ratings. We found no large systematic differences between the populations of participants, indicating that perceptual similarity of motions relies on a basic perceptual process common to all humans.[4]

Since we interpolated the motion parameters to generate some of the gaits we examined the relationship between interpolation of the parameters and the resulting similarity judgements. While the relationship is not linear, we found it to be smooth and monotonic. This suggests that though the psychological motion space is not metric, it is locally well behaved.

To summarize, we tested similarity judgements against the metric properties and found evidence that the judgements do not conform to the non-degeneracy and triangle inequalities. This means that we cannot treat similarity judgements as approximations of the distance between gaits in a metric space. Comparison of the participants according to demographic and experimental variables indicated that comparing the motion of human walking figures is a process that does not require special training.

---

[3] There were eighteen regions along the Similar-Dissimilar scale demarcated with seventeen thin vertical lines. Thus the marks were placed 5.6% of the width of the scale apart.

[4] We could not test for interaction effects due to empty cells.

6. Analysis of Relationships Between Motion Spaces

In *Experiment One* the participants compared pairs of the gaits as to their similarity and described each of the gaits using eight descriptive rating scales. Combined with the parameters of the motions $\mathcal{P}(\mathcal{Q})$, we have three sets of relationships:

1. Mechanical and Linguistic Motion Spaces: which parameters $\mathcal{P}(\mathcal{Q})$ correlate with descriptions along each rating scale?

2. Mechanical and Psychological Motion Spaces: differences in which parameters correlate with similarity judgements of pairs of motions?

3. Psychological and Linguistic Motion Spaces: difference along which rating scales correlate with similarity judgements of pairs of motions?

Relationship between Mechanical and Linguistic Motion Spaces

For each participant, we determined which of the parameters influenced their ratings along the descriptive scales by computing the strength of linear correlations between the motion parameters and the descriptions. While the pattern of correlations differs for each participant, we found that each participant's ratings along each scale co-varied significantly with two to five parameters ($\alpha = 0.05$), indicating that each participant focused on particular body part movements to form their descriptions.

To determine which parameters most strongly influenced the ratings, we counted the number of participants with significant correlations for each combination of rating scale and parameter and list here those combinations which a majority of the participants (four or more out of six) had significant correlations:

fast-slow	step length and knee swing (controls the amount the foot "kicks up" as it leaves the ground).
flexible-stiff	upper torso rotation (vertical axis) and pelvis rotation (vertical axis).
smooth-bouncy	bounciness (up and down motion of the body on each step).
young-old	magnitude of arm swing (at shoulder), magnitude of elbow rotation, and knee swing.
energetic-tired	magnitude of arm swing (at shoulder), magnitude of elbow rotation, tilt of torso, knee swing, average knee bend throughout stride.
light-heavy	heel or toe strike on each step.
graceful-spastic	magnitude of elbow rotation, torso sway (front and back tilt), bounciness, and hip swing (height of leg swing as foot swings forward).
normal-strange	torso sway, bounciness, and hip swing.

These relationships are not too surprising — we carefully picked our set of descriptive scales and Bruderlin carefully picked Walker's controls.

Relationship between Mechanical and Psychological Motion Spaces

We computed the strength of the correlations between the mechanical and psychological motion spaces by approximating the distance between pairs of gaits in the mechanical motion space by the difference in their parameters, as well as the differences of the Z-scores of the parameter computed using principal components analysis [10]. To summarize our findings, we found individual parameters that correlated stronger than 0.4 for all participants, and some correlations as strong as 0.6. The most popular parameters were those controlling the height the arms were raised from the sides of the body, the bounciness of the stride, and the fixed tilt of the torso. The strongest correlations between the similarity judgements and the principal components of the parameters were along the first principal component for all participants and ranged from 0.33 to 0.72 with a median value of 0.48. This indicates that the principal components of the parameters capture the interesting variation of the gaits in both the mechanical and psychological motion spaces.

We attempted to improve on the strength of these correlations by combining the principal components of the parameters by using the City-Block, Euclidean, and Dominance distance metrics (L^1, L^2, and L^∞, respectively). The strongest correlations varied from 0.41 to 0.73, with the Dominance norm (L^∞) producing the strongest correlations for four of the six participants.

Relationship between the Psychological and Linguistic Motion Spaces

For the relationships between the psychological and linguistic motion spaces we computed the strength of the correlations in a similar fashion. The strongest correlation between dissimilarities and differences along any single rating scale varied across the participants from 0.42 to 0.68 with a median of 0.58. The strongest correlations occurred along the young-old scale for four of the participants, and along the fast-slow and energetic-tired scale for the other two participants.

These correlations indicate that the rating scales can be used to indicate the similarity of gaits: similar gaits have similar descriptions and dissimilar gaits have dissimilar descriptions. As we saw before, the participants also tended to agree as to which parameters most strongly influenced each rating scale. This leads to our next question: do the participants' linguistic motion spaces have common features? To answer this question we computed the principal components of each participant's ratings. We normalized the ratings along each scale to have zero mean and unit variance. This gives each scale equal weight and tends to equalize the participants' interpretations of the scales.

Structure of the Linguistic Motion Space

We found that all of the participant's ratings could be compressed from eight rating scales to three or four principal components by taking only those components with a variance greater than one. This cut-off corresponds to a total variance accounted of more than 80%. Additionally we found several patterns across the participants' components:

- Five participants (#2, #3, #4, #5, and #6) had a very similar first principal component which is an average of all the rating scales and describes motions as either bouncy, spastic, strange, fast, heavy, energetic, young, stiff or as smooth, graceful, normal, slow, light, tired, old, flexible.

- Four participants had a single component dominated by the young-old, energetic-tired, flexible-stiff scales with the expected orientation: young, energetic, flexible versus old, tired, stiff. These components are the second principal components of #1, #3, and #4, and the third principal component of #6.

- The third and fourth principal components tend to be dominated by one or two scales — possibly reflecting the biases of each participant.

We computed the correlations between the similarity judgements and the Z-scores of the principal components of the descriptions and found for five of the participants the strongest correlation occurred along the first principal component (min = 0.47, max = 0.74, median = 0.62), and for the sixth participant the strongest correlation was 0.32 along her second component. We attempted to improve on the strength of these correlations by combining the principal components of the descriptions using the City-Block, Euclidean, and Dominance distance metrics. We were able to exceed the strength of the correlations for only half of the participants beyond the correlations computed along the components. For five of the participants the strongest correlations were produced using the City-Block norm, for the sixth participant the Euclidean norm produced the strongest correlations.

To summarize, in *Experiment One* for each participant we found moderately strong to strong linear correlations between the three motion spaces. We also found agreements between the participants as to which motion parameters influenced their similarity judgements and their descriptions, as well as common structures in their linguistic motion spaces. In each case, when we computed the principal components of the motion space we were able to find stronger correlations between the spaces using the principal components, rather than the original dimensions.

These results validate our experimental methodology and demonstrate that although we cannot assume that the participants would have similar biases as to the similarity of two gaits or how a gait should be described, the agreements between the participants suggest that higher-level human-computer interfaces to animation systems would not need to be custom tailored for each user, rather they could be "initialized" with a set of standard controls and then refined by adjusting the standard controls, or by choosing a set of controls that reflects the user's perceptual biases.

7. Conclusions and Future Work

Computer graphics has benefited greatly from an understanding of human vision. For example, design guidelines based in knowledge of trichromacy, opponent colors, and JND measurements have informed the design of graphics hardware and software. For more complex stimuli and tasks, however, the basic perceptual abilities and bottlenecks are not well described. In the case of human figure animation, we know very little. This paper begins a process of exploring the motion spaces associated with human figure movement. We postulated two human-based representations of human figure movement, a linguistic space whose nature is determined in part by our ability to describe and categorize movements, and a psychological space more closely tied to perceptual events. Both contribute to our visual experience, and an understanding of both will support the creation of authoring and database management tools for character animation.

Experiment One examined the classification of gaits within the structure of pairs of opposite movement description terms. We found that the focus of attention varied among subjects, but that similar stimulus characteristics were salient in determining the classification of gaits, and that classification was somewhat consistent across most of our subjects and could be reduced to three to four principal components. *Experiment Two* explored the metric properties of the psychological space by asking subjects to make comparisons between a limited range of movements that were unlikely to span boundaries between multiple linguistic descriptors, but which were perceptually distinct. We concluded that similarity judgements do not have all of the metric properties. Our analysis was complicated by order effects of stimulus pair presentation, a not uncommon finding in complex perceptual tasks. Despite this, we did achieve some support for our hypothesis that the underlying perceptual evaluation was similar across subjects. The persistence of intersubject performance differences does suggest that future animation systems should be customizable not only for the user's preferences, but for their perceptual abilities and cognitive/linguistic structures as well. If our findings are correct, we can predict that this customization might be achieved by altering parameter values associated with the relative weights given to common perceptual cues without the need to add or substantially modify the nature of the cues themselves.

Our findings are preliminary, and more research will be needed before we begin to achieve our goal of creating animation environments capable of mapping between the intuitive linguistic descriptions of motions and computer representations by incorporating our understanding of the non-categorical aspects of human motions captured by the psychological motion space. Future experiments will explore the perceptual and linguistic spaces in more detail, and additional experimental controls for order effects should enable us to build models of the relationships between the three motion spaces with increasing predictive validity. In themselves, the present experiments have demonstrated that both the linguistic and psychological spaces have a level of structure and internal consistency that will support just such a parametric analysis.

Additional details of both experiments are available in the first author's doctoral dissertation [9].

References

[1] Kenji Amaya, Armin Bruderlin, and Tom Calvert. Emotion from motion. In Wayne A. Davis and Richard Bartels, editors, *Proceedings of Graphics Interface '96*, pages 222–229. Canadian Information Processing Society, Canadian Human-Computer Communications Society, May 1996. ISBN 0-9695338-5-3.

[2] Armin Bruderlin. *Procedural Motion Control Techniques for Interactive Animation of Human Figures*. PhD thesis, Simon Fraser University, School of Computing Science, March 1995.

[3] N. Burtnyk and M. Wein. Interactive skeleton techniques for enhancing motion dynamics in key frame animation. *Communications of the ACM*, 19(10):564–569, October 1976.

[4] John E. Chadwick, David R. Haumann, and Richard E. Parent. Layered construction for deformable animated characters. In *Computer Graphics (ACM SIGGRAPH 1989 Proceedings)*, pages 243–252, July 1989. Published as V23(4) of Computer Graphics.

[5] Diane Chi. *A Motion Control Scheme for Animating Expressive Arm Movement*. PhD thesis, University of Pennsylvania, Department of Computer & Information Science, June 1999. Also published at IRCS-99-06.

[6] Diane M. Chi, Norman I. Badler, and Janis Pforisch. Animating expressivity through effort elements. In *Siggraph'99 Conference Abstracts and Applications*, page 231, 1999.

[7] Dance notation bureau. http://www.dancenotation.org/, 2001. Phone: 212-564-0985, Fax: 212-904-1426.

[8] Mark L. Davison. *Multidimesional Scaling*. John Wiley & Sons, 1983.

[9] Jason Harrison. *Measuring and Comparing Human Walking Motions for Computer Animation*. PhD thesis, University of British Columbia, Department of Computer Science, December 2001. Available from http://www.cs.ubc.ca/~harrison/Thesis/Doctoral/.

[10] J. Edward Jackson. *A User's Guide to Principal Components*. John Wiley & Sons, Inc., 1991.

[11] Rudolf von Laban. *The language of movement; a guidebook to choreutics*. Boston, Plays, 1974.

[12] Rudolf von Laban and F. C. Lawrence. *Effort*. Macdonald and Evans, 1947.

[13] Jeffery Loomis, Howard Poizner, Ursula Bellugi, and John Hollerbach. Computer graphic modeling of american sign language. In *Computer Graphics (ACM SIGGRAPH 1983 Proceedings)*, pages 105–114, 1983. Published as V17(3) of Computer Graphics.

[14] Helena M. Paterson and Frank E. Pollick. Form and animacy in the perception of affect from biological motion. Poster at Vision Sciences Society First Annual Meeting, 2001. Available from the author: http://staff.psy.gla.ac.uk/~helena/.

[15] Helena M. Paterson, Frank E. Pollick, and Anthony J. Sanford. The role of velocity in affect discrimination. In *Proceedings of the Twenty-third Annual Conference of the Coginitive Science Society*, 2000.

[16] Ken Perlin. Real time responsive animation with personality. *IEEE Transactions on Visualization and Computer Graphics*, 1(1):5–15, March 1995.

[17] Cary B. Phillips and Norman I. Badler. Interactive behaviors for bipedal articulated figures. In Thomas W. Sederberg, editor, *Computer Graphics (ACM SIGGRAPH 1991 Proceedings)*, pages 359–362, July 1991. Published as V25(4) of Computer Graphics.

[18] Zoran Popović and Andrew Witkin. Physically based motion transformation. In Alyn Rockwood, editor, *Computer Graphics (ACM SIGGRAPH 1999 Proceedings)*, pages 11–20, Los Angelas, California, August 8-13, 1999. ACM SIGGRAPH.

[19] E. Rosch. Principles of categorization. In E. Rosch and B. B. Lloyd, editors, *Cognition and Categorization*. Hillsdale NJ: Lawrence Erlbaum, 1978.

[20] Charles Rose, Michael F. Cohen, and Bobby Bodenheimer. Verbs and adverbs: Multidimensional motion interpolation. *IEEE Computer Graphics and Applications*, 18(5):32–40, September/October 1998.

[21] Munetoshi Unuma, Ken Anjyo, and Ryozo Takeuchi. Fourier principles for emotion-based human figure animation. In Robert Cook, editor, *Computer Graphics (ACM SIGGRAPH 1995 Proceedings)*, Annual Conference Series, pages 91–96, Los Angeles, California, 6-11 August 1995, August 1995. ACM SIGGRAPH, Addison Wesley.

[22] Munetoshi Unuma and Ryozo Takeuchi. Generation of human motion with emotion. In Nadia Magnenat-Thalmann and Daniel Thalmann, editors, *Computer Animation '91*, pages 77–88, Geneva, Switzerland, 1991. Springer-Verlag.

[23] David Zeltzer. Representation of complex animated figures. In *Proceedings of Graphics Interface '82*, pages 205–211, 1982.

A Novel Multi-resolution Anthropometrical Algorithm For Realistic Simulation and Manipulation of Facial Appearance

H. K. Hussein
Ain Shams University,
Faculty of Science,
Math. and Comp. Sc. Dept.,
Abbassia, Cairo, Egypt

A. Bastanfard and M. Nakajima
Graduate School of Inf. Sc. & Eng.
Tokyo Institute of Technology
2-12-1 O-okayama, Meguro-ku,
152-8552, Tokyo, Japan

Abstract

Facial appearance changes associated with aging are affected with a variety of cues to age. These changes include the quantity and the color of hair, the length of the nose and ears, skin elasticity and the texture of skin (size of pores, prevalence of wrinkles, etc.). An attempt to mimic such changes by computer is an aspiring goal and challenging task. This paper proposes a novel algorithm with two techniques as a key solution for such a challenge by capturing such a variety of cues to age. These techniques discuss the facial deformation based on the face anthropometrical theory and simulate facial textures such as stubble and wrinkles with multi-resolution wavelets discriminated technique. Given some neutral face "C", the idea is to capture two features of "C" with advancing years. The first is the geometric deformation details like anthropometrical data change that developed in the anthropometrical theory. The second is the facial textures given in "C" after passing years. Then, together with warping technique we map these features to any other particular face in order to generate more expressive and convincing facial appearance. Comparisons with existing methods are drawn, advantages of our proposed techniques over previous methods are examined and validation of our approach is also given by discussions and illustrations of some experimental results.

Keywords: Wavelets, Multi-resolution analysis, Texture discrimination, Image map.

1. Introduction

Creating realistic renderings of human faces with animation has an endeavor in computer graphics for nearly three decades [12,13] and remains a subject of current interest. Applications of human face modeling and animation are founded in sophisticated human-computer interfaces, interactive games, multimedia titles, VR applications and in a broad variety of production animations. As we are humans, we are easily able to categorize a person's face and are often able to be quite precise in this estimation. Reproducing visual aging effects by computer is a difficult and time-consuming task because of the complex and individual shape of the face, the subtle and spatially varying reflectance properties of skin and the intricate deformations of the face during aging process. Animating a familiar object from a single image with aging or under some source of variation requires a handle on how to capture the image space created by that source of variation. In principle, three main elements have to be considered in facial aging: aging wrinkles, skin texture variations and facial shape changes. This paper shows how to simulate and predict aging accounting for these three elements. Our approach is motivated by a research on two studies. The first is the human texture perception and the multi-resolution analysis of wavelets for simulating the facial textures like stubble and wrinkles. The second is the face anthropometrical theory for simulating the facial deformation details with aging. The rich description of human geometry that developed in the anthropometrical theory provides an invaluable resource for human modeling in computer graphics. Anthropometrical studies like [21,22,9] report statistics on reliable differences in shape across faces. More details of this simulation technique will be given in section 4.1. On the other hand, the ability to delineate objects in the visual world depends partly upon the perception of textural consistency and difference. The theory of texture perception attribute preattentive texture discrimination to differences in first-order statistics of stimulus features such as orientation, size and brightness of constituent elements [19,25,33,15]. Daugman [18] has determined that the 2D Gabor filters are members of a class of functions achieving optimal joint resolution in the 2D space and frequency domains. They have also been found to be a good model for two-dimensional receptive fields of simple cells in the striate cortex. Computer applications of a set of Gabor filters to a variety of textures found to be preattentively discriminable produces results in which differently textured regions are distinguished by first-order differences in the values measured by filters [38]. From this point of view a novel multi-resolution wavelets discriminated technique for facial textures simulation will be discussed in section 4.2.

The paper is organized as follows. Section 2, reviews some of the prior researches in facial textures and skin modeling with some discussions of the problems of simulations. Section 3, provides a brief summary of the facial anthropometrical theory which we have used. Section 4, introduces our proposed techniques for facial deformation, wrinkle simulation and aging animation. Some experimental results with discussions are given in section 5. Finally, conclusion and direction for future work are discussed in section 6.

2. Prior Research and Problems

Recent endeavors provided solutions to the problems of facial animation and produced some attractive examples in terms of realism. Realism in face modeling and animation remains an aspired goal and its task becomes more challenging when wrinkle formation and facial aging are considered. The area of facial aging simulation has received relatively little attention in the computer graphics community and researchers discussed it from different point of view namely, geometric models, physically-based models and biomechanical models using either particle system or continuous system. For instance, Ishii et al. [36] proposed a geometric model of micro wrinkle, which uses a curved surface based on a polygon for expressing folds and ridges. Other extensions and improvement methods have been reported in [39,41,29,28,20]. On the other hand the idea of changing object appearance with only image information has been investigated recently by various researchers in both computer vision and graphics. Liu et al. [42] used the image ratio between a neutral face and an expression face of the same person to modify a different person's neutral face image and generate facial expression details. Given a face under two different lighting conditions and another face under the first lighting condition, Shashua et al. [4] used quotient image to generate an image of the second face under the second lighting condition. Stoschek [3] incorporates image morphing into the image synthesis process for photo-realistic re-rendering of faces at arbitrary illumination and pose directions. Another class of techniques based on morphing and their extensions were discussed in [8,2,5,1]. There were a few efforts for the dynamic model of wrinkles. Viaud et al. [24] have presented a generic hybrid model for the formation of expressive wrinkles, where bulges are modeled as spline segments. On the other hand, there is no method in which the texture image modified as a function of skin deformation. A physically based approach [10] can offer a better simulation of wrinkle formation, but if it requires geometrical modeling of the wrinkles it may be expensive. Texture mapping offers a good simulation of static wrinkles, but constructing visually interesting bump maps requires practices and artistic skills [20]. Based on an assumption that a family has some self-similarity, cloning method and aging simulation in a family [39] generate aging wrinkles on the faces of the son and daughter. Although, this method offered a good simulation of skin aging and wrinkles, its assumption may not be satisfied for all families because similarity can not be recognized in all families. Caricaturing technique [2,8] suffers from average face dependency and needs a collection of multiple images of different faces to form the average one.

The original contribution of this paper compared with the previous mentioned work is given in terms of the following advantages. First, the proposed techniques are efficient in time complexity, simple to implement, relatively easy and reliable in which they require only one source image without a need to collect a lot of images. Second, they are local. By local we mean that, wrinkling effects caused by deformations are confined the deformed areas. Third, they provide a simple way to capture the geometrical details founded in the real world objects without any constraints and map them smoothly to other real world objects. Finally, their computations are fast enough for an interactive environment.

3. Theory of Face Anthropometrical Measurements

Up to now, little has been done to simulate the facial appearance with advancing years. It is quite cumbersome process which is related to the change of physical structure and biological composition in body tissues. By a research on the theory of the face anthropometrical measurements, we concluded that, the form and values of these changes could be measured according to face anthropometrics [21,22,9]. Our idea describes a similar use of anthropometrics in the simulation of facial deformations for computer graphics applications. Anthropometrics theory is the biological science of human body measurement. Its evaluation begins with the identification of particular locations on a subject, called landmark points defined in terms of visible or palpable feature (skin or bone) on the subject. Farkas [21,22] used a wide set of measurements for describing the human face. Such measurements consist a total of 47 landmark of point for describing the face. Figure 1, illustrates some of them.

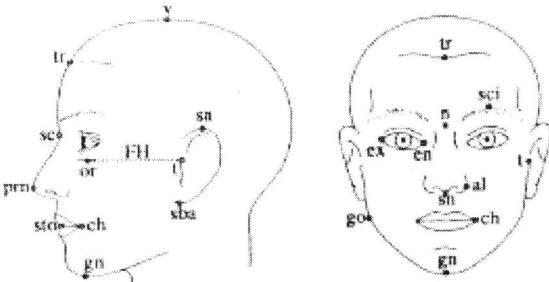

Figure 1 Anthropometrical landmarks on the face [21,9].

The landmarks are typically identified by abbreviations of the corresponding anatomical terms. For instance, the inner corner of the eye is "en" for endocanthion, while the top of the flap of cartilage (the tragus) in front of the ear is "t" for tragion. Farkas [21,22] included some types of facial measurements, which illustrated in figure 2. In figure 2, "en-ex" refers to the shortest distance between the landmarks at the corner of the eye, "v-tr" refers to the vertical distance between the top of the head and hairline, and "ch-t" refers to the tangential distance from the corner of the mouth to the tragus. More details can be found in [21,22].

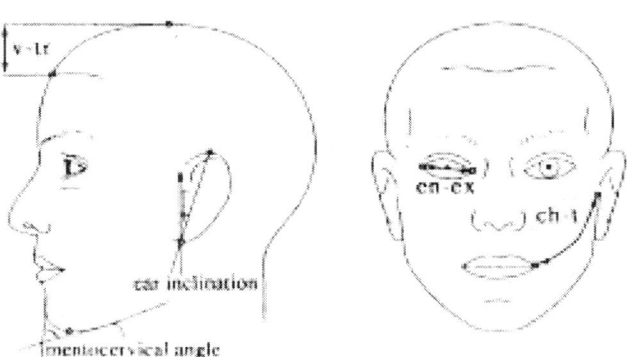

Figure 2 Anthropometrical measurements [21,9].

4. Our Proposed Algorithm

The quest for improved realism is always an important goal for computer graphics. One major difficulty in this process is the extreme complexity of real objects which exhibit many subtle variations over their entire surface. One of such variations is the cumulative aging that affects all real objects. Advancing age in humans often is accompanied by progressive deterioration of various physiological processes and morphological entities. This section explores a new algorithm with two techniques for realistic simulation and manipulation of facial appearance based on a previously discussed anthropometrical theory and multi-resolution wavelets discriminated technique.

4.1 Anthropometrical Facial Features Deformations Technique

As people become older their faces are subject to many changes. Visual acuity losses in the elderly probably are the best known of the age-related change. If one asks the question, after passing years how many variations are there in the face?, and which features will be changed with age?. Face anthropometrical theory founded the answer and showed us all of the features that have variations with advancing years. It classified the aging process into four groups, where each group has some feature variations with advancing years [17,21,23,16,30]. For instance, Weale [30] reports that after age 40, humans may lose as much as 4 cycles/degree per decade of their life. In addition, progressive changes in skin texture, hair color, nose, ears, as well as loss of hair (balding) also occur with advancing years which in turn affects the overall appearance of the face. Such changes are a function of some threshold, which is given in terms of age, sex, weight, and other parameters. For example, there is some threshold for hair receding [35], and there is some coefficient for cartilage growth with aging [17,23,16]. The idea for the facial feature deformation technique is based on the way of integrating such items in order to indicate the age of a person with other aging artifacts. Burson et al. [26] computed the difference of the aligned images of a young face and an old face. Given the image of a new neutral face to be aged the difference image is warped and added to this new face to make it look older. Our idea is built on such a technique. The advantage is that, instead of computing such differences, we capture such variations from the study of the previously discussed face anthropometrical theory. The problem for the facial feature deformation technique can be formulated mathematically as follows: Given two neutral faces M and N of two aligned surfaces S_1 and S_2 such that for every point on M, there is a corresponding point on N which has the same meaning like, (eye corners, nose tip, mouth corners, etc.). Let M^* denotes the image of M after deformations due to aging. Assume that N^* be the unknown image of the face N with the same aging effects (deformations) as M^*. Since human faces have approximately the same geometrical shape then, the facial feature deformations can be formulated as follows:

$$\frac{M^*(x,y)}{M(x,y)} = \frac{N^*(x,y)}{N(x,y)} \Rightarrow N^*(x,y) = N(x,y)\frac{M^*(x,y)}{M(x,y)} \qquad (1)$$

Where (x,y) are the coordinates of the pixels in the given images. The idea of our technique is to capture these ratios with aging from the face anthropometrics measurements theory. Anthropometrics measurements made a variety of statistical investigations possible on the reliable differences in shape across faces within a group of subjects. Subjects have been grouped on the basis of gender, race, age, attractiveness, etc. Besides the statistics on measurements, statistics on the proportions between measurements have also been derived. These proportions give useful information about the correlations between features with aging process. Means and variances for the measurements within a group tabulated in [17,21,16] effectively provide a set of measurements, which virtually capture all of the variations that can be occurred in the group. Taking into account the parameters of the given neutral face N and its unknown image N^* after deformations due to aging given in equation (1), the process of our algorithm can be summarized in the following three main steps:

- Identify the landmark point measurements or features of the given face using the anthropometrical landmarks measurements.
- Capture the calculated features change ratios due to aging R=M^*(x,y)/M(x,y), obtained according to the face anthropometrics measurements [17,21,16].
- Compute equation (1) by moving the features of N along R and warp the image accordingly [40].

In our implementation, we used linear warping over the feature points Delaunay triangulation, which we can combine with a one-to-one constraint algorithm to prevent the warped image folding [7]. The process of our algorithm resembles image metamorphosis (morphing) [1], but unlike morphing which changes the identity of the subject during the morph, by this method the identity is maintained across the transformation, as it will be shown in the experimental results.

4.2 Wavelets Facial Textures Simulation Technique

Face modeling and animation considering wrinkle formation and aging are an aspiring goal and a technical challenge. Facial aging exhibits not only facial features deformations as previously discussed but also subtle changes in the facial textures like stubble and wrinkles. These details are important visual cues but they are difficult to synthesis. Since these details are difficult to synthesis then intuitively, the best choice is to capture these details and map it to any other particular person's face in order to generate more expressive and convincing facial appearance. Geometrically, the difference between an old person's skin surface "M1" and a young person face "M2" is that, the older one has more bumps than the younger one. Thus, the goal is based on the way of how to capture such bumps of "M1" and map it to "M2" in order to make it look realistically older. We formulated this problem mathematically by developing a function say F such that

$$F(M1, M2) = \hat{M}2 \tag{2}$$

Where $\hat{M}2$ is the new form of the image M2 with the same facial features (bumps) of M1. For the function F, we present a novel multi-resolution wavelets discriminated technique for capturing such facial textures.

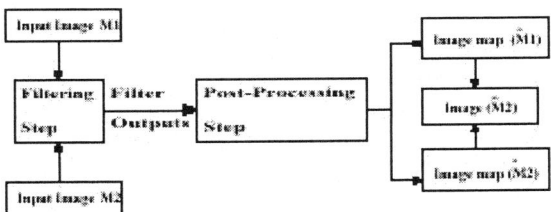

Figure 3 General structure algorithm outline.

In our approach we developed a formula for the desired function F, to be consist of two processing steps: (1) filtering step followed by (2) post-processing step. Given images M1 and M2 of two aligned surfaces S_1 and S_2 respectively, the filtering step produces a filter outputs or (filter responses) of both M1 and M2. Then, by applying the post-processing step a smooth discriminated feature vector image or simply image map of M1 and M2 namely, $\overline{M}1$ and $\overline{M}2$ are respectively obtained as illustrated in figure 3.

Based on the two processing steps of the function F, figure 4 shows the flowchart of the action of F on both M1 and M2 to obtain the required image $\hat{M}2$, where $\hat{M}2 = M2\left(\overline{M}1 / \overline{M}2\right)$.

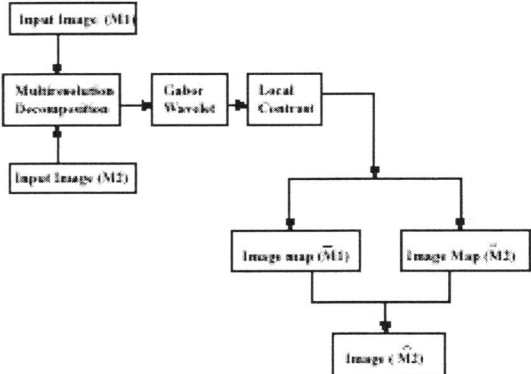

Figure 4 Algorithm flowchart structure steps.

The choice of the two processing steps of the function F is motivated by research on multi-resolution wavelets analysis and human texture perception and discrimination. Current theories of texture discrimination are based on the fact that two different textures are often producing a different distribution of responses in a bank of (orientation and spatial-frequency selective) linear filters. In aging a similar concept occurs where, the distributions of responses in a bank of linear filters of two facial textures at different age are different. Our idea is derived from this concept where, almost all of the spatial information characterizing a facial textured image can be captured in the first order statistics of an appropriately chosen set of linear filter outputs. Since wavelets [11,27,32] offer an elegant technique for representing the levels of details presented in an image and quickly captures the essence of the image data with only a small set of coefficients, this implies that wavelets use should give visually realistic results. Therefore, it will be a best choice for our purpose. In what follows, we will explain the mathematics behind the overall structure steps of the previously mentioned proposed function F.

4.2.1 Multi-resolution Wavelets Decomposition

Over the last few years, many constructions of wavelets have been introduced both in the mathematical analysis and in the signal processing literature [6,27,31]. The connection between the signal processing and the mathematical analysis was made by the introduction of multi-resolution analysis and the fast wavelet transform [32]. Multi-resolution representation is very effective for analyzing the information content of images and for providing a simple hierarchical framework for interpreting the image information [6,32]. It reorganizes the image information into a set of details appearing at different resolutions. Given a set of increasing resolutions $(r_j)_{j \in Z}$, the details of an image at the resolution r_j are defined as the difference of information between its approximation at the resolution r_j and its approximation at the lower resolution r_{j-1}. A multi-resolution decomposition enables us to have a scale-invariant interpretation of the image where, at different resolutions the details of an image generally characterize different physical structures of the image. The starting point for multi-resolution analysis is a nested set of vector spaces $\{V^0 \subset V^1 \subset V^2 \subset \Lambda \; V^j \subset \Lambda \}$, as j increases, the resolution of functions in V^j increases. The basis functions for the spaces V^j are known as scaling functions. From signal processing point of view, this means that, the approximation of a signal at a resolution 2^{j+1} contains all necessary information to compute the same signal at a smaller resolution 2^j. In signal processing context, wavelets originated in the context of subband coding or more precisely quadrature mirror filters [27,31]. The resulting coefficients describe the features of the underlying image in a local fashion in both frequency and space. Since the wavelets are local in space and frequency, then from this point our idea is derived to use a discrimination smoothing filters with little smoothing in the areas containing aging effects like stubble and wrinkles and strong smoothing in the remaining areas. Wavelets are computationally attractive as the associated transform is linear in the number of pixels [11]. From the mathematical point of view of the wavelets, a multi-resolution analysis is built using two basis functions, a scaling function and a wavelet function each of which satisfy some refinement relation [6,27,31]. Therefore, a linear image transform represents an image as a weighted sum of basis functions. That is, the image M (x, y) can represented as a sum over an indexed collections of functions, $g_i(x,y)$ given as:

$$M(x, y) = \sum_i y_i g_i(x, y) \tag{3}$$

Where, y_i is the transform coefficients. These coefficients are computed from the signal by projecting onto a set of projection function $p_i(x,y)$:

$$y_i = \sum_{x,y} p_i(x, y) M(x, y). \tag{4}$$

In many image processing applications, an image is decomposed into a set of subbands. The subbands are computed by convolving the image with a bank of linear filters. Each of the projection functions are a translated copy of one of the convolution kernels. In our case the multi-resolution decomposition is performed on each image to generate a number of visual channels, each containing the response of a particular receptive field. The multi-resolution decomposition is built by low pass filtering and decimating the original image. We call each of these images the base image for a particular level of the decomposition. This means that, for each of the images "M1" and "M2", the function F is decomposed into a set of functions F_i, where the domain of each function F_i is a subset of F, as F_i's need only be a function of the information contained in the low spatial frequency bands of its input image M_k for some k. An intuitive proof of this is given by induction. Consider a new image M', which is generated from an image M by removing its high frequencies by low pass filtering with a Gaussian kernel. With just M' and without knowledge of the additional information in M, one could still consider generating a new image M'_{new}, which is similar in its appearance to M'. Thus, the process of generating M'_{new} from M' is independent of the highest frequency band of M. This argument can be repeated to show that M''_{new} can be generated from M'' without knowledge of M' and so on. F_i is then given by:

$$F_i\left(M \overbrace{\Lambda`}^{n-times}\right) = F_i[L_i(M), L_{i+1}(M), \Lambda, L_n(M)] = L_i(M_{new}) \qquad (5)$$

where $L_i(M_{new})$ is the ith special frequency octave or equivalently the ith level of the laplacian pyramid decomposition. Note that the original image can always be recovered by inverting the sequence of operations as exemplified above.

4.2.2 Gabor Wavelets and Local Contrast

The development of Gabor wavelets was motivated by the fact that Gabor wavelets have been shown to resemble the receptive field profile of simple visual cortex cells which can perform joint spatial frequency analysis. In order to briefly describe Gabor wavelets and provide a rationale for this research, the 2-D Gabor wavelets, the short time Fourier transform (STFT) and Gabor transform need to be explained first. A 2-D Gabor function is a plane wave with some frequency and orientation within a two dimensional Gaussian envelope. Its spatial extent, frequency and orientaion preferences as well as bandwidths are easily controlled by some parameters used in generating the filters [25]. The Gabor element function g(x,y) is a 2-D Gaussian envelope modulated by a sinusoid with the frequency λ and orientation θ, defined mathematically as follows:

$$g(x,y) = \exp\left(-\frac{C^2 + \gamma^2 D^2}{2\sigma^2}\right)\cos\left(2\pi \frac{C}{\lambda} + \phi\right) \qquad (6)$$

Where, $C = x\cos\theta - y\sin\theta$, $D = x\sin\theta + y\cos\theta$, λ specifies the wavelength of the cosine factor of the Gabor function, $1/\lambda$ represents the special frequency of the cosine factor in equation. (6), θ specifies the orientation of the normal to the stripes of the Gabor function, ϕ specifies the phase offset of the cosine factor of the Gabor function, σ is the variance of Gaussian distribution in both x and y directions and γ specifies the eccentricity of the Gaussian factor. The half-response spatial frequency bandwidth b (in octaves) of linear filter with an impulse response is defined as:

$$b = \log_2 \frac{\left(\sigma/\lambda + 1/\pi \sqrt{\frac{\ln 2}{2}}\right)}{\left(\sigma/\lambda - 1/\pi \sqrt{\frac{\ln 2}{2}}\right)} \tag{7}$$

The ratio σ/λ determines the special frequency bandwidth of simple cells and thus the number of parallel excitatory and inhibitory strips zones, which can be observed in their receptive fields. For example, figure 5(a) shows an intensity map of a receptive field function $(\sigma = 0.9, \lambda = 15, \theta = 90, \phi = 10, b = 0.7)$ with a particular position, size, orientation and symmetry. The corresponding spatial frequency response is shown in figure 5(b). On the other hand, wavelets theories introduce the concept of scale, which is analogous to the concept of frequency in Fourier analysis. The Fourier transform $R(\omega)$ is defined as follows:

$$R(\omega) = \int_{-\infty}^{\infty} r(t) \exp(-j\omega t) dt, \tag{8}$$

Where r(t) is the time basis signal and $\exp(j\omega t) = \cos(\omega t) + j\sin(\omega t)$.

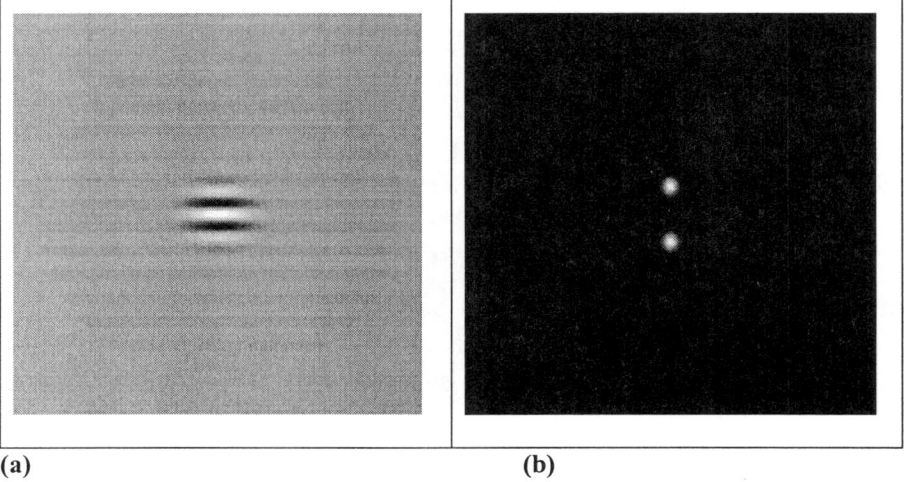

(a) (b)

Figure 5 An illustration of the 2-D Gabor function in (a) space and (b) its corresponding spatial frequency domain.

The Fourier transform can only provide signal information in the frequency domain without any localized references to the time domain. Thus, with Fourier transform, it is not possible to do joint spatial/spatial-frequency analysis. In contrast, the short time Fourier transform (STFT) can achieve this function and it is defined as:

$$STFT(\tau,\omega) = \int s(t)g(t-\tau)\exp(-j\omega t)dt \qquad (9)$$

From this definition, the STFT can be interpreted as the Fourier transform of a signal that is windowed by the function $g(t-\tau)$. The STFT with a Gaussian window is called Gabor transform. The Gabor transform can be regarded as a signal being convolved with a filter-bank whose impulse in the time domain is Gaussian modulated by sine and cosine wave. As the frequency ω of the sine and cosine function changes, a set of filters with the same window size is constructed. The problem with the STFT or Gabor transform is that the size of the window in the time domain is fixed and thus results in a fixed resolution in both spatial and frequency domains. Therefore, the STFT and Gabor transform are suitable for analysis of stationary signals, which is not suitable for the facial textures. This problem can be overcome by the wavelet transform. A wavelets is defined as:

$$h_{b,a}(t) = \frac{1}{\sqrt{a}} h^*\left(\frac{t-b}{a}\right) \qquad (10)$$

A continuous wavelet transform CWT is defined as:

$$CWT_{b,a} = \frac{1}{\sqrt{a}} \int_{-\infty}^{\infty} h^*\left(\frac{t-b}{a}\right) s(t)dt \qquad (11)$$

Where, s (t) is the signal, a and b are the dilation and translation factors respectively and h(t) is called the mother wavelet. The wavelet transform is decompose the signal s(t) into the set of wavelet functions. The wavelet transform obtains a flexible resolution in both time/spatial and frequency domain through the factors a and b. In our proposed technique, the Gabor wavelet function used for facial texture simulation was same as [14] used and is defined as:

$$h(x,y) = \exp\left[-\alpha^{2j}\frac{x^2+y^2}{\sigma^2}\right]\exp\left[j\pi\alpha^j(x\cos\theta + y\sin\theta)\right] \qquad (12)$$

Where ($\alpha = \frac{1}{\sqrt{2}}$, $j = \{0,1,\Lambda\}$) and $\theta \in [0,2\pi]$. The different choices of frequency j and the orientation θ constructed a set of filters. As the frequency of the sinusoid changes, the window size will be changed. For example, when j is changed from 0 to 3, the sinusoid frequency is reduced whereas the Gaussian window size increases. More details on Gabor wavelets can be found [14,25,37]. A local contrast calculation produces contrast images that describe the response of an ensemble of neurons to a particular spatial frequency and orientation. We call these images the channel images as they represent different channels of the visual system. In this stage, the channel probability maps from the higher levels of the pyramid are up sampling to match the resolution of the lowest level of the pyramid. In summary and by referring to equation (2), if both M1 and M2 are aligned then, their intensities in the area with non-facial cues to age should be very close (i.e. the correlation is high), while their intensities in the area with potential facial cues to age are different. Therefore, the two processing steps of the function F substitute the high frequency components of M2 with those from M1. The high frequency components of the difference between the images M1 and $\overline{M}1$ in M1 are normalized by $\overline{M}2$ in order to cancel the intensity scale difference between the low frequency components of M1 and M2. The aging processes of the proposed technique show that, how one can capture the image space created by some source of variation from a single image and a smooth in the image space domain is correspond to a smooth in the geometrical space domain. As a result, it yields images with realistic looking facial textures simulation without needing to model each facial textures as a separate element. Finally, for image reconstruction, the original image can always be recovered by inverting the sequence of operations as exemplified above.

5. Experimental Results and Discussion

Several simulations for manipulating the facial appearance with animation have been performed based on our proposed techniques. Figures 6(a)-(b) demonstrate two facial appearance manipulation using the anthropometrical features deformations technique. By merging both of the proposed techniques, figure 7 shows an animation sequence with more expressive and convincing facial appearance with advancing years. From the experimental results one can see that in compared with morphing, the neutral face identity is maintained during the animation as previously discussed in the last paragraph of section 4.1. The proposed techniques have been implemented using Java^{TM} and an OpenGL compatible version of Java3D.

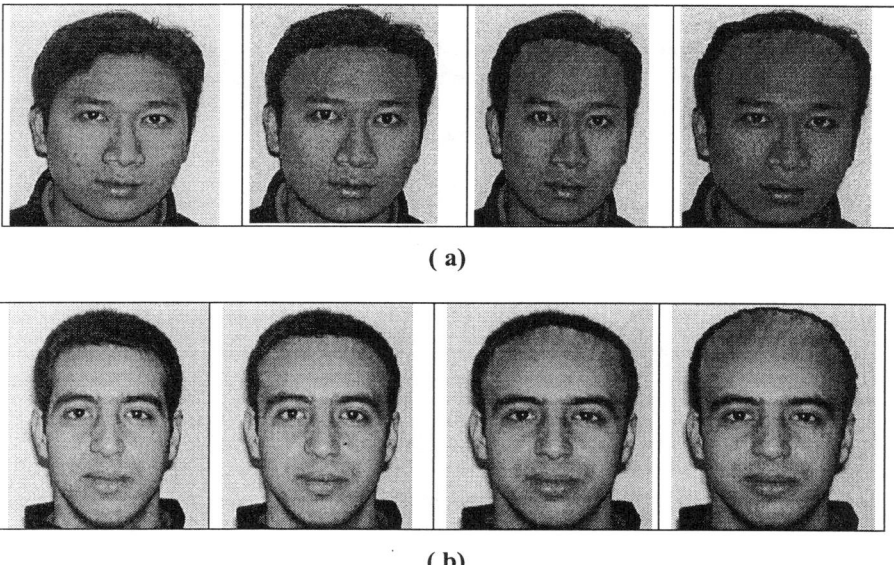

Figure 6 Facial appearance manipulation results with facial features deformations simulation technique.

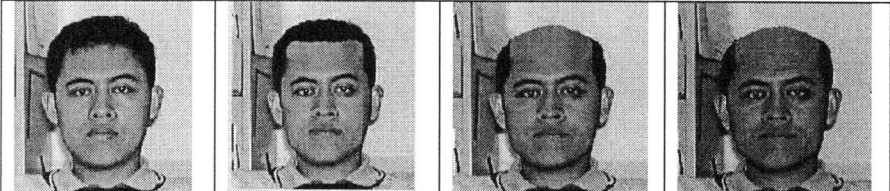

Figure 7 Facial appearance manipulation results with facial features deformations and facial textures simulation techniques.

6. Conclusions and Future Work

Modeling and rendering of realistic faces with facial appearance manipulations are difficult task and becomes more challenging when facial textures such as stubble and wrinkles are considered. In this paper we have presented a new idea as a key solution for such a challenge via two proposed techniques. Our idea is motivated by a research on two studies. The first is the human texture perception and the multi-resolution analysis of wavelets for simulating the facial textures like stubble and wrinkles. The second is the anthropometrical theory for simulating the facial features deformations with advancing years. The advantages of the proposed techniques over the previous proposed methods are given in terms of the following advantages. First, the proposed techniques are efficient in time complexity and simple to implement due to the use of a sequence of simple image processing operations. Second, the proposed techniques are reliable in which they require only one source image without a need to collect a lot of images. Third, they provide a simple way to capture the geometrical details of the real world objects without any constraints and map it smoothly to other real world objects without a need to any practice or artistic skills. Finally, their computations are fast enough for an interactive environment and has potential to be practically useful tool for graphics applications. On the other hand, the process of facial appearance manipulation is the complex one. It depends not only on the structure of the initial face but also on many aspects of one's life, including climatic, psychological and other parameters. Consequently, for more realistic visual aging effects with facial appearance further research effort is still needed. In our future work will focus on two categories. First, we would like to extend our algorithm based on spherical Wavelets [34] by using what they refer to as a lifting scheme. Second, extending our proposed techniques based on neural network.

Acknowledgements

Sincere thanks go to Dr. Sahar Mohammed Ali, the visiting researcher at Tokyo Institute of Technology and a staff member of Ain Shams University, Faculty of Science, Mathematics and Computer Science Department, Cairo, Egypt, for the continuous guidance during the preparation for this research work and helpful mathematical
- discussions on Wavelets.

References

[1] Hassanien A., Karam H. and Nakajima M. "Image metamorphosis transformation of the facial images using elastic body spline", Signal Proc. Inter. Journal, ELSEVIER Publisher, Vol. 70, No. 2, pp. 129-137, 1998.
[2] Duncan A. and David I., "Manipulating facial appearance through shape and color'", IEEE Computer Graphics and App.., Vol. 15, No. 5, pp. 70-76, 1995
[3] Stoschek A., "Image-based re-rendering of faces for continuous pose and illumination directions", IEEE International Conf. on CVPR, pp.582-587, 2000.
[4] Shashua A. and Tammy R., "The Quotient Image: Class-based re-rendering and recognition with varying illuminations", IEEE Transaction PAMI, Vol. 23 No. 2, pp. 129-139, 2001.
[5] George A. and Hole G., "The influence of feature based information in the age processing of unfamiliar face", Perception, Vol. 27, pp.295-312, 1998.
[6] Jawerth B. and Sweldens W., "An overview of wavelet based multi-resolution analysis", SIAM Review, Vol. 36, No. 3, pp. 377-412, 1994.
[7] Tiddeman B., Duffy N. and Rabey G., "A general method for overlap control in image warping", Computers and Graphics, Vol. 25, No. 1, pp. 59-66, 2001.

[8] Burt D. and Perrett D., "Perception of age in adult Caucasian male faces: computer graphic manipulation of Shape and color information", Proc. Royal Soc. London B 259, pp.137-143, 1995.

[9] Douglas D., Metaxas D., Stone M., "An anthropometric face model using Variational Techniques", Proc. of SIGGRAPH'98, pp. 67-74, 1998.

[10] Terzopoulos D. and Waters K., "Physically-based facial modeling and animation", Journal of Visualization and Computer Animation, Vol. 1, pp. 73-80, 1990.

[11] Stollnitz E., Derose T. and Salesian D., "Wavelets for computer graphics: A]primer (Parts 1 and 2)", IEEE Computer Graphics and Applications, Vol. 15, No. 5, pp. 76-84, 1995.

[12] Parke F., "Parametric model for facial animation", IEEE Computer Graphics and Applications, Vol. 2, No. 9, pp. 61-68, 1982.

[13] Parke F. and Waters K., "Computer facial animation", A. K. Peters, 1996.

[14] Naghdy G. and Ogunbona P., "Texture analysis using gabor wavelets", IS&T/SPIE 2657 Sym. Electronic imaging, pp. 74-84, 1994.

[15] Karam H., Hassanien A. and Nakajima M., "Visual simulation of texture/non-texture image synthesis", IEEE Computer Graphics International, CGI`2000, Switzerland, Geneva, pp. 343-351, 2000.

[16] Kwon H. and Lobo N., "Age classification from facial images", Computer Vision and Image Understanding, Vol. 74, No. 1, pp. 1-21, 1999.

[17] Cheng J., Stephen M., Perkins W. and Hamilton M., "Perioral Rejuvenation", Proc. of Facial Plastic Surgery Clinics of North America , Vol.8, No. 2, pp.223, MAY 2000.

[18] Daugman J., "Uncertainty relations for resolution in space, spatial frequency and orientation optimized by two-dimensional visual cortical filters", Journal of the Optical Society of America A, Vol. 2, pp. 1160-1169, 1985.

[19] Malik J. and Perona P., "Preattentive texture discrimination with early vision mechanisms", Journal of the Optical Society of America A, Vol. 7, No. 5, pp. 923-932, 1990.

[20] Boissieux L., Kiss G., Magnenant-Thalman N. and Kolar P., "Simulation of Skin aging and wrinkle with cosmetic insight", Computer Animation and Simulation, pp.15-27, 2000.

[21] Farkas L., "Anthropometry of the Head and Face", Raven Press, 1994.

[22] Farkas L., "Anthropometric facial proportions in medicine", Thomas Books, 1987.

[23] Mark L., Pittenger J. and Hines H., "Wrinkle and head shape as coordinated source of age-level information", Perception and Psychophysics, Vol. 27, No. 2, pp. 117-124,1998.

[24] Viaud M. and Yahia H., "Facial animation with wrinkles", 3rd Workshop on animation, Eurographics`92, Cambridge, Springer-Verlag, 1992.

[25] Turrner M., "Texture discrimination by Gabor functions", Biolological Cypernetics, Springer Verlag, Vol. 55, pp. 71-82, 1986.

[26] Burson N. and Schneider D., "Methods and apparatus for producing an image of a person's face at a different age", United States Patent 4276570, p. 1-14, 1981.

[27] Rioul O. and Vetterli M., "wavelets and signal processing", IEEE Signal processing, pp. 14-38, 1991.
[28] Eric P., Pierre P. and George D., "Surface aging by impacts", Proc. Graphics Interface`2001, pp. 175-182, 2001.
[29] Marschner R., Guenter B. and Raghupathy S., "Modeling and Rendering for Realistic Facial Animation", In Proceedings of 11th Eurographics Workshop on Rendering, Czech Republic, June 2000.
[30] Weale R., "Senile changes, cell death and vision", In Sekuler R., Kline D. and Dismukes K. (Eds.), Aging and human visual function, pp. 161-171, NY, 1982.
[31] Mallat S., "A wavelet tour for signal processing", 2nd Edition, Academic Press, 1999.
[32] Mallat S., "A theory for multi-resolution signal decomposition: The wavelet representation", IEEE Trans. PAMI, Vol. 11, No. 7, pp. 674-693, 1989.
[33] Jeremy S., "Multi-resolution sampling procedure for analysis and synthesis of texture images ", In Proc.of SIGGRAPH`97, pp. 361-368, 1997.
[34] Peter S. and Wim S., "Spherical Wavelets: efficiently representing functions on the sphere", In Proc. of SIGGRAPH`95, pp. 161-172, 1995.
[35] Ezaki T. and Kasori Y., "Bilateral temporoparietal flaps in the treatment of Male baldness", Aesth. Plast. Surg., Vol. 19, pp. 41-47, 1995.
[36] Ishii T., Yasuda T., Yokoi S. and Toriwaki J., "A generation model for human skin texture", Proc. of CGI`93, pp. 139-150,1993.
[37] Lee T., "Image representation using gabor wavelets", IEEE Trans. PAMI, Vol. 18, No. 10, pp. 959-971, 1996.
[38] Randen T. and John H., "Filtering for texture classification: A comparative study", IEEE Trans. PAMI, Vol. 21, No. 4, pp. 291-309, 1999
[39] Lee W., , Wu Y., Magnenat-Thalmann N., "Cloning and aging in a VR family", The Visual Computer, Vol. 5, No. 1, pp. 32-39, 1999..
[40] George W., "Digital image warping", IEEE Computer Society Press, 1990.
[41] Wu Y., Kalra P., Moccozet L. and Magnenat-Thalman N., "Simulating wrinkles and skin aging", The Visual Computer, Springer Verlag, Vol. 15, pp. 183-197, 1999.
[42] Liu Z., Shan Y. and Zhang Z., "Expressive expression mapping with ratio images", Proc. of SIGGRAPH'2001, pp. 271-276, 2001.

Real-time animation of running waters based on spectral analysis of Navier-Stokes equations

S. Thon and D. Ghazanfarpour
Laboratory MSI - Limoges University
16, rue Atlantis
87068 Limoges Cedex, France
thon@ensil.unilim.fr, ghazanfa@ensil.unilim.fr

Abstract
In order to simulate realistically the complex behaviour of water, the best way is to use Computational Fluid Dynamics (CFD) equations such as the Navier-Stokes equations. However, these equations require too much computation time and memory to be used for real time animation of large water scenes such as running waters. In this paper, we propose a model for real time animation of running waters based on spectral analysis and synthesis of Navier-Stokes equations.

Keywords: Natural phenomena, running waters, Navier-Stokes equations, spectral analysis, real time animation

1. Introduction

The modeling of natural phenomena is an important domain of research in Computer Graphics. Water is an important natural phenomena because of its omnipresence in our everyday life. Water has been represented in Computer Graphics in many situations, mainly in the case of ocean waves [6] [10] [2] [17] [3] [13] [16] but also waterfalls [12] [5] or splashes [9] [7].
A small number of models for running waters such as brooks, rivers or torrents have been proposed in Computer Graphics. Chiba et al [1] proposed a particle-based simulation allowing collisions between water particles and obstacles for representing complex water currents, but the equations used for describing the particles motion do not allow turbulent effects such as eddies or vortices. Xu et al [18] used hydraulic equations for simulating water currents and waves in a channel, and we proposed in [14] a simple and visually realistic model based on a procedural animated 3D texture, but neither of these models take into account interactions between water and obstacles. Neyret and Praizelin [8] concentrate on the simulation of quasi-stationary

waves and ripples in brooks in the vicinity of obstacles and banks by using hydrodynamics laws, but without taking into account turbulent phenomena.

In order to represent more realistically the complex behavior of water, we could use physical models from Computational Fluid Dynamics (CFD) such as the Navier-Stokes equations. However, under their complete 3D form, these equations are too time and memory consuming to be used in the case of large water surfaces.

In [15], we proposed a semi-physical model of running waters using the less consuming 2D Navier-Stokes equations to simulate the horizontal water motion as well as a pseudo random function to simulate its vertical motion. However, this model was not fast enough to allow real-time animation. The main problem is that solving the Navier-Stokes equations during the animation loop, even under their 2D form, requires too much computation time.

In this paper, we propose a model that allows real time animation of running waters, with interactions between water and obstacles as well as turbulent effects. The idea is to precompute in a first step a set of 2D velocity fields with the 2D Navier-Stokes equations and then to use these precomputed values during the animation step, without having to solve the Navier-Stokes equations anymore. However, if we directly use this set of precomputed velocity fields, a vast amount of memory will be needed. In order to reduce the memory usage, the main feature of this paper is to transform the precomputed time evolving velocity fields in the frequency domain by a fast Fourier transform (FFT) and then to compress the obtained spectra by neglecting frequency components having low energy levels. We show that important simplifications of the spectra can be achieved while preserving the main features of the velocity fields. Therefore, we can store a set of velocity fields with a very limited number of selected frequency components. During the animation, for each time step we synthesize a new velocity field in real time by using an inverse spectral transform of the selected frequency components. In order to track the motion of individual fluid elements, particles are injected in this time evolving velocity field. In order to represent the water surface, patches textured with water like animated textures are associated to the injected particles and rendered in real time with OpenGL.

The remainder of the paper is organized as follows. The streambed creation process is briefly described in section 2. The stream model is presented in section 3 and decomposed into the precomputations step (section 3.1) and the real time animation step (section 3.2). We conclude and give ideas for future works in section 4.

2. Streambed

2.1 Streambed creation

In order to represent running waters, we should first create a streambed. We use the reverse erosion method for landscape creation that we proposed in [14]. This method is very intuitive and easy to use for a designer. First, the designer explicitly defines the stream trajectory with a Bézier curve with an arbitrary number of control points (figure 1a). Next, the cross section of the bed is obtained by a second Bézier curve having six control points, swept along the stream trajectory. The positions of these six control points are computed according to parameters given by the user, namely the width, the depth and the bank width of the streambed (figure 1b). The shape of the cross section is modified in the meanders to take into account the effects of bank erosion by water, by moving the second Bézier curve control points positions. The positions of these control points are also perturbed by user defined pseudo random functions in order to alter in a more realistic way the regularity of the cross section along the trajectory. The landscape is build around this streambed with a fractal technique (figure 1c). Obstacles are placed in the streambed (4 boulders in the case of figure 1c) to study interactions between water and obstacles. Once this streambed has been created, we can fill it with our stream model. The landscape is rendered with OpenGL as a set of triangles.

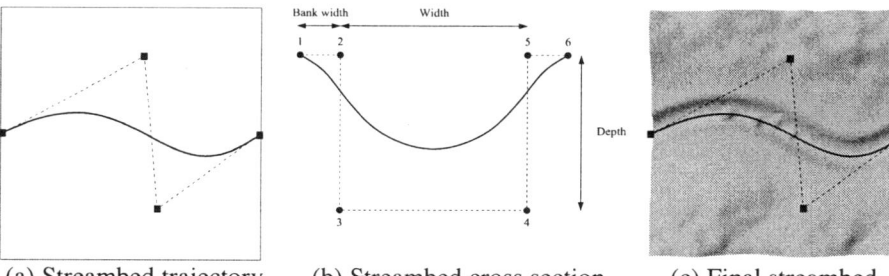

(a) Streambed trajectory   (b) Streambed cross section   (c) Final streambed

Figure 1. Streambed creation.

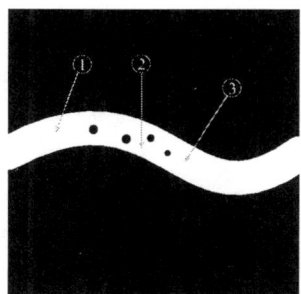

Figure 2. In the following sections, we study evolution in time of velocity for fluid cells numbered 1, 2 and 3.

2.2 Fluid domain creation

In order to simulate the horizontal fluid motion in the streambed with the 2D Navier-Stokes equations (section 3.1), we have to create a 2D fluid domain. This domain is a fixed uniform 2D binary grid composed of obstacle cells and fluid cells (figure 2). Fluid motion will be studied with the Navier-Stokes equations only in the fluid cells of the grid. This grid is obtained from a 2D horizontal slice of the streambed, taken at water rest level. The size of the grid is the same that the size of the terrain (512x512 cells for figure 2). A fluid cell in the binary grid corresponds to a streambed cell in the terrain. All other cells in the binary grid are obstacle cells.

3. Stream model

Our objective is to design a running water model that can be animated in real-time. We also want realistic interactions between water and obstacles as well as turbulent effects. The semi-physical model that we proposed in [15] does not allow real-time animation, because we solved the time consuming 2D Navier-Stokes equations at each time step during the animation loop. In this paper, we propose a stream model that is build upon two steps. During the first step, we precompute velocity values with the 2D Navier-Stokes equations (section 3.1). The second step is the real time execution that makes use of these precomputed values (section 3.2).

3.1 Precomputations

3.1.1 Overview

Like our previous model [15], we want to use a time evolving 2D velocity field given by the 2D Navier-Stokes equations, in order to take into account the interactions between water and obstacles as well as the turbulent effects. However, the computation of the Navier-Stokes equations, even under its 2D form, takes too long to allow real-time animation.

A first solution could be to precompute a set of velocity fields by using the 2D Navier-Stokes equations, before entering the main animation loop. This precomputed velocity fields would then be used cyclically during the real time animation step. Such an approach is not physically correct, but allows visually realistic results. However, the storage of these precomputed velocity fields is highly memory consuming. Indeed, for the example of the fluid domain of figure 2, we have 32200 fluid cells. If we precompute the evolution of the 2D velocity (2 floats=8 bytes) for each fluid cell over 256 time steps, the amount of memory needed is 32200x256x8=63 MB. This is too much if we consider that the aimed platform is an average personal computer with 128 MB of RAM, for example in the case of a video game.

So, instead of using directly this set of precomputed velocity fields, we propose to deduce from this data a procedural model requiring less memory. In order to design this procedural model, we use the spectral analysis during the precomputations step to study the evolution of velocity vectors along the time. This procedural model will allow to synthesize a new velocity field at any time during the real time animation step. Thus, this precomputations step can be decomposed in three parts:

1. **Computation of the 2D Navier Stokes equations:** we solve the 2D Navier-Stokes equations in a loop of N iterations in order to obtain a set of N 2D velocity fields. In practice, we precompute a set of 256 velocity fields (section 3.1.2)
2. **Spectral transform of the velocity fields:** we compute the 1D FFT of the evolution over the N time steps of the 2D velocity[1] for each fluid cell, in order to obtain a 1D spectrum of N components for each fluid cell (section 3.1.3)
3. **Spectral simplification:** in order to reduce the need of memory, we simplify the obtained spectra by only storing the most significant components of each spectrum (section 3.1.4)

This precomputations step is done once and the results (the components retained for each spectrum) are saved in a file. Thus, it is not necessary to do this precomputations each time we run the program.

3.1.2 Navier-Stokes equations

The Navier-Stokes equations are the governing laws of fluid dynamics. These equations describe the behavior of fluids with a set of partial differential equations formed by the momentum equations (equations 1 and 2) and the continuity equation (equation 3). We only use the 2D form of these equations:

Momentum equations:

$$\frac{\partial u}{\partial t} + \frac{\partial p}{\partial x} = \frac{1}{Re}\left(\frac{\partial^2 u}{\partial x^2} + \frac{\partial^2 u}{\partial y^2}\right) - \frac{\partial(u^2)}{\partial x} - \frac{\partial(uv)}{\partial y} + F_x \quad (1)$$

$$\frac{\partial v}{\partial t} + \frac{\partial p}{\partial y} = \frac{1}{Re}\left(\frac{\partial^2 v}{\partial x^2} + \frac{\partial^2 v}{\partial y^2}\right) - \frac{\partial(uv)}{\partial x} - \frac{\partial(v^2)}{\partial y} + F_y \quad (2)$$

Continuity equation:

$$\frac{\partial u}{\partial x} + \frac{\partial v}{\partial y} = 0 \quad (3)$$

Where u and v are the horizontal velocity components along x and y axis, t is the time, p is the pressure, Re is Reynold's number, F_x and F_y are horizontal components along x and y axis of forces applied to the fluid.

These 2D equations are numerically solved in time by finite difference approximation on the fixed uniform 2D grid covering the whole fluid domain built in section 2.2. Thus, we obtain velocities values (u,v) as well as pressure p for each fluid cell of the 2D grid. The resolution method is described in [15]. A good practical introduction to the numerical resolution of the Navier-Stokes equations can be found in [4].

---

[1] We treat 2D velocity vectors (u,v) as complex numbers (u = real part and v = imaginary part), so the 1D FFT is a transform of complex numbers.

3.1.3 Spectral transform of the velocity fields

We compute the 1D FFT of the evolution over the N time steps of the 2D velocity for each fluid cell. Thus, we obtain a 1D spectrum of N components for each fluid cell. Some examples of spectra are given on figure 3 for the fluid cells numbered 1, 2 and 3 of figure 2.

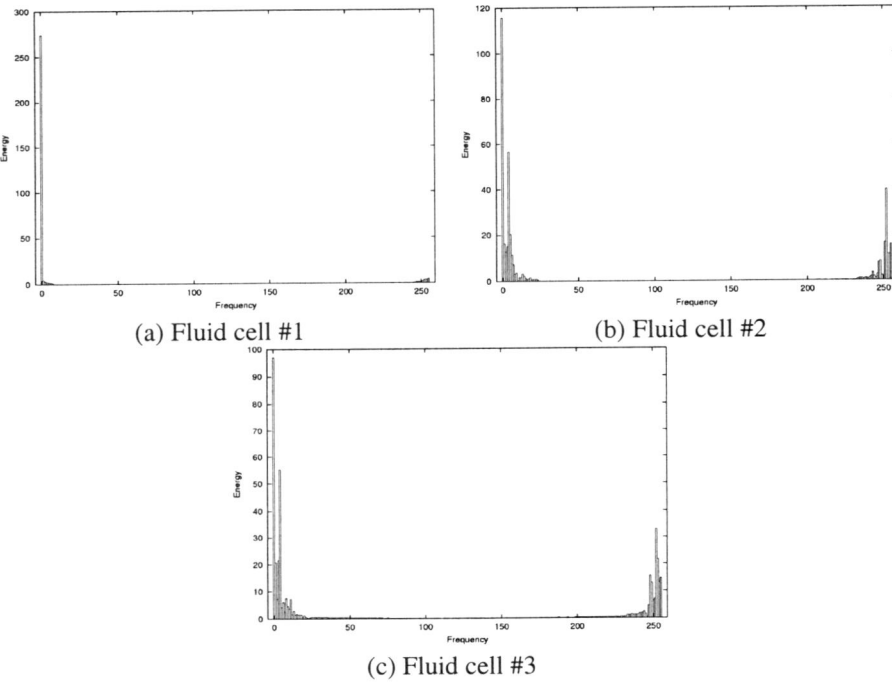

Figure 3. Spectra of time evolving velocity for fluid cells 1, 2 and 3 for 256 time steps.

We can see on figure 3 that few components of these spectra are really significant, many components have a very low energy. One of the main ideas of this paper is to simplify this spectra by only selecting the most significant components.

3.1.4 Spectral simplification

We propose to simplify the previously computed spectra by reducing their number of components. For each spectrum, we select only the N_f frequency components having the highest energy such that their energy sum is greater or equal to a percentage x given by the user of the total energy of this spectrum.

Efficient compression ratio can be obtained. With few components we can synthesize (section 3.2.2) time evolving velocity vectors close to the original signal.

For the example of figure 2, only 5 components per fluid cell on average are sufficient. More frequency components are necessary for the synthesis of velocity in turbulent areas (figure 6 and 7) than in more laminar areas (figure 5), because the time evolution of velocity is more complex in turbulent areas.

3.2 Real time animation

3.2.1 Overview

Once the precomputations step is done, we can achieve a real time animation of the stream. The animation main loop can be decomposed into three parts, executed at each time step:

1. Synthesis of a new 2D velocity field with the simplified spectra (section 3.2.2) (figure 4a)
2. Study of particles motion in this velocity field (section 3.2.3) (figure 4b)
3. Display of water surface by associating patches textured with water like animated textures to the particles (section 3.2.4) (figure 4c)

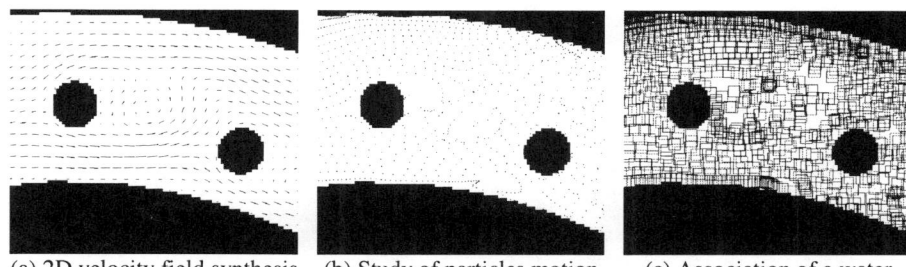

(a) 2D velocity field synthesis (b) Study of particles motion (c) Association of a water patch to each particle

Figure 4. The three parts of the animation main loop on a close up of figure 2.

3.2.2 Velocity field synthesis

During the real time animation step, we synthesize for each time step a new velocity field by using the precomputed frequency components. Thus, for each fluid cell of the fluid domain, we synthesize at time t a 2D velocity vector $\vec{V}(v_x, v_y)$ with equations 4 and 5.

$$v_x = \sum_{i=1}^{N_f} \left(X_i . \cos\left(f_i . 2\pi \frac{t}{N} \right) - Y_i . \sin\left(f_i . 2\pi \frac{t}{N} \right) \right) \tag{4}$$

$$v_y = \sum_{i=1}^{N_f} \left(X_i . \sin\left(f_i . 2\pi \frac{t}{N} \right) + Y_i . \cos\left(f_i . 2\pi \frac{t}{N} \right) \right) \tag{5}$$

Where N_f is the number of frequency components retained after spectrum simplification for this fluid cell, N is the number of precomputed time steps, f_i is the frequency of the ith frequency component, X_i and Y_i are the complex frequency components.

We can see on figure 5 to 7 that with only few frequency components we can synthesize time evolving velocity vectors that are very close to the original ones. This allows two advantages:

- Velocity fields can be computed quickly, because only few frequency components have to be summed in equations 4 and 5. For the example of figure 2, we synthesize on a Pentium III 933 MHz a complete velocity field with 5 frequency components per fluid cell on average about 9 times per second. In comparison, it takes about 7 seconds to obtain a single velocity field by direct resolution of the 2D Navier-Stokes equations over the same fluid domain. The increase in speed with our spectral synthesis method compared to a direct resolution of the 2D Navier-Stokes equations is then of a magnitude of 63.

- The method is low memory consuming. For each fluid cell, we have to store the following data: cell position (x,y) (8 bytes), number of frequency components (4 bytes) and an array of N_f frequency components defined by X_i, Y_i, f_i (N_f x 12 bytes). So, for the example of figure 2, as in average 5 frequency components out of 256 are needed to synthesize a time evolving velocity vector for each fluid cell, the model only needs 2.3 MB (32200x(8+4+5x12)=2318400 bytes). In this case, the original amount of data (63 MB) can then be compressed by a ratio of 27.

3.2.3 Particles motion

During the animation main loop, in order to study the horizontal motion of the stream, we track the movement of individual fluid particles in the synthesized time evolving 2D velocity field. Particles are injected at regular time intervals at the source of the stream. The number of particles injected at the same time is given by the user. The computation of the position of one particle at time $t_{n+1} = t_n + \delta t$ given its position $(x^{(n)}, y^{(n)})$ at time t_n is accomplished in two steps:

1. In the first step, we determine the velocity $(u^{(n)}, v^{(n)})$ in the stream at particle position $(x^{(n)}, y^{(n)})$. Since velocities (u,v) are synthesized by our method only for discrete points of the 2D stream grid, we compute the velocity at particle position by a bilinear interpolation of the velocities of the four points of the grid surrounding the particle.

2. Once the particle velocity is known, we compute its new position at time t_{n+1} with the forward Euler method:
$$x^{(n+1)} = x^{(n)} + \delta t . u^{(n)}, \quad y^{(n+1)} = y^{(n)} + \delta t . v^{(n)} \qquad (6)$$
If the new position of a particle is outside the fluid domain or in an obstacle cell, then this particle is deleted from the particles list.

For the example of figure 2, we study the motion of about 28000 particles, which takes about 0.075 s on a Pentium III 933 MHz.

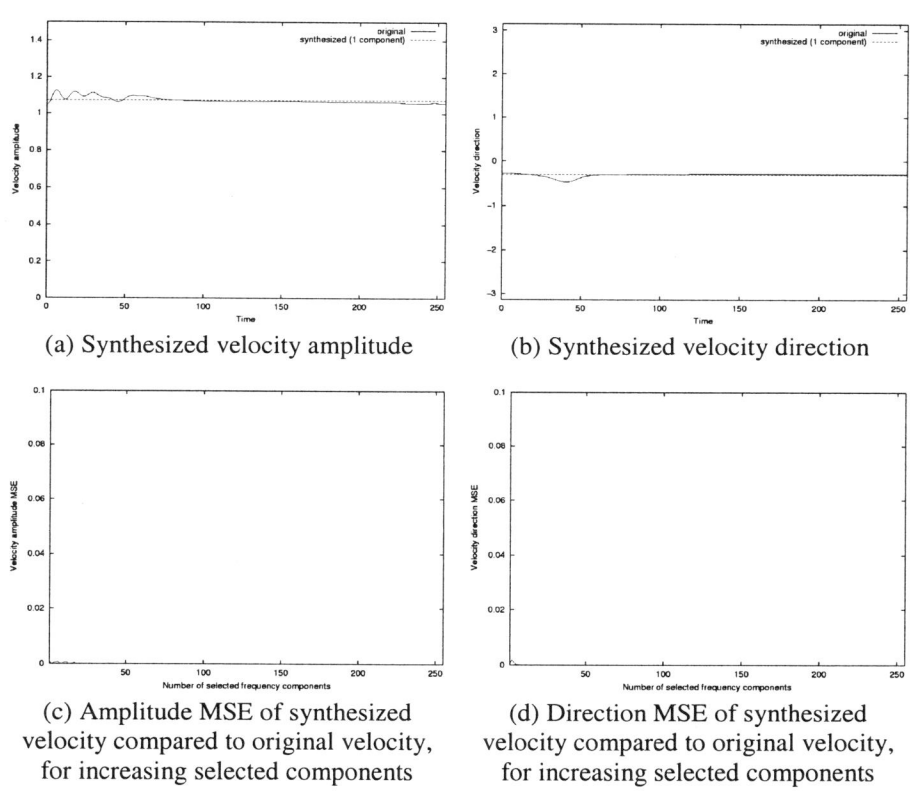

(a) Synthesized velocity amplitude

(b) Synthesized velocity direction

(c) Amplitude MSE of synthesized velocity compared to original velocity, for increasing selected components

(d) Direction MSE of synthesized velocity compared to original velocity, for increasing selected components

Figure 5. Velocity synthesis for fluid cell #1.

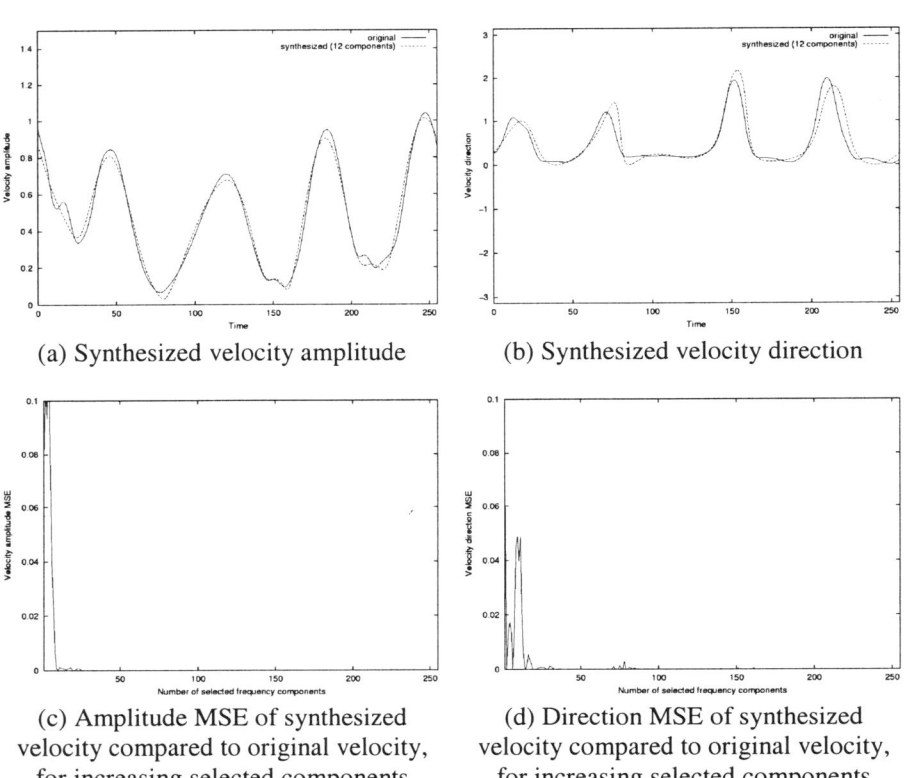

Figure 6. Velocity synthesis for fluid cell #2.

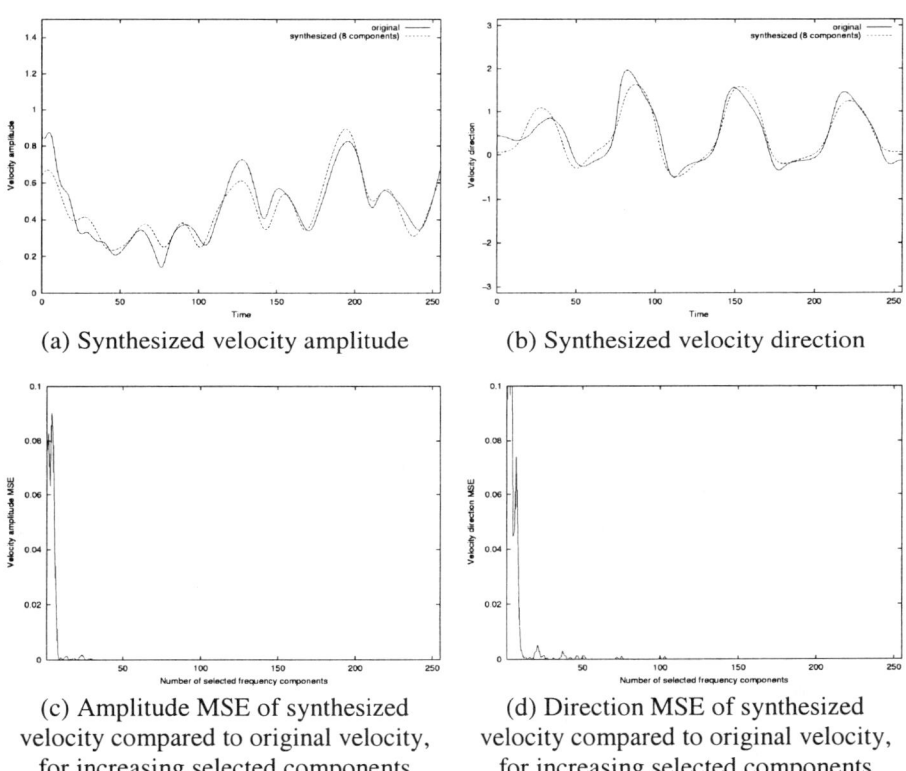

Figure 7. Velocity synthesis for fluid cell #3.

3.2.4 Water surface display

In order to display the water surface, we associate to each particle injected in the velocity field a patch textured with a water like animated texture. This patch is a planar quadrilateral lying on the horizontal water plane and centered on the position of its associated particle. The animated texture mapped to the patches is taken in a set of precomputed time evolving textures that loop in time. The textures are slices of a 3D Perlin turbulence function [11] (figure 8). In practice, we use 64 textures with a resolution of 64x64. By cycling these textures with time, we obtain for each mapped patch a realistic water like animation.

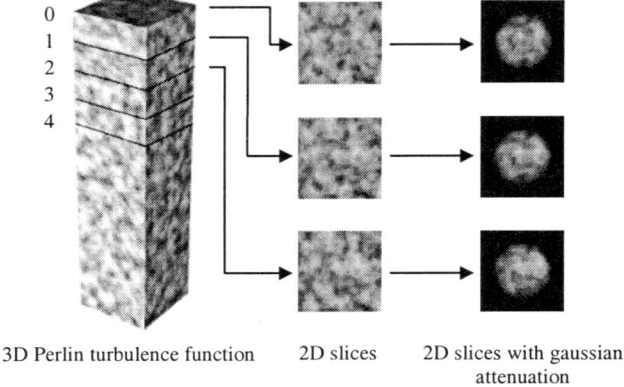

Figure 8. Water like textures obtained from slices of a 3D Perlin turbulence function.

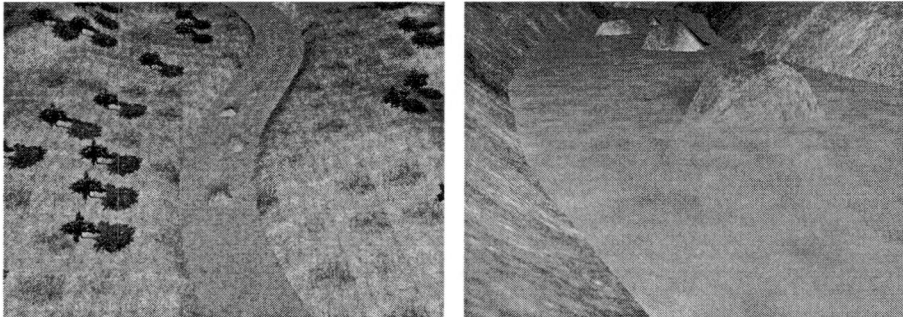

Figure 9. Running water animated in real time and rendered with OpenGL.

The textures applied to the patches have alpha channel in order to obtain translucent water surface. This alpha channel is attenuated by a gaussian curve centered on the patch, so that the alpha channel is null on the borders of the patch. Thus, patches borders are not visible and overlapping patches can blend without artifact. The textured patches are displayed in real time with OpenGL (figure 9).

More realistic results could be obtained by using these textures as bump maps, instead of simple color textures like we do.

4. Conclusions and future works

We have proposed a running water model based on the spectral analysis of the Navier-Stokes equations. This model is based on two steps. In a first step, we precompute a set of time evolving 2D velocity fields with the 2D Navier-Stokes equations. We transform this data in the frequency domain and simplify it by only selecting the most representative frequency components. The second step corresponds to the real time animation loop during which we synthesize velocity fields with the selected precomputed frequency components. Thus, it is possible to synthesize velocity fields without having to solve the time consuming Navier-Stokes equations during the animation loop. Computations are fast enough to allow real time animation. The simplified spectral representation of the data requires little memory storage.

Our model is not physically correct, but our objective is only to obtain visually realistic results. However, since our velocity field synthesis process depends on precomputations, the velocity field can not be dynamically modified during the animation to simulate the action of new forces, like for example the drop of a stone in the water.

As future works, we plan to work on both animation and rendering. We need to find even faster animation methods. Moreover, we have mainly focused in this paper on animation. For more realism, we plan to work on real time realistic rendering of water.

References

[1] Chiba N., Sanakanishi S., Yokoyama K., Ootawara I., Muraoka K., Saito N., *"Visual simulation of water currents using a particle-based behavioural model"*, Journal of Visualization and Computer Animation, Vol 6, pp 155-171, 1995.

[2] Fournier A., Reeves W., *"A simple model of ocean waves"*, Computer Graphics (Siggraph '86 proceedings), Vol 20, No 3, pp 75-84, 1986.

[3] Gonzato J.C., Le Saec B., *"A phenomenological model of coastal scenes based on physical considerations"*, Computer Animation and Simulation, pp 137-148, 1997.

[4] Griebel M., Dornseifer T., Neunhoeffer T., *"Numerical simulation in fluid dynamics: a practical introduction"*, Society for Industrial and Applied Mathematics, 1998.

[5] Mallinder H., *"The modelling of large waterfalls using string texture"*, The Journal of Visualisation and Computer Animation, Vol 6, No 1, pp 3-10, 1995.

[6] Max N., *"Vectorized procedural models for natural terrain: waves and islands in the sunset"*, Computer Graphics (Siggraph '81 proceedings), Vol 15, No 3, pp 317-324, 1981.

[7] Mould D., Yang Y.H., *"Modeling water for computer graphics"*, Computers and Graphics, Vol 21, No 6, pp 801-814, 1997.

[8] Neyret F., Praizelin N., *"Phenomenological Simulation of Brooks"*, Eurographics Workshop on Animation and Simulation, pp 53-64, 2001.

[9] O'Brien J.F., Hodgins J.K., *"Dynamic simulation of splashing fluids"*, Proceedings of Computer Animation '95, pp 198-205, 1995.

[10] Peachey D.R., *"Modeling waves and surf"*, Computer Graphics (Siggraph '86 proceedings), Vol 20, No 3, pp 65-74, 1986.

[11] Perlin K., *"An image synthesizer"*, Computer Graphics (Siggraph '85 proceedings), Vol 19, No 3, pp 287-296, 1985.

[12] Sims K., *"Particle animation and rendering using data parallel computation"*, Computer Graphics (Siggraph '90 proceedings), Vol 24, No 4, pp 405-413, 1990.

[13] Thon S., Dischler J.M., Ghazanfarpour D., *"Ocean waves synthesis using a sea spectrum controlled turbulence"*, Proceedings of Computer Graphics International, pp 65-72, 2000.

[14] Thon S., Dischler J.M., Ghazanfarpour D., *"A simple model for visually realistic running waters"*, Eurographics UK 2000 Conference Proceedings, pp 81-86, 2000.

[15] Thon S., Ghazanfarpour D., *"A semi-physical model of running water"*, Eurographics UK 2001 Conference Proceedings, pp 53-59, 2001.

[16] Thon S., Ghazanfarpour D., *"Ocean waves synthesis and animation using real world information"*, Computers and Graphics, Vol 26, No 1, 2002.

[17] Tso P.Y., Barsky B.A., *"Modeling and rendering waves: wave-tracing using beta-splines and reflective and refractive texture mapping"*, ACM Transactions on Graphics, Vol 6, No 3, pp 191-214, 1987.

[18] Xu Y., Su C., Qi D., Li H., Liu S., *"Physically based simulation of water currents and waves"*, Computers and Graphics, Vol 21, No 3, pp 277-280, 1997.

Rendering

Factoring a Specular Reflection Field Into Added Diffuse Reflection Fields

A. L. Thomas
Spatial Model Based Animation and Machine Vision Group
School of Engineering and Information Technology
University of Sussex

Abstract

This paper presents the first stages in exploring an hypothesis that would appear to support a shape from shading, reconstruction algorithm from time series image sequences. The hypothesis arises from a demonstration that stereo contoured images of a diffuse reflection surface can be used to reconstruct a reasonably accurate three-dimensional contour model of the original surface. When the same approach is applied to a true mirror then the reconstructed surface becomes that of the reflected scene. However, if the mirror is dirty, this reconstruction breaks down giving neither the mirror surface nor the scene surface. If the two reflection components from the dirty mirror, from the scene and from the mirror surface, assuming each to obey Lambert's Law, can be separated then it should be possible to apply the original simple algorithm to each image-factor to define two three dimensional surfaces. This paper explores a way in which a time series sequence of images such as a video or film, or stereo images might be used to factor a specular reflecting surface into an equivalent set of added "Lambertian" surfaces.

Keywords: machine vision, shape capture, shape from X, specular-reflection.

1. Introduction and Background

1.1 Shape from Illumination Contours

If a matte surface which obeys Lambert's Law of reflection, is being viewed from different positions then the same points on the surface will, by definition, have the same perceived brightness from each viewing position. Contours of surface brightness obtained from images captured from different viewing points can, where this is true, be triangulated to give the three-dimensional surface positions belonging to the contour illumination values. This means that if a viewing position is moving parallel to the image plane then the projection of the contour position will move at a corresponding rate along the viewing surface matching the motion of the viewing position in the way illustrated in Figure 1

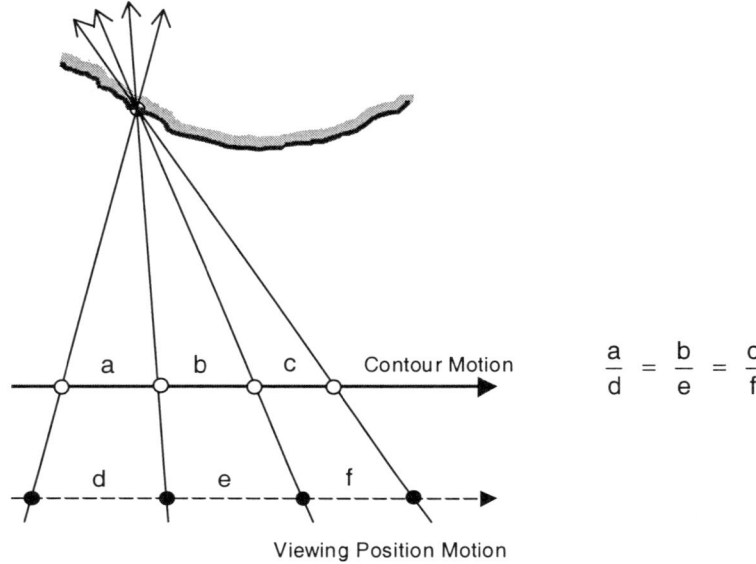

Figure 1: *uniform motion of a contour line*

If the surface of an object obeys Lambert's law of reflection then it is possible to triangulate the contour distribution of surface illumination from two stereo images to reconstruct the shape of the original surface.

A polar or rose diagram of the brightness of a matte surface seen from different directions will be that shown in Figure 2.

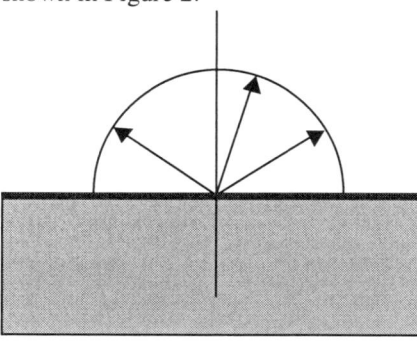

Figure 2: *matte surface reflection-distribution for a point*

If a component of a surface's reflection is specular, then as a first approximation it is possible to consider the surface as a true mirror for this specular component. This allows its reflection to be considered as a matte surface reflection from an image on a different surface to the mirror in the way shown in Figure 3.

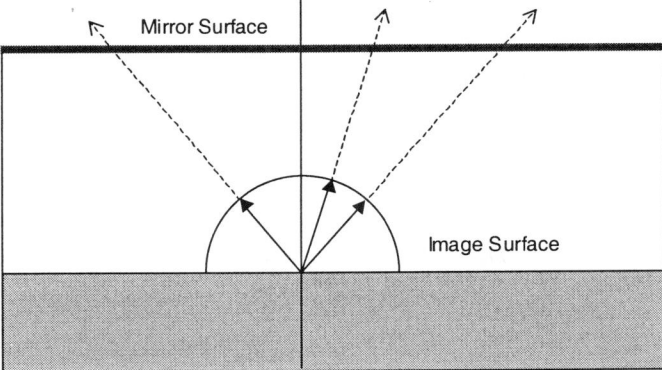

Figure 3: *mirror reflection from a virtual image*

However if the surface exhibits both matte and mirror reflection characteristics then the resulting polar diagram for a surface point could be constructed in the way shown in Figure 4.

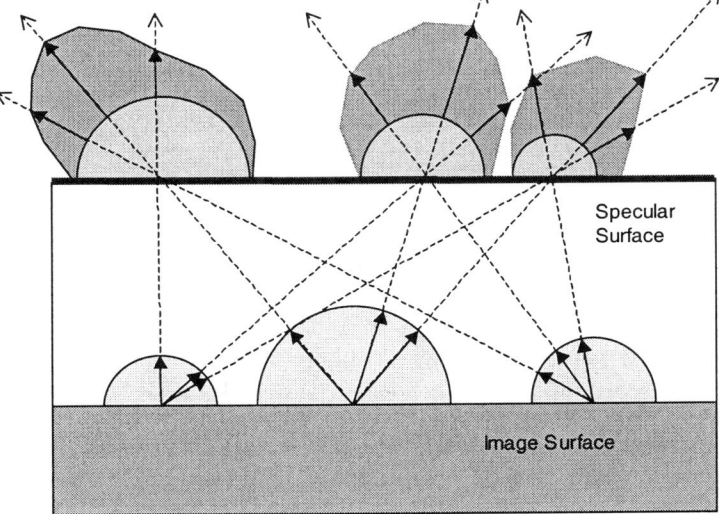

Figure 4: *specular reflection as the addition of two diffuse reflections*

There seemed to be two ways in which the separation of the component surfaces and their illumination or brightness distributions might be achieved. The first was to try to capture the movement of the component patterns of the two distributions in a holistic way. The second was to unravel the contributions of the two surfaces locally, in a geometrical piecewise manner.

D. Vernon [2] has started to explore the first approach using Fourier transforms of overlaid added images, moving relative to each other with a uniform velocity. The key idea was that the magnitude of the frequency components of the two patterns would stay the same, but the changing relative spatial positions of the patterns, would change their phases in the Fourier transform. This allowed each frequency element from the combined image to be treated as the vector sum of the frequency elements from the two separate images. Following this approach there was sufficient information in four composite images to algebraically separate two added, overlaid images. Six composite images allowed three added images to be separated, eight separating four and so on. However this process used square, plane, images, and did not therefore directly support shape reconstruction.

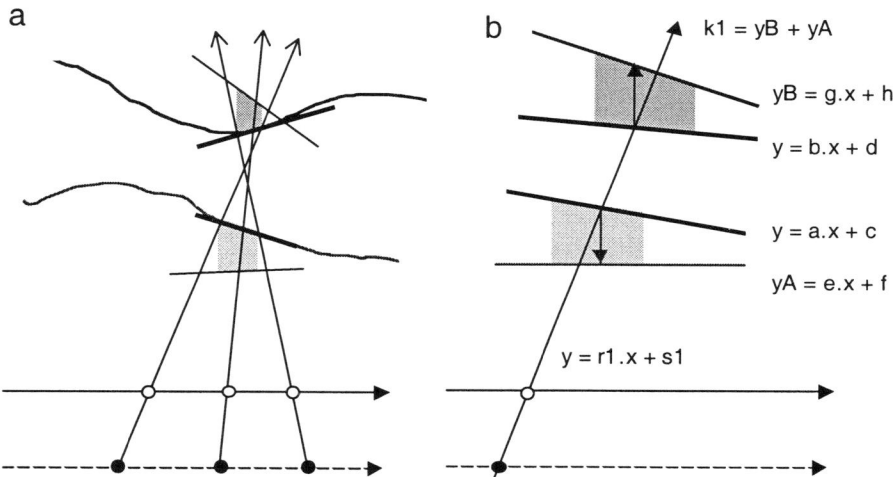

Figure 5: *two surface illumination-distributions combined in one image distribution*

If over a small local region of a surface, the surface is assumed to be planar and its brightness is assumed to have a linear gradient along the surface for its diffuse reflection component. If the same is assumed for the virtual surface of the reflected image for the specular component of the reflection, then there are 8 unknowns to be calculated from measurement data for viewing positions taken along a raster line. These are the coefficients of the line equations for the intersection of the surfaces and a plane through the raster line and viewing point, and the corresponding linear brightness distribution along each surface line. In Figure 5b, the unknowns are {a, b, c, d, e, f, g, h} and the values {r, s, k} are measured values dependent on the viewing ray. This would appear to require at least 8 equations, generated from 8 independent viewing positions. This in turn would require at least, the values from 8 adjacent pixel positions in the same image. The problem this poses is that projecting these 8 point values out into a scene will cover too wide a surface extent for the linear assumptions, used to set up this analysis model, to remain valid. There are two ways in which this situation can be improved, firstly by using stereo images from two cameras, reducing the spread of the 8 independently measured point values. The second is using time series data from a moving camera, which again will allow independent measurements to be taken from a closer cluster of point values on surfaces in the scene space. However, the situation is more complex, because the equations in the unknowns are not linear. For one viewing ray shown in Figure 5b, the resulting equation becomes:

$$k1 = yA + yB = g \cdot \frac{(d-s1)}{(r1-b)} + h + e \cdot \frac{(c-s1)}{(r1-a)} + f$$

Multiplying out this equation gives cubic terms in the unknowns. However, if the final image of a surface is considered to be made up from two overlaid images: the projections from two matte surfaces, then a contour of a particular value will not necessarily move in a way that directly corresponds with the motion of the viewing position. It appeared possible that the differences in its motion could provide the information necessary to define the contributing surfaces and their illumination.

1.2 The Parallel Surfaces Case

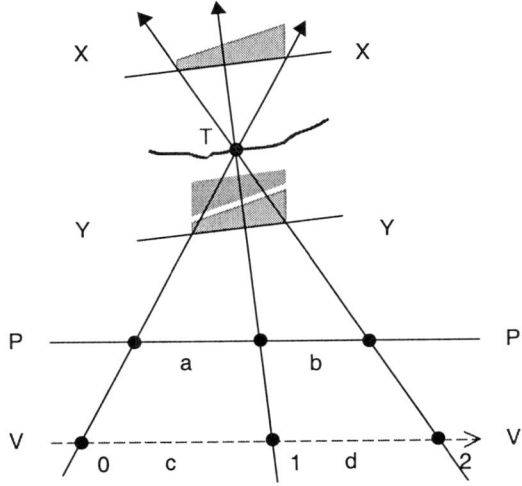

Figure 6: *triangulation of a surface point from three viewpoints*

However, even where a contour moves in direct correspondence with a viewing point, it does not necessarily imply a single matte surface. Figure 6 shows a viewing surface PP and three different viewing positions V0, V1, and V2. The corresponding three projections of a surface point T are shown on the plane PP. These points will all have the same illumination value if T is a matte surface exhibiting diffuse reflection. If the viewing position moves parallel to the image plane PP, the distance between the picture-plane's projected-positions: P0 and P1: a, and P1 and P2: b, will be in the same ratio as the distances moved by the viewing point from V0 to V1: c, and V1 to V2: d. However, this means that if two parallel surfaces had opposite and compensating illumination distributions of the form shown for lines XX and YY then the projected positions P0, P1 and P2 would still retain the same illumination value, viewed from V0, V1 and V2. There is not enough information in the distribution of illumination values in the image plane to distinguish these two different situations: a single matte surface from two compensating parallel matte surfaces, when the projection rays through matching illumination values are concurrent in this way. However, the situation is different if the viewing rays, through matching illumination values do not pass through a common point, as shown in Figure 7.

1.3 The Oblique Surfaces Case

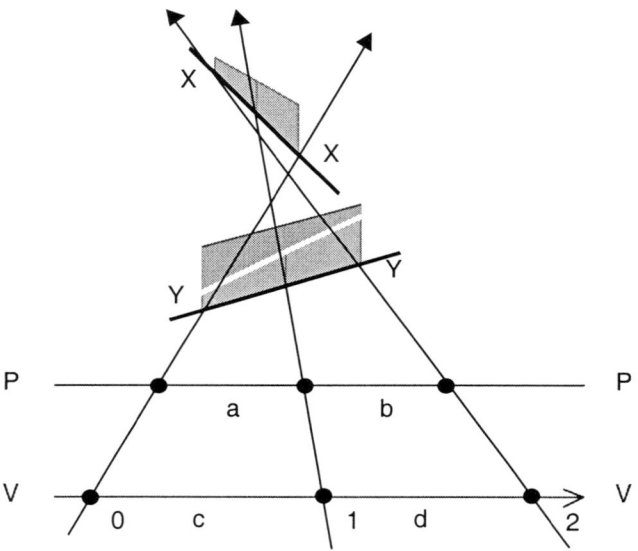

Figure 7: *non-concurrent matching-contour rays*

In Figure 7 the relationships which can create this new situation are shown. In this case no single matte surface can create the effect shown, however, there are many pairs of surfaces which will create the same distribution of matching illumination values in an image sequences obtained from a time series of viewing positions. If two plane surfaces, each with an appropriate, uniform illumination gradient, are considered then the relationships shown in Figure 7 could result. The rays linking the viewing positions and matching contour lines need no longer intersect as the triangulation of a single surface point.

Given the simplifying assumptions: plane surfaces, and uniform illumination gradients on these surfaces, a geometric construction can be set up to construct a set of surfaces which can compensate for each other in the required way. This can be based on a single point 'A' placed in the way shown in Figure 8. This point as the apex of the triangle ABC can be used to define the set of possible plane surface pairs such as XX, YY, which would generate the contour-line motion in the image plane associated with the viewing point sequence B-D-C. If the triangle ABC is divided into two sub triangles by linking a point D on BC back to the apex A. Lines drawn parallel to the triangle base BC through points F and E will then cut the sides of these construction sub-triangles in segments labeled c, d, e, f, so the following ratios are equal:

$$\frac{a}{b} = \frac{c}{d} = \frac{e}{f}$$

If an arbitrary, initial sloping surface YY is then drawn in through a point F. Construction lines through points J and M parallel to the triangle side AB can then be drawn in, and where they cut the line YY new points K and N can be labeled. Two new viewing rays DK and CN can then be drawn in as shown.

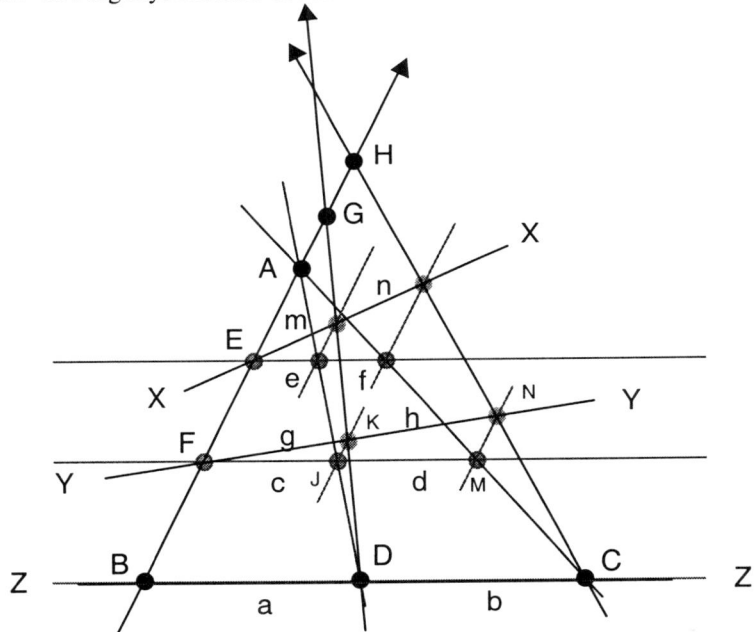

Figure 8: *constructing contour rays from an arbitrary initial surface YY.*

The property of this construction is that any lines parallel to the base BC drawn across the triangle ABC will allow a new set of non-parallel lines like XX to be drawn in, where the key property of this construction is that it sets the ratios:

$$\frac{a}{b} = \frac{c}{d} = \frac{g}{h} = \frac{e}{f} = \frac{m}{n}$$

The motivation for this construction is as follows. If over the small region of the surfaces spanned by the three rays, their illumination gradients are assumed to be constant then the slopes of the surfaces will determine the changes in the relative positions of these contour line rays seen from the different viewing points. These surfaces will have to be placed relative to each other so that the ratios of the distances between their intersection points with contour viewing rays are constant. Given that each ray is projected through a contour line with the same illumination intensity value, the following relationships hold:

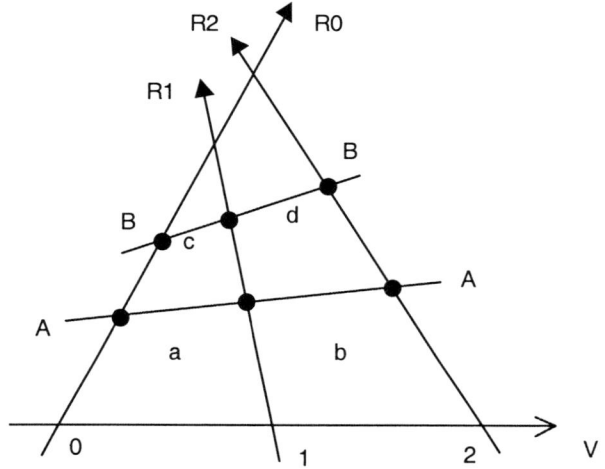

Figure 9: *matching ratios on non-parallel lines*

Along ray R0: $A0 + B0 = k;$ (1)   k: equal, summed illumination
Along ray R1: $A1 + B1 = k;$ (2)   intensities from the two
Along ray R2: $A2 + B2 = k;$ (3)   surfaces along different
                                     viewing-rays

Therefore

$(A0-A1)+(B0-B1) = 0;$ subtracting (2) from (1)
$(A1-A2)+(B1-B2) = 0;$ subtracting (3) from (2)

$\Delta A.a + \Delta B.c = 0;$ where ΔA and ΔB are the gradients
$\Delta A.b + \Delta B.d = 0;$ along AA and BB respectively

$$-\frac{\Delta A}{\Delta B} = \frac{a}{c} = \frac{b}{d}$$ therefore $\frac{a}{b} = \frac{c}{d}$

This final relationship corresponds to that set up by the geometric construction shown in Figure 8.

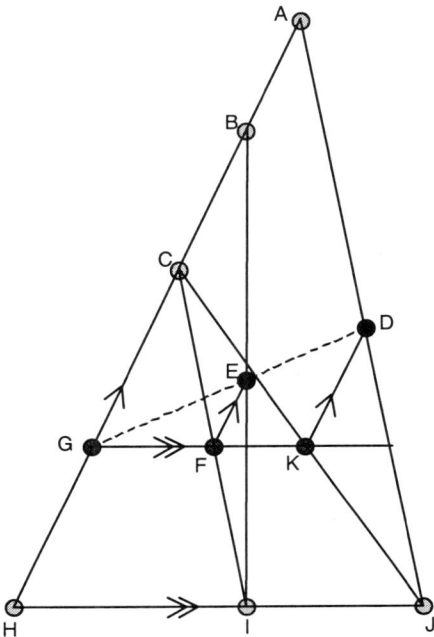

Figure 10: *reconstructing an oblique plane surface from three contour rays*

In triangles CBI and FEI

$$\frac{FE}{CB} = \frac{FI}{CI}$$ from similar triangles

In triangle CAJ and KDJ

$$\frac{KD}{CA} = \frac{KJ}{CJ}$$ from similar triangles

Therefore $$\frac{FE}{KD} = \frac{CB}{CA}$$

In triangles CHJ and CGK

$$\frac{HJ}{GK} = \frac{CH}{CG}$$ from similar triangles

Therefore

$$\frac{HI}{GF} = \frac{HJ}{GK}$$

In triangle CIJ and CFK

$$\frac{FI}{CI} = \frac{KJ}{CJ}$$ from similar triangles

Hence $$\frac{FE}{CB} = \frac{KD}{CA}$$

By Construction

$$\frac{CB}{CA} = \frac{HI}{HJ}$$

In triangles CGF and CHI

$$\frac{HI}{GF} = \frac{CH}{CG}$$ from similar triangles

Hence

$$\frac{GF}{GK} = \frac{HI}{HJ} = \frac{CB}{CA} = \frac{FE}{KD}$$

Hence in Figure 10, triangles GEF and GDK are similar and so GED is a straight line.

2. Reconstructing Surfaces from Contour Rays

The construction process to generate a particular set of compensating surfaces, which will match the arbitrary starting surface YY, shown in Figure 8 is simpler than the reverse operation shown in Figure 10. Given three contour rays, there is an infinite set of families of related surfaces, each of which could give the required relationships to generate the given contour motion sequence. This can be illustrated in Figure 11 by changing the position of the initial surface YY and repeating the construction of XX. In Figure 11 the choices of the first surface and the positions of the construction point A and the viewing points B, D and C, are used to define the appropriate relationship between three rays and a family of surfaces. In Figure 10, only the rays HA, IB and JA are given, so a variation of the construction is necessary to determine the possible families of related surfaces, which are capable of generating them.

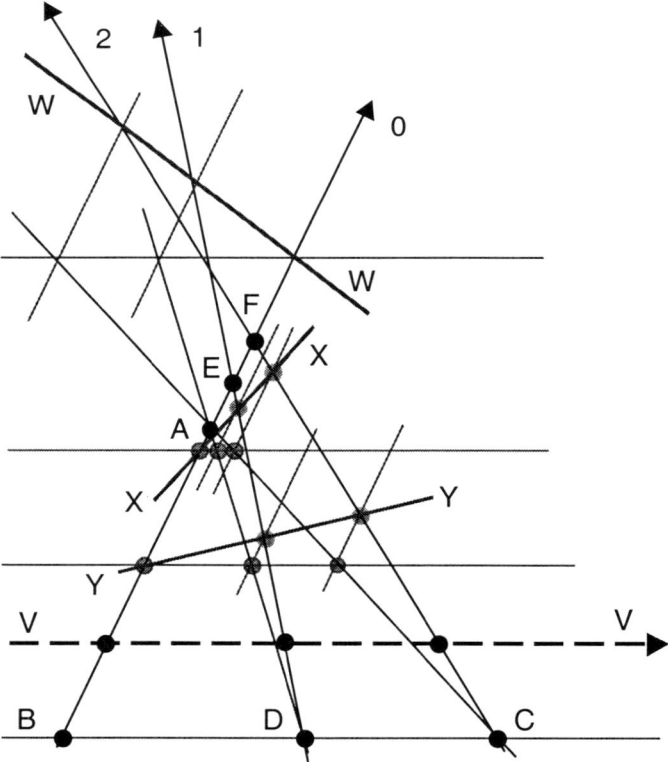

Figure 11: *constructing surfaces from given viewing rays*

In Figure 11, if the second two rays intersect the first ray in the points E and F, the construction triangle can be set up by drawing its base line BC, through any point B, parallel to the image plane or parallel to the trajectory of the viewing points. (Shown as the line VV in Figure 11). The apex of the triangle is then a point A on the first ray, placed so that the distance ratios AE: EF are the same as BD: DC. Any horizontal line cutting this triangle will intersect the lines BA, DA, and CA and be cut into segments having lengths in this same ratio. These segments can then be projected back onto the viewing rays in the way shown in Figure 11 to locate the family of surfaces such as WW, XX and YY. The choice of the point B determines this family of lines. Each B will give an infinite set of potentially matching surfaces.

If four rays through the corresponding contour lines seen from four viewing positions are analysed together then it is possible to limit the position of the base line of the construction triangle to a single position. This will give one construction triangle hence will produce only one family of related surfaces capable of generating the given contour positions, rather than an infinite number of them.

In Figure 12, the viewing rays R0, R1, R2 and R3 define positions F G and H. The base line BC for the construction triangle will be parallel to the viewing plane and the line of motion of the viewing positions. This means that the line BC can only be set up if it can be placed so that the ratio of DE: EC is the same as the ratio FG: GH. This would appear to locate a unique position for the line BC, either above or below the point F. Once this line has been located then the position of A will have to be selected so that the ratio AF: FG is the same as the ratio BD to DE. Since A can be located anywhere along the ray R0, there seems to be no restriction on doing this. From this reasoning it is clear that four rays will define an infinite set of matching surfaces.

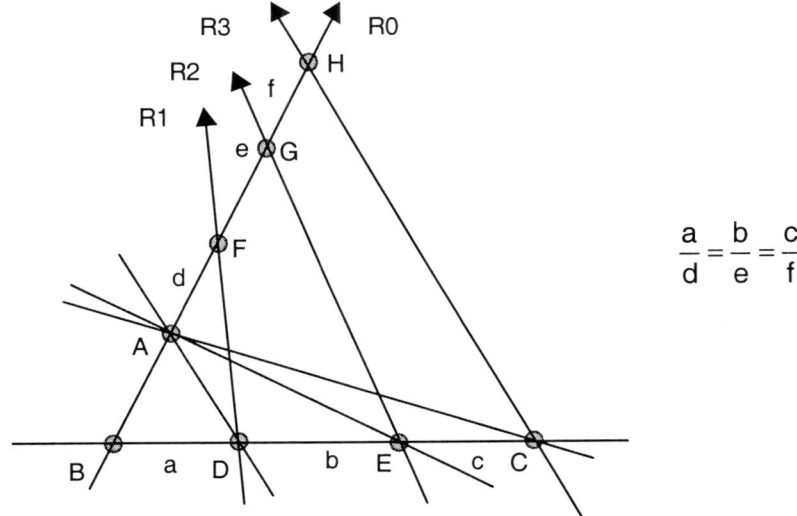

Figure 12: *four corresponding contour, viewing rays*

The next task, if possible, is to reduce the choice of surfaces from an infinite set of possibilities to a more manageable number. If two closely spaced contours in the same neighbourhood in each image in the time sequence, are processed in the same way, then only surfaces from the first set which match surfaces from the second set will be eligible candidates

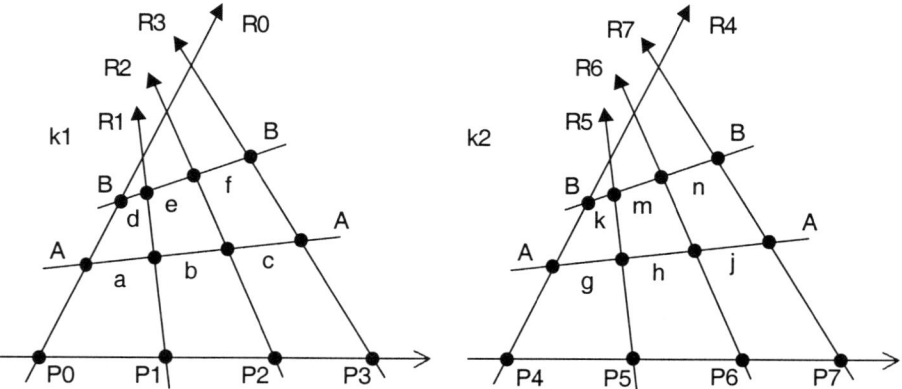

Figure 13: *two sets of rays for contour-values k1 and k2*

Along R0:	A0 + B0 = k1;	Along R4:	A4 + B4 = k2;
Along R1:	A1 + B1 = k1;	Along R5:	A5 + B5 = k2;
Along R2:	A2 + B2 = k1;	Along R6:	A6 + B6 = k2;
Along R3:	A3 + B3 = k1;	Along R7:	A7 + B7 = k2;

Therefore where ΔA and ΔB are the illumination gradients along AA and BB respectively

$$\Delta A.a + \Delta B.d = 0; \qquad \Delta A.g + \Delta B.k = 0;$$
$$\Delta A.b + \Delta B.e = 0; \qquad \Delta A.h + \Delta B.m = 0;$$
$$\Delta A.c + \Delta B.f = 0; \qquad \Delta A.j + \Delta B.n = 0;$$

$$-\frac{\Delta A}{\Delta B} = \frac{a}{d} = \frac{b}{e} = \frac{c}{f} = \frac{g}{k} = \frac{h}{m} = \frac{j}{n}$$

$$\frac{a}{b} = \frac{d}{e} \qquad \frac{a}{c} = \frac{d}{f} \qquad \frac{a}{g} = \frac{d}{k} \qquad \frac{a}{h} = \frac{d}{m} \qquad \frac{a}{j} = \frac{d}{n}$$

The problem with this approach is that there is no reason why the construction triangles for the surfaces in Figure 13 should be common to both contour sets. However it is possible to relate the geometry of the two construction triangles from the relationship between the two contour rays R0 and R4, in Figure 14, since they are both taken from the common viewing position V0.

3. An Algebraic Equation for Illumination Compensating Surfaces

In Figure 14 a general line XX is defined from the first set of contour rays relative to the position S0 using parameter $\lambda 1$, and from the second set of contour rays relative to the position S4 using parameter $\lambda 2$. Given these equations for the line XX, and given the rays (V0, P0) and (V0, P4), the positions of the intersections between the line and the rays, S0 and S4, can be used to relate the parameters $\lambda 1$ and $\lambda 2$ in the following way.

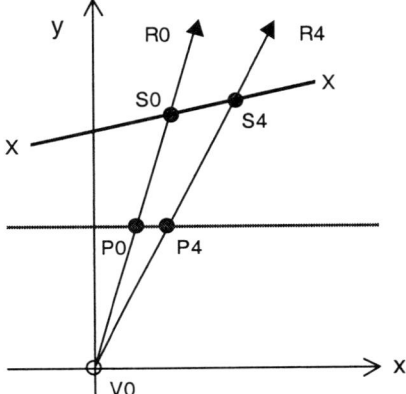

Figure 14: *relating two contour sets*

Equation for line XX : $\quad y = g.x + c$

Equation for ray R0 : $\quad S0 = \lambda 1.V0 + (1 - \lambda 1)P0 \quad$ from contour value k1

Equation for ray R4 : $\quad S4 = \lambda 2.V0 + (1 - \lambda 2)P4 \quad$ from contour value k2

Therefore :

$$g = \frac{(S0y - S4y)}{(S0x - S4x)} = \frac{\lambda 1.(V0y - P0y) + P0y - \lambda 2.(V0y - P4y) - P4y}{\lambda 1.(V0x - P0x) + P0x - \lambda 2.(V0x - P4x) - P4x} = \frac{A.\lambda 1 + B.\lambda 2 + C}{D.\lambda 1 + E.\lambda 2 + F}$$

where: $\quad A = V0y - P0y \qquad B = V0y - P4y \qquad C = P0y - P4y$

$\qquad\qquad D = V0x - P0x \qquad E = V0x - P4x \qquad F = P0x - P4x$

Given four contour rays from four consecutive viewing points the simplest algebraic approach was to follow these geometric constructions, step by step. Firstly, evaluate vertices of the construction triangle, and then use these to find the general equation for the family of surface section-lines passing through a general point S0 on contour ray R0. Figure 15 illustrates a transformation to the basic diagram, which simplifies the algebraic treatment of the geometrical constructions outlined above, by shearing the display space to make contour ray R0 vertical and perpendicular to the triangle base BC.

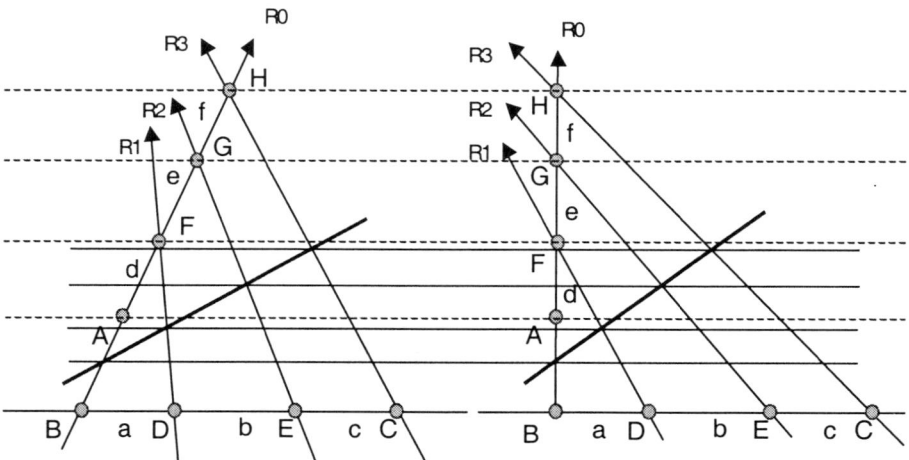

Figure 15: *transforming the display space*

In Figure 16 the surface line XX and the contour viewing-rays are transformed by a shearing operation, where x values are changed to make R0 vertical, but all the corresponding-point y values are kept the same. The first step is to intersect the rays R1, R2 and R3 with R0 to give the points F, G and H. The second step is to evaluate the position of the line BC so that the ratio FG: GH is the same as the ratio DE: EC.

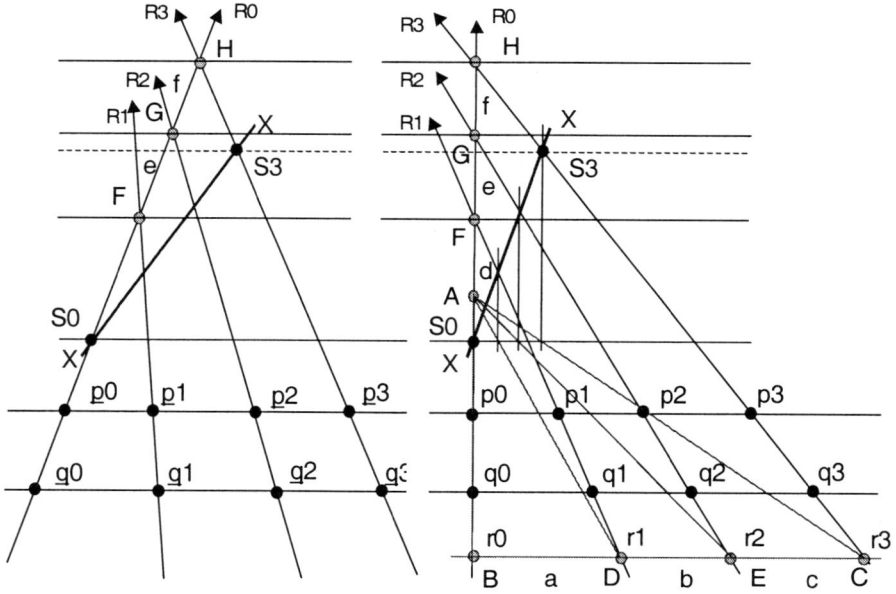

Figure 16: *calculating construction triangle vertices*

This will allow the ratio of BD to DE to be determined. The third step is to locate the point A on BH making the ratio AF: FG the same as BD: DE. Once the point A has been calculated then the equations of the lines AD, AE and AC are determined.

These lines can then be intersected with a horizontal line through S0, to give the x locations of vertical construction lines whose intersection with the original viewing rays will lie on the required line XX. Finally the inverse shear transformation applied to these points will then allow the general equation for the line XX to be evaluated for the original layout.

Step 0: Setting up the Co-ordinate Axes: The Shear Operation

It is convenient to make q0 the origin of the co-ordinate system. If q0 is not the origin of the co-ordinate system then there needs to be a translation operation to make q0 the origin. Similarly, if the picture plane is not parallel to the x-axis then a rotation is needed to make it so.

Once these initializing transformations have been done, the final step is to shear the display space to make the contour viewing ray R0 line up with the y-axis. The following homogeneous matrix defines the shear transformation and its inverse, needed to do this:

$$[x \; y \; 1] \begin{bmatrix} 1 & 0 & 0 \\ -\frac{px0}{py0} & 1 & 0 \\ 0 & 0 & 1 \end{bmatrix} = [x \; \underline{y} \; 1]$$

and

$$[x \; \underline{y} \; 1] \begin{bmatrix} 1 & 0 & 0 \\ \frac{px0}{py0} & 1 & 0 \\ 0 & 0 & 1 \end{bmatrix} = [x \; y \; 1]$$

However, if q0 is the origin and the x-axis is along the line of motion of the viewing positions (q0, q1, q2, q3) and it is parallel to the image plane, where the corresponding "k^{th} value" contour projection for these viewing positions are at positions (p0, p1, p2, p3). The various construction points can be initialized from the digitized-input, measured points in the following way.

    py = py0;

    px0 = 0.0;   px1 = px1 − px0;   px2 = px2 − px0;   px3 = px3 − px0;

    qy = 0.0;

    qx0 = 0.0;   qx1 = qx1 ;   qx2 = qx2;   qx3 = qx3;

Step 1: The intersections of Ray R0 with R1, R2 and R3

Line joining (q_i and p_i)

$$y = \frac{(py - qy)}{(px_i - qx_i)} \cdot x + \frac{py.(px_i - qx_i) - px_i.(py - qy)}{(px_i - qx_i)}$$

$$0 = (py - qy)x - (px_i - qx_i)y + px_i.qy - py.qx_i$$

Lines DF, EG and CH joining ($q1$ and $p1$), ($q2$ and $p2$) and ($q3$ and $p3$) for (q_i and p_i)

where $x = 0.0 \quad qy = 0.0 \quad fy_{i=1} = gy_{i=2} = hy_{i=3} = \dfrac{py.qx_i}{(qx_i - px_i)}$

Step 2: Locating points on the base line BC of the construction triangle ABC

For line BH joining ($q0$ and $p0$) $\quad x = 0:$ where $\quad y = ry \quad rx0 = 0$

For lines DF joining ($q1$ and $p1$), EG joining ($q2$ and $p2$) and CH joining ($q3$ and $p3$)

where $\quad y = ry \quad qy = 0.0 \quad rx_i = \dfrac{(px_i - qx_i).ry + py.qx_i}{py}$

In Figure 17 line BC has to be placed to maintain the following relationship

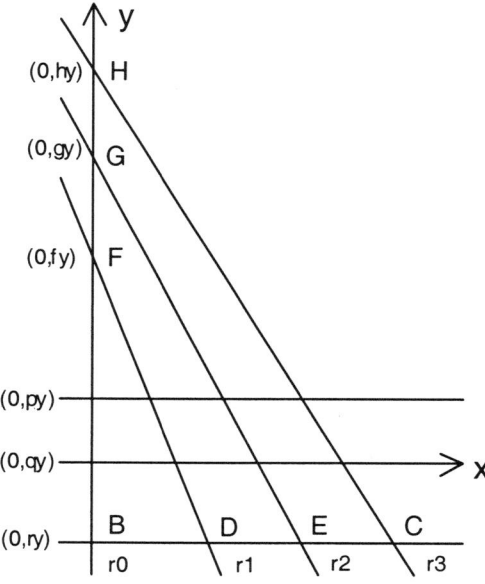

Figure 17: *calculating construction triangle vertices*

$$\frac{(rx3-rx2)}{(rx2-rx1)} = \frac{(hy-gy)}{(gy-fy)}$$

if $(rx3-rx2)(gy-fy) = (rx2-rx1)(hy-gy)$

then $\underset{1}{fy}.(rx2-rx3) + \underset{2}{gy}.(rx3-rx1) + \underset{3}{hy}.(rx1-rx2) = 0$

where $px_{ij} = px_i - px_j$

$\underset{1}{fy}.[(px23-qx23)ry + py.qx23]$

$\qquad + \underset{2}{gy}[(px31-qx31)ry + py.qx31]$

$\qquad\qquad + \underset{3}{hy}[(px12-qx12)ry + py.qx12] = 0$

Let $A = fy.qx23 + gy.qx31 + hy.qx12$

and $B = fy.px23 + gy.px31 + hy.px12$

$$ry = \frac{-py.(fy.qx23 + gy.qx31 + hy.qx12)}{(fy.px23 + gy.px31 + hy.px12) - (fy.qx23 + gy.qx31 + hy.qx12)} = \frac{A.py}{A-B}$$

substituting back

$$rx_i = \frac{A}{A-B}.(px_i - qx_i) + qx_i = \frac{A.px_i - B.qx_i}{A-B}$$

Step 3: Locate Point A

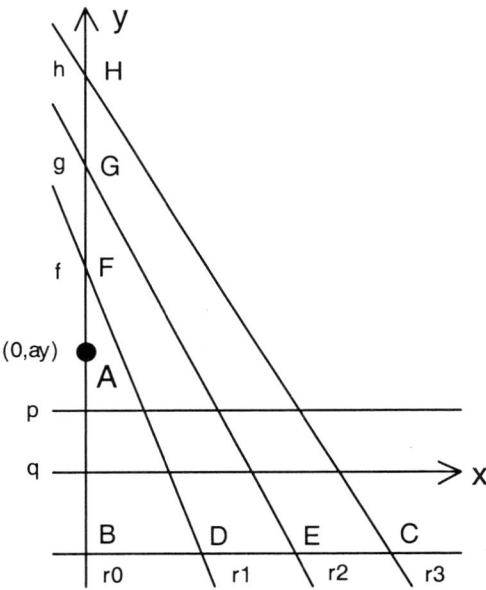

Figure 18: *calculating construction triangle vertices*

Point A has to maintain the following relationship

$$\frac{(rx2 - rx1)}{(rx1 - rx0)} = \frac{(gy - fy)}{(fy - ay)}$$

$$(rx2 - rx1)(fy - ay) = rx1.(gy - fy)$$

$$rx2.fy - rx1.gy = (rx2 - rx1)ay$$

$$\frac{A}{A-B}.fy.(A.px2 - B.qx2) - \frac{A}{A-B}.gy.(A.px1 - B.qx1)$$

$$= \frac{A}{A-B}.ay.(A.px2 - B.qx2 - A.px1 + B.qx1)$$

Regrouping $\quad (A.px2 - B.qx2 - A.px1 + B.qx1) = (A.px21 - B.qx21)$

Hence $\quad ay = \dfrac{fy.(A.px2 - B.qx2) - gy.(A.px1 - B.qx1)}{(A.px21 - B.qx21)}$

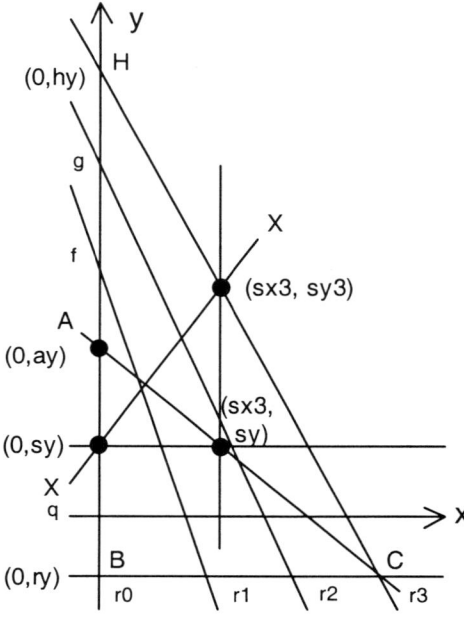

Figure 19: *calculating construction triangle vertices*

Step 4: Establish Line Equation AC from (rx3, ry) to (0, ay)

$$0 = (ry - ay)x - rx3.y + rx3.ay$$

Step 5: Determine sx3 from Line AC

$$\text{if } y = sy \qquad sx3 = \frac{rx3 \cdot (sy - ay)}{(ry - ay)}$$

Step 6: Determine sy3 from Line CH. Line CH from (rx3, ry) to (0, hy)

$$0 = (ry - hy)x - rx3 \cdot y + rx3 \cdot hy$$

substituting for $x = sx3$

$$sy3 = \frac{(ry - hy)sx3 + rx3 \cdot hy}{rx3} = \frac{1}{rx3} \cdot (ry - hy) \frac{rx3(sy - ay)}{(ry - ay)} + hy$$
$$= \frac{(ry - hy)(sy - ay)}{(ry - ay)} + hy$$

Step 7: Inverse Shear Transform (sx0, sy0), (sx3, sy3)

$$\left(\frac{sy \cdot px0}{py0}, sy \right) \rightarrow$$
$$\left(\frac{rx3 \cdot (sy - ay)}{(ry - ay)} + \left[\frac{(ry - hy)(sy - ay)}{(ry - ay)} + hy \right] \cdot \frac{px0}{py0}, \frac{(ry - hy)(sy - ay)}{(ry - ay)} + hy \right)$$

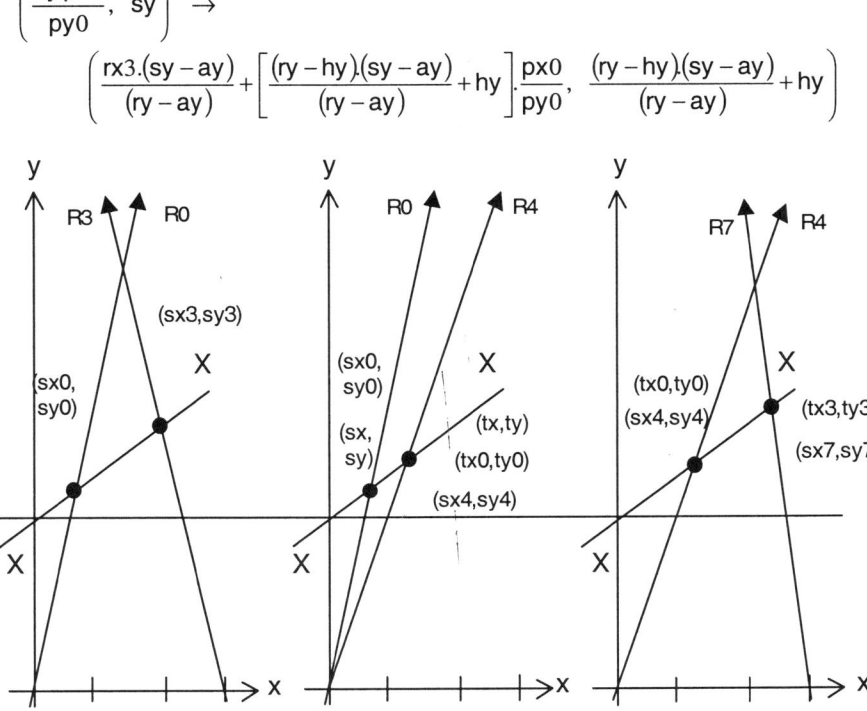

Figure 20: *relating the various point-labeling schemes*

Gradient XX:

$$g = \frac{(sy3-sy0)}{(sx3-sx0)} = \frac{(sy4-sy0)}{(sx4-sx0)} = \frac{(ty-sy)}{(tx-sx)} = \frac{(ty3-ty0)}{(tx3-tx0)} = \frac{(sy4-sy7)}{(sx4-sx7)}$$

Substituting in the known values:

Gradient XX: $\dfrac{(ty-sy)}{\left(\dfrac{ty.px4}{py4} - \dfrac{sy.px0}{py0}\right)} = \dfrac{py0.py4.(ty-sy)}{(ty.px4.py0 - sy.px0.py4)}$ (1)

$$\frac{\left(\dfrac{(ry-hy)(sy-ay)+hy.(ry-ay)}{(ry-ay)} - sy\right)}{\left(\dfrac{rx3.(sy-ay)}{(ry-ay)} + \dfrac{(ry-hy)(sy-ay)+hy.(ry-ay)}{(ry-ay)} \cdot \dfrac{px0}{py0} - \dfrac{sy.px0}{py0}\right)} \equiv \frac{(N)}{(D)}$$

N: $\dfrac{sy.(ay-hy)-ry.(ay-hy)}{(ry-ay)}$

D: $\dfrac{py0.(sy-ay).rx3 + (ay-hy)(sy-ry).px0}{py0.(ry-ay)}$

Gradient XX: $\dfrac{(ay-hy)(sy-ry).py0}{(py0.(sy-ay).rx3 + (ay-hy)(sy-ry).px0)}$ (2)

Step 9: Equate Gradient Expressions

$$\frac{py0.py4.(ty-sy)}{(ty.px4.py0 - sy.px0.py4)} = \frac{(ay-hy)(sy-ry).py0}{(py0.(sy-ay).rx3 + (ay-hy)(sy-ry).px0)}$$

Cross-multiply and factor out sy and ty where py0 = py4 = py:

$$sy^2.[rx3.py] + sy.[-rx3.ay.py] + sy.ty.[(ay-hy)(px4-px0) - py.rx3]$$
$$+ ty.[ry.(ay-hy)(px0-px4) + py.rx3.ay] = 0$$

Renaming Coefficients of sy and ty:

$A.sy^2 + B.sy + C.sy.ty + D.ty = 0$

$$ty = \frac{-sy.(A.sy+B)}{(C.sy+D)} \quad \text{for contour value k1} \quad (3)$$

Equating the slopes of the second set

$ty^2.[nx3.py]+$
$ty.[-nx3.my.py]+$
$sy.ty.[(my-ky)(px0-px4)-py.nx3]+$
$sy.[ny.(my-ky)(px4-px0)+py.nx3.my]=0$

$E.ty^2 + F.ty + G.sy.ty + H.sy = 0$

$$sy = \frac{-ty.(E.ty+F)}{(G.ty+H)} \quad \text{for contour value k2} \quad (4)$$

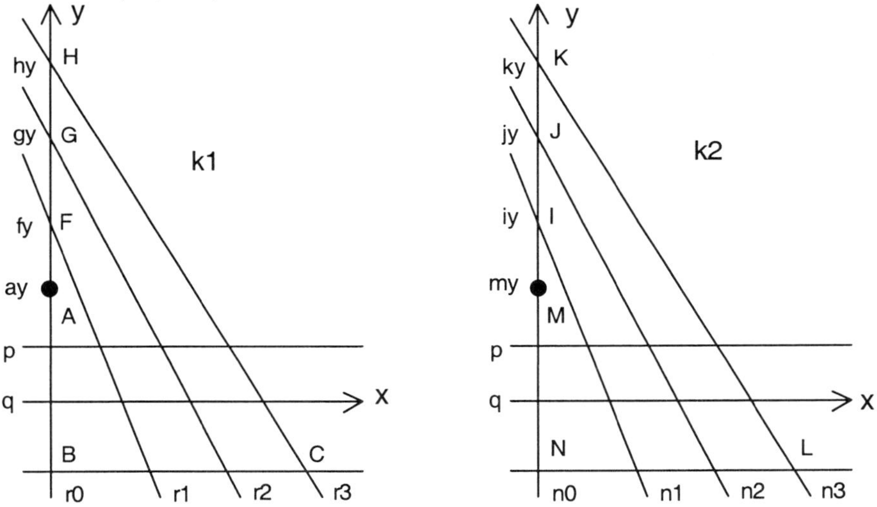

Figure 21: *relating the two contour values*

Step 10: Reduce unknowns to sy. Substitute formula (3) into (4)

$$ty = \frac{-sy.(A.sy+B)}{(C.sy+D)} \rightarrow sy = \frac{-ty.(E.ty+F)}{(G.ty+H)}$$

$$sy = \frac{\frac{sy.(A.sy+B)}{(C.sy+D)}\left(E.\frac{-sy.(A.sy+B)}{(C.sy+D)}+F\right)}{\left(G.\frac{-sy.(A.sy+B)}{(C.sy+D)}+H\right)}$$

$$sy\left(G.\frac{-sy.(A.sy+B)}{(C.sy+D)}+H\right) = \frac{sy.(A.sy+B)}{(C.sy+D)}\left(E.\frac{-sy.(A.sy+B)}{(C.sy+D)}+F\right)$$

$$(-G.sy.(A.sy+B)+H.(C.sy+D))(C.sy+D) = (A.sy+B)(-E.sy.(A.sy+B)+F.(C.sy+D))$$

Multiply out and collect powers of sy:

$$\begin{pmatrix} sy^3.(A^2.E-A.C.G)+ \\ sy^2.(C^2H-B.C.G-A.D.G-A.C.F+2A.B.E)+ \\ sy.(2C.D.H-B.D.G-A.D.F-B.C.F+EB^2)+ \\ (D^2.H-B.D.F) \end{pmatrix} = \begin{pmatrix} a.sy^3+ \\ b.sy^2+ \\ c.sy+ \\ d \end{pmatrix} = 0$$

This gives a cubic in sy, so there will be either three real roots, or one real root and two complex roots to this equation. At the most therefore, there will be three possible locations and gradients for the surfaces, which might contribute to the moving pattern of contour lines in a local neighbourhood of a scene image. Assuming the initial approximations are appropriate! The next step in this examination is to code this algorithm and apply it to simulated illumination data, then to apply it to the more complicated data from image sequences of real objects.

Step 11: Simulate two surfaces with constant illumination gradients

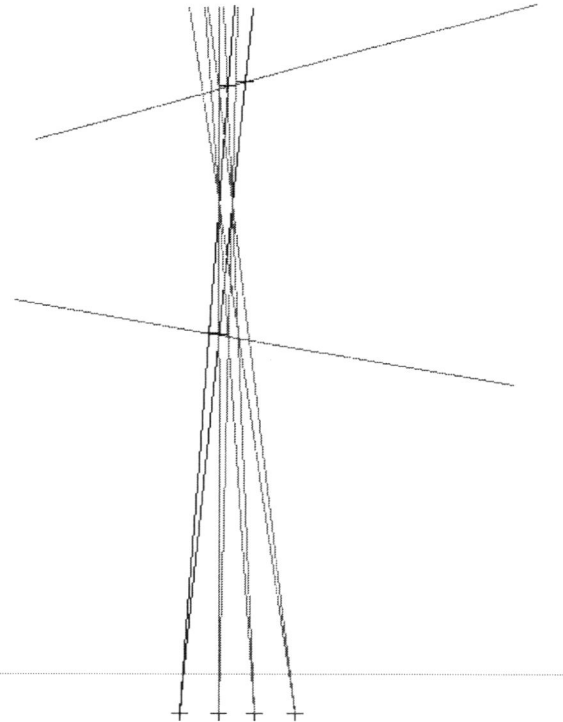

Figure 22: *generating matching contour rays from two surfaces: computer output*

In Figure 22 the first step of the simulation is illustrated. Two surfaces are defined with linear illumination gradients. Two initial viewing rays are defined and the contour value of each is determined. A grid of illumination values is then calculated on the display surface, for each viewing position, and the contour-value positions, which match the illumination values of the two original viewing rays, calculated from these grid values. The crossed-over, contour-rays give the projections of the same contour values for each of the four viewing points. In this case the illumination gradients were very similar to each other. This is shown by the way that these crossing points lie mid way between the two surface section lines.

Step 12: Reconstruct the surfaces from the image time series data

The next step was to use the pixel value data from the image sequence calculated in this simulation, for the given viewing positions, and see how closely, if at all, the reverse calculation could be carried out, to estimate the surface positions that were used to generate the images. Where the viewing rays were kept closely together the results were surprisingly good.

```
please enter viewing point
please enter viewing point
please enter picture plane
please enter contour ray R0 end point
 248.37745 182.69056
 250.15803  79.02153
please enter contour ray R4 end point
 252.58479 184.23808
 255.64045  77.49365
surface 0  12.00000  78.00000  29.21214  30.80802
surface 1  34.00000  99.00000  51.81569  53.76300
 contour values:    81.02783  84.57102
 grid values for each viewing point
 242.34351 534.00000   81.02783
 249.96384 534.00000   81.02783
 258.53601 534.00000   81.02783
 264.25039 534.00000   81.02783
 242.57252 534.00000   84.57102
 250.19297 534.00000   84.57102
 258.76526 534.00000   84.57102
 264.47971 534.00000   84.57102
 fy1 values 1-2-3 -421.41158-421.05324-420.81372
 fy2 values 1-2-3 -421.54776-421.17918-420.93280
 ry  values 0 -914.46257
 fy  values 0 -421.72916
 rx3 values 3  -26.98088
 ry  values 0 -929.02774
 fy  values 0 -421.87440
 rx3 values 3  -27.76259
         3  roots of the cubic
 182.69049
  79.02148
 -23617768.54990|
                    computer output
```

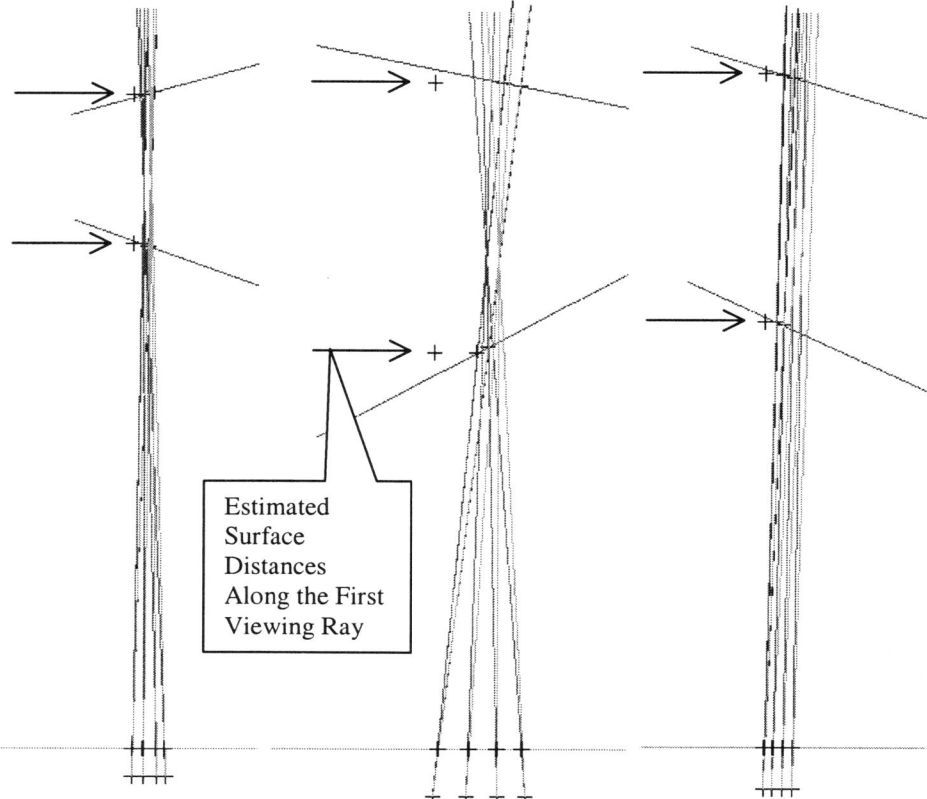

Figure 23: *surface factoring algorithm: estimating surface depths along an initial viewing ray: computer output*

However, the assumptions on which these results are based, will only hold over a very small neighborhood in a scene. What is promising about the work is that it seems applicable to those parts of a scene which are smoothly illuminated, that cannot be handled by alternative means of shape capture such as matching edges or other readily located texture based features [6].

Step 13: Reconstructing the illumination functions

Although the main objective of this study was to find a way for estimating local surface shape, in principle it can be extended to estimate the linear illumination functions assumed in the previous analysis. Having calculated the (sx[i], sy[i]) co-ordinates of the intersection of the first contour viewing ray with possible surfaces, the intersections with the second contour viewing ray (tx[i], ty[i]) can be calculated using equation 3 in step 9. From these points the equations of the surface section lines can be calculated. Assuming two surfaces in Figure 24, labeled A and B, then four arbitrary contour rays for contour values k1, k2, k3 and k4, can be intersected with these surface lines to give the series of points (p1a, p2a, p3a, p4a) and (p1b, p2b, p3b, p4b). From these the illumination functions at the top and bottom of Figure 24 can be set up.

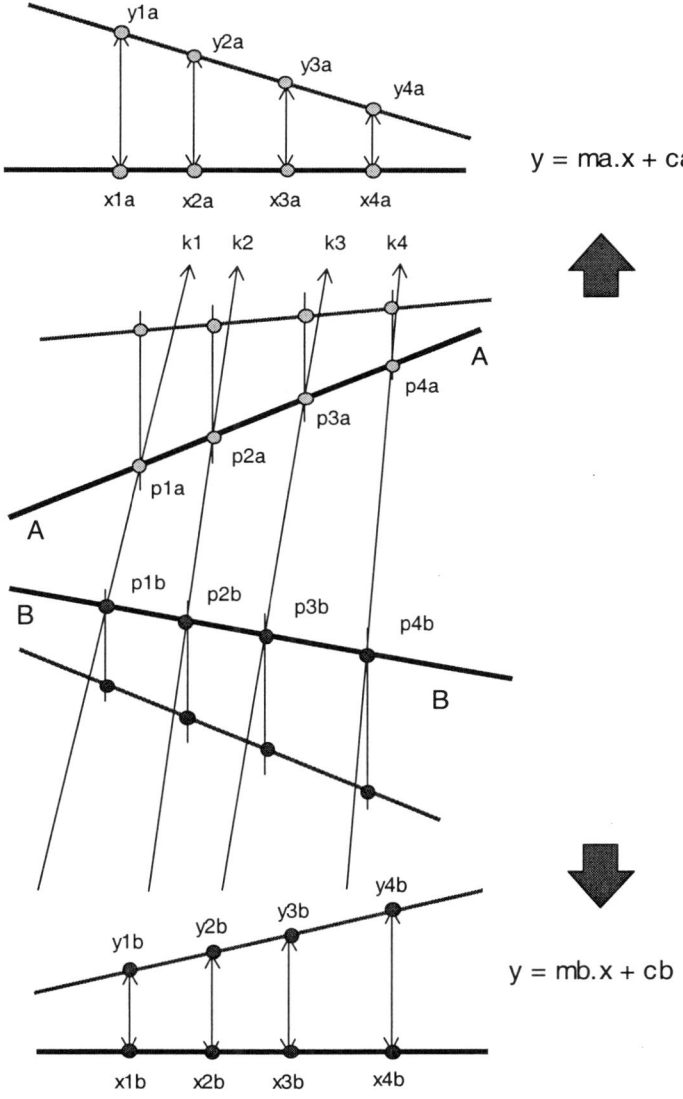

$y = m_a.x + c_a$

$y = m_b.x + c_b$

Figure 24: *calculating illumination distribution functions*

In Figure 24 the x values from the intersection of the four contour rays: k1-k4, with the surfaces AA and BB when substituted into the illumination function equations give eight equations with twelve unknowns (y1a, y2a, y3a, y4a, y1b, y2b, y3b, y4b, ma, ca, mb, cb). However, there are four more equations k1 = y1a+y1b; k2 = y2a+y2b; k3 = y3a+y3b; k4 = y4a+y4b; that are applicable. This gives:

$$ya1 = ma.xa1 + ca = k1 - mb.xb1 - cb;$$
$$ya2 = ma.xa2 + ca = k2 - mb.xb2 - cb;$$
$$ya3 = ma.xa3 + ca = k3 - mb.xb3 - cb;$$
$$ya4 = ma.xa4 + ca = k4 - mb.xb4 - cb;$$

These relationships at first sight appear to be sufficient to estimate the local illumination values and their gradients when they are needed.

Step 14: Calibration with reality

The next stage in the work is to apply the algorithm resulting from this theoretical analysis of time series images, to see where it works and where it fails, using real scene images and the corresponding real scene geometry. Even if this theoretical result proves insufficient in its current simple form, for estimating true surface distances, it seems to be an important result. It shows that given the appropriate assumptions from context based knowledge, substantial information appears to exist in an image sequence for filtering out specular reflection in local areas of a scene.

4. Conclusions

The approach followed in this paper is probably not the most general or flexible way of executing the mathematics. It is the consequence of having to unpick the problem in simple steps, when entering the apparently sufficient set of initial equations into an algebra system failed to produce usable results! The initial statement of the task seemed simple enough but there were a series of projective geometry relationships, which meant that variables that initially appeared independent were in fact interrelated.

It is not yet clear what the assumptions of linearity will cause to happen if they are not satisfied in a real system. Either the results will be totally false, or as is hoped, over a small region, only slightly in error, and amenable to statistical refinement. More analytical and experimental work is currently in progress. What is presented, is the first step in tackling a problem that for a long time has appeared impenetrable. In order to make progress a scene's surfaces have only been factored into surface pairs, and the approach that has been implemented is probably only capable of handling two surfaces.

However, just as accurate planetary orbits had to be modeled by many epicycles; and Fourier transforms representing complex functions required a long series of simpler functions added together; it seems likely that an accurate model of a specular reflection field could require the sum of many "Lambert" reflection fields. However, a relevant, related operation exists in radiosity calculations in image synthesis work. Multiple reflections from surface to surface can be calculated by inverting a matrix using an iterative process. This corresponds to chasing rays from surface to surface, and in most cases the attenuation of the light energy at each reflection, means that only a few cycles of the iteration are necessary in most cases (that are not multiple mirror systems!) to obtain reasonably accurate results. If the approach emerging in this paper is set up appropriately, then possibly only a few multiple reflecting surfaces with their matte virtual images will be necessary to match reality!

An alternative idea to extending this approach by using higher order surface factorization to improve accuracy, is the idea that what the eye sees or perceives as surface depth is determined over a local region by a simple processing scheme of the form analyzed in this paper. In other words it may not be an accurate estimate of depth that is obtained merely a self-consistent reconstruction of shape over a local region. Initially this idea was rejected, remembering basic physics experiments using parallax to determine the location of the images of pins, with mirrors and lenses. However, on further thought it seems that this is an idea which also needs further testing.

The place where the approach outlined in this paper is most likely to find an application is in the reconstruction of smooth evenly lit surfaces, in other words where there are no edges or texture features to support accurate triangulation. The pin in the parallax experiments gave true depth estimates using its edges rather than its internal illumination distribution. The idea that the perception mechanism is responsible for the surfaces we see, in the absence of edge information would seem to be supported by the way clouds of water vapour can appear as objects with distinct bounding surfaces. Walking through a fog or mist, there often appears to be a collection of false or virtual interleaving surfaces blocking long distance views. If this is true then factoring specular surfaces into two or three matte surfaces may be more than enough for the emerging three-dimensional display delivery systems to provide realistic dynamic lighting effects.

This work is a study that is one in a series being undertaken to support a model based 3DTV project [1, 4]. It is an extension of an idea that evolved from a *"shape from shading"* study [3]. It will hopefully provide, at a minimum, one more useful technique in the machine vision toolbox [5, 6]. Where the approach produces consistent results when applied to film and video image sequences, it will also contribute to the post-production industry's capabilities for generating special effects.

5. Acknowledgements

Collaboration with Dr J. Patterson and Dr P. Sieberts from Glasgow University's Computer Science department, on an EPSRC funded project: "Faraday: Models from Movies". Professor Hirschfeld in Sussex University's Mathematics department helped to develop the initial geometrical construction that allowed the required relationship between viewing rays and surfaces to be generated graphically.

6. References

1. A.G. Serrano, H. Sue, A. L. Thomas and H. Wei. *"Model-Based Interactive TV: Scene Capture and Transmission, Density Distribution Functions for Bandwidth Reduction"*. in *"Digital Content Creation"*, ed. Rae Earnshaw and John Vince. *Springer.* 2001, pp 229-271

2. D. Vernon, *"Removal of superimposed reflections from dynamic image sequences"*, in *"Irish Machine Vision and Image Processing Conference and Eight Ireland Conference on Artificial Intelligence"*. Magee College, University of Ulster. 10-13 September 1997.

3. A. L. Thomas, *"Speculation on virtual surfaces in machine vision systems"*. in *"Irish Machine Vision and Image Processing Conference and Eight Ireland Conference on Artificial Intelligence"*. Magee College, University of Ulster. 10-13 September 1997, pp 55-60

4. A. L. Thomas, *"Scene capture and modelling for three dimensional interactive stereo television broadcasting"*. in *"Digital Convergence: The Information Revolution"*. John Vince and Rae Earnshaw Eds. Springer 1999. pp 220-253

5. Olivier Faugeras, *"Three-Dimensional Computer Vision"*, The MIT Press, London, 1993

6. Richard Hartley and Andrew Zisserman, *"Multiple View Geometry in Computer Vision"*, Cambridge University Press, 2000.

A hardware based implementation of the Multipath method

Roel Martínez*, László Szirmay-Kalos• , Mateu Sbert*

*Institut d'Informática i Aplicacions, Universitat de Girona
{roel,mateu}@ima.udg.es

• Department of Control Engineering and Information Technology, Technical University of Budapest
szirmay@iit.bme.hu

Abstract

This paper presents a depth buffer hardware implementation of the multipath algorithm for radiosity. The implementation makes use of bundles of parallel lines implemented with the OpenGL's depth buffer. The new algorithm is compared with the earlier painter algorithm implementation and we conclude that the proposed technique can result in half a magnitude of speed increase, and can render the indirect illumination in moderately complex scenes in a few seconds.

keywords: Radiosity, depth buffer, OpenGL, Monte Carlo.

1. Introduction

Global illumination algorithms compute the single reflection of the light many times to simulate the multiple reflections. To obtain a single reflection at a point, the estimate of the incoming radiance is multiplied by the probability of the reflection and the product is integrated taking into account all the possible incoming directions. Consequently, global illumination is basically a numerical integration problem.

Local Monte-Carlo approaches sample the domain of the integration randomly using a probability density $p(x)$, evaluate the integrand $f(x)$ here, and provide the f/p ratio as the primary estimate of the integral. This estimate is accurate if we can find p that precisely mimics f, i.e. it makes f/p as flat as possible. This strategy, which is commonly referred as importance sampling, places more samples where the integrand is large. Since in practice p can be very far from the integrand, the

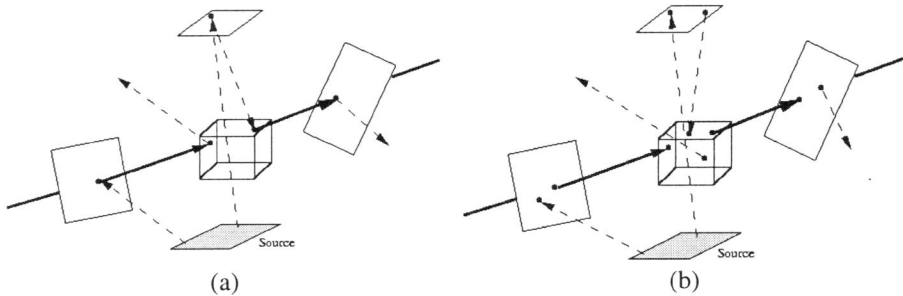

Figure 1. (a) Random walk simulation with global lines. A global line (the thick continuous one) makes two paths advance at once. Considering bi-directionality of the global lines, two other paths will also advance in the reverse direction of the line. (b) Note that the exit point on each patch is random.

estimator may have high variance. Thus to get an accurate result many independent primary estimators should be used to compute the secondary estimator as their average.

Global Monte-Carlo methods do not rely on the hope to find good sampling density. Instead, they take advantage of the fact that it is usually easy to evaluate function f at a well structured set of sample points $x_1,...,x_n$. The emphasis is on that the simultaneous computation of $f(x_1),..., f(x_n)$ is much cheaper than the individual computation of $f(x_1),...,$ and $f(x_n)$ by a local method, thus in this way we can have much more samples for the same computational effort. The disadvantage of this technique is that finding a probability density that simultaneously mimics the integrand at many points is very difficult, thus practical methods usually use uniform sampling probability. In this way, global methods are implemented using global uniformly distributed lines, in contraposition to "local" lines, generated from sampled points in the scene.

The multipath algorithm [9],[10] belongs to the family of global lines algorithms which has seen a further developing in [1],[2],[12],[13].

The objective of this paper is to demonstrate that it is possible and worth to implement the multipath method using hardware acceleration techniques, particularly the OpenGL's depth buffer.

The rest of the paper is organized as follows. In section 2 we present the multipath method with single lines and also with bundles of lines. In section 3 we introduce the depth buffer hardware implementation. In section 4 we show our results and finally present the conclusions.

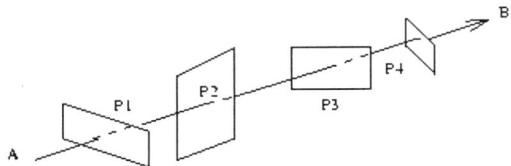

Figure 2. The global line *AB* will transport power from patch *P1* to *P2* and from patch *P3* to patch *P4*. Patches *P1* and *P4* are on the walls of the interior scene. Considering bi-directionality, the line will also transport power from *P2* to *P1* and from *P4* to *P3*.

2. Multipath method

2.1 Previous work

Global lines were first used in rendering by Buckalew in [3]. In [8] Sbert showed the intimate relationship of global lines to radiosity and used them to develop a full matrix radiosity method. The multipath algorithm for radiosity [9],[10] eliminated the need for computing the form factors explicitly, and was shown in [10] that it could be interpreted as a random walk algorithm. In [9],[10] the multipath was implemented with bundles of parallel rays, but the coherence properties have not been exploited. Meanwhile, Neumann [6] presented independently the transillumination algorithm, that has been further developed by [11], [12] and [13] in order to generalize it also for non-diffuse environments. These methods used the painter algorithm to generate global lines in bundles.

2.2 Multipath algorithm with single lines

The multipath algorithm, described in [9],[10] uses segments of global lines to build random walks that mimic classic random walks with infinite path length (see figure 1) The main differences between multipath and a classic (local) random walk approach are the source probability selection, the simultaneous advance of different paths thanks to global lines, and transporting different logical paths in a single geometrical one. The multipath method is only efficient in "smoothed" scenes, with emittance occupying a larger part of the scene and more or less equilibrated. For this reason a *first shot* distributing direct illumination before applying the algorithm is necessary (see also [4] and [14]).

Multipath algorithm casts a predetermined number of random global lines using, for instance, pairs of random points on an enclosing sphere. Each line will produce an intersection list, and the list is traversed taking into account each successive pair of patches (see figure 2). Each patch (if not emitter) stores two quantities. One records the power accumulated, and the other the unshot power. For every pair of patches along the intersection list, the first patch of the pair will transmit its unsent power to

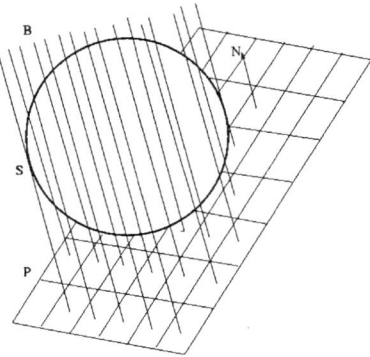

Figure 3. Bundle of parallel lines, where S is the sphere that wraps the scene, B is the bundle of lines, P is the projection plane, orthogonal to S and N is the normal to the projection plane.

the second patch of the pair. So the unshot energy of the first patch is reset to zero, and the two quantities at the second patch, the accumulated and the unsent energy, are incremented. In the case of a source a third quantity is also kept, the emitted power per line exiting the source. This power is precomputed in the following way: Given the number of lines to cast, the forecast number of lines passing through any source is found. This can be done with Integral Geometry methods [7]. The division of the total source power by this number of forecast lines gives the predicted power of one line. Then, if the first patch of a pair is a source patch, the power transported to the second patch of the pair will also include this predicted power portion.

2.3 Multipath with bundles of parallel lines

In [5] the multipath method has been extended to transfer radiosity with bundles of parallel lines, which takes advantage of the ray-coherence. The bundle of parallel lines is simulated using a general purpose polygon filling algorithm, called the painter algorithm.

The bundle of parallel lines is created as follows (see figure 3) First the scene is wrapped in a sphere. Then a random point is selected on the surface of the sphere, and an orthogonal plane to the sphere is obtained. We call this plane the *projection plane*. The direction of the bundle of parallel lines is defined perpendicular to the plane. The projection plane is associated with XY coordinates and is decomposed to n by m pixels.

Every pixel originates a line, and all patches that are projected in the same pixel are used in order to compute the exchange of energy between them, having sorted them according to their z values.

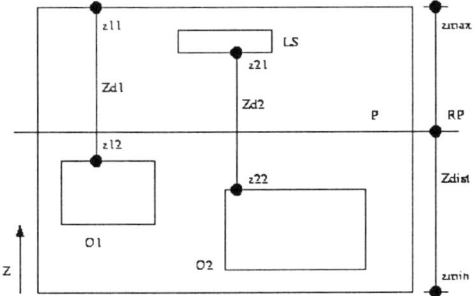

Figure 4. The probability that the plane *P*, orthogonal to Z-axis, crosses between object *O1* and the ceiling is given by the distance between the object and the ceiling *Zd1* divided by the maximum distance in the scene *Zdist*. Also, the probability that *P* crosses between *O2* and *LS* is given by *Zd2/Zdist*.

3. A new algorithm

3.1 Representative projection

Suppose that in the global direction the maximum distance of the patches from the projection plane is between Z1 and Z2. Let us generate a uniformly distributed random number z between Z1 and Z2 and place a clipping plane at z. The clipping plane will be that one which is orthogonal to the global direction and is at distance z from the reference and can be considered as a translated projection plane. Defining a window on the clipping plane to include the projection of all patches, let us run two depth buffer hardware renderings, one with GREATER and the other with LOWER settings, together with the enabling and disabling the two half-spaces on the two sides of the clipping plane. Reading back the images we have a set of mutually visible pixels (patches), which can be used to exchange energy. Note that here a patch exchanges energy only with a given probability. This probability is proportional to their distance in z. Thus for each pair of pixels (that simulates a global line segment) the energy exchange is divided by this probability.

3.2 Probability that a plane crosses between two patches

Suppose that in a scene (see figure 4) we generate a global random direction. This direction defines the Z-axis of the scene. In figure 4 the Z-axis is parallel to the scene wall just for the sake of simplicity. The Z coordinates of all scene patches are between *zmax* and *zmin*, which are the maximum and minimum Z values of the scene. Let us generate a uniformly distributed random number z between *zmax* and *zmin* that defines a random point *RP*, and a plane *P* orthogonal to the Z-axis is placed at *RP*. Now, what is the probability that the plane *P* crossed between the points *z12* and *z11*? Suppose, for example, that the point *z12* is on object *O1* and the point *z11* is on the ceiling. The probability is the distance between *z12* and *z11*, *Zd1*,

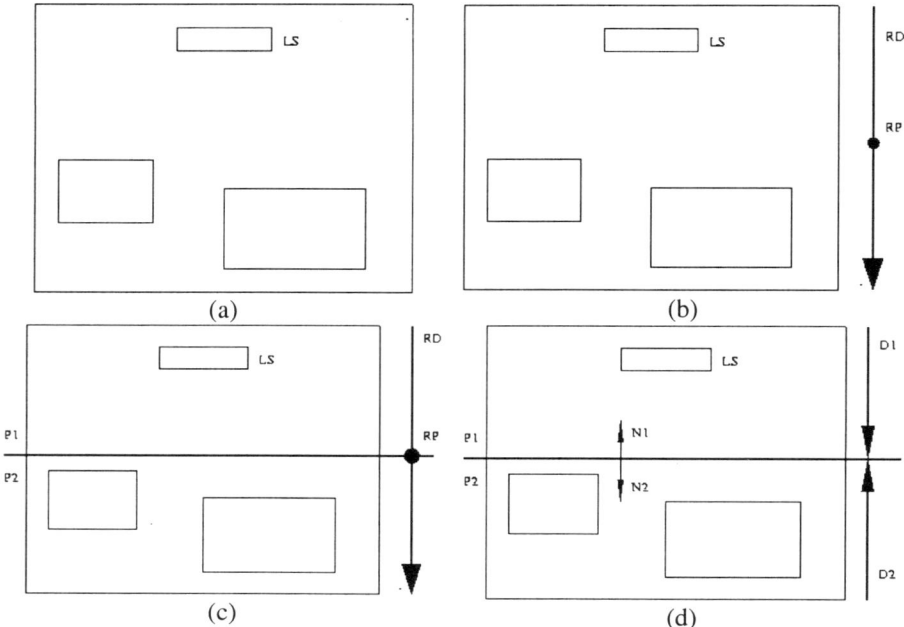

Figure 5. (a) A simple scene with two object and a light source (**LS**) (b) A random direction **RD** and a random point **RP** are selected. In this case, for simplicity, **RD** is parallel to one of the scene axis. (c) A plane with two opposite normals (**P1** and **P2**) is created incident to **RP**, and are decomposed into *n×n* pixels. (d) A projection directions (**D1** and **D2**) are defined. **D1** has the same direction than **RD** and **D2** is opposite to **D1**.

divided by the maximum Z distance (*zmax-zmin*) in the scene, *Zdist*. The probability that the plane P crossed between the points *z22* and *z21* is *Zd2/Zdist*. Note that the OpenGL pipeline scales the Z values to be in [0..1] before writing them into the z-buffer. It means that at the end of the transformation pipeline *Zdist*=1, thus the calculation of the probabilities needs only one addition.

3.3 Implementation

The bundle of parallel lines is obtained as follows: First, a random direction D_r is selected. This direction defines the Z-axis. Then a random point P_r between the minimum and maximum values of Z is selected (see figure 5(b)). The window plane, i.e. the projection plane, is defined incident to P_r and orthogonal to D_r (see figure 5 (c)), which will be used two times with two opposite viewing directions. All patches are projected onto the projection plane from the two directions using the OpenGL's depth buffer (see figure 6). Finally, the exchange of power is computed between the corresponding pixels of the two rendering steps (see figure 7). This is summarized in the following algorithm.

```
begin sendBundle
    Compute a random direction RD (defining the Z-axis)
    Compute a random point RP between minimum and maximum values of Z
    Create two opposite projection planes (orthogonal to RD,
    defined at RP and nxn size)
    Define the projection directions
    Clear the projection planes
    Project allPatches_vector onto projection plane 1
    Project allPatches_vector onto projection plane 2
    For i=0 to projectionPlaneWidth do
        For j=0 to projectionPlaneHeight do
            coord1 = i * projectionPlaneWidth + j
            index1 = projectionPlane1[coord1]
            coord2 = i*projectionPlaneWidth+projectionPlaneWidth-j-1
            index2 = projectionPlane2[coord2]
            compute Z distance between allPatches_vector[index1] and
            allPatches_vector[index2] using the Zvalues in the depthBuffer
            Exchange power between allPatches_vector[index1] and
            allPatches_vector[index2] divided by the Z distance
        endFor
    endFor
end
```

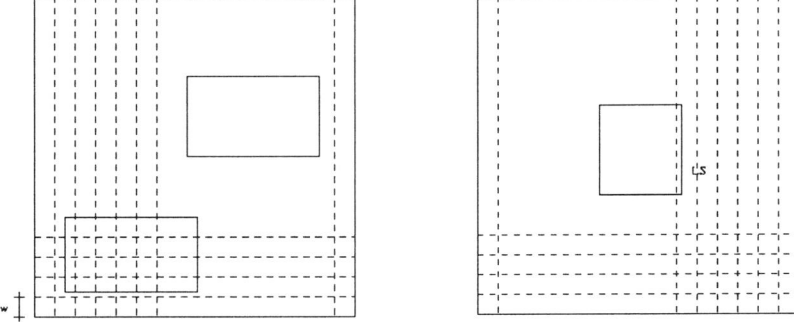

Figure 6. After all patches (see figure 5(a)) are projected onto the projection planes, the result is (a) lower section and (b) upper section of the projected scene, where w is the pixel width of the projection plane.

The discretized projection planes are represented by matrices with $n \times n$ pixels (n is defined by the user) and they store the closest patch IDs that are projected onto them. The two polygons identified by the IDs in the corresponding positions (for the two projection planes, see figure 7) will exchange power. The exchange power function is similar to the multipath single line implementation, explained in section 2.2. The only difference is that now the power is divided by the probability that a

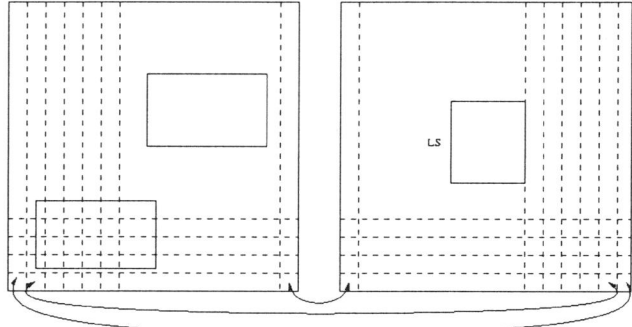

Figure 7. Exchange of energy between two projection planes.

plane crosses between two patches. This probability is given by the sum of the two Z values as read out from the z-buffer.

4. Results and discussion

We have implemented the presented algorithm in C++ and run the program on an SGI Octane computer with a MIPS R12000 270 MHZ IP30 processor. A complete rendering consists of the computation of the first-shot, i.e. the determination of the direct illumination, and the multipath step that computes the indirect illumination. The first shot step was implemented with local lines, although a hardware based implementation is also available in [14]. In this step were used 4 million local lines. We evaluate here the performance of the multipath step since the proposed algorithm alters only this phase of the computation. We used two particular test scenes. The "big room" scene (figure 9) consists of 1130 polygons that have been subdivided into 27282 patches. The "office" scene (figure 11) contains 547 polygons decomposed into 26322 patches. The size of the depth buffer matrices is 100x100 pixels for both test scenes. It means that every bundle of parallel lines has 10,000 global lines. The new algorithm could render these scenes in 5.8 and 5.7 seconds respectively, while the program implementing the painter algorithm needed 41 and 37 seconds respectively. This corresponds to a speed up of 7. In figures 8(b) and 10 are plotted the number of bundles vs the time in seconds for the "big room" and the "office" scenes, respectively. The performance of the depth buffer implementation is clearly better than the painter implementation.

In figure 8(a) we see that the error for a different number of bundles is practically the same, in both depth buffer and painter algorithms, with a very slight advantage, for a small number of bundles, for the painter's implementation. This difference is because the probability that a plane crosses between two patches is very small when the distance between them is small too. For example, in figure 9(a) the table patches near the wall (that is not visible in the image) received almost no energy and in figure 9(b) the same table patches have better illumination results.

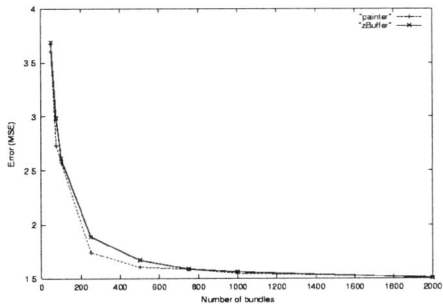 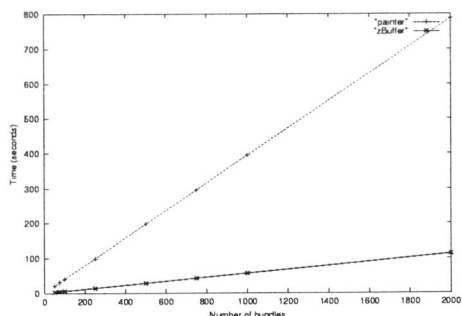

Figure 8. Comparison of multipath method using the painter's algorithm vs the OpenGL's depth buffer implementation. It is plotting (a) the number of bundles vs error and (b) the number of bundles vs the time in seconds, for the "big room" scene.

Figure 9. The images of the "big room" scene were obtained with Multipath with OpenGL depth buffer (upper) and with painter's algorithm (lower). Both images were generated with 4 million local rays for the first shot and 100 bundles for the indirect illumination. The rendering of the upper image took 5.75 seconds and the lower one 40.72 seconds on a SGI Octane.

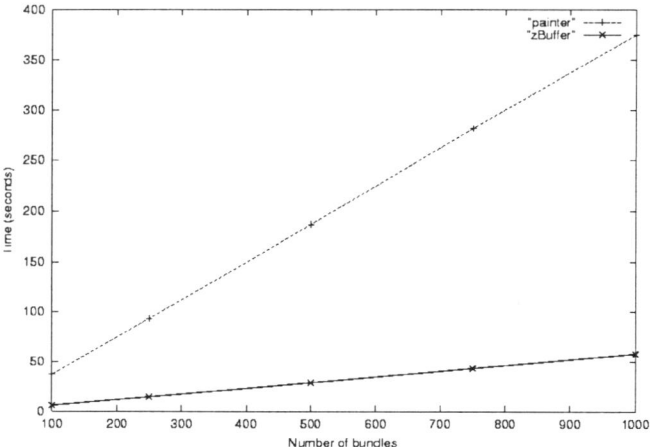

Figure 10. Comparison of multipath method using the painter's algorithm vs the OpenGL's depth buffer implementation. It is plotting the number of bundles vs the time in seconds for the "office" scene.

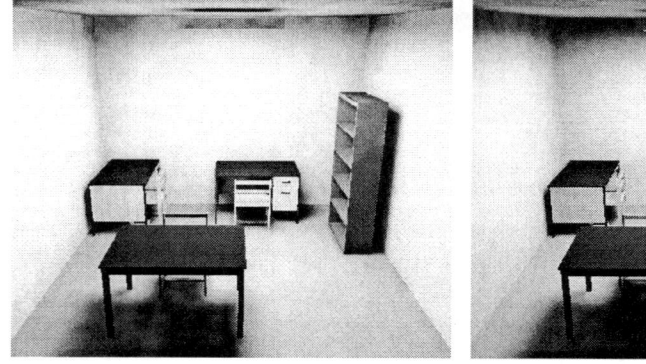

Figure 11. The images of the "office" scene were obtained with Multipath with OpenGL's depth buffer (left) and with painter's algorithm (right). Both images were generated with 4 million local rays and 100 bundles. The second step took, for the left one, 5.8 seconds and the right one 37.3 seconds in a SGI Octane.

On the other hand, the depth buffer implementation shows better results in open spaces. For example, in figure 9(a) the ceiling looks better than it looks in figure 9(b). Also in figure 11(a) and (b) we can see the difference between the ceilings' illumination.

5. Conclusions and future work

In this paper we have presented a hardware based OpenGL depth buffer implementation of the multipath algorithm. The new algorithm exploits the coherence of the scene and instead of tracing many independent rays, it uses global ray bundles to transfer the radiosity. Note that a single bundle may correspond to a lot of bi-directional rays, which can be traced efficiently. We demonstrated that the tracing of this bundle can be computed by the graphics hardware. On an SGI Octane computer this exploitation of the graphics hardware increased the rendering speed by 7 times, and made it possible to render moderately complex radiosity scenes in a few seconds.

Future work will be addressed to improve the results in areas where the distance between the patches is small. On the other hand, non-diffuse multipath version or other related global line Monte Carlo methods are also ideal target for using OpenGL depth buffer hardware implementations.

6. Acknowledgements

This project has been funded in part with grant number TIC2001-2416-C03-01 of the Spanish Government, a Spanish-Hungarian Joint-Project, National Scientific Research Fund of Hungary (OTKA ref. No.: T029135), the Eötvös Foundation and the IKTA-00101/2000 project. Thanks go to Gonzalo Besuievsky for modeling the test scene and to Frederic Pérez for his valuable comments.

References

[1] Bekaert Ph., "Hierarchical and Stochastic Algorithms for Radiosity", Ph. D. Dissertation, Department of Computer Science, Katholieke Universitiet Leuven, Leuven, Belgium, 1999.

[2] Besuievsky G., Pueyo X., "Making Global Monte Carlo Methods Useful: An Adaptive Approach for Radiosity", Congreso Espanol de Informática Gráfica CEIG'97, Barcelona, Spain, 1997.

[3] Buckalew C., Fussell D., "Illumination networks: Fast realistic rendering with general reflectance functions", Computer Graphics, (SIGGRAPH'89 Proceedings), 23(3), July 1989, pp. 89-98.

[4] Castro F., Martínez R., Sbert M., "Quasi Monte Carlo and extended first shot improvement to the multi-path method for radiosity", Proceedings of SCCG'98, Budmerice, Slovakia, April 1998.

[5] Martínez R., Szirmay-Kalos L., Sbert M., "Adaptive Multipath with Bundles of Parallel Line", Visual2000, 3rd International Conference on Visual Computing, Mexico D.F., September 18-22, 2000.

[6] Neumann L., "Monte Carlo Radiosity" Computing, Springer-Verlag 1995. 55, pp. 23-42

[7] Santaló L. A., "Integral Geometry and Geometric Probability". Addison-Wesley, New York, 1976.

[8] Sbert M., "An integral geometry based method for fast form factor computation". Computer Graphics Forum (Eurographics'93), 12(3): C409-C420, September 1993.

[9] Sbert M, Pueyo X., Neumann L., Purgathofer W., "Global multipath Monte Carlo algorithms for radiosity", The Visual Computer, 1996.

[10] Sbert M., "The use of global random directions to compute Radiosity. Global Monte Carlo Techniques". PhD. dissertation, Universitat Politécnica de Catalunya, Barcelona, March 1997.

[11] Szirmay-Kalos L., Fóris T., Neumann L., Csébfalvi B., "An analysis to quasi-Monte Carlo integration applied to the transillumination radiosity method", Computer Graphics Forum 16(3):271-281, 1997.

[12] Szirmay-Kalos L., "Global Ray-Bundle tracing", Proceedings of the 9th Eurographics Workshop on Rendering Vienna, June 1998.

[13] Szirmay-Kalos L., "Stochastic Iteration for Non-diffuse Global Illumination", Eurographics'99 Proccedings, Milano, September 1999.

[14] Szirmay-Kalos L., Sbert M., Martínez R., Tobler R., "Incoming first-shot for non-diffuse global illumination", Proceedings of SCCG 2000.

Fuzzy Random Walk

Francesc Castro, Miquel Feixas, Mateu Sbert
Institut d'Informàtica i Aplicacions. Universitat de Girona

Abstract
Random walks applied to radiosity use random lines to simulate the distribution of luminous power. Noise effects in the final image are inherent in these methods. We present an improvement that reduces this noise, avoiding the sharp transitions between every patch and its coplanar neighbours, and obtaining a smoother final image with a negligible increase in computational cost.
The main idea involved in our improvement is the distribution of a part of the incoming to a patch power between its neighbours. That is, part of the power splats the neighbour patches. Our approach is based on Information Theory concepts, as uncertainty. Reductions of the mean square error to less than a half have been obtained in our tests.

Keywords: Random Walk, Radiosity, Splatting, Uncertainty

1 Introduction

Random walks are used in rendering, and particularly in radiosity, to simulate the distribution of power in a scene [1]. Random lines simulate the interreflections of light between the patches in which the scene is discretized. One of the main drawbacks of these methods is the high number of lines needed to obtain an acceptable result. Undersampling produces an undesired noise effect in the resulting images. This effect can be reduced obviously by increasing the number of paths and so the computational cost, but our interest is to reduce the noise by other means.

The fuzzy random walk introduced in this article obtains a sensitive reduction of the noise effects in the final image with a very low increase of computational cost. This improvement is based on the idea of splatting part of the power carried by a line to the neighbour patches of the receiver patch.

We borrow from Information Theory the concept of uncertainty of an event. Uncertainty just indicates how difficult is an event to happen. In our case, the event is the intersection of a patch by a random line. So, if the uncertainty of an intersection is high, a notable fraction of power will be splatted, and vice versa.

This paper is organized as follows. In next section we will briefly refer to previous work. The description of our contribution is in section 3. Section 4 presents the results, both error graphs and images. Finally, in last section we present the conclusions and future work.

2 Previous work

We have incorporated our idea to the radiosity context, and specifically to breadth-first shooting random walk [1] where each iteration simulates one bounce of the light (the first iteration deals with the primary power, and so on).

[6] presents a Monte Carlo ray tracing approach applied to non-diffuse environments in which noise effects are reduced by considering the knowledge of the neighbourhood of the paths (footprints).

Random walks applied to global illumination suppose the transmission of particles (or photons) using random lines. Each line communicates two points in the scene, and power is transmitted between these points. This communication can be seen as an information transmission and so it can be studied from Information Theory point of view [2] [4] [3]. We borrow from Information Theory the concept of uncertainty of an event. If the probability of an event k is p_k, its uncertainty is given by

$$-log_2 p_k \qquad (1)$$

The uncertainty means how difficult is the event to happen. If the probability of the event is close to 1, the uncertainty is close to zero, and conversely, if the event is very unlikely, its probability is close to zero and its uncertainty is very high.

3 Fuzzy random walk

Radiosity random walks distribute the power between the patches using random lines. Each random line carries some amount of power from the patch where the line is origined to the hit patch.

The idea involved in fuzzy random walk is the distribution of part of incoming power to the neighbour patches of the hit patch (splatting), obtaining a reduction of the aliasing in the resulting image.

We have to determine the percentage of incoming power that has to be splatted. A first naive idea could be the distribution of a fixed percentage, but it is not difficult to see that there are some situations in which it seems more natural to splat part of the power to the neighbours, for instance when the area of the receiver patch is small in relation with the distance from the origin. It can be observed in Fig. 1: the distribution of power from the blue box to the patch i in the table probably needs less splatting than the distribution from the light to the pink box, since in this last case the determination of patch j

as receiver patch is more accidental than the first case (note that the patches in which is divided the pink box are smaller than the ones in the table, and moreover the distance of the intersection is clearly bigger in the second case).

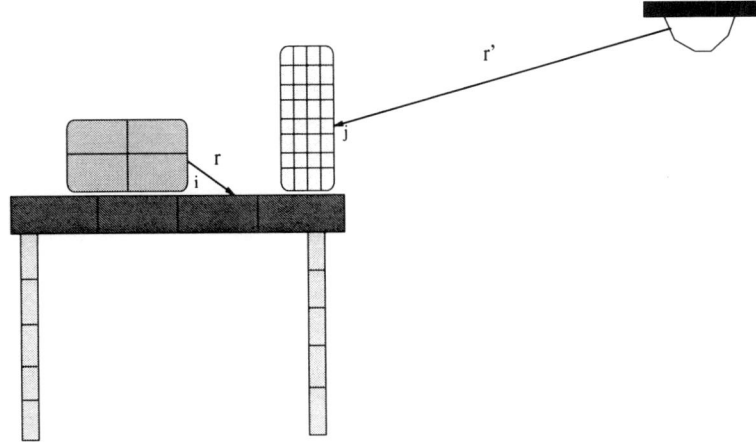

Figure 1: *The determination of patch j as receiver patch is more accidental than in the case of patch i.*

To deal with a more accurate distribution, we borrow from Information Theory the concept of uncertainty (see section 2). In the case of the radiosity random walk, we consider the probability of a line exiting from a point i to hit patch j. This is the fraction of visibility of patch j from point i (without considering any occlusion). If we consider the hemisphere of radius R (being R the distance between point i and patch j) and centered in point i, the probability can be seen as the ratio of the projection of patch j over the hemisphere and the area of the hemisphere:

$$\frac{A_j cos\theta}{2\pi R^2} \quad (2)$$

where θ is the angle between the normal of patch j and the line (note that this approximation can lead occasionally to values greater than one; in this case, we set the uncertainty to zero) (see Fig. 2).

The idea of how much accidental is a patch intersection matches completely with the concept of uncertainty. So it is natural to consider the uncertainty of every intersection (see equation (3)) in the determination of the percentage of power that has to be splatted.

$$-\log_2 \frac{A_j cos\theta}{2\pi R^2} \quad (3)$$

This value will be high if the intersection is unlikely (i.e. if the projection of patch j is small in relation with the distance of the intersection). Conversely,

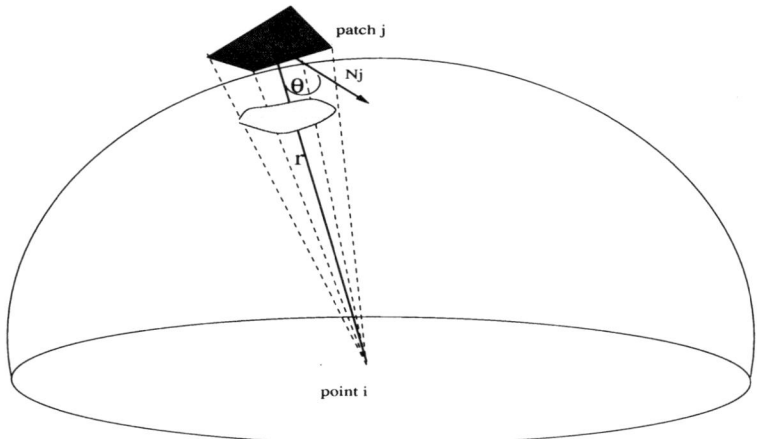

Figure 2: *Projection of patch j on the hemisphere of radius R centered in patch i*

if it is very probable to reach patch j with a random line originated in i, the uncertainty will be lower. In this last case, we consider that the distribution of power that carries out the line is more accurate than in the first case. So, the uncertainty is a good measure of how accurate the distribution of power is: the lower the uncertainty, the higher the accuracy. Then it is reasonable to establish the percentage of power that has to be splatted to the neighbour patches in function of the uncertainty. We map the uncertainty to a value between 0 and 1 that corresponds to the fraction of power that should be splatted. This is done using the following heuristic: if the uncertainty is lower than a threshold α we map to 0; if it is greater than another threshold β we map to 1 ($0 < \alpha < \beta$)); and if it is between α and β we map to the corresponding value between 0 and 1.

Note that occlusions are not taken into account in the computation of the uncertainty. This introduces an error and a bias in the final results. However, this error does not have any important repercussion, because there is a compensation in the power received for every patch, favoured by the fact that we are not using point sources.

We also have to distribute the splatted power between the neighbour patches. Fig. 3 gives us an idea of how it is done. We distribute power to the eight coplanar neighbour patches (if they exist). The amount of power that is distributed to each neighbour is given in equation (4). This corresponds to the naive idea of distributing more power to the patches that are closer to the intersection point. Note that this expression is similar to the Epanechnikov kernel used in density estimation [5].

$$w_k = \frac{1}{7} \frac{\left(\sum_{i=1}^{8} d_i^2\right) - d_k^2}{\sum_{i=1}^{8} d_i^2} \tag{4}$$

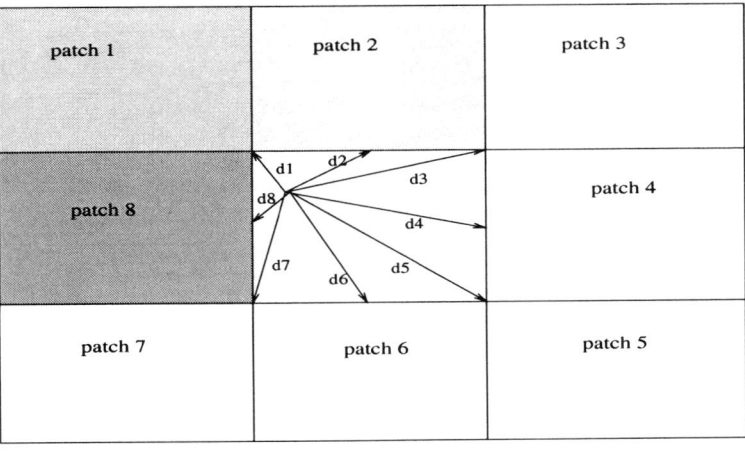

Figure 3: *The distribution of power to the neighbour patches is related to the position of the intersection point.*

4 Results

A notable reduction of the aliasing is observed with the new method, being the increase in cost nearly negligible. The application of splatting introduces a small bias that produces an unnoticeable effect on the resulting images. To avoid the bias effects in the comparisons, we have computed the error by comparing each image with its respective reference image.

Different values of the thresholds α and β (see Section 3) have been tested, given good results with $\alpha = 5$ and $\beta = 15$. We have used two different scenes[1]:

- **Scene OFFICE**

This scene represents an office with several desks, chairs and shelves. It is subdivided in approximately 7000 patches. In Fig. 6 (right) we note that incorporating fuzzy random walk the Mean Square Error (MSE) is reduced to approximately a half with a small increase of cost. We can see visual differences

---
[1] Images are available on ima.udg.es/~castro

in Fig. 4, where the image on the right has been obtained using fuzzy random walk with only a very small increase of execution time respect to the more noisy image on the left (without splatting).

(a)

(b)

Figure 4: *Scene OFFICE. (a) Classic random walk. Number of lines: 514000. Execution time: 27 sec. (b) Fuzzy random walk. Number of lines: 511000. Execution time: 30 sec.*

- **Scene ROOM**

This scene represents a room with a table, some chairs and a desk. Some small objects have been placed on the table and on the desk. It has been subdivided in approximately 25000 patches. The graph in 6 (left) presents a behaviour similar to the one in the previous scene. The image in Fig. 5 shows the reduction of the aliasing (right). The increase of cost respect to the image obtained with the classic random walk (left) is small.

5 Conclusions and future work

Fuzzy random walk has obtained a notable reduction of the noise effects in the resulting images with a very small increase of computational cost. The power arriving to a patch is splatted to the neighbour patches according to the uncertainty of the hit event. This splatting is done in each iteration of the breadth-first shooting random walk algorithm. Note that the redistribution of power done in an iteration affects the unshot power for the next iteration.

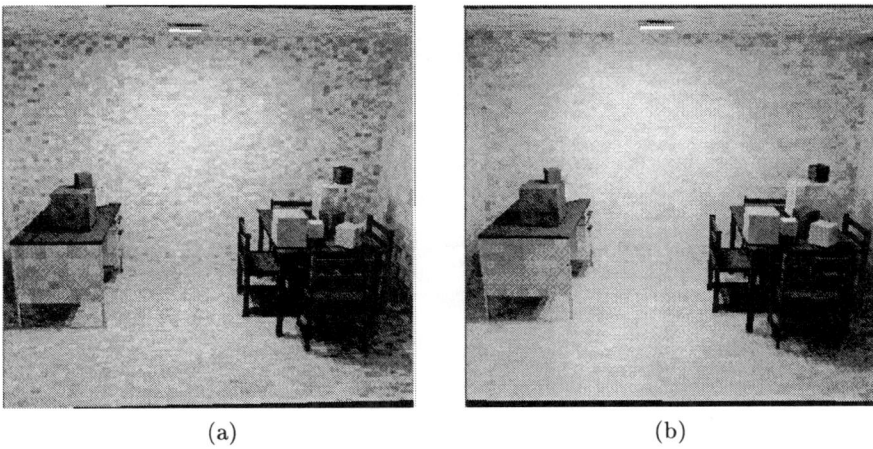

Figure 5: *Scene ROOM. (a) Classic random walk. Number of lines: 1433000. Execution time: 63 sec. (b) Fuzzy random walk. Number of lines: 1407000. Execution time: 70 sec.*

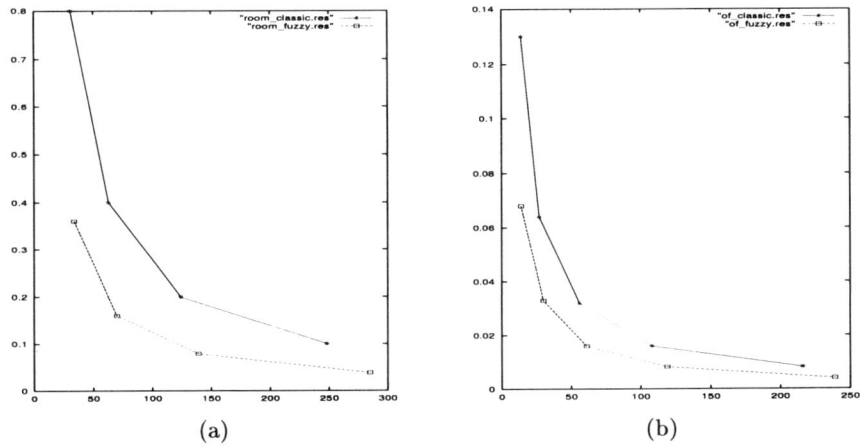

Figure 6: *(a) Scene ROOM. Time-MSE plot. (b) Scene OFFICE. Time-MSE plot. Continous line is classic random walk, dashed line is fuzzy random walk.*

Improvements will go along the lines of changing the heuristics that determine the fraction of power that has to be splatted and how much power goes to each neighbour patch.

6 Acknowledgements

This project has been funded in part with a Spanish-Austrian Joint Action n. HU2000-0011, grant number TIC 2001-2416-C03-01 from the Spanish Governement and grant number 2001/SGR/00296 from the Catalan Governement.

References

[1] P. Bekaert. Hierarchical and stochastic algorithms for radiosity. *Ph.D. thesis. Katholic Univ. of Leuven*, 1999.

[2] T.M. Cover and J.A. Thomas. *Elements of Information Theory*. Wiley, 1991.

[3] M. Feixas, E. Acebo, P. Bekaert, and M. Sbert. An information theory framework for the analysis of scene complexity. *Computer Graphics Forum (proc. Eurographics'99, Milan, Italy)*, 18, N.3:95–106, 1999.

[4] A.S. Glassner. *Principles of Digital Image Synthesis, Vol.2*. Morgan Kaufmann Pubilishers, Inc., 1995.

[5] B.W. Silverman. *Density Estimation for Estatistics and Data Analysis*. Chapman and Hall, 1986.

[6] F. Suykens and Y.D. Willems. Path differentials and applications. *Proceedings of Eurographics Workshop on Rendering*, 2001.

Shadow Mapping for Hemispherical and Omnidirectional Light Sources

Stefan Brabec   Thomas Annen   Hans-Peter Seidel

Computer Graphics Group
Max-Planck-Institut für Infomatik
Stuhlsatzenhausweg 85, 66123 Saarbrücken, Germany
{brabec, tannen, hpseidel} @ mpi-sb.mpg.de

Abstract

In this paper we present a shadow mapping technique for hemispherical and omnidirectional light sources using dual-paraboloid mapping. In contrast to the traditional perspective projection this parameterization has the benefit that only a minimal number of rendering passes is needed during generation of the shadow maps, making the method suitable for dynamic environments and real time applications. By utilizing programmable features available on state-of-the-art graphics cards we show how the algorithm can be efficiently mapped to hardware.

Keywords: Shadow Algorithms, Shadow Mapping, Dual-Paraboloid Mapping, Graphics Hardware.

1 Introduction and Background

One of the most challenging effect in the field of real time rendering is the accurate and fast calculation of shadows. For most applications, e.g. in computer games, shadows are still problematic due to their *global* nature. In order to decide if a given surface pixel can be seen by a light source one has to check a large number of potential occluders that may block the path from light to surface.

Although there are a large number of shadow algorithms, only a small subset of algorithms are really appropriate for real time rendering. Nearly all techniques in this subset can further be categorized into two main *branches* of algorithms: Those which are based on Crow's *shadow volumes* approach [3], and those that are variants of Williams' *shadow mapping* technique [13].

Both categories have their pros and cons: The shadow volume approach is capable of producing very accurate shadows due to the object space calculation. For each (possible) blocker object, a semi-infinite shadow volume is constructed which defines the volume in which all pixels inside cannot be seen by the light source. Although the actual shadow volume *in-out* test can be accelerated by using graphics hardware, the CPU still has to perform the time-consuming task of constructing the actual shadow volumes.

The shadow mapping technique on the other hand does not need any CPU time at all since all steps can by directly implemented on the graphics hardware itself (which will be explained in more detail later). Shadow mapping works on a sampled depth map of the scene, taken from the view of the light source. The actual shadow test is then a very simple operation that compares a surface pixel's depth value with the appropriate entry in the depth map. In contrast to the shadow volume approach, shadow mapping does not directly depend on the scene's complexity. All objects that can be rendered can also be used for shadow mapping, which makes this algorithm suitable for a wide range of applications. The disadvantage is of course the quality of shadows, which is directly related to the sampling of the scene. As pointed out by Reeves et. al. [9], sampling artifacts occur during the generation of the shadow map as well when performing the shadow test. To eliminate these artifacts [9] proposed a filtering scheme that softens shadow boundaries.

One main argument that often leads people to prefer shadow volumes over shadow mapping is the limited *field-of-view* when generating a suitable shadow map for a given point light source. In cases where a point light source radiates over the complete hemisphere or even omnidirectional, traditional shadow mapping (using only a single depth map) fails.

The only solution to this problem so far is to use more than one shadow map. In the worst case, up to six shadow maps must be used to cover the complete environment [4]. Although these maps can be represented as a cube map (resulting in a single texture lookup when performing the shadow test), this approach still requires up to six rendering passes when generating the shadow maps, making it unsuitable for interactive or real time applications.

In this paper we present a method to perform shadow mapping for hemispherical and omnidirectional point light sources using only one (hemispherical) or two (omnidirectional) rendering passes for the generation of the shadow map and one final rendering pass to perform the shadow test. Similar to the traditional shadow mapping technique, all steps of the algorithm can be implemented using graphics hardware.

2 Shadow Mapping

As described by [13] the traditional shadow mapping algorithm consists of two steps. In the first pass, a shadow map is generated by rendering the scene as seen by the light source and depth values of the front most pixels are stored away in this map. In the final step the scene is rendered once again, this time from the camera's point of view. During this pass the coordinates of visible surface points are transformed to the light source coordinate system. To check whether a given pixel can be seen by the light source one has to compare the depth value of the transformed pixel with the depth value stored in the corresponding shadow map entry. If the shadow map has a depth value which is less than the actual one, the pixel is blocked by an occluder in between. Otherwise the pixel is lit by the light source.

A hardware implementation for this algorithm was proposed by [10]. Using automatic texture coordinate generation it is possible to have homogeneous texture coordinates (s, t, r, q) that are derived from the eye-space coordinate system. In conjunction with a texture matrix (which is a 4×4 matrix applied to these texture coordinate) one can implement the necessary transformation to the light source coordinate system including the perspective projection.

In order to perform the shadow test, a dedicated texture mapping mode is needed that compares the entry at $(s/q, t/q)$ in the shadow map with the computed depth value (r/q). The result of this operation is coded as color $(0, 0, 0, 0)$ or color $(1, 1, 1, 1)$. In addition to this shadow test mode, the graphics hardware has also to support a way of storing depth values as textures.

In OpenGL [11] all of these capabilities are supported by two extensions [8]: The *depth_texture* extensions introduces new internal texture formats for 16, 24, or 32 bit depth values. The *shadow* extensions defines two operations ($\leq$ and $\geq$) that compare (r/q) with the value stored at $(s/q, t/q)$.

For a long time these extensions were only supported on high-end graphics workstations. Recently also consumer-class graphics cards (e.g. NVIDIA GeForce3) provide this functionality.

3 Shadow Mapping for Hemispherical and Omnidirectional Light Sources

As stated in the previous sections shadows generated with the traditional shadow mapping algorithm are limited to the view frustum used when generating the shadow map, as depicted in Figure 1(a).

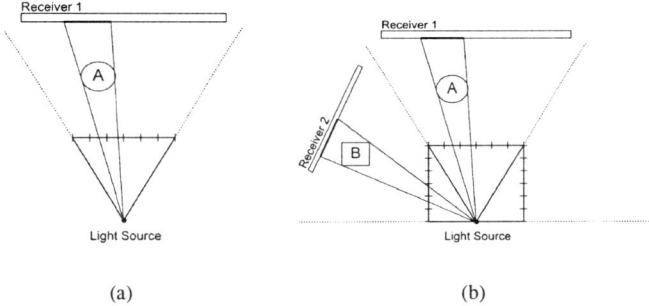

(a)   (b)

Fig. 1. (a): Traditional shadow mapping frustum. (b): Multiple shadow maps for field-of-view of 180° (hemispherical).

Since all relevant occluder geometry is inside the frustum shadows are generated as expected. This setup is useful if the light source has a spotlight characteristic (only objects inside the spotlight cone are illuminated) but fails if the light source is hemispherical or omnidirectional (*field-of-view* $>=$ 180°). The trivial solution to handle such cases would be to use a number of shadow maps that together cover the whole environment seen by the light source.

Figure 1(b) shows such a setup for a light source with a viewing angle of 180°(hemispherical). In order to cover Object A as well as Object B the environment needs to be subdivided in a cube like manner where a separate shadow map is used for each side of the cube[1]. While this setup can be efficiently rendered if the graphics hardware supports cube map textures (as explained in [4]) the generation of the (up to six) shadow maps is still too expensive.

The solution to this problem is quite simple: In order to minimize the cost of generating shadow maps we have to find a way of computing a shadow map that covers the whole field-of-view of the given light source. Since the sampling rate should be somehow constant to avoid changes in shadow quality we have to choose a parameteri-

---

[1] Since only one hemisphere will be lit, only five sides of the cube are needed.

zation that fulfills this criterion and that is also easy to compute (hardware-accelerated rendering).

We can find such parameterizations in the field of environment mapping, which approximates global illumination by pre-computing a so called *environment map* [1] which is later used to determine the incoming light for a given direction (reflection vector). Although there exist a vast number of 3D-to-2D mappings (used to *flatten* a panoramic environment into a 2D texture map), only a small subset are really appropriate for hardware accelerated rendering:

Spherical Mapping. For a long time this was the *standard* parameterization used to represent environment maps [5]. This parameterization can be simple explained by imagining a perfectly reflecting mirror ball centered around the object of interest. Although this parameterization only has one point of singularity, the sampling rate since pixels get extremely distorted towards the perimeter of the flattened sphere.

Blinn/Newell Mapping. A different parameterization of the sphere was proposed by [1]. Here 2D coordinates (u, v) are computed using a longitude-latitude mapping of the direction vector. Although this approach does not introduce as much distortion as the previous sphere mapping technique, it is not commonly used due to the expensive longitude-latitude mapping (which involves computing $arctan$ and $arcsin$).

Cube Mapping. As already mentioned in previous section, the cube map parameterization [12] is very popular since it does not require any re-warping to obtain images for the cube faces. Recent graphics hardware (e.g. NVIDIA, ATI) directly support texture fetching using cube maps. Again the main disadvantage are the number of rendering passes during the generation phase, making this method nearly unusable for dynamic environments.

(Dual-) Paraboloid Mapping. Another parameterization was proposed by [6]. Here the analogy is the image obtained by an orthographic camera viewing a perfectly reflecting paraboloid. When compared to sphere or cube mapping, this parameterization introduces less artifacts because the sampling rate only varies by a factor of 4 over the complete hemisphere. For 360°views, two parabolic maps can be attached back to back.

When comparing these different environment mapping techniques, it becomes obvious that the parabolic parameterization would be among the best choices for hemispherical and omnidirectional shadow maps due to the following properties:

- Sampling ratio varies only by a factor of 4.
- One map covers one hemisphere (number of generation passes ?)
- Easy to implement (described later)

In the next sections we will describe the concept of paraboloid mapping in detail, first using the mathematical interpretation and later with respect to graphics hardware (implementation).

3.1 Theory of Paraboloid Mapping

As described by Heidrich et al. [6], the image seen by an orthographic camera facing a reflecting paraboloid

$$f(x,y) = \frac{1}{2} - \frac{1}{2}(x^2 + y^2) \qquad , x^2 + y^2 \leq 1, \qquad (1)$$

contains all information about the hemisphere centered at $(0,0,0)$ and oriented towards the camera $(0,0,1)$. This function is plotted in Figure 2(a). Since the paraboloid acts like a lens, all reflected rays originate from the focal point $(0,0,0)$ of the paraboloid.

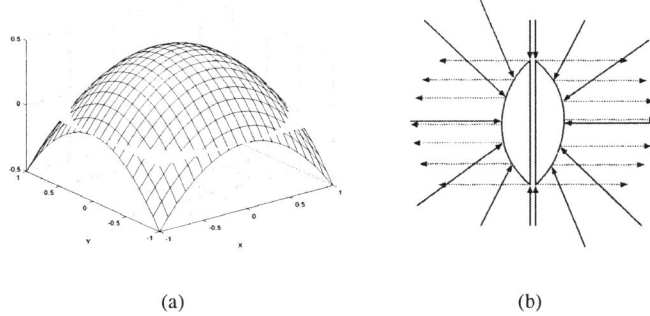

(a) (b)

Fig. 2. (a): Paraboloid $f(x,y) = \frac{1}{2} - \frac{1}{2}(x^2 + y^2)$. (b): Using two paraboloids to capture the complete environment.

In order to capture the complete environment (360°), two paraboloids attached back-to-back can be used, as sketched in Figure 2(b). Each paraboloid captures rays from one hemisphere and reflects it to one of the two main directions.

To use the paraboloid as a 3D-to-2D mapping scheme all we have to do is finding the point $P = (x, y, z)$ on the paraboloid that reflects a given direction $\vec{v}$ towards the direction $d_0 = (0, 0, 1)$ (or $d_1 = (0, 0, -1)$ for the opposite hemisphere). Using Equation 1 we find the normal vector at P to be

$$\vec{n} = \frac{1}{z}\begin{pmatrix} x \\ y \\ 1 \end{pmatrix} . \qquad (2)$$

Since the paraboloid is perfectly reflecting we simply calculate the halfway vector $\vec{h}$ which is equal to $\vec{n}$ up to some scaling factor. Using $\vec{h}$ and Equation 2 we can now formulate the 2D mapping of $\vec{v}$:

$$\vec{h} = \vec{d_0} + \vec{v} = k \cdot \begin{pmatrix} x \\ y \\ 1 \end{pmatrix} \quad v_z \geq 0. \qquad (3)$$

For $v_z < 0$ d_0 gets replaced by d_1 which corresponds to the other hemisphere (paraboloid).

3.2 Dual-Paraboloid Shadow Mapping

As shown in Equation 3 the paraboloid mapping can be used to parameterize one hemisphere using 2D coordinates (x, y). This 2D coordinates can of course also be used to perform a shadow map lookup. Instead of computing a perspective projection $(x/z, y/z)$ all we have to do is to use the new mapping instead.

It is clear that this won't work alone because we still need some scalar value representing the depth of a pixel for the actual shadow test. Since the dual approach already divides the environment into positive and negative z regions, we can get along by just using the distance between the given surface point and the center of the paraboloid $(0, 0, 0)$. This way we extended the original paraboloid mapping to be a 3D-to-3D mapping which retains all information relevant for shadow mapping.

Hemispherical Point Light. In the case of a point light source with a field-of-view of 180° one paraboloid map is capable of storing all relevant depth information that can be seen by the light source. The shadow map is generated by first calculating the transformation that translates the light's position to $(0, 0, 0)$ and rotates the light direction (main axis) into either d_0 or d_1. For all surface points in front of the light source we compute the 2D coordinates (x and y of halfway vector scaled to $z = 1$) and store the point's distance to the origin (light source) at that shadow map position.

During the actual shadow test surface points get first transformed to the new light source coordinate system. If the transformed point is in front of the light source we calculate the paraboloid coordinates and compare the stored depth value with the actual distance of the point to the origin. The point is now in shadow if the stored depth value is less than the actual computed one. Otherwise the point is lit.

Omnidirectional Point Light. For light sources that illuminate the complete environment (360°) we have to use the dual-paraboloid approach since one paraboloid map only covers one hemisphere. To generate these two maps we compute the transformation that brings the point light to the origin $(0, 0, 0)$. For all surface points we first have to check which map is responsible for storing the information. Based on the sign of the z component we choose either the *front-facing* [2] paraboloid with $d_0 = (0, 0, 1)$ or the *back-facing* one with $d_1 = (0, 0, -1)$. After this test the shadow map position and entry is computed as before (using either d_0 or d_1 to compute the halfway vector) and stored in the selected shadow map.

When performing the shadow test all we have to do is to transform the surface point to the light source coordinate system, choose the corresponding shadow map and $d_{0/1}$ based on the sign of the z component and do the shadow map test as in the hemispherical case.

4 Implementation

Heidrich et. al. [6] showed that dual-paraboloid environment mapping can be implemented on standard graphics hardware (e.g. using OpenGL [11]). Since they used a pre-processing step to compute the environment map it is not obvious how paraboloid maps could be generated for fully dynamic environments. One, although very time consuming way would be to first generate a cube map (six rendering passes) and re-sample those images as described in [2]. Although this could be implemented using graphics hardware it would still be too slow for real time applications.

To speed up this generation phase the obvious way would be to render an image using the paraboloid mapping instead of the perspective projection normally used. Rasterization hardware renders triangles by perspective correct interpolation (homogeneous coordinates). Since this part of the hardware is fixed, we cannot directly map pixels to new positions as the paraboloid mapping would require.

---

[2]The terms *front-* and *back-facing* are non significant and only used to divide the environment into two regions.

However we can accept this linear interpolation if we assume that the scene geometry is tessellated fine enough. In this case we can simply transform the vertices of triangles according to the paraboloid mapping since the interpolated pixels won't differ too much from the exact solution due to the fine tessellation.

Mapping vertices according to the extended paraboloid mapping (2D coordinates and depth value) can easily be implemented using the so called programmable vertex engines [7] available on state-of-the-art graphics cards (e.g. NVIDIA GeForce, ATI Radeon). These vertex programs operate on a stream of vertices and replace the former fixed vertex pipeline (transformation, lighting, texture coordinate generation etc.) by a user-defined program. These programs are usually directly evaluated on the graphics hardware resulting in high speed and high flexibility.

4.1 Generation of Paraboloid Shadow Maps

Implementing the generation phase for one paraboloid shadow map using vertex programming is straight forward since the programming model supports all operations needed. However we have to be careful about numerical stability. Since we want to include only those pixels that a really part of the hemisphere belonging to the chosen z axis (d_0 or d_1) we have to find a way of culling away unwanted pixels. Theoretically this test could be based solely on the range of valid coordinates $x^2 + y^2 \leq 1$ (Equation 1). For the implementation this fails due to numerical problems: When using $d_0 = (0, 0, 1)$ the normalization for points with $z \to -1$ the would break down due to the singularity at this point. If we would hand down these *undefined* x and y coordinates to the rasterization engine it would result in an undefined polygon being rasterized. The solution to this is a per-pixel culling test. During generation of the shadow map we calculate an alpha value based on the z coordinate of the transformed vertex. This alpha value is mapped to unsigned value $[0; 1]$ by an offset of 0.5. Using the alpha test we can now cull away pixels based on the sign of the z coordinate which corresponds to either the front- or back-facing hemisphere being rendered.

With this scheme we can now implement a vertex program to generate a paraboloid shadow map for one hemisphere d_0 according to the following pseudo-code[3]:

$P' = M_{light} \cdot M_{model} \cdot P$
$P' = P'/P'_w$
output alpha $= 0.5 + \frac{P'_z}{z_{scale}}$ /* for alpha test */
len$_{P'} = \|P'\|$
$P' = \frac{P'}{len_{P'}}$
$P' = P' + d_0$ /* halfway vector */
$P'_x = \frac{P'_x}{P'_z}$ /* x paraboloid coordinate */
$P'_y = \frac{P'_y}{P'_z}$ /* y paraboloid coordinate */
$P'_z = \frac{len_{P'} - z_{near}}{z_{far} - z_{near}} + z_{bias}$ /* distance */
$P'_w = 1$
output position $= P'$

First the incoming vertex is transformed and normalized by its w component. Next, an alpha value $\in [0; 1]$ is computed by scaling the z component by some user-defined constant (e.g. light's far plane z_{far}) and biasing it by 0.5 to conserve the sign of z. Using

---
[3]Instead of the assembler code we choose a more readable form here.

an alpha test function $\alpha \geq 0.5$ pixel values belonging to the opposite hemisphere d_1 are culled away.

Finally, we compute the paraboloid coordinates P'_x and P'_y as described previously. For P'_z we assign the scaled and biased distance from P' to $(0,0,0)$. Due to the precision of the depth buffer we have to use appropriate scaling and biasing factors here, similar to the selection of near and far clipping plane when using a perspective projection[4]. To avoid self shadowing artifacts we also have to move the z component slightly away from the light source using a bias value z_{bias} (similar as in [9]).

Generating a shadow map for the opposite hemisphere d_1 is trivial since we only have to flip the sign of P'_z after the transformation step and use the parameterization of d_0 as before:

$P' = M_{light} \cdot M_{model} \cdot P$
$P'_z = -P'_z$
...

4.2 Shadow Mapping with Paraboloid Shadow Maps

Implementing the shadow test using paraboloid mapping is as trivial as the generation step. In the case of an omnidirectional point light we compute the mappings for P'_0 (direction d_0) and P'_1 (direction d_1) and assign these as texture coordinates for texture unit 0 and 1. This step requires an additional scale and bias operation since texture coordinates need to be in the range of $[0;1]$.

In addition to this we also have to compute a value for selecting the right paraboloid map. By computing an alpha value based on the sign of the z component of P'_0 we can later select the appropriate texture map by checking $\alpha \geq 0.5$.

Finally the *normal* OpenGL vertex operations (camera transformation, perspective projection, lighting, additional texture coordinates etc.) are applied.

In pseudo-code the vertex program for rendering from the camera view using two paraboloid shadow maps will look like this:

$P'_0 = M_{light} \cdot M_{model} \cdot P$
output alpha $= 0.5 + \frac{P'_{0,z}}{z_{scale}}$
...
$P'_0 = P' + d_0$ /* hemisphere $(0,0,1)$ */
...
texcoords$_0 = 0.5 + 0.5 \cdot P'_0$ /* texcoords $\in [0;1]$ */
$P'_1 = M_{light} \cdot M_{model} \cdot P$
...
$P'_1 = P' + d_1$ /* hemisphere $(0,0,-1)$ */
...
texcoords$_1 = 0.5 + 0.5 \cdot P'_1$ /* texcoords $\in [0;1]$ */
normal OpenGL calculation for
lighting and vertex position

During the texturing stage we select the appropriate shadow test result depending on the computed alpha value:

---

[4]Computing the distance to the origin means that we have near and far clipping *spheres* instead of planes.

```
if(α ≥ 0.5)then
  res = tex₀    /* 1 for lit, 0 for shadow */
else
  res = tex₁    /* 1 for lit, 0 for shadow */
endif
output_RGB = res · full illumination +
    (1 − res) · ambient illumination
```

This can be implemented using programmable texture blending (e.g. NVIDIA's register combiners [8]) which is available on all state-of-the-art graphics cards.

For hemispherical point lights only one texture unit is used for shadow mapping and the result of one *if*-clause sets $res = 0$ (one hemisphere always in shadow).

5 Results

We implemented and tested our shadow mapping technique on an AMD Athlon Linux PC equipped with a NVIDIA GeForce3 64Mb graphics card using OpenGL as a graphics API. This cards supports vertex programs, programmable texture blending and also multi-texturing with up to four texture units. This way we can include the shadow test when rendering the final scene while still having two (or three) texture units left for the scene's textures.

As stated in previous sections, the number of rendering passes is two for hemispherical point lights (one shadow map generation and one final rendering pass) versus three for a omnidirectional light source (two for generating two hemispherical shadow maps and one final rendering pass using two texture units for the shadow test).

Figure 3 shows a scene illuminated by an omnidirectional point light source located in the middle of the room. This scene was directly imported from 3D Studio Max and only the wall polygons have been tesselated further (each wall subdivided into 64 quads) to avoid the interpolation problems addressed in Section 4. On a GeForce3 this scene can be rendered in real time (> 30 frames per second) including dynamic update of shadow maps at each frame (three rendering passes in total).

Figure 4 shows the results for a hemispherical light source located at the top of the room. As in Figure 3 only the surrounding walls and the floor polygon had been further subdivided. In this example an additional texturing unit is used to include the scene's textures in the final pass. This scene can also be rendered at real time rates (one shadow map generation pass and one final pass).

Both examples had been rendered using a resolution of 512 by 512 pixels for both, shadow maps and final image. Shadow quality can be further improved by generating high resolution maps using offscreen buffers.

6 Conclusion

In this paper we have shown that the dual paraboloid approach presented by [6] can easily be adopted for shadow mapping. This approach is well suited for hemispherical and omnidirectional light sources. By utilizing advanced graphics cards features the algorithm runs completely in hardware and uses only a minimal amount of rendering passes.

Although the algorithm fails for very large polygons due to the linear interpolation performed during rasterization this is in most cases no problem: For games and other

Fig. 3. Left: Scene illuminated by an omnidirectional point light (located in the middle of the room). Middle column: The two paraboloid shadow maps used (shown as grey scale images). Right column: The two hemispheres as seen by the light source.

Fig. 4. Left: Scene illuminated by a hemispherical point light. Right column: Shadow map and light source view (paraboloid mapping).

interactive applications most geometry is already very high-detailed. The only exception to this are large polygons representing walls, floor, ceiling etc. These polygons could either be further tesselated or simply ignored during the shadow map generation phase. Later is valid in cases where the visible part of the scene is bounded by such polygons, meaning those parts of the scene won't cast visible shadows anyway.

Since our method differs from the traditional shadow mapping approach only in terms of parameterization, we are able to apply all known quality improvements (e.g. per centage closer filtering [9]) without any efforts.

7 Acknowledgements

We would like to thank Prof. Wolfgang Heidrich of the University of British Columbia, Canada, for valuable discussions on this topic.

References

[1] J. F. Blinn and M. E. Newell. Texture and reflection in computer generated images. *Communications of the ACM*, 19:542—546, 1976.
[2] David Blythe. Advanced graphics programming techniques using opengl. SIGGRAPH Course, 1999.
[3] Franklin C. Crow. Shadow algorithms for computer graphics. In *Computer Graphics (SIGGRAPH '77 Proceedings)*, pages 242–248, July 1977.
[4] Sim Dietrich. *Shadow Techniques*. NVIDIA Corporation, 2001. PowerPoint Presentation available from http://www.nvidia.com.
[5] Paul Haeberli and Mark Segal. Texture mapping as a fundamental drawing primitive. *Fourth Eurographics Workshop on Rendering*, pages 259–266, June 1993. Held in held in Paris, France, 14-16 June 1993.
[6] Wolfgang Heidrich and Hans-Peter Seidel. View-independent environment maps. *1998 SIGGRAPH / Eurographics Workshop on Graphics Hardware*, pages 39–46, August 1998. Held in Lisbon, Portugal.
[7] Erik Lindholm, Mark J. Kilgard, and Henry Moreton. A user-programmable vertex engine. *Proceedings of SIGGRAPH 2001*, pages 149–158, August 2001. ISBN 1-58113-292-1.
[8] NVIDIA Corporation. *NVIDIA OpenGL Extension Specifications*, October 1999. Available from http://www.nvidia.com.
[9] William T. Reeves, David H. Salesin, and Robert L. Cook. Rendering antialiased shadows with depth maps. In *Computer Graphics (SIGGRAPH '87 Proceedings)*, pages 283–291, July 1987.
[10] Marc Segal, Carl Korobkin, Rolf van Widenfelt, Jim Foran, and Paul Haeberli. Fast shadow and lighting effects using texture mapping. In *Computer Graphics (SIGGRAPH '92 Proceedings)*, pages 249–252, July 1992.
[11] Mark Segal and Kurt Akeley. *The OpenGL Graphics System: A Specification (Version 1.2)*, 1998.
[12] Douglas Voorhies and Jim Foran. Reflection vector shading hardware. *Proceedings of SIGGRAPH 94*, pages 163–166, July 1994. ISBN 0-89791-667-0. Held in Orlando, Florida.
[13] Lance Williams. Casting curved shadows on curved surfaces. In *Computer Graphics (SIGGRAPH '78 Proceedings)*, pages 270–274, August 1978.

A Sky Light Illumination Model in Specular Environment

Tomohisa Manabe, Kazufumi Kaneda, Hideo Yamashita
Department of Information Engineering,
Graduate School of Engineering, Hiroshima University

Abstract
The paper proposes a method for rendering realistic images of outdoor scenes taking into account both direct sky light and reflected sky light caused by specular surfaces, such as windowpanes. In the proposed method, objects reflected in windowpanes of buildings can be also rendered considering the effect of sky light. The proposed illumination model for sky light reflected by specular surfaces makes the rendered images more realistic. The proposed method can also generate images quickly, even when a viewpoint, solar position and/or weather conditions are altered, using basis functions to express sky light illuminance. Several images of outdoor scenes demonstrate the usefulness of the proposed method.

Key Words: Sky light, reflected sky light, mirror reflection, photorealistic images, basis functions

1. Introduction

In recent years, computer graphics has become an indispensable technique for both architectural design and visual environmental assessment. Using computer graphics, we can visualize outdoor scenes under various weather conditions at any time of a day, and easily evaluate the visual impact of a certain construction or structure. To make the evaluation more accurate and reliable, photorealistic images are required. To generate photorealistic images of outdoor scenes, for example, it is important to consider such natural light, as direct sunlight and sky light [1] (see Fig. 1).

(a) (b)

Fig. 1 Illumination models of direct sun light and sky light
(a) Only direct sun light; (b) Taking into account sky light.

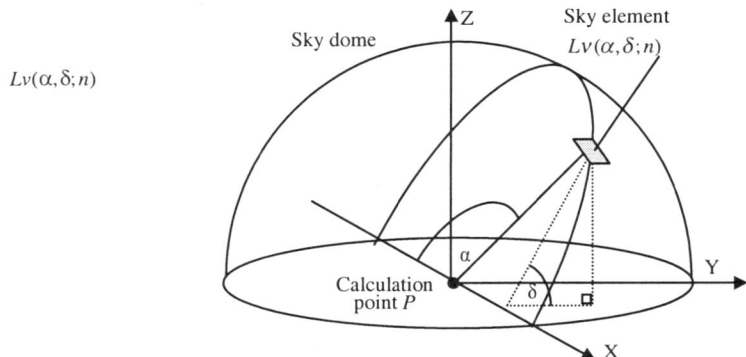

Fig. 2 Calculation of illuminance due to sky light.

In addition, it is necessary to generate images as fast as possible from any viewpoints under various weather conditions, as several alternative plans should be compared in the design process. Also, animation is often required.

A method for rendering outdoor scenes taking into account sky light was first developed by Nishita, et al. in 1986 [1]. By extending the method further, a method for calculating specular reflection due to sky light was developed [2]. Calculating illuminance due to sky light is computationally expensive, because it requires the integration of illuminance from all over the hemispherical light source, i.e., the dome of the sky (see Fig. 2). To reduce computation time, a method employing graphics hardware was proposed [3]. Although a single image can be generated faster using the method, sky light illuminance must be calculated from scratch each time, the viewpoint, weather conditions, or solar position are altered. Therefore, a great deal of time must be spent generating multiple images or animation. To address the problem, a fast method for calculating sky light illuminance was proposed by Nimeroff, et al [4]. The method calculates sky light illuminance due to the CIE standard luminous intensity distribution of the sky using basis functions. The method was further improved by taking into account spectral distribution of sky light [5][6] and weather conditions [7]. Using a the method in [7], realistic images under any kinds of weather conditions can be quickly calculated from any viewpoints.

Nevertheless, the method still has unsolved problems, including the fact that the sky light cannot be considered in the rendering of objects reflected in windowpanes of a building, and illuminance due to sky light reflected by windowpanes (called "reflected sky light" in the following discussion) cannot be calculated. To generate more photorealistic images of outdoor scenes, such lighting effects caused by the interaction of sky light with windowpanes should be also considered.

This paper proposes a method for solving problems that should be addressed in the process of generating images for architectural design. The proposed method renders both buildings reflected in windowpanes and outdoor scenes taking into account both sky light and reflected sky light. The proposed method can also calculate photorealistic images quickly, using basis functions to express sky light illuminance.

2. Calculation of illuminance due to sky light

Assuming the sky is a hemisphere with a large radius and its center located at calculation point, P, illuminance due to sky light, $I_{skylight}$ is calculated by integrating illuminance from sky elements with intensity distribution, L_V, with respect to the entire hemisphere [1] (see Fig. 2).

$$I_{skylight} = \int_0^\pi \int_0^\pi H(\alpha,\delta;P) Lv(\alpha,\delta) \sin^2 \alpha \sin \delta \, d\delta \, d\alpha , \qquad (1)$$

when (α,δ) expresses direction of the sky element in the local coordinates whose origin is a calculation point, and $H(\alpha,\delta;P)$ is the visibility function that gives 1 if the direction of (α,δ) is visible from the calculation point, and otherwise 0. Extensive calculation time is required for integrating illuminance taking into account the visibility of each sky element. Illuminance due to sky light cannot be calculated in advance, because intensity distribution, L_V, of the sky dome changes depending on solar position and weather conditions.

To solve the problem of intensity distribution of the sky, L_V, is transformed into a Fourier series, and basis illuminances, B_{lm} corresponding to each basis function of a Fourier series are calculated in advance [6].

The illuminance due to sky light can be calculated quickly by the weighted sum of the basis illuminances, even if the intensity distribution of the sky is altered.

$$I_{skylight}(P, Lv, \mathbf{n}) = \sum_{l=0}^{N} \sum_{m=0}^{N} w_{lm}(Lv, \mathbf{n}) B_{lm}(P) , \qquad (2)$$

where $\mathbf{n}$ is a plane normal at calculation point, P.
In this paper, we use the basis illuminances to render both objects reflected in windowpanes, and those illuminated by windowpane-reflected sky light.

3. Rendering objects reflected in windowpanes

Windowpanes exist in most structures in outdoor scenes, and some buildings are covered with film-coated glass to reflect sunlight. These windowpanes have the effect of mirror reflection, i.e., objects are reflected in the windowpanes, and in turn, direct sunlight and sky light reflected by the windowpanes illuminate objects. To generate photorealistic images, we also have to take into account sky light with respect to objects reflected in windowpanes. In this section, we discuss a method for calculating sky light illuminance of objects reflected in windowpanes.

In the proposed method, surfaces of objects are divided into small quadrilateral patches in what we will call the preprocess, and basis illuminances are calculated at the vertex of each of the quadrilateral patches.

In the rendering process, illuminance due to sky light is calculated using basis illuminances at the vertices of the quadrilateral patches, and illuminance at arbitrary points in a quadrilateral patch is interpolated from the illuminance at the four vertices. In the proposed method, a raytracing technique is employed to find an intersection of a ray and an object reflected in windowpanes, and illuminance due to sky light is then calculated at the intersection.

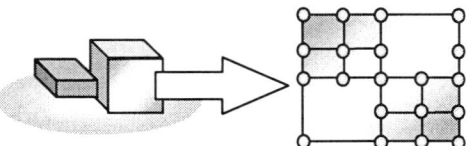

Fig. 3 Surface is subdivided into small quadrilateral patches.

3.1 The process of the proposed method

The process for rendering objects reflected in windowpanes taking into consideration sky light effects is described as follows.

* Preprocess: Calculation of basis illuminances

In the preprocess, each objects surface is recursively subdivided into small quadrilateral patches using a quadtree, and basis illuminances are calculated at each vertex of the quadrilateral patches (see Fig. 3). If the value of the first term of the basis illuminances, which is proportional to the visible areas of the sky, differs from those of the other three vertices, the patch is divided again. The adaptive subdivision makes the calculation of sky light illuminance accurate and efficient.

* Rendering

Step 1: Calculation of illuminance due to sky light

In the first step of rendering, illuminance due to sky light is calculated by the weighted sum of the basis illuminances calculated in the preprocess. In other words, after specifying solar position and weather conditions, intensity distribution of the sky [7], and weight coefficients for each basis illuminance are calculated [6]. Then, the weighted sum of basis illuminances at each vertex of the quadrilateral patches gives the illuminance from sky light at each vertex of the patches.

Step 2: Calculation of illuminance at the intersection between a ray and objects

We employ a raytracing technique to find the intersection between a given ray and objects reflected in windowpanes. Figure 4 shows a detailed flow of this step.

First, a primary ray is shot from a given viewpoint, and the intersection between the ray and the object is calculated.

(A) In the case of diffuse surfaces

If the object intersected by the ray does not have a mirror reflection, the four vertices of the quadrilateral patch intersected by the ray are found (see Fig. 5). Illuminance at the intersection is calculated by interpolating illuminances at the four vertices after the weighted sum of basis illuminances. Illuminance due to direct sunlight at the intersection is also calculated, and the illuminances due to sky light and direct sunlight are added to compute the color of the calculation point.

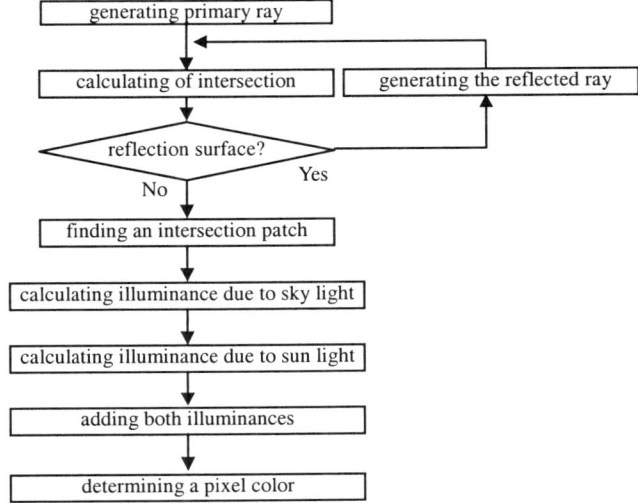

Fig. 4 Flow of illuminance calculation.

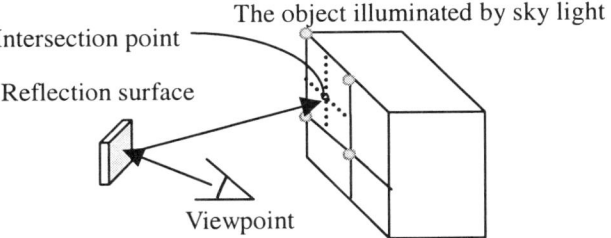

Fig. 5 Calculation of intersected patch by using raytracing method.

(B) In the case of surfaces with mirror reflection

If the object intersected by the ray dose have a mirror reflection, the reflected ray (called the secondary ray) is calculated, and an intersection between the secondary ray and other objects is calculated. When the secondary ray intersects with a diffuse surface, illuminance at the intersection is calculated in the same way as were the diffuse surfaces described in the previous case. If the intersection of the secondary ray takes place on a surface with a mirror reflection, the process is repeated, thereby generating the third ray. This recursive process make it possible to render multiple objects reflected in windowpanes while taking into account the lighting effects of sky light.

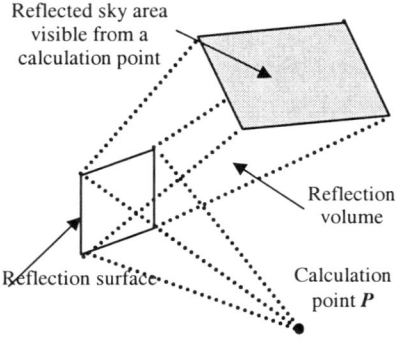
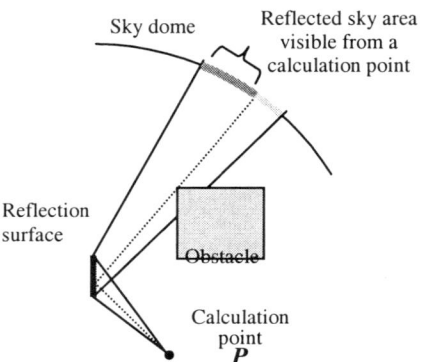

Fig. 6 Reflection volume and reflected sky area visible from a calculation point.

Fig. 7 In this case, the obstacle exists in the reflection volume.

4. Reflected sky light

Direct sunlight and sky light are reflected by windowpanes and illuminate other objects. The effect of direct sunlight reflected by windowpanes (called reflected direct sunlight in the following discussion) is remarkable and more impressive than that of reflected sky light. However, the effect of reflected sky light is also important, especially in urban areas. Neither direct sunlight nor reflected direct sunlight reach the ground in the case of towering buildings, while reflected sky light illuminates such areas as effectively as sky light. In this section, a method for calculating illuminance from reflected sky light is described.

To calculate illuminance from reflected sky light, the area of the sky visible from a calculation point through a windowpane is extracted, and the integration of Eq. 1 is executed with respect to the reflected sky area visible from a certain viewpoint. The reflected sky area visible from that viewpoint can be calculated as an intersection between a reflection volume and the sky dome (see Fig. 6). We also should pay attention to obstacles. If other objects exist in the reflection volume, the area hidden by the obstacles needs to be eliminated from the reflected sky area (see Fig. 7). However, a complicated algorithm and extensive calculation time are required to clip a reflection volume in 3D geometrical space.

To solve the problem, we employ a hemi-cube to extract a reflected sky area visible from a calculation point. In other words, objects in a scene are projected onto the surfaces of the hemi-cube using graphics hardware, and the reflected sky area is approximated as the area of the screen that is not covered with the projected objects. Before the projection, calculation point, P, is moved to a symmetric position with respect to the reflection surface. Objects existing in the half space where the calculation point is located are also copied to the other half space in symmetrical fashion with respect to the reflection surface (called "a reflection model in the mirror" in the following discussion) (see Fig. 8). Note that objects in the half space where the reflection model in the mirror is copied to are removed in advance of the process.

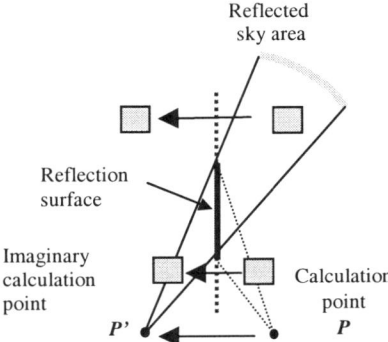

Fig. 8 Calculation of reflected sky area.

The proposed method also uses basis illuminances to calculate illuminances from reflected sky light. The basis illuminances are calculated using the reflected sky area described above. Finally, illuminance due to reflected sky light is added to illuminance due to sky light that reaches directly to objects. To distinguish from basis illuminances for calculating illuminance from direct sky light, basis illuminances for calculating illuminance from reflected sky light is called simply "basis illuminances due to reflected sky light."

4.1 The procedure

A procedure for calculating illuminance due to reflected sky light is described below.

* Preprocess

For each reflection surface, a reflection model in the mirror is constructed, and for each vertex of quadrilateral patches, basis illuminances due to reflected sky light are calculated, after reflected sky areas visible from a calculation point are obtained by the following preprocess.

Step 1: Calculation of reflected sky area visible from a calculation point

Reflected sky area visible from a calculation point through a reflection surface should be calculated taking into account the obstacles that hide the sky reflected in the windowpane. The proposed method uses graphics hardware with a reflection model in the mirror to compute the reflected sky area quickly.

Step 1.1: Calculation point, P, is moved to the symmetric position, P', with respect to the reflection surface. Then, the hemi-cube whose center is located at the imaginary calculation point, P', is set. Each surface of the hemi-cube is associated with a projection screen, and the screen is initialized with white, which signifies 'invisible area.'

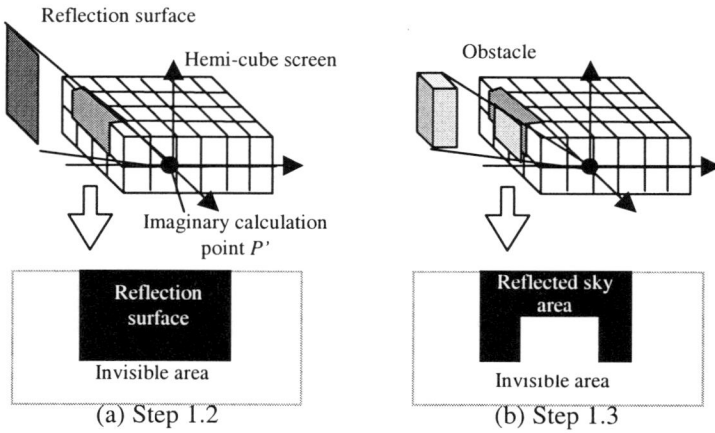

Fig. 9 Calculation of reflected sky area using a hemi-cube.

Step 1.2: The reflection surface is projected onto the hemi-cube screens with black, which signifies the sky area visible from the calculation point through the reflection surface (see Fig. 9(a)).

Step 1.3: All objects consisting of the reflection model in the mirror are projected onto the hemi-cube screens with white. After projection, the black area is the reflected sky area taking into account obstacles (see Fig. 9(b)).

Step 2: Averaging pixels of the screen

The resolution of the hemi-cube screens should be high to prevent an aliasing problem when projecting the objects, while the basis functions to express the intensity distribution of the sky are continuous functions and do not have such high frequencies. It takes a long time to calculate basis illuminances, if we use the hemi-cube screens with high resolution, because the calculation time is proportional to the number of pixels in the screens. To address the problem, the resolution of the screens is decreased by applying an averaging filter. The optimal resolution depends on the terms of the basis functions. We examined the optimal resolution by changing compression rates, such as 1/2, 1/5, 1/10, and 1/20. The result of this experiment is shown in Fig. 10. This experiment shows that the resolution of the hemi-cube screens can be compressed to a level of 1/10 without great loss of accuracy. In this case, the calculation time is reduced by nearly two-thirds.

Step 3: Calculation of basis illuminances

Basis illuminances due to reflected sky light are calculated using the reflected sky area obtained in the previous step. The proposed method uses the same approach developed in [6], but we modify the term of the basis functions. That is, the 0-th term of a Fourier series is also used in the proposed method, because the proposed method uses a hemi-cube instead of a band source for the visibility test of the sky.

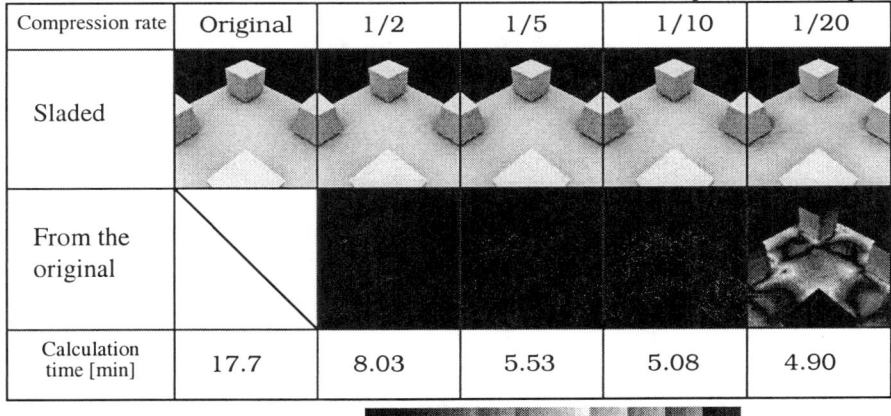

Compression rate	Original	1/2	1/5	1/10	1/20
Sladed					
From the original					
Calculation time [min]	17.7	8.03	5.53	5.08	4.90

Fig. 10 Examination of accuracy and calculation time corresponding to resolution.

Illuminance due to reflected sky light at the calculation point is given by the following equation.

$$I_{skylight}(L_V, P') = \int_0^\pi \int_0^\pi H(\alpha, \delta, P')\rho(P')f(\alpha, \delta, L_V) d\alpha d\delta . \quad (3)$$

L_V: intensity distribution of sky light
ρ : reflectivity of the surface at a calculation point
$H(\alpha, \delta, P')$: visibility function, that gives 1 if the sky in the direction (α, δ) is visible, and otherwise 0.

Illuminance function, f, is defined in the local coordinate (α, δ) and is expressed by the following equation.

$$f(\alpha, \delta, L_V) = L(\alpha, \delta, L_V)\sin^2\alpha \sin\delta , \quad (4)$$

where L is an intensity distribution function of the sky at local coordinate (α, δ).
Applying Fourier cosine transformation to the illuminance function and approximating in N-th terms,

$$f(\alpha, \delta, L_V) = \sum_{l=1}^N \sum_{m=1}^N w_{lm}(L_V)\cos(l\alpha)\cos(m\delta) , \quad (5)$$

$$w_{lm}(L_V) = \frac{2}{\pi}\int_0^\pi \int_0^\pi f(\alpha, \delta; L_V)\cos(l\alpha)\cos(m\delta)d\alpha d\delta . \quad (6)$$

In the proposed method, the integration over the sky hemisphere for Eq. 3 is discretized to the pixels of the hemi-cube screens.

$$I_{skylight}(L_V, P') = \sum_{\vec{D}}^{\Omega} \rho(P')H(\vec{D}, P')f(\alpha(\vec{D}), \delta(\vec{D}), L_V)\delta A \Delta \vec{D} , \quad (7)$$

where $\vec{D}$ is each pixel position of the hemi-cube screens, and Ω indicates the integration of all pixels. Azimuth angle, , α and elevation angle, δ, express the direction of the vector from imaginary calculation point, P', to $\vec{D}$ in a local coordinate system. δA is a solid angle of each pixel, and $\Delta \vec{D}$ is the area of sky element of $\vec{D}$. Substituting Eq. 5 in Eq. 6,

$$I_{skylight}(L_V, P') = \sum_{\vec{D}}^{\Omega} \rho(P') H(\vec{D}, P') \sum_{l=0}^{N} \sum_{m=0}^{N} w_{lm}(L_V) \cos(l\alpha(\vec{D})) \cos(m\delta(\vec{D})) \delta A \Delta \vec{D}$$

$$= \rho(P') \sum_{l=0}^{N} \sum_{m=0}^{N} w_{lm}(L_V) \left\{ \sum_{\vec{D}}^{\Omega} H(\vec{D}, P') \cos(l\alpha(\vec{D})) \cos(m\delta(\vec{D})) \delta A \Delta \vec{D} \right\}$$

$$= \rho(P') \sum_{l=0}^{N} \sum_{m=0}^{N} w_{lm}(L_V) B_{lm}(P') \qquad (8)$$

$$B_{lm}(P') = \sum_{\vec{D}}^{\Omega} H(\vec{D}, P') \cos(l\alpha(\vec{D})) \cos(m\delta(\vec{D})) \delta A \Delta \vec{D}. \qquad (9)$$

In the proposed method, basis illuminances, B_{lm}, due to reflected sky light is calculated by Eq. 9. That is, the pixel values of the hemi-cube screens are used as the values of visibility function, $H(D,P')$, in Eq. 9.

* Main process

Step 4: Calculation of illuminances due to reflected sky light at vertices of patches

In the main process, solar position and weather conditions are specified, and the intensity distribution of the sky, L_V, is computed by a method developed in [8]. Weight coefficients, w_{lm}, for basis illuminances are calculated by Eq. 6. Illuminances due to reflected sky light at the vertices of the quadrilateral patches are calculated by the weighted sum of the basis illuminances due to reflected sky light, w_{lm}, using Eq. 8.

Step 5: Rendering

Illuminance due to reflected sky light at an arbitrary point in a patch is interpolated using the illuminances at four vertices of the patch. Calculating illuminances due to direct sunlight and direct sky light using the traditional method developed in [7], the illuminance at the calculation point is finally given by adding all the illuminances due to direct sunlight, direct sky light and reflected sky light.

5. Implementation

The proposed method is implemented in SOFTIMAGE as plug-in software (called "a shader"). SOFTIMAGE has no function to deal with sky light. Implementing the proposed method as well as an illumination model for sky light [7], the system can generate photorealistic images of outdoor scenes taking into account both solar position and weather conditions.

The flow of the process where the proposed method is implemented is shown in Fig. 11. To generate images as fast as possible when changing a viewpoint, solar position and/or weather conditions, both basis illuminances due to direct skylight and reflected sky light are computed in a preprocess.

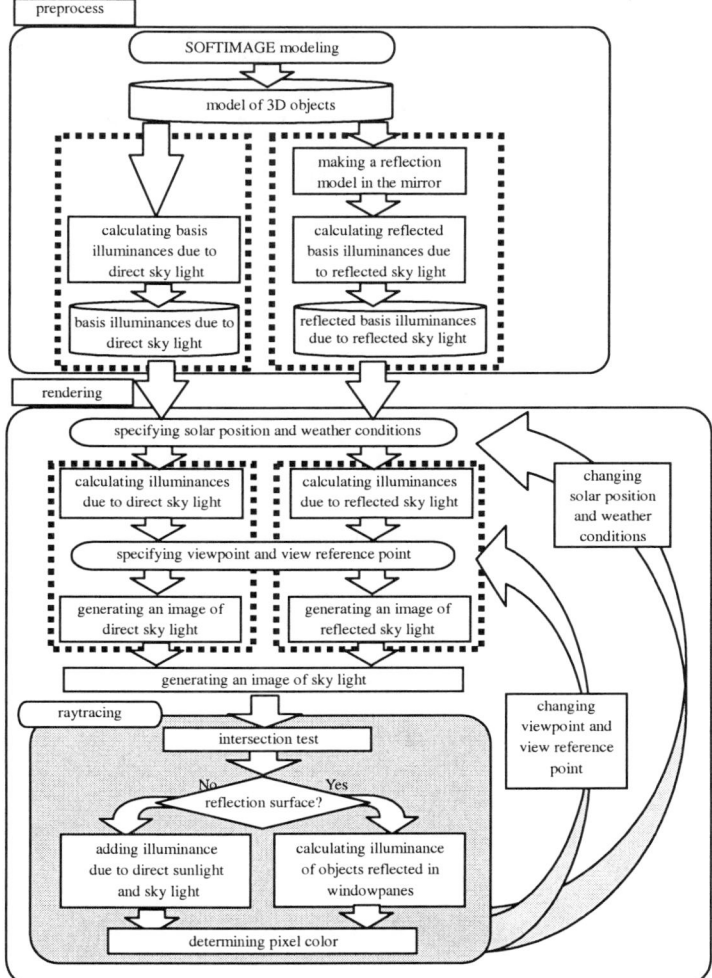

Fig. 11 The process flow.

In the preprocess, a 3D object model is processed in two pipelines to calculate basis illuminances due to direct sky light and reflected sky light. In the pipeline for calculating reflected basis illuminances, a reflection model in the mirror is generated in the manner described in Section 4.

In the main process, specifying solar position and weather conditions, both illuminances due to direct sky light and reflected sky light at each vertex of the quadrilateral patches are calculated in the two pipelines. Next, specifying a viewpoint and a view reference point, two images rendered with direct sky light and reflected sky light are generated in the respective pipelines, and these two images are merged into a single image.

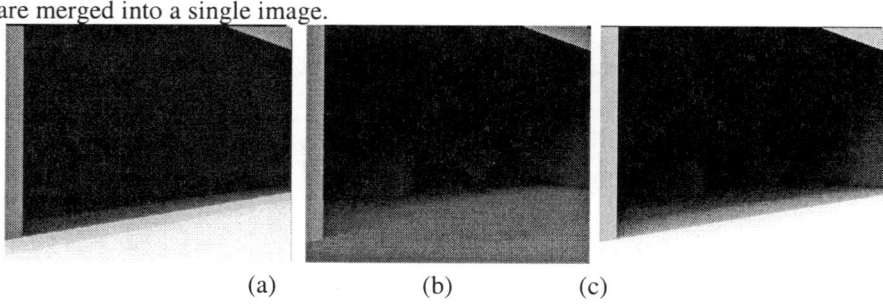

Fig. 12 Example images used a simple model. (a) Traditional method; (b) Luminance due to reflected sky light; (c) The proposed method.

Note that objects reflected in windowpanes have not been rendered in the image. The objects reflected in windowpanes are rendered in the following raytracing process. In the raytracing process, depending on surface attributes of intersections between a ray and objects, illuminance due to direct sun light or illuminance of objects reflected in windowpanes is calculated. We use a SOFTIMAGE renderer to calculate illuminance due to direct sun light, and use the method described in Section 3.1 to calculate illuminance of objects reflected in windowpanes. Finally, all the components of direct sun light, objects reflected in windowpanes, and direct and reflected sky light are added to an image.

In the proposed method, when a viewpoint and/or a view reference point are changed, only images rendered with direct sky light and reflected sky light are calculated from the pre-calculated illuminances at each vertex of patches, because the illuminances due to direct sky light and reflected sky light do not change. Only when solar position and/or weather conditions change are illuminances due to direct and reflected sky light at each vertex of patches re-calculated.

6. Examples

Several images of outdoor scenes are rendered by the proposed method. We use a simple model to examine the proposed method. Figure 12(a) is an image generated by the traditional method [7], taking into account direct sun light and direct sky light. Figure 12(b) shows illuminance due to reflected sky light proposed in Section 4. Figure 12(c) is an image generated by the proposed method. Both direct sky light and reflected sky light, as well as direct sun light, are taken into account in the image. Comparing Figs. 12(a) through (c), the effect of sky light reflected by the windowpanes plays an important role in rendering a photorealistic image.

To demonstrate the usefulness of the proposed method, we use a more complex model. The top and front views of buildings are shown in Fig. 13. Two of the buildings are built close to each other, and both buildings have windowpanes. Direct sunlight does not illuminate the entrance of one of the buildings, because the other building shuts out direct sunlight, although both direct and reflected sky light illuminate the entrance.

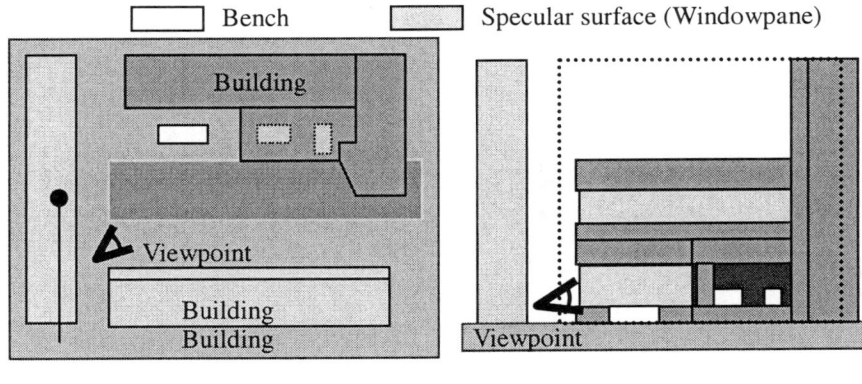

(a) Top view   (b) Front view

Fig. 13 Model of building.

Table 1 Setting of image generation.

	Traditional method [7]	The proposed method	
		Direct sky light	Reflected sky light
Number of sky area samplings	100	300	300
Number of patches	9934	26696	20384
Number of basis illuminances	3x3	5x5	5x5

Table 2 Calculation time of image generation.

	Traditional method [7]	The proposed method	
		Direct sky light	Reflected sky light
Preprocess [min]	11	36	32
Rendering [sec]	30	80	

Figure 14(a) is an image generated by the conventional method [7]. The image takes into account direct sunlight and direct sky light. Objects reflected in the windowpanes are rendered taking into account only direct sunlight. Figure 14(b) shows illuminance due to reflected sky light. Figure 14(c) is an image generated by the proposed method. Both direct sky light and reflected sky light are taken into account in the image. Sky light is also considered in the objects reflected in windowpanes. Comparing Figs. 14(a) and (c), it is obvious that the effect of sky light reflected by the windowpanes plays an important role in realistic rendering. In order to show the effect clearly, we do not use texture mapping.

Several parameters and the number of quadrilateral patches are shown in Table 1, and the time required to generate the image in Fig. 14(c) is shown in Table 2. The resolution of the image is 720x610 pixels, and the images were generated on an SGI O2 R10000/150MHz.

It took about 30 minutes to calculate basis illuminances in the preprocess. Once the preprocess is carried out, an image can be generated in about 80 seconds, taking into account both direct and reflected sky light. The time required to calculate an image

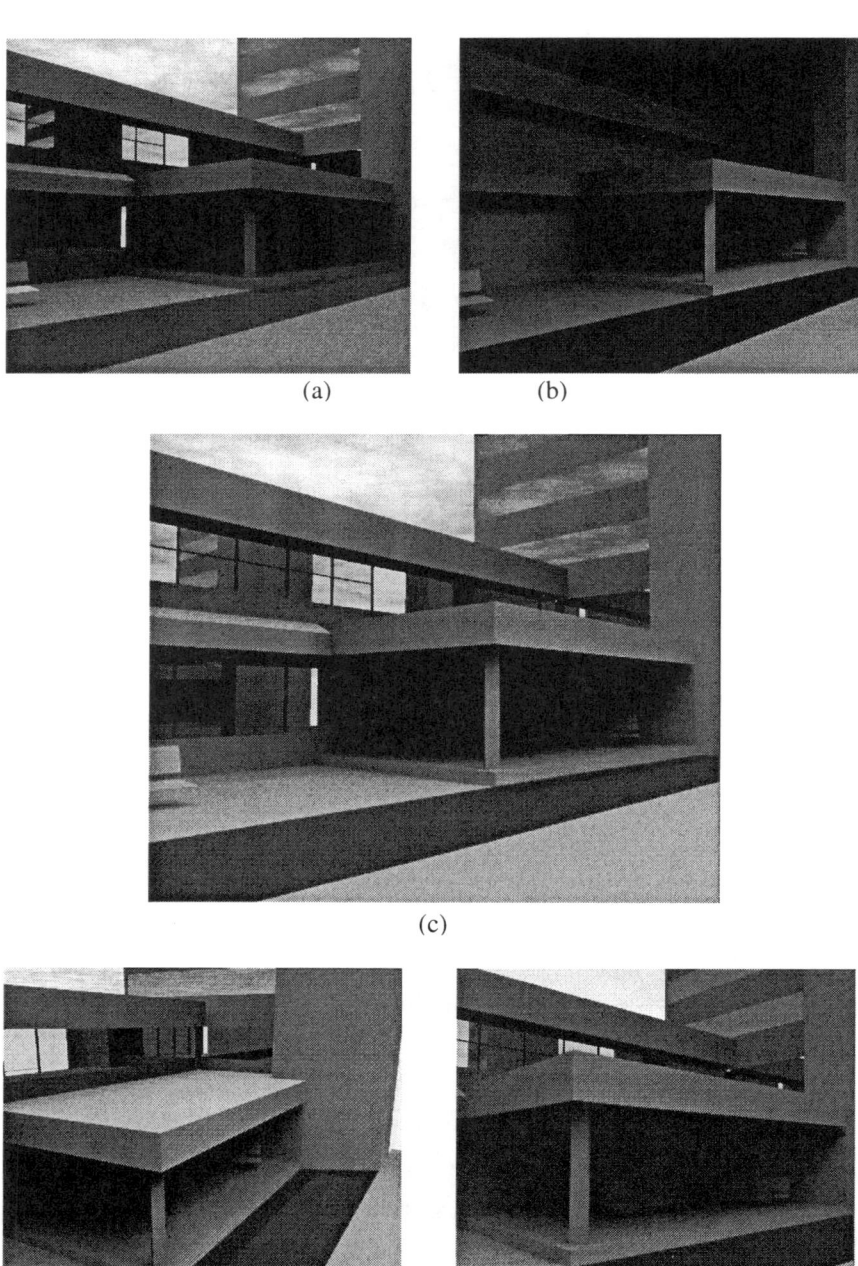

Fig. 14 Example images. (a) Traditional method; (b) Luminance due to reflected sky light; (c) The proposed method; (d) Different viewpoint; (e) Different solar position and weather condition.

by the traditional method [7] was about 30 seconds. Therefore, it took about 50 seconds in total to compute the sky light illuminance of objects reflected in windowpanes and the illuminance due to reflected sky light. It took about 100 minutes to calculate an image using the method developed first [1], which uses band sources for integrating illuminance due to sky light.

Figure 14(d) shows an image with a different viewpoint, and Figure 14(e) shows an image with different solar position and weather conditions. It took only about 80 seconds, even when the viewpoint, solar position and/or weather conditions were altered. The proposed method is useful for generating a sequence of images and animation.

7. Conclusions

We have proposed a method for rendering realistic images of outdoor scenes taking into account both direct and reflected sky light. Objects reflected in windowpanes of buildings can be rendered in consideration of the effect of sky light, and an illumination model for reflected sky light makes the images more realistic. Using basis illuminances, the proposed method can also generate images quickly, even when the viewpoint, solar position and/or weather conditions changed.

References

[1] T. Nishita and E. Nakamae. "Continuous Tone Representation of Three Dimensional Objects Illuminated by Sky Light", *Computer Graphics* **20**(4): 125-132 (1986).

[2] K. Kaneda, T. Okamoto, E. Nakamae, T. Nishita. "Photorealistic Image Synthesis for Outdoor Scenery under Various Atmospheric Conditions", *The Visual Computer* **7**(5&6): 247-258 (1991).

[3] K. Tadamura, E. Nakamae, K. Kaneda, M. Baba, H. Yamashita and T. Nishita. "Modeling of Skylight and Rendering of Outdoor Scenes", *Computer Graphics Forum* **12**(3): 189-200 (1993).

[4] Nimeroff, J. S., Simoncelli, E., and Dorsey, J. "Efficient Re-rendering of Naturally Illuminated Environments", Proceedings of 5th Eurographics Workshop on Rendering, 359-373 (1994).

[5] Y. Dobashi, K. Kaneda, H. Yamashita, and T. Nishita. "A Quick Rendering Method for Outdoor Scenes Using Sky Light Luminance Function Expressed with Basis Function", The Journal of The Institute of Image Electronics Engineers of Japan **24**(3): pp 196-205 (1995) (in Japanese).

[6] Y. Dobashi, K. Kaneda, H. Yamashita and T. Nishita. "Method for Calculation of Sky Light Luminance Aiming at an Interactive Architectural Design", Computer Graphics Forum 15(3): pp 109-118 (1996).

[7] K. Tomita, K. Kaneda, H. Yamashita and Y. Dobashi. "A Fast, Accurate Rendering Method of Outdoor Scenes Using an All-weather Skylight Model", The Journal of The Institute of Image Electronics Engineers of Japan **28**(4): pp 349-357 (1996) (in Japanese).

[8] R. Perez, R. Seals, J. Mickalsky. "All-Weather Model for Sky Luminance Distribution – Preliminary Configuration and Validation", *Solar Energy* **50**(3): pp 235-245 (1993).

High Quality Final Gathering for Hierarchical Monte Carlo Radiosity for General Environments

Frederic Pérez   Ignacio Martín   Xavier Pueyo
GGG/IiiA-UdG

Abstract

Aiming at rendering high quality images robustly for general environments with simple algorithms, we use a two-pass method that accounts for the global illumination. In this paper we present the integration of a new gathering procedure in the rendering pass, that uses the approximate results obtained by a particle tracing method, an extension of the Hierarchical Monte Carlo Radiosity (HMCR) algorithm. Results from our implementation demonstrate the efficient generation of high quality images using the technique presented herein.

Keywords: Global illumination, two-pass methods, Monte Carlo radiosity.

1. Introduction

This paper addresses the production of high quality images considering the global illumination in general environments. For such a goal, we use of a two-pass algorithm that is based on Hierarchical Monte Carlo Radiosity (HMCR) [2] and ray tracing incorporating a local gathering procedure. The resulting algorithm is easy to implement and robust. Currently our implementation treats the interaction of light between isotropic participating media and diffuse or specular (or a combination of both) surfaces. The present work is based on a previous two-pass algorithm [7], enhancing it by constructing better *Link Probabilities* [8, 11], that constitute *probability density functions* (*PDFs*) based on the results of the HMCR step. These PDFs are used to accelerate the convergence of a Monte Carlo integration process, to estimate the reflected (or scattered) radiance.

The remainder of the paper is organized as follows. First, a brief overview of the two-pass algorithm is presented in Section 2. Next, the extended HMCR step and the final gather using importance sampling are reviewed from [7], emphasizing the differences of the approach taken here, in Section 3 (first pass) and Section 4 (second pass). Results are shown in Section 5. Finally, conclusions and future directions are discussed in Section 6.

2. Outline of the Two-pass Algorithm

The extension of the HMCR algorithm [3] to account for surfaces with a combination of diffuse plus specular components, and for participating media, constitutes the first pass of the algorithm. The surfaces' diffuse component is handled as in HMCR, whilst the specular component is handled by following the path of particles through bounces until they eventually hit a diffuse surface (with no specular component), interact with a medium, or quit the scene. Particles interact randomly within participating media, according to the transmittance function that is based on the media's extinction coefficient. The meshes related to surfaces and volumes are adaptively refined, together with the implicit link structure.

The rendering step is an extended ray tracer assisted by a gathering procedure that uses Link Probabilities to accelerate the convergence of illumination estimations. For each pixel, a Link Probabilities object is constructed from the *pushed* links arriving at the viewed leaf element(s) l. For scenes in vacuum, l can be the one directly viewed or a mirrored one (or both, for general BRDFs); on the other hand, if the scene contains participating media then there is a potential set of leaves for which Links Probabilities are set. The variance of the estimators is reduced by means of the use of PDFs that are approximately proportional to the kernels of the integrals of the reflectance (for surfaces) and the scattering equations (for participating media).

3 First pass: Extended HMCR

3.1 HMCR Basics

Bekaert et al. developed HMCR, which is an extension of discrete Monte Carlo Radiosity (MCR) that incorporates hierarchical refinement and clustering [3]. In MCR algorithms, lines are generated, connecting mutually visible points x and y. Each of these lines represents a sample contributing to the form factor between the patch containing x and the patch containing y. This contribution to the form factor is immediately translated into an energy transfer between the patches. In HMCR, for each sample line, the level of the element hierarchies at x and y is determined so that the energy transfer is considered appropriate, instead of simply taking the patches containing points x and y (Figure1).

The essential difference between Hierarchical Radiosity (HR) [4] and HMCR is that at each refinement step, in HR *all* the sub-elements containing x and y are recursively refined, whereas in HMCR only the sub-elements containing x and y are considered for further refinement. The same refinement criteria and strategies as in HR can be used to check whether a candidate interaction between elements containing x and y is admissible, and, if not admissible, how it should be refined. The HMCR adaptively refined mesh and (implicit) link structure is very similar to those in HR, but are lazily constructed as needed during form factor sampling rather than beforehand as in HR.

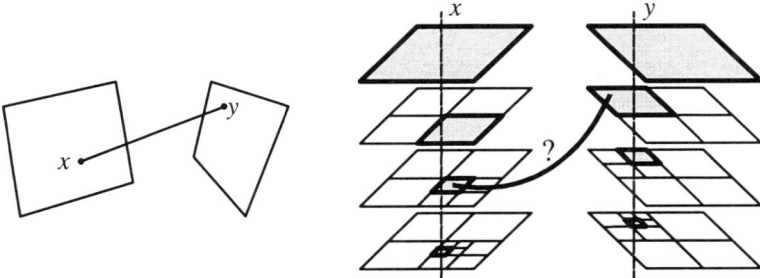

Figure 1: HMCR: for each sample line connecting two points x and y, the level of the element hierarchies at x and y is determined as being appropriate for computing the light transport from x to y [3].

3.2 HMCR for Participating Media and Surfaces with Specular Component

To handle participating media, the HMCR was modified so that the local lines can interact not only at surfaces but also in the volumes containing the media. A sampling process is established to find the points of interaction of the particles within the volume like in the Monte Carlo light tracing by Pattanaik et al. [6]. Using the *Absorption Suppression* strategy, at the interaction points the particles always scatter and reduce their flux multiplying it by the albedo Ω. The local lines end at the first interaction point, updating the unsent power of the receiving volume element at the level specified by the refiner. As in the case of the HMCR for surfaces, a refinement criterion is set to decide at which level of the hierarchies the transport of energy is appropriate. Currently we deal with isotropically scattering media, therefore when a leaf volume element is selected to shoot its unsent power, the local lines follow a uniform distribution in the space of directions.

The integration of surfaces with specular component in their BRDF in the HMCR algorithm is very easy. When a particle hits one of these surfaces, apart from the refinement and transfer of energy taking place for the diffuse component, it is also bounced following the direction of the perfect reflection/refraction taking into account the normal at the hit point. The power of the particle is weighted in the bounce by the spectral "color" of the specular component. (In the case of a "white mirror", the spectral color would be (1, 1, 1) in RGB space, so the weight for the three channels is 1, and the particle would not loose energy. A "green mirror" would absorb the red and blue components, and only the green component of the particle's power would remain for the bounced particle.) The particle keeps bouncing as long as hits surfaces with specular component. As an example, we have built a room scene (Figure 2), a kind of simplified replication of one of the scenes of E. Veach's dissertation [13], containing both direct (lamp on the right) and indirect illumination (lamp on the left, pointing upwards). The wall on the right has both (gray) diffuse and specular components. The direct illumination can be noticed on this wall as a gray contribution to the illumination imposed over the mirrored illumination. This will be more easily seen with the execution of the second pass (Figure 6). The first pass took 25.26 seconds to compute the solution, shown on the right of Figure 2. (All timings given in this paper are on a PC Linux SuSe with a PIII 550MHz processor.)

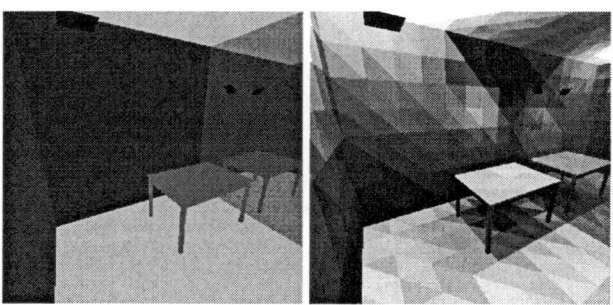

Figure 2: The room scene: (Left) The input scene. (Right) The result of the HMCR step (flat-shaded).

4 Second Pass: Ray Tracing Assisted by Local Gather

The ultimate goal of the rendering step is to compute good estimates of eye radiances. For such a task, a ray tracing is modified to use the results of the HMCR step to estimate indirect illumination, as explained below. In scenes in vacuum, the radiances reaching the eye are those from the visible surfaces, governed by the reflectance equation (for a point x in a direction ω_o):

$$L_r(x, \omega_o) = L_e(x, \omega_o) + \int \rho_{bd}(x, \omega_o, \omega_i) L_i(x, \omega_i) \cos\theta \, d\sigma_{\omega i}$$

being L_e the self-emanating radiance, $\rho_{bd}(x, \omega_o, \omega_i)$ the BRDF at x for incoming direction ω_i and outgoing direction ω_o, and L_i the incident radiance. The integral part of the reflectance equation can be split into three components: a perfectly specular part (L_{spec}), direct illumination (L_{dir}) and indirect illumination (L_{ind}). Dropping the parameters, we have:

$$L_r = L_e + L_{dir} + L_{spec} + L_{ind}$$

The self-emission L_e is directly available from the scene description, so it causes no problems. The L_{dir} component can be computed for example by sampling the light sources directly. Alternatively, it can also be computed in conjunction with L_{ind} as explained below (our implementation offers both possibilities). The L_{spec} component is computed by following the viewing path. A reflected ray is traced to retrieve the incoming energy at the interaction point. This energy is weighted accordingly by the specular fraction of ρ_{bd}.

The computation of the L_{ind} component is more laborious. L_{ind} is estimated by using the solution of the HMCR step. A straightforward approach is to use the results of the HMCR pass directly, or perhaps after Gouraud shading, as Bekaert et al. do [3]. However, this leads to disturbing artifacts like over estimating lighting in shadow areas and light leaks. A better—though more costly—solution is to use the HMCR results to estimate L_{ind} (or $L_{dir} + L_{ind}$) with a gathering procedure, by means of Link Probabilities to accelerate its convergence [8, 11], using the sets of links stored in the first pass. This is a gathering process similar to other final gathering schemes. (For overviews on final gathering refer to [11, 12, 2].) Our final gather procedure differs from others by the fact that we set a different PDF for each viewed point (not for patches) and they are adaptively modified to better match the incoming distribution of energy (to alleviate visibility problems) [8].

In order to implement the gathering procedure, in [7] the HMCR step collected links explicitly when transferring energy, and a Link Probabilities instance was constructed from the *pushed* links arriving at the leaf elements related to the interaction points. Note that the stochastic nature of the HMCR step gives a chance to miss links, mostly when dealing with very small patches (of tiny objects, for example). This leads to underestimation of irradiance, and also discontinuities in the illumination function across boundaries of patches. This is fixed by delaying the link construction to the rendering phase—the HMCR step not storing links at all. Now, in the rendering pass, for a gathering point x, the links are reconstructed by refining the scene against x, perhaps subdividing patches in this process. We use the same refinement schema as the refinement of HMCR, taking into account that now we do not consider element-to-element refinement but point-to-element refinement. This refinement thus establishes the set of links that serves as a basis for the Link Probabilities objects. Finally, the Link Probabilities are sampled to estimate the irradiance at the interaction points to obtain a better estimate of L_{ind} at last.

An example of the result of the refinement procedure is depicted in Figure 3, for the room scene. Yellowish lines represent links with higher probability in the related Link Probabilities object (see Section 4.1 for the basics of Link Probabilities). As expected, the links with highest probabilities for the example point are those related to the visible light source. It should be noticed that delaying the link construction to the second pass saves computation time of the HMCR step because it does not have to collect links. In our room scene example, this represents the 4.4% of the time of the first pass. Unfortunately, the refinement needed per gathering point increments the time of the second step. (This can be alleviated by discarding the elements with very low illumination, with the consequence of more biased results.) Notice that the refinement is mandatory to fix the problems of under estimated illumination and discontinuities in the illumination between patches. This is shown in Figure 4, where we have rendered images for a zoom on a corner of the table of the room scene, collecting links in the HMCR step and delaying link construction to the second step, using the refinement per gathering point. We can see, in false-color, the zones of the images that differ the most. The mentioned discontinuities can be easily seen at the lines joining certain patches, due to the fact that missed different links. Also it can be seen that using the refinement per gathering point, the penumbra area has been improved substantially.

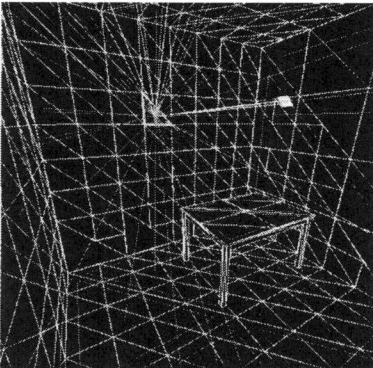

Figure 3: Mesh obtained by the execution of the HMCR step for the room scene, plus links established for an example point after refinement.

Figure 4: (From left to right) Zoom of the table corner, showing the mesh; result of the rendering step using links collected in the HMCR step; result of the rendering step using links established by the refinement procedure; differences in false color.

For scenes including participating media, care must be taken because of the transmittances through the media and the source radiances inside the media. The rendering step must then solve the *integral transport equation*:

$$L(x) = L_{ri}(x) + L_m(x) = \tau(x_0, x) L(x_0) + \int_{x_0}^{x} \tau(u, x) \kappa_t(u) J(u) du$$

being $\tau(x_0, x) = \exp(-\int_{x_0}^{x} \kappa_t(u) J(u) du)$ the *transmittance* from x_0 to x, $L_{ri}(x)$ the *reduced incident radiance*, due to the radiance of a background surface (if any), and $L_m(x)$ the *medium radiance*, due to the contribution of the source radiance J within the medium [9]. The radiance at the background surface, $L(x_0)$ is estimated as explained above.

To estimate $L_m(x)$, a set of *interaction points* is chosen along the line of sight (jittered samples along the pierced participating media). As in the case of scenes in vacuum, the estimates of the source radiances resulting from the first pass could be used directly to estimate L_m. However, if a more accurate image is required, a gathering strategy is used at those interaction points in the media, similar to the gathering for points in surfaces.

4.1 Link Probabilities Basics (PDFs Based on Links)

The Link Probabilities refer to the discrete PDFs constructed in the domain of the given links. The set of links established for a given point with the refinement procedure represents its sources of illumination. Each link is given a certain probability by means of estimating the irradiances coming from each link, and normalizing their sum. A sample (reflected/scattered) direction is obtained by first sampling the resulting PDF to choose a link. If the link's sender is a surface, then its related solid angle can be sampled to get a source point [1, 14]. If the link's sender is a participating medium, we sample the related volume according to the volume measure. In any case, sample directions that do not hit the link's sender are rejected.

We use PDFs that adapt themselves as the execution progresses (i.e., as each instance is sampled) to resemble with better accuracy the incoming irradiance from the set of related links. A situation where constant PDFs can work poorly is shown in Figure 5; adapting the PDFs by taking into account the number of failures (choosing a direction that does not hit the link's sender) with respect to the number of attempts to get a sample direction once a link is sampled reduces the variance of the estimator. As a consequence, the quality of the result is improved.

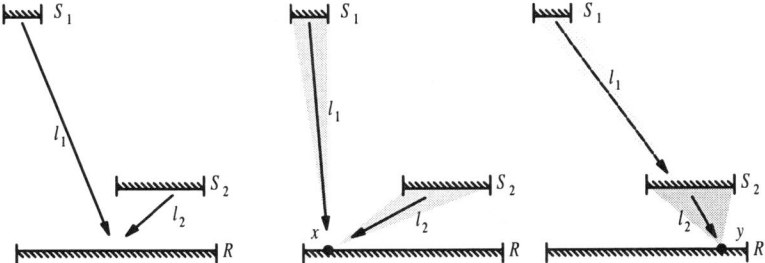

Figure 5: (Left) HMCR set two links arriving at leaf R. (Middle) At point x the PDF must consider both links. (Right) The PDF at point y should ideally set to zero the probability of link l_1 since sender S_1 is fully blocked.

5 Results

In Figure 6 we show a set of images obtained by progressively doubling the number of samples in the second pass for the room scene. Obviously, it can be seen that the noise is reduced as long as more samples are used. The timings of this set of images are shown in a logarithmic plot in Figure 7, with the image resolution fixed to 400*400 pixels. It can be observed that the rendering time is not doubled as the number of samples is doubled (this hypothetically doubling in the rendering time is shown in dashed lines). This is due to the refinement procedure made for the gathering points, and to the construction of the related Link Probabilities object. When using more and more samples, this cost is amortized, so the timing curve approaches the doubling of time.

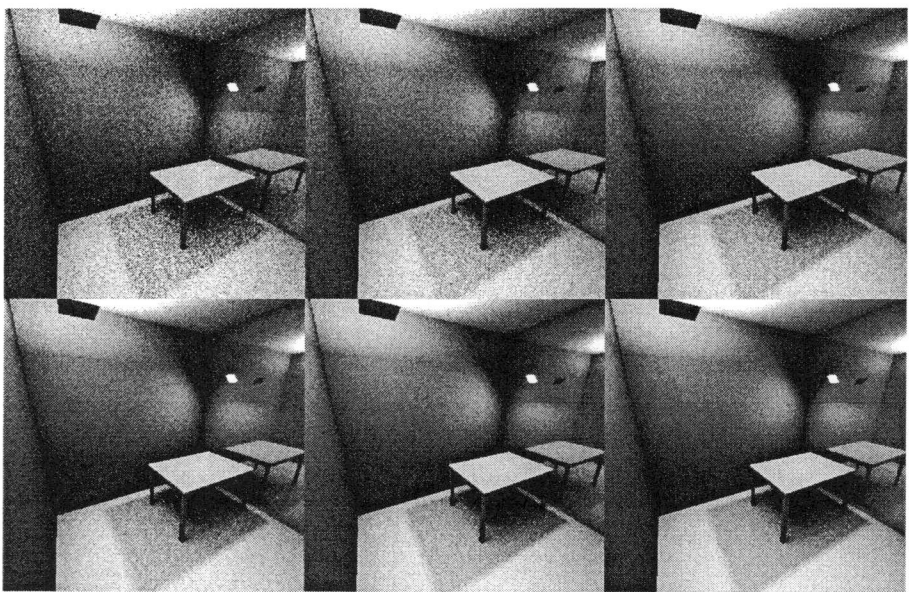

Figure 6: (From left to right and from top to bottom) Results of the second step using 4, 8, 16, 32, 64 and 128 samples per pixel for the room scene.

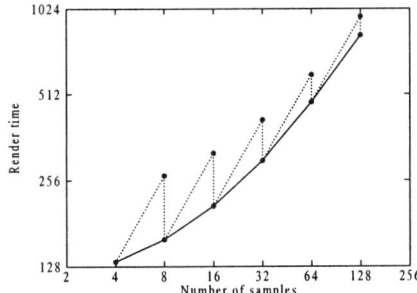

Figure 7: Rendering time per number of samples of the set of images of Figure 6.

As a second test we used the office of [7], that contains specular surfaces (attenuated mirrors on a wall, and at the door), and diffuse plus specular components of the BRDF for the top of a table. Notice that most of the illumination comes to the ceiling, since there is only a single lamp pointing upwards. Running the HMCR algorithm takes 19.25 seconds for a rough estimate of the global illumination. (Previously, though, when collecting links in the HMCR pass, we were forced to shoot more lines to get also an acceptable set of links, so it took 67 seconds.) The resulting radiances of the patches are also shown on the left of Figure 8. Notice again that this solution (or after applying Gouraud shading) does not show illumination features like shadows close to the bottom of the table's legs, etc. However, after executing the rendering step gathering energy at interaction points, those features are captured, as shown on the middle of Figure 8 (built in 551.6 seconds). (When collecting links in the first pass, though, the second step only took 461 seconds, but some areas–mostly small patches on chairs–had underestimated illumination, which is fixed now.) For this image, of a resolution of 400*400 pixels, 16 samples have been used for estimating $L_{dir} + L_{ind}$. Some noise is still perceptible, for instance in Figure 8 (right), at the corner made by the two walls and at the region of the wall close to the desk. This noise was worse when collecting links in the first pass. Again, this undesirable effect can be reduced by using more samples at gathering points, especially at critical points, instead of using a fixed number of samples. The noisy points can be detected for instance by controlling the variance of the estimation. Also, considering the visibility in the refinement procedure for the gathering process would help substantially (see Section 6).

Figure 8: Office room with indirect illumination: (Left) The result of the HMCR step. (Middle) Solution after the second pass. (Right) Solution after the second pass for a second view.

Finally, we have tested our algorithm with a more complex model, a kitchen scene (shown on the left of Figure 9). This scene has two large windows that act as diffuse light sources. The extended HMCR step took 12 seconds to compute a rough solution of the global illumination (middle of Figure 9). Notice that currently our implementation of the HMCR pass does not deal with clusters for light exchange, and thus there are patches that have not received any hit (so they have no energy), for example in the vase. However, this solution is still usable by the rendering step, that spent 1651 seconds to compute an image of 400*400 pixels, with 64 samples per pixel. Two more views, that took 1794 and 1891 seconds respectively, are shown in Figure 10.

Figure 9: The global illumination is roughly computed for a kitchen model (left—courtesy and copyright of LightWork Design Ltd.) with the extension of the HMCR algorithm (middle—shown flat-shaded). Finally, with the use of our local gathering procedure, we obtain a high quality image (right).

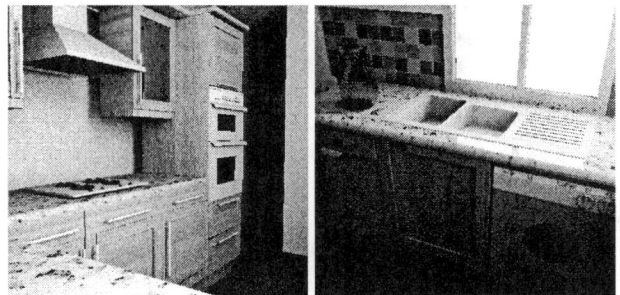

Figure 10: Two more views of the kitchen, after the second step.

6 Conclusions and Future Work

We have presented a new scheme for the final gathering enabling the computation of high quality images, based on the HMCR extended algorithm, using importance sampling, by means of Link Probabilities. This method provides good results for very different lighting conditions.

The work presented here constitutes the basis of a more ambitious project, using an efficient two-pass algorithm for a large range of possible input scenes. To this end, after running executions for participating media (since the implementation is already finished for both surfaces and media), we envisage dealing with the issues discussed below.

Cheaper Rendering Step. The coherence of the radiances at the image and scene spaces has to be exploited to avoid excessive or unnecessary sampling. Key scene points have to be identified, so that interpolation (when some criteria is met) could be used, potentially saving high computation times. This would reduce the number of LP objects that are constructed.

Better LP construction. Currently the refinement procedure in the rendering step does not take into account visibility, relying on the adaptiveness of the Link Probabilities to handle occlusion. We should investigate the inclusion of the visibility in the refinement, in such a way that does not increase prohibitively the rendering time. Also we consider the use of shaft culling for objects O with high illumination to quickly discard receivers that do not see O. For glossy (not perfect specular) BRDFs, the refinement should take into account the BRDF for the outgoing direction. For the estimation of the irradiance, the use of Quasi-Monte Carlo random sequences would improve its convergence.

Caustics and General Materials. Caustics could be easily rendered by identifying the paths that cause them. In the HMCR pass, when bouncing off of glossy objects, the illumination caused by the related particles should be stored separately, for instance using a photon map (this would allow caustics on participating media) [5]. In the rendering step, when estimating L_{ind}, the caustic component could be added by retrieving it, with density estimation if using a photon map.

So far our implementation deals with surfaces with a combination of purely diffuse plus purely specular components, and for isotropic scattering media. In order to handle glossy surfaces and anisotropically scattering media, the directionality of the radiant properties has to be represented. The HMCR step could use Illumination Samples [10], storing them only for glossy/anisotropic objects. When one of these objects was chosen to shoot its unshot energy, the related Illumination Samples would be combined with the BRDF or phase function to draw reflected/scattered directions. For the visualization of the results of the HMCR step the final set of illumination samples can be used to reconstruct eye radiances. Another possibility would be to construct directional distributions based on the illumination samples for faster rendering from different viewpoints.

Natural Lighting. We are actively working on an extension of the HMCR pass that integrates sun and sky light. Apart from allowing the rendering of scenes directly lit by natural sources, we consider illumination through light pipes.

Acknowledgements

This work is supported by the ESPRIT Open LTR project 35772 "SIMULGEN", Simulation of Light for General Environments, by the CICYT's TIC2001-2392-C03-01, and by 2001/SGR/00296. Many thanks to Neil Gatenby (LightWork Design) for the kitchen model, to Nicolas Holzschuch for his VRML translation, and to Philippe Bekaert for his *fig* to *cgm* translator (that was used for this document).

References

[1] J. Arvo. "Stratified Sampling of Spherical Triangles." In *Computer Graphics Proceedings, Annual Conference Series, 1995 (ACM SIGGRAPH '95 Proceedings)*, pages 437-438, 1995.

[2] Ph. Bekaert, Ph. Dutré, and Y. D. Willems. "Final Radiosity Gather Step Using a Monte Carlo Technique with Optimal Importance Sampling." Technical Report CW275, Department of Computer Science, Katholieke Universiteit Leuven, Leuven, Belgium, November 1998

[3] Ph. Bekaert, L. Neumann, A. Neumann, M. Sbert, and Y. D. Willems. "Hierarchical Monte Carlo Radiosity." In G. Drettakis and N. Max, editors, *Rendering Techniques '98 (Proceedings of Eurographics Rendering Workshop '98)*, pages 259-268, New York, NY, 1998. Springer Wien.

[4] P. Hanrahan, D. Salzman, and L. Aupperle. "A Rapid Hierarchical Radiosity Algorithm." In *Computer Graphics (ACM SIGGRAPH '91 Proceedings)*, volume 25, pages 197-206, July 1991.

[5] H. W. Jensen and P. H. Christensen. "Efficient Simulation of Light Transport in Scenes with Participating Media Using Photon Maps." In *Computer Graphics (ACM SIGGRAPH '98 Proceedings)*, pages 311-320, 1998.

[6] S. N. Pattanaik and S. P. Mudur. "Computation of Global Illumination in a Participating Medium by Monte Carlo Simulation." *The Journal of Visualization and Computer Animation*, 4(3):133-152, July - September 1993.

[7] F. Pérez, I. Martín, and X. Pueyo. "Hierarchical Monte Carlo Radiosity for General Environments." Technical Report IiiA 02-01-RR, Institut d'Informàtica i Aplicacions, Universitat de Girona, Spain, 2002.

[8] F. Pérez, I. Martín, F. X. Sillion, and X. Pueyo. "Acceleration of Monte Carlo Path Tracing in General Environments." In *Proceedings of Pacific Graphics 2000*, Hong Kong, PRC, October 2000.

[9] Jos Stam. Multi-Scale Stochastic *Modelling of Complex Natural Phenomena*. PhD thesis, University of Toronto, Dept. of Computer Science, 1995.

[10] M. Stamminger, A. Scheel, X. Granier, F. Pérez, G. Drettakis, and F. Sillion. "Efficient Glossy Global Illumination with Interactive Viewing." *Computer Graphics Forum*, 19(1):13-25, 2000.

[11] W. Sturzlinger. "Optimized Local Pass Using Importance Sampling." In *WSCG 96 (Fourth International Conference in Central Europe on Computer Graphics and Visualization)*, volume 2, pages 342-348, Plzen, Czech Republic, 1996. University of West Bohemia.

[12] C. Ureña and J. C. Torres. "Improved Irradiance Computation by Importance Sampling." In J. Dorsey and Ph. Slusallek, editors, *Rendering Techniques '97 (Proceedings of the Eighth Eurographics Workshop on Rendering)*, pages 275-284, New York, NY, 1997. Springer Wien. ISBN 3-211-83001-4.

[13] E. Veach. *Robust Monte Carlo Methods for Light Transport Simulation*. PhD thesis, Stanford University, December 1997.

[14] C. Wang. "Physically Correct Direct Lighting for Distribution Ray Tracing." In David Kirk, editor, *Graphics Gems III*, pages 307-313. Academic Press Professional, Boston, MA, 1992.

New Contrast Measures for Pixel Supersampling

Jaume Rigau, Miquel Feixas, Mateu Sbert[1]
Institut d'Informàtica i Aplicacions, Universitat de Girona
17071–Girona, Spain

Abstract
Ray tracing is a straightforward and powerful image synthesis technique but usually requires many rays per pixel to eliminate the aliasing or noise in the final image. However, not all the pixels in the image require the same quantity of rays. In this paper we introduce new measures for supersampling refinement criteria, based on colour and geometry. These measures use the entropy, one of the most relevant Information Theory concepts. All the new measures are compared with other classic contrast measures.

Keywords: contrast, entropy, pixel quality, pixel sampling, supersampling.

1 Introduction

Although ray tracing is a straightforward and powerful image synthesis technique, it usually requires many rays per pixel to eliminate the aliasing or noise in the final image. However, not all the pixels in the image require the same quantity of rays. The edge of an object, the contour of a shadow, and a high illumination gradient will require a much better treatment than a region with almost uniform illumination. To this effect, many pixel supersampling refinement criteria have been defined in the literature [6].

The measures used in these criteria are based on intensities (image space) and also on geometry (object space). They are also useful for an adaptive subdivision of image space for progressive refinement [9]. Some of them have been recently applied in the image based rendering field for weighting pixel colour for reconstruction [10] and adaptive sampling strategies [4, 5], and creating a priority schema for sampling in interactive rendering [13].

In this paper we will introduce new measures for supersampling refinement criteria, using both colour and geometry. These measures are based on Information Theory concepts. The new measures will be compared with classic contrast measures [8].

---
[1] jaume.rigau|miquel.feixas|mateu.sbert@udg.es

The organization of this paper is as follows: in section 2 we present some previous work, in section 3 we introduce new pixel colour and geometry quality measures, in section 4 we define new pixel colour and geometry contrast measures, in section 5 we show a supersampling example, and finally we present our conclusions.

2 Previous work

Many supersampling refinement measures have been defined in the literature. For a complete survey see [6]. These measures are based on colour intensities (image space based) and/or geometry (object space based).

In [8], Mitchell presents one of the most widely used intensity measures [2], the *contrast*, defined by

$$C = \frac{I_{\max} - I_{\min}}{I_{\min} + I_{\max}} \qquad (1)$$

where $I_{\min}$ and $I_{\max}$ are the minimum and maximum light intensities respectively. As each sample value consists of three separate intensities for red, green, and blue, Mitchell computes a separate contrast for each one and supersampling is done if any contrast is higher than a given threshold. Red, green, and blue thresholds are set to 0.4, 0.3 and 0.6 respectively, based on the relative sensitivity of the visual system.

In [13], Simmons uses a *priority* value based on the above concepts (contrast and perception) [8, 6]:

$$p_c = 0.4 \frac{r_{\max} - r_{\min}}{r_{\min} + r_{\max}} r_{avg} + 0.3 \frac{g_{\max} - g_{\min}}{g_{\min} + g_{\max}} g_{avg} + 0.6 \frac{b_{\max} - b_{\min}}{b_{\min} + b_{\max}} b_{avg} \qquad (2)$$

where min, max, and *avg* represent the minimum, maximum, and average values respectively for r, g, and b colour components.

On the other hand, a useful and simple geometric measure for refinement is *depth difference*, used recently in image based rendering [4, 5, 10] and interactive rendering [13]. Depth difference is given by

$$p_d = 1 - \frac{d_{\min}}{d_{\max}} \qquad (3)$$

where $d_{\min}$ and $d_{\max}$ represent minimum and maximum distance.

In [11] we presented view-dependent information theory quality measures for pixel sampling and scene discretization in flatland. These measures are based on a definition for the mutual information of a line [12].

3 Pixel quality

In this section we introduce a new pixel quality measure, the pixel entropy.

This measure will be defined from the information provided by the rays passing through a pixel. Let us consider that each pixel ray that hits a scene point gives us information about the distance and orientation of the hit surface with respect to the eye point and the colour of the hit point. From these informations, two different quality measures are defined, pixel colour entropy and pixel geometric entropy, based on the colour and geometry (distance and orientation) respectively.

Entropy is a relevant Information Theory measure [1, 3]. The *entropy H* of a *discrete* random variable X with values in the set $\{x_1, \ldots, x_n\}$, is defined by

$$H = -\sum_{i=1}^{n} p_i \log p_i \qquad (4)$$

where $p_i = Pr[X = x_i]$, the logarithms are taken in base 2, and $0 \log 0 = 0$ by continuity. As $-\log p_i$ represents the *information* (or surprise) associated with the result x_i, the entropy gives the average information of a random variable. When the logarithm is taken in base 2, the unit of information is called a *bit*. The value of H is from 0 to $\log n$. The maximum value is reached when all the probabilities have the same value ($\frac{1}{n}$), and the minimum value when one of the probabilities is equal to 1.

3.1 Pixel colour entropy

Although our main objective is to define pixel colour entropy, we give a global definition of entropy concerning all the rays passing through the image plane. We consider that each colour consists of different components or channels, and each one ranges from 0 to 1. Without loss of generality, in the majority of cases our colour measures will refer to a single component of the spectrum.

Let us consider the probability of each image plane ray as its colour fraction with respect to the sum of the colours of all the rays. Thus, the *image plane colour entropy* is given by

$$H_T^c = -\sum_{i=1}^{N} r_i \log r_i \qquad (5)$$

where N is the total number of image plane rays, and r_i represents the colour fraction of ray i.

If P is the number of pixels of the image plane, then $N = \sum_{i=1}^{P} N_{p_i}$, where N_p is the number of rays traversing a pixel. Thus, *pixel colour entropy* is defined by

$$H^c = -\sum_{i=1}^{N_p} p_i \log p_i \qquad (6)$$

where p_i represents the colour fraction of ray i with respect to the sum of the colours of all the rays passing through a pixel. Obviously, pixel entropy ranges from 0 to $\log N_p$, and maximum pixel entropy is obtained when the colour of all the pixel rays is the same.

Using the properties of entropy [3] it is easy to see that image plane entropy and pixel entropy can be related in the following way:

$$H_T^c = \sum_{i=1}^P q_i H_i^c - \sum_{i=1}^P q_i \log q_i = \sum_{i=1}^P q_i H_i^c + H_I^c \tag{7}$$

where $q_i = \sum_{j=1}^{N_{p_i}} r_j$ is the *importance* (sum of probabilities) of pixel i, H_i^c is the colour entropy of pixel i, and H_I^c is the *importance entropy* of the image plane calculated from the importance of each pixel.

Thus, the global entropy of the image plane is the sum of all the pixel entropies, weighted by the importance of each pixel, and the importance entropy obtained from the importance of each pixel.

We can also observe that the entropy increases with the number of rays. In order to give a pixel quality measure between 0 and 1, the pixel entropy can be normalized with $\log N_p$. Thus, *pixel colour quality* of a colour component can be defined by

$$Q^c = \frac{H^c}{\log N_p} \tag{8}$$

If we consider all the colour components, the *pixel colour quality* can be given by

$$\mathbf{Q}^c = \frac{\sum_{i=1}^n Q_i^c}{n} \tag{9}$$

where n is the number of colour components. Thus, pixel colour quality can be interpreted as a measure of the colour *homogeneity* or *uniformity* of the rays passing through the pixel. This measure will enable us to define, in the next section, a new colour contrast measure for pixel supersampling. Note that the larger the number of rays the more accurate the quality measure.

Figure 1(b) uses a temperature map (the red colour corresponds to the highest quality, the blue colour to the lowest) to show the colour quality of all the pixels of an image. We can observe a low colour quality in shadow areas and edges.

3.2 Pixel geometric entropy

Similar concepts introduced in the above section can be defined in this one with respect to a geometric measure. In order to avoid repetitions we will only give the most basic definitions.

The geometric information of each ray is given by the angle θ which the normal forms at the hit point with the ray and by the distance d between this point and the eye. We take $\frac{\cos\theta}{d^2}$ as a geometric factor of a ray [12]. This value provides a geometric quality measure of a scene point from the observer point of view.

Let us consider the probability of each image plane ray as its geometric fraction, with respect to the sum of the geometric factors of all the rays. Thus, *image plane geometric entropy* is given by

$$H^g_T = -\sum_{i=1}^{N} r_i \log r_i \qquad (10)$$

where r_i represents the geometric fraction of ray i.

Pixel geometric entropy is defined by

$$H^g = -\sum_{i=1}^{N_p} p_i \log p_i \qquad (11)$$

where p_i represents the geometric fraction of ray i with respect to the sum of the geometric factors of all the rays traversing a pixel.

Finally, *pixel geometric quality* is defined by

$$Q^g = \frac{H^g}{\log N_p} \qquad (12)$$

In figure 1(c) we show the geometric quality of each pixel of an image with a gray scaled map (the highest entropy corresponds to the darkest part, the lowest entropy to the lightest). Observe that the edges have a very low entropy and are very well emphasized.

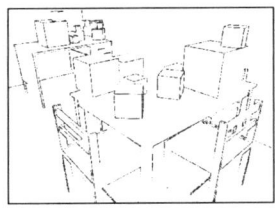

(a) Reference image   (b) Colour quality   (c) Geometric quality

Figure 1: (a) The reference image has been obtained with 8 rays per pixel. (b) Pixel colour $\mathbf{Q}^c$ and (c) geometric Q^g qualities corresponding to figure (a) are shown with temperature and gray scaled maps respectively.

4 Pixel contrast measures

In this section we present new pixel contrast measures based on pixel entropy. As the entropy represents the homogeneity of the information brought back by the rays crossing a pixel, we can define a simple measure which expresses the diversity or contrast of a pixel.

4.1 Pixel colour contrast

As we have seen, H_i^c represents the entropy or the degree of colour homogeneity of pixel i. From this measure, *pixel colour contrast* is defined by

$$C^c = 1 - Q^c = 1 - \frac{H^c}{\log N_p} \tag{13}$$

and represents the colour diversity or contrast of a pixel. Obviously, C^c ranges from 0 to 1.

We can also introduce the pixel binary contrast from minimum and maximum colour probabilities captured by this pixel. This measure is obtained from the binary entropy H_B^c of these values. So, *pixel colour binary contrast* is defined by

$$C_B^c = 1 - H_B^c \tag{14}$$

where $H_B^c = H(\frac{p_{\min}}{p_{\min}+p_{\max}}, \frac{p_{\max}}{p_{\min}+p_{\max}})$ and $p_{\min}$, $p_{\max}$ represent the probabilities corresponding to the minimum and maximum colours respectively. Obviously, H_B^c and C_B^c range between 0 and 1. This is a particular case of C^c because binary contrast only takes into account the minimum and maximum values. As we will see in our experiments, this binary measure yields more radical contrast than C^c.

Similarly to [8, 6, 13], we can obtain the global colour contrast of a pixel by averaging all the colour component contrasts weighted by their respective importances (colour average). This avoids oversampling on the areas with small colour values.

Considering all the colour components, we define the *global pixel colour contrast*

$$\mathbf{C}^c = \frac{\sum_{i=1}^n \alpha_i C_i^c \overline{c_i}}{\sum_{i=1}^n \alpha_i} \tag{15}$$

and the *global pixel colour binary contrast*

$$\mathbf{C}_B^c = \frac{\sum_{i=1}^n \alpha_i C_{Bi}^c \overline{c_i}}{\sum_{i=1}^n \alpha_i} \tag{16}$$

where the coefficients α_i weigh their respective colour component and $\overline{c_i}$ is the colour average (of component i) of all the pixel rays. In an RGB system, the colour contrast measures ($\mathbf{C}^{RGB}$ and $\mathbf{C}_B^{RGB}$) have three components with coefficients α_r, α_g and α_b. As in [8, 13], all the contrast measures calculated in this paper take $\alpha_r = 0.4$, $\alpha_g = 0.3$ and $\alpha_b = 0.6$ (see section 2).

In figures 2 and 3 we show different colour contrast temperature maps. These maps compare the heuristics (2) used in [13] (figures 2(b) and 3(b)) with measures $\mathbf{C}^c$ (figures 2(c) and 3(c)) and $\mathbf{C}_B^c$ (figures 2(d) and 3(d)). We can observe these measures present very good behaviour in critical areas (represented by warm colours) like object edges and shadow contours. With respect to figures 2(b) and 3(b), our measures are more discriminating, specially the binary contrast.

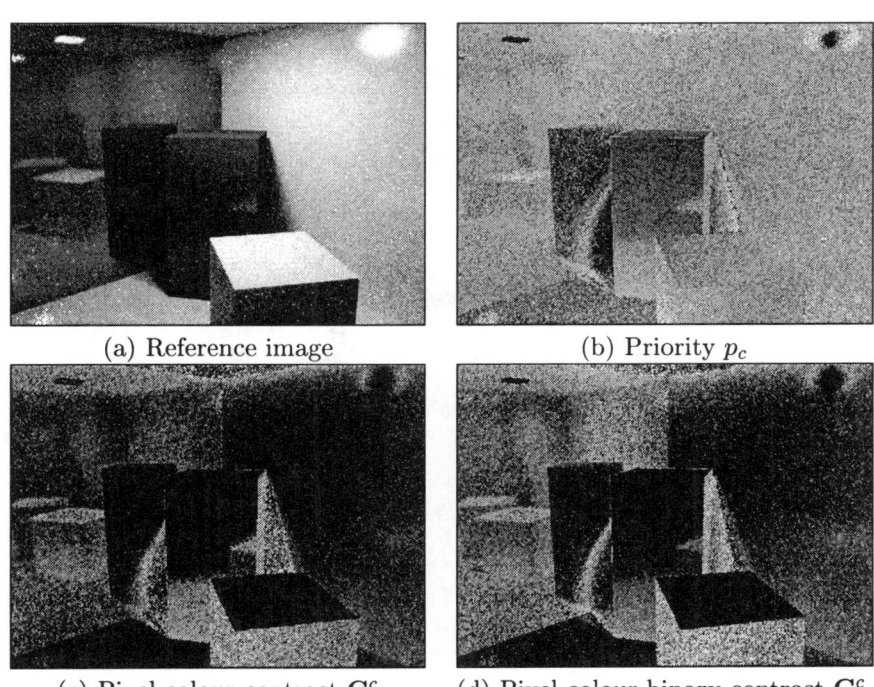

(a) Reference image (b) Priority p_c

(c) Pixel colour contrast $\mathbf{C}^c$ (d) Pixel colour binary contrast $\mathbf{C}_B^c$

Figure 2: The reference image (a) has been obtained with 8 rays per pixel. Temperature maps correspond to p_c (b), $\mathbf{C}^c$ (c), and $\mathbf{C}_B^c$ (d).

4.2 Pixel geometric contrast

As we have seen, H^g represents the entropy or the degree of geometric homogeneity of a pixel. From this measure, we define the *pixel geometric contrast* by

$$C^g = 1 - Q^g = 1 - \frac{H^g}{\log N_p} \tag{17}$$

Similarly to the above section, we introduce the pixel binary contrast from minimum and maximum geometric factor probabilities of this pixel. Thus,

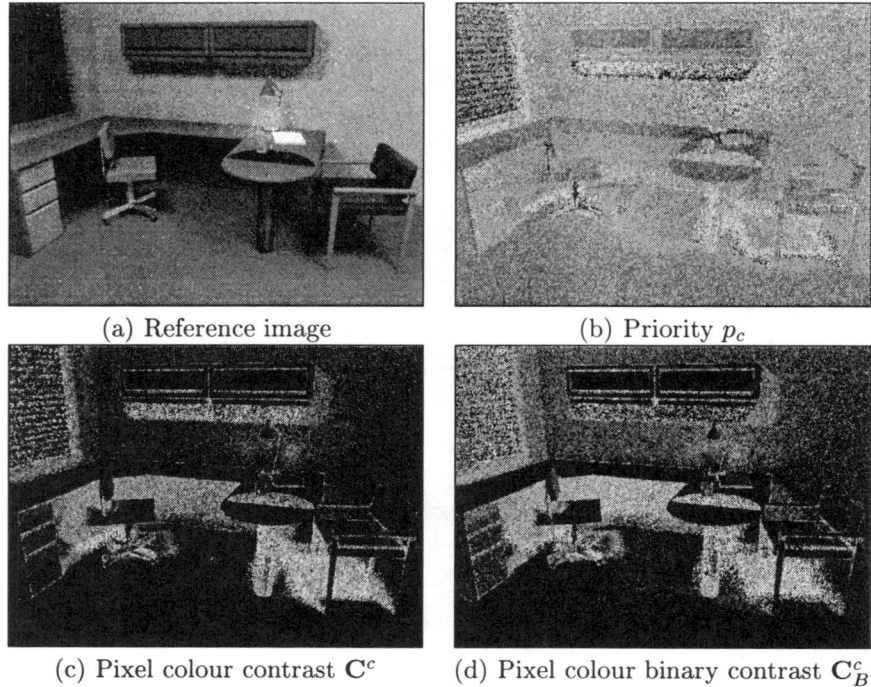

(a) Reference image (b) Priority p_c

(c) Pixel colour contrast $\mathbf{C}^c$ (d) Pixel colour binary contrast $\mathbf{C}^c_B$

Figure 3: The reference image (a) has been obtained with 8 rays per pixel. Temperature maps correspond to p_c (b), $\mathbf{C}^c$ (c), and $\mathbf{C}^c_B$ (d).

pixel binary contrast is given by

$$C^g_B = 1 - H^g_B \tag{18}$$

where $H^g_B = H(\frac{p_{\min}}{p_{\min}+p_{\max}}, \frac{p_{\max}}{p_{\min}+p_{\max}})$ is the binary entropy of the minimum and maximum geometric factor probabilities, $p_{\min}$ and $p_{\max}$.

A third case can also be considered, the *logarithmic difference contrast*,

$$C^g_L = \log p^{\max} - \log p^{\min} = \log \frac{p^{\max}}{p^{\min}} \tag{19}$$

where $p_{\min}$ and $p_{\max}$ are the minimum and maximum geometric factor probabilities of a pixel. This measure has been introduced in [11] and is based on the definition of the mutual information of a line. As we will see, C^g_L also shows a good behaviour.

In figures 4(a,b,c) and 5(a,b,c) we show different geometric contrast maps. These maps are compared with a depth difference heuristics (3) shown in figures 4(d) and 5(d). It can be seen that our measures capture the majority of edges because we take into account two components: distance and orientation.

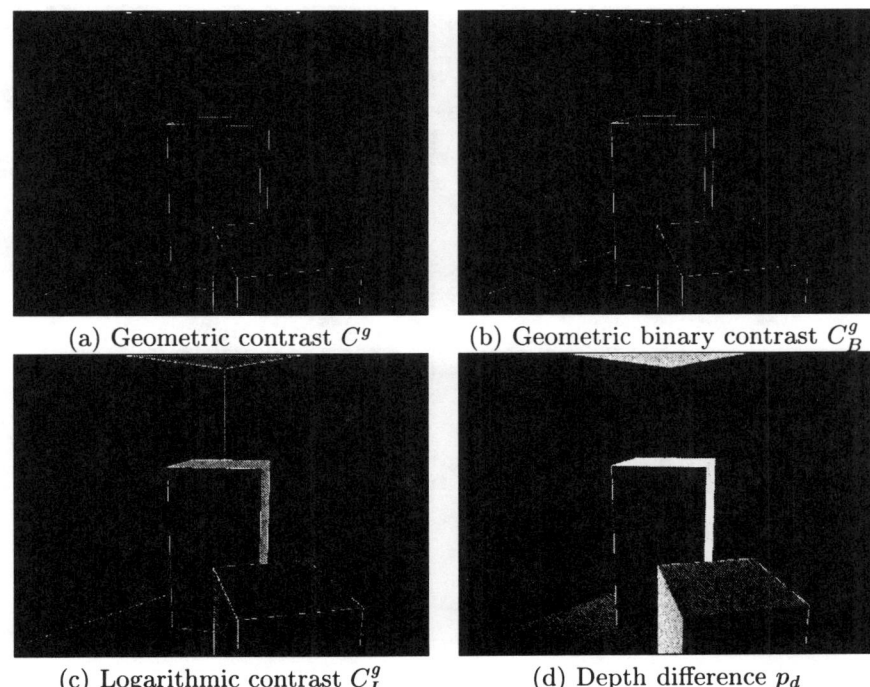

Figure 4: The reference image 2(a) has been obtained with 8 rays per pixel. Gray maps correspond to C^g (a), C^g_B (b), C^g_L, and p_d (d).

4.3 Pixel colour–geometry contrast

Finally, a combination of colour and geometric contrasts is considered. This combination enables us to graduate, with a coefficient δ between 0 and 1, the influence of both measures and is given by

$$\mathcal{C} = \delta \mathbf{C}^c + (1-\delta)C^g \qquad (20)$$

This combination can be made with any type of pixel colour contrast and geometric contrast. In general, good behaviour has been shown with binary contrasts (colour and geometric), and $\delta = \frac{1}{5}$.

In figure 6, we show two different combinations comparing priority values (figure 6(a)) to our measures (figure 6(b)).

5 Supersampling

In this section, we apply the new defined contrast measures to supersampling in stochastic ray tracing. A very simple supersampling technique, proportional

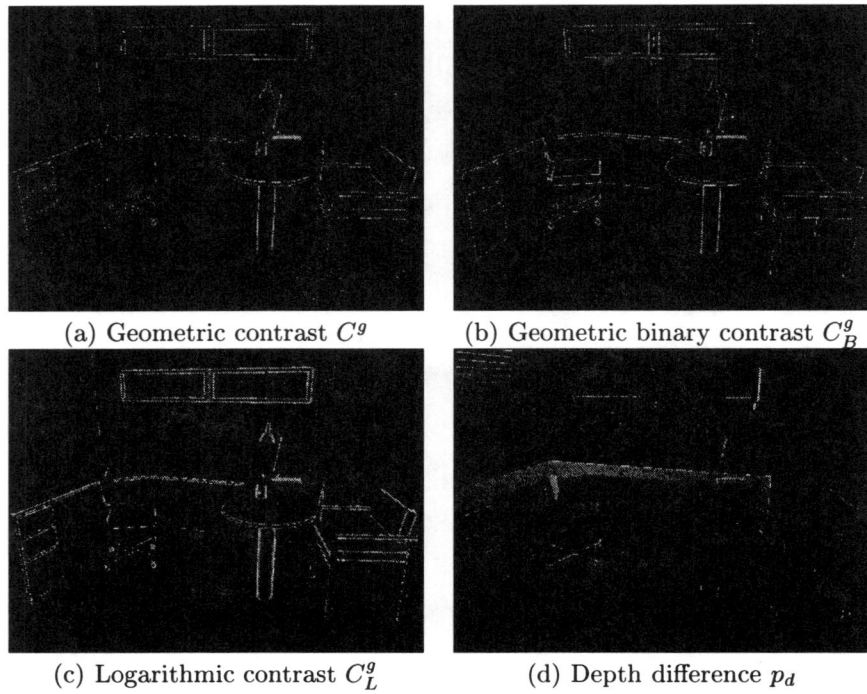

Figure 5: The reference image 3(a) has been obtained with 8 rays per pixel. Temperature maps correspond to C^g (a), C_B^g (b), C_L^g (c), and p_d (d).

to the respective temperature map, is used to show the behaviour of these measures.

In figure 7(a) we show a supersampling image obtained with an average of 32 rays per pixel in the following way. First, a uniform sampling with 8 rays per pixel has been made in order to obtain the temperature map of figure 7(b). And second, this map has been used in the supersampling process with an average of 24 rays per pixel. The contrast measure used is a colour and geometry combination with $\delta = 0.5$ based on binary contrasts. This means that the more critical the area, the more supersampled it is (warm colours), and the less critical, the more undersampled (cool colours, with a minimum of 8 rays per pixel). Two detail regions are compared from the supersampling image in figure 7(a) and a similar image obtained by uniform sampling with 32 rays per pixel: supersampling (figures 7(c,e)) and uniform sampling (figures 7(d,f)) images. We can observe a noise diminution in the supersampled regions, and a better representation of shadow contour and edges.

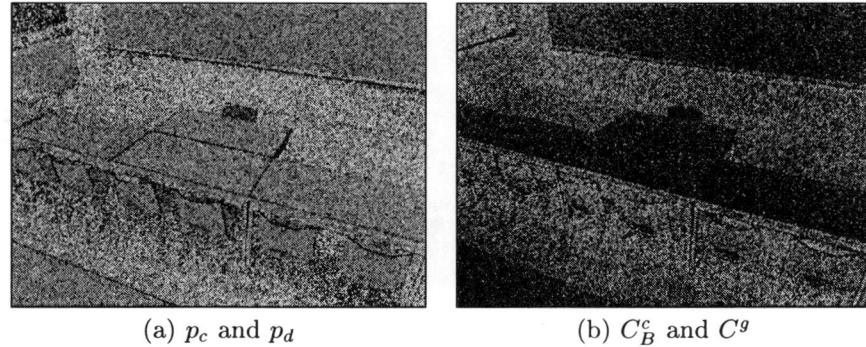

(a) p_c and p_d (b) C_B^c and C^g

Figure 6: Temperature maps of (a) p_c and p_d and (b) C_B^c and C^g with $\delta = 0.1$. The reference image has been obtained with only 4 rays per pixel.

6 Conclusions

We have defined Information Theory based measures for supersampling refinement. These measures show a very good behaviour in isolating the regions that need to be supersampled. This behaviour compares well with classic supersampling criteria. Our measures have been applied to pixel supersampling although they can be used for adaptive refinement, due to the additive properties of the entropy [3]. Our future work will be focused in this direction.

Acknowledgements

This project has been funded in part with grant numbers TIC-2001-2416-C03-01 of the Spanish Government and 2001-SGR-00296 of the Catalan Government. All the images have been obtained with the *RenderPark* [7] software and are available in *http://ima.udg.es/~rigau*. The reference scenes are from Francesc Castro (1, 7), Cornell University (2, 4), and Greg Ward (3, 5).

References

[1] R.E. Blahut. *Principles and Practice of Information Theory*. Addison-Wesley, 1987.

[2] Terrence M. Caelli. *Visual Perception: Theory and Practice*. Pergamon Press, Oxford, UK, 1981.

[3] T.M. Cover and J.A. Thomas. *Elements of Information Theory*. Wiley Series in Telecommunications, 1991.

[4] Lucia Darsa and Bruno Costa Silva. Multi-resolution representation and reconstruction of adaptively sampled images. In *Proceedings of IX*

Brazilian Symposium on Computer Graphics and Image Processing (SIB-GRAPI'96), pages 321–328, October 1996.

[5] Lucia Darsa, Bruno Costa Silva, and Amitabh Varshney. Navigating static environments using image-space simplification and morphing. *1997 Symposium on Interactive 3D Graphics*, pages 25–34, April 1997.

[6] A.S. Glassner. *Principles of Digital Image Synthesis*. Morgan Kaufmann Publishers, San Francisco (CA), USA, 1995.

[7] Computer Graphics Research Group. *RenderPark: A Photorealistic Rendering Tool*. Katholieke Universiteit Leuven, Leuven, Belgium, November 2000.

[8] Don P. Mitchell. Generating antialiased images at low sampling densities. *Computer Graphics (Proceedings of SIGGRAPH'87)*, 21(4):65–72, July 1987. Held in Anaheim (CA), USA.

[9] James Painter and Kenneth Sloan. Antialiased ray tracing by adaptive progressive refinement. *Computer Graphics (Proceedings of SIGGRAPH'89)*, 23(3):281–288, July 1989. Held in Boston (MA), USA.

[10] Kari Pulli, Michael F. Cohen, Tom Duchamp, Hugues Hoppe, Linda Shapiro, and Werner Stuetzle. View-based rendering: Visualizing real objects from scanned range and color data. In Julie Dorsey and Philipp Slusallek, editors, *Rendering Techniques'97 (Proceedings of the 8th Eurographics Workshop on Rendering)*, pages 23–34, New York (NY), USA, June 1997. Springer-Verlag Vienna-New York. Held in St. Etienne, France.

[11] Jaume Rigau, Miquel Feixas, Philippe Bekaert, and Mateu Sbert. View-dependent information theory measures for pixel sampling and scene discretization in flatland. In *Proceedings of Spring Conference on Computer Graphics'01*, pages 173–180, Los Alamitos (CA), USA, April 2001. IEEE Computer Society. Held in Budmerice, Slovak Republic.

[12] Jaume Rigau, Miquel Feixas, and Mateu Sbert. Information theory point measures in a scene. Research Report IIiA–00–08–RR, Institut d'Informàtica i Aplicacions, Universitat de Girona, Girona, Spain, 2000.

[13] Maryann Simmons and Carlo H. Séquin. Tapestry: A dynamic mesh-based display representation for interactive rendering. In Bernard Péroche and Holly Rushmeier, editors, *Rendering Techniques 2000 (Proceedings of the 11th Eurographics Workshop on Rendering)*, pages 329–340, New York (NY), USA, June 2000. Springer-Verlag Vienna-New York.

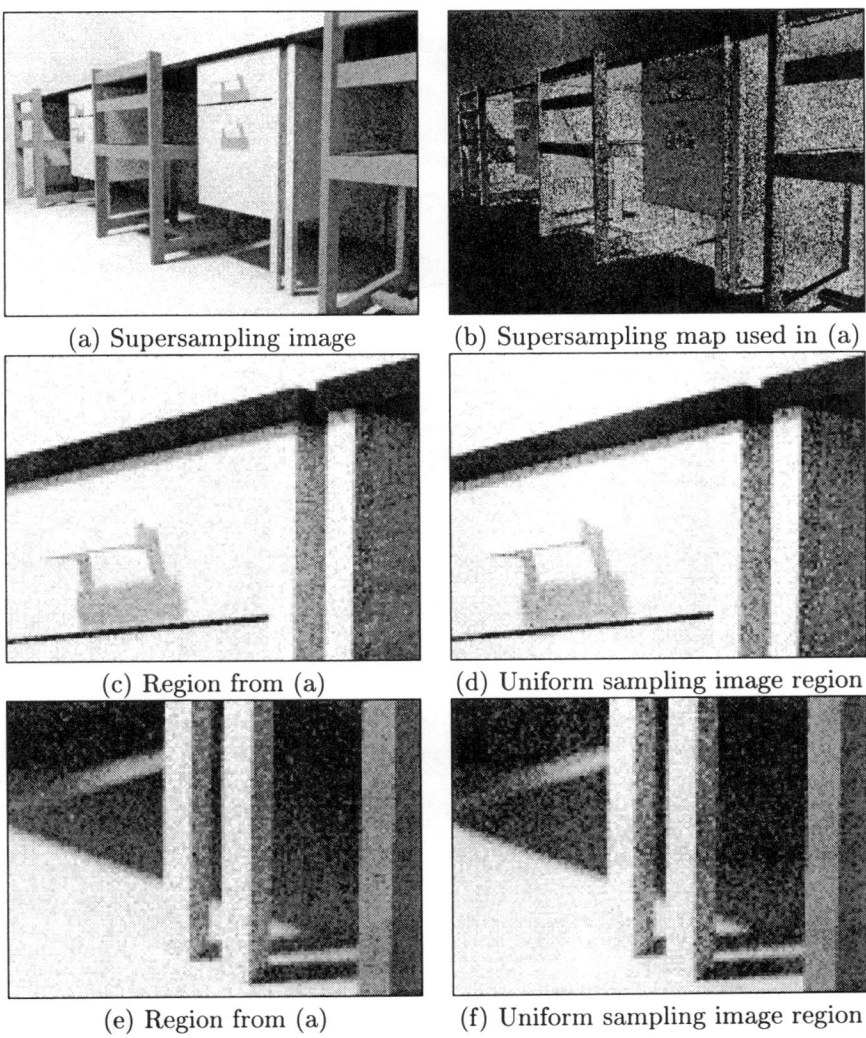

(a) Supersampling image (b) Supersampling map used in (a)

(c) Region from (a) (d) Uniform sampling image region

(e) Region from (a) (f) Uniform sampling image region

Figure 7: Supersampling image (a) with an average of 32 rays per pixel, obtained using the temperature map in (b), calculated with the first 8 rays. Detail regions from (a) are shown in (c) and (e). They are compared with the same regions, (d) and (f) respectively, taken from an uniform sampling image with 32 rays per pixel.

Visibility maps. A topological structure for fast antialiased ray tracing

J. Grasset, D. Plemenos, O. Terraz
University of Limoges, MSI laboratory
grasset@msi.unilim.fr, plemenos@unilim.fr, terraz@unilim.fr

Abstract

In this paper, a new method to get efficient antialiased ray tracing is presented. The proposed method is based on the use of a visibility map, a topological structure of the scene, depending on the point of view. After construction of the visibility map of a scene, simplified ray tracing is performed taking into account surfaces sharing an edge in a pixel, and producing highly antialiased images. The whole process, map construction and simplified ray tracing, is fast, compared to traditional ray casting algorithms.

Keywords: visibility maps, ray tracing, antialiasing.

1. Introduction

Visibility computation is widely used in computer graphics, from actual visibility determination to fields like form factors computation or shadowing. In this paper, we propose a construction method of a topological and vectorial structure storing the polygons or part of polygons seen from a given point of view. We describe a simple application – a fast antialiased raytracing, and then extensions and further works are proposed.

2. Previous works

Lots of visibility computations or hidden parts removal algorithms have been proposed, and various extensive surveys have been made, like [Dor94] for object-space methods, or [Dur00] on the whole research field. Some methods use sampling (for instance, the classic Z-Buffer [Cat74], A-Buffer [Car84], ray-casting [App68] and ray-tracing [Whi80]), and work in image-space. The aim is to compute what is seen in each pixel of the image. These approaches are usually quite robust and easy to implement. Their main drawback is that some artefacts may occur because of lack of precision. Others methods use object-precision computations, like in [WA77], [HH84] or [TA98], and compute sets of visible polygons. This improves the precision of the result, but there are usually problems of numerical approximations.

Some of these visibility computations benefit, or even require, that polygons are processed in depth order. A good way to get this sort is to use a BSP tree, proposed by [FKN79]. This method computes an *a priori* depth sort, in a pre-processing stage. Then the order of polygons for a specific viewpoint is obtain by a simple tree traversal. Improvements have been proposed to reduce the number of polygons splits, i.e. the final size of the tree, for instance in [CW96].

A mathematical description of the topological structure used can be found – among others - in [Lie91]. A study on Boolean operations between maps using half-edges labelling, related to the way the visibility is computed by the method presented here, have been proposed in [Caz96].

3. Visibility map

3.1 Map constructing

The structure we use is a map, made of half-edges connected by α_0 and α_1 links.

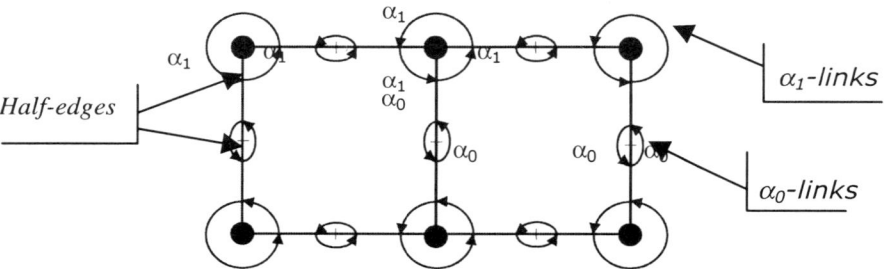

Figure 1 : *a map.*

The figure 1 shows a map example. Edges are –naturally- made of two half-edges connected by an α_0-link, and they are joined to make a vertex by α_1-links. These α_1-links are in trigonometric ordering.

The visibility map is built in several stages :
- depth sorting of the polygons of the scene, for the current viewpoint
- projection of these polygons into the viewing plane
- determination of every « full inclusion » among all the projected polygons
- computation of all the intersections between segments in the viewing plane, topological organisation from the resulting intersections, and labelling
- hidden edge removal according to labels
- search for inclusion between the sets of connected faces

3.2 Depth sort and first including search

Since the depth sort of the polygons of the scene is modified each time the position of the camera changes, it is interesting to use a BSP tree. Sorting the polygons is then achieved with a simple tree traversal, which is very fast. The polygons are affected a number that is their rank in the sort and that we call, abusively, their depth. The higher the depth is, the further the polygon is (or is supposed to be) from the camera.

Once the polygons are arranged in depth order and numbered, they are projected into the viewing plane. Each projected polygon inherits the depth of the related scene polygon : we use the word depth for these polygons too, even if they are all in the viewing plane. They are stored as faces of the map. The half-edges of each face are labelled with the depth number of the face. At this time, the faces are all independent, with a unique label : this can be represented as a set of layers whose rank number is the depth of the face it supports.

When all the faces have been created, the first step is to search for all the existing « full inclusions », i.e. all the cases where a face is wholly in another one (possibly sharing edges or part of edges and vertices). For such inclusion, the option is :
- If the included face is deeper than the including one, it is removed from the list of faces to process. It is, in fact, the projection of a polygon of the scene hidden by another one. So it is a face we are not interested in, since we are searching for visible parts of the scene.
- If the including face is deeper than the included one, both faces are kept and the inclusion is stored in the topological structure (figure 2).

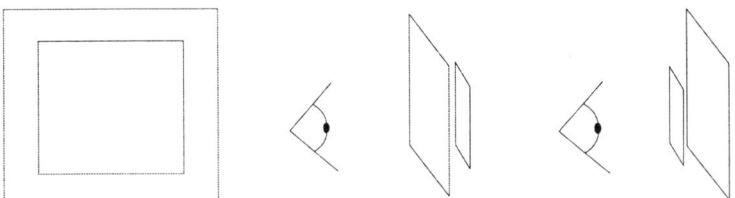

Figure 2 : *an inclusion and its two possible interpretations.*

3.3 Computation of segments intersections

It is mainly on this stage that the map is built. The aim is to determine the way the faces are connected, so it is necessary to find every intersection or superposition between edges. The different situations are (figure 3):
- point intersection between two interiors (meaning segments except their ends)
- segment intersection between colinear segments, i.e. situations of superposition.
- point intersection occurring on existing vertices, these may be superposition of two vertices or inclusions of a vertex in a an interior.

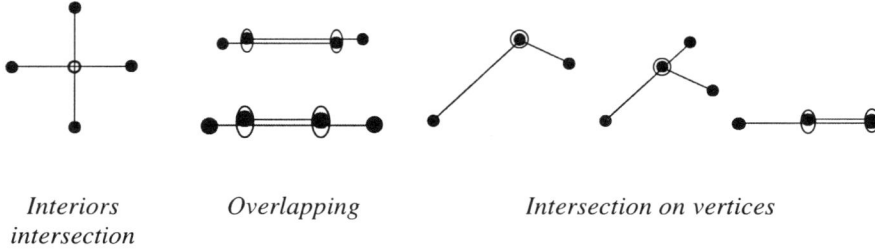

Interiors   Overlapping   Intersection on vertices
intersection

Figure 3 : *examples of intersections*

For each of these configurations, specific operations have to be done to create a correct map. Superposition results in half-edges removal, and vertices creation or merging leads to α_1-link creation or update. All the suppression operations have to insure that no depth information needed for the following steps is lost.

Depth labels are maintained according to inheritance rules applied when half-edges are merged (and, by the way, suppressed) or created. Because we are looking for visible polygons only, when two half-edges are merged the depth label given to the result is the smallest one : it is related to a closer part of the scene than the other half-edge. When there is a creation, the approach is to take into account that an edge is a border between two half-planes whose depths are given by the half edges. So, determining the depth label of a newly created half-edge is the same as searching the depth of the area it is associated with : that is what is actually done. For instance, to deal with a point intersection between two interiors, we first compute the depth of the area in each « quadrant » from the depth of the four previous half-planes, and this way we obtain the correct half-edges labels (figure 4).

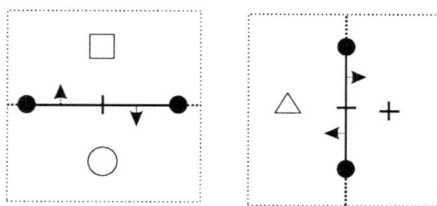 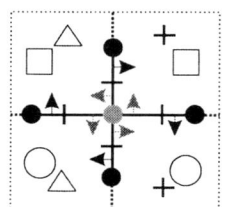

Intersecting edges, represented each on one layer. The half-planes that they separate are marked with symbols (actually these are depth labels, given by half-edges).

The intersection has been processed. Each « quadrant » inherits of two half-planes ; the new half-edges are labelled according to them.

Figure 4 : *labels determination for newly created half-edges.*

3.4 Hidden edges removal

When all the intersections have been detected and the topological operations have been done, the map is correct. In particular, there are no pending edges, all the faces are well-defined. So the next step is to give each face its depth label, according to the depth labels of the half-edges related to it. The rule is very simple : the label of the face is the smallest of its half-edges labels. In fact, summing up the half-edges labels gives a set of layers describing the face, and we are looking for the upper one. It is important to notice that this set of layers is not complete, some of them may be missing because of previous edges merging, but the depth labels inheritance rules guarantee that the upper layer is the correct one.

Once all the faces are labelled, all the half-edges are given the label of the face they are related to. The hidden edges removal is simply the removal of all the edges whose two half-edges have the same depth label. These suppressions of edges are followed by topological updates. In fact, if the two half-edges of an edge have the same depth label, it means that the same polygon is seen of the both side (because the « depth » is the rank in the depth order and is unique). Consequently, it means that the edge is hidden by the polygon.

3.5 Final inclusions determination

After the removal of hidden edges, some faces may have become included in other ones. It is necessary to look for such situations, whether to suppress included faces (if they are hidden) or to store this inclusion into the topological structure. This research is fasten by the topological data. Actually, we only have to find inclusion between connected sets. To do this, some properties are useful :
- there is no intersection between the connected sets,
- as a result : if a point of a connected set C_1 is inside a connected set C_2 it means that C_1 is wholly inside C_2.
- and more precisely : if a connected set C_1 is inside a connected set C_2 it means that C_1 is wholly included in a single face of C_2
- for two connected sets C_1 and C_2, only the following cases have to be tested :
  - an inclusion of C_1 in C_2 : it is enough to check if a point of C_1 is inside C_2
  - an inclusion of C_2 in C_1 : the same kind of test can be made.
  - Independency of C_1 and C_2.

Configurations with no inclusion are detected very quickly. At the opposite, if a connected set is inside another one, it is necessary to find in which face is the inclusion. This process is longer, but once again it is enough to check a point of the included set with each face until the including one is found.

When an inclusion is detected, all the faces in the included connected set that have a higher depth label than the including face are removed : they are hidden. The faces that have a lower depth label are to be kept and are stored in the map.

After this step, the creation visibility map is completed.

3.6 Computation times

The table below presents a few results, but for some implementation reasons, (mainly disk swapping) larger scenes are not processed in significant times yet.

Scene	Number of polygons	Visibility map creation
Test 1	757	3.6 s
Test 2	1200	8.2 s
Test 3	3333	81 s
Test 4	5140	254 s

Table 1 : First results on some test scenes.

The number of polygons given here is the one produced by the BSP tree.

Figure 5 : some test scenes.

3.7 Discussion

Inclusions and intersections determination require numeric approximations. For instance, a threshold value is used to decide if two vertices are overlapping. There is the same problem to decide whether a point is in a segment or not, and more generally to resolve which type of intersection is detected (for example, to decide if a segment is inside another one or if if is the same segment). Since topological operations are different according to the type of the intersection, these approximations have to be processed very carefully.

As a good result of the accuracy needed for these geometric operations, the topological structure offers interesting properties. Pending edges, no faces reduced to a point or to an edge, no crossed face, etc... are avoided. These features are important for the easiness of development and the stability of the applications that use the visibility map.

The computation times given here can be highly improved by the use of better algorithms for segments intersections and inclusions detections. It would be better too to compute at the same time intersections and inclusions, because some operations are performed twice.

4. Accelerated ray tracing from the visibility map

4.1 Main costs of classic raytracing

We focus on scenes made of non reflecting opaque polygons, so classic raytracing is restricted to these conditions.

For such scenes, raytracing has to search for the closest polygon each ray hits. The usual way to do so is to check the intersection of each ray with every polygon of the scene. This is the highest time cost for large scenes.

Antialiasing is needed to improve visual quality of raytraced pictures. If a pixel of the screen contains the image of more than one polygon – usually two for the edges -, the aim is to find the percentage of the pixel showing each polygon. The raytracing method to do this is supersampling ([Mit87]), meaning the division of pixels into subpixels : the pixel color is the average of the colors of its subpixels. The precision depends on the subdivision rate : nine or sixteen subpixels are usually used. This process is expensive because of the high number of rays it needs to cast.

4.2 Benefits of the visibility map for raytracing

The visibility map offers a very important gain in computation time for ray tracing. The polygon hit by each ray is known immediately. The cost of the intersections research is minimal: it is enough to compute the intersection point of the ray with the hit polygon. The position of the edges and the polygons that they separate are given by the map too : the antialiasing can be done quickly and efficiently.

With the map, the computation time for raytracing depends on the number of activated pixels in the image and on the light model used. In the classic approach, its depends also on the number of polygons of the scene : for the map-based method, this factor occurs only during the map creation.

4.3 Image of the map

To be able to quickly use the data it contains, the visibility map is drawn in a grid that has the same dimensions as the image to be processed. The elements of the grid are structures that includes :
- the identifier of the polygon lying « before » the edge (according to the raytracing sweeping),
- the identifier of the polygon lying after the edge
- the percentage of the pixel covered by each of these polygons.

This image of the edges of the visibility map is drawn using a scan-line algorithm. For each line, the ordered active edges list is updated easily because there can only be insertion or suppression as there is no more intersection that would lead to edges swap. Then the grid elements that are on the real edge, even « very slightly », are activated. Consequently, the image of the edges seems thicker than if it was drawn by usual algorithms (the Bresenham's one for instance).

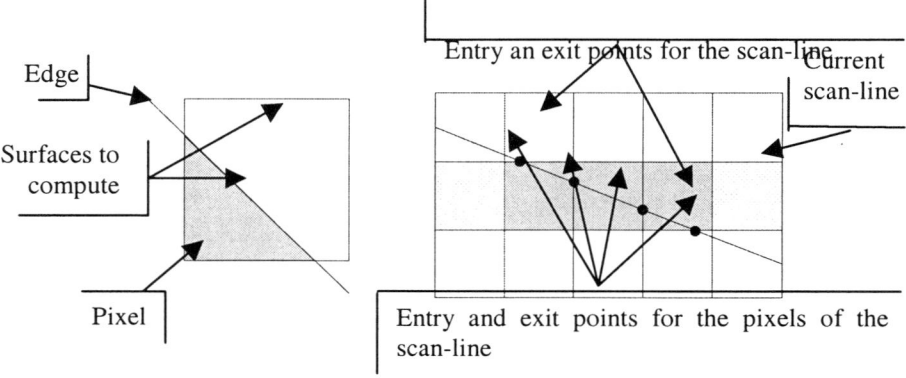

Figure 6 : *Antialiasing – Case of a pixel (left) and case of a scan-line (right).*

To get the percentage of each polygon in a pixel, the area of the pixel lying before the edge (of after, that is the complementary) is computed. To do this, it is assumed that the scan-line has a thickness of 1 (meaning its height is one pixel), and the point where the real edge enters in it and the point where it exits are computed. In this interval of the scan-line, all the grid elements have to be updated : for each one the entry point and the exit point are defined, and then the corresponding surface is processed.

The entry and exit points determination is incremental, the difference between these points corresponds to the slope of the edge.

4.4 Raytracing

The raytracing is done by scanning at the same time the image of the vibility map and the pixel grid. The image of the map gives information about the current polygon, that is the polygon hit by the current ray. This is updated each time an edge is crossed. If the current pixel is the image of an edge, a ray is shot to each of the two polygons, and the final color is the average of the corresponding colors wheighted by the percentage stored in the image of the map.

The vertices of the map require a particular operation. For each of them, the area of every part of polygon visible in it is precisely computed. A ray is casted for each of these areas, and the pixel color is the weighted average of the colors obtained by these rays.

4.5 Results

For the reason mentioned in section III.6, no significant results can be presented for larger scenes. Nevertheless, the few examples below show clearly the benefit of the map, and the interest of not to depend on scene polygons number when rendering.

The rendering parameters (camera position, light models...) are the same for both raytracings. The image resolution is 800×600 pixels. The classic ray-tracing implemented here only use the BSP tree for the optimisation. The comparison with other optimisation must be done (with bounding boxes hierarchy for instance).

Scene	Number of polygons	Map creation	Raytracing on map	Classic raytracing
Test 1	400	1.8s	3.4s	116s
Test 2	750	3.6s	10.5s	511s
Test 3	1200	8.2s	9.4s	714s

Table 2 : rendering times

4.6 Discussion

The computation times are much shorter than with classic raytracing, even if the construction of the visibility map is included. If a set of renderings are done from the same viewpoint, in which cases the visibility map does not change, the proposed structure makes possible to perform several ray tracing renderings in reasonable times. This can be applied to change the image size, to crop it, to modify some objects colors, etc..., and to view the results quite quickly.

On the other hand, some raytracing features are not preserved in our approach. It is not possible to cope with refractions or non polygonal objects, because for these applications it would be necessary to use non polygonal faces in the map. Some other features are not yet implemented or have not been wholly studied, but they can be included in the map, like, for instance, reflections, discussed in the next section.

Topological data allow an efficient antialising, with a very good visual quality, because it stores the polygons lying on both sides of each edge. Nevertheless some improvements have to be done. The first one is about configurations where two edges or more cross a pixel. In such cases our algorithm is currently incomplete. The second one is about the interest of some very precise computations. Actually, surfaces of polygons inside a single pixel are processed very carefully, and these values are used to weight averages of colors. But the colors themselves are approximations : they are processed as if there was only one color on the part of the polygon seen in the pixel, and that is wrong. So it would be interesting to study which approximations are visually reasonable for the surfaces computations, to fasten and simplify the antialiasing from the map.

The main drawback of the proposed method is the programming complexity and the large structure needed. These are, unfortunately, intrinsic features, that cannot be basically improved.

5. Extensions – Others applications

5.1 Labelling extension

We have proposed an hidden surfaces removal based on labelling, dedicated to scenes made of opaque, non reflecting, polygons. As already mentioned, if this approach is thought to as the interpretation of a set of labelled layers, the aim is to find which layer is on top. That is why in some of the previously described processes, only the closest elements are kept. On the other hand, if polygons were transparent, it would necessary to maintain data on all the layers contributing to a face of the map. So, to extend our approach we need to store lists of labels, and to have such a list for every half-edge. The main changes in the algorithm would be the following :
- when edges overlap, the remaining half-edges inherit all the labels of the merged half-edges
- for newly created half-edges, each of them inherits all the labels of the half-plane it is related to
- the final labelling of the faces of the visibility map is done by merging all the labels lists of its half-edges

This labelling extension causes problems to be studied, mainly due to the memory cost of such a structure.

5.2 Applications

The visibility map, as presented here, can be used for other applications than ray tracing. We are studying its use for fields where the understanding of which part of the scene a part of an image is related to is important. These may be user helps, or computer vision for instance.

The extension that we introduced, with the description of all the layers contributing to a face, makes possible to take into account scenes with transparency, reflections, or shadows. This can be apply to produce richer pictures in rendering based on a visibily map. Non-photorealistic rendering may benefit too of the precise knowledge of edges or shadows areas.

6. Conclusion

We have introduced an approach to create a topological structure representing the projection of the visible parts of a three-dimensional scene, for a given viewpoint. This structure is called visibility map. We have proposed an application to a accelerated raytracing, with efficient antialiasing.

The main research perspectives are the labelling extension -to take into account transparency, reflection or shadow-, the study of other types of rendering, and the use of a visibility map in understanding of scenes or pictures.

References

[App68] A.Appel *"Some techniques for shading machine rendering of solids"*, AFIPS 1968 Spring Joint Computer Conference, volume 32, 1968.

[Car84] L.Carpenter *"The A-Buffer, an antialiased hidden surface removal method"*, Computer Graphics (SIGGRAPH'84 proceedings), 1984

[Cat74] E.E.Catmull *"A subdivision algorithm for computer display of curved surfaces"*, Ph.d. thesis, 1974

[Caz96] D.Cazier *Opérations booléennes entre cartes topologiques* Ph.D. thesis, Strasbourg University, 1996

[CW96] H.M.Chen, W.T.Wang *"The feudal prioriy algorithm on hidden-surface removal"*, Computer Graphics, 1996

[Dor94] S.Dorward *"A survey of object-space hidden surface removal"*, International Journal of Computational Geometry and Applications, 1994

[Dur00] F.Durand *"A multidisciplinary Survey of Visibility"*, SIGGRAPH'2000 courses notes, 2000

[FKN79] H. Fuchs, Z. M. Kedem, B. F. Naylor *"On visible surfaces generation by a priori tree structures"*, ACM 1979.

[HH84] P.S.Heckbert, P.Hanrahan *"Beam tracing polygonal objects"*, Computer Graphics (SIGGRAPH'84 proceedings), 1984

[Lie91] P.Lienhardt *"Topological models for boundary representation : a comparison with n-dimensional generalized maps"* Computer-Aided Design, vol 23, n°1, 1991

[Mit87] D.P.Mitchell *"Generating antialiased images at low sampling densities"* Computer Graphics (SIGGRAPH '87 proceeding, Jul. 1987).

[TA98] S.Teller, J.Alex *"Frustrum casting for progressive interactive rendering"*, Technical Report TR-740, MIT, 1998

[WA77] K. Weiler, P. Atherton *"Hidden surface removal using polygon area sorting"*, , SIGGRAPH, ACM Computer Graphics, 1977.

[Whi80] T.Whitted *"An improved illumination model for shaded display"*, CACM, 1980

Realtime Shading of Folded Surfaces

B.Ganster   R. Klein   M. Sattler   R. Sarlette

{ganster, rk, sattler, sarlette}@cs.uni-bonn.de

University of Bonn
Institute of Computer Science II
Computer Graphics
Römerstrasse 164
53117 Bonn, Germany

Abstract

In this paper we present a new, simple, and efficient way to illuminate folded surfaces with extended light sources in realtime including shadows. In a preprocessing step we compute the parts of the surrounding environment that are visible from a set of points on the surface and represent this information in a binary visibility map.
The illumination of the scene, i.e., incoming light from different directions, is encoded in an environment map. This way, extended light sources and complex illumination conditions of the surface can be simulated. The binary visibility information stored in the visibility maps is used during runtime to calculate the incoming and outgoing radiance in the direction of the viewer for each sample point. Various reflection models like the Phong or Lafortune model can be incorporated into these calculations. After computing the radiance values in each sample point, the surface is shaded using simple Gouraud interpolation.
Using the pre-computed visibility information, the whole shading and even the change of lighting conditions can be simulated in realtime by modifying the environment map. As an extension to the environment map we support additional point light sources whose parameters and positions can also be manipulated in realtime. Several examples of mesh illumination and shading are demonstrated.

keywords: folded surfaces, cloth shading, shadowing, illumination

1 Introduction & previous work

In this work we aim at real time shading of surfaces such as cloth, which possibly contain holes and complex folds, under realistic illumination conditions. The surface is given as a triangle mesh. The appearance of a surface point is given by the radiance leaving the point in the direction of the viewer. According to the rendering equation [8, 12], this radiance is obtained by integrating the incoming radiance over all incoming directions at the vertex v. These directions are typically represented by a hemisphere, $H(v)$, centered around v's surface normal.

The problem of shading folded surfaces, especially cloth, was addressed by Stewart [1]. The main idea of his algorithm is a preprocessing step, which computes 3D *visibility cones* for each vertex point, which are used to determine the parts of the environment "seen" by this point. The cones are stored for each vertex and used to evaluate the direct primary irradiance at runtime by doing several intersection tests. The local illumination model described in [9] is used to calculate the resulting irradiance value.

Stewart reduces the calculation of the 3D visibility cones to a number of 2D visibility computations by slicing a polygonal mesh with parallel planes. If the illumination comes from a point light source, it is sufficient to test whether the point lies in the visibility cone. If a uniform diffuse area light source illuminates the surface, the area light source is intersected with the visibility cone and a contour integral around the boundary of the part of the source inside the cone yields the direct primary irradiance [4]. If the surface is illuminated by a uniform diffuse spherical source that surrounds the surface, a contour integral can be applied to the boundary of the visibility cone in the same manner as that of the area source. Although the results presented by Stewart are convincing, the necessary computation of intersection areas and the evaluation of the integrals prevent the use of complex shaped light sources and changing lighting conditions in real time. To overcome these problems we propose to use *binary visibility maps* instead of the Stewart's visibility cones. These binary visibility maps are computed in a preprocessing step as follows: we proceed by considering a finite set of directions on the hemisphere $H(v)$ belonging to a vertex v. For each such direction we determine whether the environment is visible or occluded by the surface, and accordingly set the binary value at the corresponding position in the visibility map. Following the work of Stewart [1] we neglect the incoming light from directions occluded by the surface itself. Only light from directions in which the outside environment is visible contributes to the radiance of a surface point. To discretize the directions we evaluated three different models: a hemicube, a single plane and a subdivision of the hemisphere into rectangles using spherical coordinates. This way, we can accurately handle all extended light sources whose projection onto the hemisphere, the hemicube or the single plane can be approximated with sufficient accuracy by the visibility map. To illuminate the surface we encode realistic lighting conditions in a global environment map. During the rendering process, the radiance values stored in this environment map are used to calculate the outgoing radiance in direction of the viewer for each vertex of the mesh. For the computation various reflectance models of the surface can be applied. The next section contains an overview over the algorithm. Section 3 deals with the preprocessing phase, explains the visibility tests and the methods and models that were used. The rendering part is explained in section 4. In section 5 benchmarks of the preprocessing step and the rendering are presented.

Example images can be found in the appendix.

2 Algorithm outline

This section gives a brief outline of our algorithm:

- Preprocessing
    - For each vertex v of the mesh we compute the visibility map by rendering the scene using v as eye point and the normal n of the mesh in v as viewing direction. Pixels of the visibility map not covered by the mesh encode their corresponding direction in the hemisphere.
    - The visibility maps are computed and stored for each vertex.
- At runtime
    - The radiance with respect to the observers' position is calculated for each vertex using a standard reflection model. The vertex visibility map is used to determine whether the radiance from a certain direction contributes to its radiance value.
    - The positions of point light sources are transformed into the coordinate system of the visibility map. It is subsequently decided whether the point light source contributes to the illumination of the vertex or not. This can easily be performed using the visibility map.
    - Finally, we assign the calculated radiance values to their vertices and perform a Gouraud interpolation.

3 Preprocessing

During the preprocessing phase we generate the visibility maps for each vertex of the mesh.

3.1 Computation of visibility maps

We compare three different ways to encode a visibility map: the hemicube [2], a single plane [3] and the hemisphere discretized into a rectangular grid. To obtain the visibility map in a vertex v the mesh is projected by a central projection with center v to one of these models (see figure 2). The hemicube, the hemisphere and the single plane are centered around v's surface normal n. The single plane is oriented perpendicularly to n. If the environment cannot be seen in a certain direction, the visibility of this direction in the visibility map is set to the RGB value $(0, 0, 0)$, otherwise the direction itself is encoded in an RGB value. As we restrict ourselves to a cube model of the environment map, the RGB value (x, y, n) is given by the x and y coordinate

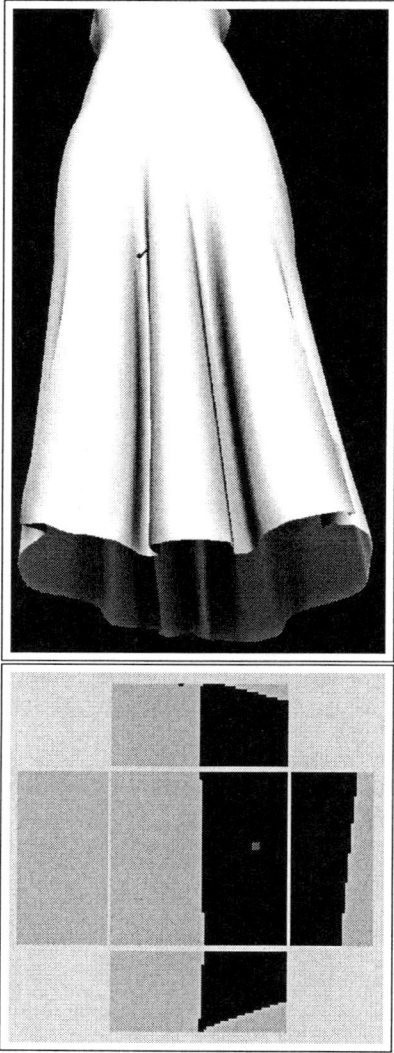

Figure No 1: Visibility test. The top image shows the mesh with a vertex (blue dot) inside a fold. The vertex is marked by its red normal. The bottom image shows the visibility map of this vertex. The model used for the visibility map is a hemicube with a resolution of 64×64 pixels for the top side of the cube and 64×32 for the sides. The figure shows the unfolded hemicube. For simplicity in this picture the directions in which the environment can be seen are coded by black and not by the direction itself. The directions where the environment cannot be seen are drawn in green. The red dot shows a projected point light source. In this example the light source can be seen by the specified vertex. Therefore the vertex is lit.

in the picture of the n-th side of the cube of the environment map. The numbering of the sides is as follows: The top face is numbered 0, the bottom face 5, the front face 1, the right face 2, the back face 3 and the left face 4.

Figure 1 shows a sample mesh and the corresponding visibility map for one vertex. A hemicube model is used with a resolution of 64×64 for the top and 64×32 for the sides. The top image shows the mesh with a vertex (blue dot) inside a fold. The vertex is marked by its red normal. The bottom image shows the unfolded hemicube for the above mentioned vertex. For simplicity in this picture the directions in which the environment can be seen are coded by black and not by the direction itself. The directions where the environment cannot be seen are drawn in green. The red dot shows a projected point light source. In this example the light source can be seen by the specified vertex. Therefore the vertex is lit.

The resolution of the visibility maps is $n \times m$. We experimented with values $n, m \in [4, 256]$. The resolution can be defined by the user. For good results we recommend $n \times m \geq 64$, as the possible resolution of the outgoing radiance in a vertex is limited by this number in case of diffuse lighting of the environment. For a resolution less than 64 this results in blotchy images. The central projection for all three models can be computed using standard ray tracing. For the hemicube and the single plane standard OpenGL rendering can be applied. However, using standard OpenGL rendering to project the mesh onto the sphere is complicated and involves specific hard to implement clipping steps. Details on this can be found in [10].

For a static mesh the visibility map is fixed and is stored together with the coordinates and the material parameters (reflectance parameters) of a point.

3.2 Comparison of Methods

Let **v** be the vertex of the mesh we determine the visibility map for. We evaluated the following methods for generating the visibility maps.

1. *OpenGL-Rendering*: We rendered the mesh using a triangle stripped display list of all triangles in the mesh.

2. *OpenGL-Rendering with triangle pre-selection*: In a first step, all triangles of the mesh are sorted into a three-dimensional grid. Then, triangle strips are generated for all triangles contained in a certain cell using a straightforward stripping algorithm. Finally, the triangle strips are stored in display lists. During the rendering of the mesh, we call the display lists of only those voxels that are within a given distance from the vertex **v**. This distance is given in units of the maximum dimension of the mesh. See table 1.

3. *Raytracer*: For every discretized direction of the visibility map we test all triangles of the mesh for an intersection with the ray leaving the point in that direction.

Method	Model	Resolution	Running time (sec)	Distance (ums)
Triangle Rasterizer	HC	8x8	28.4	2.0
	HC	16x16	30.0	
	SP	8x8	4.3	
	SP	16x16	5.0	
	HS	16x4	51.5	
	HS	32x8	54.7	
Triangle Rasterizer with triangle preselection	HC	8x8	15.2	1/6
	HC	16x16	17.0	
	SP	8x8	3.1	
	SP	16x16	3.7	
	HS	16x4	15.0	
	HS	32x8	20.6	
Raytracer with triangle preselection	HC	8x8	120.0	1/6
	HC	16x16	457.9	
	SP	8x8	32.2	
	SP	16x16	104.3	
	HS	16x4	33.3	
	HS	32x8	110.6	
Raytracer with grid traversal	HC	8x8	27.1	2.0
	HC	16x16	103.8	
	SP	8x8	9.3	
	SP	16x16	46.1	
	HS	16x4	7.2	
	HS	32x8	26.8	

Table No 1: Overview of the running times of the visibility calculation routines. Abbreviations used: HC= hemicube, SP= single plane, HS= hemisphere. UMS=units of mesh size.

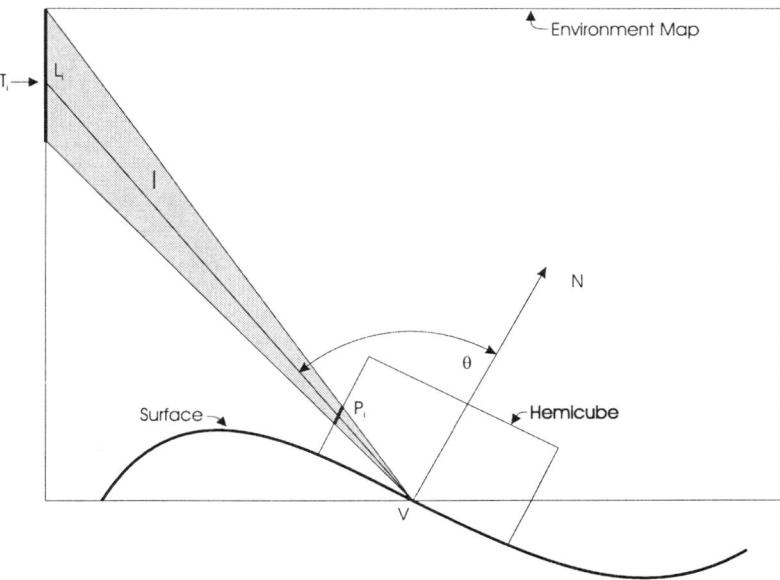

Figure No 2: The mapping between the *binary visibility* map of vertex v and the global environment map T_i is encoded in each pixel P_i of the visibility map itself. The environment patch T_i emits L_i in the direction I. θ is the angle between the surface normal N in v and the direction I of the incoming radiance. For simplicity, only a side view is shown.

4. *Raytracer with triangle preselection*: Similarly to OpenGL rendering with triangle pre-selection, we sort all triangles of the mesh into a three-dimensional grid and test only triangles in gris cells close to **v**.

5. *Raytracer with grid traversal*: We test only triangles lying in grid cells passed by the ray.

Table 1 summarizes the run times for all combinations of methods and models. The computations were performed on an Intel Celeron 800 MHz machine with a NVIDIA TNT2 graphics card. To evaluate the core speed of the visibility calculation routines, we do not include the rendering of the environment map into the measurements, i.e. we do not encode the directions. The table demonstrates quite clearly that OpenGL rendering with triangle preselection in singleplane mode and raytracer with grid traversal in hemisphere mode are the fastest techniques for the preprocessing step.

The singleplane model is efficient, however it has the disadvantage that the aperture angle must be less than 180 degrees, so only part of the half space is evaluated.

Therefore, the model may miss some small folds.

Using the Hemicube model is relatively slow compared to the singleplane model, because five pictures must be rendered for each point (the other models only need to render one image). On the other hand, it is more accurate than the single plane model and in contrast to the hemisphere it can be hardware-accelerated.

The table also shows that the OpenGL runtime only slightly depends on the resolution of the images that are generated. The situation is radically different in case of the raytracer, the double resolution needs twice as many rays.

4 Realtime Rendering

During the realtime rendering the outgoing radiances have to be computed for every vertex of the mesh.

4.1 Illuminating the surface using an environment map

As already mentioned, we restrict ourselves to cube maps. For the results the 24bit RGB pictures are generated by hand (see Appendix). For real applications they can be generated using high dynamic range images from the real world environments. The resolution of the environment map is adapted to the resolution of the visibility map in such a way that one texel in the environment map corresponds to approximately one pixel of our visibility map.

4.1.1 Calculating the outgoing radiance

The outgoing radiance in vertex v at the surface location x in direction of the viewer has to be computed. According to the rendering equation [3] the amount of incident light reflected towards the viewer has to be gathered. For this purpose, the incident radiance of each pixel is weighted by the Δ-form factor of the pixel itself and then used as incoming radiance of a reflection model. The Δ-form factors are derived from the rendering equation as following [12]:

$$L_o(x,\vec{\omega}) = L_e(x,\vec{\omega}) + \int_S f_r(x, x' \to x, \vec{\omega}) L_i(x, x' \to x) V(x, x') G(x, x') dA' \quad (1)$$

with:
L_o: outgoing radiance $[Wm^{-2}sr^{-1}]$
L_e: emitted radiance $[Wm^{-2}sr^{-1}]$
f_r: BRDF $[sr^{-1}]$
L_i: incident radiance $[Wm^{-2}sr^{-1}]$
$\vec{\omega}'$: incidence direction
$\vec{n}$: normal at the surface location x
x': another surface location
$\vec{n}'$: normal at x'

dA': differential area at x'
$(x' \to x)$: radiance leaving x' in the direction towards x
S: set of all surface points

$$V(x,x') = \begin{cases} 1 & : \quad x \text{ and } x' \text{ are mutually visible} \\ 0 & : \quad \text{otherwise} \end{cases} \qquad (2)$$

$$G(x,x') = \frac{(\vec{\omega}' \cdot \vec{n}')(\vec{\omega}' \cdot \vec{n})}{\|x' - x\|^2} \qquad (3)$$

For the evaluation of the hemicubes we assume, that every surface in the model is Lambertian, so that the reflected radiance is constant in all directions. This reduces equation (8) to:

$$\begin{aligned} B(x) &= B_e(x) + \int_S f_{r,d}(x) B(x') V(x,x') G(x,x') \, dA' \\ &= B_e(x) + \frac{\rho_d(x)}{\pi} \int_S B(x') V(x,x') G(x,x') \, dA' \end{aligned} \qquad (4)$$

B: radiosity (outgoing) $[Wm^{-2}]$
ρ_d: diffuse reflectance for a Lambertian surface ($\rho_d = \pi f_{r,d}(x)$)

Discretizing:

$$B_i = B_{e,i} + \rho_i \sum_{j=1}^{N} B_j F_{ij} \qquad (5)$$

The form factor F_{ij} from differential area dA_i to differential area dA_j is

$$F_{ij} = \frac{1}{A_i} \int_{A_i} \int_{A_j} \frac{V(x,x') G(x,x')}{\pi} \, dA_j \, dA_i \qquad (6)$$

Delta form factors for the hemicube pixels: (A hemicube pixel covers the area ΔA, the visibility information ist encoded into the pixels):

$$\Delta FF = \frac{G(x,x')}{\pi} \Delta A \qquad (7)$$

For the hemicube model the Δ-form factors for top and side faces are computed analog to [11].

The contribution of one pixel in the visibility map of x is computed using the radiance stored in the corresponding texel of the environment map. This radiance is weighted by the Δ-form factor of the pixel and then used as input of a local illumination model, which is Lambertian reflection in our algorithm. Note that for real-world environment maps no Δ-form factor has to be applied to the outgoing radiance stored in the environment map, since it is already encoded in the corresponding real-world picture. Due to the superposition property of light the total amount of radiance leaving the vertex in direction of the viewer is then easily obtained by summing the contributions of outgoing radiance of all pixels of the visibility map not marked as occluded. Note that the incident radiance corresponding to a pixel is taken from the environment map using the texel of the environment map encoded in the visibility map, see Figure 2. Note, that the Δ-form factors have to be computed only once and can be reused for every vertex. After calculating the radiance values for all vertices, the mesh can be rendered using a standard OpenGL-Renderer with Gouraud interpolation.

For the point light source any desired illumination model can be incorporated into the algorithm.

4.1.2 Dynamic environment maps

Due to the above calculations, our algorithm allows the dynamic modification of the illumination condition in realtime by using different cube maps. For example, if we want to rotate the surface in the environment, a rotated cube map is generated.

5 Results

Figure 3 and 5 show the static mesh of a cloth illuminated by virtual light encoded in hand made cubic environment maps (figures 4,6). The environment maps faces represent uniformly emitting light sources. In all pictures, the relative position of the model with respect to the environment map is fixed. In order to visualize the effect of the different lighting conditions, the whole scene including the environment map is rotated. We take snapshots from several viewing positions. Note how the radiance especially in the foldings descents from the illuminated to the dark side. Folds pointing towards the light source are fully illuminated. The situation is even more apparent if we use the faces of the environment map as colored light sources, see figure 6. Figure 8 shows a textured mesh of parts of the Grand Canyon based on satellite altitude data with 66049 vertices. In the left image pre-computed shadows calculated with a hemicube model are used. In the right image no illumination is used. The visual impression of the left images reveals a greater depth impression due to the self-shadowing in the faults.

Due to the vertex based shading it is necessary that the resolution of the triangle mesh provides sufficiently high fidelity. An additional point light source is used in figure 8 with the Utah teapot mesh. The spout casts a shadow on the pot (left image).

The images in figure 9 show a spaceship consisting of 18720 vertices. Self-shadowing is visible in the propulsion units, at the cockpit and under the wings.

6 Conclusions and Future Work

The algorithm presented is able of illuminating folded surfaces with extended light sources in realtime. The illumination conditions can be changed at runtime.
So far our meshes cannot be deformed in realtime. This would require a complete new set of visibility maps at every frame. At the moment, our preprocessing step needs at least about 3 seconds of runtime, using the hemiplane model, which is not enough to achieve interactive frame rates. A possible optimization could be to update only the parts of the mesh which have changed. Furthermore, it might be possible to further exploit graphics hardware acceleration for the preprocessing step. Future versions of our method should use high dynamic range images for the environment maps, which, at this state, consist only of RGB images. This will increase the realism of effects simulated by the environment illumination. Moreover, a local illumination model described by Stewart and Langer [9] can be applied to estimate secondary irradiance. The use of this model yields perceptually acceptable shading without resorting to an expensive global illumination step.

7 Acknowledgements

We would like to thank Markus Wacker from the University of Tuebingen for the mesh we used in our examples and our colleague Marcin Novotni for useful hints and corrections. Some of the used models were provided by www.3DCAFE.com.

References

[1] A. James Stewart. *Computing Visibility from Folded Surfaces*, Elsevier Preprint, 1999.

[2] J. D. Foley, A. van Dam, S. K. Feiner, and J. F. Hughes. *Fundamentals of Interactive Computer Graphics*, Addison Wesley, second edition. 1990.

[3] Micheal F. Cohen, John R. Wallace. *Radiosity and Realistic Image Syynthesis*, Morgan Kaufmann Publishers, Inc. 1993.

[4] Peter Shirley. *Realistic Ray Tracing*, A K Peters. 2000.

[5] T. Whitted. *An Improved Illumination Model for Shaded Display*, Communications of the ACM, vol.23, no. 6. 1980.

[6] F. C. Crow. *Shadow Algorithms for Computer Graphics*, SIGGRAPH 77. 1977.

[7] L. Williams. *Casting Curve Shadows on Curved Surfaces*, SIGGRAPH 78. 1978.

[8] J. T. Kajiya. *The rendering equation*, Computer Graphics, vol. 20, no.4. 1986.

[9] A. James Stewart. and M. S. Langer *Towards accurate recovery of shape from shading under diffuse lighting*, IEEE Transactions on Pattern Analysis and Machine Intelligence, vol. 19, no.9, 1997.

[10] B. Ganster *Efficient cloth shading*, Diploma Thesis, University of Bonn, 2002.

[11] Michael F. Cohen and Donald P. Greenberg *The Hemi-Cube: A radiosity solution for complex environments*, SIGGRAPH 85 Proc., vol. 19, no.3, 1985.

[12] H.W. Jensen *Realistic Image Synthesis Using Photon Mapping*, A K Peters, 2001.

8 Appendix

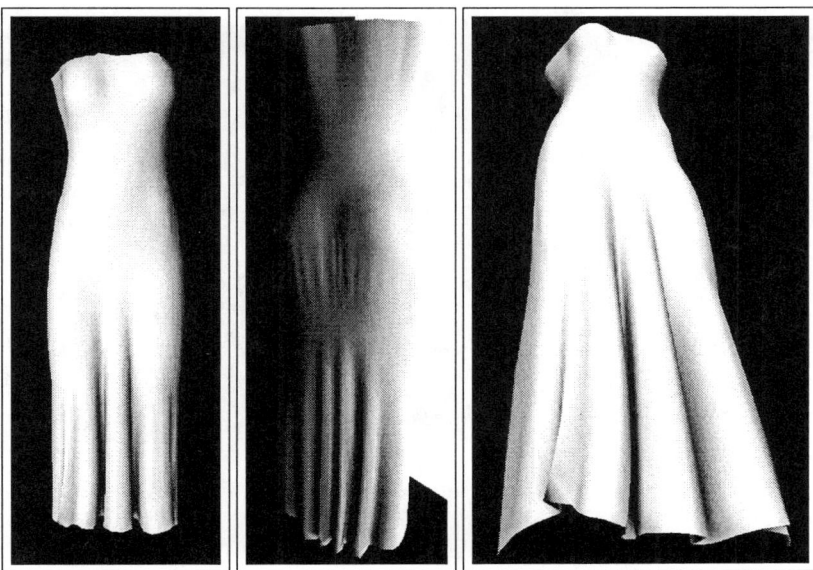

Figure No 3: These three images show a folded dress consisting of 3120 vertices. The left image shows a frontal view of the dress. Due to the pre-computed shadowing the folds in the lower part of the dress are clearly visible. In the center image, the back of the dress is shown, slightly rotated against the front side of the environment cube. The right image is rendered using another point of view, showing the folds in more detail.

Figure No 4: Environment cube map used for the rendering of the above images, with only the front side white.

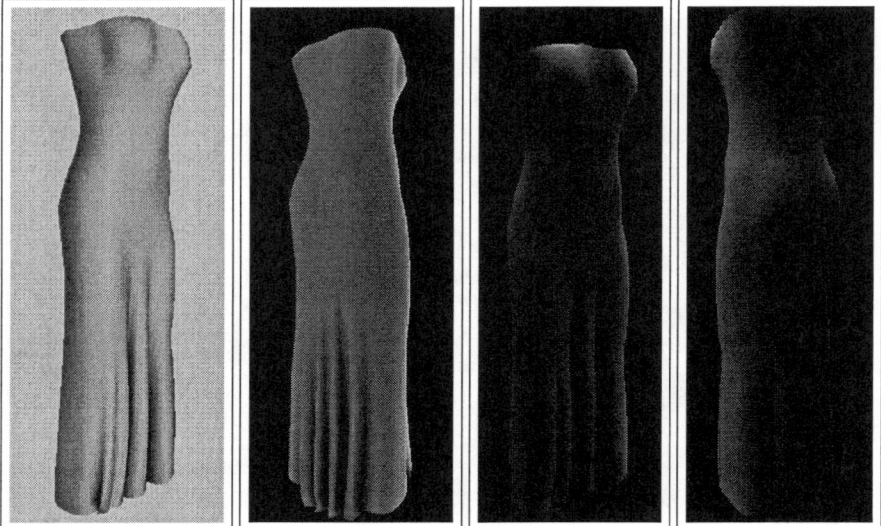

Figure No 5: These images show the effects of the usage of the environment faces as colored light sources. The mesh used, is the same as in figure 3. The corresponding environment maps are shown in figure 6. The reflection of the different light sources can be distinguished from each other in the folds.

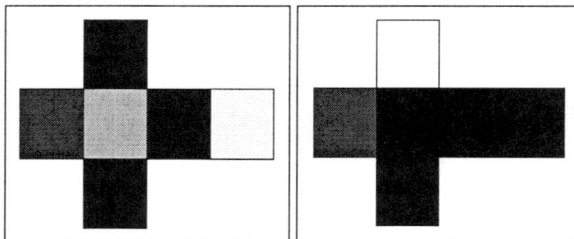

Figure No 6: Environment cube maps used for the rendering of the above images. For the two left images top and bottom are black. Sides are red, green, blue and yellow. For the two right images left and right are blue and red, the top is white and the rest is colored black.

 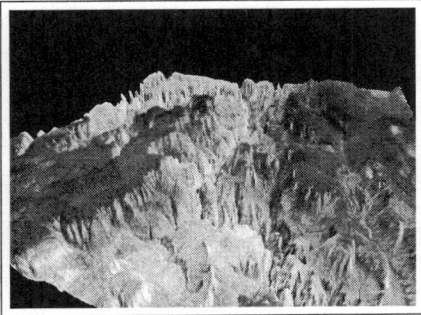

Figure No 7: These images show a textured mesh of parts of the Grand Canyon based on satellite altitude data with 66049 vertices. In the left image pre-computed shadows calculated with a hemicube model are used. In the right image no illumination is used. The visual impression of the left images reveals a greater depth impression due to the self-shadowing in the faults.

Figure No 8: The Utah teapot. The mesh consist out of 3907 vertices and is illuminated with a point light source (yellow dot) in front of the teapot (left image). The light source visibility is calculated on a per vertex basis, as described in the paper. The right image shows the teapot with the light source moved above it. Self shadowing is also visible in both images.

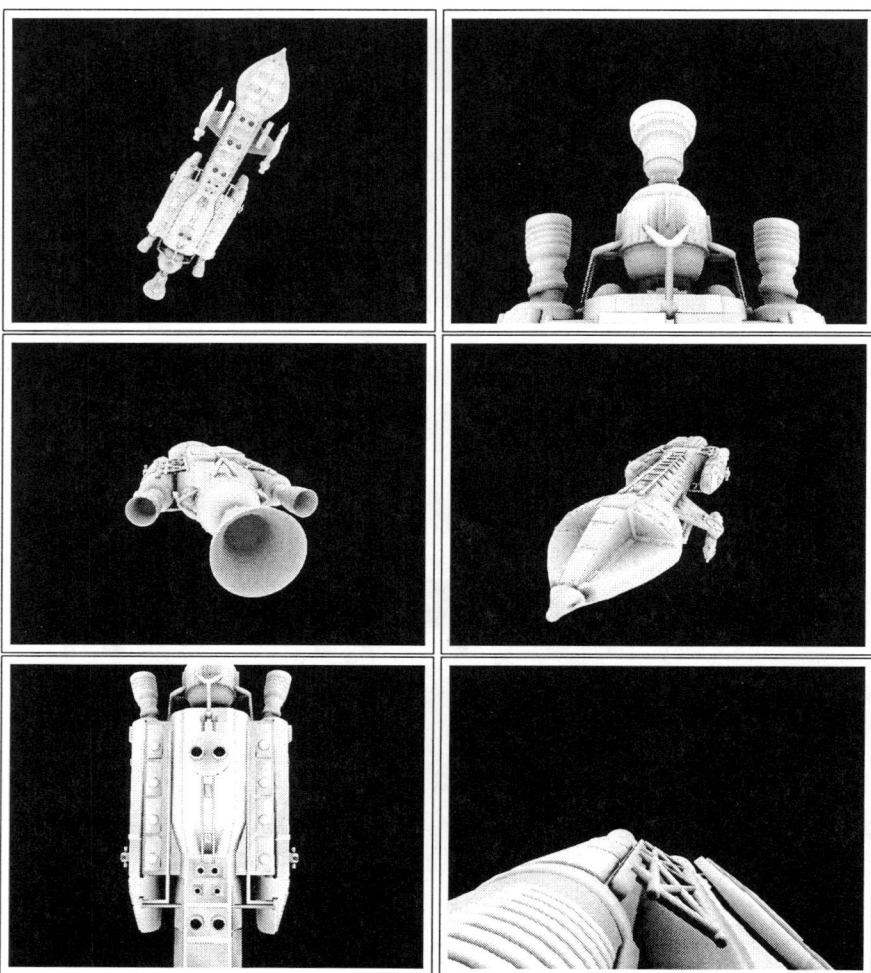

Figure No 9: These images show a spaceship model with 18720 vertices, provided by www.3DCAFE.com. A hemicube model with a resolution of 64 × 64 pixels for the top of the cube and no additional point light sources were used. Self-shadowing is visible in the propulsion units, at the cockpit and under the wings.

Rendering Natural Waters: Merging Computer Graphics with Physics and Biology

E. Cerezo, F.J. Serón

Advanced Computer Graphics Group (GIGA)
Computer Science Department
Technical School of Engineering
University of Zaragoza
C/ Maria de Luna 3, E-50015 Zaragoza, Spain
ecerezo@posta.unizar.es
seron@posta.unizar.es
http://giga.cps.unizar.es/

Abstract

The creation and rendering of realistic water scenes is one of the challenging tasks in Computer Graphics. To reproduce the illumination and colour inside water bodies an algorithm capable of dealing with media with anisotropic and multiple scattering has to be used. We have developed a simulation system based in the discrete ordinates method to solve the problem of light transport in general participating media. We discuss its application to the rendering of images of natural waters, a difficult task due to the different components that determine their optical behaviour. A couple of simple images calculated in different waters are presented. Results indicate the relevant role played by the spectral behaviour of the absorption and scattering coefficients and by the correct treatment of the phase function in the process of image generation.

Keywords: Participating Media, Discrete Ordinates, Global Illumination, Bio-optical models

1. Introduction

Research on the rendering of natural scenes, such as clouds, water, trees, terrain, fire, has become increasingly wide spread. In particular, the creation and rendering of realistic water scenes is one of the challenging tasks in Computer Graphics. Most of the work that has been done is concerned with the effects of the reflection and refraction of light on the water surface: shafts of light, caustics...[1], [2], [3]. Great effort has been taken in studying atmospheric conditions to know how much sunlight and skylight reaches the water surface and the problem of wave generation [4], [5], [6]. However, realistic rendering of water scenes requires the transport of light within the water body to be properly handled.

Due its complexity, when considering light transport in water strong simplifications are usually made (single scattering, isotropy, homogeneous media...). Nishita et al. [7] study the colour of sea surface as viewed from outer space; they include in their model the scattering due to water molecules, but they make an analytic quasi-single scattering approximation. Premoze et al. [8] also consider the problem of light transport, but they have centred their work in the simulation of the appearance of the water surface. Therefore, when carrying the light transport they also make important simplifications: they solve a mono-dimensional equation (the radiance in the medium will depend only on the depth). They do not try to simulate the radiance due to scattering; they estimate it using some empirical equations that relate the radiance just below the air-water surface with the light coming from the sun. Tadamura et al. [9] study the colour of water in applications of lightning design. They are the only ones that consider the presence of light sources within the water (usually, only illumination due to the sun and the sky is considered). But when performing the light transport they only consider single scattering and no illumination of objects inside the water due to scattering. Jensen et al. [10] generalise the bidirectional Monte Carlo ray-tracing method to scenes containing participating media and apply it to render scenes with water. They calculate volume photon maps and use them in the rendering stage to estimate the radiance due to scattering within the media. It is a very general method able to consider non-homogeneous media and anisotropic scattering with complex geometries. With certain media the savings in memory is substantial, compared with some finite element methods, but when applying it to render water the memory increases, specially if the highly-peaked marine scattering behaviour has to be reproduced. So, it can be concluded that the transport of light in water has generally been made aplying strong restrictions to the medium with the only exception of systems using non-deterministic methods such as Monte Carlo.

Our work focuses on the simulation of the transport of light in water in the more general case: non-homogeneous medium, anisotropic scattering and multiscattering. We have applied the method of Languénou et al. [11] that is based on the discretization of the participating medium in finite volumes (voxels) and on the use the discrete ordinates method to handle directions. Finite volume element techniques are not as flexible as Monte Carlo ones, but they are undoubtedly faster and more effective for simple scenes. We have generalised the method to the case of objects and light sources inside the medium. The presence of light sources considerably increases the complexity of the light transport problem: the illumination does not only depend on the depth, so pure 3D calculus has to be performed. The illumination of the objects due to direct but also scattered light has to be taken into account.

The use of realistic medium parametrizations and a proper handle of the spectral dependence of the medium characterising parameters is also essential. It should be pointed out that the behaviour of marine waters is drastically different of that of pure water. This is caused by the presence of several components in these waters (dissolved salts, dissolved organic compounds, plankton...). The spectral absorption and scattering coefficients as well as the scattering phase functions are strongly affected by these components: the illumination and colour of the water is consequently determined by their presence. The resolution of the transport problem within the water is a prerequisite for the solution of many problems such as the synthesis of realistic underwater images, the underwater visibility, the capture of satellite images, the biologic productivity studies, or the thermodynamics of stratified media in submarine environments.

The structure of this paper is as follows: in Section 2 the radiative transfer equation which describes the behaviour of light in a participating medium is presented, whereas in Section 3 our simulation system is outlined. Section 4 analyses the oceanic medium as participating medium and presents the bio-optical models used to parametrize it. Section 5 discuss the problems that arise due to the special scattering characteristics of the oceanic medium and presents a study of simple images obtained for different waters. In Section 6 conclusions and future work are discussed.

2. Working with Participating Media: the Radiative Transfer Equation

As radiation travels through a participating medium it undergoes three kinds of phenomena: absorption, which causes a diminishment of the intensity, emission, which increases intensity and scattering which causes a redirection of energy. There are two types of difficulties when studying the radiation in this kind of media. First of all, emission, absorption and scattering do not only take place in the medium boundaries, but within any point of the medium. A complete solution of the exchange of energy requires knowledge of the physical properties and the intensity of radiation within every point of the medium. A second difficulty comes from the spectral effects due to the dependence of the characterising parameters with the wavelength, making it necessary a detailed spectral analysis.

The equation that governs the transfer of energy in this kind of media is the radiative transfer equation –RTE–:

$$\frac{dL_\lambda(S,\theta,\varphi)}{dS} = -a_\lambda(S)L_\lambda(S,\theta,\varphi) + a_\lambda(S)L_{\lambda emis}(S,\theta,\varphi) - \sigma_\lambda(S)L_\lambda(S,\theta,\varphi) \quad (1)$$
$$+ \frac{\sigma_\lambda(S)}{4\pi} \int_{w_i=4\pi} L_{\lambda_i}(S,\theta_i,\varphi_i)\Phi_\lambda(S,(\theta_i,\varphi_i) \to (\theta,\varphi))dw_i$$

$L_\lambda(S,\theta,\varphi)$ is the radiance, ie, the power per unit of projected area perpendicular to the ray per unit of radiation length and solid angle in the direction (θ,φ). The equation gives its local variation when traversing a distance dS. The meaning of the different terms at the right of the equation is as follows:

- The first term refers to absorption: $a_\lambda(S)$ is the so-called absorption coefficient (the fraction of energy lost per unit length, dimension m^{-1})

- The second term corresponds to self-emission: $L_{\lambda emis}(S, \theta, \varphi)$ is the radiant energy emitted, due to spontaneous or stimulated emission

- The third term represents the reduction of the radiance along the propagation direction because of scattering (out-scattering): $\sigma_\lambda(S)$ is the scattering coefficient (dimensions m^{-1})

- The last term accounts for the in-scattering, ie, the increase of radiance along the propagation direction due to the scattering of radiance coming from other directions. $\Phi_\lambda(S, (\theta_i,\varphi_i) \to (\theta,\varphi))$ is the phase function which describes the angular distribution of the scattered energy.

Another important parameter for characterising the medium is the extinction or attenuation coefficient, which is the sum of the absorption and scattering coefficients:

$$K_\lambda = a_\lambda + \sigma_\lambda \qquad (2)$$

The inverse of the attenuation coefficient is called attenuation length (dimension m). In Table 1 the parameters characterising a participating medium are summarised. Their spectral dependence should be noted.

a_λ	Absorption coefficient
σ_λ	Scattering coefficient
$K_\lambda = a_\lambda + \sigma_\lambda$	Extinction coefficient
$\Phi_\lambda((\theta_i, \varphi_i) \to (\theta, \varphi))$	Scattering Phase Function
$l_\lambda = 1/K_\lambda$	Attenuation length

Table No. 1. Coefficients characterising a Participating Medium

In this work we do not consider self-emission ($L_{\lambda emis}=0$), so equation (1) simplifies:

$$\frac{dL_\lambda(S)}{dS} = -K_\lambda L_\lambda(S) + \frac{\sigma_\lambda}{4\pi} \int_{w_i=4\pi} L_\lambda(S, \theta, \varphi) \Phi_\lambda(S, (\theta_i, \varphi_i) \to (\theta, \varphi)) dw_i \qquad (3)$$

Boundary conditions have to be added to the equation, basically void conditions (no incoming radiances) or surface reflection conditions:

$$L_{ë}(è_r,\varphi_r) = E_{ë}(è_r,\varphi_r) + \quad (4)$$

$$\int_0^{2\delta}\int_0^{\delta/2} f_{brdf}((è_i,\varphi_i) \to (è_r,\varphi_r))L_{ë}(è_i,\varphi_i)\cos è_i \sin è_i dè_i d\varphi_i$$

where E_λ is the energy emitted in the (θ_r,φ_r) direction and f_{brdf} is the bidirectional reflectance function.

3. Solving the RTE: our Simulation System

3.1 The General Framework: the Discrete Ordinates Method

In order to solve the radiative transfer equation, different methods have been proposed. Restricting them to those capable of dealing with the more general and realistic case of multi-scattering (a ray may undergo several scattering events), there are the following families of methods: zonal methods, Montecarlo methods and flux methods, that include the P-N or spherical harmonics methods and the multiflux or discrete ordinates methods. In Table 2 the different methods and relevant works are outlined. A good review of these methods can be found in [12].

Zonal	[13], [14], [15]
Monte Carlo	[16], [17]
Spherical harmonics	[18], [19]
Discrete Ordinates	[11], [20], [21]

Table No. 2. Different methods to deal with Participating Media

We have chosen the discrete ordinates method to solve the radiative transfer equation because it is general, it poses no restrictions to the medium characteristics and is computationally feasible. It is based on the angular discretization of the solid angle about a location over a finite number of directions.

Angular discretization. The integral over solid angles in equation 3 is replaced by sums over a discrete set of directions. Therefore, the variation of the radiance along direction V_m will be given by (λ subscripts have been omitted for clarity):

$$\mu_m \frac{\partial L_m}{\partial x} + \xi_m \frac{\partial L_m}{\partial y} + \eta_m \frac{\partial L_m}{\partial z} = -KL_m + \frac{\sigma}{4\pi} \sum_{t=1}^{n_d} w_t \Phi_{tm} L_t \qquad (5)$$

where n_d is the number of discrete directions, (μ_m, ξ_m, η_m) are the director cosines of direction V_m, and w_t is the weight associated to direction V_t, $m, t \in [1, n_d]$ provided that $\sum_{t=1}^{n_d} w_t = 4\pi$. Angular discretization can be uniform or not.

Spatial discretization. Furthermore, to transform the differential equation into an algebraic one, a spatial discretization is performed: the medium is subdivided into voxels of constant physical properties. In fact, what is computed in the algorithm is not the radiance of the voxel for each direction but the Source Term [22], which in our case reduces to:

$$G_m = \frac{\sigma}{4\pi} \sum_{t=1}^{n_d} w_t \Phi_{tm} L_t \qquad (6)$$

This term represents the gain of radiance in direction m owing to in-scattering. The radiances of the voxel faces and the source term for each of the discrete directions are constant inside the voxel so the RTE (equation 3) can be analytically integrated along a path of length s inside the voxel, obtaining:

$$L_m(s) = L_m(0)e^{-Ks} + \frac{G_m}{K}(1 - e^{-Ks}) \qquad (7)$$

which is the basis of the transfer of energy inside the voxel.

3. Resolution Method

Our algorithm is based in the work of Languénou et al.[11] and has been presented elsewhere [23]. Our main contribution to the method has been its generalization so that the system is able to:

- include objects and sources inside the participating medium
- use realistic medium parametrizations
- consider inelastic processes
- validate the results to assure that they are not only qualitatively but quantitatively (physically) correct; in particular the energy absorbed in each of the voxels is also calculated.

The work presented in this paper focuses in the second point. Nevertheless, for completeness, we outline here the general structure of the resolution algorithm.

The resolution method is iterative. First of all, an initialisation step corresponding to the first order of scattering is performed. Then, in the iterative process, each of the iterations corresponds to one scattering. The results of this process are the source terms in each direction in each voxel of the medium and the radiances in the medium's boundaries. Some of these boundaries are "physical" (for example the seabed or the air-water surface in a marine scene) and other just "geometrical" or "non-physical" (they simply delimit the simulation volume). The iterative process follows the one in [11], but a proper handling of the surfaces and objects within the medium has been incorporated. Therefore, those aspects will be emphasized.

The First Step: "Loading" the Medium and the Objects. First of all, the source terms in each voxel are initialised taking into account the contribution of each illuminating source. Direct illumination on the physical boundary surfaces of the medium (seabed, air-water surface...) and on the objects within the water is also computed. These radiances are incorporated as boundary conditions when dealing with the next orders of scattering. For the moment, all surfaces are considered as having Lambertian properties.

The Iteration Process: Computing the Multi-Scattered Light Field. Afterwards, for every single direction a complete traversal of the matrix of voxels is carried out:

- A direction V_m $m \in [1, n_d]$ is selected

- The traversal is done beginning in one of the 8 extreme voxels. It is important for the traversal to follow the "energy flux sense": for a direction with direction cosine >0 the sweep should be done increasing voxel indexes and for one with direction cosine <0, inversely

- In each voxel (for the direction being considered):

  1. The direction classifies the six voxel faces into three incoming and three outgoing faces. The radiance of an incoming face will be: zero if the face belongs to a "non-physical" boundary (void boundary condition) or a reflected radiance if it belongs to a "physical" surface or the outgoing radiance of the adjacent voxel

  2. The previous source term contribution and the incoming radiances are used to calculate an average radiance L_m in the voxel (assumed constant within the voxel)

  3. This average radiance L_m is used to calculate the outgoing radiances. This calculus is done using the equation of energy transfer inside the voxel (equation 7)

4. L_m is also used to calculate the increments of the source terms for the discrete directions due to scattering (calculation of the next order of scattering):

$$\Delta G_t + = \frac{\sigma}{4\pi} w_m \Phi_{mt} L_m, \forall t \in [1, n_d] \qquad (8)$$

- Each time a "physical" surface (either belonging to a boundary or to an object) is encountered the radiance of the surface is stored

- Once all the voxels have been treated, next direction is considered

- After having followed all directions, the next order of scattering is considered, initiating again the traversal of the medium for each discrete direction anew.

With this iterative process, the energy initially loaded when initialising the voxels' source terms is propagated throughout the medium. When the contributions to the radiances of the boundaries and to the voxels' source terms are negligible, convergence is met and the resolution process is stopped.

3.3 Storage of Results and Rendering Stage

As already pointed out, all the magnitudes we work with are spectral ones: the source spectrum is divided into intervals, so that one calculation is carried out for each of the discrete wavelength values. To avoid storing the source terms for each direction, an expansion in spherical harmonics is performed in each voxel.

To obtain the images a simple ray-tracer adapted to voxelised participating media (based in [24]) has been used. Every time a ray travels inside a voxel a distance s, equation 7 is used. The expansion coefficients stored in each voxel are used to interpolate the source terms in new directions when rays are cast in the rendering stage. In this stage we obtain the spectrum corresponding to each pixel of the image, no the RGB value. So, two additional problems have to be solved: the pixel's spectrum has to be converted in to an RGB triplet and all colour information (such as the objects' textures) has to be transformed into spectra. To solve the first problem we have used the CIE colour matching functions [25] and for the second one we have used a method similar to [26].

4. The Ocean as Participating Medium

4.1 Light in the Sea

Oceanic medium can be viewed just as a participating medium: light is scattered and absorbed as it travels through the water. The global effect is the attenuation of the intensity of light which has important consequences: it is a limiting factor for the development of life in water and it it strongly limits visibility making it necessary the use of artificial light beyond certain depths: seeing ranges vary from scarcely one meter in contaminated waters to 30 or 60 meters in very clear ones. So, the design of underwater imaging systems is interesting not only in oceanography but in many different areas such as the marine archaeology, the construction of petrol platforms or the maintenance of submarine cables. The design of these kind of systems can not be based in a trial-and-error scheme because fabrication and placement of underwater systems is extremely expensive. Computer models can play here an important role, allowing an underwater imaging system designer to experiment with different imaging strategies as a function of water quality. The specific case we are trying to solve is related to the problem of tracking submarine cables. Our participating media resolution module would be used to validate and fine tune the digital image treatment system to track power cables (such as the ones that comprise the system of electric energy transport between islands). In these systems, cables are located by means of a sequence of images captured by a camera mounted on an AUV (Autonomous Underwater Vehicle). These images are analysed by appropriated digital imaging systems. Due to the difficulties and the expense of obtaining these kind of images, our application could serve as a device to obtain simulated underwater images to study the performance of different digital imaging systems. A simulation system capable not only to generate images but also radiometric magnitudes, as is our case, will be even more useful.

4.2 Characterising Parameters: Bio-optical Models

The interesting issue about natural waters and, in particular, about the oceanic medium, is that electromagnetic radiation interacts not only with the water but with materials dissolved or suspended in it. This makes ocean phenomenologically rich [27]. Seawater consists in pure sea water, dissolved organic compounds (generally referred to as yellow matter or CDOM -coloured dissolved matter-) and particulate matter both organic (viruses, colloids, bacteria, phytoplankton) and inorganic (created primarily by weathering of terrestrial rocks and soils) [28]. Each of these components contributes in some fashion to the values of the optical properties of a given water body. Bio-optical models try to predict optical properties of water from the concentration of biogenic components. Chlorophyll is a pigment present in all planktonic plants and its concentration in mgm^{-3} is commonly used as the relevant optical measurement of phytoplankton abundance.

Waters can be divided into two categories:

- Case 1 waters, in which the concentration of phytoplankton is high compared to nonbiogenic particles, so that optical properties can be correlated to chlorophyll concentration

- Case 2 waters, where that correlation does not exist or can not be established.

Roughly 98% of the world's open ocean and costal waters fall into the case 1 category. Estuarine or near-shore waters belong to case 2 category.

Absorption. Water is nearly "opaque" outside the near-ultraviolet to near-infrared wavelengths, henceforth, attention can be restricted to this narrow band. These wavelengths overlap with the wavelengths of the sun's maximum energy output and with a corresponding window in atmospheric absorption. It is this astounding overlap of energy source and open window that has enabled aquatic life to develop. Dissolved salts make seawater a much better conductor of electricity than is pure water, what causes a much higher absorption at very long wavelengths. Yellow matter, detritus and phytoplankton contribution to absorption is relevant. Specially important is the contribution of phytoplankton cells due to their pigments which are strong absorbers of visible light. Absorption by chlorophyll (the most important one) is characterized by strong absorption bands in the blue and in the red with very little absorption in green.

So, depending on the concentrations of dissolved substances, phytoplankton, and detritus, the total spectral absorption coefficient of a given water sample can range from almost identical to that of pure water to one which shows orders-of-magnitude greater absorption than pure water. Morel [29] has proposed a bio-optical model for the spectral absorption coefficient of case 1 waters. All contributions to the absorption coefficient are parametrized in terms of the chlorophyll concentration C (mg m^{-3}):

$$a(\lambda) = [a_w(\lambda) + 0.06 a_c^*(\lambda) \, C^{0.65}][1 + 0.2 \exp(-0.014(\ddot{e} - 440))] \tag{8}$$

$a_w(\lambda)$ is the absorption coefficient of pure water (m^{-1}) and $a_c^*(\lambda)$ is non-dimensional chlorophyll-specific absorption coefficient. λ is the wavelength expressed in nm. Chlorophyll concentrations for various waters range from 0.01 mg m^{-3} in the clearest open ocean waters, to 10 mg m^{-3} in productive coastal upwelling regions, to 100 mg m^{-3} in estuaries or lakes.

Scattering. A commonly employed bio-optical model for the total scattering coefficient is that of Gordon and Morel [30]:

$$b(\lambda) = \left(\frac{550}{\lambda}\right) 0.30 C^{0.62} \tag{10}$$

where λ is in nm and C is the chlorophyll concentration in mg m^{-3}.

The phase function can be modelled with two terms:

$$\tilde{\beta}(\Psi) = \frac{b_w(\lambda)}{b(z,\lambda)} \tilde{\beta}_w(\Psi) + \frac{b_p(\lambda)}{b(z,\lambda)} \tilde{\beta}_p(\Psi) \tag{11}$$

the first one corresponding to the contribution of water molecules and the second one corresponding to particles contribution. The phase function that characterizes scattering in pure sea water is:

$$\tilde{a}_w(\Psi) \equiv 0.06225(1 + 0.835\cos^2\Psi) \qquad (12)$$

which is very similar to Rayleigh scattering (almost isotropic) except for the 0.835 factor, attributable to the anisotropy of the water molecules. Nevertheless, as soon as there is a slight amount of particulate matter in the water –always the case for even the clearest water- the phase function becomes highly peaked in the forward direction, and the scattering coefficient increases by at least a factor of ten. The particles cause at least a four-order-of-magnitude increase in scattering between 1° and 90°. Table 3 compares several optical properties for pure sea water and for three different water samples. These data show how greatly different even clear ocean water is from pure sea water. The last column gives the angle Ψ such than one half of the total scattering occurs at angles between 0 y Ψ. This angle is rarely greater than 10° in natural waters.

water	a (m^{-1})	b (m^{-1})	$\Psi(1/2b)(°)$
pure sea water	0.0405	0.0025	90.00
clear ocean	0.114	0.037	6.25
coastal ocean	0.179	0.219	2.53
turbid harbour	0.366	1.824	4.68

Table No. 3. Selected optical properties for different water samples

Figure 1 shows the so-called particle phase function. Highly peaked forward phase functions are characteristic of diffraction-dominated scattering in a polydisperse system (a system containing particles of many different sizes). With regard to the continuous rise even for very small angles, it may be attributed to turbulence.

The scattering coefficient for the water molecules is given by:

$$b_w(\lambda) \equiv 16.06 \left(\frac{\lambda_0}{\lambda}\right)^{4.32} \beta_w(90°; \lambda_0) \qquad (13)$$

And the scattering coefficient due to particles can simply be obtained from:

$$b_p(z,\lambda) \equiv b(z,\lambda) - b_w(z,\lambda) \qquad (14)$$

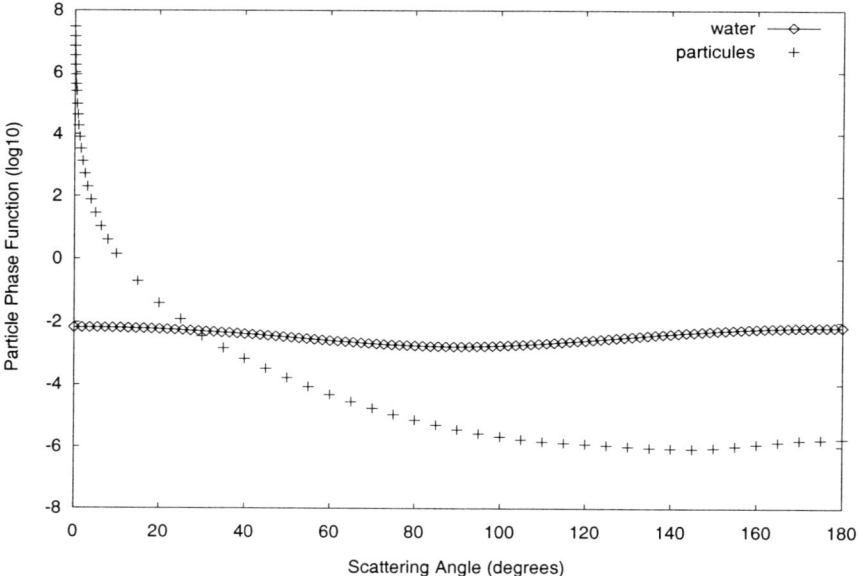

Figure No. 1. Particle Phase Function

5. Studying Different Waters

5.1 Adapting our System

The use of highly-peaked forward scattering phase functions give rise to two kind of problems:

- If the source terms are not a smooth function of direction, the expansion in spherical harmonics does not work

- If the strong scattering directionality (which means that the angular deviations in the light rays are small) has to be appropriately treated it is necessary to work either to add many more discrete directions to the uniform discretization, or to work with non-uniform discretizations. It should be noted that the privileged scattering direction is different from one voxel to another and is determined by the position of the voxel relative the light source (see Figure 2).

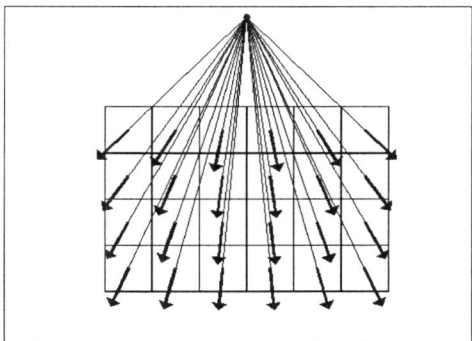

Figure No. 2. Characteristic directions

To cope with these difficulties and trying to maintain memory requirements as low as possible, we have made two major changes in our simulation strategy:

- Instead of calculating the spherical harmonics expansion in each voxel, we maintain the source term information in each direction. Instead of interpolating, the concept of "importance" is used to calculate the contribution of each of the source terms in the direction of the ray in the rendering step: the source terms in each direction will contribute according to their magnitude and to their distance (in terms of the cosine of the angle) to the ray direction;

- In each voxel, a new "characteristic" direction is added to the quadrature (painted bold in Figure 2): the direction is determined by the centre of the voxel and the position of the source (we work, for the moment, with punctual sources). As the rest of the phase function is "smooth", in the uniform discretization less directions are necessary. The characteristic direction allows to calculate more precisely the first scattering contribution (the most important one) without increasing too much the needs of memory. In the iterative multiscattering process the energy corresponding to the characteristic directions is also distributed throughout the medium.

5.2 Results

An incandescent light source has been placed at a distance of 1 meter from the seabed above the object. A grid of 25x25x25 voxels and a uniform quadrature of 74 directions (plus the characteristic direction) has been used. In order to account for the wavelength dependence of the final colour image the visible spectrum is divided up into 16 values that range from 400 to 700 nm in 20 nm increments. Four different simulations, each of them corresponding to waters with different chlorophyll concentrations, have been carried out and are presented in Figures 3, 4 , 5 and 6.

494

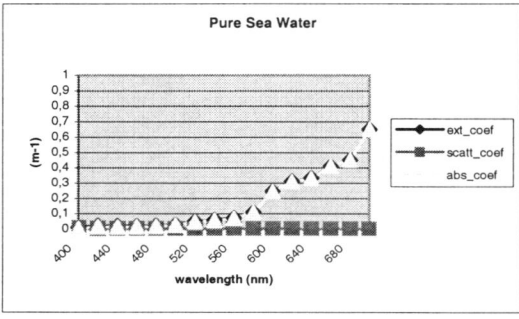 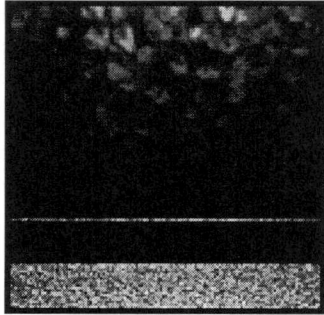

Figure No. 3. Pure sea water: strong absorption at red wavelengths, very little scattering

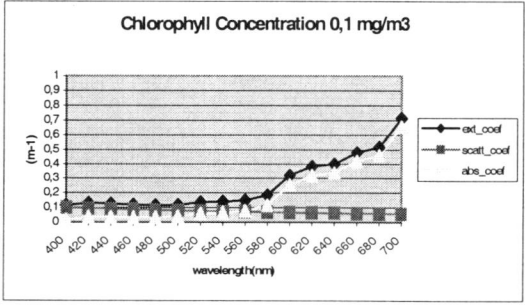 

Figure No. 4. Sea water with very low phytoplankton abundance: scattering increases and colour begins to "move" to green

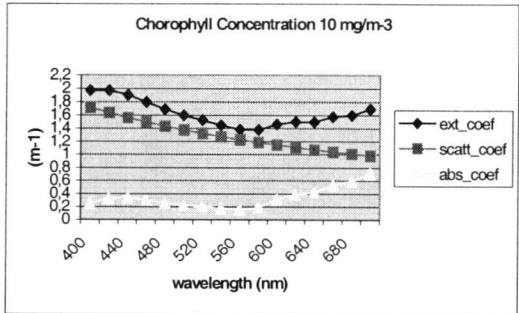 

Figure No. 5. Sea water with important phytoplankton abundance: greater absorption at blue wavelengths, increase of scattering, strong decrease of visibility

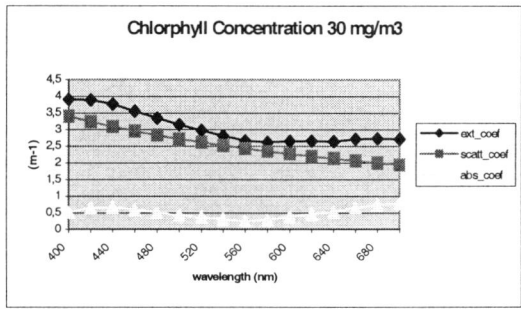

Figure No. 6. Sea water with very high phytoplankton abundance: strong absorption at blue wavelengths and heavy scattering

6. Conclusions and Future Work

A couple of simple images calculated in different waters are presented. Results indicate the relevant role played by the spectral behaviour of the absorption and scattering coefficients and by the correct treatment of the phase function in the process of image generation.

This study is part of a wider research line developed by the GIGA (Advanced Computer Graphics Group of the University of Zaragoza) to simulate the behaviour of light in participating media (not only in the visible part of the spectrum). In the case chosen, the visible range, the method developed is used to generate underwater images. The following improvements could be done in this specific area:

- Study of factors such as the nature of the sea bead (algae, sand...) and the spectral radiance on the water surface, due to the sun and the sky contribution

- Consideration of possible inelastic phenomena

- Study of non-homogeneous media.

*This work has been partly financed by the Spanish "Comisión Interministerial de Ciencia y Tecnología" (contracts number TIC2000-0426-P4-02 and TIC2001-2392-C03-02).

References

[1] Shnyia M., Saito T., Takahashi, T., *"Rendering Techniques for Transparent Objects"*, Proceedings of Graphics Interface'89, pp 173-181, 1989.

[2] Watt M., *"Light-Water Interaction using Backward Beam Tracing"*, Computer Graphics Vol 24, No 4, pp 377-385, 1990.

[3] Nishita T., Nakamae E., *"Method of displaying Optical Effects within Water using Accumulation Buffer"* SIGGRAPH'94 Conference Proceedings, ACM SIGGRAPH, pp 373-380, 1994.

[4] Fournier A., Reeves W.T., *"A simple model of ocean waves"*, Computer Graphics Vol 20, No 4, pp 75-84, 1986.

[5] Ts'o P.Y., Barsky B.A., *"Modeling and rendering waves: Wave-tracing using beta-splines and reflective and refracting texture mapping"*, ACM Transactions in Graphics Vol 6, No 3, pp 191-214, 1987.

[6] Peachey D.R., *"Modeling waves and surf"*, Computer Graphics Vol 20, No 4, pp 65-74, 1986.

[7] Nishita T., Sirai T., Tadamura K., Nakamae E., *"Display of the Earth Taking into Account Atmospheric Scattering"*, SIGGRAPH'93 Conference Proceedings, ACM SIGGRAPH, pp 175-182, 1993.

[8] Premoze S., Ashikmin M., *"Rendering Natural Waters"*, Proceedings of 8th Pacific Conference on Computer Graphics and Applications (PG'00), Hong-Kong, China, 3-5 October (2000), pp 23-30, 2000.

[9] Tadamura K., Nakamae E., *"Modeling the colour of Water in Lightning Design"*, in Earnshaw & Vince (eds.), Computer Graphics: Developments in Virtual Environments: Academic Press, pp 97-114, 1995.

[10] Wann Jensen H., Christensen P.H., *"Efficient Simulation of Light Transport in Scenes with Participating Media using Photons Maps"*, SIGGRAPH'98 Conference Proceedings, ACM SIGGRAPH, pp 311-320, 1998.

[11] Languénou, E., Bouatoch, K. Chellem, M.: *"Global Illumination in Presence of Participating Media with General Properties"*, in Photorealistic Rendering Techniques, Sakas, Shirley, Müller (eds.), Springer, pp 71-86, 1995.

[12] Pérez F., Pueyo X, Sillion F.X., *"Global Illumination Techniques for the Simulation of Participating Media"*, Proceedings of the Eight Eurographics Workshop on Rendering, Saint Etienne, France, pp 309-320, 1997

[13] Rushmeier, H., Torrance, E., *"The Zonal Method for Calculating Light Intensities in the Presence of a Participating Medium"*, Computer Graphics Vol 21, No 4, pp 293-302, 1987.

[14] Bhate N., *"Application of Rapid Hierarchical Radiosity to Participating Media"*, Proceedings Of ATARV-93: Advanced Techniques in Animation, Rendering and Visualization, Bilkent University, July, 1993.

[15] Sillion, F.X., *"A Unified Hierarchical Algorithm for Global Illumination with Scattering Volumes and Object Clusters"*, IEEE Transactions on Visualization and Computer Graphics, Vol 1, No 3, pp 240-254, 1995.

[16] Pattanaik S.N., Mudur S.P., *"Computation of Global Illumination in a Participating Medium by Monte Carlo Simulation"*, The Journal of Visualization and Computer Animation Vol 4, No 3, pp 133-1152, 1993.

[17] Blasi P., LeSaec B., Schlick C., *"A rendering algorithm for discrete volume density objects"*, Computer Graphics Forum Vol 12, No 3, pp 201-210, 1993.

[18] Kajiya J.T., von Herzen B.P., *"Ray-tracing volume densities"*, Computer Graphics Vol 18, No 3, pp 165-174, 1984

[19] Bhate N., Tokuta A., *"Photorealistic volume rendering of media with directional scattering"*, in N. Max (editor), Proceedings of the Third Eurographics Conference on Rendering, Bristol, England, May 1992, pp 227-245, 1992.

[20] Patmore C., *"Simulated Multiple Scattering for Cloud Rendering"*, in Graphics, Design and Visualization: Proceedings of the International Conference on Computer Graphics-ICCG93-, Mudur & Pattaniak (eds.), Elsevier Science Publishers, pp 29-40, 1993.

[21] Max N., *"Efficient Light Propagation for Multiple Anisotropic Volume Scattering"*, in Sakas G., Shirley P., Müller S. (eds.), Photorealistic Rendering Techniques: Springer, pp 87-104, 1995.

[22] Siegel H., Howel J.R., *"Thermal Radiation Heat Transfer"*, Third edition. Hemisphere Publishing Corporation, 1992.

[23] Cerezo E., Serón F.J., *"Synthetic Images of Underwater Scenes: A First Approximation"*, Proc. Of the 9-th International Conference in Central Europe on Computer Graphics, Visualization and Computer Vision (WSCG'2001), Plzen (Czech Republic), pp 395-402, 2001.

[24] Amanatides J., Woo A., *"A Fast Voxel Traversal Algorithm for Ray Tracing"*, in Eurographics'87, Conference Proceedings, Maréchal G. (editor), Elsevier Science Publishers, pp 3-10, 1987.

[25] http://www.cie.co.at/ciecb/

[26] Wandell B.A., *"The synthesis and analysis of color images"*, IEEE Transactions on Pattern Analysis and Machine Intelligence, Vol. 9, No 1, pp 2-13, 1987.

[27] Spinrad R.W., Carder K.L., Perry M.J. (eds.), *"Ocean Optics"*, Oxford Monographs on Geology and Geophysics. Oxford University Press, 1994.

[28] Mobley C.D., *"Light and water: Radiative Transfer in Natural Waters"*, Academic Press, 1994.

[29] Morel A., *"Light and marine photosynthesis: a spectral model with geochemical and climatological implications"*, Prog. Oceanogr., Vol 26, pp 263, 1991.

[30] Gordon H.R., Morel A, *"Remote Assesment of Ocean Color for Interpretation of Satellite Visible Imagery, a Review"*, Lecture Notes on Coastal and Estuarine Studies, Vol 4, Springer Verlag, 1983.

A System for Image Based Rendering of Walk-throughs

Gaurav Agarwal   Dinesh Rathi   Prem K. Kalra
Subhashis Banerjee

Department of Computer Science and Engineering
Indian Institute of Technology
New Delhi, 110016, India
email: {pkalra,suban}@cse.iitd.ernet.in

Abstract

We present a method for rendering novel views from a set of reference views under the assumption that scene surfaces can be approximated by planar patches. We use a set of sparse correspondences between the reference views to determine homographies through different planar patches using a clustering technique. We also obtain a segmentation of the scene in terms of planar regions visible from at least two views. Such segmentations explicitly resolve the visibility issues in novel view generation. We present results on rendering of realistic walk-through sequences for both indoor and outdoor scenes which demonstrate the applicability of our method.

1 Introduction

Recently, the problem of image based rendering has attracted considerable attention [2, 8, 12, 14, 4, 1], wherein the environmental map for rendering of novel views are maintained in terms of a set of images instead of explicit geometric and photometric models of a scene. In this paper we address the problem of generation of a sequence of novel views of a scene from a set of reference views. We assume that i) the scene surfaces can be approximated by planar patches (a common situation), and ii) every region in a target view is visible from at least two reference views; and develop a complete walk-through generation system starting from a set of sparse correspondences between the reference views. We consider the situation where the scene can have multiple occluding boundaries. We generate an intermediate representation of the scene in terms of planar patches which enables on-line rendering of novel views in an automatic manner. We also present a simple visibility analysis algorithm to determine which parts of a target novel view are visible in which parts of the reference views. As a consequence, we can explicitly resolve the visibility issues of image based rendering - those of *folds*, where multiple points of the reference images map on to a single point in a target image, and *holes*, where a region occluded in a reference image becomes visible in a target image. Our method is based on segmentation of the scene in terms of homographies between regions in the reference images through the planar patches.

1.1 Previous work

Laveau and Faugeras [8] present a method of representing a 3D scene as a collection of reference images and their pairwise epipolar geometries. They propose a 2D ray-tracing algorithm which start from each point in the target image and locate the corresponding points in the reference images, from which the intensity information can be transferred. In case multiple world points map on to the same pixel in the target image, their method can resolve the ambiguity by depth ordering and can thus account for *folds*. Their method does not require explicit 3D reconstruction but require dense disparity maps and the pairwise epipolar relationships.

McMillan and Bishop [12] (see also [10, 13, 11]) use the "plenoptic function" (which is a parametrized representation of all visible rays from a camera) originally proposed in [2] to compute aggregate image warps from reference images to target images. In [10, 13] they assume that the projective depth of every point is known and compute the aggregate warp using the projective depth and known camera positions. In [12] they acquire panoramic reference images on cylindrical manifolds, which serve as plenoptic models, and compute the aggregate warp from the cylindrical epipolar geometries and dense angular disparity maps. In all the above methods they follow an order of painting the target images by moving towards the epipoles in the reference images which preserve the correct occlusion-compatible depth order [11]. This "painter's" ordering result in target images free of *folds*. However all these methods require dense correspondences in some form.

In another significant approach to image based rendering Chen and Williams [3], and, Seitz and Dyer [14] use view interpolation to generate a target view from reference views. Chen and Williams [3] use image flow fields and local neighborhood analysis to reconstruct arbitrary target views with some constraints on gaze angle. Seitz and Dyer [14] show that a target view corresponding to a virtual camera can be generated by linear interpolation of the reference views provided the optical center of the target view lies on the line joining those of the reference views. In both these methods the visibility issues (*folds*) are resolved by z-buffering using disparity values. The view morphing method of Seitz and Dyer [14] has the restriction that the monotonicity of matches must be preserved between corresponding epipolar lines of the two reference views, i.e., the infinite line joining no two visible points P and Q should intersect the base-line between the reference views.

In a recent approach Lhuillier and Quan [9] present an algorithm for joint triangulation of matched regions in reference views and obtaining dense correspondences without using epipolar geometry. They use the joint view triangulation to interpolate a novel view. They do not discuss how they resolve the visibility issues but their results appear to be remarkably good when it comes to handling occlusions.

All the above methods require dense correspondences between the features in the reference views for rendering the novel views. Such correspondences are hard to obtain automatically, especially when the reference images differ in scale and illumination due to forward zooming motion (common in walk-throughs) or large baseline separations. Providing dense correspondence information manually is a tedious process and often require simplifying assumptions (like planarity, as in our case) for interpolation. In most of the above methods occlusion is handled either by a painting order or by z-buffering. While the painter's methods may result in unnecessary re-painting of target image regions, z-buffering is known to be memory inefficient. Laveau and Faugeras [8] explicitly compute the correct depth ordering in case multiple world points project on to the same image point on to the target view, but they need dense correspondences to do so.

In contrast, we automatically compute homographies between planar scene patches from a small set of seed correspondences (typically 15 to 20) which can either be provided manually or may even be computed automatically. The homographies through the planar patches provide the implicit interpolation necessary for rendering the novel views. Further, we explicitly compute a segmentation of the scene in terms of visibility from the reference views. As a consequence, we can explicitly resolve the visibility issues and no re-painting or z-buffering is necessary.

The rest of the paper is organized as follows. In Section 2 we give the system overview. In Section 3 we present our clustering algorithm for detecting homographies through all planar scene patches. In Section 4 we present our method for joint view segmentation for each planar patch. In Section 5 we present our algorithm for rendering a novel view. In Section 6 we present results on walk-through generation and finally, in Section 7 we conclude the paper.

2 System overview

We consider the problem of rendering target views along a specified walk-through path from a set of reference views $V_r, r = 1, \ldots, n$. We assume uncalibrated cameras, and, without loss of generality, set the camera matrix corresponding to the first camera to $\mathbf{P}_1 = [\mathbf{I} \mid \mathbf{0}]$. The camera matrices corresponding to the other reference views can then be chosen as $\mathbf{P}_r = [\mathbf{M}_r \mid \mathbf{e}_r]$ for $r = 2, \ldots, n$ [7]. Here $\mathbf{e}_r$ is the epipole in V_r with respect to the first camera and $\mathbf{M}_r = [\mathbf{e}_r]_\times \mathbf{F}_r$, where $\mathbf{F}_r$ is the fundamental matrix between the first and the rth view. The epipolar geometry and the camera matrices are computed in the standard way using the 8-point algorithm from a small number of seed correspondences [7].

In the off-line stage we compute a panoramic representation for each planar patch in the scene. The panoramic representation is computed using a segmentation of jointly visible parts of each plane from pair-wise analysis of reference images. The jointly visible parts are determined using

1. Computing homographies through planar patches using a clustering technique, and
2. A subsequent segmentation of planar regions visible in two reference views.

In the on-line stage of rendering of walk-throughs we perform a visibility analysis which based on the panoramic representations and the epipolar geometry.

It is often convenient to specify the path of the walk-through (the path followed by the camera centers of the novel views) in Euclidean terms. For this purpose, we assume that the camera centers of the reference views lie on a plane (a horizontal plane) and provide a 2D projective transformation between the projective representations of the camera centers and the rough Euclidean positions. The projective representations of the target novel views along the walk-through path are then approximated as convex combinations of the cameras corresponding to the reference views [14].

3 Determining homographies through planar patches using clustering

Images of world points lying on a plane are related to the corresponding image points in a second view by a 2D (planar) homography [5, 7]. Writing the first camera as $\mathbf{P} = [\mathbf{I} \mid \mathbf{0}]$ and a second camera as $\mathbf{P}' = [\mathbf{M} \mid \mathbf{e}']$, the homography induced by plane defined by $\pi^T \mathbf{X} = 0$ with $\pi = (\mathbf{v}^T, 1)^T$ is given as

$$\mathbf{H} = \mathbf{M} - \mathbf{e}' \mathbf{v}^T \qquad (1)$$

and is completely determined by correspondences of four points on the plane. For the four point homography to be a plane induced homography the consistency condition $\mathbf{He} = \mathbf{e}'$ must be satisfied.

Figure 1: Three reference views (View 1, View 2 and View 3)

In what follows we briefly describe our algorithm for determining homographies through different planar patches using a clustering technique. We use the Harris corner detector [6] to detect corners in the two images. Suppose the corner detector returns a set S_m of m corners in the first image. From the above set we select a small subset S_n of n of reliable seed matches such that they are uniformly distributed over the images. For reference images obtained from widely disparate view points it may be necessary to hand pick these seed correspondences. We use RANSAC [7] on this small set of point correspondences to determine homographies through different planar patches as follows:

Algorithm:

1. Select 4 point correspondences from the set S_n of n correspondences randomly such that the image distances of the four points are less than a preset threshold (we give a chance for the four points to be chosen from the same region).

2. Compute the homography between the two images using these 4 points. Verify that $\mathbf{He} = \mathbf{e}'$ within a tolerance; otherwise select a different set of four points.

3. Transfer the set S_m of detected corners in the first image to the second using the homography computed in the above step. Determine a subset $S_k \subset S_m$ of size k corners which fall within a distance threshold of corners in the second image and also satisfy the epipolar constraint $\mathbf{x}'^T \mathbf{F} \mathbf{x} = 0$.

4. If the number k is greater than some threshold T, then re-compute the homography using all the k corners by least-squares (include the newly found correspondences). Otherwise, repeat the above steps with a new choice of the 4 points. If the number k remains less than T after N trials, use the largest consensus set to compute the homography. We also record the region of support of the homography in the two images as the convex cover of the set S_k of k points.

5. Remove the correspondences that have been accounted for from both sets S_m and S_n. If the remaining correspondences (out of n) are above a threshold (minimum number of correspondences required per plane), repeat the steps above to find another homography through a new planar patch.

Figure 2: Corner matches between views 1 and 3 corresponding to the three planar patches. The matches corresponding to each patch are shown with different symbols.

Let the homographies found using the above procedure be $\mathbf{H}_i, i = 1, \ldots, l$ and their regions of support be S_i. Each of these homographies represent distinct planar patches in the scene. In Figure 1 we show three reference images used to test our novel view generation scheme. In Figure 2 we show the matches (out of S_m) in reference views 1 and 3 projected on view 3 through the homographies corresponding to three planes. We have cropped the floor because no reliable seed correspondences could be found in this region. The above algorithm correctly determines the homographies through the two doors and the back plane. The entire scene between the doors and above the floor get represented by a single homography because of their small relative depth separation compared to the distances from the cameras. In the next section we present our scheme for segmentation of the scene regions visible in both the reference views using the homographies computed above.

4 Segmentation of planar regions visible in two reference views

The segmentation algorithm is described as follows:
Algorithm:
For each of the homographies $\mathbf{H}_i, i = 1, \ldots, l$ computed above do the following:

1. Select in the first image a region somewhat larger than its region of support S_i computed above. In our experiments we have enlarged each region S_i by 10 pixels in all directions.

Figure 3: The joint view segmentations projected in view 3

2. Warp the intensity information of the enlarged regions (selected above) towards the second image using H_i and compute a difference (color) image. Segmentation of the dark regions in the difference image gives the final region of support for the homography in both views. We obtain the final segmentation by region-growing. In cases where the occluding boundaries are known to be straight lines, the region boundaries are refined by edge detection.

In Figure 3 we show the difference images computed after warping the enlarged regions of support for each homography in the first image towards the third. These are the common regions visible in both the reference views.

We do the above analysis pair-wise between all reference views. Finally for each planar patch visible from at least two views, we create a panoramic representation [15] P_i by registering the intensity images using the homographies found by each pair-wise analysis. We create the representation on the image plane in which it occupies the largest area. Each panoramic representation P_i represents the union of all regions of a planar patch that are visible from at least two reference views. Note that this panoramic representation is a conceptual device and need not be explicitly rendered. It is merely a data structure threading the pair-wise common segments corresponding to a planar patch through the corresponding homographies. In Figure 4 we show the panoramic representation of the back plane created from all the reference views (3 of which are shown above) for illustration.

5 Visibility analysis for rendering of a novel view

In order to render a novel view with a known camera matrix, we first need to establish the homographies between the novel view image plane and the panoramic representations P_i of each planar patch. Since all camera matrices and the pair-wise epipolar geometries are known, these homographies can be computed in any of the two ways.

Figure 4: The back plane panorama

1. For each planar patch P_i compute the explicit representation of the plane π from the reference views using Eqn. 1. Once π is known, use the epipolar geometry between the patch P_i and the target view to compute the homography using Eqn. 1 again.
2. Transfer at least four points (usually several more) for every planar patch from two reference views to the target view using the *trifocal tensor* [7], and use least-squares to compute the homography between the panoramic representation and the target view image plane.

Both the methods give good results in practice. Let the homography from the novel view to the ith panoramic patch be $\mathbf{H}_i$.

We also create a representation of all detected planar patches on any one of the reference images, say V_p, and estimate the homographies induced by each planar patch between V_p and the target view. Let these homographies be $\mathbf{G}_i$. We also estimate the epipolar geometry between V_p and the target view. The rendering algorithm can then be described as follows:

Algorithm:

1. For each pixel $\mathbf{x}$ in the target image compute the transfer $\mathbf{H}_i\mathbf{x}$ to the panoramic representation of each planar patch using the respective homographies $\mathbf{H}_i$ and determine whether the transferred point lies within the panoramic image segment.
2. If $\mathbf{H}_i\mathbf{x}$ lies within the corresponding panoramic image segment for only one value of i, then transfer the color information from $\mathbf{H}_i\mathbf{x}$ to $\mathbf{x}$. In such a case there is no ambiguity and the ray back-projected through $\mathbf{x}$ in the target view intersects only one finite plane of common visibility.
3. Suppose $\mathbf{H}_i\mathbf{x}$ lies within the corresponding panoramic image segment for more than one value of i. This indicates that the ray back-projected through $\mathbf{x}$ intersects more than one plane in the visible domain (see Figure 5). Then, for each of these planar patches,

transfer **x** to the reference image V_p using the homographies $\mathbf{G}_i$ corresponding to these patches.

4. Now, since all these points on V_p are corresponding points of **x** through different planar homographies $\mathbf{G}_i$, they must lie on an epipolar line in V_p. Clearly, the correspondence closest to the epipole occludes all others (Figure 5). Determine the plane for this correspondence and transfer the intensity information from the corresponding position of the panoramic representation of this planar patch on to **x**. Note that even when the epipole is a point at infinity, the relative ordering for occlusion holds.

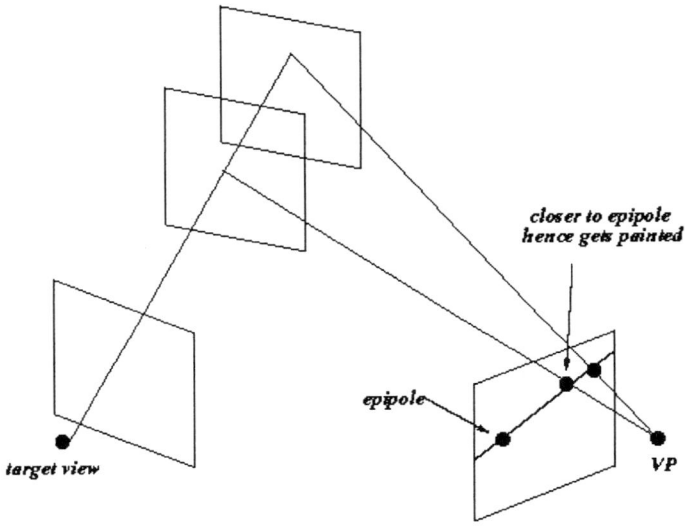

Figure 5: Occlusion handling

In case **x** doesn't correspond to any pixel in any of the panoramic representations of the planar patches there will be a *hole* at **x**. Note that this would indicate one or both of the following cases:

1. The assumption that every region in the target image is visible from at least two reference views is falsified, or,
2. The segmentation of jointly visible regions (described above) is incorrect.

In either of the above cases manual intervention will be necessary to modify the segmentation.

Note that the rendering algorithm explicitly accounts for resolution of occlusions, and no re-painting or z-buffering is required. Consequently, there can be no *folds*.

6 Results

In Figure 6 we show twelve views of the results of a walk-through along a zig-zag path towards the door (see at http://www.cse.iitd.ernet.in/vglab/demo/visibility/labscene.mpg). In this

Figure 6: Some views of the rendered walk-through sequence

example, no manual intervention other than hand picking of approximately 25 initial correspondences was necessary. In Figure 5 we show the rendering of a sequence of novel views with the two end views as reference images (these reference images have been obtained from the web-site http://www.inrialpes.fr/movi/people/Lhuillie/demo3.html; see also [9]).

7 Conclusion

We have engineered a complete system for image based rendering of scenes with planar patches starting from a small set of point correspondences using standard and well tested techniques from computer vision. We exploit "spatial coherence" where a scene in the reference image(s) is subdivided into planar patches that are mapped onto the target image through homographies. The main features of the system are i) only a small set of initial correspondences are required, ii) visibility is resolved explicitly, and no re-drawing or z-buffering is necessary, and iii) the method is largely automated, though it may require some manual intervention during the off-line segmentation stage. The method can easily be extended to deal with panoramic reference views [15]. The results demonstrate the robustness of the method.

References

[1] *Image-Based Modeling, Rendering, and Lighting*, SIGGRAPH Course 39, *SIGGRAPH*, 1999.

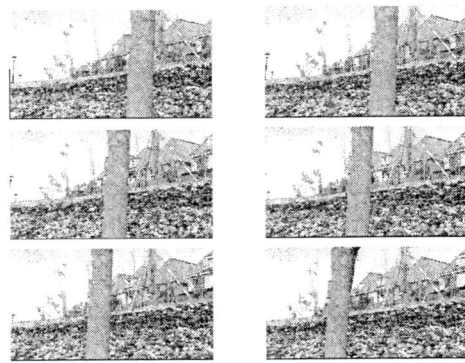

Figure 7: Rendering of an outdoor scene from the two end reference views

[2] E. H. Adelson and J. R. Bergen, "The Plenoptic function and the Elements of Early Vision," *Computational Models of Visual Processing*, Chapter 1, Edited by Michael Landy and J. Anthony Movshon. The MIT Press, Cambridge, Mass. 1991.

[3] S. E. Chen and L. Williams, "View Interpolation for Image Synthesis," *SIGGRAPH*, 1994.

[4] P. E. Debevec, C. J. Taylor and J. Malik, "Modeling and Rendering Architecture from Photographs," *SIGGRAPH*, 1996.

[5] O. Faugeras, *Three-Dimensional Computer Vision: A Geometric Viewpoint*, The MIT Press, 1996.

[6] C. Harris and M. Stevens, "A Combined Corner and Edge Detector," *Proc. 4th Alvey Vision Conference*, pp. 153-158, 1988.

[7] R. Hartley and A. Zisserman, *Multiple View Geometry in Computer Vision*, Cambridge University Press, 2000.

[8] S. Laveau and O. D. Faugeras, "3-D Scene Representation as a Collection of Images and Fundamental Matrices," INRIA, Technical Report No. 2205, 1994.

[9] M. Lhuillier and L. Quan, "Image Interpolation by Joint View Triangulation," *CVPR*, 1999.

[10] L. McMillan, *An Image-Based Approach to Three Dimensional Computer Graphics*, Ph.D thesis, University of North Carolina at Chapel Hill, 1997 (Technical Report TR97-013).

[11] L. McMillan, "Computing Visibility Without Depth," *UNC Technical Report*, TR95-047, University of North Carolina, 1995.

[12] L. McMillan and G. Bishop, "Plenoptic Modeling: An Image Based rendering System," *SIGGRAPH*, 1995.

[13] L. McMillan and G. Bishop, "Shape as a Perturbation to Projective Mapping," *UNC Technical Report*, TR95-046, University of North Carolina, 1995.

[14] S. M. Seitz and C. R. Dyer, "View Morphing," *SIGGRAPH*, 1996.

[15] R. Szeliski, "Image Mosaicing for Tele-Reality Applications," *DEC and Cambridge Research Lab. Technical Report,*, CRL 94/2, 1994.

Visual Interaction

ns:
Interaction in Virtual Worlds: Application to Music Performers

J. Esmerado, F. Vexo, D. Thalmann
Computer Graphics Lab
Swiss Federal Institute of Technology
EPFL-LIG 1015 Lausanne

Abstract

We present a model for the representation of the interactions between virtual human figures and virtual objects in 3D virtual scenes. These interactions can depend on externally provided information not being limited in their complexity. The representation model for virtual humans is modular and provides tools for representation of the interaction know-how pre-requisite. Timing constraints are relevant in this model and concurrency and synchronism are used to insure the adequacy of the resulting animations of virtual humans and associated interacted objects. Resulting gestures are derived from an adapted application of Inverse Kinematics methods.

Keywords: Virtual Scenes, Virtual Humans, Virtual Objects, Interaction, Inverse Kinematics, Musician Simulation.

1. Introduction

Populated virtual environments have been a wide research topic in recent years. Among the possible trends within this field there is the quest for realism and believability. In virtual environments, believability depends on several factors such as an accurate rendering of the visual properties of the scene constituents. Believability can depend also on the accuracy and naturalness of the possible events and actions taking place in the virtual scene. Events may result from actions produced by active scene constituents, such as autonomous virtual humans (AVH) and the accuracy of these actions and associated events depends on the adopted underlying model for the virtual scene.

One of the expected important types of actions is of the interaction type. In this work we are especially interested in the representation of interactions between autonomous virtual humans and other scene constituents named *virtual objects*. Virtual objects can exhibit several levels of morphological and motion inducing methods nature complexity. Some virtual objects can exhibit self-animation

properties; other virtual objects require virtual human guidance to perform in an adequate, believable manner. The latter corresponds to the case of virtual human/virtual object interaction based on information about the object and its standard use.
In order to handle the variety of elements that can be part of a virtual scene and their relationships in a comprehensive and semantically adequate manner, an integrating scene content model is necessary.

This paper presents a proposal of a comprehensive model for representing the content of virtual scenes. This model is meant to facilitate capturing the relationships and semantics of virtual scene contents and to provide a framework for the effective representation of interactions between elements in the virtual scene. This is model is based on an object-based approach to enable reaching any level of particularity for a given scene constituent.

2. Context

2.1 Proposed 3D Scene Model

In a virtual scene, it is possible to distinguish the constituents, (henceforth referred to as *elements*), actions and events. Elements can be non-animated (or *static*), or animated. Elements can also correspond to virtual objects (including a particular case, the background images or *décor*) and virtual humans. Virtual Humans can exhibit either autonomous behavior or be 3D representatives of real world users (real-user avatars). Virtual Objects can range from simple non-animated, non-deformable types of object to deformable, self-animated and reactive ones.

In virtual scenes, events can derive essentially from actions performed by active elements in the scene and is typically associated with the beginning and ending of some relevant activity [9]. Specially interesting for an external observer is witnessing realistically simulated interactions in virtual scenes. The level of complexity of the interaction will be able to draw a corresponding level of interest of an observer [3][6]. For this reason, one of the principal objectives of our model is to facilitate the representation of sophisticated interactions in virtual scenes taking place in an automatic way.

In our model, we are interested in representing mainly, but not only the visual properties of the scene elements. This way, visual properties of elements are identified as their *shape* and a particular shape can be associated to an element for rendering purposes.

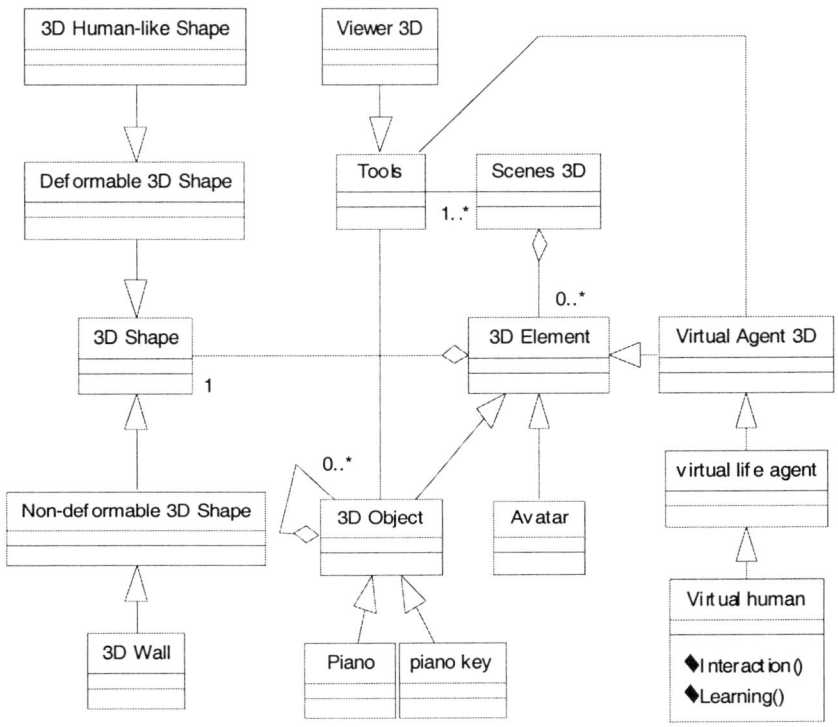

Figure 1: 3D Scene Content Model

The representation of Virtual Objects must encompass all the range of their possible levels of variety and complexity along with common properties such as properties related to their morphology. For reaching an acceptable degree of realism the object representation should contain representations of forms of behavior that relate to the physical properties of that object. This can become particularly useful when events such as interactions between the object and other scene elements take place. This way, in many cases a virtual object should be capable of performing self-animation, that is, to generate its own forms of reaction from its internal representation.

The internal representation of self-animation may need to accept input from the surrounding scene. Controlled self-animation corresponds to a situation where another scene entity (generally a virtual human) is commanding or at least guiding the object's animation. In our model it is considered as too costly for rendering time to base interactions representation strictly on the simulation of physical contact. The consequence is that commanding a virtual object corresponds to starting and ending each of the object's animations, being the object's internal animation representation that takes charge in-between. An autonomous animation of an object corresponds in short to a behavior from the object. An object can be composed from several sub-objects or parts, forming a more complex whole. Each of those components is an object in its own right that can possess a similar set of attributes to the main encapsulating object.

Figure 1 shows an example of the integration of elements in the scene their explicit associated shape properties and the possibility of defining objects from other objects.

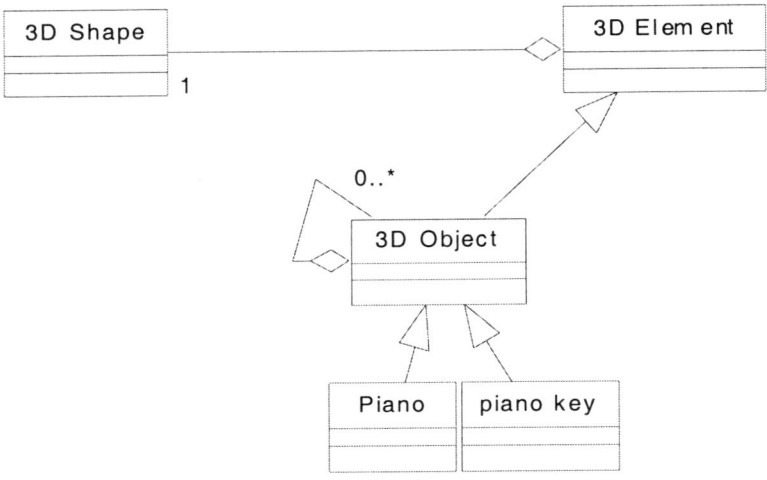

Figure 2: **Virtual Object Model**

A virtual human model must contain the necessary elements allowing it to be visualized in a realistic manner while possessing the characteristics enabling an informed, varied and autonomous type of interaction with its surroundings. This latter aspect entails the need to associate to the virtual human the necessary resources to allow for forms of perception, interpretation, reasoning and gesture generation adapted to the situations generated in virtual scenes. We call the latter intellectual attributes. These may encompass a vast set of properties or criteria. For this reason we will narrow down the discussion of mental properties representation to those attributes that are relevant for the representation of virtual human interaction skills.

For representing skills it becomes necessary to represent knowledge [8]. Knowledge is generally applied using also information data and all those elements must be stored or *memorized*. Limited duration memory data is considered as part of a

Volatile Memory whereas lifelong data is stored in a Permanent Memory region. All information that must become part of a virtual human's patrimony is a permanent memory item. That is for example the case of skills. In Volatile Memory items like recollections of encountered objects in the scene, objects currently being carried, etc. These items are associated to a maximal duration and can also be discarded when they stop being relevant.

Interaction skills are normally associated to one or more objects. To facilitate representing the need of an object a dedicated *known objects list* is proposed in order to quickly determine whether an encountered object permits the impending execution of one of the virtual human's skills. By crosschecking the encountered object's type identifier with the *known objects list* it is possible to determine a list of associated skills and by matching with all available skill preconditions to see if the skill execution can proceed.

For ease of representation of the list of objects being carried at a given time by a virtual human a memory *inventory* list is also introduced.

2.1.1 Skills Representation

Skills Representation

{

Executable skill types to choose from:

- Identification Skill Model
- Independent Basic Skills (Walk, Dance, Music, etc.)
- Procedural Skills (linked to Virtual Object)

Additional possible characterization data objects per skill:

- Skill Level
- Time Influence on Skill Level (law of evolution)
- Skills Dependence on VO
- Skill Dependence on other Skills

}

Among virtual object-related skills, some simplifying modeling choices are adopted:

- The levels of necessity of a given object can increase/decrease over time account for the increased longing for performing a particular Skill.
- The Pre-processing of the scene is required for identification of the objects present that are concerned by skills. This mechanism can be limited to a perimeter around the Autonomous Virtual Human (AVH).
- A filtering mechanism discards the useless objects (those with no skill associated for the current AVH).

A *pseudo-code* for Interesting *Object Selection Mechanism* is as follows:

```
if ( FoundObject IN ListofSkillRequiredObjects ) { //
        FoundObject -> LocatedObjectList
        if ( FoundObject IN NeedList ) { // Especially Necessary Object
                if ( FoundObject == AVAILABLE ) { // Not taken by other interacting VH
                        GetReferencePositionAndPostureToAdopt()
                        MarkObjectAsTakenByCurentVH( FoundObject )
                        StartInteractionSkill()
                }
                else { // Object taken...
                        while (NOT tooLong() ) {
                                if ( OtherObjectSameTypeInKnownLocation() )
                                {
                                        // There's still some hope...
                                        GotoSameTypeObjectOldLocation()
                                        if ( StillThere() AND AVAILABLE ) {
                                                StartFromTheBeginning()
                                        }
                                        else {
                                                ContinueSearchfor Objects()
                                        }
                                }
                                QuitCurrentlyActivatedSkill()  // Liberates resources associated to the current skill
                        }
                }
        }
}
```

A *Need* List allows the virtual human to give preference to certain types of objects among those that were identified in its neighborhood. The intersection of this list with the available objects allows for possible Need-list entry satisfaction. The object in question must be marked as *free* to become associated to a virtual human and must also be marked as *portable* for the current AVH in order to be able to be picked-up by it. The complete representation of a Need concept would entail abstract needs derived from rules like 'people must wear a helmet before going into a construction site'. A skill that requires a missing object cannot be activated until that object is localized and *captured* (associated to the virtual human). It can happen that a skill requires more than one object and this should associate to a single missing object a very high priority during search and identification phases.

There are two important notions: *Interesting* object, which corresponds to objects within the set of skill-related objects in the Autonomous Virtual Human's current skill list, and the notion of *Especially Necessary* object, which corresponds to the contents of a special list within the Autonomous Virtual Human model, representing an object need to be fulfilled as soon as possible. This avoids having to manage a representation of a growth of need over time or some other equivalent method.

2.1.2 General approach for modeling virtual object interaction skills

As depicted from the diagram in Figure 3, our general approach to skill modeling consists firstly of taking all the necessary data from adequate sources such as information providing objects in the scene and converting that data into a skill-usable data format if required. Once all the necessary data (including knowledge data) is available in a convenient format, interaction skill data generation can take place using adequate reasoning mechanisms.

The results may consist mainly on animation data and also the required results or specific effects on the interacted object. As depicted Figure 3, the interaction module feeds a synchronization mechanism that enforces the simultaneity of the resulting animations on the Autonomous Virtual Human embodiment and also on the interacted Virtual Object, along with possible interaction results or products such as sound generation, lighting effects, etc.

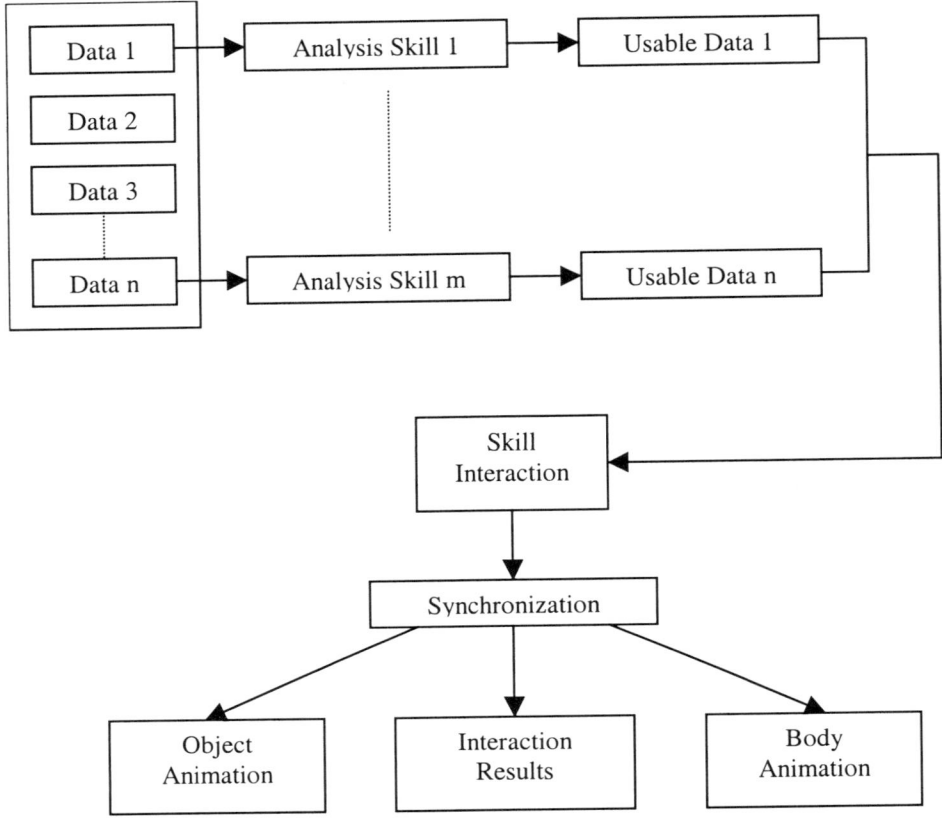

Figure 3: General Interaction Model

3. Application Example: Virtual Pianist

As a demonstration example for the usage of our proposed model we chose the case of a virtual pianist. This demonstration is chosen as an illustration of what a complex interaction case may involve and of how the proposed model tools are used in order to solve the interaction simulation problem. In this case, the virtual scene must contain at least a Piano virtual object a Pianist autonomous virtual human and a virtual scorebook in order to provide the necessary music input. No music score data is initially associated to the virtual human.
The particular demands posed by this type of interaction include:

- Pianist must act within a very strict timeline due to music dependence. Music is essentially a sound-time form of activity.
- The contact surface of the key (piano mobile component) is very restricted. The finger as arm extremity should accompany the motion of the key
- The speed associated to those motions should reflect the produced sound volume.

The interaction between finger and piano key is dependent from music data input. It has to be automatically decided by a specialized Expertise. It is also dependent on the availability of a carried object containing music data, a music score object.

3.1 Permanent Memory Content

Interaction skills always obey a general pattern described as follows:
- Approach the Virtual Human to the Virtual Object to be interacted and place the Virtual Human embodiment and/or the Virtual Object at a suitable distance according to the skill specification.
- Execute the skill interaction with the virtual object.
- Restore the previous Virtual Object state and abandon its immediate surroundings.

For a piano playing interaction to take place in a virtual scene the virtual human must possess dedicated skills as described in the following.

3.1.1 Piano Playing Skill Execution Model

The piano playing skill general model normally follows this sequence:

- Locate piano virtual instrument
- Check if music input is already available for the Virtual Human
- If there is music input available proceed as follows:
- Place music Input Object if it exists and is necessary
- Make Virtual Human install itself at a suitable position in front of the instrument. Hands and arms float closely over the keyboard without possibility of contact
- Music Playing Skill Execution phase
- Remove music Input Object if it exists
- Virtual Human abandons the location in front of the instrument

3.2 Music Playing Skill Execution Phase

The piano skill Execution model generally obeys the following procedural pattern:

- Transform Note Input into structured note data
- Generation of a music interpretation
- Hand/Finger attribution to the note
- Schedule time for note execution
- Feed time and note to the instrument model
- Feed finger and time to the Virtual Human animation unit
- Generate animation for Virtual Pianist
- Generate animation for Virtual Piano
- Check end of execution for each time-scheduled note set for both Virtual Pianist and Virtual Piano

3.2.1 Fingering Attribution Skill

This capability is a skill that does not refer to interaction directly. It corresponds to the execution of an abstract model according to which it is possible to attribute fingers to keys given, at least notes and rhythm.
General models for tackling this problem have been proposed. Their tendency is to rely on mathematics [7]. Our approach seeks to approach near real-time performance, as in real life sight-reading. It is a rule-based system approach enriched with meta-rules, heuristics and search mechanisms. The method consists of applying pre-defined fingering knowledge as much as possible. This technique corresponds to isolating parcels of the stream of notes that match a partial predefined solution. Frequently, there may be more than one possible solution. In a rule-based approach, the preferred solutions are those that solve for the largest number of notes. Heuristics are applied for guiding those choices especially concerned with frontier conditions between partial solutions to help disambiguate conflicts and provide a satisfactory overall solution for each case [5][11][8].

The used rules are about permitted fingering sequences, exceptional situations and physical *convenience* rules. In music, some special 'rules' apply to certain pre-defined situations. When piano music is the focus, several identifiable higher-level musical elements possess their own set of possible fingerings and thus these elements should be clearly identified beforehand. This identification allows the use of rules that mention those consecrated musical units, in general harmonic elements. Element examples include chords, the arpeggios, tremolos, octaves, octave scales, broken chords, harmonic intervals and scales. There's also general knowledge on how certain harmonic interval successions in fact can also be seen as broken chords.

3.3 Scorebook and Music Data Representation

A virtual human interacting with a virtual piano object is based on musical input. To be able to provide different music pieces at different points in the scene without the need to store all that information in the virtual human itself we introduce the virtual scorebook in the scene. A pianist virtual human can then use the musical information contained in this object to guide its interaction with an available virtual piano.

If a scorebook is present in a suitable position with respect to the virtual human and the piano, or if a scorebook is part of the virtual human's inventory then a link is created between this object and the virtual human so that the processed music data can be transferred.

The model for the scorebook virtual object derives from the general object representation model and more specifically contains references both to a MIDI source data file and to the proprietary format used for the animation processes.

Concerning music data, the requirements of an automatic music-based instrument plus virtual human animation system are not directly met by the MIDI specification as defined. The reasons that dictated the adoption of an alternative representation for the music data are as follows:

- In order to be able to implement a reasoning scheme based on music data there is a great convenience of being able to structure such data thus forming when possible higher level data structures that allow a more comprehensive vision about the music properties. If we only dispose of raw one-by-one note data there is a strong limitation as to the variety of rules one can write about music content. In other words structuring music data is the key to dispose of an effective music analysis tool.
- In order to be effective, at a given point in time the animation system should promptly know which and how many notes are active in a structured way, independently of MIDI internal file structure considerations such as number of intervening tracks and the partitioning of notes among those tracks.
- The needs of an automatic choice of fingerings (attribution of hands and fingers to the set of notes being play at each moment) also imposes that at each instant in time we should be able to take a theoretical snapshot of the keyboard state and that we can do the same for any number of instants preceding or coming after the current instant. This is due to the input requirements of the expert knowledge approach typically associated to this type of choice making.
- The body motions generated by a real virtuoso pianist can reach high speeds, especially at the finger level. To be able to emulate a real-time interaction it is necessary to limit the minimal duration of a musical event, otherwise the system would be forced to frequently discard motions that cannot be rendered during a given time lapse in order to keep up with a given musical pace. Since in that case musical notes would still be rendered, it would be senseless to be forced to discard frequently the corresponding animation.

Our approach for structuring musical data consists of the following fundamental steps:

Notes are collected and their durations noted, along with their starting times, independently of their MIDI track origin.

We estimate the minimal duration of a single note.

The previous choice allows also for a representation of the music content in a fixed rate basis. The minimal time duration is used to define a "music frame" duration time unit. This way all notes can be represented over time in an integrated manner as multiples of the specified minimal time duration.

This representation allows representing the processed MIDI content as entries into a table where each entry corresponds to one single minimal time duration. The played notes can be represented as part of as many consecutive table entries as necessary to represent their total duration. The representation as a table allows to immediately knowing the past present and future of the notes being used and therefore is a valuable tool for the automatic generation of fingerings.

4. Implementation

Currently an implementation of a Virtual Pianist playing on a Virtual Piano using data from a Virtual Score book exists based on the proposed Scene Content Model. This implementation is meant to provide a more general Music Simulation Platform integrating any number of musicians playing assorted instruments. Languages C/C++ are used both on Unix and Windows platforms. On Windows, proprietary VHD++ platform development tools are used essentially for rendering.

The visual rendering is issued through a separate lightweight process, which controls also accessory aspects like viewpoint positioning and the *camera motion*. This allows a convenient positioning of the observer. The sound rendering is not sensitive to this positioning yet, though.

The synchronized animations are shown to the observer through the visual rendering process. The animation of the scene elements is done through synchronized lightweight processes (Posix threads) that react on a quarter of a second basis in time for the rendering process to do its image updates. Also synchronized with the animation of the scene elements (piano and pianist) the piano sound rendering thread operates based on the concept of a minimal duration for a single note. Every single note has to be represented as a multiple of the minimal note duration.

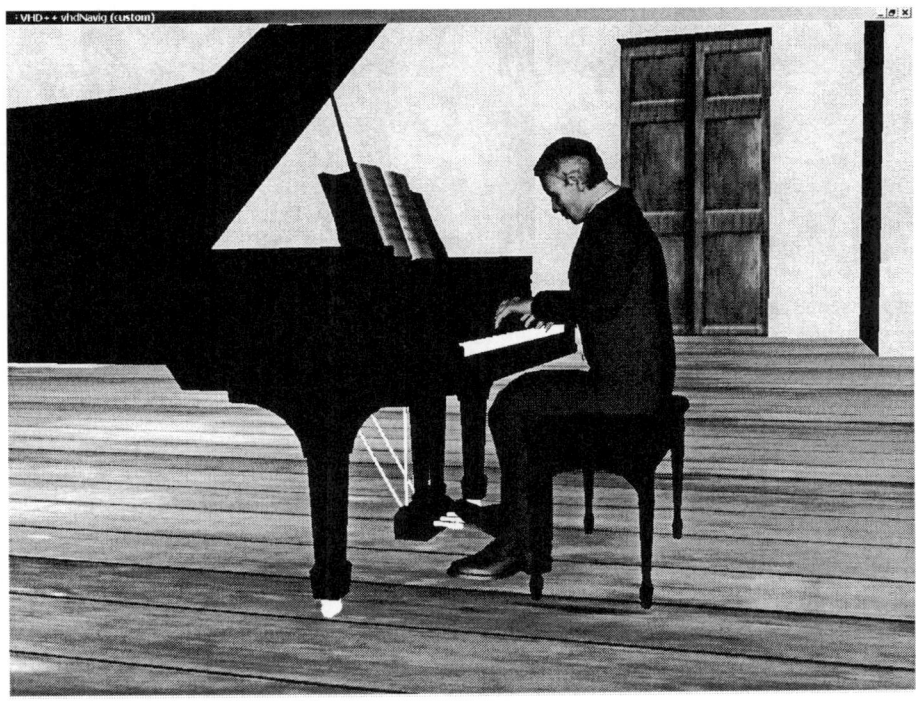

Figure 4: Virtual pianist interacting with virtual piano.

In our implementation, music data usage is prepared before any animation takes place. This can be viewed as a *learning* phase, or pre-processing.

The piano learning process is intimately related to the musical piece being played, as it would be in a real pianist case. In our case learning means learning the gestures for the playing of a specific music piece. To this end a piano-learning routine is centered on one function where the necessary know-how to generate the standard representation of the body articulation angles for each animation frame is represented. This corresponds to a modular representation for the know-how of a specialist.

The main implementation aspects covered by the pianist-related know-how function are:
- Collecting of relevant note information (current, past and future)
- Attribution of hands and fingers to every note in the current time slot (as dictated by the internal music table representation entry) and
- Generation of the gestures corresponding to the playing of the target notes using the attributed fingers taking into account as many positioning factors as the internal skill representation of the pianist allows to.

The first activity, finger attribution to keys, was addressed by using a system based on rules. This system may be as comprehensive as required by the particular application demands, thus providing an ever-extendable refinement, which can provide multiple solutions, that can be ordered and selected using heuristic criteria.

Our music representation structure facilitates this type of analysis for rules condition matching, contrary to the original MIDI format given the fact that all the content is directly available. For each instant in time, the solutions found depend on the current set of notes to be played but should also depend on recent past notes and also future notes to be played in order to generate the most natural possible gestures/solutions. Obviously, there is normally no unique ideal solution to this type of problem. In our implementation we only strive to produce reasonably well-formed solutions, since in general there is no unique absolutely "correct" solution to the fingering problem, anyway. There are no special duration restrictions to this phase since the resulting finger attributions are generated "off-animation" and stored away in the knowledge memory of the associated virtual human for later usage.

The second, gesture generation, uses inverse kinematics techniques to generate the final gestures associated to the placement of the fingers on the desired (virtual) keys, these being in their pressed-down position [1]. The inverse kinematics algorithm conversion is normally insured by the specification of a number of controlling points (end-effectors) situated at the fingertips and wrists of the virtual human pianist [2][4][10]. The resulting gestures are combined with in-between gestures and interpolated so that a smooth gesture sequence and transitions results [12][6].

The learning phase is meant to produce adequate gestures from the available input and corresponds to a modular part that is replaceable. This modularity property is one of the important points of the object-oriented design of our model. The criterion to abide by is that the output has to be in any case a sequence of gestures adapted to the external musical input. Once the off-animation learning process has produced the set of gestures that correspond to the musical data the animation activity can take place when needed.

The animation phase deals with the interaction simulation. Both the acting element (the virtual human pianist) and the virtual object being acted upon have to be animated in a coherent manner with one another. If the object is composed of observable moveable parts this aspect becomes even more obvious from an observer point of view. We realized that a more physical-based approach involving real time collision detection was not fast or reliable enough at this time of writing if our aim includes also preserving the intelligibility of the music sound rendering. According to the proposed model, we produce the synchronized, independent animations of the player's embodiment and the musical instrument, both synchronized with the output of music sound. Each of these three activities is launched in parallel, their key events being synchronized with one another.

5. Conclusions

We proposed a model for the representation of the content of virtual 3D scenes populated by virtual humans and containing objects that may exhibit complex features.

In this work we have proposed a model for representing the contents of virtual scenes aimed at facilitating the representation of the interactions between virtual humans and virtual objects in those scenes. This model proposal results from the need of having an integrated approach to represent 3D scene content extensible enough to encompass future developments and additions while already providing a frame work for integrating a new virtual human - virtual object skilled interaction modeling. These skilled virtual humans interactions can be modeled taking time into account. Time dependence is a key aspect for the correct representation of many interaction activities especially when both interacting parties exhibit visual animation behaviors and this why we pay special attention to finding solutions to tackle this particular problem.

In our demonstration application we have one virtual human agent (a virtual pianist) that is capable of interacting (playing) with one virtual object (a virtual piano) in an autonomous way. As sole input to the interaction there's yet another object (a virtual scorebook). The scorebook role in the scene is to stock musical data that a virtual pianist can extract and use as input for an educated learning phase and subsequent playing phase. This musical input data from the scorebook is also used for generating the piano animation and corresponding sound production.
One of the most relevant characteristics of the piano-playing problem is the synchronization aspect of music playing animation.
In order to model the synchronization mechanism it is necessary that the data that serves as a basis for the control assumes a suitable format. In our demonstration case the musical input provided is associated with the scorebook scene component. Originally this data comes in MIDI format. However, MIDI format, though structured, does not directly provide a directly usable data source format adapted to our needs: In fact, our needs include the convenient ability to dispose of a list of all the events that take place at the same time and to know exactly what that time is. MIDI does not directly provide data in this format since it is a sequential description of events that may be scattered across multiple independent tracks.

The learning procedure is meant to produce adequate gestures from the available input and corresponds to a modular part that is replaceable. This modularity property is one of the important points of the object-oriented design of our model. The criterion to abide by is that the output has to be in any case a sequence of gestures adapted to the external musical input. Once the off-animation learning process has produced the set of gestures that correspond to the musical data the animation activity can take place when needed. The use of interpolation techniques can further smooth resulting gestures out.

The demonstration application validates the usefulness of the proposed model for interactions in virtual scenes. By introducing improved expert interaction know-how modules the resulting interactions can be further improved in gesture variety and believability.

References

Baerlocher P., Boulic R., *Task-Priority Formulations for the Kinematic Control of Highly Redundant articulated Structures*, In Proceedings of IROS, Victoria, Canada, 323-329, 1998.

Baerlocher P., *Inverse Kinematics Techniques of the Interactive Posture Control of Articulated Figures*, PhD Thesis, Swiss Federal Institute of Technology at Lausanne (EPFL), Lausanne Switzerland, 2001.

Becheiraz P., *Un Modele Comportamental et Emotionnel pour l'Animation d'Acteurs Virtuels*, PhD thesis, Swiss Federal Institute of Technology at Lausanne (EPFL), Lausanne Switzerland, 1998.

Boulic R., Rezzonico S., Thalmann D., *Multi Finger Manipulation of Virtual Objects*, Proceedings of the ACM Symposium on Virtual Reality Software And Technology, VRST, 67-74, 1996.

Caicedo A., Thalmann D., *Intelligent Decision making for Virtual Humanoids*, Workshop of Artificial Life Integration in Virtual Environments, 5th European Conference on Artificial Life, pp.13-17, Lausanne, Switzerland, September 1999.

Emering L., *Human Action Modeling and Recognition for Virtual Environments*, PhD Thesis, Swiss Federal Institute of Technology-EPFL, Lausanne, Switzerland, 1999.

Funge J., *AI for Games and Animation: A Cognitive Modeling Aproach*, A.Peters, Natick, MA, 1999.

Haton J-P et all, *Le raisonnement en Intelligence Artificielle: techniques, modèles et architectures pour les systèmes à base de connaissances*, InterEditions, Paris 1991.

Macedonia M., Brutzman D., Zyda M., Pratt D., Barham P., Falby J., Locke J., *NPSNET: A Multi-Player 3D Virtual Environment Over The Internet*, Proc. 1995 Symposium on Interactive 3D Graphics, NY:ACM, pp. 93-94, 1995.

Tolani D., Badler N., *Real-Time Inverse Kinematics of the Human Arm*, Presence 5(4), 393-401, 1996.

Turban E., *Expert Systems and Applied Artificial Intelligence*, Macmillan Publishing Company, 1992.

Wiley D., Hahn J., *Interpolation Synthesis for Articulated Figure Motion*, Virtual Reality Annual International Symposium, Albuquerque, New Mexico, March, 1997.

Enhancing Archive Television Programmes for Interactivity

Mark Carey BSc   Alf Watson BSc, PhD   Dave Paget BSc.

University of Sunderland

Abstract

The emergence of digital television has seen an increase in the amount of available channels. The television industry faces the task of filling these schedules on stations that often broadcast for 24 hours a day. One resolution has been the use of archive material.

Digital television has also led to the implementation of interactive services, supplementing programmes as broadcast and also offering stand alone services, providing access to shopping facilities and games and trivia quizzes.

With the advent of interactive services, the audiences expectations of the delivery of programmes has increased, but the increased funding required for new services and programmes is becoming difficult.

Research has been developed to combine a cost-effective answer for the provision of programmes for digital channels whilst implementing the new emerging technologies.

We propose the development of an interactive environment, designed from archive material. This will push forward interactivity disseminated via broadcast, in allowing the user full navigation of the environment through 360 degrees, creating the experience of 3D viewing.

By using archive material we are able to reduce costs as the process introduces the re-purposing of an existing commodity, with the combination of a new technology. It is envisaged that the new environment can recreate a full archive programme or in the early stages of development, interactive scenes to supplement the material as broadcast

Keywords: Archive Material, Virtual Environments, Immersive environments, Digital Puppets, 3D, Interactivity, Navigation,Digital television, Enhancement, Animation.

1.0 Introduction

The aim of this paper is to introduce a working methodology for the creation of an interactive 3D environment, utilising and enhancing archive programmes, for broadcast via interactive television (iTV) [1].

The working methodology has been created in response to the analysis of the requirements of individual archive programmes [2], and has led to the development of a new set of production values that can be applied to the processes involved in the creation of the interactive 3D environment. The production processes that have been applied to the research are discussed and illustrated throughout the paper.

The reality of achieving the recreation of an entire archive programme was minimal given the size of the production team and the available hours and resources which could be given to the project. For this reason it was determined that the recreation of a single scene within the selected material would be the most viable application of the methodology. This enables the facilitation of the development of a working model to demonstrate the results of the undertaken research and its further potential expansions and implementations, which can be produced on a larger scale than that which have been presently available. It is envisaged that this would eventually lead to the process being applied to a complete recreation of a full archive programme.

The methodology created within the research could also be applied to creating 3D interactive extras to be distributed within 2D television programmes. Potential outlets include DVD and CD-ROM, which are good examples of existing technologies that have developed and utilised interactivity and navigation.

All methods discussed are derived from archive sources and develop a re-purposing of materials.

2.0 Archive Television Programmes

The production process utilises archive television programmes as its source for design and texture of the environment.

Table 1

The rationale for using archive material are:
• Low overheads; as there is little or no requirement to record new information, which would entail the creation of sets and the hiring of actors both of which can be costly. This also reduces the mount of required production time for the project.
• It is an existing material and therefore easily accessible
• The process of conversion to a 3D iTV environment, re-purposes archive material and uses a commodity that may otherwise have remained in storage. [2]
• Gives a purpose to retaining and utilising material. [2]
• Presents excellent results with a quicker execution time to that of a new production, while demonstrating the possibilities of interactive 3D environments for television broadcast.
• Archive material can provide a ready made audience base if the programme being converted has a cult following in the audience it attracts.

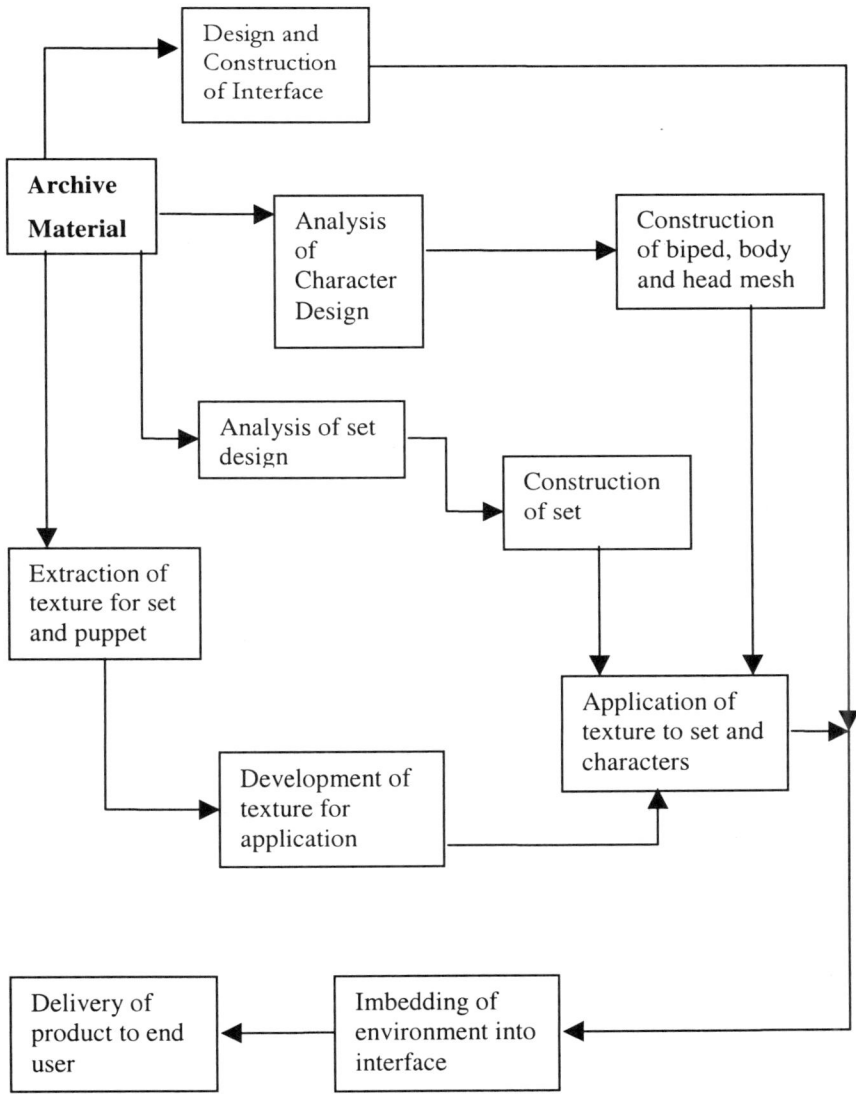

Figure 1 Flow chart of production process for recreation of 2D archive material to 3D interactive environment

Archive material that has a long run of programmes can be ideal for use in the production process, and should be considered in the selection of material.

Table 2

Reasons for selecting a long running established archive programme:
• A good wealth of material from which to choose individual productions and scenes
• The increased possibility of recurring sets allowing the availability of more angles and different shots of the set.
• The possibility of good supplementary material
• Good production files for the archive material, which may include drawing concepts of sets that were not constructed or ideas for inclusion in the programme that can now be adapted to the programme.
• The possibility that the missing fourth wall of the set will be seen at some point in the series history to give a representation of how it should look when being created as part of the 3D environment. The production drawings may also provide a representation of this area even though it was never created.
• If particular textures or shots of sets do not appear in one programme from the series, there is the possibility that it can be extracted from another programme instead and adapted for use in the current production.

When the original material was recorded the set in which the story is developing is likely to have been constructed of only two or three walls. In a normal room there is a basic layout of four walls. With there only being a maximum of three walls in a set there is a missing fourth area. In the course of the research this has been termed as the missing fourth wall. It was from this area that the production would have been shot. By giving a 360 degree view capability to the user, the missing fourth wall has to be created.

While reasons for using archive material have been detailed above there is also a need to identify the right kind of archive footage, something that will adapt better to the processes involved in production of the 3D environment. From this selection a set of new production values are derived, which determine the overall design, look and navigation of the set.

Table 3

Production Values arising from the working Methodology:
1.) Depth of understanding of the archive material
2.) No complexes, including set designs, and shot constructions
3.) No redundant characters
4.) Basic Lighting
5.) The inclusion of new creative input
6.) Script and Story Lines for adaptation, simple with few complexes
7.) The use of sources supplementary to archive footage
8.) Implementation of interfaces and interactions to exploit potential of material
9.) Access of scenes in a non linear viewing capacity, non-chronological
10.) The provision of control of point of view to the audience
11.) Links from the environment to information in conjunction with CD-ROM or Web Site capabilities.
12.) Inclusion of imbedded interactivity in some way rewarding the user.

By following these new production values and the methodology, the successful creation of an interactive 3D environment for iTV is achieved.

3.0 Required elements for inclusion in an iTV environment

Table 4

Elements required as part of a 3D, iTV environment:
1. The full navigation of the environment by the end user through 360 degrees.
2. A Photo-Realistic appearance in order to capture the belief of the audience [3]
3. Ease of navigation of both the environment and the interface
4. A programme, that better lends itself towards the enhancements being implemented.
5. Good supplementary materials to the existing archive material being used.
6. The creation of photo-realistic characters, which are lip-synced to audio material extracted from the archive source. [5,6,7]

The combination of the above elements provides the realisation of a believable 3D interactive environment. The environment must be user friendly, easily accessible and immerse the viewer.

The production process is unique in its delivery of a navigable 3D interactive environment for broadcast television. [3,10]

4.0 Creating Navigation for an iTV environment

Navigating within 3D environments is not a new idea, but its implementation to interactive television is relatively new.

Exploration of 3D environments can be experienced:

- online in artificial environments created for interactivity between users, represented in the environment as avatars

- in computer games again through the use of avatars.

While these environments can be photo-realistic or artificial in appearance, there is no definition of the overall look as they are generally created as new productions. In using archive material to construct the iTV environment a benchmark is established based on user expectations based upon the aesthetic of the original programme

When using an avatar to navigate within a game, the user has the ability to change events that occur through the paths the avatar follows or the actions they undertake. Whilst this can be partially applied to the iTV environment, there is already existing action and a story line in place restricting the opportunities available to change the path of events. While this may limit the amount of influence the user has upon events, there are other opportunities to be exploited. These can include the manipulation of point of view to a greater degree than that offered in computer games, and is a new development to the delivery of television programmes, as well as linking material into DVD-ROM, CD-ROM and web-sites. This would prove useful for material intended for dissemination via the Internet for display on a digital set top box or Web TV.

The developments of computer games and online artificial environments lay much groundwork in researching developments that can be expanded or adapted to iTV environments. [4]

The methods of dissemination of 3D material for iTV are often complex and varied.

Approaches include:
- stereoscopic images through the use of glasses, making objects appear to come out of the screen
- hologramatic representations which the user physically moves around in order to experience views from all angles.

These forms of interactive 3D are delivered with the content creator having greater control over the views and angles than that provided to the audience.

The proposal of this project is to continue to deliver 3D environments on current 2D screens whilst offering greater interactivity. The interactive experience is realised through the navigation of the environment offered to the viewer. [4]

When considering the navigational needs of the environment for the end user, a simplistic structure of control was implemented. In previous experiments in the navigation of the environment, controls were assigned to the keyboard, but this proved cumbersome in operation and none intuitive to a test audience.

As the environment was being designed for interactive television, experiments were undertaken in testing the intuitiveness of various methods of control for the audience. Our experiments suggested that the replication of a remote control handset proved the intuitive navigation control.

The user is given the option of buttons on the control, as would be the case for a normal television controller, except with this remote being a virtual creation the user has to click on the button with the mouse.

While the remote is virtual it still provides a possible outlay for future expansion of technology that can be applied to this form of iTV, and suggests possible buttons that would need to be included as part of a new controller should one be manufactured.

The controls provided to the user are:
- Pan left
- Pan right
- Pan up
- Pan Down
- Zoom in
- Zoom out

In the creation of the remote the buttons for the functions have to remain as separate items to the actual main controller image.

Figure 2 An example of the remote control handset used for navigation of the environment

If the images are not kept separate to one another, all of the images on the controller would be assigned to only one control function because essentially there would only be one image to apply to the functions. By keeping them separate it is possible to layer the images over one another to compile the overall image. This means that each image can be assigned to a different control function and resolve the problem, whilst still providing the complete remote image to the user.

The given controls provide the user with the capability of moving through 360 degrees around the set, allowing any possible viewpoint of the set to be realised. There is also the capability of being able to zoom into the scene and towards the actors to bring the user closer to characters.

Navigation is also required in the user interface that the environment is imbedded into. This navigation is similar to that experienced on DVD, meaning that it can be easily adapted for use in navigation via a remote control handset or with the use of mouse if the product is displayed via a PC. [1,10]

5.0 Texturing

Texture is important to the look of both the set and the characters. By using archive material the texture in the 3D iTV environment must match that represented in the original source. This also means that the textures being applied are photo-realistic which is a necessity in order to keep continuity between the archive material and environment as well as providing a believable representation to the user. Part of this realisation comes from good lighting conditions and it is possible to add artificial lights to the environment in order, to better match the condition of the original footage. [4,10]

There is also the opportunity of allowing the user to set their own lighting conditions and alter the appearance of the set. The lighting pattern applied to the set by the production team acts as a default, which can be reset by the user to return conditions to a normal level.

While the main textures are taken from the visual footage there are sometimes problems in getting good angles or clear shots of parts of sets that do not often appear on the screen. In this case archive material with good supplementary materials can be of an advantage.

Table 5

Ideal sources of supplementary material are:
• Publicity material, mainly in photography which may have come from books or magazines. • Direct photographs possibly taken by visitors to the set or members of the production cast and crew that have not been publicised but still provide an excellent source of information. • Telesnaps; a set of photographs taken off screen at the time of original transmission and then sold to cast and crew as representations of their work, particularly useful in future development possibilities arising from this work.

While the items listed above provide ideal supplements to the original archive material it is not always possible to access these materials or that the supplements exist for every programme. If the case arises where there is little or no supplementary material available, it falls to the production team to create, from new design, the unknown construction areas and for the design to match that of the archive material.

When several sources are available for use in production, those of the archive footage and the supplementary materials, the techniques for capturing the materials differ, depending upon which source is being used. The supplementary materials are scanned and video footage captured through a video capture card. Both of these methods convert the material to image files, which can then be edited for use within the environment.

This may include

- cropping the image to the correct size for the plane it is being applied to

- any adjustments necessary to make them as accurate a representation of the archive source. This may include touch up work and cleaning of the image.

Once the image is satisfactory it then requires a depth of field. This enhances the 3D environment and adds to the depth and reality of the perspective, which would be lost if the captured 2D images was applied.

Depth in the images is achieved by loading them into a 2D to 3D photographic tool and then pinning around the area of the image to be included as part of the texture. The more parts of the area that are pinned the greater the depth applied. In the conversion from 2D to 3D, the image can be manipulated to the point where the perspective becomes a frontal view.

The need to adjust the perspective arises from the original image captured. If the image is a frontal view when captured, there is no need to manipulate, just the addition of depth. Whilst capturing images in a frontal view saves time, the ability to be able to change the view when the image is captured from a different angle overcomes potential limitations in having to find specific images in a front view point only. [8]

The viewpoint of the texture relates to the viewpoint applied to the plane in the environment at its creation. If the plane has been created in a right hand viewpoint the application of the texture would also have to be applied from a right hand viewpoint in order to match that of the plane. Through the settings of the package used and for ease of closely matching the viewpoint of the texture and the plane, the frontal view perspective has been used. The planes were created in this perspective and the textures adapted accordingly. When the navigation of the environment is enabled, changing the view around the plane also changes the representation of the texture.

In applying the texture to the plane it is helpful if the dimensions of the two, match. If the texture's pattern is not quite right for the plane's area, it is possible to increase or reduce this through use of tiling.

6.0 Construction

The construction of the set arises from an analysis of the chosen set, from the archive material, for recreation as the 3D environment. It is important to try and pick from the material as many shapes as possible. In general walls are rectangular or square in appearance, while windows may range from round to square or even triangular! It is important to pin these down as it helps to choose the correct shape to use within the 3D modelling package.

Each identified shape is constructed separately and can then be moved to positions next to other constructed shapes to form the main basis of the set layout.

The set chosen in our examples is of a simpler design than some, but the process at present lends itself better to basic layout and simple lighting set ups. The set is also symmetrical and therefore a little bit easier to match up the shapes and in the defining of wall sizes.

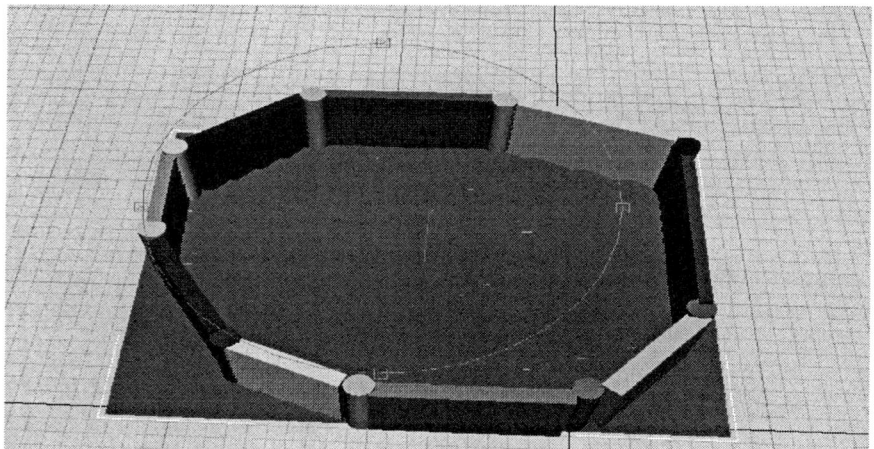

Figure 3 The untextured and unrendered set from above.

The planes are adjusted to the correct heights, widths, and lengths, so that the set takes the appearance of that in the original archive material except it is now in a 3D environment.

The construction also takes into account the need to create the missing production area and this can open possibilities for expansion of the set for new exploration and content creation in delivery to the user. This new production does not require new material to be recorded as it can all be created in the modelling environment and textured through the adaptation of those already taken from the archive material for use in the rest of the set. [8]

When the set resembles the desired layout, texture can be applied to complete the appearance. Texture is applied to the set through use of a simple drag and drop procedure over the planes and shapes already constructed.

Figure 4 A rendered version of the textured set

7.0 Digital Puppets

The creation of the digital puppet is perhaps more important than the realisation of the set. Audiences identify with characters and look to them for explanations and the development of story lines. For this reason characters have to be highly detailed and convey to the audience that the are witnessing the same set of actors that they have associated with previously in the archive material. [9, 3]

In the creation of a digital puppet the following is required:
- The creation of a believable looking head mesh
- Recreation of a body mesh for application to the biped
- The creation of a biped for the application of a body and animation in walk-paths which are applied directly to the biped.

7.1 Creating a characters head

Two methods of constructing a head have been developed in experimentation for the project. This has included an automated version relying on software to create the main mesh, and a manual process whereby a head mesh has been created and textured by the production team in the modelling package relying less on the automated generation of software. [5]

In both processes two shots of a person or character are required in order to calculate the whole head. This is one frontal shot and one profile shot.

The automated creation is achieved by a software package that generates the head into a 3D model from the 2D frontal and profile images supplied. The head is produced as a textured model and items such as hair, hats, jewellery and spectacles can be added to the mesh at a later stage.

If we were creating a new production, the required shots of the actors being modelled would be easy to obtain, but in the case of archive material the required shots must be found from the sources available.

While it may be possible to rehire an actor for a photo shoot to model the head, it may not be the most practical solution. Reasons for this are:

- Age; an actor may now be several years older than when they appeared in the programme and look rather different, or sadly an actor may have passed away.
- Rehiring actors is costly and would greatly raise the expenditure required.
- The project aim is to source all material from archive footage therefore adding weight to the necessity of material and its re-purposing.

The manual process of developing a 3D head mesh requires the user to sculpt the head in the modelling package, using shapes and planes in the same way to the creation of the set. The shapes are moved in the environment to positions next to one another to the resemblance of a human head. This requires a good analysis of a person's head and great skill from the designer constructing the mesh. It is a very difficult process to get right and in terms of time and quality of results the automated method is seen as being the better of the two.

The manual process also relies on the operator to texture the head. This is achieved by deconstructing the mesh from 3D to a flat 2D image. This image can then be exported to a graphics tool to apply the textures captured from the original images of the actor that were used in the creation of the head mesh. When applied the head can be reconstructed back to a 3D mesh, complete with texture.

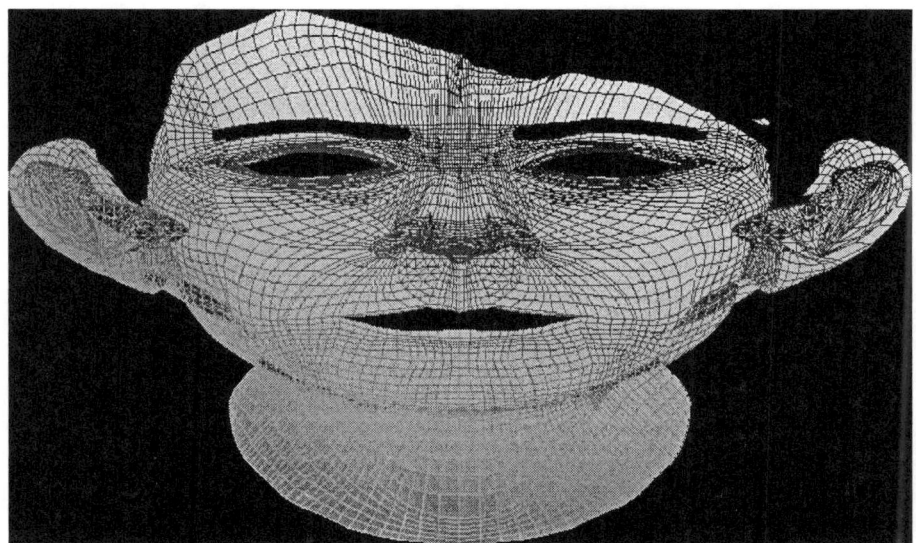

Figure 5 The head mesh deconstructed from a 3D model to a 2D Planar map

I

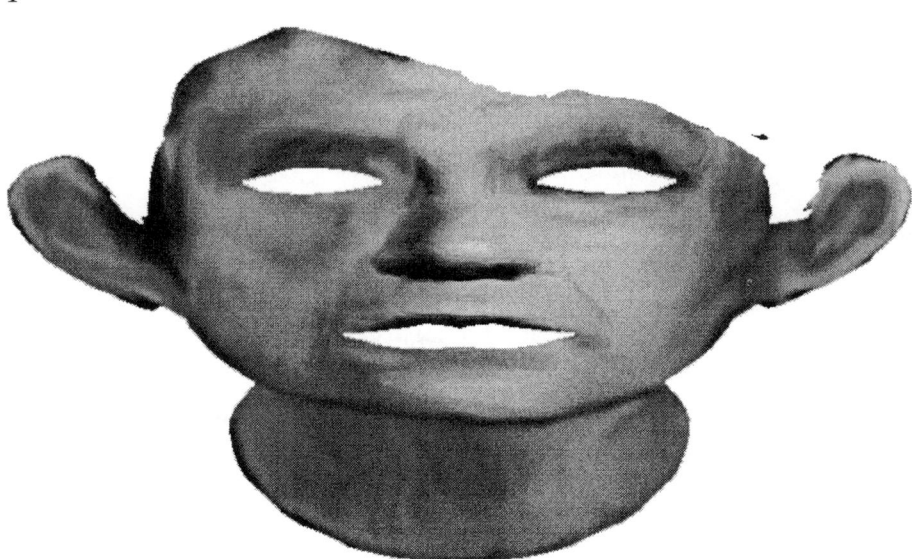

Figure 6 The texture as applied to the Planar map

Figure 7 The finished head, applied a biped complete with body mesh.

The 3D mesh is attached to either the body mesh to form one overall mesh, or applied directly to the biped structure as a separate mesh from the body.

The creation of a suitable body mesh has been achieved through a manual process of construction, as so far a suitable automated process has not been discovered, unlike that use in the creation of the head mesh. [6,7]

The manual process of creating the body use shapes within the package to construct the various parts of the anatomy. Like the head mesh they too have to be applied to the biped. This enables the movement of the body mesh, as it is actually the biped that creates the movement and the attached mesh changes shape to match the biped through the various movements it uses.

For the body to look realistic it must have texture applied, as in the case of both the head and the set. The body mesh texture is skin and clothing of the character.

Clothing and skin textures can be added to the body mesh by either:
- dragging and dropping as used in texturing of the set

or
- by deconstructing the mesh to a 2D planar map and applying the texture in a photographic package like that undertaken in the manual creation of the head mesh.

When the character is complete it can be placed within the set environment and animated to walk around and react according to the story line in the archive material. The animation must match the movements of the character in the archive material and follow the audio material extracted from the archive source. [6,7,8]

The most successful results in the animation of a walking character have been through the use of applied walk paths. The walk path can be applied to the biped from on eof several available presets, or the user has the ability to create their own. In initial experimentation, the preset walk paths were applied to the characters, but as progress has developed individual walk paths have been implemented.

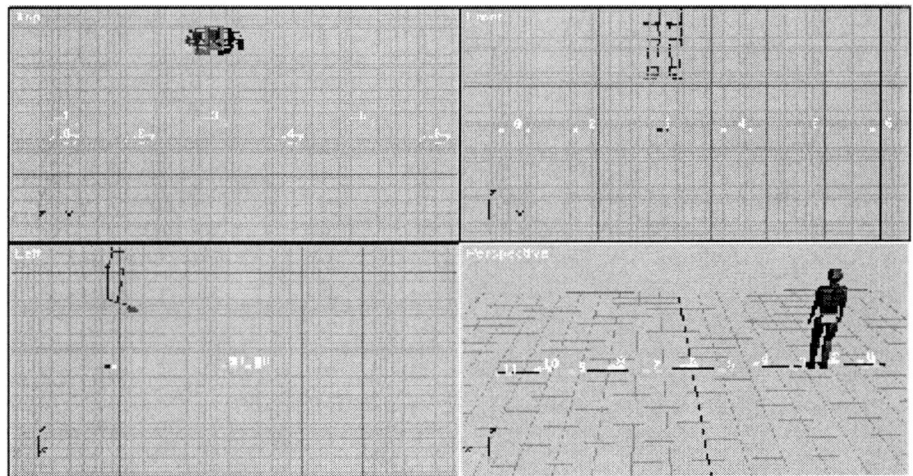

Figure 8 A biped on a walk path. Neither the head or body mesh is applied to the biped.

The walk path is useful for bipedal characters, but there is also a need to animate none bipedal characters as well as other parts of bipedal anatomy not animated by the walk path. These movements are implemented through use of key frame animation. The required movements are enabled through adjusting the part of the anatomy or object at key frames, determined by the point at which the particular animation is required.

The position of the anatomy or object at the start of the animation sequence is selected in the first key frame. A second key frame is selected and the anatomy moved to the position of the final frame of the sequence. The transition between the two key frames is calculated by the package to provide the full animation, without the need to painstakingly create it, frame by frame.

Key frame animation is also used for interactivity where the user may click an item in the environment and a piece of animation is enable such as the opening of a door or a window.

While the function to activate the sequence would not be implemented in the modelling environment, the resultant animation would, and needs to be planned at this stage, before the environment is exported in to the multi-media authoring package.

Figure 9 An untextured set complete with textured biped. The biped is still in the experimental stages of production.

8.0 User Interfaces

The user interface is the final implementation to the overall environment. The interface allows navigation of the environment and displays graphical and textural information to the user. This may include character biographies, instructions on the navigation of the environment and links to CD-ROM's, web sites and streaming media. [4,10]

The control of the imbedded environment is also part of the interface. The controls for navigation are discussed in a previous section of this paper. The design of the interface is based upon the archive programme and designed to be as simple as possible in its navigation by the user.

The over all look can still be complex but must not confuse its intended audience.

Interactive Television

To navigate: please use the controller below by clicking a button in either the PAN, ZOOM or MODE categories

To exit this show: please click the POWER button

To continue: select one of the view MODEs.

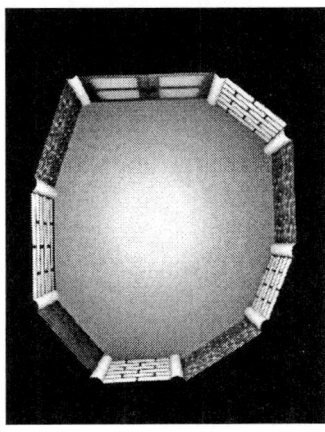

Figure 10 An example of the interface. The controller is on the left of the screen with the text around it explaining how it works. The image on the right is a representation of the environment. When the environment is accessed by the user, a larger version is presented for navigation.

9.0 End Product

Once everything is compiled in the authoring package the finished article can be saved out as a .exe file. In this form it is ready to be used either as a broadcast product or more probable at this stage of development, a Web TV product. This will allow either the streaming of the media, or the download of the overall file where the user is free to interact, and view the material off line.

10.0 Conclusion

While interactive services are still developing they do not currently allow true integration of interactivity between events that unfold on screen and that of the users actions.

Currently, the trends have been towards the use of interactive services as stand alone products such as games services and shopping facilities, or have been applied to programmes that are informative more than entertaining, such as sports events, news programming and documentaries.

While the use of increased data provision is provided, there has been much use of allowing the viewer to select the camera of their choice from those offered by the broadcaster, but there is still not the option of perspective choice.

The research to date has taken a different genre to those currently offered and chosen instead to follow a drama serial.

This work shows possibilities for future development within broadcasting and video dissemination to new levels of interactivity that so far remain to be experienced in this form by a mass audience.

The methodology arising from the undertaken research is still a work in progress, but the basics that have so far been achieved show that there are positive benefits to be gained for the television industry and the end user that can be further expanded to make an even better product.

References

1. Kotsis, N., Lambert, R.B. and McGregor, D.R. 1999. *"Implications of Television over the Internet."* Digital Convergence: The Information Revolution pp 313 – 325, Springer Verlag, 1999, ISBN 1-85233-140-2.

2. Chenot, J-H., Drewery J.O and Lyon, D. 1998. *"Restoration of Archived Television programmes for digital broadcasting".* IBC 98 (Amsterdam), September 1998. IEE conference publication pp 26-31. www.bbc.co.uk/rd/pubs/papers

3. Kanade, T., Rander, P. and Narayanan, P.J. 1997. *"Virtualized Reality: Constructing Virtual Worlds from Real Scenes".* January – March 1997. IEEE Multimedia pp 34 – 46.

4. Thomas, G. and Storey, R. 1999. *"Tv Production in the year 2005".* June 1999. Montrueax Symposium 99 records pp. 234 –238. www.bbc.co.uk/rd/pubs/papers

5. Goto, T., Kshiragar S. and Magnenant – Thalmann, N. 2001. *"Automatic Face Cloning and Animation".* May 2001. IEEE Signal Processing Magazine pp 17 – 25.

6. Plankers, R. and Fua, P. 2001. *"Tracking and Modelling People in Video Sequences".* March 2001. Computer Vision and Image Understanding Volume 81 Number 3 pp 285 – 302.

7. Moslund, T.B. and Granum, E. 2001. *"A survey of Computer Vision-Based Human Motion Capture".* March 2001. Computer Vision and Image Understanding Volume 81 Number 3 pp 231 – 268.

8. Moezzi, S., Tai, L, and Gerard, P. 1997. *"Virtual View Generation for 3D digital video".* January – March 2001. IEEE Multimedia pp. 18 – 25.

9. *Actors".* Virtual Worlds and Multimedia pp.113 – 126.

10. Price, M. and Thomas, G. 2000. *"3D Virtual Production and Delivery using* Magnenant – Thalmann, N. and Thalmann, D. 1993. *"The World of Virtual MPEG-4".* IBC 2000 (Amsterdam). 8 – 12 September 2000. IEE Conference Publication. www.bbc.co.uk/rd/pubs/papers

Author Index

Agarwal, G. 497
Albrecht, I. 281
Annen, T. 395
Arevalo, M. 103
Atmosurkato, I. 181
Banerjee, S. 497
Bastanfard, A. 313
Beets, K. 149
Bergeron, R.D. 213
Booth, K.S. 293
Borodin, P. 199
Brabec, S. 395
Carey, M. 527
Castro, F. 387
Cezero, E. 479
Chiba, N. 121
Claes, J. 149
Drago, F. 121
Esmerado, J. 509
Feixas, M. 265, 387, 437
Fisher, B.D. 293
Fiume, E. 165
Ganster, B. 463
Ghazanfarpour, D. 331
Goto, T. 3
Grasset, J. 451
Graybeal, J.W. 77
Haber, J. 281
Harrison, J. 293
Hasegawa, J. 237
Heidrich, W. 265
Huang, Z. 181
Hussein, H.K. 313
Jern, M. 63
Jiang, J. 37
Kalra, P.K. 497
Kaneda, K. 407
Kang, M.J. 3
Klein, R. 199, 463
Kojekine, N. 137
Kuchar, O.A. 77
Laramee, R.S. 213
Leow, W.K. 181

Luible, C. 103
Magnenat-Thalmann, N. 3, 103
Manabe, T. 407
Martin, I. 423
Martinez, R. 375
McGee, D.R. 77
McQuerry, D.L. 77
Miyazaki, S. 237
Nakajima, M. 313
Novak, P.L. 77
Novotni, M. 199
Paget, D. 527
Peddie, J. 91
Perez, F. 423
Plemenos, D. 451
Protopsaltou, D. 103
Pueyo, X. 423
Rathi, D. 497
Rigau, J. 437
Sarlette, R. 463
Sattler, M. 463
Savchenko, V. 137
Sbert, M. 265, 375, 387, 437
Seidel, H-P. 281, 395
Seron, F.J. 479
Szirmay-Kalos, L. 375
Tang, W. 245
Terraz, O. 451
Thalmann, D. 23, 509
Thomas, A.L. 347
Thomas, J.J. 77
Thon, S. 331
van Reeth, F. 149
Vazquez, P-P. 265
Vexo, F. 509
Wan, T.R. 245
Watson, A. 527
Yamashita, H. 407
Yasuda, T. 237
Yokoi, S. 237
Zhang, H. 165
Zhou, L. 181